W9-COS-545

A conservative approach to economic growth has dominated policy circles for close to two decades. This approach holds that the key to restoring economic growth lies in reducing the size and role of government in the market economy through deregulation of the financial sector, privatization, and lower taxes. The contributors to this book argue that the principles of "trickle down" economics are of dubious validity, and have led to economic stagnation, high unemployment, and increasing inequality. They develop a new perspective on macroeconomic policy, one affirming that egalitarian and democratic economic structures are not only compatible with economic revival, but in fact offer the best hope for sustainable growth of living standards. Their alternative recognizes that markets have an important role to play, but only within the framework of macroeconomic stability, corrections of market failures, and egalitarian rules of the game.

Macroeconomic policy after the conservative era

UNU World Institute for Development Economics Research (UNU/WIDER) was established by the United Nations University as its first research and training centre and started work in Helsinki, Finland, in 1985. The principal purpose of the Institute is policy-oriented research on the main strategic issues of development and international cooperation, as well as on the interaction between domestic and global changes.

UNU World Institute for Development Economics Research (UNU/WIDER)
Katajanokanlaituri 6B
00160 Helsinki, Finland

Macroeconomic policy after the conservative era

Studies in investment, saving and finance

EDITED BY
Gerald A. Epstein
and
Herbert M. Gintis

Department of Economics
University of Massachussets, Amherst

CAMBRIDGE
UNIVERSITY PRESS

Published by the Press Syndicate of the University of Cambridge
The Pitt Building, Trumpington Street, Cambridge CB2 1RP
40 West 20th Street, New York, NY 10011-4211, USA
10 Stamford Road, Oakleigh, Melbourne 3166, Australia

First published 1995

Printed in Great Britain at the University Press, Cambridge

A catalogue for this book is available from the British Library

Library of Congress cataloguing in publication data applied for

HC
59.15
m3
1995

ISBN 0 521 46290 8 hardback

CE

To our parents,
Samuel and Wanda Epstein and
Gerson and Shirley Gintis.

Contents

ix

Contributors

V. Bhaskar, Reader in Economics, Delhi School of Economics, Delhi University, Old Campus, Delhi, 100007, India.

Samuel Bowles, Professor of Economics, University of Massachusetts, Amherst, MA 01003.

Robert Boyer, Senior Research Economist, CEPREMAP, 14, rue du Chevaleret, 75013 Paris, France.

Robert Eisner, William R. Kenan Professor of Economics, Department of Economics, 2003 Sheridan Road, Evanston, IL 60208–2400.

Andrew Glyn, Professor of Economics, Corpus Christi College, Oxford University, Oxford, OX1 HJF.

David M. Gordon, Professor of Economics, New School for Social Research, 65 Fifth Ave., New York, NY 10003.

Christopher Heye, Department of Political Science, Bldg. E53, MIT, Cambridge, MA 02139.

Manuel Pastor Jr., Associate Professor of Economics, Occidental College, Los Angeles, CA 90041.

J. Mohan Rao, Associate Professor of Economics, University of Massachusetts, Amherst, MA 01003.

Peter Skott, Associate Professor of Economics, University of Aarhus, Aarhus, 8000 Aarhus C, Denmark.

Acknowledgements

The efforts and advice of many people and organizations contributed to the creation of Macroeconomic Policy After the Conservative Era. We are especially indebted to the World Institute for Development Economic Research, its parent organization the United Nations University, and its far-sighted leader Lal Jayawardena. The idea for such a book and the organization of a conference on the subject is due to Professor Stephen Marglin of Harvard University, whose encouragement sustained us through the long process of commissioning, reviewing, and revising manuscripts. We are also indebted to Kevin Crocker, Dan Gintis, Edward McPhail, Elspeth McCusker and Anne Rix for research and editorial assistance, and to John Haslam and the staff of the *Cambridge University Press* for their faith in this project, as well as rendering the process of production as painless as possible.

Part one

Introduction

1 Macroeconomic policies for sustainable growth

Gerald A. Epstein and Herbert Gintis

In recent years, economic policy in the United States, Great Britain, and other developed third world economies has been based on a set of conservative principles of dubious validity. Latin America, Africa, and parts of Asia remain mired in economic stagnation, and they have been joined by the United States as a low-growth, heavily indebted nation. Meanwhile, unemployment remains high in much of Europe, and economic inequality is increasing. This volume offers a critique of and alternatives to this dominant policy orthodoxy.

According to the policy consensus of the 1980s, fostered by the electoral successes of conservative parties, developed in major universities, and implemented by international lending agencies, government is the obstacle, not the facilitator of economic growth, while increased economic equality and democratic accountability impede economic growth.

Among the tenets of this macroeconomic orthodoxy, three are especially prominent. First, government budget deficits are detrimental to the economy, since they absorb national saving, raise interest rates, and thus dampen the pace of domestically financed private investment. Balanced budgets, it follows, are necessary to the restoration of healthy economic growth. More generally, policies that reduce savings *ex ante* – egalitarian redistributive policies, for example – retard business investment.

A second tenet is that government intervention in product, financial, and labor markets is economically inefficient. Hence industrial and financial deregulation provide potent opportunities for increasing allocational efficiency and restoring productivity growth. Similarly, according to this view, government support of labor and collective bargaining slow innovation and raise the rate of unemployment.

A third tenet is that government ought not to interfere with international product and financial movements. According to this view, controls on capital flows should be avoided, since the international reallocation of saving to regions of high investment returns is both globally efficient and essential to the recipients' economic development. Recipient countries, in turn, should not impede capital outflows, on the ground that such policies discourage capital inflows and protect inefficient government policies from the vote of no confidence of the marketplace (World Bank, 1991).

The widespread acceptance of this policy orthodoxy in the 1980s was based not on empirical evidence of its effectiveness, but rather was a violent reaction against the previous Keynesian and social democratic orthodoxies that held sway during the stretch of vigorous world economic growth in the period from the conclusion of the Second World War to the 'stagflationary' era of the mid 1970s. This Keynesian/social-democratic consensus, differing more in degree than in kind among countries, was inspired by a set of beliefs that stand in sharp contrast to current accepted wisdom: that economic egalitarianism is complementary to economic growth, that high wages spur aggregate demand and foster a healthy and skilled work force, and that organized labor promotes industrial stability and productivity growth.

For policy makers of a Keynesian persuasion, good government is a prime instrument of economic growth: government spending helps maintain full employment, automatic stabilizers dampen the business cycle, regulation of financial markets prevents financial crises and channels credit in socially productive directions, and the regulation of international capital movements afford nations the policy autonomy they require to achieve economic objectives (Marglin and Schor, 1990).

While poor performance has tarnished the reputation of the conservative policy orthodoxy, there is no simple return to the past. Indeed, critics have identified critical weaknesses of the Keynesian/social-democratic perspective – most importantly its focus on stabilization as opposed to growth, its inadequate treatment of efficiency–equity issues, its distaste for market competition and seeming tolerance of a bloated state sector, and its apparent bias in favor of influential, oligopolistic segments of business and labor. Moreover, economic life has changed; contemporary economic problems cannot be solved through a wholesale revival of doctrines whose success depends on conditions that are currently only of historical interest. Among these now defunct conditions is the inevitability of growth, the unimportance of environmental concerns, the position of organized labor at the center of progressive change, and the preeminence of domestic over international issues in trade and finance.

We develop here a new perspective on macroeconomic policy, one affirming that egalitarian and democratic economic structures are not only compatible with economic revival, but, in fact, offer the best hope for sustainable growth of living standards. By contrast, continuing the policies of conservative economics will only deepen the economic stagnation and inequality we are witnessing in many parts of the globe.

This task begins with Andrew Glyn's documentation of the failures of the conservative approach to economic policy, and then turns to an empirical investigation of the determinants of investment and saving. The results, developed in papers by Christopher Heye, V. Bhaskar and Andrew Glyn, Manuel Pastor, David Gordon, and Robert Eisner suggest that the dominant policy paradigm, which views increased private and public saving as the key to restoring growth, has little empirical support. A policy oriented to increasing private and public investment directly is more likely to succeed in both advanced capitalist and developing economies.

In the next section, Peter Skott, J. Mohan Rao, and Gerald Epstein analyze financial deregulation and suggest that the free market prescription to deregulate domestic and international financial markets are unlikely to deliver large benefits, and may even engender significant instability, in both the advanced capitalist and developing countries.

With the shortcomings of conservative policy, the important question is what alternatives exist? Samuel Bowles and Robert Boyer cast doubt on the viability of the traditional progressive policy, "wage-led growth," in contemporary internationally open economies. But in the concluding section, the chapters by David Gordon, Gerald Epstein, and Herbert Gintis, and Samuel Bowles and Herbert Gintis, suggest that egalitarian and democratically oriented policies, such as asset-based redistribution and social infrastructure investment, offer a significant opportunity to overcome the agency and coordination problems besetting contemporary economies.

From golden age to gilded age

Conservative economics promised to restore the high rates of economic growth enjoyed by the industrialized economies in the 1950s and 1960s, but which gave way to stagnation, inflation, and political instability in the 1970s. This promise has been unkept, and no institutional structure has been developed to replace the arrangements that fostered economic growth in the post-war period.

The 1950s and 1960s were a golden age of economic growth in the western world (Glyn, Hughes, Lipietz, and Singh, 1990; Maddison, 1989). OECD rates of growth of real GNP averaged 4.9 percent annually between 1960 and 1973. During this period, productivity growth averaged a robust 3.3 percent per year in manufacturing and 2.2 percent in the business sector overall, for the period 1960–73 in OECD countries (Glyn, chapter 2, table 2.1). These high rates of economic growth gave way however to an era of stagflation in the 1970s, during which GNP grew by only 2.7 percent, unemployment rose to an average of 4.2 percent, and inflation averaged 11.3 percent (Glyn, chapter 2, and OECD, 1991).

The fall of golden age growth was initially attributed by most economists to external shocks, primarily sharp increases in energy prices, with the implication that once these shocks were absorbed, golden age growth would reappear. An alternative analysis, based on the insights of Marx, Kalecki, and Keynes, countered that the problems were more structural than the shock theory implied (Marglin and Schor, 1990). As a result, far from a mere pause, the new period marked the collapse of the golden age.

This alternative approach views the capitalist economy as facing a set of conflict and coordination problems, the resolution of which is a precondition of sustained growth. During the golden age, these conflict and coordination problems were controlled by a set of institutions, sometimes called a social structure of accumulation or system of regulation, that worked together to maintain appropriate levels of production, saving, investment, and economic growth (Aglietta, 1976; Gordon, 1978; Bowles and Gintis, 1982; Bowles, Gordon, and Weisskopf, 1990).[1]

A social structure of accumulation includes arrangements that shape the domestic macro economy by managing the level of output, employment, and growth. To be successful, these arrangements must maintain a high level of aggregate demand and channel a sufficient share of output to investment to support rapid productivity growth. During the golden age, aggregate demand management, counter-cyclical monetary and fiscal policy, as well as the automatic stabilizers provided by the welfare state, were the key elements of this system.

A social structure of accumulation also includes arrangements that govern the international economy. Central here are mechanisms to maintain stable exchange rates, trading regulations, and terms of trade, as well as adequate flows of international credit and sources of external aggregate demand. The hegemony of the United States in the post-war period, symbolized by the Bretton Woods System and dollar-centered fixed exchange rate system, was the central feature of this international order.

A third dimension in the golden age social structure of accumulation was the set of arrangements governing capital–labor relations. Institutions that minimize and resolve conflicts between capital and labor are conducive to high rates of growth. In the OECD countries, a variety of such methods were practiced, usually involving public support for organized labor and government-sponsored arbitration of industrial disputes.

A final set of necessary elements in a social structure of accumulation are the mechanisms for eliciting the requisite behavior on the part of individual agents, the "rules of coordination." Here the mechanisms by which the actions of corporations, banks, the state, labor, and other actors are brought in line with each other and the exigencies of the economy as a whole are central. The price mechanism has been the central coordinating rule, profits guiding the allocation and accumulation of capital, and wages the motivation and allocation of labor. Other mechanisms, for example, government regulation of the financial system, are important to varying degrees in different countries and time periods.

When these various arrangements function well, individually and in concert, the economy generates high rates of productivity growth and investment. When they do not, the economy falters. In the 1950s and 1960s, the system of regulation operated well, but its very success tended to undermine its functioning. The decline of the golden age can be attributed to the rupturing and eventual collapse of these arrangements.

Domestically, the low unemployment rates and income security provided by the welfare state contributed to a squeeze on profits in many of the industrialized economies (Bowles and Gintis, 1982). Internationally, the relative decline of United States power and the increases in oil prices in 1973 and 1979 that resulted partly therefrom, contributed to a further profit squeeze and decline in investment rates in the OECD countries. These domestic and international difficulties, in turn, caused a retreat from Keynesian demand management policies, by the late 1970s further undermining the system of regulation (Epstein and Schor, 1990).

The relative decline of the power of capital *vis-à-vis* labor, and of the United States relative to other countries, led to a virtual counter-revolution throughout the industrialized countries. With the elections of Ronald Reagan in the United States and Margaret Thatcher in England, and the perceived failure of Francois Mitterrand's expansionary policy in the early 1980s in France, a new policy of restoration set in. Domestic macroeconomic policy shifted to fiscal austerity and tight money. Industrial relations shifted to confrontation and anti-union activities on the part of management and government. The rules of coordination shifted to deregulation of product and financial markets. Internationally, the United States reasserted dominance through a massive military build up.

Conservative economic policy: can it achieve a new golden age?

As Glyn documents in chapter 2, conservative policies were successful in restoring the business dominance in the major industrialized countries. Union activity declined, profit shares increased, and inflation fell dramatically. However these policies were less successful in improving overall economic performance.

First, economic inequality increased. The share of the top 20 percent of the income distribution increased dramatically in most countries, while the share of those in the bottom 20 percent fell substantially. Second, economic growth was not restored. Investment rates, growth rates, unemployment rates, and productivity growth, with a few exceptions, failed to show much improvement overall in the 1980s. Finally, significant signs of underlying strain, particularly in the deregulated financial sectors, suggest that the seeds of further macroeconomic problems were sown during this period.

Despite these apparent failures, a policy consensus has coalesced around its major themes. Analytically, this consensus stresses the links among saving, investment, and finance and their connection with productivity growth. According to this view, increased investment in plant and equipment presupposes an increase in saving, both private and public. The key to increasing private saving is redistribution to the wealthy, while the key to increasing public saving is government austerity. Finally, the key to creating the proper incentives for saving and investment is that financial markets be permitted to function with a minimum of government regulation.[2]

David Gordon, in chapter 3, identifies an important weak link in this logic: increasing private saving, *ceteris paribus*, does little to increase private investment. Gordon provides strong evidence, using both single equation and simultaneous equation time-series models for the United States, that direction of causation is in fact reversed: investment generates saving, but not vice versa. His results further suggest that attempts to increase saving will reduce output while policies to increase investment raise output.

Saving fails to generate investment in part because increased personal saving does not appear to alter the financial constraints affecting investment. According to Gordon, the neoclassical line of causation from saving to the cost of capital and then to the level of investment is not operative, at least in the United States. This is consistent with the view that savings of institutions, such as corporations, are more important for investment than that of households (Marglin, 1984). Hence, if investment is the key to productivity growth, then redistributing income to the wealthy to generate more saving is not likely to increase productivity.

Robert Eisner's analysis in chapter 4 casts doubt on another plank in the conservative economic platform: namely, that increasing government saving, for instance by cutting budget deficits, will increase total saving in the economy. Eisner first points out that conventional measures of the budget deficit can be extremely misleading. But more important, his econometric results suggest that increases in government savings do not increase the pool of saving. Indeed, *increases* in government spending are more likely to increase total saving and investment, at least in the United States.

If regressive redistribution and austerity do not increase saving and investment, what about financial deregulation, the third plank of conservative macroeconomic policy? Peter Skott, in chapter 9, develops a model, building on the work of Hyman Minsky, suggesting that unregulated financial markets can lead to instability in saving and investment. J. Mohan Rao, in chapter 10, develops a model of financial markets applicable to developing countries that further casts doubt on the assumption that unregulated financial markets allocate credit properly.

In a similar vein Manuel Pastor, in chapter 8, presents econometric evidence that in the context of the Latin American debt crisis, unregulated financial markets and debt creation undermined rather than promoted the investment process. His study of the relation between debt accumulation and investment in Latin American countries in the 1970s and 1980s finds that the "debt overhang" (the amount of debt accumulated over and above what is likely to be serviced) significantly reduced private investment in Latin America. His study indicates that finance does indeed matter for investment, but that unregulated finance may lead to excessive debt that hinders productive investment.

The theoretical premises of the new policy consensus

The conservative policy orthodoxy is based on an agency-theoretic analysis of the government and a Walrasian analysis of the market (Epstein and Gintis, chapter 13). In conservative political economy the government has limited and biased information concerning economic opportunities, and public officials, rather than maximizing social welfare, act in their own interests. In particular, the theory of rent-seeking behavior suggests that interventions will generally benefit the powerful. While it may be possible to devise incentive mechanisms ensuring that public officials' interests agree with social interests, rent-seeking behavior renders it likely that such mechanisms will be shunned in favor of others that pander to whatever groups currently have access to positions of political power. Hence, government failure is the rule, not the exception.

We believe that this approach is accurate in identifying the agency problems facing the formation and execution of macroeconomic policy, but incorrectly denies that these problems cannot be handled by instituting the proper rules of the game in democratic decision making and accountability. Despite agency problems in the public sector, there is no doubt but that the state has been a critical instrument in contributing to the emergence and success of capitalist economies since the Industrial Revolution.

In contrast to its Machiavellian view of the public sector, conservative policy orthodoxy accepts an idealized Walrasian model of market behavior, in which market failure is the exception. Prices are assumed universally to clear markets, information is abundant and symmetric, Say's Law holds, agency problems are absent, and there are no externalities of importance. Hence, in the marketplace, power is absent, resources are allocated efficiently, full-employment stability is the norm, and natural resources are effectively managed without government interference.

An extensive body of contemporary microeconomic theory belies this Walrasian view of economic life. Information asymmetry and problems with the enforcement of contractual exchange lead to a situation in which prices fail to clear markets and rationing prevails. In such a world, power is prevalent, unemployment is the norm, and effective demand a determinant of economic well being. In short, the market is riddled with agency problems and requires an agency theoretic analysis as deep as that of the public sector (Epstein and Gintis, chapter 13).

The new Keynesian alternative

If the conservative approach is found wanting both theoretically and empirically, what of the Keynesian alternative, emphasizing demand management to maintain full employment and economic growth? Though some Keynesian arguments are compelling, the Keynesian consensus is excessively sanguine concerning both the government and the market. On the one hand, as the conservative analysis suggests, there are serious agency and informational problems with government intervention, and differential access to political influence, based on wealth and class position, severely bias state policy.

On the other hand, there are fundamental flaws in the basic Keynesian faiths that demand management can produce full employment, and that under conditions of full employment the market operates as suggested by the Walrasian model. The market, for Keynesians, has only one basic flaw: it is unstable, generating depression and unemployment. Government policy correspondingly, has only one basic task, that of maintaining aggregate demand. In the words of new Keynesian, N. Gregory Mankiw (1991, p. 6):

The basic questions of macroeconomics are: "What causes output and employment to fluctuate?" and "How should monetary and fiscal policymakers respond to these fluctuations?"

It is now clear, however, that the long-term levels around which such fluctuations occur are considerably more important than the fluctuations themselves. Political influence and agency problems prevent the maintenance of full employment and high levels of investment and productivity growth through demand management, as evidenced by the "full-employment profit squeeze" that contributed to the downfall of the golden age. Keynesians, in short, are strong in the realm of short-term demand management, but possess no compelling long-run approach to macroeconomic policy. Yet the most pressing contemporary macroeconomic problems lie in the long run, including increasing growth rates, average rates of factor utilization, and improving the distribution of income and wealth. In the long run we are all dead, but our children, our children's children, and our nations, are not.

Wage-led growth and structuralist macroeconomics

Economists unhappy with these traditional approaches have developed an alternative "structuralist macroeconomics," integrating Keynesian insights with the intellectual tradition of Marx and Kalecki.[3] This approach treats the distribution of income and power as determinants of macroeconomic outcomes rather than as by-products of more fundamental economic processes. The structural and Keynesian approaches share a great deal. Both emphasize the importance of the rules of the game rather than the pattern of individual decision making in determining such basic macroeconomic variables as saving and investment. Moreover, their common focus on institutions and income distribution lead them to stress the role of profits in the determination of saving and investment, an element missing from the neoclassical approach.

Structural and Keynesian macroeconomic models, though they share these concerns, diverge in other respects. Structural models focus on capital–labor conflict over wages and productivity, investment and output being determined by the outcome of the conflict. Here causation goes from real wages and productivity to profits, and from profits, given the difference in savings propensities out of wages and profits, to investment. Hence saving determines investment in the long run, as in the neoclassical model. Also an increase in wages, by lowering profits, lowers investment and growth, again as in the neoclassical model.

Despite this communality of views, the mechanisms of the conflict over wages and productivity vary from analysis to analysis. In some models, employment rents and unemployment, the latter determined partly through business influence on macroeconomic policy, are important mechanisms of the struggle over wages, work effort, and profits (Bowles and Gintis, 1982; Marglin, 1984; Schor, 1985). Whereas the structural model, true to its Marxian roots, views the capitalist as a contestant over a share of the pie, the Keynesian model views the capitalist as an investor. Guided by animal spirits, the Keynesian capitalist invests, thus generating the profits and saving needed to finance this investment. Investment thus determines profits, with real wages as a residual. A central Keynesian assumption is that the supply of funds adjusts to capitalists' investment needs *in advance* of the realization of profits. With this assumption, investment determines saving, and a wage increase leads to higher consumption, more profits, and consequently higher investment and saving, counter to the neoclassical view.

These two models are evidently incompatible as they stand. They may be reconciled through an approach first suggested by Kalecki, in which the assumption that firms determine output through profit maximization is dropped, but the assumption that capacity utilization responds to aggregate demand is retained. In this model, aggregate demand affects the profit rate through capacity utilization, but the real wage is not determined entirely by capacity utilization, as in Keynes' general theory.

A Kaleckian hybrid of Keynes and Marx, a macroeconomic model where profits determine output through the investment and consumption functions, and output determines profits through the process of labor extraction, can be derived (Marglin and Bhaduri, 1990; Bowles and Boyer, 1990; Bowles and Boyer, chapter 5; Gordon, chapters 3 and 12). In this model, redistributing income to wages can in principle raise aggregate demand, output, employment, and investment – a stagnationist regime or "wage-led growth." However it is also possible that such redistribution leads to a decline in investment – an exhilarationist regime or "profit-led growth."

In this context, the neoclassical economists and structuralist macroeconomists might both expect to find a redistribution of income to profits to lead to more investment and output in some situations. Unlike neoclassical economists, however, this approach opens the possibility that redistribution toward wages can increase employment, investment, and growth.

The chapters in the present volume by V. Bhaskar and Andrew Glyn (chapter 7) and Samuel Bowles and Robert Boyer (chapter 5) report empirical results suggesting that the Marx–Keynes–Kalecki focus on profit-led investment is well founded. But the strength of the relationship varies significantly from country to country. As Bhaskar and Glyn note, while profitability is important for most of the countries, there is no simple association between increasing profits and increasing investment in their data.

Christopher Heye's analysis in chapter 6 may provide a clue to this lack of consistent results on profitability. His results indicate that expectations are important in the determination of investment, a point stressed by Keynes but often overlooked in the modern literature. Similarly, though the structuralist perspective makes it clear that financial accommodation plays a central part in an investment driven model of growth, financial factors that might mediate and even disrupt the relationship between profits and investment have not been sufficiently well modeled or estimated.[4] Variations in financial structure, either through variations in the degree of credit rationing or in the nature and degree of financial instability induced by financial deregulation, may help explain variations in the response of investment to changes in the profit rate.

Just as there is no apparent simple relationship between increasing profits and investment, which casts doubt on the generality of profit-led growth, Bowles and Boyer in chapter 5 find mixed evidence for the "stagnationist" or wage-led model as the basis for a progressive strategy for restoring economic growth. They present estimates of the effects of increases in real wages on aggregate demand and hence on employment in a sample of OECD countries. Their results suggest that in some countries, increases in real wages can lead to increases in aggregate demand (contrary to the neoclassical and supportive of Keynesian analysis) but that in other countries, increases in real wages reduce aggregate demand. Indeed, they find that when the open economy effects of increased wages on exports are taken into account, in a number of cases a positive association between real wages and aggregate demand became negative.

According to Bowles and Boyer, while the negative impacts of wage increases have been widely exaggerated in policy circles, wage increases do not *by themselves* constitute a viable strategy for supporting increases in employment. However, as they suggest, higher wages do increase productivity. This suggests that, in the proper context, more egalitarian policies may provide the basis for sustainable increases in living standards.

Fairness and sustainable growth

If conservative policy seems to be empirically and theoretically weak, and both traditional Keynesian and Marx–Keynes–Kalecki approaches do not give sufficient guidance for a progressive macroeconomics, what macroeconomic alternatives can give proper guidance for policy? Some of the chapters in this volume point to the development of an alternative macroeconomics which builds on the analysis of Marx, Kalecki, and Keynes described above, but one which also attempts to move beyond them. Some of the chapters discussed previously, especially those of Heye and Skott, suggest adding the Keynesian idea, modified by Minsky, of financial instability to our analysis of macroeconomic dynamics to be taken into account when framing solutions. Doing so will help us understand the key link between saving and investment provided by finance, a link that is still underdeveloped, though apparently increasingly important.

The chapters in the final section of the volume stress the importance of coordination and agency problems as central components of an analysis of macroeconomic problems and solutions.

The chapters by David Gordon, Gerald Epstein and Herbert Gintis, and Samuel Bowles and Herbert Gintis suggest that more egalitarian policies may be central to generating sustainable increases in living standards. However, their main contribution may not be through increases in aggregate demand, as in the Keynes–Kalecki approach, but rather through their positive impacts on productivity growth. These egalitarian policies enhance productivity by solving agency and coordination problems in the economy and are likely to be a better form of "supply-side" economics than the conservative policy of regressive redistribution and deregulation.

Gordon (chapter 12) identifies an important channel through which redistribution of income, wealth, and power can both improve the functioning of the economy and help to overcome the limits of the full-employment profit squeeze. He argues that economic stability and sustainable growth require the reduction of coordination problems and conflicts. Coordination problems and conflicts, he suggests, lead to weak productivity growth and investment, even if other aspects of the macroeconomic structure, in particular the distribution of income, are appropriate in terms of their effects on aggregate demand or in eliciting work effort. Egalitarian redistribution can play a positive role in reducing these obstacles, independent of their effects on demand. Rather than by generating aggregate demand, egalitarianism can play a role by inducing cooperation.

In addition to aggregate demand and coordination problems, Epstein and Gintis in chapter 13 identify agency problems, both in the economy and in the state, as obstacles to sustainable growth. Agency problems in credit markets, the firm, and the state lead to misallocation of resources and unemployment. In the public sector, agency problems lead to misallocation of public resources and perverse macroeconomic policy. Epstein and Gintis argue that these agency problems, along with traditional concerns of structuralist macroeconomics, must be taken into account when analyzing and proposing policies. For example, they suggest that market competition is important not because markets "get the prices right," but because markets act as enforcement mechanisms to reduce agency problems in the state and the economy. Similarly, they suggest that egalitarian economic policy, in particular asset-based redistribution, can improve the functioning of the economy, by providing incentives for accumulation of human capital and innovation, in addition to promoting democratic accountability and social policy in the public interest.

Finally, Bowles and Gintis in chapter 14 show that asset-based redistribution can contribute to the solution of coordination problems. They note that economic growth requires a strong state sector, but such a state poses the threat of redistributing wealth in response to populist pressures. The wealthy may thus prefer a weak state in an unhealthy economy to a strong state in a healthy economy, and the strength of this preference is likely to increase with the degree of economic inequality. Moreover, they suggest that the level of cooperation, which contributes to low-cost solutions to coordination problems, increases with the degree of economic equality. They also argue that economies with highly unequal asset distributions generate inefficient incentive structures, since those who bear the costs of undertaking productivity enhancing activities tend under such conditions not to have claims on the fruits of their activities, the result being high monitoring costs and low effort. They argue on agency-theoretic grounds that there exist egalitarian productivity-enhancing asset redistributions, and give possible examples thereof.

A progressive strategy for restoring economic growth

The policy guidelines flowing from our analysis suggest, in line with our analysis of the decline of the golden age, that a restoration of sustainable growth will require the creation of a new set of institutions capable of overcoming the conflict, coordination, and agency problems endemic to capitalist economies. This book points to significant elements of such a structure.[5]

First, long-term growth requires a commitment to the development of human, social, and environmental resources, and hence to an egalitarian social policy, broadly defined. An educated and healthy labor force will be the hallmark of successful economies in the coming years, and the strategic redistribution of income is a major, though certainly not the only, means to this end. Redistribution must, however, be broadly conformable with incentive compatibility. We therefore suggest increased reliance upon wealth and estate taxation rather than upon income taxation. Similarly, we prefer the expansion of worker ownership (e.g., through favorable tax treatment) to income supports as an incentive compatible form of asset redistribution.

Second, our analysis supports the Keynesian notion that investment determines savings, rather than vice versa. Since the key to restoring faltering growth is restoring the rate of investment, and since investment depends on the expectation of future aggregate demand, both government demand and the use of automatic stabilizers must be maintained at relatively high levels. In particular, there is no necessary inverse relationship between government budget deficits, total saving, and investment. In the past the *composition* rather than the *level* of government expenditure (e.g., inordinate levels of military expenditure) has impeded economic growth. Public investment in human and physical infrastructure ought to be a high priority. Moreover the maintenance of adequate levels of profitability need not unduly compromise redistributive objectives if there is a redistribution of assets in the form of worker ownership.

Third, financial regulation must be aggressively pursued in implementing economic policy. Financial deregulation offers few of the benefits that have been attributed to it in recent years (Dymski, Epstein, and Pollin 1993). Informational asymmetries and the instability of expectations make financial regulations necessary to the smooth functioning of asset markets. Moreover, agency-theoretic conditions, in particular the absence of third-party enforcement of debtor–creditor relationships, imply that unregulated capital markets give rise to extensive credit rationing and a misallocation of resources. Systematic attention must be given to the correction of market failures in this area. Similar attention must be applied to the government as well: financial regulation should be engineered in such manner as to be circumscribed, accountable, and tamper proof, in the absence of which such missteps as the Savings and Loan debacle in the United States are likely.

Fourth, competitive markets promote economic growth by allowing society to identify inefficiencies, obliging economic actors to reveal information, and inducing a high level of performance on the part of labor and management. Thus, in relation to markets, governments should lay down the basic rules of the game, including property rights, within which competitive economic behavior is carried out, and these rules should be carefully structured so as not to interfere with productive efficiency.

Finally, macroeconomic policy may usefully include restraints on international capital mobility, where such mobility renders stabilization or growth policies difficult to execute. The conservative policy orthodoxy argues for financial openness on tenuous grounds, that of the efficient allocation of capital on a world scale. There is little evidence, however, that open financial markets work in the neoclassical manner (Epstein, chapter 11). The absence of third-party enforcement in cross-national financial transactions renders the Walrasian model an unlikely source of correct insight into international financial theory. Indeed empirical research, some of which is presented in this volume, indicates that financial flows cannot be understood as responses to the differential marginal efficiency of investment in different countries (Epstein and Gintis, 1992; Schor, 1992; Epstein, chapter 11). Rather, the threat of "capital flight" serves to constrain governments intent on implementing otherwise socially desirable objectives.

Notes

1 An overview of these institutional arrangements is presented in Marglin and Schor (1990), chapter 1, and elaborated in Glyn, Hughes, Lipietz, and Singh (1990).

2 World Development Report (1991). See Hatsopoulos, Krugman, and Summers (1988) for a concise statement of this position.

3 The term "structuralist macroeconomics" is offered by David Gordon in chapter 12. See also Rowthorn (1982), Marglin (1984), Marglin and Bhaduri (1989), Bowles and Boyer (1990), and Taylor (1985). See Marglin and Bhaduri (1989), for further discussion of the points in this section.

4 See however Crotty and Goldstein (1992), Fazzari, Hubbard, and Petersen (1988), and Skott, chapter 9.

5 See also Marglin and Schor (1990) and Banuri and Schor (1992).

2 Stability, inegalitarianism, and stagnation: an overview of the advanced capitalist countries in the 1980s

Andrew Glyn

As already discussed in chapter 1, the 1980s saw a profound shift in economic policy in the advanced capitalist countries (the ACCs) from the norms which had governed the "golden age" (see Marglin and Schor, 1990). Full employment could no longer be guaranteed but would be left to market processes, government deficits would be eliminated to hold back inflation or release resources for private investment, profitability had to be restored to reinstate the business investment previously "crowded out," and the egalitarian trends represented by the seemingly inexorable rise in government welfare spending had to be halted, if not reversed. This lurch in the stance of policy making throughout the capitalist world represented at bottom an attempt to claw back from workers some of the gains that the long period of high employment had brought them in terms of wages, working conditions, and welfare. These gains were blamed for the deterioration of economic performance from the later 1960s through the 1970s. The obvious response from employers was to try, through economic policy and legislation, to restore their power in the factories, discipline at the wage-bargaining table, and control over the level of state spending.

The purpose, then, of this chapter is to throw some light on the fundamental question: did the change in policy stance represent a viable new pattern of development? Judged by output growth the 1980s was hardly spectacular, with Europe slowing down further as compared to the "intershock period" of 1973–9 (table 2.1). The long period of expansion after 1982 saw much slower output growth (outside the USA) than in the golden age. The stagnation of the early 1990s was more pronounced in Europe and Japan than that of the early 1980s, and could not be blamed on an external oil shock.

But such continuity of output growth between the intershock period and the 1980s conceals very significant changes in other facets of

Table 2.1. *The growth slowdown, 1960–93:* average annual percentage growth rates of total output (GDP)

	1960–73	1973–9	1979–90	1979–82	1982–90	1990–3
USA	4.0	2.4	2.6	– 0.1	3.6	1.2
Europe	4.8	2.6	2.0	0.9	2.7	0.6
Japan	9.6	3.6	4.3	3.7	4.5	2.1
OECD	4.9	2.7	2.8	0.8	3.5	1.1

Source: OECD, *Historical Statistics* and *Economic Outlook.* Figures for 1993 are OECD forecasts (July 1993).

economic performance. This chapter begins by charting, necessarily briefly, the extent to which the most obvious indicators of heightened conflict in the seventies (inflation, industrial unrest, profit squeezes, and government deficits) were reversed in the 1980s. Inflation declined, profits recovered, government finances improved, and strikes were at low levels. Judged by these indicators at least, substantial success in restoring domestic economic stability was achieved. Partly as a result of pursuing this objective, but also to sharpen market incentives, there was a conscious shift away from egalitarian policies. Section 2 contrasts the abandonment of full employment in the countries of the European core with the much more favorable employment record of both "corporatist" countries in Northern Europe and some of the more *laissez faire* economies, notably the USA. Compared to the diverse employment record, cuts in expenditure on social welfare and reductions in the progressiveness of the tax system represented a very widespread reversal, or at least halting, of the egalitarian thrust of policies typical of the golden age. The policy shift toward the free market was not, however, without its problematic elements even for the owners of capital. Section 3 outlines the troubling indicators at the end of the 1980s of financial instability in both the domestic and international spheres. So capital accumulation in the 1980s took place against this backdrop of reduced domestic conflict, a pronounced policy shift toward inegalitarianism, and increasing financial strains. Section 4 shows that the investment recovery of the 1980s left rates of accumulation well below those of the golden age, especially in Europe. Moreover the pattern of investment was twisted away from manufacturing and toward service sectors, mostly closely linked to domestic consumption booms and insulated from international competition. Section 5 places the further stumbling in growth after 1990 in the context of the patterns of development emerging in the 1980s and reports on the continued adherence of international organizations such as the OECD and IMF to the policy prescriptions they had zealously pursued over the previous decade.

1   The reduction of conflict

Throughout the later 1960s and the 1970s the ACCs experienced a period of heightened conflict over distribution. Periods of accelerating inflation reflected the reluctance of workers to accept the growth of living standards implied by productivity growth and terms of trade movements combined with pressure on governments to preserve high employment by accommodating the expansion of credit. Profit squeezes took place when employers were constrained, by competitive conditions or demand, from passing on such higher wage increases as price rises. Budget deficits reflected, in part, reluctance by governments to impose higher taxation to finance the growing weight of social expenditure, fearing that distributional conflict would be exacerbated as workers sought to offload the burden through wage negotiations. Strikes signaled the often fraught relations between employers and workers (see Armstrong *et al.*, 1991 for one interpretation along these lines).

Whilst there are country-specific features at work, these indicators are nevertheless helpful in underlining the turbulence of the seventies and the degree of stabilization in the eighties. Appendix table 1A provides data (where available) for each of twenty-one OECD countries; for conciseness the text tables in this and the following section show averaged data for the OECD as a whole, the USA, Japan, a group of seven European "core" countries, and a group of five "corporatist" countries.[1] The data are shown for the "intershock" period 1974-9 as a whole, the eighties as a whole, and the final year of the period which is helpful to signal trends within the 1980s.

Inflation

Inflation was lower after 1979 (averaging 5.2 percent per annum) than before (8.8 percent per annum) and this was true in almost every country, with a rather similar fall in the USA, Japan, and Europe (table 2.2).

Inflation was lower in 1990 (4.4 percent) than during the eighties as a whole and this was true of most countries, with Europe showing the biggest fall (from the highest level). Double digit inflation persisted only in Greece and Portugal. The main factors behind the slowdown of inflation were the tight monetary and fiscal policies pursued, implying the reality or threat of higher unemployment. Weaker commodity prices,

Table 2.2. *Inflation:* GDP deflator (average annual percentage growth rates)

	1973–9	1979–90	1990
USA	8.8	5.2	4.4
Europe core	9.7	5.7	3.8
Corporatists	9.5	6.5	4.5
USA	8.0	4.6	4.1
Japan	8.1	1.9	2.1

Source: Appendix table 1A.

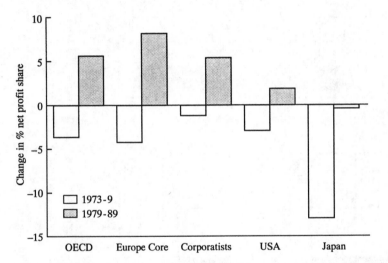

Figure 2.1   Manufacturing profit shares, 1973–89
Source: Appendix table 1A.

especially oil after 1986, played a modest role (Gilbert, 1990; Coe *et al.*, 1988) and in any case partly reflected the tight policies pursued by the OECD countries.

Profits

Fifteen out of seventeen countries saw a decline in the profit share in the sensitive and important manufacturing sector between the years 1973 and 1979 (figure 2.1). Between 1979 and 1987 the profit share expanded everywhere but Japan.

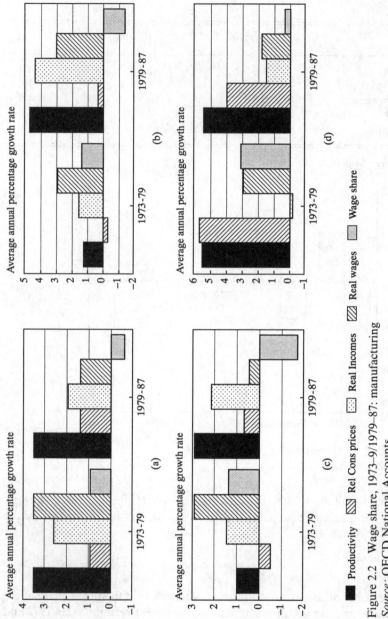

Figure 2.2 Wage share, 1973–9/1979–87: manufacturing
Source: OECD National Accounts.
(a) OECD (b) UK (c) Sweden (d) Japan

■ Productivity ▨ Rel Cons prices ▨ Real Incomes ▨ Real wages ▨ Wage share

The profit recovery was strongest in Europe (the UK, Netherlands, Belgium, and Sweden all recording increases of some 10 percentage points, together with Australia), and this more than reversed the squeeze of the intershock period, making up also for some of the decline at the end of the golden age. The profit share may increase either because productivity growth accelerates or because real wage growth slows down.[2] Figure 2.2 shows that for the OECD as a whole the dominant factor in the decrease of the wage share (increase of the profit share) was the slowdown in the (pre-tax) real wage growth; Sweden exemplifies this pattern. The UK was exceptional in that a very strong profit recovery occurred despite a steady growth of real wages, the source of higher profits being the Thatcher "productivity miracle" (see Glyn, 1992b). Overwhelmingly, however, it was "wage moderation" which funded the reversal of the profit squeeze, though under very different circumstances in different countries – unemployment averaging around 2.5 percent in Sweden and 10 percent in the Netherlands.

Despite very similar growth rates of real wages to that in Europe, and a faster growth of productivity, the profit share in Japanese manufacturing did not recover. The explanation was the continued rapid rise in the relative price of consumer goods in Japan (see figure 2.2). This meant that even a modestly growing real wage required a constant share of manufacturing value added going to workers if they were to afford the rapidly rising relative prices of consumer goods, such as food and housing, supplied from outside the manufacturing sector. The slow growth of real wages occurred despite a tight labor market. There was a slightly slower growth rate of the working age population than in the 1960s and the reserves of labor which could be drawn out of agriculture were much diminished. Even an increase in women's participation in paid work did not prevent the ratio of job offers to vacancies exceeding unity in 1989 for the first time since 1974.

Budget deficits

The budget story (table 2.3) is a little more complicated than for inflation and profits. Most governments incurred bigger deficits in the 1980s (averaging 3.3 percent of GDP) than in the intershock period (2.5 percent) – the upward trend in deficits continued well into the 1980s (the UK and Germany were notable exceptions). The later 1980s saw a rather general reversal of the rising trend in budget deficits; by 1990 the average deficit was down to 1.6 percent of GDP with spectacular reductions in a number of countries (Ireland, Sweden, Denmark, Japan, and the UK). Average

Table 2.3. *Budget balances* (general government, % GDP)

	1974–9	1980–90	1990
OECD	− 2.5	− 3.3	− 1.6
Europe core	− 4.2	− 5.0	− 3.6
Corporatist	0.2	− 0.3	1.8
USA	− 1.4	− 3.5	− 4.1
Japan	− 3.4	− 1.1	3.0

Source: See appendix table 1A.

ratios of public debt to GDP peaked in 1987 and were falling sharply in some countries (the UK, Australia, Sweden, and Japan). But a number of others had stubbornly large deficits (Italy, Belgium, Netherlands, and Greece) throughout the 1980s, with public debt in Italy reaching, and in Belgium easily exceeding, GDP.

Strikes

In Japan, the USA, and the European core countries the 1980s brought fewer strikes than the intershock period, and in each case strike incidence was less at the end of the 1980s than during the period as a whole (figure 2.3). In Italy and the UK, the two most strike prone countries in Europe in the intershock period, strike rates in 1990 were around one quarter of those for the period 1973–9; and the same broad pattern held in Canada and Australia which also had very high strike rates in the intershock period. The corporatist countries represent one partial exception in that both Finland (the most strike prone of them) and Sweden (whose figures are dominated by a few major disputes) experienced more days occupied in strikes in the 1980s than in the 1970s (though still few in absolute terms). Of the peripheral European countries both Spain and Greece suffered extensive strike waves at the end of the 1980s and this bumps up the (unweighted) OECD average.

Conclusions

With due allowance for individual exceptions (especially the southern European countries) the overall patterns are rather consistent across the USA, Japan, the European core, and the corporatist countries. The conflict which had previously been manifested in high inflation, profit squeezes, budget deficits, and strikes was widely moderated in the 1980s

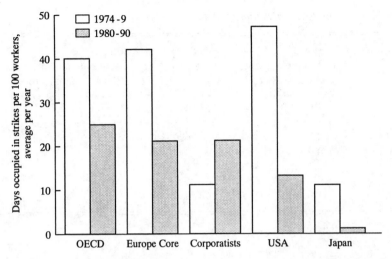

Figure 2.3   Strikes, 1973–90
Source: See appendix table 1A.

as inflation declined, profits recovered, the government's finances stabilized, and strikes were at low levels. Moreover this stabilization was not
simply a cyclical phenomenon; the faster growth at the end of the 1980s
did not bring a rapid increase in inflation, more strikes, or renewed profit
squeezes. If restoration of these dimensions of domestic economic stability was the key task of the change in policy regime, being seen as a
precondition for improved economic performance, then the provisional
verdict must be one of considerable success. The next section looks at the
trend away from egalitarianism in the 1980s, partly as a by-product of
restoring domestic stability, but also as a deliberate policy for the
heightening of market incentives.

2   Inegalitarianism

Reducing domestic conflict does not necessarily have to take inegalitarian
forms. In principle inflation may be reduced at high employment levels
through acceptance by the trade union movement of the real wage trend,
made "feasible" by productivity and terms of trade movements, together
with the profit requirements for adequate investment. Even if an increase
in profitability is called for, the extent to which this leads to extra
consumption for higher income groups may be curtailed through dis-
couragement of dividend increases and the taxation of capital gains.
Budget deficits could be closed by an increase in taxation falling hardest

Table 2.4. *Unemployment, employment*

	Unemployment Average % rates			Employment % of population % per annum change	
	1974–9	1980–9	1990	1973–9	1979–88
OECD	4.2	7.4	6.8	− 0.1	− 0.1
Europe core	4.4	7.9	6.5	− 0.5	− 0.4
Corps	3.0	4.3	4.6	0.7	0.5
USA	6.7	7.2	5.4	0.9	0.7
Japan	1.9	2.5	2.1	0.1	0.2

Source: Appendix table 2A.

on top income groups. Strikes could be reduced if such policies were seen as the resolution, on labor's terms, of the conflict generated by slow growth. The alternative, inegalitarian pattern, would involve higher unemployment, together possibly with legislation to weaken trade unions, enforcing the unwinding of inflation whilst profitability was improved. Strikes, perhaps after a period of defensive conflicts, would fall despite lower real wage growth. Profit increases would be reflected in rapid increases in (lowly taxed) capital gains on shares, whilst consumption from unearned incomes was further boosted by high (real) interest rates. Budget deficits would be closed primarily by cuts in welfare spending with top income groups benefitting from tax cuts. It is the latter inegalitarian pattern of response which dominated the OECD in the 1980s, although with some strikingly different patterns in the corporatist countries. Following the pattern of section 1, summary tables of relevant indicators are provided in the text, extracted from the more or less comprehensive, country-by-country data given in Appendix tables 2A and 3A.

Unemployment and employment

The rise in unemployment was one of the most prominent features of the ACCs in the 1980s; whilst the basic function of such a rise is to weaken labor's bargaining position overall, unemployment has the additional inegalitarian consequence of unloading a disproportionate share of the costs of slower growth on to the minority who lose their jobs. During the 1980s the unemployment rate averaged 7.5 percent in the OECD, nearly half as much again as during the intershock period. Whilst the rise in unemployment was sharpest in Europe, only a handful of countries (Australia, Sweden, and the USA) ended the 1980s with a lower rate than in 1979; and in all these cases the average rate was higher in the 1980s than in the intershock period.

As argued elsewhere (Rowthorn and Glyn, 1990), unemployment is not a comprehensive measure of employment performance. In terms of the employment rate (non-agricultural employment as a percentage of the non-agricultural population of working age) the corporatist countries scored even more strongly in the 1980s than when unemployment is considered. Whilst North America and Australia also recorded strong increases in the employment rate, only the corporatist countries (other than Denmark) achieved both low unemployment and rapid employment growth. The European core countries continued to show quite marked declines in the employment rate.

Description of the availability of work must be complemented by analysis of the pattern of pay. The distribution of earnings for UK male manual workers has been remarkably constant since the 1880s; between 1979 and 1990 the ratio of earnings for a worker 10 percent below the bottom fell from 68 percent of the median to 64 percent, whereas for a worker 10 percent below the top the ratio increased from 148 percent to 159 percent (Gregg and Machin, 1993). Such trends occurred also for women workers, non-manual workers, and those outside manufacturing, and there were increased differentials between manual and non-manual workers. In the USA the trend toward greater earnings inequality started around the late 1960s (Levy and Murnane, 1992) and involved both greater demand for skilled workers and greater differentiation in earnings for those of given qualifications. Increases in earnings inequality in the 1980s appear to have been very general (see Davis, 1992), including Sweden where trade union policy had secured sharp reductions in inequality in the 1970s. Deliberate government policy to deregulate the labor market played a role in increasing wage dispersion; for example the weakening of the Wages Council system in the UK increased wage dispersion in low-paid industries, whilst the strongly binding minimum wage system in France appears to have contributed to much smaller increases in pay inequality there.

One aspect of wage dispersion for which there are systematic data, and which was the target of deliberate policy, is the female/male differential (figure 2.4). In the 1970s, eight countries showed substantial increases in the ratio of female to male hourly earnings in manufacturing (increases of around 10 percentage points in the UK, Sweden, Ireland, and Denmark); Japan was the only country to display a fall. In the 1980s, only Greece and Norway notched up significant increases (the latter from a high starting

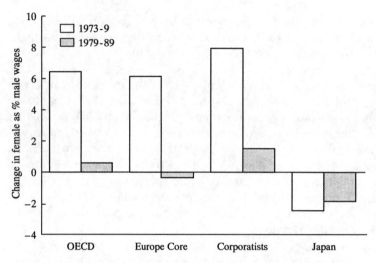

Figure 2.4   Female/male wage differentials
Source: See appendix table 1A.

point). Patchy data (OECD *Employment Outlook*, 1990) point also to a downward trend in skill differentials in the 1960s and/or 1970s, measured either as the ratio of non-manual to manual earnings (Japan, Australia, Italy) or of monthly salaries to weekly wages (Sweden, Finland, Denmark); these trends were generally halted in the 1980s and in some countries increases in differentials were pronounced (Germany, Italy, the UK, Norway).

Social expenditure and taxation

One of the strongest features of the 1970s was the rise in the share of government spending; in the 1980s the rise was very generally halted (figure 2.5). Although this is a broader category than welfare expenditure, it was the expansion of the welfare state, and then attempts to cap this expansion, which dominate the trends in total spending. The halt to the rise in government spending occurred even in the corporatist countries where the increase had been sharpest in the 1970s.

Marked cuts (1 percent of GDP or more) in the share of social expenditure are confirmed for the UK, Germany, and Netherlands between 1979 and 1989; large reductions in total government spending suggest that substantial cuts in the more limited category of social expenditure also occurred in Belgium, probably Australia, Sweden, and New Zealand.[3] Other countries (including France, Italy, Norway, Finland,

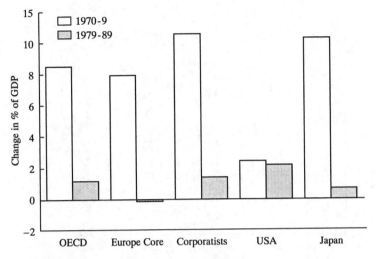

Figure 2.5   Government expenditure, 1970–89
Note: Excludes debt interest.
Source: See appendix table 2A.

Greece, and Spain) showed continuing strong increases in government expenditure over the 1980s, though the trend usually flattened out in the later part of the period. Whilst the uniformity of strong upward trends in social expenditure disappeared in the 1980s, the group which seems to have definitely reversed the pattern is a mixed one, containing both Northern European countries with very high initial shares of social expenditure, together with the UK, Australia, and New Zealand with low initial shares.

Cuts in the top rate of income tax occurred in every country except Switzerland, and averaged 17 percent for the OECD. The UK and the USA led the way with cuts of 40 percent, in both countries the overall effective degree of progressiveness of the direct tax system was already very meagre (Appendix table 3A).

Wealth and poverty

Reduced taxation of high incomes must have contributed to the increased share of the highest income group (20 percent of the population) which occurred in seven out of eight countries; again the rise was greatest in the UK. Income data exclude capital gains. Figure 2.6 provides a measure of capital gains on shares; the ratio of equity prices to workers' earnings is a simple indicator of the importance of capital gains in relation to earned income.

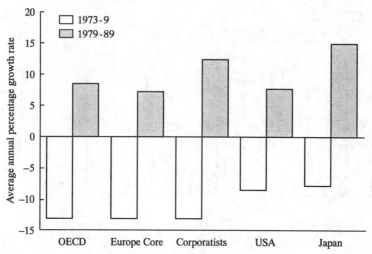

Figure 2.6   Share prices relative to wages
Source: See appendix table 2A.

Every OECD country showed a rise in this indicator over the period 1979–89; the average rise being more than 8 percent per year (implying real share prices rose some four times as fast as real earnings). This reversed the even faster downward trend in this indicator between 1973 and 1979. Rises in stockmarket prices after 1979 were strikingly higher in Japan and in the corporatist countries (particularly Sweden and Finland) than in the rest of Europe and the USA.[4] As well as indicating gains for property relative to labor such rises in share prices are suggestive of the degree of confidence, within capital markets at least, as to the durability and dynamism of economic stabilization and recovery.

Finally there were quite marked increases in poverty in five out of eleven EEC countries, for which the EEC assembled data, and also in the USA; Ireland showed the biggest rise with the UK having the greatest increase of the higher-income countries (see Appendix table 3A). While numbers in poverty in both the USA and UK used to be closely tied to macroeconomic conditions (real income growth and unemployment), in the 1980s these historical relationships broke down and poverty rose much more than could be accounted for by overall economic conditions (Cutler and Katz, 1991; Gregg and Machin, 1993).

Conclusions

The various dimensions of distribution considered here, despite data which are frequently patchy in concept and coverage, point generally in the direction of increased inequality in the 1980s. Data for the overall distribution of household income (which should reflect earnings inequality, employment opportunities, unearned income, taxes, and benefits) show large increases in inequality in the UK and the USA and a very general trend for inequality to decline less rapidly (as in some corporatist countries), or rise more rapidly, than in the 1970s (Atkinson, 1993). The trends discussed earlier for capital gains and for government expenditure on welfare programs reinforce this conclusion.

The employment picture is the most complicated; as argued in detail elsewhere (Glyn, 1992a) the maintenance of relatively high employment in the context of slower growth after 1973 could be achieved in a number of ways. At one extreme, the "market" solution of low real wage is increases and expanded job opportunities in the market sector. At the other, more interventionist end, subsidies to preserve jobs in the market sector are combined with heavy taxation accepted by workers to finance expansion of public-sector jobs. The former, to which the USA approximates, represents a rough and ready egalitarianism, or spreading of the misery, which is the rougher the more pronounced are earnings differentials (as in the more *laissez-faire* systems, see Rowthorn, 1992). The latter is the conscious, social-democratic egalitarianism exemplified by Sweden in the 1970s and early 1980s, but generally somewhat reined in during the later 1980s as limits to the compression of take-home pay were reached. The most inegalitarian outcomes in terms of employment took place in the European core (and peripherals) where neither market pressures nor collective discipline sufficed to prevent unemployment rising sharply.

Cuts in expenditure on social welfare, reductions in the progressiveness of the tax system, increased weight of unearned income and capital gains in the 1980s represented a reversal of the egalitarian trend, even in those countries where commitment to full employment was consciously preserved. Obviously such reversals were from a range of starting points, so that for example the cut in government spending in Sweden still left it amongst the largest spenders on social welfare. Moreover many of the gains made during the "golden age" were only nibbled at rather than comprehensively reversed. Thus expenditure on social welfare at the end of the 1980s was frequently double the share of GDP at the beginning of the 1960s, and in no country much under 150 percent of that starting point; similarly the extent to which women's pay was below men's was generally much less at the end of the 1980s than in the 1960s, even in those countries where the 1980s saw some reversal of the trend toward reduced differentials. With this proviso there can be no dispute that a central feature of the 1980s was a general reversal of the long-term trend toward greater equality.

3   Financial instability

The effect of the free play of market forces was felt most dramatically in the financial sector. A post mortem conducted by the Bank for International Settlements put the "major expansion of credit during the decade" down to

a relaxation of credit constraints in the financial industry in the wake of both market-driven and policy-determined structural changes. The end result of those changes was greatly to increase competitive pressures in the industry and to broaden the range of borrowing opportunities . . . market forces were primarily responsible for the increased competition between banks and securities firms in the United States which fuelled the debt-financed takeover wave . . . By contrast, deregulation was especially broad in Sweden, Norway and Finland, which moved from a system where credit was rationed to one of open competition, all in the space of a few years in the mid-1980s. A similar process took place in Australia in the early 1980s. Deregulation was also extensive in the United Kingdom, where (direct and indirect) restrictions on credit were abolished and greater competition between banks and building societies was encouraged . . . In Japan deregulation has been more gradual, but as from the mid-1980s restrictions on corporations' access to international markets were relaxed and deposit rates freed, while less regulated non-bank credit institutions thrived. (BIS, 1993, pp. 165–7)

Deregulation was supposed to increase the competitiveness of financial markets and thus improve resource allocation. But the most important effect was vastly inflated asset prices; in Sweden and Finland real asset prices (commercial and residential property and shares) on average trebled in the 1980s; in Japan residential, commercial property, and equities rose in real terms by 74 percent, 86 percent, and 166 percent in the second half of the 1980s (BIS, 1993, p. 161). Between the peak and around the end of 1992 real asset prices fell 50 percent in Finland, 36 percent in Japan, 31 percent in Sweden, and 10–15 percent elsewhere (with the exception of Germany where, according to the BIS, the financial system underwent little structural change and there were no major fluctuations in asset prices). In the international sphere the abolition of exchange controls, and a retreat from official intervention in exchange markets, increased the volatility of major currencies. This made returns from real investments dependent on export revenues less secure.

Consumer debt

Easier access to credit and limited growth of real incomes encouraged rapid increases in consumer borrowing. Between 1979/80 and the late 1980s, the household savings ratio fell by 7 percentage points or more in

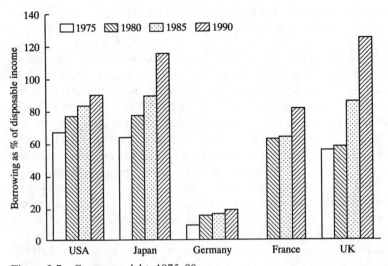

Figure 2.7   Consumer debt, 1975–90
Source: OECD, *Economic Outlook*, 1988, 1993.

Norway, Italy, Sweden, the UK, France, and Finland; this implied consumer expenditure rising around 1 percent per year faster than household income. Only Japan and Germany, together with its immediate neighbors in the "Deutsche-Mark Zone," more or less maintained savings ratios. The rise in borrowing to finance this consumption, together with increases in mortgage debt, led to very rapid increases in total household debts. By 1990 they frequently approached, or exceeded in the case of the UK, 100 percent of disposable incomes (figure 2.7). Only Germany and Italy of the G7 countries remained immune from this surge in personal borrowing.

Combined with high real interest rates (from 1982 onwards these consistently stayed within the range of 2–7 percent in most ACCs) additional borrowing increased debt service burdens. In the UK the share of household disposable income paid as debt interest doubled from 4.1 percent in 1978 to 8.6 percent in 1989. Many borrowers were unable to meet these commitments and repossession of houses reached record levels.

Corporate borrowing and the financial sector

Since capital accumulation declined alongside the fall in profitability, corporations could continue financing a high proportion of their investments from internal funds, and during the 1980s as a whole borrowing was less than in the 1970s. At the end of the 1980s, however, the investment recovery led to sharply increased borrowing by both Japanese and UK corporations (some 10 percent and 4 percent respectively of GDP in 1989–90).

In Japan, Germany, and France the proportion of companies income paid out in the form of interest payments was similar at the end of the 1980s to 1979; US corporations, however, paid out much more in interest (31 percent of gross profits in 1988 as compared to 24 percent in 1979). Encouraged by the tax concessions for debt interest the development of the "junk bonds" market in high risk, high yielding fixed interest securities enabled US companies to substitute fixed interest borrowing for funds previously supplied by shareholders. When the market collapsed in early 1990, it left many companies in a situation where a sharp downturn in their profits would leave them unable to meet their interest payments, making bankruptcy likely. UK firms, as well, suffered at the end of the decade from very high interest rates.

A careful assessment of the corporate financing position in the USA raised the following possible scenario:

Bankruptcies or financial distress amongst some major firms could contribute to a liquidity crisis in several ways. Perhaps most important would be the effect of such news on . . . fragile confidence . . . More directly the legal proceedings initiated by bankruptcy would freeze the liabilities of the failing firms, converting assets that the firms' creditors may have previously considered to be fairly liquid into illiquid assets and worsening the illiquidity problem of the creditors. Similarly, major bankruptcies might contribute to cash-flow problems of the firms' suppliers and customers. As the liquidity crisis of the 1930s seriously disrupted the ability of the banks to function, a corporate liquidity crisis could disrupt the production and investment activities of firms. In such a situation, the liquidity of nonfinancial firms and banks would be closely intertwined . . . (Bernanke and Campbell, 1988, p. 96)

The fragility of US corporate financing was compounded by a potentially more menacing situation in the financial sector itself. The US Savings and Loans Institutions (the "Thrifts") incurred enormous losses as a result of speculative investments permitted by financial deregulation. The analysis of the cost of resolving the "Thrift Crisis" also concluded gloomily that "the problems among thrifts have obscured from public view a taxpayer obligation for failed banks that in other times would be highly unsettling" (Brumbaugh et al., 1988, p. 283). The authors explain that "given the large number and asset size of weak banks, the extent to which . . . accounting techniques hide market value losses, it is possible that losses in the commercial banking industry could eclipse those in the thrift industry" (ibid., p. 250). These losses, stemming from agriculture, real estate, and the oil industry within the USA, and from lending to the

LDCs, reduced the capital of many major banks to a perilously low level. Total support for the banks and thrifts (generally allowing them to restructure or merge) averaged 1.3 percent of GDP in the USA for the five years 1988–92, with the government providing half the funds accounting for over one fifth of the US budget deficit. In Norway, Sweden and Finland bank support operations were costing some 2 percent of GDP in the early 1990s. In Japan non-performing loans represented 40 percent of banks' first tier capital (BIS, 1993, pp. 170–4).

International finance

The collapse of the fixed exchange rate system in 1973 did not have the disastrous consequences for international trade sometimes predicted. Exchange rates between the major currencies have fluctuated considerably on a day-to-day basis, despite government intervention to smooth out "disorderly" markets, but studies suggest that this has had little effect on the volume of overseas trade. Much more serious have been the trends in exchange rates from year to year. Floating rates "should" balance out inflation rate differences, preserving real competitiveness. But in the 1980s financial flows came to dominate foreign exchange markets rather than trade flows; of an estimated $420 billion crossing the world's foreign exchanges each day in 1987, more than 90 percent represented financial transactions unrelated to trade. As funds moved into dollars, attracted by high US interest rates, a soaring dollar pushed unit costs in the US up by 38 percent relative to those of its competitors between 1980 and 1985. The US merchandise deficit, which had averaged $21 billion per year during the years 1975–81 leapt to an average of $133 billion per year during the period 1984–8. Sterling's rise, 46 percent between 1978 and 1980, was even greater.

Like all speculative surges, the rise of the dollar had to come to an end. The bubble burst in mid 1985 and two years later it had fallen by 30 percent. In February 1987 the Group of Seven agreed, under the Louvre Accord, to defend the dollar at around the current rate, and then spent, according to the IMF, upwards of $150 billion doing so. But the period since the Louvre Accord has been far from successful in terms of stabilizing effective exchange rates. There continued to be substantial fluctuations in the real values of the US dollar, yen, and pound. Only the mark and franc maintained some zone of stability, linked to one another inside the European monetary system and appearing as a centre of gravity around which the other major currencies fluctuated.

The deep disruption caused by the huge exchange rate swings of the 1980s put the supporters of financial deregulation on the defensive. The

Bank for International Settlements noted in response to criticism of destabilizing financial flows:

short-term capital flows, including transactions in long-term assets for short-term speculative purposes, may at times have a strong destabilising impact on the exchange market. Moreover, it is certainly true that, as a result of the increasing global integration of national markets, these destabilising capital flows can assume vast proportions. The fragility of the US financial system in the face of this kind of interest rate increases that could be necessary to stave off a dollar collapse, this threat to the dollar represented a major source of instability, however, is not new controls and impediments which would also curtail the stabilising capital flows and exchange rate transactions, but more stable national economic policies and their better international co-ordination. (BIS, 1988, p. 178)

The bank noted that the continued US deficit implied that "the cumulative amount of position-taking in favour of the dollar necessary to finance this deficit will be very large. Even marginal attempts to reduce these huge open positions [holdings] in dollars could entail major exchange market pressures" (ibid., p. 179).

Conclusions

The financial system of the ACCs, both its domestic patterns and its international linkages, present a strikingly less reassuring picture than do the indicators of the intensity of conflict over distribution reviewed in section 1. The basis for renewed capital accumulation which seemed to have been indicated by reduced inflation and restored profits, and was reflected in increasing inequality, coexisted with severe financial strains. The overall impact on the scale, pattern, and effects of capital accumulation form the subject of the next section of this chapter.

4   Capital accumulation

Business investment

Business investment collapsed during 1974–5 and its recovery during the rest of the intershock period was modest by golden age standards. The growth rate of the business capital stock slid down from 5.4 percent per annum during 1973 to 4.4 percent per annum during 1979; the decline was greatest in Japan and least in the USA (see table 2.5). Manufacturing suffered from an even sharper decline, especially in Europe where the growth rate of the capital stock halved between 1973 and 1979 to 2 percent per annum.

The three years of very slow growth after 1979 saw fixed investment

Table 2.5. *The accumulation rate, 1960–89:* average annual percentage growth rates of capital stock

	1960–73	1973–9	1979–89	1979	1983	1989
Business						
USA	3.7	3.7	3.5	4.3	2.8	3.5
Europe	5.2	3.8	2.9	3.6	2.6	3.4
Japan	12.4	6.6	7.3	6.6	6.5	9.4
ACC	5.0	4.1	3.9	4.4	3.2	4.6
Manufacturing						
USA	4.0	3.9	2.3	4.1	1.3	2.1
Europe	5.1	2.4	1.3	2.1	0.8	2.0
Japan	12.4	5.4	6.3	4.9	5.4	7.6
ACC	5.5	3.6	2.9	3.5	1.9	3.2

Source: Armstrong *et al.* (1991), tables A5, A6.

stagnate. By 1983 the growth rate of the business capital stock had sunk to 3.2 percent per annum and manufacturing to 1.9 percent. In Europe the manufacturing capital stock was growing by less than 1 percent per annum. There was a strong increase in investment after 1982, but the much vaunted "investment boom" lagged behind the average growth of investment during both recessions and recoveries in the 1960s. Nevertheless coming after a decade of weak investment, the recovery pushed up the growth rate of the capital stock. For the ACCs as a whole the rate of accumulation in business recovered to 4.6 percent per annum in 1989 and to 3.2 percent in manufacturing. For business the rate of accumulation was still around one fifth (Japan) to one third (Europe), below the 1973 rate; in manufacturing the shortfall was larger (one quarter for Japan to one half for Europe).

Whilst the decline in accumulation up to the early 1980s broadly follows the decline in profitability, the subsequent pattern of recovery does not. In Japan where the rate of profit fell the most after 1973 and recovered the least, the rate of accumulation has recovered the most and by the end of the 1980s was not very far below the 1973 rate.[5] In Europe where the years of stagnation and mass unemployment by and large restored profitability, the recovery of accumulation has been very tentative. The USA saw less pronounced trends in profits and investment.

Part of the explanation for buoyant Japanese investment probably lies in the fact that, despite its sharp fall, the profit rate in Japan appears to have still been higher than elsewhere (though conclusions must be tentative due to the difficulty of making comparisons of profitability across countries where methods of calculation differ). Since 1973 the average rate in business has been higher than in the other major countries with the most comparable estimates (16 percent in Japan as compared to 11 percent in Germany and the USA, and 6 percent in the UK). Moreover the profit rate has been much more stable in Japan than in most of the other countries, which is an important factor in maintaining capitalist confidence.[6]

The lack of relation between profit recovery and investment response in the 1980s is confirmed by data for other countries. Japan is by no means the only "perverse" case; Canada and Norway secured rapid increases in investment without profit recoveries, whereas a sharp profit increase in UK manufacturing failed to secure an investment boom. There is no consistent pattern across countries between the profit recovery in the 1980s and the growth of manufacturing investment.[7] The more sophisticated analysis in Armstrong et al. (1991) confirms that profitability is but one influence on investment amongst others and suggests that increasing profitability is neither necessary nor sufficient to secure an increase in investment.

It seems probable that the particular weakness of manufacturing investment, the sector where international competition was extremely strong and increasing in the 1980s, owes something to the financial instability discussed earlier. Substantial year-to-year swings in effective exchange rates have rendered returns from manufacturing more uncertain as compared to sectors more protected from competition. It also increased the attractiveness of direct investment to service markets overseas rather than in exports; such inward direct investment grew twice as fast as imports into OECD countries during the 1980s, and especially fast in the USA whose exchange rate fluctuated spectacularly.

In a number of countries the period since 1979 has seen a strong twist in the pattern of investment away from manufacturing toward distribution and the financial sectors. In the UK, between 1979 and 1989 investment in industry and agriculture stagnated, that in distribution rose by two thirds, and that in finance more than trebled. In the USA investment seems to have been even more twisted away from manufacturing and toward distribution and finance (figure 2.8). In France, Germany, and Scandinavia there was much less bias against manufacturing (though amongst the Scandinavian countries Sweden's investment in finance and distribution grew twice as fast (96 percent) as in manufacturing (46 percent)).[8]

In addition to business investment three other categories of expenditure which are relevant to long-run growth potential should also be considered – government infrastructure investment, education spending, and expendi-

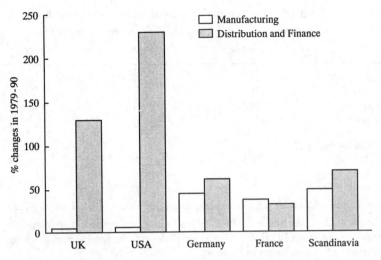

Figure 2.8   Sector investment
Source: OECD National Accounts, Germany, data for 1979–90.

ture on research and development (R and D). Government investment (which is a broader category than infrastructure investment as it includes housing, hospitals, and so forth) fell in the OECD from an average of 3.4 percent of GDP in 1979 to 2.8 percent in 1989. In many countries (UK, Germany, Sweden, Belgium, Denmark, Australia, and New Zealand) the cut was by more than one third and most probably included a severe decline in infrastructural investment.

Education spending fared rather better than infrastructure; out of eleven countries with data (including the USA and the UK) the Netherlands was the only one to report a substantial decline in the share of education spending in GDP. With demographic factors generally favorable, real spending per student rose by some 1.1 percent per annum on average in the OECD countries, though this was down from 1.8 per annum in the second half of the 1970s. Country experience was very diverse: in the USA spending per student accelerated from 0.6 percent per annum to 4.2 percent per annum; in the UK it continued to decline at about 2 percent per annum; whilst in Japan and Sweden it fell after 1980, having risen more than 4 percent per annum in the later 1970s. R and D spending is one of the few features of the 1980s which might suggest improved future growth. Real R and D spending rose on average at 5.6 percent per annum in the period 1980–5 compared to 3.9 percent per annum, during the 1970s; Germany and the UK were notable exceptions with slowdowns in R and D growth.[9]

Table 2.6. *Productivity growth* (average annual percentage growth rates)

	USA	Japan	Europe
Business			
1960–73	2.2	8.6	4.8
1973–9	0.0	2.9	2.6
1979–90	0.5	3.0	2.2
Manufacturing (hourly)			
1960–73	3.3	10.2	6.0
1973–9	1.2	4.5	4.0
1979–90	2.6	4.8	3.0

Note: US manufacturing figure for 1979–90 is a new series apparently giving much slower growth than the old one (3.6% p.a. for 1979–89). Europe is an unweighted average of growth rates for nine countries.
Sources: OECD, *Economic Outlook*, June 1992, table 48; BLS, *Monthly Labour Review*, April 1993, December 1992, table 50.

Investment and productivity growth

A slowing down of the pace of investment not only represents slower growing demand, but also hampers productivity growth. On average the much slower productivity growth of the intershock period was no more than maintained, and in Europe generally productivity growth declined (table 2.6).

The decline in productivity growth as compared to the golden age was particularly large in Japan (5–6 percent per annum slowdown in both business and manufacturing) and rather less elsewhere (1.5–3 percent per annum in Europe and in US business). The usual pattern (see Armstrong *et al.*, 1991, chart 14.3) was for productivity growth to slow down as much as, and usually rather more than, the growth of fixed capital per worker. So whilst the general factor behind the productivity slowdown was the decline in accumulation, even the investment which did take place yielded smaller productivity gains.[10]

Marked accelerations in productivity growth in manufacturing in the 1980s were confined to a very few countries – the UK and the USA, where manufacturing investment was stagnant, and probably Finland, where it was more buoyant. In these cases productivity recovered from intershock stagnation and approached golden age, pre-1973, rates of growth. For the business sector as a whole it appears that only in New Zealand did productivity growth show a sharp increase in the 1980s (but from − 1.2 to

1.8 percent per annum) and only there was it within 1 percentage point of the pre-1973 growth rate. Productivity growth in services was generally slower in the 1980s than the 1970s, let alone the 1960s. The twist in investment toward the service sector noted for a number of countries does not seem to have yielded considerable productivity gains. In particular, a recent OECD study (Englander and Mittelstadt, 1988) noted the failure of productivity growth to recover in the "information-intensive" service industries – retail and wholesale trade, transport and communication, finance and business services – citing misinvestment and time for staff to be trained to use the technologies as possible explanations.

The most spectacular case of productivity recovery was represented by UK manufacturing where hourly productivity growth accelerated from 1.1 percent per annum during 1973–9 to 4.2 percent per annum for 1979–89. The fact that this reflected rationalization rather than modernization is indicated by the very weak manufacturing investment noted above. Careful examination (Oulton, 1990) suggests that the "shock effect" of the very severe manufacturing recession in the UK (output fell by 14 percent between 1979 and 1981) was the major factor behind the productivity recovery. The largest and most unionized plants bore a disproportionate share of the closures and showed the biggest increase in productivity. Firms shed the excess labor which was the legacy of the intershock period when slow growth was combined with union and government pressures toward job maintenance. The most dramatic examples of rationalization took place in nationalized industries, steel, and coal, after long and bitter strikes. In the UK coal industry productivity more than doubled after the 1984–5 miners' strike; by 1989 employment was one third of the level seven years before as "uneconomic" pits were closed and productivity driven up in the rest. In the private sector the pattern of confrontation with the labor force and subsequent rationalization was less dramatic. Even if more "cooperative" attitudes from workers and unions persisted in the UK, it is unlikely that rapid productivity growth could have been maintained without a much higher level of industrial investment than was forthcoming, even before the recession which began in 1990.

Productivity growth which derived from rationalization, with output stagnant and employment falling, had a strongly inegalitarian impact in the UK. The main sufferers were those who lost their jobs, and remained unemployed or took worse paid jobs. Workers in UK manufacturing who kept their jobs achieved real wage increases of nearly one quarter in the decade after 1979; but the total real wage bill stagnated, real profits grew much faster than wages, and dividends grew faster than profits. By 1989

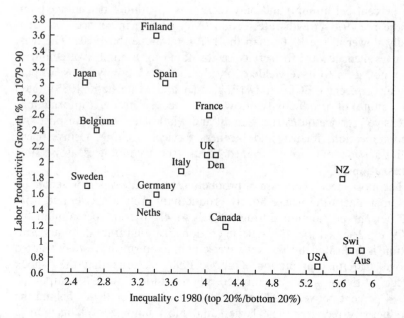

Figure 2.9   Inequality and productivity, 1979–90
Source: OECD, Economic Outlook, World Development Report.

real dividends were 56 percent higher in UK manufacturing than in 1979, whereas the total real wage bill was nearly 10 percent lower (Glyn, 1992b). Far from providing the incentives for higher productive investment (and thus long-term expansion of output and jobs) this redistribution from labor was squandered in consumption from capital gains and in speculative overinvestments in some service sectors.

There is the general belief that increasing inequality is justified in order to secure a faster rate of growth. However the prestigious *World Development Report 1991*, put out by the World Bank often criticized for paying insufficient attention to inequality, noted that "there is no evidence that saving is positively related to income inequality or that income inequality leads to higher growth. If anything, it seems that inequality is associated with slower growth" (p. 137). This conclusion is confirmed by more elaborate statistical testing (see Alesina and Rodrick, 1992). Whilst the World Bank's figures refer mainly to developing countries, the same relationship holds also for the ACCs (see figure 2.9). The economies with the most unequal income distribution at the beginning of the 1980s, like the USA and Switzerland, showed far slower productivity growth in business during the subsequent decade than did countries like Japan,

Belgium, and Sweden where incomes are apparently most evenly distributed.[11] Whilst some policies simultaneously worsen income distribution and raise growth of productivity in a restricted sector of the economy (as the example of UK manufacturing discussed earlier shows), the general case for increasing inequality to raise growth receives no empirical support. Yet the return of stagnation in the early 1990s saw a redoubling of the demands from the IMF and other international organizations for the inegalitarian policies of the 1980s as the final section will show.

5   Into the 1990s

The expansion of the later 1980s was rather moderate. Only in 1984 and 1988 did OECD growth exceed 4 percent, and in neither of these peak years did it reach the *average* growth rate of 1960–73. Growth slowed to 0.7 percent in 1991 and to 1.5 percent in 1992 as the USA recovered, but was expected to slip again in 1993 as the German economy (including the East) declined by some 2 percent. The sharpest decline was in Finland where GDP fell by 10 percent between 1990 and 1992 as markets in the ex-USSR collapsed; the most protracted decline was in Sweden where GDP fell by around 2 percent per annum for 1991, 1992, and 1993 as a particularly extravagant credit boom collapsed. With unemployment in 1994 anticipated at 17 percent in Finland and more than 7 percent in Sweden, the superior employment performance of the corporatist countries appeared liable to disintegrate.

Much attention has been devoted to falling consumption, as households increased their savings rates in order to repay debts. Sweden and the UK were the most extreme cases, with the proportion of disposable income being consumed falling by 9 percent in two years in Sweden (OECD, *Economic Outlook*, June 1992, table 35). Business investment played a very important role in the slowdown, falling by 7 percent in the USA in 1991 (the biggest fall since 1975), and by 9 percent in the UK (the biggest post-war fall). Even Japan, where investment had grown very fast in the later 1980s (see section 4), saw reduced business investment in 1992 and 1993 (the first falls since 1975) and Germany's reunification investment boom of 1989–91 (the strongest since the 1960s) subsided, with the fall in investment in 1993 expected to be the largest since 1974.

One contributory factor to the investment slowdown was that the easy credit conditions of the later 1980s were reversed as banks restricted their lending in order to restore their balance sheets and make good mounting bad debts. The OECD noted that: "Structural problems have been less pronounced in European credit markets than in those of the USA and Japan. Nevertheless debt burdens did reach dangerous levels in the UK . . . In some Nordic countries, banks suffered serious asset quality deterioration" (OECD, *Economic Outlook*, June 1992, p. 17).

The OECD and IMF redoubled efforts toward fiscal consolidation and market deregulation. Reflecting the rise in government deficits as growth slowed and as (in Sweden and the UK for example) tax rates were cut,[12] the OECD called for reduced public borrowing in order not to crowd out private investment once the OECD economies picked up; the IMF believed that tighter budgets (preferably by cutting government expenditure rather than increasing taxation) soon lead to higher output and employment "as both supply and demand increase in response to increased efficiency, productivity and income growth" (1992, p. 16).

Both organizations argued, in practically identical terms, for more labor-market deregulation; for example the OECD said that "high costs of hiring and firing, minimum wage requirements and wage bargaining systems unsuited to local market conditions seem – in spite of sporadic reforms – to be obstacles to prompt labour market adjustments and thus to the creation of jobs" (OECD, *Economic Outlook*, June 1992, p. xi).

Conclusions

This chapter has documented the important stabilization of domestic conflict in the ACCs in the 1980s, as witnessed by the decline in inflation rates, budget deficits, strike levels, and a rather widespread restoration of profitability of the 1980s (section 1). Furthermore the earlier trend toward egalitarianism was moderated or reversed in most countries (section 2). In the European core countries the availability of employment declined; the reduction in inequality of earnings, especially of women's pay, was generally halted or reversed as was the upward trend of spending on the welfare state, the progressiveness of the tax system was reduced, there were very large capital gains from shares and poverty tended to rise. The central planks of orthodox, financial and social discipline combined with greater incentives, notably failed to lay the basis for a durable expansion at the end of the 1980s.

The investment recovery which took place in the 1980s left rates of accumulation, especially in Europe, well below those achieved in the golden age. Manufacturing investment has been particularly weak and generally unresponsive to the recovery of profitability. A number of countries saw an important twisting of the pattern of investment toward distribution and finance, sectors particularly linked to domestic consumption booms and relatively insulated from increasingly intense and, with seesawing exchange rates, decreasingly predictable international competition. Productivity growth was generally weak in manufacturing, with the notable exception of the UK and a few others, where fierce rationalization was successfully carried through, but with strongly inegalitarian consequences. In services, where much investment was concentrated, productivity growth was very slow (section 4). The expansion of the later 1980s was propped up and distorted by an unsustainable credit expansion (section 3). Unwinding the resulting patterns of financial fragility, especially in the USA, Japan, the UK, and Scandinavia, is acting as a continuing deflationary impetus, with unemployment set to rise in the mid 1990s above its 1980s peak.

The fundamental question posed by the analysis in this chapter is why did the process of domestic stabilization fail to lay the basis of a more sustained and durable recovery? Two factors seem particularly important. Increased power of labor brought about by the golden age boom was an essential component of the increasing problems in the ACCs for nearly twenty years after the mid 1960s (see Armstrong *et al.*, 1991). Even though the labor movement has been very severely weakened in the 1980s, it still remains an important force, especially in Germany which plays such a central role in Europe. A longer and deeper process of stabilization, involving further radical weakening of trade unions, may be necessary before employers would be confident that strong growth and high employment could be sustained without a return of wage pressure, rising inflation, and profit squeezes. Until this stalemate is resolved the fundamental thrust of government policies is likely to remain cautious and hesitant. Secondly, international economic relations, only alluded to in this chapter, have become increasingly unstable. Fluctuations in exchange rates have repeatedly thrown into disorder the relative competitiveness of producers within the ACCs. Emerging competition from producers in the far east, especially China, and prospectively from Eastern Europe, have added an extra dimension to the unpredictability of future market trends. With investment in the traded-goods sector held back by all these uncertainties, the limitations of finance and commerce as engines of growth were revealed in the collapse of the 1980s upswing.

The liberal policies of the 1980s were aimed above all at domestic stabilization. Despite some successes they have clearly failed to put in place a convincing system for regulating conflict within and between individual countries.

Appendix   See pages 46 to 51 inclusive.

Table 1A. Indicators of conflict, 1973–90

	Inflation Average annual rates %			Profit shares Manufacturing change in % points		Strikes Days occupied per 100 workers annual averages			Budget balances General govt. % GDP annual averages		
	1973–9	1979–89	1990	1973–9	1979–89	1974–9	1980–90	1990	1974–79	1980–90	1990
OECD	8.8	5.2	4.4	−3.7	5.6	40	25	13	2.5	−3.3	1.6
Euro core (Ger., Fra., It., UK., Bel., Neth., Switz.)	9.7	5.6	4.6	−4.3	8.1	42	22	10	4.2	−5.4	−4.3
Corps. (Swe., Fin., Nor., Den., Aus.)	9.5	6.4	4.7	−1.3	5.4	11	21	14	0.8	−0.2	0.8
USA	8.0	4.6	4.1	−3.0	1.8	47	13	17	1.4	−3.5	−4.1
Japan	8.1	1.9	2.1	−13.0	−0.5	11	1	0	3.4	−1.1	3.0
Sweden	10.6	8.1	9.4	−7.3	11.1	3	17	2	1.3	1.1	3.8
Finland	12.6	7.4	5.2	5.2	3.9	24	41	43	2.8	0.4	1.4
Norway	8.2	6.9	4.5	−0.3	−0.5	7	10	8	2.1	5.0	2.6
Austria	6.1	3.9	2.5				0	0	2.1	−2.9	−2.2
Denmark	10.2	5.9	2.1	−2.8	6.9	9	17	2	0.2	−2.6	−1.4
Switz.	3.7	4.0	5.3				0	0			
Belgium	8.1	4.3	3.0	−13.6	14.1	24			5.8	−9.1	5.4
Neths.	7.4	2.6	2.9	0.0	15.8	2	2	4	2.3	−5.7	−5.3
Germany	4.7	3.1	3.4	−3.1	2.5	3	3	1	−3.0	−2.1	−1.9

France	10.9	6.8	3.0	−4.6	2.1	21	8	5	−1.1	−2.1	−1.7
Italy	17.1	11.3	7.5	2.7	3.1	130	62	30	−9.2	−10.9	−10.6
UK	16.1	7.4	6.8	−7.0	10.8	54	37	8	4.1	−2.3	−1.0
Ireland	14.0	7.6	1.3	−1.5			38	6	8.4	−8.5	1.8
Spain	18.4	9.8	7.3			124	65	25	−0.7	−4.3	3.9
Greece	15.5	18.0	19.3				106	361	−2.4	−11.8	−18.6
Portugal	19.9	18.2	14.3		10.7		16	0	−5.3	5.9	5.0
Canada	9.2	5.4	3.0	−0.7	2.3	99	45	29	−1.7	−4.5	−3.8
Australia	12.3	8.0	3.9	−3.2	11.0	72	34	20	−2.0	−1.0	1.1
NZ	13.2	11.0	4.4	−8.4	5.6	30	42	17			

Note: All averages for groups of countries are unweighted (except OECD inflation and budget); only those countries without gaps in data are included.

Sources: Inflation (GDP deflator), OECD, *Historical Statistics 1960–90*, plus OECD, *Economic Outlook*, June 1993.
Profits (net profit share in manufacturing). Armstrong *et al.*, 1991 plus OECD, *Historical Statistics* adjusted for self-employment (and depreciation where necessary).
Strikes (days occupied per 100 employees), whole economy, Dept. of Employment Gazette, December 1992 and earlier issues.
Budget balance (general government net lending) OECD, *Historical Statistics* and *Economic Outlook*.

Table 2A. Indicators of egalitarianism, 1973–89

	Unemployment Average % rates			Employment (Emp/Pop) % p.a. changes		Female/male wages changes in ratio (%)		Government spending % of GDP changes		Share prices/wages % p.a. changes	
	1974–9	1980–9	1990	1973–9	1979–88	1970–9	1979–89	1970–9	1979–89	1973–9	1979–89
OECD	4.2	7.4	6.8	−0.1	−0.1	6.4	0.6	8.5	1.2	13.2	8.4
Euro core (Ger., Fra., It., UK, Bel., Neth., Switz.)	4.4	7.9	6.5	−0.5	−0.4	6.1	−0.3	7.9	−0.1	13.1	7.1
Corps. (Swe., Fin., Nor., Den., Aus.)	3.0	4.3	4.6	0.7	0.5	7.9	1.5	10.5	1.3	−13.3	12.2
USA	6.7	7.2	5.4	0.9	0.7			2.4	2.1	−8.7	7.5
Japan	1.9	2.5	2.1	0.1	0.2	−2.5	−1.9	10.2	0.6	−8.0	14.7
Sweden	1.9	2.4	1.6	1.2	0.3	9.3	0.2	18.3	2.4	−10.1	17.8
Finland	4.4	4.9	3.3	0.5	0.7	4.9	1.5	6.2	2.5	−15.9	17.7
Norway	1.8	2.8	5.1	1.8	0.6	5.4	6.2	9.4	4.3	−17.4	9.3
Austria	1.5	3.3	3.5	−0.1	0.2			8.3	0.7	−11.3	6.4
Denmark	5.5	8.0	9.6	0.1	0.5	12.0	−1.8	10.3	2.7	−11.8	10.0
Switz.	0.3	0.6	0.6	−1.0	−0.4	1.2	1.6	8.6	0.6	−9.5	4.5
Belgium	6.3	10.8	7.5	−0.7	−0.5			11.2	4.7	−15.6	7.2
Neths.	4.9	9.7	7.3	−0.9	−0.1	8.3	−1.5	11.3	−3.2	−12.4	10.6
Germany	3.2	5.9	4.9	−0.8	−0.6	3.2	0.0	8.3	2.8	−6.7	5.2

France	4.5	9.0	9.1	-0.3	-0.9			6.4	3.9	-13.4	7.3
Italy	6.6	9.5	9.9	0.3	-0.1			4.0	6.4	-25.5	9.4
UK	5.0	10.0	6.5	-0.1	-0.3	11.5	-1.2	5.3	-0.9	-8.7	5.6
Ireland	7.6	15.6	14.0	-0.5	-1.4	10.5	3.1	7.2	-0.5	-11.0	2.9
Spain	5.2	17.5	16.0	-2.3	-1.1			10.1	6.0	-33.9	7.4
Greece	1.9	6.6	7.9					6.3	12.2		
Portugal	6.0	7.3	5.7					14.6	3.8		
Canada	7.2	9.3	8.1	0.7	0.8			4.2	1.4	-8.4	2.7
Australia	5.0	7.5	6.8	-0.9	0.3			6.9	1.9	-9.9	5.4
NZ	0.8	4.6	7.9	0.2	-0.9				3.2		

Sources: Unemployment rate (standardized where possible), OECD, *Historical Statistics and Economic Outlook.*
Non-agricultural employment rate (% of non-ag. population) calculated from OECD, *Labour Force Statistics*, 1989.
Female/male hourly earnings, manufacturing OECD, *Employment Outlook*, 1988, table C1, updated from ILO, *Yearbook of Labour Statistics 1989/90.*
Government expenditure 1979–89, Oxley, 1990, table 9 (excludes subsidies and interest). 1970–9 Total government expenditure less interest (most countries) less military for USA, Saunders and Klau, 1985.
Share prices/money wages: ratio of industrial share prices to average earnings, IMF, *Financial Statistics.*

Table 3A. Indicators of egalitarianism, 1980s

	Tax progressiveness late 1970s	Top tax change in income tax (%) c. 1980–c. 1989	Poverty % Pop < 50% of median incomes late 1970s	Poverty change 1979-85	Top 20% change in share of incomes (%) late 70s mid 1980s	Equality of incomes Rank late 1970s	Employment (Emp./Pop) % 1979	Female/male Wages % 1979	Social expenditure % GDP 1980
OECD	11	−17	13	1.3	1.2		65.1	73.7	23.3
Euro core (Ger., Fra., It., UK., Bel., Neth., Switz.)	9	−14	9	1.1	1.2		62.8	72.0	26.6
Corps. (Swe., Fin., Nor., Den., Aus.)	14	11	8				71.3	82.9	28.3
USA	5	37	17	2.3	2.0	9	66.8		18.0
Japan	5	−25			0.6		68.0	50.4	16.1
Sweden	20	14	5		0.9	1	79.7	89.3	33.2
Finland	15	−7					67.8	75.3	22.9
Norway	20	−19	5			2	72.7	80.5	24.2
Austria	10	12					62.4		26.0
Denmark	5	4	13	2.3			73.9	86.4	35.1
Switz.	20	0	8			5	78.8	65.9	19.1
Belgium	20	17	8	−0.7			56.4		33.9
Neths.	5	11	9	0.8	1.3	7	56.9	80.1	31.8
Germany	5	−3	5	1.7	−0.8	3	64.8	72.8	26.6

France		−3	18	−0.2	0.6		61.7		30.9
Italy		−22	9	2.3	1.8		51.1		23.7
UK	5	−43	8	2.8	3.0	4	70.2	69.1	20.0
Ireland	15	−19	17	5.1			53.9	66.7	23.8
Spain		−9	20	−0.5			48.1		15.6
Greece		−13	24	−0.2					12.6
Portugal		−40	28	0.2					17.5
Canada	5	18	12			6	65.3		19.5
Australia	15	−16	12			8	64.4		17.3
NZ	20	33					73.4		22.4

Note: All averages for groups of countries are unweighted.

Sources: Tax: difference in direct tax, including social security, as % of incomes at 3 times average and at average levels, calculated from OECD, *The Income Tax Base*, 1990.

Change in top rate of income tax: OECD, *Economies in Transition.*

Share of top 20% income recipients in income: Boltho (1990).

Poverty: % of population in households with incomes (adjusted for family size) less than 50% of median, Buhmann (1988) and O'Higgins and Jenkins (1990).

Equality: rank based on average of 5 measures, Buhmann (1988).

Female/male wages and employment rate, see Appendix table 2.

Notes

Revised version of paper prepared for WIDER project on Savings, Investment and Finance. My thanks to Wendy Carlin, Gerry Epstein, Herb Gintis, and other members of the project for comments.

1 The European core consists of Germany, France, Italy, UK, Belgium, Netherlands, and Switzerland; the corporatist countries are the Scandinavian countries and Austria (see Pekkarinen *et al.*, 1992). Averages for groups are unweighted in order to reflect "typical" country experience (except for figures for total OECD in tables 2.1, 2.2, 2.4).

2 In such a comparison productivity has to be adjusted for the change of consumer prices (which deflate real wages) relative to manufacturing value added prices (which deflate manufacturing output and productivity). Such changes in relative prices reflect a host of factors such as terms of trade, indirect taxation, productivity growth in manufacturing, and services; these vary substantially between countries (during 1979–87 consumer prices grew 4 percent faster in Japan than manufacturing value added prices and 0.2 percent slower in Denmark) and across time (in the USA the difference increased from 0.5 percent per year during 1973–9 to 2.5 percent per year during 1979–87).

3 The problem with these data is that they include government consumption and investment on traditional public goods (defence, public administration) and on economic services and infrastructure (but not debt interest). Substantial cuts (around 1 percent of GDP) in subsidies occurred in a number of countries (the UK, Finland, Greece, Ireland, Norway, New Zealand, Portugal); whilst not included in welfare spending such subsidies usually have a strong egalitarian function in maintaining jobs, or reducing the prices of essential elements of consumption. All the 1980s data on government expenditure are from Oxley *et al.* (1990, tables 9 and 10).

4 Estimates in Glyn (1992a) suggest that consumption out of property incomes declined as a share of marketed output between 1973 and 1979, but rose sharply during 1979–86, especially in the European core countries.

5 The profit rate recovery depended on the output–capital ratio as well as the profit share; in the 1980s the downward trend in output–capital ratios was halted as the prices of capital goods grew more slowly than output prices. By 1987 the profit rate in Europe was at its 1973 level in both business and manufacturing, though still somewhat below its 1960 peak; in Japan the business profit rate was around two thirds, and the manufacturing rate less than one half of 1973 rates. US rates were around one fifth to one third below 1973 rates. See Armstrong *et al.*, 1991, chapter 14 for more detail.

6 All these data are for pre-tax profits. Taxation of corporate profits seems to have been lower in Japan than in the USA or Germany, but not relative to the UK. But there have been no cuts in profits tax in Japan which could explain the buoyant accumulation there (Armstrong *et al.*, 1991, table 14.12).

7 Data in Ford and Poret (1990) show that business investment growth accelerated sharply (more than 2 percent per year) after 1979 in Finland, Japan, Sweden, Switzerland, Belgium, and the UK (as compared to growth during 1970–9); however it slowed down sharply in Norway, Denmark, Greece, and Ireland. Putting these data beside OECD calculations for the profit share in business (OECD, *Economic Outlook*, December 1990, table 55), which is less than ideal being gross of capital consumption and including housing rents, suggests a similar lack of relation between profit recovery in the 1980s and investment response to that in manufacturing (neither the investment share, nor the growth rate of business investment nor its acceleration in the 1980s is significantly correlated with the profit share in business at the beginning of the 1980s nor its change during the 1980s).

8 Data for finance investment may include assets leased out to other sectors (except for the UK where it is possible to correct for this).

9 Data on government investment and education spending are from Oxley *et al.* (1990), on R and D from Englander and Mittelstadt (1988).

10 Romer (1987) presents a theoretical model where productivity growth depends, because of economies of scale, far more closely on capital accumulation than the growth-accounting tradition allows; this seems consistent with the long-run relationship between growth of capital per worker and of productivity shown in Romer (1989) and Glyn *et al.* (1990). Englander and Mittelstadt (1988) also provide evidence that the contribution of capital accumulation to the post-1973 productivity slowdown is greater than growth accounting indicates; they also emphasize the role of slow output growth, itself partly a reflection of weak investment.

11 Data for sixteen OECD countries from *World Development Report 1991*, table 30 on the ratio of incomes received by the top 20 percent and bottom 20 percent and from OECD *Economic Outlook*, December 1991, table 48 for productivity growth in the business sector. The inequality data exclude undistributed profits (or the capital gains they give rise to), but certainly suggest that inequality in the distribution of personal incomes is not, as is often asserted, associated with faster growth (through, for example, greater availability of savings from the rich, or greater work effort from top managers, etc.).

12 Government deficits had been pared down from 4.4 percent of GDP in 1983 to 1 percent in 1989; by 1992 they were back to nearly 3 percent of GDP, and ratios of debt to GDP were back on the increase (OECD, *Economic Outlook*, June 1993).

Part two

Savings, investment, and employment

3 Putting the horse (back) before the cart: disentangling the macro relationship between investment and saving

David M. Gordon

With persistent stagnation afflicting the advanced economies since the late 1960s and early 1970s, economists and policymakers have turned more and more urgently to the problem of sluggish investment. If stagnant investment could be energized, then both productivity growth – through supply-side effects – and output growth – through the Keynesian multiplier – would be likely to rebound as well.

In many of the advanced economies, further, a widespread policy consensus has emerged about how best to revitalize investment: According to a broad range of conservative and neo-liberal economists, private saving must be enhanced in order to provide the funds necessary for expanded investment. And if it proves difficult to augment private saving, as many believe will be the case in economies like the United States, then dramatic increases in net government saving must also be imposed.[1] Lawrence Summers and Chris Carroll provide a compact distillation of this prevailing policy consensus for the case of the United States (1987, pp. 608, 635): "Without an increase in national saving, and given the increasing reluctance of foreign investors to hold American assets, it is unlikely that even current levels of investment can be maintained . . . Unless new ways of encouraging private saving can be found, it may be necessary for the federal government to run chronic budget surpluses in coming years." One way or the other, according to this broad policy consensus, private and public consumption must be contained: "The important point," Hatsopoulos, Krugman, and Summers write for the US case (1988, p. 307), "is to realize that any other policies cannot work unless the United States also restrains its consumption growth."[2]

The early proposals of the Clinton Administration in the United States underscore the powerful sway of this analytic and ideological position. Having campaigned for the Presidency with promises of "putting people first," the new President unveiled an economic program which featured

57

budget austerity as its centerpiece. The Administration's first budget proposals vowed by 1997 to cut the federal budget deficit by roughly 2 percent of GNP (Executive Office of the President, 1993, table 3-1). The rationale for such fiscal austerity could not have been clearer (ibid., pp. 9–10): "Large, sustained budget deficits mean that we must either reduce our investment at home or borrow the money overseas. This drain on our savings has caused anemic domestic investment . . ."

The core economic foundation of this policy consensus, obviously, is that saving must be boosted *in order to* stimulate investment. At a purely superficial level, two kinds of argument are mobilized to support this apparently self-evident proposition.

First, the standard national-income accounting identity is marshalled to emphasize the tightness of the saving–investment relationship. Using standard notation, after standard rearrangements, we can write

$$I \equiv S + G^n - X^n \tag{1}$$

where, at the aggregate level, I is investment, S is private saving, G^n is net government saving (equal to government tax revenues minus government spending) and X^n is net exports. Assuming that net exports do not play a crucial role in equilibrating national saving and investment,[3] it follows *ex post* that investment cannot increase without simultaneous and commensurate increases in either private saving and/or the net government surplus.

Second, it is widely observed that there is a close cross-national relationship between national investment rates and national savings rates (see, for example, Summers, 1988, pp. 361–4). This pattern has suggested to many mainstream economists that an individual country cannot boost its investment share without first permissively increasing its own net national saving rate.

The moment we move beyond these superficial observations, however, it becomes clear that they are insufficient by themselves to support the prevailing policy wisdom. The accounting identity in equation (1), once again ignoring the potential equilibrating effect of net exports, tells us only that investment must equal private and public saving *ex post*. It does not tell us that we must *first* increase saving before we can *subsequently* expand investment. The relationship between net national investment and net national saving, further, tells us only that they vary closely together across countries, not that net investment rates in some countries are higher than in others *because* net national saving rates in those countries are higher.

Indeed, given what little this raw material can tell us, one could just as easily argue that conventional policy wisdom has stood economic behavior on its head. If investment must equal saving *ex post*, it could obviously be the case *ex ante* that investment changes first and that saving comes subsequently into balance with investment, rather than the other way around. And if investment and saving move closely together over time and across countries, it could be the case that variations in investment *predetermine* variations in saving rather than changes in saving predetermining changes in investment.

We can learn very little, in short, about the necessity of the prevailing policy wisdom from simple observations of the definitional relationship between saving and investment. We are left, then, with more fundamental questions about the contours of that relationship: Does saving "cause" investment? Does investment "cause" saving? Are they simultaneously determined? Can their macro relationship be disentangled?

In addressing those questions, this chapter argues that the prevailing policy consensus has misunderstood the macroeconomic relationship between investment and saving. I argue, indeed, that the determination of investment is *prior* to the determination of saving, suggesting the need for a clear alternative to the prevailing policy wisdom that raising the saving rate is a necessary condition for revitalizing investment. Concentrating on the empirical case of the US economy in the post-World War II era, I advance this argument in four principal sections.

I first present *prima facie* quantitative evidence that investment leads saving, and not the other way around, through a sequence of Granger causality tests.

Taking this *prima facie* empirical evidence at its face value, I next focus on the economic logic of a heterodox theoretical argument that investment predetermines saving, highlighting the critical role of distribution and finance in determining the relationship between investment and saving.

Given the central importance of distribution and finance for this heterodox analytic argument, the third section briefly pursues two econometric exercises: (a) It explores the relative quantitative importance of distribution in the determination of investment and saving, reviewing the specification and estimation of non-neoclassical consumption and investment functions in which, indeed, the distribution of income between capital and labor plays a significant role in conditioning both investment and saving. (b) It also tests for the influence of various kinds of financial constraints on the determination of investment, exploring the possibility that investment is *not* constrained by the supply of loanable funds.

The final section seeks more systematically to disentangle the complex macroeconomic relationships between investment and saving. Building on the results of the econometric explorations in section 3 and making use of both vector autoregression (VAR) and structural models, I present a variety of additional quantitative evidence which further strengthens the a priori expectation that investment predetermines saving and not the other way around.

The chapter concludes with a brief discussion of the policy implications of standing the investment–saving relationship right side up. Once we put the horse back in front of the cart, evidently, the case for a progressive policy alternative to right-wing/neo-liberal austerity regimes looks substantially more plausible and promising.

1   Investment leads saving: the superficial evidence

We can begin by affirming that there is, indeed, a problem which warrants investigation. There can be little question that investment has stagnated in the advanced countries since the early 1970s or that, reflecting the income accounting identity reproduced in equation (1), saving has declined alongside it.

Basic trends in investment and saving

Table 3.1 provides a spare introduction to those trends. It presents cycle averages for net investment and net national savings rates, expressed as a percentage of gross domestic product, for the OECD economies and for the United States for the period from 1960 (when the consolidated OECD data series begin) through 1988.[4] Following the high levels of investment and saving at the end of the post-war boom, in the 1960–6 and 1967–73 cycles, net investment and net saving declined steadily and substantially over the next two cycles.[5]

Next, for a closer though still superficial glimpse of the relationship between investment and saving, I turn to the data for the United States. It is possible, of course, that conventional national income measures of investment and saving for the United States do not track the macro magnitudes with which public policy should be primarily concerned. Important recent contributions have suggested, indeed, that saving rates are not as low in the US as the standard national income definitions and data would indicate.[6] But I have chosen here to focus on the standard measures of net saving in order to confront the conventional wisdom on its own turf: Even if better measures of saving might reveal a higher national saving rate in the US, bearers of the mainstream message might

Table 3.1. *Net investment and net national saving rates: OECD economies and the United States, cycle averages, 1960–88*

Cycle	Net capital formation as % of GDP		Net national saving as % of GDP	
	OECD	US	OECD	US
1960–6	12.6%	8.9	13.0	9.8
1966–73	13.2	8.9	13.8	9.3
1973–9	11.5	7.5	11.4	7.7
1979–88	8.4	5.2	7.8	3.6

Note: Net capital formation defined as gross fixed capital formation, including private, government (excluding military) and non-profit sectors, minus consumption of fixed capital. Net national saving defined as national disposable income minus total (private and government) final consumption and consumption of fixed capital. By these definitions, net capital formation equals net national saving minus the national surplus on current transactions and a statistical discrepancy. *Source:* OECD (1990).

nonetheless continue to argue that *still higher* saving rates would be necessary in order to stimulate more rapid investment. It may be the case *not only* that saving rates in the US are not as low as presumed, as others have already argued, *but also* that augmenting saving rates will not substantially boost the pace of investment – the possibility directly explored in this chapter.

Once one accepts (for the purposes of discussion) the conventional definitions of saving in the data for the United States, the choice of aggregate magnitudes for investigation can be made fairly simply.

On the investment side, since two of the principal problems to which policy concern has been directed involve sluggish productivity growth and eroding US international competitiveness, one wants in the first instance to concentrate on a series which tracks most closely those investments enhancing labor or total factor productivity. As a result, it seems appropriate to exclude from consideration depreciation expenditures, inventory investments, and residential investment – none of which significantly effects longer-term improvements in productivity. Controlling for inflation as well as focusing on domestic investment, one is therefore led to concentrate primarily on *real net fixed domestic non-residential investment*, a standard series for net investment in almost all policy discussions about US macro performance.

Some might want to quarrel, however, with the choice of *net* rather than *gross* investment. It is certainly true that the division of total invest-ment expenditures between net investment and depreciation may be some-what arbitrary, reflecting accounting practices at least as much as economic behavior. And it may be true, further, that replacement investment incor-porating more modern vintages of capital can potentially enhance long-term productivity growth. If we are interested in the temporal and behav-ioral relationship between investment and saving, nonetheless, exclusive attention to gross investment may introduce a near tautology into the dis-cussion. Since, at least in conventional US national accounting definitions, exactly the same flows measuring depreciation (or "capital consumption allowances") are included in the value of *both* gross investment *and* gross business saving, and since depreciation is fairly large relative to net invest-ment (and net business saving), a very high contemporaneous correlation between gross investment and almost any definition of gross saving would be introduced into the analysis as an artifact of definitional conventions. It seems prudent, therefore, to concentrate primarily on net (fixed domestic non-residential) investment and to test, along the way, how our conclu-sions might differ if we considered gross investment instead.

On the saving side, most mainstream policy discussion builds on neo-classical expectations that decisions by private households about personal saving establish the conditions within which other macro relations are determined and to which government policy decisions about net govern-ment saving must ultimately respond. It seems appropriate for these discussions, consequently, to concentrate primarily on data for *real per-sonal saving*, taking note where appropriate of movements in real net government saving.

It is true, of course, that neoclassical economists also consider *total private saving*, defined as the sum of personal and business saving, since the distinction between households and firms is often treated as a veil and indi-vidual agents are assumed to optimize total private (rather than merely household) saving. I will nonetheless concentrate primarily on personal saving for two reasons: First, most policy discussion does, indeed, pay attention almost exclusively to personal (rather than total private) saving. Second, for reasons explored in detail below, the relationship between business saving and investment is interpreted through very different theo-retical lenses by neoclassical and heterodox economists. It will therefore be necessary to treat that relationship separately in order to be able to distin-guish properly between alternative theoretical and policy approaches. Where necessary, nonetheless, I shall look at the behavior of measures of *real net private saving*, defined as the sum of personal and net business saving, in order to keep track of that alternative aggregate measure.

Table 3.2. *Net investment and personal savings for the United States: net fixed non-residential investment and personal saving as percent of potential output, cycle averages, 1955.4–1989.2*

	Net investment (% of pot. output)	Personal saving (% of pot. output)	Net private saving (% of pot. output)
1955.4–1959.2	2.8%	4.6	7.6
1959.2–1966.1	2.8	4.0	7.0
1966.1–1973.1	3.8	5.0	7.4
1973.1–1978.4	3.0	5.5	8.2
1978.4–1989.2	2.6	3.7	5.0
Full period	2.8	4.6	6.7

Note: Net investment is real net fixed domestic non-residential investment. Personal saving is gross private saving minus undistributed (adjusted) corporate profits and capital consumption allowances (all in real terms). Net private saving is gross private saving minus capital consumption allowances (in real terms). Potential output is real potential gross national product.
Source: See Data appendix.

Here as throughout the rest of the quantitative analysis in this chapter, I concentrate on quarterly data for periods extending between business-cycle peaks (in order to control as well as possible for cyclical fluctuations). I have chosen to begin the full analysis with the first complete business cycle after the Korean War, beginning with its initial peak in 1955.4. The quantitative analysis extends through the peak at the end of the long 1980s cycle.[7] In order to control for increases in the scale of the economy, I normalize all aggregate flow data by dividing by potential output.[8]

Table 3.2 thus presents in the first two columns cycle averages for US net investment and personal saving (normalized on potential output) for the period from 1955.4 through 1989.2. (The third column also tracks net private saving.) As noted for the different OECD measure of net investment in table 3.1, US net investment rates peaked in the 1966–73 cycle and then declined steadily through the next two cycles. As commonly noted, personal saving rates dropped dramatically in the 1980s cycle. Net private saving rates dropped by roughly comparable margins during the 1980s as well. It is interesting to note, finally, that net investment peaks earlier (in the 1966.1–1973.1 cycle) than does either personal or net private saving (which both peak in the 1973.1–1978.4 cycle).

The temporal relation between net investment and personal saving

What can we conclude about how these series for net investment and personal saving (or net private saving) vary together over time?

There is a standard econometric technique for testing formal hypotheses about the time-series relations between two variables, commonly known as pairwise *Granger causality tests.*[9] By regressing X on its own lags as well as on lags of Y, and then reversing the test by stipulating Y as the dependent variable, one can provisionally infer something about the temporal priority of X and Y. More formally with such tests, for example, one concludes that X *does not Granger-cause* Y if one can accept the null hypothesis that all of the lagged values of X can be excluded from the regression with Y as the dependent variable.[10] The results of these tests do not imply anything about actual cause and effect, in a more fundamental behavioral sense, but merely test for the possibility that one variable may lead another in a limited statistical sense.

The classic terrain for the application of such Granger-causality tests involves the bivariate relationship of output and the money supply, prefigured by the long-standing (though now quiescent) debate between Keynesians and monetarists.[11] Given the importance of recent policy discussion about the relation between investment and saving, it would appear equally intriguing to apply Granger-causality tests to that time-series relation as well.[12] I turn now to a series of such tests for the United States. I concentrate on the Granger relation between the series for net non-residential investment and personal saving previously highlighted in table 3.2, although I also check the robustness of the estimated results by additionally testing for pairwise Granger-causality between personal saving and both net *residential* and net *total* investment as well as for between net private saving and net investment.

Because I am interested here primarily in abstracting from the obvious short-term simultaneity between investment and saving and in drawing attention to longer-term relationships, I concentrate here on the relationship between investment and saving over a period longer than two years. Table 3.3 reports on the results of these Granger-causality tests for various lag lengths ranging from two years (eight quarters) through five years (twenty quarters). The two main sets of columns report the tests for the two alternative directions of determination between normalized personal saving and alternative measures of normalized net investment, with the left-hand set ((1)–(3)) testing the null hypothesis that net investment is not Granger-caused by personal saving and the right-hand set ((4)–(6)) testing the null hypothesis that personal saving is not Granger-caused by net investment. Within those sets of columns, results are reported for

Table 3.3. *The temporal relation of net investment and personal saving: Granger-causality tests on the pairwise relation between net fixed investment and personal saving normalized on potential output, various lag lengths, 1955.4–1989.2*
(Probability at which to reject null hypothesis of no Granger-causality)

No. of quarters included in test	Net investment not Granger-caused by personal saving			Personal saving not Granger-caused by net investment		
	(1) Non-res.	(2) Res.	(3) Total	(4) Non-res.	(5) Res.	(6) Total
8	x	x	x	0.04	0.02	0.01
12	x	x	x	0.09	0.03	0.06
16	x	x	x	0.06	0.04	0.04
20	x	x	x	0.07	0.06	0.05

Note: "x" indicates a worse than 0.10 statistical probability that one can reject the null hypothesis of no Granger-causal relation between the two variables. In each pairwise test, lags of both variables in the bivariate pair are included for each quarter up to the lag length reported for the respective rows.
Source: Author's estimations. See Data appendix for variable definition and sources.

three alternative definitions of (normalized) net investment: non-residential investment (the series of most direct concern to us here), residential investment, and total investment. For each column, results are reported for four different lengths of lag inclusion.

Given the complexity of macroeconomic interdependencies, Granger-causality test results are often fairly ambiguous. The results reported in table 3.3 are surprisingly unambiguous. For every lag length and every definition of net investment, as columns (1)–(3) show, we can nowhere reject the null hypothesis that net investment is not Granger-caused by personal saving, indicating that we do not lose any statistical information by excluding (normalized) personal saving as an independent variable from a regression with (normalized) net investment as the dependent variable regressed on past values of itself. Sharply in contrast, columns (4)–(6) indicate that we can uniformly reject, for at least a 10 percent level of significance, the hypothesis that personal saving is not Granger-caused by net investment. This means that we would lose information in tracking the time-series pattern of net personal saving if we ignored its temporal covariation with past values of net investment.

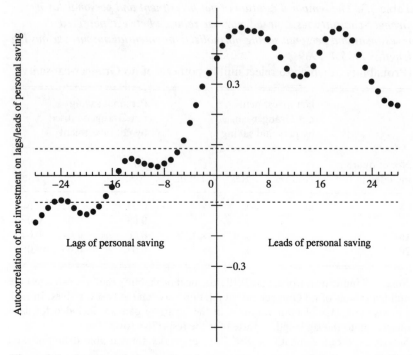

Figure 3.1   Autocorrelations of net investment on personal saving: normalized net fixed non-residential investment on normalized personal saving
Note: Dotted lines indicate threshold of statistical significance for autocorrelations.

In slightly less forbidding language, in short, these tests strongly support the hypothesis that net investment leads personal saving, that net investment is indeed determined *prior* to personal saving. While the tests are merely bivariate and only begin to scratch the surface of the complex macro interactions between investment and saving, they nonetheless provide *prima facie* empirical evidence casting doubt upon the prevailing conventional wisdom that net investment has stagnated in the United States at least in part *because* of logically and/or temporally prior declines in personal saving.

Figure 3.1 graphically illustrates these results by plotting the cross-correlations between current values of (normalized) net non-residential investment and lags and leads for values of (normalized) personal saving from zero to twenty-eight quarters. The graph further dramatizes the extent to which real net fixed domestic non-residential investment appears to lead real personal saving: Ignoring the short period (up to eight lags/leads) in which both investment and saving are co-determined with aggregate capacity utilization, the autocorrelations of net investment with *lags* of personal saving are nowhere positive and significant while the autocorrelations of net investment with *leads* of personal saving are everywhere positive and significant.

The results are not as clear cut if one moves to different definitions of investment and saving – but for reasons which clarify rather than muddy these initial impressions.

We can consider first the difference between trends in net and gross investment. According to mainstream economics, if the availability of funds is crucial as a constraint on business investment decisions, reductions in the flow of personal saving would exert downward pressure on business spending both for replacement investment and for new investment alike. But the data for the US for the post-war period actually suggest, quite to the contrary, an opposite sign of association in the relationship of personal saving with (a) net investment and (b) replacement investment, respectively: Net investment is *positively* associated with leads of personal saving, while depreciation is *negatively* associated with leads of personal saving. For example, while (as figure 3.1 shows) the cross-correlation between net non-residential investment and lags and leads of personal saving is everywhere *positive* and significant between a lag of four quarters and a lead of twenty-four quarters, the comparable cross-correlations between non-residential depreciation and lags and leads of personal saving are everywhere *negative* and significant between a lag of ten quarters and a lead of twenty-four quarters.

The explanation apparently builds on the following sequence of connections: Suppose we are examining an economy with stagnating net investment and, at least partly as a consequence, declining productivity growth, as was true for the US economy after the mid 1960s.[13] This would make it likely, other things equal, that the capital–output ratio would be increasing as the productivity of capital lagged.[14] Since depreciation expenditures are primarily determined by trends in the real (lagged) capital stock, we would therefore expect that the depreciation–output ratio would rise in turn. But if net investment was stagnating during this same period and if net investment partly determines net personal saving (for reasons to be explored below), we would find that the saving–output ratio would also be declining.[15] This would leave us with the pattern reported above: positive correlations between declining normalized net investment and declining normalized personal saving but negative correlations between rising normalized depreciation and declining normalized personal saving.[16] Were we to look only at gross investment, these different directions of association would be masked.

We can also consider the relationship between net investment and net private saving, incorporating net business as well as personal saving into the analysis.

Here, as with the difference between net and gross investment, the results reflect two relatively independent dynamics. It is not the case, as neoclassical economists might have it, that net business saving is simply a mirror for personal saving, rising when it falls and vice versa: There is nowhere a significant negative correlation between (normalized) real personal saving and real net business saving between zero and twenty-four lags. Whereas it remains true, as with the Granger-causality tests presented in table 3.3, that we can accept the hypothesis that net private saving does not lead net investment for lags from eight to twenty quarters, there is no longer any evidence that net investment leads net private saving over the same period. One possible explanation for this shift in results is fairly straightforward: According to heterodox economists, net business saving, as a component of before-tax corporate profits and unlike personal saving, is considered to constitute one of the most important determinants of corporate investment. If net investment leads personal saving but is partly led by corporate profitability, then we would indeed expect the analysis of the relation of net investment to net private saving to be muddied. In any case, pending further exploration of the relation between corporate profitability and corporate investment, there is no more evidence that saving leads investment if we consider net private saving than if we confine our attention to personal saving alone.

To conclude this first section, it would be reasonable on empirical grounds to conclude that net investment leads personal saving. Most neoclassical economists, at least in their policy pronouncements, appear to anticipate the opposite direction of determination. Does the empirical observation that net investment appears to lead personal saving make sense on theoretical grounds? Or is it little more than an empirical artifact, an anomaly resulting from the conjuncture of logically disconnected statistical trends?

2   Alternative accounts of the investment/saving relation

This way of posing the problem of the relationship between investment and saving echoes an earlier debate in economics between Keynesian and pre-Keynesian economists. Prior generations of pre-Keynesian economists had stressed the central importance of saving as the autonomous factor in the investment–saving pair, while Keynes argued that saving was a passive "determinate" of the system (Keynes, 1936, p. 183).[17]

But much has happened in economics since Keynes. Focussing on recent explorations in macro analysis, I briefly examine in this section alternative theoretical grounds for one or another logical expectation about the aggregate relationship between investment and saving. I begin with a review of neoclassical analyses of that relationship and then present an alternative structuralist perspective.

The neoclassical story

Despite all the many alternative strands of neoclassical macroeconomics, analytic expectations about the determinants of aggregate investment and saving are fairly standard. In most synthetic discussions, investment decisions made by firms are assumed to depend on aggregate income and the prevailing interest rate (as a central component of the "cost of capital services" confronting the firm).[18] According to the prevailing life-cycle/permanent income models of consumption, personal saving decisions are also thought to depend on fluctuations in (permanent disposable) income and the interest rate (as a measure of the intertemporal rate of discount facing households) as well as on personal wealth.[19]

In the first instance, then, it may indeed be reasonable to expect that investment and personal saving are simultaneously determined through the joint determination of aggregate income and the real interest rate. If so, abstracting from the influence of other exogenous factors affecting either investment and/or saving, one could not easily separate the chicken from the egg: Investment could not increase unless saving increased, and *vice versa*. In this respect, prevailing neoclassical views are inveterately Keynesian.

In the medium term, of course, it makes little sense to abstract from the influence of other exogenous factors affecting investment or saving. And here, neoclassical economists appear to place paramount priority on savings propensities. Stephen Marglin (1987, p. 986) observes:

In the longer period the [neoclassical] economist falls back on very different arguments: the mainstream of the profession takes accumulation to be determined by saving propensities, with nary a side glance at investment demand. That Japan has over the last quarter century devoted 30 per cent of gross output to fixed capital formation and Great Britain 20 per cent is conventionally explained in terms of higher Japanese saving propensities, not in terms of a greater propensity to invest.

If saving propensities change, interest rate (or quantity) adjustments will elicit the warranted level of investment in response. The possibility of autonomous changes in investment "propensities" is rarely acknowledged.

But how does this general and relatively generic concentration on saving propensities lead to an applied policy emphasis on reduced consumption and/or net government spending?[20]

Probably the easiest way to approach that question is by process of elimination. In the conventional income-accounting identity, there are three principal components of net national saving which must equal net national investment: net business saving, personal saving, and net government saving.

Of the three, net business saving receives the least attention in conventional discussions. Business saving is itself equal to net after-tax corporate retained earnings, or the undistributed portion of the net after-tax flow of corporate profits. There could be three ways in which net business saving could increase – through an increase in before-tax profit flows, through a decrease in profit-tax rates, or a decrease in the dividends pay-out rate. But the second by itself cannot produce an increase in net national saving, since an uncompensated reduction in corporate tax revenues would result in an exactly equal increase in the net government deficit, leaving total national saving untouched. This leaves the possibility of increasing net national saving by increasing the before-tax flow of business profits or reducing dividend payouts.

But these possibilities are largely ignored by neoclassical economists because, in a real neoclassical economy, the before-tax profit rate or profit share has virtually no status as a relevant analytic category (see, for example, Desai, 1987). Either net profit is simply assumed to disappear in competitive equilibrium. Or the rate of return is assumed to be equal to the marginal productivity of capital, itself technologically determined. Or the rate of return is viewed as the price, measured by the rate of interest, necessary to induce investors to save – in which case the problem of the rate of profit essentially collapses into the issue of personal saving propensities. In any of these cases, in standard textbook discussions, the before-tax flow of net corporate profits is not an economic category upon which policy is thought to be capable of having much impact.

Which leaves, by elimination, only personal saving and net government saving. And since government policymakers are not regarded as "economic individuals" in their own right, they are assumed to respond recursively to circumstances independently generated by the activities of individual agents in the private market economy. This leads to an analytic priority on the determination of personal saving, with its corresponding emphasis (beyond the short run) on personal saving propensities. If households could be induced (at given levels of national income) to consume less and save more, then greater investment would be possible unless and only if other exogenous pressures forced government policymakers to soak up those additional savings through increased net government deficits.[21]

An alternative structuralist story

In traditional Keynesian macroeconomics, investment, rather than saving, assumed paramount logical priority. Skott (1989, p. 115) summarizes the sequence of determination: "Keynesian theory has always regarded investment as a key variable. Firms decide the level of investment, and income and saving then adapt to bring about the *ex post* identity between saving and investment.

But numerous problems with traditional Keynesian formulations have raised doubts about this sequence of determination. In order to explore the possibility of reinstating something like that logic of determination, if not necessarily the Keynesian perspective within which it was formerly situated, many heterodox economists have recently begun to construct an alternative perspective which seeks to synthesize crucial insights of both neo-Keynesian and Marxian traditions. As in my other chapter in this volume, I shall refer here to this perspective as "structuralist macroeconomics."[22] This perspective is inclined to revive traditional Keynesian expectations that investment autonomously stimulates output and saving. The analysis of the roles of distribution and of finance, among other factors, is central for this inclination.

The role of distribution

In this emergent heterodox perspective, the distribution of income between classes (or factor shares) plays a decisive macroeconomic role. The logic of this argument is summarized in the spare structuralist macro model presented in Gordon (chapter 12, this volume). For ease of reference, I reproduce a slightly modified version of that same model here in table 3.4, decomposing gross investment into net investment and depreciation (since net investment will be examined econometrically in the next section) and presenting a model of a "closed" economy by treating (normalized) net exports as exogenous (since net exports do not figure centrally in the analysis of saving and investment pursued here). The reader should refer to my other essay for elaboration of the logic of such a structuralist model (as well as references to the relevant literature).

Figure 3.2(a) illustrates the determination of equilibrium in the model. For ease of comparison with other standard presentations of the heterodox perspective, I assume for generality a simple upward-sloping profit

Table 3.4. *Simple reduced-form structuralist model of a real closed private economy*

(4.1)	$\phi \equiv C_\phi + \Gamma^n_\phi + d_\phi + Z_\phi$	
(4.2)	$C_\phi = a_0 + a_1\phi + a_2\pi + a_3 Z_C,$	$a_1 > 0, a_2 < 0$
(4.3)	$\Gamma^n_\phi = \beta_0 + \beta_1\phi + \beta_2 r + \beta_3 Z_I,$	$\beta_1, \beta_2 > 0$
(4.4)	$\pi = \gamma_0 + \gamma_1\phi \qquad + \gamma_3 Z_\pi,$	$\gamma_1 > 0$
(4.5)	$r \equiv \pi \cdot \phi \cdot q^*_k$	
(4.6)	$d \equiv \lambda_d K^n_{-1}$	
(4.7)	$K^n \equiv K^n_{-1} + \Gamma^n_\phi \cdot Q^* - d$	
(4.8)	$q^*_k \equiv Q^*/K^n$	
(4.9)	$S_\phi \equiv \phi - C_\phi$	

where $X_\phi \equiv X$ normalized on potential output (Q^*)
  $Z_i \equiv$ Exogenous variable(s) affecting endogenous variable i
  $\phi \equiv$ Aggregate capacity utilization $(\equiv Q/Q^*)$
  $C \equiv$ Real consumption expenditures
  $I_n \equiv$ Real net investment
  $d \equiv$ Real depreciation expenditures
  $\pi \equiv$ Profit share of output
  $K^n \equiv$ Real net capital stock
  $q^*_k \equiv$ Potential output–capital ratio $(\equiv Q^*/K^n)$
  $S \equiv$ Real saving

function rather than the non-linear profit function introduced in my further specification of the model in my other chapter in this volume.

The condition of aggregate output/income balance, normally expressed at this level of abstraction as the requirement of the equality between investment and savings, gives us a "utilization function" represented on the graph as $\phi(\pi)$, with its slope derived by taking the derivative of ϕ in the balance condition relation with respect to π.[23] The system is closed and equilibrium determined by adding a profitability function to the graph, expressed here as the $\pi(\phi)$ curve.[24] Point a in figure 3.2(a) represents the equilibrium combination of the profit share and capacity utilization toward which this system tends. Once π^* and ϕ^* are determined, then S_ϕ^* and I_ϕ^* follow directly from equations (4.2)/(4.9) and (4.3)/(4.5) respectively.

What does such a simplified representation tell us about the macro relationship of investment and saving? Two principal lines of exploration seem most relevant.

First, it could be that a change in the exogenous variables in either the aggregate accounting balance equation (4.1) or the profitability equation

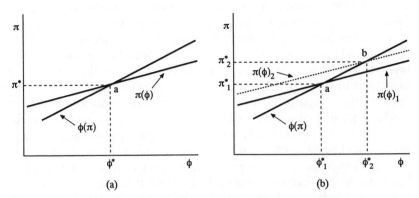

Figure 3.2   Simple structuralist model of real closed private economy

(4.4) could drive the system. Figure 3.2(b) illustrates the effects of a change in Z_π (in equation (4.4)) strongly favorable to profits. The $\pi(\phi)$ curve shifts upward, resulting in a new equilibrium at point b – with higher values of both the profit share and capacity utilization. Given the signs stipulated in equations (4.2) and (4.3) (and the identity for saving in (4.9)), this would result in increases in the (normalized) flows of both investment and saving. Whether investment appeared to "lead" saving or vice versa would depend on the lags (if any) on the coefficients on profitability and utilization in the investment and consumption equations.[25]

Second, it could be that the exogenous variables in the investment and consumption equations ((4.3)–(4.2)) and/or the coefficients in those equations change autonomously, leading in the short to medium term to an autonomous change in either investment and/or saving. But, the *ex post* identity between saving and investment must be honored. How does saving respond to an autonomous change in investment or vice versa?

In the standard neoclassical story, of course, the interest rate (or the real value of household wealth) secures the necessary adjustment. What plays the equivalent role in the kind of simplified structuralist story presented here? Structuralists place considerable weight on the likelihood of relatively stable saving and consumption relations, so the more interesting question involves the effects of autonomous changes in investment. What happens, for example, when "investors' spirits" soar – represented here by either a favorable change in Z_I or an increase in one of the structural parameters in equation (4.3)?[26]

An increase in investment will certainly stimulate an increase in aggregate demand, which would bring about a subsequent increase in saving.

But what effects would an increase in investment have on profitability? Here, recent structuralist analyses point to alternative possible effects, depending in particular on the level of aggregate utilization at which the economy was operating. If the economy was operating at relatively low levels of utilization, for example, it could certainly be the case that an increase in investment, triggering an increase in aggregate demand, would improve the efficiency of firms' production, leading to an increase in productivity and thus, other things being equal, to an increase in the profit share. If so, the initial increase in investment would unambiguously lead to an increase in saving. If not, then the story is more complicated.

But, whether the story is simple or more complicated, could an initial burst in investors' expectations ever be realized? If saving had not already increased, where would investors get the money to gratify their more ebullient expectations? This leads, of course, to the question of finance.

The role of finance

Many if not most structuralists respond simply and emphatically that credit systems in capitalist economies tend to be accommodating, effectively providing capitalist firms with as much money as they need for their investment plans.[27] Marglin (1987, p. 989) summarizes the logic of this position:

> The main point, in two words, is credit money. The process of expanding investment can get started with no accompanying increase in desired saving if capitalists are assumed to have access to an accommodating banking system which one way or another can create claims on scarce resources out of whole cloth. Here the psychology of financial capital joins the psychology of industrial capital, for unless the financiers share the optimism of industrialists, there is no way, absent those mythical cash hoards, by which investment can increase without a contemporaneous increase in desired saving ... The consequent increase in profits provides the wherewithal to retire debt as it becomes due.

Once we turn to finance, indeed, it becomes evident that the crucial disagreement between the neoclassical expectation that saving "calls the tune" and the structuralist argument that investment can potentially drive the economy, as Skott notes (1989, p. 116), "concerns the investment function rather than the saving function."

Were the neoclassical view appropriate, on the one hand, we ought to be able to find direct or indirect evidence of a credit market constraint on investment: We should be able to find, for example, that the supply of bank funds (or bank net assets) is positively associated with investment – with a squeeze in banking funds eventually imposing a squeeze on firms' investment expenditures. Or, to pursue the interest rate channel of effect, we ought to be able to find not only (a) that interest rates negatively affect investment but also and crucially (b) that the flow of personal saving negatively affects interest rates.

Were the structuralist perspective plausible, on the other hand, we would expect to find little or no evidence of direct or indirect credit squeezes on investment, since this approach presumes that investors can and do borrow nearly at will.

These differences in expectations about the investment/credit relation can be at least partially tested econometrically. I pursue some of those tests in the following section.

3   Testing hypotheses on the role of distribution and finance

Based on the theoretical discussion of the previous section, it would appear that there are at least two necessary conditions for the plausibility of a structuralist account of the investment/saving relation. First, we should be able to find evidence that distribution matters in the determination of saving and investment. Second, we should be able to find evidence that investment expenditures are effectively free of direct or indirect credit constraints resulting from movements in personal or public saving. This section briefly reports on econometric tests of each of those two necessary conditions.

The effects of distribution on investment and consumption

Can we confirm something like the consumption and investment functions introduced in equations (4.2) and (4.3) in table 3.4? Does profitability have a positive effect on investment and a negative effect on consumption?

Consumption and saving

I begin with consumption and saving. Since both mainstream and structuralist analyses view saving as a residual, it makes the most sense to test behavioral hypotheses about the influence of distribution on the determination of consumption. Here, two versions of the structuralist hypothesis can be tested. (1) We can test a reduced-form expression, following the logic of equation (4.2), in which the profit share itself is hypothesized to have a negative effect on consumption.[28] (2) We can test structural hypotheses about different propensities to consume out of various income sources, especially including wage and salary income and income from ownership of capital assets. I test both of these versions here for aggregate (normalized) real consumption expenditures for the US economy for the period from 1955.4 through 1989.2.

(1) I first derive a reduced-form specification for consumption – expressed as a function of distributive shares rather than direct income flows – based primarily on two relevant perspectives in the prevailing structuralist macro literature.

(a) We can begin with the simple Cambridge hypotheses about different consumption propensities from wage and salary and capital income.[29] First express consumption as a function of factor incomes and capital income as a function of profits (where all variables are expressed in real terms)

$$C = a_1 + a_2 W + a_3 R, \qquad 1 \geq a_2 > a_3 \geq 0 \tag{2}$$

$$R = \beta_1 + \beta_2 \Pi, \qquad 1 \geq \beta_2 > 0 \tag{3}$$

where C is real aggregate consumption, W is real wage and salary income, R is real income from owned capital assets, and Π is corporate profits.[30] Normalizing all variables on real potential output (Q^*) and substituting from (3) into (2), we get

$$C_\phi = a_1 + a_2 W_\phi + a_3(\beta_1 + \beta_2 \Pi_\phi) \tag{4}$$

where a ϕ as subscript indicates that a flow variable is normalized on real potential output. Then, making use of the formal factor-share identity that $W_\phi \equiv \phi - \Pi_\phi$ (where $\phi = Q/Q^*$) and regrouping, we get

$$C_\phi = (a_1 + a_3\beta_1) + a_2 \phi + (a_3\beta_2 - a_2)\Pi_\phi \tag{5}$$

or

$$C_\phi = a_1 + a_2 \phi + a_3 \Pi_\phi \tag{6}$$

where $a_3 = (a_3\beta_2 - a_2)$. Since $a_2 > a_3$ and $1 \geq \beta_2 > 0$ by assumption, $a_3 < 0$ and consumption will be a negative function of the profit share (of potential output).

In a world with government taxes and transfers, of course, consumption depends on after- rather than before-tax and transfer flows. We should thus modify the aggregate income identity to take account of taxes, transfers, and other leakages from aggregate income. We can now write, instead of $\phi \equiv W_\phi + \Pi_\phi$

$$(\phi - d_\phi - T^p_\phi) \equiv \phi^{na} \equiv W^a_\phi + \Pi^a_\phi + Y^{tp}_\phi + Y^0_\phi \tag{7}$$

where the superscript a indicates after-tax flows, d is depreciation, T^p is total personal tax payments, ϕ^{na} is after-personal-tax net capacity utilization, Y^{tp} is personal transfer income, Y^0 represents other leakages from after-tax net aggregate income (such as excise taxes), and, as before, the subscript ϕ indicates a flow variable normalized on potential output. Rewriting (2) with consumption as a function of after-tax income, substituting for W^a, normalizing and rearranging, we then get a final operational expression for a reduced-form Cambridge consumption function to replace (6). We can now write for magnitudes expressed after tax

$$C_\phi = a_1 + a_{21}\, \phi^{na} + a_3 \Pi^a{}_\phi + a_{22}\, Y^{tp}{}_\phi + a_{23}\, Y^0{}_\phi \tag{8}$$

where, as before, $a_{21} > 0$ and $a_3 < 0$. Presuming a higher than average propensity to consume out of personal transfer income and a neutral or negative effect of other leakages ($Y^0{}_\phi$) on consumption, we would expect a hierarchy of expected coefficients: $1 \geq a_{22} > a_{21} > 0 \geq a_{23} > a_3$.

(b) Such a formulation of the Cambridge hypothesis supposes instantaneous adjustment of consumption to changes in income. But the structuralist perspective would propose, at least for the vast majority of households dependent on wage and salary income, a highly inertial quality to consumption. Marglin (1984, chapters 7, 17, and 18) formalizes this heterodox expectation by proposing a "disequilibrium" model of consumption: The large majority of households will seek to achieve a target level of consumption – in an advanced economy presumably a level of real consumption which grows modestly over time – and will adjust current consumption to the relationship between recent and target consumption. This hypothesis can be formulated in several different ways. One convenient expression builds on the relationship between current consumption and recent rates of change of consumption (where variables in bold are expressed as continuous rates of change)

$$C_\phi = b_1 C^0 + \theta(C_{t-1} - C^0), \qquad \theta < 0;\ 1 > b_1 > 0 \tag{9}$$

where C^0 indicates trend consumption. According to this formulation, two dynamic adjustment effects should have an important influence on consumption: (i) current consumption would inertially reflect the influence of recent trends in consumption ($1 > b_1 > 0$); and (ii) current consumption would be reduced below (above) warranted levels, other things equal, if circumstances had permitted consumption recently to grow more (less) rapidly than the target rate of growth of consumption ($\theta < 0$).

One could reasonably supplement this formulation of the disequilibrium hypothesis with two "rainy day corollaries." (a) If unemployment is expected to increase, then working households will be likely to reduce current consumption in order to protect against potential future income losses. (b) In an economy where disequilibrium saving can take a variety of forms, if recent disequilibrium adjustments have resulted in an increase in net household assets, then current consumption would positively adjust to take advantage of the income stream generated by that incremental net household wealth.[31]

Combining the reduced-form Cambridge expression (8) with the disequilibrium hypothesis in (9) and its rainy-day corollaries, we arrive at a final reduced-form consumption function suitable for econometric estimation

$$C_\phi = a_1 + a_{21}\,\phi^{na} + a_3\,\Pi^a{}_\phi + a_{22}\,Y^{tp}{}_\phi + a_{23}\,Y^{to}{}_\phi$$
$$+ b_1\,C^\circ + \theta\,\tilde{C}_{t-1} + b_2 u + b_3\,A^{nh}{}_\phi \qquad (10)$$

where $\tilde{C}$ is the derivation of consumption growth around its trend rate of growth ($\equiv [C_{t-1} - C^\circ]$), u is the unemployment rate, $A^{nh}{}_\phi$ is real net household wealth normalized on potential output), and, as derived above, $1 \geq a_{22} > a_{21} > 0 \geq a_{23} > a_3$; $1 > b_1 > 0$; $\theta < 0$; $b_2 < 0$; and $b_3 > 0$.[32]

In estimating equation (10), I have also included a few other variables in order to control for autonomous changes or "shocks" in other concrete factors which might otherwise affect consumption behavior.[33] Table 3.5 reports on the results of econometric estimation of a reduced-form heterodox consumption function.[34]

Column (1) begins with the sparest possible version, including only the elements of equation (8) as well as trend (normalized) consumption. The results are consistent with heterodox expectations, with a negative coefficient on the profit share (significant at 5 percent). Since lagged trend consumption is a right-hand variable, the steady-state propensities are calculated by assuming trend consumption equal to current consumption, moving the trend term to the left-hand side of the equation, and dividing back through by $(1 - b_1)$. This results in an average propensity to consume out of income (net after-tax capacity utilization) of 0.98; and a negative effect of profitability on consumption of 0.18.

Column (2) reports the results of estimating equation (10) while column (3) reports the standardized "beta" coefficients for the regression. At a purely superficial level, the equation obviously succeeds: The equation has a high adjusted R^2 while the coefficients on all variables included in the regression have the expected signs and are significant at least at the 1 percent level. To save space in the table, the results for the vector of dummy variables are not reported; coefficients on all of those variables included in the equation are also significant at the 1 percent level with varying signs and relative magnitudes of effect on the dependent variable.

Several results of this estimation deserve further comment:

First, the principal hypotheses of the structuralist approach to consumption are all confirmed, with negative and significant coefficients on the profit share and on the deviation of consumption growth from trend. Here, the steady-state propensity to consume out of after-tax income is

0.68 while the steady-state negative effect of profitability on consumption is 0.25, close to the steady-state effect on profitability reported in column (1).

Second, the hypothesis of a hierarchy of coefficient values on the components of after-tax income is confirmed, with the coefficient on normalized transfer income clearly the highest, followed by the coefficient on net after-tax capacity utilization (or, in more familiar terms, normalized disposable income) and then, both with negative signs, the coefficients on the profit share and other leakages from gross before-tax income.[35]

Third, the beta coefficients reported in column (3) reveal one striking surprise. As one might have expected, the beta coefficients on trend consumption, net after-tax utilization, and net personal wealth are all relatively large. But the beta coefficients on the distributional variables suggest that, while distribution matters in the determination of consumption, the heterodox literature may have overlooked the most important distributional variable. While the beta coefficient on the after-tax profit share is smaller than those for trend consumption, net after-tax utilization, and net personal wealth, the beta coefficient on normalized transfer income is by far the largest in the entire equation. The effect of distribution on the macro economy is mediated not only by private-sector determinations, one might evidently conclude, but also by government interventions affecting the distribution of income.

(2) Households do not directly determine their consumption expenditures on the basis of enterprise profits. They make decisions, rather, on the basis of wage and capital income actually received and disposable for consumption or saving. We should also turn, then, from the reduced-form consumption function derived in the preceding paragraph to its structural equivalent.

Having already incorporated the several foundations for equation (10), derivation of a structural version of that equation is straightforward. We dispense with equation (3), the linkage which expresses income from capital assets as a function of profits, and work directly with equation (2). This evidently results in an expression corresponding to equation (10) in which, instead of the terms for net after-tax utilization and the normalized profit share, we incorporate terms for normalized disposable wage and salary (W^a_ϕ) and capital income (R^a_ϕ)

$$C_\phi = a_1 + a_{21} W^a_\phi + a_3 R^a_\phi + a_{22} Y^{tp}_\phi$$
$$+ b_1 C^\circ + \theta \check{C}_{t-1} + b_2 u + b_3 A^{nh}_\phi \tag{11}$$

Here, our principal interest lies in the range of magnitudes for the three

Table 3.5. *Estimated consumption equations: real personal consumption expenditures (normalized on real potential output), US economy, 1955.4–1989.2*

Independent variables	Symbol	Lags[a]	Dep. var. C_ϕ (1)	C_ϕ (2)	Betas (3)	ΔC_ϕ (4)
Constant	a		0.02 (0.68)	0.05 (5.00)	—	0.001 (2.38)
Trend norm. consumption[b]	C_ϕ^0	1	0.33 (5.06)	0.45 (16.92)	0.34	−1.25 (7.82)
Dev. consumption growth[b]	$\tilde{C}$	3	—	−0.22 (7.95)	−0.07	−0.06 (3.15)
Net after-tax capacity utilization	ϕ^{na}		0.66 (12.65)	0.37 (16.99)	0.38	—
Normalized after-tax profits	Π^a_ϕ	12	−0.12 (1.97)	−0.14 (4.84)	−0.07	—
Normalized transfer income	Y^{tp}_ϕ		0.84 (12.29)	0.91 (18.87)	1.11	—
Normalized residual income	Y^o_ϕ		−0.22 (4.59)	−0.15 (8.73)	−0.12	—
ΔNorm. prod. after-tax earnings	ΔW^{ap}_ϕ		—	—	—	0.23 (4.26)
ΔNorm. non-prod. after-tax earns.	ΔW^{an}_ϕ		—	—	—	0.20 (3.64)
ΔNorm. transfer income	ΔY^t_ϕ		—	—	—	0.68 (7.04)
ΔNorm. after-tax capital earns.	ΔR^a_ϕ	1	—	—	—	0.13 (2.39)
Norm. net personal wealth[b]	ΔA^{nh}_ϕ	1	—	0.01	0.32	0.01

Variable	Symbol	Lags				
ΔAfter-tax real mortgage rate	Δi^a_y	4	—	(6.72)	—	(2.34)
%Δ Unemployment rate	u	1, 2 / 0–4, 7	—	—	−0.49	−0.002 (3.64)
%Δ Consumer expectations	Φ	9	—	−0.16 (25.20)	0.04	−0.07 (4.68)
%Δ Family share of households	l_f	9, 10 / 9, 13, 16	—	0.01 (5.41)	0.10	0.02 (4.21)
%Δ Married family share	l_m	2, 7, 12 / 1	—	1.86 (8.84)	—	1.00 (5.90)
%Δ Food/crude prices	p_{ax}	1, 3, 4 / 3	—	−0.93 (8.21)	−0.16	−1.71 (6.91)
%Δ Food/crude prices, 1980s	$p_{a\bar{x}}$	2, 3, 5–7 / 2, 5	—	−2.88 (6.71)	−0.30	−0.19 (3.19)
%Δ Earners' income inequality	σ_w		—	0.25 (11.25)	0.10	−1.23 (4.51)
Norm. Vietnam War pressure	$G_{VIET\phi}$	8 / 4	—	0.48 (18.68)	0.16	0.10 (3.86)
MA(1)			0.64 (9.47)	−0.81 (6.28)	—	−0.70 (7.41)
R²			0.920	0.996	—	0.846
SER			0.006	0.001	—	0.002
D.W.			1.304	2.018	—	2.030

Notes: [a] When lags are different between columns (2) and (4), lags for (2) are in the first row for the respective variables while lags for (4) are in the second row.

[b] Variable is entered in (4) in difference form.

Notes: Numbers in parentheses are t-statistics; threshold for significance at 1% = 2.38. A vector of dummy "shock" variables, not reported here, is also added to both regressions.

coefficients on the components of disposable income. Our expectations in this case are that $1 \geq a_{22} > a_{21} > a_3 \geq 0$.

I have made three alterations of equation (11) for the purposes of direct estimation. First, in order to allow for the possibility that working and affluent households have different propensities to consume out of wage and salary income, I have decomposed total wage and salary income into production worker and non-production worker components. Second, because the more formal derivation of this model (in Gordon, 1994) relies on a neoclassical model of consumption for affluent households in which interest rates matter, I have added the after-tax real mortgage interest rate as an additional influence on intertemporal allocation. And third, in order to improve the precision of the tests for differences among the respective coefficients on the components of disposable income, I have taken differences of the key variables in equation (11) because the hypothesis of a unit root in the dependent variable, normalized real consumption expenditures, cannot be decisively rejected.[36]

Column (4) of table 3.5 reports on estimation of this modification of equation (11). The adjusted R^2 is much lower than in column (3) because the dependent variable is differenced. The coefficients on the components of disposable income are arrayed as hypothesized, with the coefficient on normalized transfer income by far the largest and the coefficient on capital income smaller than the others. The difference between the consumption propensities out of wage and salary and capital income (roughly 0.10) is somewhat smaller than the corresponding "steady-state" estimates in columns (1) and (2). As with the equation reported in column (2), distribution matters here most because of the differential influence of transfer income: While one can decisively reject the hypothesis that the coefficient on normalized transfer income is the same as the other three, one can only reject the hypothesis that the coefficients on production worker wage and salary income and on capital income are different at the 20 percent level.

With these several results, we can generally confirm the plausibility of the heterodox approach to the determination of consumption and saving. While distribution appears to matter more because of the high propensity to consume out of transfer income than because of differential propensities to consume out of wages and profits, one can nonetheless confirm the hypothesis of different consumption/saving propensities out of profits and wages, especially in the reduced-form consumption equations. Should we confirm that distribution matters for investment as well, then these results for consumption are strong enough to allow us to affirm the potential usefulness of analyzing the determination of macro equilibrium through the interaction of distribution and utilization, as outlined in table 3.4 and figure 3.2.

Investment

What about investment? With many fewer gyrations than for consumption, we can simply test an operational version of equation (4.3) above in which profitability as well as demand factors determine investment. Here, the logic of equation (4.3) is implemented with only a couple of additional twists.

First, expected profitability is formalized as expected *relative* profitability, taking into account not only the expected average rate of return on investment but also the opportunity cost of that investment – as represented by some real after-tax interest rate or by a more inclusive measure of the cost of capital services. We should thus look not merely at $I = I(r^\theta, \phi^\theta)$ but more explicitly at $I = I[(r^\theta/i_o), \phi^\theta]$, where i_o is the opportunity cost of investment.

Second, in order to promote comparability with more typical Keynesian investment functions, the influence of expected demand is formalized by a normalized analogy with the usual multiplier and accelerator terms – by which both the level and rate of change of capacity utilization affect normalized investment.

Third, even if we focus exclusively on net investment, ignoring replacement investment, we may still need to consider the vintage effects of a variable pace of technological innovation. When the speed of technological innovation quickens, for example, firms are likely to increase new investment, beyond levels warranted by their established pattern of response to profitability incentives, in order to replace older vintages of capital more rapidly than usual. If the volume of depreciation is estimated in aggregate data by assuming constant rates of depreciation over time, as is the case for the United States, this will result in additional measured net investment that is due only to the failure of conventional measures of capital consumption. One can further postulate, therefore, that normalized net investment will be a positive function of the rate of change of an index of disembodied technical innovation, Ψ.

These three stipulations result in a simple linear implementation of equation (4.3)

$$I^n{}_\phi = a_1 + a_2 r^a + a_3 i_o + a_4 \phi + a_5 \dot{\phi} + a_6 \Psi,$$
$$a_2, a_4, a_5, a_6 > 0, \quad a_3 < 0 \tag{12}$$

where r^a is the after-tax of corporate profitability, i_o is the cost of capital services, ϕ and $\dot{\phi}$ are the level and rate of change of capacity utilization, and Ψ is the rate of change of an index of technical innovation.[37] In implementing this simple investment equation, I have included a vector of dummy variables to test for various "shock" effects, such as the influence

Table 3.6. *Estimated investment equations: real net fixed non-residential investment (normalized on real potential output), US economy, 1955.4–1989.2*

Independent variables	Symbol	Lags	(1)	(2)	(3)	(4)
Constant	a		−0.03 (4.53)	−0.03 (4.68)	−0.03 (4.40)	−0.03 (4.79)
Capacity utilization	ϕ	4	0.08 (11.66)	0.08 (11.63)	0.08 (11.48)	0.09 (11.29)
%Δ Capacity utilization	$\dot{\phi}$	1–3	0.36 (7.54)	0.36 (7.43)	0.35 (7.47)	0.36 (7.58)
After-tax profit rate	r^a	4	0.13 (6.77)	0.14 (6.46)	0.14 (6.18)	0.13 (6.68)
Cost of capital services	i_0	8	−0.12 (16.72)	−0.11 (12.56)	−0.12 (15.20)	−0.12 (16.71)
%Δ Index of tech. inn.	ψ	7, 9, 14	0.10 (4.50)	0.14 (4.43)	0.14 (3.95)	0.14 (4.53)
%Δ Index, tech. inn., 1980s	ψ_-	11, 23	−0.32 (8.43)	−0.26 (6.91)	−0.32 (8.39)	−0.27 (5.20)
Steel strike	Θ_{STL}	4	−0.003 (2.31)	0.003 (2.44)	−0.003 (2.09)	−0.003 (2.25)
Wage–price guideposts	Θ_{GP}	1, 9, 18	0.02 (4.71)	0.02 (4.63)	0.02 (4.62)	0.01 (4.24)
Investment tax credits	Θ_{ITAX}	13	−0.004 (4.26)	−0.004 (4.13)	−0.004 (4.19)	−0.004 (4.28)
Nixon-round controls	Θ_{NIX}	2, 4, 6, 8, 11, 13, 15, 18	0.01 (4.33)	0.01 (4.33)	0.01 (4.29)	0.01 (4.37)

			(1)	(2)	(3)	(4)
Federal reserve shock	Θ_{FED}	1, 13, 15	-0.002 (2.57)	-0.002 (2.55)	-0.002 (2.55)	-0.002 (2.56)
1955 tax reform effect	Θ_{TP0}	13	0.004 (4.99)	0.004 (4.96)	0.004 (4.93)	0.004 (4.88)
1964 tax reform effect	Θ_{TP1}	3,17	0.001 (2.74)	0.001 (2.71)	0.001 (2.70)	0.001 (2.56)
1968 tax reform effect	Θ_{TP2}	8	0.001 (1.94)	0.001 (1.80)	0.001 (1.94)	0.001 (1.72)
1978 tax reform effect	Θ_{TP4}	2, 8, 10, 14	0.002 (4.12)	0.002 (4.08)	0.002 (4.04)	0.002 (4.16)
1981 tax reform effect	Θ_{TP5}	9, 14	-0.001 (7.83)	-0.001 (6.90)	-0.001 (7.78)	-0.001 (5.50)
1986 tax reform effect	Θ_{TP6}	2, 8	0.001 (4.00)	0.001 (3.93)	0.001 (3.98)	0.001 (3.92)
Norm. personal saving	S_ϕ	8	—	0.02 (0.82)	—	—
Norm. government deficit	G^n_ϕ	10	—	—	0.004 (0.23)	—
Norm. net foreign capital	Γ^x_ϕ	8	—	—	—	0.05 (1.32)
	MA(1)		-0.26 (2.18)	-0.22 (1.85)	-0.26 (2.20)	-0.23 (1.98)
	R^2		0.970	0.970	0.970	0.971
	SER		0.002	0.002	0.002	0.002
	D.W.		1.888	1.905	1.885	1.907

Notes: Numbers in parentheses are t-statistics; threshold for significance at 1% = 2.37.

of the 1963 investment tax credits, and have allowed for structural change in the effect of technical innovation during the 1980s.

The results of quarterly estimation of equation (12) are reported in column (1) of table 3.6. All of the principal behavioral hypotheses are confirmed, with coefficients of the expected sign and significant at 1 percent. Of central interest, the coefficient on the after-tax rate of corporate profitability is positive and significant at 1 percent.[38]

Financial constraints

The second necessary condition for the plausibility of a structuralist view of the investment/saving relationship involves the role of finance. For the neoclassical view to hold, we ought to find that credit-market constraints should have a direct or indirect influence, *ceteris paribus*, on the flow of investment. For the structuralist view to hold, by contrast, we should find little or no evidence of such effects.

Table 3.6 reports on a series of tests for the direct influence of credit-market effects within the framework of the simple structuralist investment function derived above.[39]

Column (2) tests for the direct influence of variations in real normalized personal saving: The neoclassical story might expect a strong positive effect, but the coefficient on the saving variable is insignificant, with a t-statistic less than 1.0, while the rest of the equation remains robust after its inclusion.

Column (3) reports on the results of including normalized government saving: Neoclassical emphasis on "crowding out" might lead one to expect a strong positive effect, but this direct test for the effects of public saving is no more successful than that for private saving.

Column (4) tests for the influence of the net inflow of foreign capital: While the effect is positive, as expected, it is also quite weak, with a coefficient barely significant at the 10 percent level.

These additional results reported in table 3.6 focus on hypotheses about the direct effects of finance on investment. The traditional neoclassical story would be just as likely, however, to focus on the indirect effects of saving on investment, running from saving through the cost of capital services to the rate of investment.[40] Since the cost of capital services indeed has the expected negative coefficient in the results reported in table 3.6, is it possible that one or another measure of saving has a negative relationship with this measure of credit-market influence – with increased saving helping reduce the prevailing interest rate – thus providing confirmation of an indirect effect of saving on investment?

Since the measure of the cost of capital used here, conforming to standard specification, is a composite variable including the discrete effects of the relative price of capital goods, the expected rate of return on capital assets, and the tax treatment of fixed investment, I have not constructed behavioral models of the determination of the cost of capital services. Instead, I have performed much simpler Granger-causality tests for the influence of various components of saving on this measure of the cost of capital. Without much qualification, we can conclude from these tests that there is no evidence of a negative association between any of the principal components of saving and the cost of capital. (a) We can accept the null hypothesis that the cost of capital services is not Granger-caused by normalized real personal saving for tests on lags (at four-quarter intervals) from four to twenty-four quarters. (b) We can partially reject the hypothesis that the cost of capital services is not Granger-caused by normalized net government saving, but the effect is the opposite of that anticipated by the crowding-out hypothesis. In the near-term (up to a lag of twelve quarters), there is evidence that net government saving and the cost of capital services Granger-cause each other, but the relationship is positive, not negative. This is probably due to a direct tax effect, not to credit-market "crowding in": The higher the rate of taxation of fixed investment, other things equal, the higher will be measured net government saving and, simultaneously, the costlier will be capital borrowed to finance net investment. Indeed, at even longer lags (from twelve to twenty-four quarters), we can accept the hypothesis that net government saving is Granger-caused by the cost of capital services, suggesting that changes in tax treatment of investment continue to show up in estimates of government net saving, while we can now accept the null hypothesis at the 20 percent level or better that the cost of capital services is *not* Granger-caused by net government saving. (c) We can also accept the null hypothesis that the cost of capital services is not Granger-caused by the normalized net inflow of foreign capital for tests on the full range of lags (at four-quarter intervals) from four to twenty-four quarters.[41]

There is, in short, virtually no evidence that credit-market conditions directly or indirectly influence investment in ways which would support the prevailing neoclassical hypothesis that variations in saving condition variations in investment. Much more detailed analysis of the operations of credit markets would be necessary to reach any stronger conclusions, but there is at least no reason, on the basis of these preliminary glimpses of financial effects, to reject the structuralist view that the supply of saving does not constrain the flow of investment.

4   Models of the relation between investment and saving

The results in the previous section are merely single-equation results. The relationship between investment and saving, according to either neoclassical or structuralist accounts, involves several possible channels of determination. We must examine more than single-equation evidence in order to pursue this effort at disentangling the investment–saving relation.[42]

In this section I report on two such efforts at modeling the investment–saving relation more completely. The first allows for the possibility of either the neoclassical or the structuralist account, relying on a synthetic vector autoregression (VAR) model including variables highlighted by both perspectives. The second relies more explicitly on the structuralist perspective, building and simulating a compact operational version of the simple structuralist model first presented in table 3.4 in section 2.

An a-theoretical VAR model of investment and saving

We can study the investment–saving relation by including key variables highlighted by both neoclassical and structuralist perspectives in an a-theoretical VAR model. If we select variables inclusively, we can allow either or both theoretical accounts to reveal themselves in the interrelationships within that estimated model.[43] I pursue such an exercise here for the full period from 1955.4 to 1989.2.

Given the sharp constraints on degrees of freedom in VAR models, one obviously wants to make parsimonious choices of the variables which ought to be included in any VAR model. In the case highlighted by the discussion in section 2, both neoclassical and structuralist perspectives would agree on the need to include variables representing normalized personal saving, normalized net fixed non-residential investment, and the aggregate rate of capacity utilization. Neoclassical theory would further stipulate the inclusion of the cost of capital services, of importance for investment, and a real interest rate which presumably helps mediate the relation between saving and investment. The structuralist perspective introduced in sections 2 and 3 would argue for the inclusion of a measure of profitability, capturing the central effects of distribution, and the cost of capital services as an additional influence on investment.

I have therefore chosen to work with a VAR model including six endogenous variables representing the union of the sets of variables identified by these two perspectives, including measures of normalized real personal saving, normalized real net fixed non-residential investment, the aggregate rate of capacity utilization, the after-tax rate of corporate profitability, the cost of capital services, and the real three-month

Treasury bill rate. In order to encompass as much as possible of the full period over which investment and saving are simultaneously determined along with capacity utilization, I have estimated VAR equations with one to eight lags of each of the six endogenous variables as well as a linear time trend.

There are two principal kinds of experiments one can perform with a VAR model which should be of interest for our discussion here. First, one can subject the VAR system to a (standard-deviation) shock of each included variable in turn and then simulate the model forward over a substantial number of periods, tracing the reverberations of that single-variable shock throughout the full system. This test allows one to explore, for example, the effects on investment of a shock in saving. Second, one can subject the system to shocks in all the variables, simulating the effects of all those shocks over a significant time period, and trace how much of the cumulative effects in each variable are due to shocks in itself and to shocks in the other endogenous variables.

In performing these experiments, the order of inclusion of the variables in the system is crucial, since the first-included variables are credited with whatever common error components are shared with variables subsequently entered into the system. In order to give innovations in saving the best possible chance of having a significant effect throughout the simulated system, I have chosen to include saving as the first variable in the system, followed in turn by investment, utilization, profitability, the cost of capital services, and the real interest rate.[44]

Table 3.7 reports the cumulative effects of shocks to saving and investment within this estimated and then simulated system.

The first pair of columns ((1)–(2)) traces the effects on personal saving and investment of a standard-deviation innovation in personal saving, with the cumulative responses expressed as a percentage of each variable's own mean value for the full period of estimation. As column (1) shows, saving is cumulatively responsive to its own innovations, with a cumulative effect equal to 34.1 percent of the period mean of saving after sixteen quarters and to 56.4 percent after thirty-two quarters. But, as column (2) makes clear, investment is largely unresponsive to this same innovation in personal saving, with the cumulative response never reaching more than 12.3 percent (after twenty-four quarters). This is the system equivalent to our finding in section 1 that investments is not Granger-caused by saving.

By contrast, we find in the second pair of columns ((3)–(4)) that both investment *and* saving are cumulatively responsive to an innovation in investment. After thirty-two quarters, the cumulative response of investment to its own innovation (in (4)) is roughly as large as the cumulative response of saving to its own innovation (in (1)), although the response

Table 3.7. *Response of investment and saving to innovations: cumulative responses of net investment and personal saving to innovations in net investment and personal saving, estimates from 6-variable VAR system, 1955.4–1989.2*

	Cumulative responses to innovations expressed as % of variable's own mean			
	Response to st. dev. shock in saving		Response to st. dev. shock in investment	
Quarters elapsed	Saving (1)	Investment (2)	Saving (3)	Investment (4)
8	18.4%	8.6	21.7	42.3
16	34.1	10.0	36.5	34.9
24	45.3	12.3	43.5	41.8
32	56.4	10.7	49.1	58.4

Note: Impulse response (this table) and variance decomposition (table 3.8) based on estimated VAR system including six endogenous variables and a linear time trend. The six endogenous variables comprise, in the order of inclusion for estimation of impulse responses, normalized personal saving, normalized net non-residential investment, aggregate rate of capacity utilization, net after-tax NFCB profit rate, cost of capital services, and real Treasury bill rate.

Source: See Data appendix for variable definition and documentation.

comes earlier – presumably reflecting the importance of sudden shifts in investors' expectations, on the investment side, and the relatively inertial quality of the determination of consumption and saving, on the other. In relatively sharp contrast with the results reported in column (2), however, saving is much more responsive to an innovation in investment (in (3)) than vice versa; cumulatively over the full thirty-two quarters, indeed, saving is nearly as responsive to an innovation in investment as it is to an innovation in itself ((3) versus (1)).[45]

Table 3.8 presents results of the second kind of VAR experiment. All of the endogenous variables in the same VAR model are subjected to a standard deviation shock at the base period. For each subsequent quarter, the resulting simulated "error" in the respective endogenous variables, expressed for convenience as the variance in the variable from its baseline trend, is decomposed into the error due to its own innovations and the error due respectively to innovations in each of the other endogenous variables. (By definition, the own- and other-variance

Table 3.8. *Investment, saving and utilization responses to system shocks: Variance decomposition of responses to innovations in all variables in a 6-variable VAR system, 1955.4–1989.2*

Percent of variable's variance due to innovations in respective variable[a]

	% Decomposition of variance for Saving				Investment				Utilization			
Quarters elapsed	Sav. (1)	Invest. (2)	Util. (3)	Other[b] (4)	Sav. (5)	Invest. (6)	Util. (7)	Other (8)	Sav. (9)	Invest. (10)	Util. (11)	Other (12)
4	71.3	10.0	11.3	7.4	3.4	88.8	2.5	5.4	6.4	24.0	49.7	19.9
8	38.5	31.0	22.3	8.2	4.2	79.1	3.2	13.6	5.8	20.5	32.9	40.8
16	37.9	31.0	22.4	8.7	2.9	54.3	9.0	33.8	3.8	34.3	18.9	43.0
24	35.6	27.2	26.9	10.3	2.3	42.1	20.9	34.6	2.8	35.4	18.5	43.3
32	32.1	23.0	32.0	12.9	2.1	38.8	26.6	32.5	5.4	32.2	18.2	44.2

Notes: [a] Sums across four columns for any single variable may not add to 100% due to rounding error.
[b] "Other" variables include the rate of profit, the cost of capital services, and the 3-month Treasury bill rate.
Notes and Sources: See above for table 3.7.

components sum to 100 percent.) If a variable is largely exogenous to the system, the percentage of its variance due to its own innovation will remain quite high over a long period of simulation. If a variable is heavily conditioned by other endogenous variables, the percentage of its error due to its own innovation will start at 100 percent (or close to it) but decline fairly quickly as the portion attributable to innovations in other variables begins to rise.

Columns (1)–(4) of table 3.8 report the variance in saving attributable to the respective endogenous variables for periods from four to thirty-two lags. Beginning at 100 percent in the first quarter, the portion of saving's variance due to its own innovation drops to only 38.5 percent after eight quarters and then begins to level off. The portion due to investment rises quickly to 31.0 percent after only eight quarters and then begins relatively to give way to the components due to capacity utilization and the other three variables in the system.

In relatively sharp contrast, turning to columns (5)–(8), the portion of investment's variance due to its own innovation remains quite high after eight quarters (79.1 percent) before beginning to reflect the influence of capacity utilization and the contributions of profitability, the cost of capital, and the real interest rate. Notably, the portion due to the innovation in saving (column (5)) never rises above 4.2 percent (after eight quarters).

The final set of four columns reports results of the same exercise for capacity utilization. Here, clearly, there is relatively little inertial effect of utilization's innovation on itself. But the influence of saving remains scant, reaching a peak of only 6.4 percent. By sixteen quarters, more than three quarters of the variance of utilization is due to investment and the other three endogenous variables.

The results in table 3.8 thus provide a relatively compact (if also a-theoretical) guide to the relationship between investment and saving. After eight quarters, the relative contribution of the investment innovation to saving's variance (31 percent) is more than seven times greater than the relative contribution of the saving innovation to investment's variance (4.2 percent). Looking at the decomposition of utilization's variance, similarly, the relative contribution of the investment innovation after sixteen quarters (34.3 percent) is nine times greater than the relative contribution of the saving innovation (3.8 percent).

A structuralist model of investment and saving

While the results of these experiments with a VAR model are interesting, they fail to provide much guidance about *how* investment affects saving –

much less to offer some clues about prospectively promising policy initatives.

In order to overcome those limitations, we need to turn toward simulations based on a less a-theoretical structural model of the joint determination of investment and saving. For these purposes, I have chosen to work from the simple structuralist model presented in table 3.4. The aim of this final exercise is to provide a behaviorally meaningful systemic representation of the relationship between investment and saving which, however simplified, can begin to approximate the results of real-world initiatives to boost both investment and saving.

The basic structure of the model presented in table 3.4 is retained, with all flow variables normalized on potential output. The model builds on the estimated consumption and investment equations presented respectively in column (2) of table 3.5 and in column (1) of table 3.6. Profitability is treated as an exogenous variable, dropping the behavioral representation included in equation (4.4), as is the cost of capital services. Instead of assuming a given rate of depreciation, as in equation (4.6), normalized non-residential depreciation expenditures are determined stochastically, with a simple behavioral relation expressing depreciation as a function of the normalized capital stock and linear and geometric time trends.[46]

In addition to the other endogenous identities presented in equations (4.5)–(4.9) in table 3.4,[47] it is further necessary to determine real net personal wealth endogenously since it plays an important role in the consumption equation and since, obviously, cumulated net worth reflects past saving behavior. The nominal change in personal financial wealth is itself determined by adding saving and accumulated capital gains on equity and subtracting household demand for money balances as well as a statistical discrepancy.[48] The level of real personal wealth is then determined by deflating the sum of nominal personal financial wealth and personal money stocks and adding to it the real value of personal residential assets. Capital gains on equity and the value of residential structures are treated as exogenous variables, while normalized household money demand is determined by a simple behavioral equation using, as independent variables, lagged money demand, lagged trend consumption, the lagged rate of change in unemployment, and a vector of dummy variables reflecting changes in personal income tax rates.[49]

Such a simple structural model can hardly pretend to represent a full and encompassing behavioral representation of the post-war US economy.[50] It has the advantage, nonetheless, of an explicit and operational representation of all of the main channels through which a structuralist macroeconomic perspective could analyze the interactions between investment and saving. And with such representation, it allows us to perform some simulations of the kinds of policy experiments representing neoclassical and structuralist approaches to boosting investment and saving.[51]

Neoclassical policy proposals are easily represented. In general, mainstream policy analysts hope for either a change in personal saving propensities, exogenously increasing the flow of personal saving, or a tax on consumption, in order to boost net government saving without impinging upon personal saving. I have represented the second policy imperative by increasing total government tax revenues by the equivalent of a flat, across-the-board, one standard deviation's change in personal tax payments, reducing personal disposable income by an equal amount; I have called this the "consumption tax" experiment. In order to represent an entirely exogenous shift in personal saving by a roughly equivalent amount, I have simply "forgiven" or erased personal interest payment obligations, increasing household saving – at given levels of income – by an average quarterly amount roughly equivalent to the reduction in personal disposable income involved in the "consumption tax" experiment; I have called this the "saving windfall" experiment. According to the neoclassical story, one or the other initiative should augment total saving, whether public or private, and eventually stimulate investment in turn.

According to the structuralist story sketched in the second part of section 2, two different kinds of "shocks" might result in increases in both saving and investment. First, if there were an autonomous shift in profitability – resulting, for example, from a positive "shock" to productivity with wages held constant – both saving and investment would increase under the conditions stipulated by the structuralist model depicted in figure 3.2. Second, a favorable shift in investors' expectations would autonomously boost investment and, consequently, saving. I have represented the first kind of "shock" by an autonomous 50 percent increase in the flow of after-tax profits, an amount roughly equivalent in dollars to the average simulated shocks representing the neoclassical story; I have called this the "productivity windfall" test.[52] And to represent the effects of an autonomous shift in investors' expectations, I have estimated a version of the investment equation presented in column (1) of table 3.6 which seeks to model investors' expectations by including a term for the interest-rate spread, and simulated the effect of a favorable shift in investors' expectations equivalent to 1.5 times the standard deviation of the interest-rate spread variable. (This amount was calibrated to provide a simulated boost to investment roughly half the magnitude of the investment stimulus resulting from the "productivity windfall.") I have called this the "investors' spirits" experiment.

Table 3.9. *Structural simulation of shocks to investment and saving:
percent deviation of net investment, saving, and utilization from
benchmark simulation, estimated in simulations of structuralist model,
1955.4–1989.2*

	Average deviation from baseline simulation, expressed as % of variable's baseline mean, full period			
Simulation	Net investment	Personal saving	Consumption	Capacity util.
(1) Saving windfall	1.3	33.9	0.6	0.4
(2) Consumption tax	− 6.3	− 31.1	− 2.9	− 2.1
(3) Productivity windfall	8.8%	5.9	− 0.6	0.02
(4) Investors' spirits	4.5	3.0	0.2	0.3

Notes: See text for description of model used for simulation.
Net investment is real net fixed domestic non-residential investment. Personal saving is gross private saving minus undistributed (adjusted) corporate profits and capital consumption allowances. Consumption is real personal consumption expenditures. Capacity utilization is the ratio of actual to potential output. All flow variables are normalized on real potential output.
Source: See Data appendix for complete variable definition and sources.

Table 3.9 presents the results of these policy "experiments." The changes were implemented for the respective exogenous variables for the full period of estimation from 1955.4 through 1989.2. They amount, therefore, to "what-if" experiments over a long "medium-term." Their estimated effects are taken from dynamic model simulations over the full period and these results are compared to those for a dynamic (baseline) simulation of the model without the policy "shocks." I have presented the results of each of the experiments for four outcome variables: normalized net fixed non-residential investment, normalized real personal saving, normalized real personal consumption expenditures, and the aggregate rate of capacity utilization. Rows (1)–(2) in table 3.9 represent the results of the neoclassical experiments, while rows (3)–(4) report the results of the structuralist tests. For each experiment, the effects are reported as the average value of the endogenous variable's deviations from a baseline simulation, without the policy experiments, expressed as a percentage of that variable's average values under the baseline simulation.

In the case of the "saving windfall" (row (1)), an autonomous increase in personal saving results, hardly surprisingly, in a huge relative increase in personal saving. But the huge increase in saving produces only a scant relative stimulus to investment – which itself eventually leads to a modest increase in consumption and utilization.

The "consumption tax" (row (2)) has an effect exactly opposite to its intended impact. While it is supposed to increase saving and investment, it has the effect (first) of reducing disposable income, which then reduces both investment and consumption, resulting in a reduction of capacity utilization which therefore contributes to the reduction in personal saving. On balance, there is no compensating stimulus provided by the increase in net government saving which the autonomous tax increase permits.[53]

We next turn to the structuralist experiments. The "productivity windfall" (row (3)) has the effects anticipated by the structuralist model. Investment is substantially boosted (by close to 10 percent of its baseline mean). The increase in both profitability – the distributional effect – and investment – the demand effect – result in an increase in personal saving. The distributional effect results in a decrease in consumption, as one would expect from the heterodox consumption function. The combined effects on capacity utilization are roughly a wash, with the average utilization rate remaining effectively unchanged. The results, in short, are those which the neoclassicals seek but are unable to secure through their own initiatives: an allocative transfer of resources from consumption to saving and investment which would presumably result in a more rapid rate of economic growth in the future.[54]

The "investors' spirits" experiment also boosts both investment and saving. Investment increases, of course, but since the shift in expectations does not come out of the wage and salary share, both saving and consumption are able to respond positively in turn. The net result is an increase in utilization much greater than that from the productivity windfall experiment.

If the policy objective is to increase both investment and saving in roughly proportionate amounts, in short, structuralist policy initiatives would appear to have much more promise than those promoted by neoclassical economists. Following the neoclassical cookbook, one can successfully increase (or decrease) saving, but nothing like the increases (or decreases) in investment necessary to preserve the investment/saving balance are forthcoming. Following structuralist suggestions, by contrast, both investment and saving can be increased in roughly balanced proportions.[55] And that, if we return to the beginning of this chapter, is the principal objective to which policy economists have been turning with increasing intensity.[56]

5   Policy implications

Seeking to boost stagnant investment, the prevailing policy consensus in many advanced countries calls for efforts to curb consumption and trim government deficits in order to fatten saving.

That policy imperative presupposes that increases in saving will, indeed, stimulate greater investment. This chapter has cast considerable doubt upon that presupposition, at least for the case of the US economy. It has suggested, instead, that efforts to boost investment directly could not only stimulate investment but also help foster the saving required, over the medium term, to help finance that investment. If this were the only issue involved in the debate over policies to boost investment and saving, the analysis presented in this chapter might appear to shift the terms of debate dramatically.

But there is still another presupposition underlying the mainstream policy consensus. One important additional reason many neoclassical economists stress the need to fatten saving is that they do not believe that anything can be done on the supply side to enhance productivity – and thereby to enhance the actual and expected rate of return on fixed investment, to bolster investors' spirits, and directly to promote more rapid investment. The sources of the productivity slowdown may not be entirely mysterious, in the minds of mainstream economists, but they remain largely insusceptible to policy initiatives. Hatsopoulos, Krugman, and Summers write (1988, p. 304), for example:

There is a further reason for focusing on the cost of capital in addressing U.S. productivity problems. Many other possible sources of productivity difficulties are much less amenable to public policy. Insofar as the productivity problem is a consequence of the depletion of good ideas . . . or the changing attitudes of workers, or the behavior of managers, there is relatively little that public policy can do to address it.

It is precisely on this point, however, that progressive policy advocates would vigorously challenge the mainstream consensus. Many of us have argued at length that sluggish productivity growth in countries such as the United States and the United Kingdom reflects the costs and burdens of a set of institutions, shaped partly by public policy, which provide ineffective support for productivity enhancement.[57] Has there been a "depletion of good ideas"? The government can help promote research and development. Have workers' attitudes become a problem? The government can help shape labor–management institutions which, through greater workplace democracy, provide much stronger worker incentives. Does the "behavior of managers" impede productivity growth? The government can help promote more efficient managerial use of available resources by taxing financial speculation, promoting real wage growth (in order to push management to make the most effective possible use of their labor), and supporting innovation and new product development.

Despite many recent advances in modern economic analysis,[58] mainstream policy analysts typically continue to work with a view of production as technologically determined, immune to social determinations, and therefore beyond the reach of public policy. That view is archaic and counter-productive. It makes much more sense, many progressives have argued, to work with a "social" rather than a "technical" model of production and profitability.[59]

And it is here that structuralist micro and macro analyses converge. It is possible, progressives argue, to enhance productivity growth by promoting more effective and democratic management and production within the firm. It is further possible, the structuralist perspective reviewed here would suggest, that enhanced productivity growth can both promote investment and foster the saving required to help finance it. Gordon (this volume), Bowles and Gintis (this volume), and Epstein and Gintis (this volume) all provide suggestions about the kind of interdependent micro and macro initiatives which could help realize this prospect.

It is reasonable to argue, in short, that neoclassical policy analysts are wrong on two out of two counts. First, promoting saving by itself is unlikely to stimulate investment. Second, public policies promoting productivity growth, with the corollary objective of stimulating investment, can work and should be pursued much more aggressively. The case for tighter austerity regimes rests on remarkably weak foundations. By contrast, the case for a progressive alternative appears substantially more persuasive.

Data Appendix   Data sources and documentation

This appendix defines and provides source documentation for all the variables used in or necessary for quarterly results reported in this essay.

I use here the following abbreviations: NIPA, National Income and Product Accounts; CB, CitiBank Database; *SCB, Survey of Current Business*, and *SA, Statistical Abstract of the United States*. All other source references here refer by author and date to sources included in the list of references for this data appendix. Unless otherwise noted, "normalized" refers to a real variable divided by real aggregate potential output (defined below). Unless otherwise noted, all rates of change are logarithmic rates of change and all discrete differentials in the regression tables are calculated as arithmetic first differences.

Outcome variables

Net investment and depreciation

Quarterly data for real gross fixed investment are provided in NIPA Table 1.1: line 7. However, data on *net* non-residential and residential investment are only available on an annual basis. It is nonetheless possible to derive quarterly figures for these series with considerable accuracy.

(1) Using the Chow-Lin interpolation procedure (Chow and Lin, 1971), I have estimated a quarterly series for real non-residential depreciation by interpolating the annual series for real non-residential depreciation (NIPA 5.3:8) on a constant, a time trend, and aggregate capacity utilization (see below). Since non-residential depreciation is highly trended, with relatively little cyclical variation, the potential distortions within any given year from such quarterly interpolations are likely to be minimal. The procedure further constrains the average annual values of the interpolated quarterly series to equal the corresponding annual value for the original series (the correlation between the average annual average value of the interpolated series and the original annual series, indeed, is 1.00).

(2) Given this one quarterly series for real non-residential depreciation (d_k), it is then possible arithmetically to derive quarterly estimates of the other three components of total fixed gross investment: (a) Real net fixed non-residential investment is obtained by subtracting d_k from real gross fixed non-residential investment (NIPA 1.2:8); (b) real residential depreciation (d_r) is obtained by subtracting d_k from total depreciation (NIPA 1.10:2); and (c) real net fixed residential investment is obtained by subtracting d_r from real gross fixed residential investment (NIPA 1.2:11).

These simple operations thus generate quarterly series for net investment and depreciation for both non-residential and residential components.

Saving and consumption

Nominal personal saving is taken from NIPA 2.1:30 and deflated by the implicit GNP price deflator for (NIPA 7.4:1) to equal real personal saving. Real net business saving is defined as undistributed corporate profits (with inventory valuation adjustment) (NIPA 1.14:26 + 27) deflated by the implicit GNP price deflator (NIPA 7.4:1). Real net private saving is the sum of real personal saving and real net business saving.

Real personal consumption expenditures come directly from NIPA 1.2:2.

Explanatory variables

Additional consumption variables

Trend normalized consumption is defined as an eight-quarter backward-moving average of real personal consumption expenditures (divided by real potential output). The deviation of consumption growth is the rate of growth of last period's real personal consumption expenditures minus a twelve-quarter backward-moving average of the rate of real personal consumption expenditures, beginning with the previous period.

Capacity utilization

Aggregate capacity utilization is defined as the ratio of real actual to real potential output for the aggregate economy. Real aggregate potential output is estimated by applying the method traditionally used by the Council of Economic Advisers and by updating their calculations through 1989. Method with applications through 1978 is presented in Clark (1979); data through 1978 come from unpublished data supplied by Council of Economic Advisers. Updated series and detailed documentation of estimate is available in supplementary memo, "Estimating the Rate of Capacity Utilization: Description of Methodology," available from this author. Rate of change of capacity utilization is defined as the logarithmic rate of change of capacity utilization for the private domestic non-residential sector. Net after-tax capacity utilization is aggregate capacity utilization minus normalized total depreciation expenditures $(d_k + d_r)$ and normalized total government tax revenues (NIPA: 3.1:1, deflated by NIPA 7.4:1).

Corporate after-tax rate of profits

The flow of net after-tax profits is defined as fully adjusted net corporate profits plus net interest payments minus corporate tax payments: NIPA, 1.14, 20, 29, 23 respectively). The profit share (used in the consumption equations) is after-tax profits divided by real potential output. The rate of profit (used in the investment equations) is net after-tax profits for the non-financial corporate business sector (NIPA, 1.16, 27, 35, 29 respectively) divided by net fixed capital stock plus inventories measured at their current replacement cost for the NFCB. Stock of capital defined as the (mid-year current dollar) value of the net fixed non-residential private capital stock for all industries in the non-financial corporate business sector (NFCB) of the US economy. (Mid-year estimates derived by averaging the current and previous year's end-year values.) US Department of Commerce (1987), table A6; and *SCB*, "Fixed Reproducible Tangible Wealth in the United States, 1986–89," August 1990, table 8. Stock of inventories for NFCB from unpublished work sheets provided by Bureau of Economics, Department of Commerce.

Capital–output ratio

For trends in capital–output ratio, capital is defined as stock of real net fixed non-residential private capital stock for all industries (sources same as above), and output as real GNP (NIPA 1.2:1).

Other components of aggregate income

Normalized transfer income is total government transfers to persons (NIPA: 1.9:15) deflated by the implicit GNP deflator (NIPA 7.4:1). Normalized residential income is real total GNP (NIPA 1.2:1) minus (real compensation (NIPA 2.1:2 + 8) + real capital income (NIPA 1.9:16 + 17 plus 1.14:9 + 17) + real total personal tax revenues (NIPA 3.2:2 + 3.3:2) + real depreciation ($d_k + d_r$) (all deflated by NIPA 7.4:1)) plus real transfer income (NIPA: 1.9:15 deflated by 7.4:1).

Exogenous saving and investment

The normalized real government deficit is from NIPA 3.2:31 plus 3.3:31 deflated by the government purchases implicit price deflator (NIPA: 7.4:16). Normalized net foreign investment is from NIPA 4.1:22 deflated by the fixed investment implicit price deflator (NIPA: 7.4:8).

Components of earnings

Real after-tax production and non-production wage and salary income is based on the decomposition of total employee compensation (NIPA 1.14:2) and total personal taxes between production and non-production employees (method available from author upon request). Real-after-tax capital earnings is real capital income (NIPA 1.9:16 + 17 plus 1.14:9 + 17 deflated by NIPA7.4:1) adjusted for capital's share of total personal taxes (method available from author upon request).

Net personal wealth

Real net household assets defined as Fair (1984), variable AH. Further identities used in determining real net household assets endogenously taken from Fair (1984), table A.5, eqs. 65–6.

Interest rates

Real after-tax mortgage rate defined as Fair (1984) variable RMA. Cost of capital services defined as in Chirinko (1987), with data kindly supplied by Robert Chirinko. Three-month treasury bill rate used in VAR simulations is from CB: FYGN3.

Unemployment

The rate of unemployment is the percent of unemployed in the total civilian labor force, from CB: LHUR.

Technological innovation

Defined as a multivariate factor loading on the annual rate of change of the stock of research and development capital, the annual rate of change of the stock of scientists and engineers in private industry, and the annual flow of new books published on technology. Sources and estimating method reported in Gordon (1989).

Miscellaneous control variables

Consumer expectations measured by index of consumer sentiment, from CB: HHSNTN. Family share of households and married family share based on data from *CPS*, Series P-25. Food/crude prices based on the difference between the consumer price index (CB: PZUNEW) and the consumer price index for all items less food and energy (CB: PUXX). Index of earners' income inequality defined as a weighted ratio of white male (full-time, year-round) earnings to black male and female (full-time, year-round) earnings, based on data from *CPS*, Series P-60. Vietnam War Demand "Shock" defined as original incremental outlays for national security due to the Vietnam conflict normalized on potential output. Incremental Vietnam War costs from *SA*, table 594.

Dummy "shock" variables

The Tax Reform Effect variables are defined as a value of + 1 for the quarters during the year in which significant reform of the personal income tax system took place and a value of − 1 for the subsequent four quarters. Episodes of significant tax reform based on Pechman (1987), Tables A-3, A-5. Full details of these and other dummy shock variables are available from the author upon request.

Notes

The author would like to thank Sam Bowles, Steve Marglin, and the editors of this volume for encouragement and helpful suggestions, as well as participants at an Economic Policy Institute seminar for thoughtful reactions.

1 For more background on this policy perspective, see the introduction to this volume. For a clear statement of the logic underlying the conventional policy wisdom calling for increased net saving, see Hatsopoulos, Krugman, and Summers (1988).

2 On the problem of "underconsumption," see also Hatsopoulos, Krugman, and Poterba (1989).

3 For a discussion of the likelihood that net exports and net national indebtedness do not adjust and that the identity holds for the relationship between investment and *national* saving, see Feldstein and Horioka (1980), Summers (1980), and Epstein and Gintis (1992).

4 The cycle dating corresponds to cycle peaks for the US economy, in order to maintain consistency with the rest of the analysis in this chapter. US cycle peaks are determined by peaks in the rate of capacity utilization for private non-residential business, where capacity utilization is measured by the ratio of actual to potential output for that sector. For justification of this measure and the cycle dating which results, see Bowles, Gordon, and Weisskopf (1990, chapter 4).

5 For a detailed report on investment and saving trends in the OECD countries which similarly confirms recent declines in net investment and net saving rates, see Dean *et al.* (1989).

6 For example, Eisner (1991) argues that conventional definitions of net national saving in the US data are far too narrow and that a broader definition of net national saving reveals a substantially higher net national saving rate.

Block (1990) argues that flow-of-funds data provide a clearer picture of national saving and those data suggest that net national saving actually increased during the 1980s, both relative to its own time trends and to net fixed domestic investment, suggesting "an increasing supply of personal saving relative to the amount of net private investment actually taking place" (p. 15).

For further useful discussion of these problems, see Blecker (1990).

7 As noted above (in footnote 4), business-cycle peaks are defined by peaks in a series for capacity utilization for private non-residential business. Since this series peaks when the rate of growth of real output falls below the rate of growth of real potential output, rather than when the rate of growth of real output actually becomes negative, business-cycle peaks indicated by this dating method are bound to occur before peaks designated by the usual National Bureau of Economic Research dating criteria. Thus, for example, the long 1980s business cycle peaked in the second quarter of 1989 by the method deployed here while the NBER peak did not occur until mid 1990.

8 Documentation of definitions and sources for all quarterly US data deployed in this chapter are provided in the Data appendix.

9 For a compact review of the formal specification of such tests, see Judge *et al.* (1985, pp. 667–9).

10 There are alternative specifications of such tests, with variants on the basic test including leads of one or both variables as well. I have reported here results for the traditional test including only lags of both variables, although additional tests not reported here suggest that inclusion of leads would not change the basic conclusions derived from this exercise. For formulation of alternative specifications of this type of test, see Geweke, Meese, and Dent (1983).

11 See, for example, Sims (1972).

12 However natural and intriguing such tests may be, at least for a superficial glimpse of this pairwise relation, these are the first such tests of which I am aware for either the United States or other advanced economies.

13 For an examination of the timing of stagnant net investment and the productivity slowdown in the US, see Bowles, Gordon, and Weisskopf (1990, chapters 4, 7).

14 The net capital–output ratio, defined as the ratio of the real net fixed domestic non-residential capital stock to real gross national product, increased steadily in the US economy over the four key phases of the post-war period being examined here, equaling 0.85 in 1955.4–1966.1, 0.86 in 1966.1–1973.1, 0.93 in 1973.1–1978.4, and 0.98 in 1978.4–1989.2.

15 A similar set of connections is adduced in Pieper (1989).

16 The connections underlying this explanation are strongly confirmed by the US data, with the pace of productivity growth providing the critical key to the sign of the relationship between depreciation and saving: For example, the contemporaneous correlation between (normalized) non-residential depreciation and (normalized) personal saving is positive (0.33) during the part of the post-war boom covered here when there was increasingly rapid productivity growth (1955.4–1966.1), but strongly negative (− 0.70) during the period of stagnant or declining productivity growth rates (1966.1–1989.2), resulting on balance in a smaller negative correlation (− 0.43) for the full period.

17 See Bridel (1987) for a useful review of the history of thought on this debate.

18 This provides, of course, the basis for the standard derivation of the IS-curve in traditional representations of the "grand neoclassical synthesis."

19 For a useful review of neoclassical analyses of consumers' expenditures, with a relatively complete bibliography, see Deaton (1987). It should be noted that much of the recent discussion of the behavior of aggregate consumption abstracts from the possible influence of the real interest rate on consumption. This elision largely results, however, from the assumption, for reasons of analytic convenience, that the real interest rate is constant over the period of determination of life-time consumption (as well, in part, from the considerable ambiguity in empirical studies about the relation between aggregate consumption and the real interest rate). See, for discussion of these issues, Deaton (1987, pp. 595–7).

20 In the discussion which follows, honoring neoclassical expectations about the relatively insignificant role of the net international trade balance in equilibrating investment and saving, I abstract from total saving and focus on net national saving.

21 One further complication (within neoclassical economics) involves the possibility of a behavioral feedback effect from net government borrowing to household decisions about personal saving. The idea of "Ricardian equivalence," due principally to Barro (1974), suggests that government deficits, involving lower government saving today in return for higher tax payments in the future, will generate a partly compensating increase in consumers' saving in order to help finance future increases in their or their children's tax obligations. But the empirical evidence for and against this proposition is relatively ambiguous. For a recent review, see Poterba and Summers (1987).

22 For examples of early efforts at such a synthesis, see Marglin (1984, chapters 20–1) and Taylor (1985). For a more recent review, see Taylor (1991).

23 In this simple model, this equation is derived in its conventional form by substituting from (4.9) into (4.2). Then modified (4.2) is set equal to (4.3) and solved for ϕ. The model presumes the usual stability condition that saving is more responsive to demand than investment. It is also assumed in the graph that investment is more responsive to profitability than saving, an assumption which is consistent with the empirical results reported in the following section as well as in Gordon (this volume).

24 As noted in the text, the profit function is drawn as a linear, upward-sloping curve for generality of presentation. See Gordon (this volume) for full discussion and evidence on the likely shape of the profitability function.

25 And here, again relying on superficial evidence, we would have strong reason to suspect that in the observed data investment would lead saving. Looking only at simple bivariate

correlations, investment follows changes in both the profit share and the rate of aggregate capacity utilization much more quickly than does saving. An autonomous change in profitability or utilization favorable to investment and saving would thus show up in data for investment substantially before it would manifest itself in data for saving.

26 See, for direct discussion of these problems, Marglin (1987) and Skott (1989, chapter 7).

27 See, for some basic summaries of this position, Davidson (1978) and Moore (1988).

28 I call this a reduced-form expression because the behavioral hypotheses underlying the Cambridge consumption function involve hypotheses about propensities to consume out of income which households actually receive from capital assets, which in turn are presumed to be a function of the profit share. Direct tests of the effect of the profit share on consumption thus involve a reduced-form expression which collapses the two links in the chain of determination from (a) profitability through (b) income from capital assets to (c) consumption.

29 See, for a useful review of the evolution of this view, Marglin (1984, chapter 6).

30 The assumption that $\beta_2 \leq 1$ is not especially important behaviorally but is useful for the derivation of sign expectations in equation (6) below. Assuming a simple economy with no taxes or other leakages from the residual after wages are paid, it makes sense that income from capital assets could not be larger than profits and that it might be smaller if some profits were kept as retained earnings in order to finance investment.

31 In the extreme form of the Cambridge hypothesis, working households have no saving and would be likely to accumulate no net personal wealth. As long as the marginal propensity to consume of these households is less than one, however, the possibility of net personal wealth accumulation emerges.

32 For simplicity, I have derived this version of the Cambridge equation with respect to the adjustment dynamics only for working households, neglecting the possibility of alternative adjustment dynamics for affluent households. In Gordon (1994, chapter 4), I formally postulate two classes of households, using the standard neoclassical model of life-cycle consumption to analyze the adjustment behavior of affluent households. Given the absence of disaggregated data on personal consumption expenditures for these two separate classes of households, one must aggregate the two models for a single final aggregate model of consumption behavior. The final operational equation closely resembles equation (10).

33 A skeletal list of those additional variables with sign expectations in parentheses: the rate of change in an index of consumers' expectations (+); the rate of change of an index of earnings inequality among full-time workers (+) (greater earnings inequality among wage and salary workers, other things equal, would force a higher consumption ratio among workers with relatively reduced earnings in order to maintain their target levels of consumption); the rate of change in the share of households living in "families" (as opposed to unrelated individuals) (+) (since there is likely to be a higher ratio of dependents to earners in family units than among unrelated individuals, it is likely, other things equal, that family units must devote a higher proportion of their earnings to consumption than would unrelated individuals); the rate of change of prices for food and energy (−), in order to control for adjustment to volatile shifts in those commodities; and the normalized level of incremental defense expenditures during the Vietnam War (+), in order to take into account the possible effects of unexpected spurts in demand during that military episode. I have also included a vector of dummy variables to control for the effects of other concrete shocks – including the Korean War and Nixon Round price controls, the 1959 steel strike, the mid 1960s wage–price guideposts, the 1979 shift in Federal Reserve policy, and major revisions in federal income tax provisions – while remaining agnostic about the signs of their possible effects.

34 The equations are estimated by two-stage least squares since this consumption equation is used in the small structural model used for simulation purposes in the following section and since, in that model, the level of net after-tax capacity utilization is an endogenous variable. Lag lengths in this and the other regression equations reported in tables 3.5 and 3.6 were selected by a search for the lag length which maximized the explanatory power of those respective variables.

35 Formal statistical tests confirm the hypotheses that all of these four coefficients are significantly different from each other with the sole exception of the coefficients on the profit share and normalized residual income, for which we must accept the null hypothesis of equality.

36 If both a trend and a constant term are included in implementation of the augmented Dickey–Fuller test, the hypothesis of a unit root in C_ϕ cannot be rejected at the 10 percent level though it can be rejected at the 5 percent level. If only a constant is included, the hypothesis of a unit root can be rejected even at the 10 percent level. (These results rely on a recent extension by MacKinnon (1990) of the critical values for the augmented Dickey–Fuller test as implemented in the statistical package MicroTSP v. 7.0.)

37 The reader might note that Keynesian and neoclassical approaches to investment are approximately nested within this synthetic structuralist investment equation, with the Keynesian approach imposing zero restrictions on coefficients a_2 and a_3 and the neoclassical approach imposing a zero restriction at least on a_2, if not also on a_4 and a_5. An annual version of this investment equation is explored in some detail in Gordon, Weisskopf, and Bowles (1990), with references there to some mainstream formulations which are roughly comparable.

38 In order to test most directly for the slope of the $\phi(\pi)$ curve in figure 3.2, a simpler version of the investment function can be estimated which includes only the level of capacity utilization, the level of the after-tax profit share, and the cost of capital services. In such an estimated equation, the coefficient on the after-tax profit share is 0.73, roughly four times larger than the (steady-state) coefficient on profitability in column (1) of table 3.5. This affirms the positive slope depicted in figure 3.2 and indicates the designation of the US economy during this period as a "profit-led" case.

39 In each of these tests, the lag on the additional included variable was selected by choosing the lag at which there was the largest autocorrelation between the residual of the estimated equation in column (1) and the candidate for inclusion, thus maximizing the possibility that inclusion of the selected independent variable would be warranted on econometric grounds.

40 This is, for example, the channel of effect directly stipulated in Hatsopoulos, Krugman, and Summers (1988).

41 In a neoclassical world in which perfect credit markets equilibrate the rate of return on fixed investment (here measured by the corporate rate of profit) and the cost of borrowing, it might be that the effects of saving on investment are revealed through the channel of the profit rate (which is, after all, net business saving) in addition to or instead of through the channel of the cost of capital services. Here, however, the neoclassical story would be confounded by the positive sign of profitability in the investment equation. If increased personal saving loosened credit markets and thereby lowered the cost of borrowing, and if the rate of return itself declined as an equilibrium response to that lower cost of borrowing, then the positive coefficient on the rate of profit in the investment equations would give us a net negative effect of personal saving on investment.

42 In particular, the reader should resist the temptation to draw inferences about the underlying logic of the left structuralist model introduced in section 2 from the single equation estimates presented in section 3, since the single equations focus only on specific elements of the larger model. See Gordon (this volume) for a more complete set of estimates for a spare model and Gordon (1994, chapters 4–7) for much fuller treatment.

43 On the logic of VAR models, see Sims (1980).

44 This consideration is not trivial in this system, since the cross-equation residual correlations run in some instances as high as 0.4–0.5. (The residual correlation between the equations for saving and investment, however, is less than 0.01.)

45 Since the structuralist perspective emphasizes the key role of distribution, it is further interesting to note the response of saving and investment to innovations in profitability. In results from the same experiment not reported in the table, after thirty-two quarters, the cumulative response of investment to a shock in the rate of profit is 50.6 percent of its period mean, nearly as large as for a shock in investment and almost five times larger than the effect of an innovation in saving on investment. Because the direct effect of profitability on consumption in table 3.5 is relatively weak, the effects of profitability on saving are mostly indirect, through the channel of investment–utilization–saving. And here, since the effects of profitability on investment do not begin to show up until after two years, the cumulative effects of an innovation in profitability on saving are slow but steadily increasing: Beginning at 4.4 percent after sixteen quarters, the cumulative effects of an innovation in profitability on saving rise to 21.4 percent after thirty-two quarters and 37.9 after forty-eight quarters.

46 This is important in order to allow for a feedback effect from net investment to the capital stock to depreciation to capacity utilization, of which depreciation is a component (see eq. (4.1)).

47 In US national income data, instead of the simple identity in (4.9), saving is equal to disposable income minus consumption expenditures as well as personal interest payments and personal transfers abroad.

48 The accounting identities determining the change in real net personal wealth are based on the flow-of-funds data mobilized by Ray Fair for use in his macroeconometric model. See, for the definitional identities, Fair (1984, table A-5, eqs. 65–6).

49 A variety of other definitional equations are necessary in the model merely to transform key endogenous variables into the forms in which they appear in the consumption and investment equations. Once consumption is determined, for example, algebraic transformations produce the variables recursively entering the consumption equation as lagged trend consumption and the lagged deviation of the rate of change of consumption around its trend rate of change.

50 I have not reproduced the full equations for this model for reasons of space. A full listing of the equations is available from the author upon request.

51 The simple correlation for a full-period dynamic simulation between actual capacity utilization and simulated capacity utilization is 0.97, suggesting that the structuralist model, however simple, tracks the actual economy with substantial accuracy over this large slice of the post-war period and thus provides a reasonable framework within which to conduct these policy experiments.

52 Lest this 50 percent increase in profits seem unreasonably large for such "policy" experiments, I should note that it is equivalent to a once and for all increase in the level of hourly productivity in the non-farm business sector, holding hours of work constant, of only about 2 percent.

53 This is consistent, of course, with the absence of any direct or indirect effects of net

government saving on investment in the single equation econometric exercises reported in the preceding section.

54 One should note that since productivity growth is not being modeled at this simple reduced-form level, the long-term effects of increased investment on the growth rate are not captured.

55 Since the mean baseline value of saving is higher than the mean baseline value of investment, the average deviations in rows (3) and (4) are in fact roughly proportional. In row (3), for example, the 8.8 percent change in real normalized investment is equivalent to an average of $7.176 billion (1982$), while the 5.9 percent change in real personal saving is equivalent to an average of $7.115 billion (1982$).

56 The skeptical reader might immediately wonder whether my choice of a "structuralist" model for these structural simulations has prejudiced the outcomes. But since none of the single-equation experiments reported in section 3 reveals a direct or indirect effect of saving on investment, a neoclassical structural model would be no more capable of producing investment increases commensurate with the "saving windfall," for example, than is the structuralist model whose simulations are represented in row (1) of table 3.9.

57 This chapter is already long enough and I shall not here provide detail on such progressive policy proposals. A summary of many of these arguments, with numerous additional references, is provided in Bowles, Gordon, and Weisskopf (1990, chapters 11–13).

58 See, for example, Green (1988).

59 See, on this distinction, Weisskopf, Bowles, and Gordon (1983) and Bowles, Gordon, and Weisskopf (1990, chapter 1).

4 US national saving and budget deficits

Robert Eisner

It has been widely argued that the decline of "national saving" in the United States in the 1980s was brought on by large federal budget deficits.[1] This is frequently taken as a matter of a simple accounting identity. Gross saving is the sum of private saving and public saving, the latter defined as the government budget surplus. The greater the federal deficit, it is then assumed, the greater is public dis-saving and hence the less is the arithmetic sum of private and public saving. Since national saving is merely gross saving minus capital consumption allowances, it too must then be less.

To take this accounting identity as evidence that reducing the federal deficit must raise national saving should be recognized, on even the slightest reflection, as patently absurd. It is startlingly akin to the assumption, more than half a century ago, that saving and investment would be increased if we all undertook to save more by consuming less. Perhaps! But that is exactly the proposition to be proved, or supported by empirical evidence, not assumed.[2]

The difficulty, going back to the national income accounts, is that while the saving–investment identity must hold by definition, it does not follow that changing one component of saving must change major components of investment or the total of saving–investment by the same amount or even in the same direction, as Gordon has pointed out in the preceding chapter of this volume, unless we short circuit the entire argument by assuming all other things constant. Thus, gross saving is the sum of undistributed corporate profits, capital consumption allowances, personal saving, and the total government – federal, state, and local – surplus. These (plus the statistical discrepancy) are in turn equal to the sum of gross private domestic investment and net foreign investment. Can we properly assume that raising one component of public saving by reducing the federal deficit, by raising taxes or cutting expenditures, will leave these other components unchanged? Will it increase total investment? If it does not, of course, it cannot raise total saving. The issue is complementary to that raised by Gordon in the preceding chapter

109

regarding the relations between personal and private saving and investment.

At the most obvious level, will not reducing federal grants in aid to states and localities, currently running at some $150 billion per year, in the first instance cause an equal decrease in state and local surpluses?[3] Will not increasing taxes in the first instance reduce both undistributed profits and disposable income, in the latter case, further reducing personal saving? And if, as most prevalent theory and empirical evidence suggest, consumption is reduced, may not the resultant sluggishness of demand and sales bring about reductions in business investment as well as residential housing construction, thus further reducing income and saving?

It is of course possible that slack capacity may reduce supply prices of investment goods and that a lower demand for money for transactions purposes, perhaps along with policy-induced increases in money supply, may combine to reduce the cost of capital enough to bring about an increase in investment. In principle, this would be more likely to occur if the economy were at or near full employment and full utilization of capacity, with enough pent-up demand to prevent fiscal tightening from bringing on a general slowdown. But again such results do not necessarily come automatically – except for those dogmatically committed to faith in perpetually and instantaneously clearing markets – and are not to be assumed.

We shall here examine relations involving national saving, federal budget deficits, and changes in the money supply in the United States, along with real exchange rates, to see what has actually occurred. While we shall not ignore the traditional or conventional, "official" measure of national saving, we shall consider, as well, broader measures of saving, encompassing government and household investment in all forms of tangible capital and investment in intangible capital, and measures of net foreign investment adjusted for changes in the market values of US and foreign assets.[4]

1   Issues and concepts

Is the United States rate of national saving too low? Do US budget deficits reduce national saving and hence, like termites, eat away at the foundations of future well being? The answers are, you cannot tell unless you measure right. And if saving is too low, you cannot tell what to do about it unless you know what you are talking about.

The conventional measure of "gross saving," as reported by the United States Bureau of Economic Analysis, is identically equal to the sum of gross private domestic investment and net foreign investment, minus the statistical discrepancy. On the saving side of the account, as we have indicated, it is the sum of personal saving, corporate saving (undistributed corporate profits), private capital consumption allowances, and the government budget surplus (Federal and state and local, combined).[5] The "national saving" of common parlance is then *net* saving, calculated by subtracting capital consumption allowances, as shown in table 4.1. This measure is deficient or misleading on several major counts.

First, personal saving is defined as personal income minus personal taxes (and non-tax payments), personal consumption expenditures, interest paid by consumers to business, and personal transfer payments to foreigners. The problem here is that "personal consumption expenditures" include vast amounts for consumer durables and semi-durables, which in meaningful terms would properly be counted as investment, and hence as saving.

Second, unlike in the United Nations System of National Accounts followed in much of the world, none of US government expenditures for goods and services is included in investment, which, as designated, comprises only *private* investment. Correspondingly, all government expenditures for goods and services are subtracted from government revenues in arriving at the budget surplus, which is the conventional definition of government saving.

Third, the net foreign investment figure, highly negative in recent years, reflects changes in the US net international investment position where a major component, direct investment, is measured at original cost rather than current value. Appropriate corrections, indicated by Eisner and Pieper (1990), Dewald and Ulan (1989), and now, for the US Bureau of Economic Analysis, Landefeld and Lawson (1991), very substantially reduce or eliminate the negative US position. These corrections imply a considerable increase, in recent years, in appropriate measures of net foreign investment and hence of national saving.

Fourth, while the net foreign investment measure is a particularly significant example, in general, measures of both income and saving and investment exclude the value of real capital gains and losses, so that net saving will correspond only by chance to economically relevant changes in wealth. Further, increased realization of capital gains will increase taxable income but not the conventional income of the national income accounts. By increasing income taxes, greater realized capital gains will, by conventional measures, reduce private saving while increasing public saving. Increased capital gains in themselves, aside from tax consequences, are likely to reduce the conventional measure of national saving if they raise consumption more than they raise measured income. If

Table 4.1. *Net saving and investment account, 1992* (billions of dollars)*

Gross private domestic investment	770.9	Personal income	5,056.8
		Less: Personal tax and nontax payments	627.2
Less: Consumption of fixed capital	653.5	Less: Personal outlays	4,216.1
		Personal consumption expenditures	4,093.9
Net private domestic investment	117.3	Interest paid by consumers to business	112.0
Net foreign investment	− 47.1	Personal transfer payments to foreigners	10.2
		Personal saving	213.5
		Undistributed corporate profits with inventory valuation and capital consumption adjustment	107.2
		Government surplus or deficit (−), national income and product accounts	− 281.0
		Federal	− 295.3
		State and local	14.2
		Net saving	39.7
		Statistical discrepancy	30.5
Net investment	70.2	Net saving and statistical discrepancy	70.2

Source: * Adapted from *Survey of Current Business*, April 1993, tables 1.1, 1.9, 2.1, and 5.1, pp. 8, 10, 12, and 15.

they are accompanied by more measured investment included in national income, national saving will rise.

Fifth, and of overwhelming importance for critical questions of growth for which saving matters, conventional measures exclude all saving and investment in intangible and human capital. Such saving and investment far exceed in magnitude, and very likely in importance, the private saving in tangible capital that gets so much attention.

And sixth, a major factor in the presumed decline of the widely regarded measure of *net* national saving has been the very large relative, as well as absolute, increase in depreciation or capital consumption allowances. As shown by Pieper (1989), however, this may as well be viewed as a consequence rather than a cause of declining real growth. As growth of output approaches zero, unless the capital–output ratio increases, the net saving and investment rates must also approach zero. At any point in time, the ratio of depreciation to fixed investment, and hence of net saving to gross investment and saving, may depend much more on the rate of past investment than the propensity to save.

The differences between real net national saving and the conventional measure of national saving, about which there has been so much hand wringing, are large. These differences have substantial import for international and intertemporal comparisons. With proper focus on a full, relevant measure we may still find reason for concern. The causes, however, will prove different. And so will reasonable remedies.

Take investment in transportation, as one salient example. In an earlier century in the United States, this involved in considerable part private investment in railroads. Through much of this century it has entailed huge amounts of government investment in roads and airports and private investment in automobiles. The former is financed by taxes and the latter is counted as consumption. Neither shows up as part of "saving." Is it proper then to judge our saving reduced to the extent the reduction is due to this shift from business to non-business investment?

Similar issues arise in international comparisons. France and more recently Germany have undertaken and are undertaking large amounts of investment in high-speed trains. This swells OECD figures for their total saving and capital formation. But US figures include all government investment as "government consumption." US investment in new airports and runways (however inadequate) is generally a government project and not counted in "investment." With comparable inclusion of all public and private investment, the widely commented on excess of Japanese over US saving[6] would be reduced. But then, if capital formation in education took into account hours spent in school and study and were, properly, to include the opportunity cost of students' time, Japanese

Table 4.2. *Saving measures and components, mean percents of GNP, 1971–81 and 1982–90*

Series	1971–81	1982–90	Difference
(Current dollars)			
GSD	16.82	13.29	− 3.53
CCAD	9.94	11.01	+ 1.07
NS0D	6.87	2.28	− 4.59
GPDID	16.58	15.26	− 1.32
NPDID	6.64	4.25	− 2.39
INVRAD	9.11	7.60	− 1.51
NFIDMISD	0.24	− 1.97	− 2.21
NS1D	9.35	5.62	− 3.73
INVLAND	4.11	0.35	− 3.76
NS7D	13.46	5.97	− 7.49
NFICORD	− 0.01	0.71*	+ 0.72
NS3D	13.45	7.30*	− 6.15
INVINTAD	17.02		
INVSDID	0.25		
NRD	6.57		
NRMLND	3.01		
(1982 dollars)			
GS	17.38	14.92	− 2.46
CCA	10.39	12.02	+ 1.63
NS0	6.98	2.90	− 4.08
GPDI	17.14	16.89	− 0.25
NPDI	6.75	4.87	− 1.88
INVRA	8.93	7.81	− 1.12
NFIMS82	0.24	− 1.97	− 2.21
NS1	9.17	5.84	− 3.33
INVLAN	4.11	0.35	− 3.76
NS7	13.28	6.19	− 7.09
NFICOR	− 0.01	0.71*	+ 0.72
NS3	13.27	7.50*	− 5.77
INVINTA	16.72		
INVSDI	0.27		
NR82	6.39		
NRMLN82	2.94		

Note: * 1982–89.

investment in this vital form of human capital might be seen to dwarf that of the United States.

2   Measures

The decline in conventional US national saving over the last two decades may be viewed in the movements of its components. In table 4.2, I present comparisons, for the years from 1971 to 1981 and 1982 to 1990, in current and 1982 dollars, of the major elements of conventional US "national saving" (NS0 and NS0D) and of suggested alternate measures (see definitions below), all as percents of GNP.[7,8]

We may note first that the conventional measure of national saving fell from 6.87 percent in the period 1971–81 to 2.28 percent in years 1982–90, a drop of 4.59 percentage points. This represented a drop of 3.53 percentage points in the *gross* saving rate, which was coupled with a rise of 1.07 percentage points in the rate of capital consumption. Gross saving, it may be remembered though, is identically equal to gross private domestic investment plus net foreign investment minus the statistical discrepancy. The total of these last two (NFIDMISD) fell by 2.21 percentage points, which means that gross saving available to the US to finance gross private domestic investment (GSD − NFIDMISD = GPDID) declined by only 1.32 percentage points. Gross private domestic investment in 1982 dollars as a percent of GNP, GPDI, it should be noted, was virtually unchanged, declining by only 0.25 percentage points. Real net private domestic investment as a percent of GNP, NPDI, declined by 1.88 percentage points, however, the decline reflecting almost entirely the increase in capital consumption allowances.

Net foreign investment, we have pointed out though, should correspond to changes in the market values of assets, net of liabilities, of the home country in the rest of the world and of assets, net of liabilities, of the rest of the world in the home country. Applying a net foreign investment correction (NFICORD), to make net foreign investment consistent with such changes in market values, does not make a substantial difference in the conventional measures, NFI or NS0, over the entire periods of comparison. There was, however, a substantial swing in that correction from 1981–4 to 1985–9, of 2.38 percentage points, from − 1.13 percent of GNP to + 1.25 percent, as shown in table 4.3. This suggests corresponding corrections over those years in the private, business, and government components of gross saving, the proportions depending on which sector held the assets whose market values moved differently from evaluations used in the official accounts.

A move to a comprehensive measure of saving entails relating it to a

Table 4.3. *Net foreign investment corrections*

	Percents of GNP		
	1981–4	1985–9	Change, 1981–4 to 1985–9
Net foreign investment (NFID)	− 0.77	− 2.76	− 1.99
Net foreign investment correction (NFICORD)	− 1.13	+ 1.25	2.38
Adjusted net foreign investment (NFIADJD)	− 1.90	− 1.51	0.39

comprehensive measure of investment. This is effected by taking the change in the BEA's "constant-cost net stock of fixed reproducible tangible wealth,"[9] which includes government and household fixed capital as well as that of business and non-profit institutions, multiplying it by a price deflator calculated as the ratio of current cost to constant cost net stocks, and adding the change in business inventories. The totals as percents of GNP, denoted INVRAD for investment in reproducible assets in current dollars, and the corresponding constant dollar series, INVRA, are shown in table 4.2. We then add NFIDMISD, net foreign investment minus the statistical discrepancy (NFIMSD82 in the constant dollar series) to obtain measures of national saving which include government and household net investment. These, however, are still exclusive of government and household investment in semi-durables and inventories and of all investment in land.

Substantial growth in stocks of consumer durables kept down the decline in investment in reproducible assets. From 1971–81 to 1982–90, the fall in the mean value of INVRAD was only 1.51 percentage points as compared to 2.39 percentage points for NPDID (the current United States Bureau of Economic Analysis measure of net private domestic investment, as a percent of GNP), from 9.11 percent of GNP to 7.60 percent, and only 1.12 percentage points for INVRA, in 1982 dollars. The drop in the corresponding measure of national saving, NS1D, with the inclusion of net foreign investment, was again considerable however, coming to 3.73 percentage points; the drop was 3.33 percentage points for NS1, in 1982 dollars.

We may secure a still further expanded measure of saving, NS7D or NS7 in 1982 dollars, by adding increases in the real value of land. These are calculated from the "Balance Sheets for the US Economy" prepared by the Federal Reserve's Flow of Funds division. We take the year-end values of land at market prices and deflate by year-end GNP price deflators (the average of fourth-quarter and subsequent first-quarter figures) and consider the differences in these deflated values as real saving in land. We then multiply these differences by the corresponding annual GNP implicit price deflators to get the current dollar values of saving in the form of increases in the value of land, INVLAND (INVLAN in the constant dollar series), over and above that accountable to general inflation.[10]

The saving measure, NS3D (NS3 in the constant dollar series) adds the net foreign investment correction, NFICORD (or NFICOR in constant dollars). NS3D (and NS3) are thus equal to NS7D (and NS7), including investment in land, plus the net foreign investment correction.

Our measure of investment in land (INVLAND), which may suffer from infirmities in the underlying data, indicate a sharp fall, from 4.11 percent of GNP in 1971–81 to 0.35 percent in 1982–90. This in turn brings down the current dollar measures, NS7D and NS3D, by 7.49 and 6.15 percentage points, from 13.46 percent to 5.97 percent and from 13.45 percent to 7.30 percent, respectively.

By far greatest in amount and possibly, we may suggest, in current significance at the margin, is investment in intangible capital. We fall back here on my TISA ("Total Incomes System of Accounts") estimates.[11] These were built up in some detail in current and 1972 dollars for various components of investment in education and training, research and health.[12] Constant dollar totals used in this chapter were crudely converted to 1982 dollars by dividing by the GNP 1982 dollar implicit price deflator for 1972.

The ratio of net investment in intangible capital to GNP in current dolars (INVINTAD) averaged 17.02 percent over the years 1971 to 1981. (TISA estimates, beginning in 1945 and 1946, extend only to 1981.) This may be compared to the conventional saving ratio, NS0D, of 6.87 percent for that period, the ratio of 9.35 percent for NS1D, which includes investment in all reproducible fixed capital, and the ratio of 13.45 percent for NS3D, which also includes investment in land.

We add net investment in intangible capital and the relatively small amounts of net investment by government and households in inventories and semi-durables to NS1D to get a measure of saving, NS14D, including all investment in tangible reproducible capital and in intangible capital. We add investment in land to obtain the measure, NS15D. And now the ratios of saving to GNP, as seen in table 4.4, turn really large: 26.36 percent for NS14D over the 1971–81 period and 30.47 percent for NS15D, the measure including investment in land.

Table 4.4. *Comparison of mean saving ratios, 1971–81*

Current dollars		Constant dollars	
Measure	Mean (% of GNPD)	Measure	Mean (% of GNP)
NS0D	6.87	NS0	6.98
NS1D	9.35	NS1	9.17
NS7D	13.46	NS7	13.28
NS3D	13.45	NS3	13.27
NS14D	26.36	NS14	25.88
NS15D	30.47	NS15	29.98
NS16D	32.93	NS16	32.27
NS17D	33.48	NS17	32.92
NS0D/NS14D	26.06	NS0/NS14	26.97
NS0D/NS15D	22.55	NS0/NS15	23.28
NS0D/NS16D	20.86	NS0/NS16	21.63
NS0D/NS17D	20.52	NS0/NS17	21.20

Finally, we can add saving in the form of net revaluations of tangible assets, that is, capital gains over and above those accountable to inflation. These give us ratios of national saving to GNP of 32.93 percent for NS16D and 33.48 percent for NS17D, the measure including investment in land.

We may note how far we have gone by observing that the mean for the current dollar ratios for the years 1971 to 1981 of conventional national saving, NS0D, divided by the mean for our comprehensive measure including all investment in tangible and intangible capital other than net revaluations, NS15D, is only 22.55 percent. The corresponding proportion involving the measure including net revaluations, NS17D, is 20.52 percent.

Some of the findings from these old and new measures merit high-lighting. First, despite all the complaint about the fall in conventional national saving in the 1980s decade of high budget deficits, that most critical component for domestic growth, the share of real gross private domestic investment in GNP, fell hardly at all. The drop in conventional national saving stemmed first rather from the rise in the capital consumption allowance ratio, which may be somewhat suspect itself and in any event would seem to be more the effect than the cause of a decline in growth. And it stemmed second from the decline in net foreign investment, also suspect at least in its failure to include changes in the market value of US direct foreign investment. With appropriate correction, net foreign investment, thanks in part to the decline in the value of the US dollar, in fact turned up in the latter part of the 1980s. In any event, the declines in net foreign investment that did occur would not appear to have the negative effects on domestic productivity associated with declines in real domestic investment, and hence would be of lesser consequence for economic growth.

We may also note again that the decline in real net private domestic investment, as reported by the BEA, is partially compensated by a rise in investment in consumer durables, so that the total decline in the ratio to GNP of net investment in reproducible assets, including household and government investment, is less. This, along with the very large amounts of investment in intangible capital that are in considerable part financed by government, should give pause to those who would think to curb or reverse presumed declines in national saving by either of the usual prescriptions for reducing budget deficits – raising taxes or cutting government expenditures.

Designations and definitions of elements of adjusted measures of national saving

First designations, ending in "D," denote current dollars; second designations refer to 1982 dollars.

GSD, GS	Gross saving from national income and product accounts
CCAD, CCA	Capital consumption allowances with adjustment, from national income and product accounts
GPDID, GPDI	Gross private domestic investment
INVRAD, INVRA	Net investment in reproducible assets, excluding investment in consumer semi-durables and government and household inventories
NFIDMISD, NFIMSD82	Net foreign investment minus statistical discrepancy, national income and product accounts
INVLAND, INVLAN	Net investment in land
NFICORD, NFICOR	Net foreign investment correction
INVINTAD, INVINTA	Net investment in intangible capital
INVSDID, INVSDI82	Net investment in consumer and government semi-durables
NRD, NR82	Net revaluations
NRMLND, NRMLN82	Net revaluations excluding land

Definitions and derivations of saving rates and other variables

NS0   Conventional net national saving = gross saving − capital consumption allowances with adjustment, from national income and product accounts as of March 1991

NS1   Change in total fixed reproducible capital, from "Summary Fixed Reproducible Tangible Wealth Series, 1925–89," *Survey of Current Business*, October 1990, pp. 31–2, updated to 1990 with unpublished data furnished by John Musgrave of the Bureau of Economic Analysis, plus net foreign investment minus statistical discrepancy from national income and product accounts

NS7   Change in total fixed reproducible capital plus net foreign investment minus statistical discrepancy (NS1), plus change in real value of land from Board of Governors of the Federal Reserve System, Flow of Funds Division, *Balance Sheets for the US Economy 1945–90*, March 1991, end-of-year land values deflated by average of fourth quarter and subsequent first quarter GNP implicit price deflators

NS3   Change in total fixed reproducible capital plus adjusted net foreign investment, calculated from changes in the net international investment position of the United States adjusted to market value (Eisner and Pieper, 1990), minus statistical discrepancy, plus change in real value of land

NS14   Change in total fixed reproducible capital plus adjusted net foreign investment minus statistical discrepancy plus investment in intangible capital and in government and household inventories and semi-durables from Total Incomes System of Accounts (TISA, Eisner, 1989c)

NS15   Change in total fixed reproducible capital plus adjusted net foreign investment minus statistical discrepancy plus change in real value of land (NS3), plus investment in intangible capital and in government and household inventories and semi-durables

NS16   Change in total fixed reproducible capital plus adjusted net foreign investment minus statistical discrepancy plus investment in intangible capital and in government and household inventories and semi-durables (NS14), plus total net revaluations from TISA

NS17   Change in total fixed reproducible capital plus adjusted net foreign investment minus statistical discrepancy plus change in real value of land plus investment in intangible capital and in government and household inventories and semi-durables (NS15), plus net revaluations exclusive of net revaluations on land

DMB   Change in monetary base as percent of GNP in 1982 dollars, from *Economic Report of the President*, February 1991, December averages of monetary base deflated by GNP fourth quarter implicit price deflator

ERR   Real exchange rate index, multilateral trade-weighted value of the US dollar (March 1973 = 100), adjusted by changes in consumer prices, from *Economic Report of the President*, February 1991, p. 410

PAHED6   Price-adjusted high-employment deficit as percent of GNP, the negative of PAHES6, the price-adjusted high-employment surplus as
percent of GNP, on a 6 percent unemployment basis, taken from
Bureau of Economic Analysis series published in *Survey of Current
Business* for the years from 1970 to 1990 and adjusted for "price
effects" (changes in real value of net Federal debt due to inflation), as
reported in Eisner and Pieper (1984) and Eisner (1986). The high-
unemployment surplus for years prior to 1970 was calculated as
indicated in the Data sources appendix below.

3   Deficits and conventional national saving

In searching for the influence of federal deficits on saving it is important
to distinguish it from the common effect of cyclical movements on public
and private saving. Lower GNP of course means lower national income
and almost certainly lower private saving. The associated reduction of tax
revenues and increase in transfer payments for unemployment increase
the federal deficit and thus lower public saving. A minimum necessity in
the analysis therefore is use of a cyclically adjusted measure of the deficit.

Further, conventional measures of the deficit fail to take properly into
account the role of inflation. They include nominal rather than real
interest expenditures and correspondingly do not count as a "tax" the
reduction in the real value of government debt due to inflation. I have
presented both of these corrections in earlier works[13] and offer here an
extended measure of a federal "price-adjusted high-employment deficit,"
PAHED6.

I have noted previously that higher values of a price or inflation-
adjusted, high-employment deficit, or lesser surpluses, were associated
with *greater* subsequent growth in real GNP, personal consumption
expenditures, and gross private domestic investment, but with lesser
growth, or decline of net exports over the period 1955 to 1984.[14] These
relations proved robust to the introduction of monetary variables, particularly real changes in the monetary base, which were themselves positively related to the growth of GNP, consumption, and domestic investment. The theoretical rationale for the relations, and the results, it was
explained, fit well the life-cycle theory of consumption and neoclassical
and accelerator theories of investment, reinforced perhaps by portfolio
choice considerations. Real budget deficits imply increases in wealth as
perceived by private agents in the form of government debt and thus
generate increases in consumption demand, for both domestic and foreign
goods. To the extent that some private agents are liquidity constrained,
the flow of after-tax income corresponding to budget deficits, even apart
from the wealth effect, further contributes to the private demand for

goods. The initial increases in output, or even rational anticipations of increases in output, and the greater financial wealth in turn induce an increase in demand for physical capital. It may be useful to present these relations more formally.[15]

First, real consumption may be viewed as a function of real income, real capital, real financial wealth of the private sector consisting of the domestically held, interest-bearing and non-interest-bearing government debt ("outside money") and the real rate of interest.

$$C/P = C(Y/P, K, GD/P, M_x/P, r);$$
$$0 < C_1 < 1; \quad C_2, \ C_3, \ C_4 > 0; \quad C_5 \gtreqless 0. \tag{1}$$

Then, real investment is a function of current output, the expected path of future output, the existing stock of capital and its marginal rental cost, the last a function of the real rate of interest, and the net stock of financial capital held by the private sector.

$$I/P = I(Y(t)/P(t), \ K, c, \{GD + M_x\}/P); \quad I_1, I_4 > 0; \quad I_2, I_3 < 0 \tag{2}$$

where $Y(t)/P(t)$ represents some appropriately weighted average of the series of expected real future outputs, itself a function of current and past real output.

Exports, given foreign income and wealth, are a function of real exchange rates, appropriately lagged, and imports are a function of real exchange rates (measured as a trade-weighted index of the amount of foreign currencies that can be bought for a dollar) and real income and output. Thus net exports may be written

$$NE = X/P - M/P = E(ERR_{-2}, Y/P); \quad E_1, E_2 < 0. \tag{3}$$

We then have the identity

$$Y/P = C/P + I/P + NE + G \tag{4}$$

where G denotes real government expenditures for goods and services.

The real interest rate and hence the rental cost of capital are determined by the condition of equality of money supply and money demand

$$M_s = M_d = P^*L(Y/P, i, \dot{P}^e); \quad L_1 > 0; \quad L_2, L_3 < 0 \tag{5}$$

where $\dot{P}^e$ is the expected rate of inflation (so that r, above, $= i - \dot{P}^e$).

Real net foreign investment is net exports minus net government interest payments and transfers to foreigners. The real exchange rate is then a function of the real interest rate, real net foreign investment, and the value in foreign currencies of foreign claims on US assets. This last stock is affected by both the accumulation of negative flows of net foreign investment and the changes in values of those accumulations as a result of revaluations in own currencies and changing exchange rates themselves. Briefly

$$ERR = R(r, NFI, FC); \quad R_r, R_{NFI} > 0; \quad R_{FC} < 0. \tag{6}$$

On the supply side there are production functions dependent on capital and labor. These indicate marginal rates of substitution and the elasticity of investment with respect to the rental cost of capital and the effects of increasing demand on prices and inflation. Rates of inflation are more responsive to real demand as output approaches the capacity determined by factor supply and the production function. Expected inflation and nominal interest rates may adjust more or less completely, with some lag, to actual inflation.

This model is spelled out in much greater detail, with suggested plausible parameters, in Eisner and Hwang (1993). Simulations, with these parameters, suggest that greater real structural deficits increase consumption and also increase domestic investment, where output effects generally dominate substitution effects relating to the rental cost of capital. However, they decrease net foreign investment as, depending on the monetary regime, they tend to raise real interest rates and real income. Real exchange rates ultimately adjust to keep net foreign claims from growing relative to GNP. The real deficit and the real domestically held debt also stabilize as ratios of GNP. The net effect of real structural deficits on saving – the sum of gross private domestic investment and net foreign investment – is positive.

The issue at hand, however, is not what our model generates – however plausible I find it and its parameters. It is rather what the data, applied to structural or reduced-form equations that may be drawn from the model, actually show. Government budget deficits, we must acknowledge, may bring about increases in gross private domestic investment such as those we have observed and still lower the national saving rate. Net foreign investment was in fact reduced, as imports soared, with larger budget deficits and more rapidly growing GNP. Higher real exchange rates would be expected, with some lag, further to lower net exports and net foreign investment. With the ratio of capital consumption allowances presumably little if at all affected, greater deficits could then generate gross private domestic investment and still reduce the national saving rate.

In fact, as may be seen in figure 4.1, the conventional national saving rate, which we have designated NS0, along with various expanded measures of saving, moved generally downward from early in the 1970s, and was distinctly lower in the 1980s, when budget deficits were relatively high. Figure 4.2, graphing conventional national saving and the prior year's adjusted high-employment deficit, PAHED6(− 1), would seem to

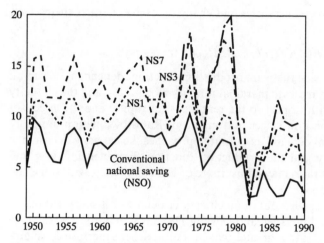

Figure 4.1   Measures of national saving (0, 1, 3, 7) as percents of GNP

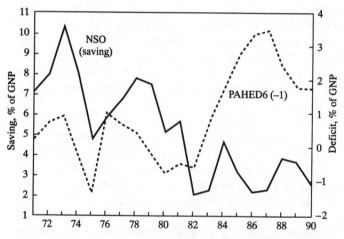

Figure 4.2   Conventional measure of national saving and lagged adjusted deficit

confirm, at least for the high-deficit 1980s, that the greater inflation-adjusted high-employment deficits were associated with less national saving. It is important, however, to look further.

Deficits add to the total debt, interest bearing and non-interest bearing, of the Federal government and consequently to the assets of the private sector (and of state and local government). As indicated above this may be expected to lead directly to more consumption and income and saving and, with accelerator and possibly portfolio effects, possibly to a higher

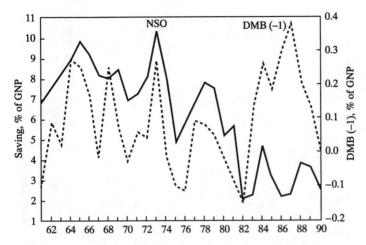

Figure 4.3   Conventional national saving, and lagged change in monetary base, DMB(− 1), as percents of GNP

proportion of income saved. To the extent the Federal Reserve buys government securities, however, part of that debt is monetized and shows up in the monetary base. It is appropriate to recognize the possible special role of monetary factors and include real changes in the monetary base, along with the deficit, in relations explaining saving. Figure 4.3 indeed offers suggestive evidence of a positive relation between real changes in the monetary base and subsequent saving. And finally, very large swings in real exchange rates over the last two decades may be expected to have substantial effects on net foreign investment and hence on national saving. They should be included in relations to be estimated.

Saving rates and deficits are both highly autocorrelated. Table 4.6 presents the results of AR(1) regressions in levels and first-difference regressions of alternative measures of national saving on the lagged inflation or price-adjusted high-employment deficit, PAHED6(− 1), real changes in the monetary base, lagged one and two years, DMB(− 1) and DMB(− 2), all expressed as percents of gross national product, and an index of the twice-lagged, trade-weighted real exchange rate, ERR(− 2), over the years 1972 to 1990. Beginning with the conventional national saving rate, NS0, we note a statistically significant coefficient of 0.887 for PAHED6(− 1). With an AR(1) coefficient (rho) of 0.984, estimates are essentially of a first-difference relation, where the coefficient of PAHED6(− 1) is 0.905; in the considerable number of other cases where the AR(1) coefficient was in the neighborhood of unity, we have reported only the first-difference regressions. Each percentage point increase in the

Table 4.6. *Adjusted budget deficits, changes in monetary base and alternate measures of real national saving, NS0, NS1, NS7, 1972–90, and NS3, 1972–89* ($NSk_t = b_0 + b_1 \text{PAHED6}_{t-1} + b_2 \text{DMB}_{t-1} + b_3 \text{DMB}_{t-2} + b_4 \text{ERR}_{t-2}$), $k = 0, 1, 7, 3$)

Variable or parameter	Regression coefficients and standard errors						
	AR(1)	First differences					
	NS0	NS0	NS1	NS7	NS7	NS3	NS3
C	− 9.501	− 0.381	− 0.395	− 0.737	− 0.699	− 0.321	− 0.321
	(135.709)	(0.253)	(0.272)	(0.756)	(0.741)	(0.942)	(0.902)
PAHED6(− 1)	0.887	0.905	1.124	2.606	2.584	2.351	2.351
	(0.368)	(0.366)	(0.393)	(1.093)	(1.074)	(1.328)	(1.279)
DMB(− 1)	8.237	8.429	9.139	16.022	15.301	9.298	9.288
	(2.178)	(2.191)	(2.354)	(6.551)	(6.356)	(8.235)	(7.778)
DMB(− 2)	5.835	6.116	7.072	3.845	—	0.039	—
	(1.849)	(1.852)	(1.989)	(5.536)		(6.818)	
ΣDMB	14.072	14.545	16.211	19.867	—	9.337	—
	(3.046)	(3.085)	(3.314)	(9.222)		(11.687)	
ERR(− 2)	− 0.135	− 0.149	− 0.146	− 0.171	− 0.152	− 0.079	− 0.078
	(0.037)	(0.041)	(0.044)	(0.122)	(0.117)	(0.148)	(0.139)
AR(1)	0.984	—	—	—	—	—	—
	(0.081)						
$\hat{R}^2$	0.808	0.618	0.657	0.446	0.465	0.195	0.253
D–W	2.728	2.826	2.837	2.226	2.044	1.625	1.624
n	19	19	19	19	19	18	18

Notes: * Significant at 0.05 probability level.

C   Constant term.

AR(1)   First-order autoregressive coefficient.

$\hat{R}^2$ Adjusted coefficient of determination.

D–W   Durbin–Watson coefficient.

n Number of observations.

PAHED6(-1)   Lagged price-adjusted, BEA 6 percent high-employment budget deficit as percent of GNP.

DMB(-1)   Lagged real change in monetary base as percent of GNP (December figures divided by fourth quarter GNP implicit price deflator).

DMB(-2)   Two-year lagged real change in monetary base as percent of GNP (December figures divided by fourth quarter GNP implicit price deflator).

ERR(-2)   Trade weighted, real exchange rate, lagged two years (March 1973 = 100).

NS0   Conventional net national saving = gross saving − capital consumption allowances with adjustment.

NS1   Change in total fixed reproducible capital plus net foreign investment minus statistical discrepancy.

NS7   Change in total fixed reproducible capital plus net foreign investment minus statistical discrepancy (NS1) plus change in real value of land.

NS3   Change in total fixed reproducible capital plus adjusted net foreign investment minus statistical discrepancy plus change in real value of land.

deficit (as a ratio of GNP) was thus associated with almost a percentage point *in*crease in conventional national saving. We may also note the significant positive coefficients for increases in the real monetary base and the expected negative coefficient for the real exchange rate. It might be inferred from these estimated parameters that an easier monetary policy would increase national saving both directly and by bringing down exchange rates. But reducing the budget deficit in itself, if these regressions for data of the last two decades can be considered relevant, would appear not to increase national saving, as has been widely argued, but rather to reduce it.

Questions may be raised about the endogeneity of variables in our least squares regressions. I can also present the results of VARs (vector autoregressions), however, that would appear to confirm the individual equation least squares results. Working with two lags of PAHED6, DMB, ERR and NS0, included in that order, we may note, from impulse response functions shown in table 4.10 and figure 4.4, that a percentage point increase in the ratio to GNP of the structural, inflation-adjusted deficit, PAHED6, was associated with a small contemporaneous decline in the national saving ratio, NS0 (of which the deficit is itself, of course, a negative component), but subsequent increases of a percentage point or more in saving over each of the next three years. The national saving rate indeed remained higher for nine more years, gradually dwindling as the initial increase in the deficit was reversed.

Over the period of our observations, innovations in the deficit – or positive shocks – were associated, with a two-year lag, with roughly equal subsequent negative movements in the deficit. If policymakers, counterfactually, had actually kept the deficit higher, the gains in saving might perhaps have been even greater and further repeated.

The VARs indicated that similar, if shorter-lived, increases in subsequent saving were associated with initial increases in the real monetary base. Increases in the real exchange rate, however, brought decreases in national saving.

4   Extended measures of national saving

As I have argued on a number of occasions,[16] our interest in national saving, as it relates to provision for the future, must certainly call for focus on much more than the conventional measure of saving. Investment in new automobiles provides future transportation sevices whether it consists of gross private domestic investment by Hertz or Avis, government purchases by a municipal police department, or private "consumption" expenditures for durable goods by households. Business, government, and

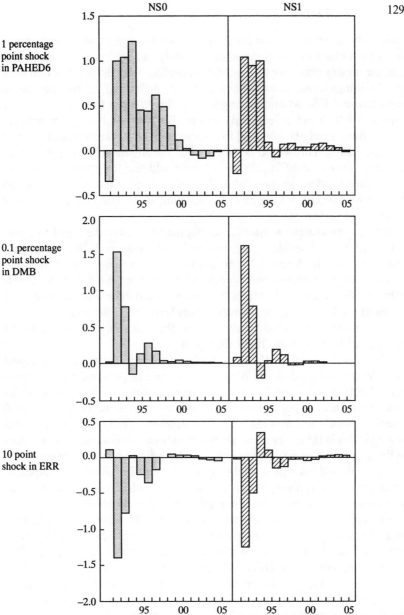

Figure 4.4 VARs with two lags, 1972–90 observations. Impulse response functions for national saving, as percent of GNP (conventional, NS0, and expanded, NS1), to 1991 shocks: one percentage point shock in price-adjusted high-employment deficit as percent of GNP (PAHED6): 0.1 percentage point shock in change in real monetary base as percent of GNP (DMB); 10 point shock in trade-weighted real exchange rate index (ERR)

Note: * Ordering is shocked variable first and saving variable last in each case.

university expenditures for research may prove a more important investment than much business spending for plant and equipment. Households
and businesses may save by investing in land and its resources as well as in
the buildings constructed above them. A good half of the decline in
conventional US national saving rate in the 1980s is to be found in the
reported fall in net foreign investment. But the net foreign investment
figures must surely be adjusted for changes in the market value of US and
foreign claims. This would be essential to get any meaningful measure of
increases in our "debt" to the rest of the world that are alleged to pose an
increasing burden on our future.[17] Only an adjusted measure of net
foreign investment, taking this into account, should go into our measure
of national saving.

Broader measures of national saving may not alter the trend to lower
rates, we have observed in the conventional measure. In fact, they generally do not. In figure 4.1, for example, we can see that saving that
includes all government and household investment in fixed reproducible
capital, NS1, while higher than the conventional NS0 was also distinctly
lower in the 1980s than previously.[18] Similarly, NS7, the measure including the saving constituted by increases in the real value of land, is higher
yet, but still lower in the 1980s than previously.

The critical question, though, is what effect on saving we can expect
from lower budget deficits. Would an increase in personal income taxes
that effects a reduction in consumer expenditures for new automobiles
and other durable goods raise national saving? The regressions of NS0
suggest it would not. But then it would almost certainly not raise national
saving if this is taken, as it should be, to include the consumer investment
in durable goods as a form of saving. If the reduction in the budget deficit
is accomplished, as well it might, by a reduction in government expenditures for roads, bridges, and airports, we may also expect that it would
also *lower* and not raise the expanded measure of national saving.

And this is indeed precisely what we observe. In table 4.7 we relate the
lagged price-adjusted high-employment deficit, PAHED6(− 1) to private
tangible investment, which we take to include, in addition to gross private
domestic investment (GDPI) and net foreign investment (NFI, not all of
the latter of which, to be sure, is "tangible"), investment in consumer
durables (CD). In AR(1) regressions over the period 1957–90, we note
highly significant positive coefficients for both the GPDI and CD components, along with the highly significant negative coefficient for NFI.
The coefficient for all of private tangible investment is a significantly
positive 0.785, suggesting that each additional percentage point of
inflation-adjusted structural deficit, as a ratio of GNP, was associated with
almost 0.8 of a percentage point *more* of private saving and investment. If

Table 4.7. *Adjusted deficit and private tangible investment* ($I_{j,t} = b_0 + b_1 \, \text{PAHED6}_{t-1}$)

I_j	Regression coefficients*						
	b_0	PAHED6$_{t-1}$ b_1	$\hat{R}^2$	D-W	rho	n
Gross private domestic	16.488	0.769	0.315	1.63	0.513	34
	(0.527)	(0.297)			(0.181)	
Net foreign	−0.250	−0.407	0.882	2.05	0.891	34
	(0.749)	(0.086)			(0.088)	
Gross	16.072	0.473	0.443	1.73	0.762	34
	(1.134)	(0.309)			(0.129)	
Consumer durables	16.052	0.299	0.931	1.57	0.989	34
	(45.080)	(0.072)			(0.059)	
Private domestic tangible	24.030	1.335	0.613	1.54	0.539	34
	(0.618)	(0.317)			(0.159)	
Private tangible	24.064	0.785	0.393	1.600	0.616	34
	(0.784)	(0.355)			(0.159)	

Notes: * Ordinary least squares with a first-order correction for serial correlation. Standard errors are shown in parentheses. Sample period is 1957–90.

Variable definitions:

PAHED6 = price-adjusted 6 percent high-employment deficit, as estimated by the BEA for the years 1970–90 and extrapolated backward by the Holloway method on the basis of the BEA middle expansion trend deficit for the earlier years, as percent of GNP. I_j = real investment of type j – GPDI, NFI, gross, and consumer durables from the BEA – taken as a percent of GNP. Private domestic tangible is the sum of gross private domestic investment and consumer durables. Private tangible is the sum of gross investment and consumer durables.

Table 4.8. *Adjusted deficit, change in monetary base, real exchange rate and private tangible investment (first differences)* ($\Delta I_{j,t} = b_0 + b_1 \Delta PAHED6_{t-1} + b_2 \Delta DMB_{t-1} + b_3 \Delta DMB_{t-2} + b_4 \Delta ERR_{t-2}$)

ΔI_j	Regression coefficients*							
	b_0	$\Delta PAHED6_{t-1}$ b_1	ΔDMB_{t-1} b_2	ΔDMB_{t-2} b_3	$\Sigma \Delta DMB$ $b_2 + b_3$	ΔERR_{t-2} b_4	$\hat{R}^2$	D-W
Gross private domestic	−0.097 (0.209)	0.734 (0.271)	6.716 (1.694)	6.207 (1.444)	12.923 (2.526)	−0.071 (0.036)	0.610	2.15
Net foreign	−0.059 (0.081)	−0.241 (0.105)	0.016 (0.658)	−0.900 (0.561)	−0.884 (0.918)	−0.032 (0.014)	0.470	2.19
Gross	−0.156 (0.204)	0.493 (0.264)	6.732 (1.652)	5.307 (1.408)	12.039 (2.462)	−0.103 (0.035)	0.528	2.40
Consumer durables	0.135 (0.063)	0.257 (0.082)	1.477 (0.513)	0.801 (0.437)	2.278 (0.765)	−0.009 (0.011)	0.525	1.70
Private domestic tangible	0.039 (0.246)	0.991 (0.318)	8.194 (1.989)	7.007 (1.695)	15.201 (2.965)	−0.080 (0.042)	0.639	1.97
Private tangible	−0.020 (0.240)	0.750 (0.310)	8.209 (1.941)	6.108 (1.654)	14.317 (2.893)	−0.113 (0.041)	0.571	2.21

Notes: * Ordinary least squares. Standard errors are shown in parentheses. Sample period is 1962–90; there are twenty-nine observations.

Variable definitions:

PAHED6 = price-adjusted 6 percent high-employment deficit as percent of GNP

DMB = change in the real monetary base as a percent of GNP (December figures divided by 4th quarter GNP implicit price deflator)

ERR = trade weighted real exchange rate (March 1973 = 100)

I_j = real investment of type j – GPDI, NFI, gross, and consumer durables, from the BEA, taken as a percent of potential GNP. Private domestic tangible is the sum of gross private domestic investment and consumer durables. Private tangible is the sum of gross investment and consumer durables.

we eliminate NFI, we find the coefficient for private *domestic* tangible investment is a considerably higher 1.335, suggesting that each percentage point more of deficit was associated with four-thirds of a percentage point more of subsequent investment.

In table 4.8, in first-difference regressions (the results of AR(1) regressions in the levels, with values of the autoregression coefficient close to unity, were similar), we add the change in the lagged change in monetary base variables, $\Delta DMB(-1)$ and $\Delta DMB(-2)$, and the change in a two-year lagged real exchange rate variable, $\Delta ERR(-2)$. Lack of consistent monetary data forces us to restrict our sample to years beginning in 1962. Further, with the available real exchange series beginning only in 1973, we arbitrarily set the values of ERR at 100 for all years prior to 1973 (March 1973 = 100). Despite these limitations, results were essentially consistent with those already reported. The coefficient of $\Delta PAHED6(-2)$ for gross private domestic investment was a still significant, positive, if reduced, 0.734; the coefficient for all private domestic tangible investment, including consumer durables, was 0.991; and the coefficient for all of private tangible investment was a still positive, and significant, 0.750. The real exchange rate variable, $\Delta ERR(-2)$ had the expected negative signs. The coefficients of $\Delta DMB(-1)$ and $\Delta DMB(-2)$ are generally positive and significantly so, consistent with the theory that their stimulative effects along with lower real interest rates will, with appropriate lags, increase domestic investment, but may, by generating more imports, reduce net foreign investment.[19] The deficit coefficient for NFI is again negative, as expected.

We also report in table 4.6 the results of regressions, in first difference form, of *net* saving, NS1, NS7, and NS3, which incorporate successively government and consumer fixed investment, investment in land, and the net foreign investment correction. The size of the positive coefficients of PAHED6(-1) are now distinctly larger, 1.124, 2.606, and 2.351 (this last only for the eighteen observations from 1972 to 1989), respectively. Coefficients of the monetary variables, DMB(-1) and DMB(-2), are again positive and significantly so for NS1, but less clear, particularly for DMB(-2), for NS7 and NS3. Coefficients of the exchange rate are negative, but significantly so only for NS1.[20]

In table 4.9, we can report the results of regressions of our broadest measures of national saving, incorporating from my total incomes system of accounts (TISA)[21] investment in intangible capital, government and household inventories and semi-durables, and net revaluations or real capital gains. Since the TISA accounts have not been extended beyond 1981, I had only ten useable observations for these regressions. Further, with the real exchange rate index only available from 1973, there would

Table 4.9. *Adjusted budget deficits, changes in monetary base and alternate measures of real national saving, NS14, NS15, NS16, and NS17, 1972–81* $(NSk_t = b_0 + b_1 PAHED6_{t-1} + b_2 DMB_{t-1} + b_3 DMB_{t-2}, k = 14, 15, 16, 17)$

Variable or parameter	Regression coefficients* and standard errors			
	NS14	NS15	NS16	NS17
C	25.689	30.126	31.154	32.268
	(1.109)	(1.324)	(2.851)	(2.109)
PAHED6(− 1)	2.180	3.424	9.179	8.591
	(1.805)	(2.049)	(2.524)	(1.983)
DMB(− 1)	16.055	20.283	23.385	21.086
	(11.412)	(14.401)	(17.412)	(13.325)
DMB(− 2)	12.866	7.801	32.724	28.398
	(10.555)	(13.384)	(17.659)	(13.051)
ΣDMB	28.921	28.084	56.109	49.484
	(12.555)	(15.481)	(24.506)	(18.428)
AR(1)	− 0.014	− 0.010	0.350	0.336
	(0.679)	(0.509)	(0.544)	(0.389)
$\hat{R}^2$	0.416	0.468	0.713	0.780
D–W	1.610	1.519	1.068	1.967
n	10	10	10	10

Notes: * Significant at 0.05 probability level.

C   Constant term.
AR(1)   First-order autoregressive coefficient.
$\hat{R}^2$ Adjusted coefficient of determination.
D–W   Durbin–Watson coefficient.
n   Number of observations.

PAHED6(− 1)   Lagged price-adjusted, high-employment budget surplus as percent of GNP.

DMB(− 1)   Lagged real change in monetary base as percent of GNP (December figures divided by fourth quarter GNP implicit price deflator).

DMB(− 2)   Two-year lagged real change in monetary base as percent of GNP (December figures divided by fourth quarter GNP implicit price deflator).

NS14   Change in total fixed reproducible capital plus adjusted net foreign investment minus statistical discrepancy plus investment in intangible capital and in government and household inventories and semi-durables.

have only been six meaningful observations in AR(1) relations and not very meaningful results if the ERR(− 2) variable had been included. Nevertheless, in all cases, it may be noted, the coefficient of the PAHED6 variable was substantially positive. In the regressions of NS16 and NS17, these positive coefficients were again statistically significant at the 0.05 level or below.[22] The DMB coefficients were uniformly positive.

We may also report the results of vector autoregressions involving the extended saving ratio, NS1. As with those for NS0, discussed above, key results of these VARs, also shown in table 4.10 and figure 4.4, are remarkably consistent with those of the ordinary least squares and AR(1) regressions we have been discussing. Positive shocks of one percentage point to PAHED6 were associated, again after slight contemporaneous declines, with positive impulse responses in NS1 of about a percentage point of GNP in each of the next three years.

As in the case of the conventional saving rate, NS0, real increases in the monetary base were also associated with increases in the expanded saving measure, NS1. Increases in the real exchange rate were similarly associated with declines in the expanded saving measure.

5   Conclusion

We purport to nothing definitive about this analysis. National saving has certainly many determinants, the impact of which may vary with the state of the economy, policy regimes, and the complicated and perhaps changing relations among current variables and the probability distributions of expectations of their future values. Results in full-scale, multi-equation, macroeconomic models may prove more persuasive to some – although not to others – than the essentially reduced forms considered in this chapter.

Table 4.9 (cont.)

NS15	Change in total fixed reproducible capital plus adjusted net foreign investment minus statistical discrepancy plus change in real value of land (NS3) plus investment in intangible capital and in government and household inventories and semi-durables.
NS16	Change in total fixed reproducible capital plus adjusted net foreign investment minus statistical discrepancy plus investment in intangible capital and in government and household inventories and semi-durables (NS14) plus total net revaluations.
NS17	Change in total fixed reproducible capital plus adjusted net foreign investment minus statistical discrepancy plus change in real value of land plus investment in intangible capital and in government and household inventories and semi-durables (NS15) plus net revaluations exclusive of net revaluations on land.

Table 4.10. *VARs with 2 lags, orderings PAHED6, DMB, ERR, and NS0 or NS1, impulse response functions to one percentage point shock in price-adjusted high-employment deficit (PAHED6), from VARs and from 100-observation samples*

From VARs Year	NS0	PAHED6	DMB	ERR
1	− 0.33	1.00	0.017	0.6
2	0.99	0.10	0.084	− 2.3
3	1.04	− 0.29	− 0.017	− 10.3
4	1.22	− 0.86	− 0.106	− 9.8
5	0.45	− 0.84	− 0.093	− 8.6
6	0.44	− 0.72	− 0.068	− 5.4
7	0.61	− 0.58	− 0.048	0.5
8	0.48	− 0.30	− 0.021	5.1
9	0.27	0.01	0.010	6.9

Year	NS1	PAHED6	DMB	ERR
1	− 0.26	1.00	0.020	1.2
2	1.03	0.28	0.086	− 0.1
3	0.93	− 0.01	0.009	− 7.7
4	0.99	− 0.55	− 0.074	− 7.8
5	0.08	− 0.59	− 0.069	− 7.5
6	− 0.09	− 0.55	− 0.054	− 5.8
7	0.06	− 0.50	− 0.043	− 1.5
8	0.07	− 0.32	− 0.026	2.7
9	0.03	− 0.07	− 0.001	5.0

From samples

NS0			NS1		
Year	Mean	Stan. err.	Year	Mean	Stan. err.
1	− 0.26	0.66	1	− 0.28	0.72
2	1.21	1.10	2	1.14	1.14
3	1.27	1.35	3	1.07	1.25
4	1.56	1.46	4	1.29	1.33
5	0.61	1.75	5	0.10	1.38
6	0.94	1.95	6	0.19	1.37
7	1.24	2.39	7	0.12	1.57
8	1.24	2.77	8	0.42	2.02
9	1.21	2.99	9	− 0.14	2.86

Cumulative	Mean	Stan. err.	Cumulative	Mean	Stan. err.
1	− 0.26	0.66	1	− 0.28	0.72
2	0.95	1.57	2	0.87	1.66
3	2.21	2.58	3	1.94	2.51
4	3.77	3.62	4	3.22	3.36
5	4.38	4.85	5	3.33	4.13
6	5.32	6.45	6	3.52	4.73
7	6.56	8.48	7	3.64	5.27
8	7.80	10.81	8	4.06	5.77
9	9.01	13.37	9	3.92	6.58

One may ask how our estimates compare with others that might justify the apparent conventional wisdom that budget deficits reduce national saving. To my knowledge – although that knowledge may well be imperfect – no appropriate, data-based estimates have been presented. Where support for the assertion has been offered it has consisted of naive comparisons of contemporaneous, conventional, actual – not prior, structural, or cyclically adjusted or inflation adjusted or investment adjusted deficits – and conventional measures of saving. In many cases the "analysis" has entailed nothing more than looking at the saving–investment identity and the naive assumption that if one component of (conventional) saving – federal government "saving" – goes up, all the other components will remain the same and therefore the total will go up.

The evidence presented here, however inconclusive all such evidence must be, does offer support to the hypothesis that, as relevant theory suggests may well be the case, real budget deficits have increased rather than decreased national saving, even by its narrow, conventional measure. With the broader, more comprehensive measures of national saving with which we should be most concerned, the effects may be greater. The solution to imagined or real problems of an insufficiency of saving[23] would not appear, on the findings from data of the last two decades, to be found in reducing or eliminating "the budget deficit." This conclusion complements that of Gordon, in the preceding chapter, that encouraging personal or private saving does not appear to increase investment.

A constructive approach would point rather to an easier monetary policy, that would raise domestic and foreign investment and, most important, to shifts of priorities in the direction of more public and private household investment[24] in both tangible and intangible capital.

Appendix   Data sources

1   High-employment surplus and high-employment GNP

The high-employment surplus is defined for a 6.0 percent rate of unemployment. The source for both series for the years beginning with 1970 is the issues of the *Survey of Current Business* of December 1983, May 1985, August 1989, and August 1990. For the years from 1955 to 1969, the high-employment surplus is estimated by taking the Department of Commerce "mid-expansion trend" cyclically adjusted series, and using Holloway's (1989) estimation procedure to convert it to a 6 percent basis. The Holloway procedure is in fact now used by the Commerce Department to estimate the 6 percent unemployment surplus.

High-employment GNP for the years from 1970 on is taken from the *Survey of Current Business* issues listed above. For the years prior to 1970, high-employment GNP is estimated as GNP6 = GNPME × [1 + 0.02(UME − 6)], where GNPME is the Commerce Department of "mid-expansion trend GNP" and UME is the percentage point unemployment rate associated with mid-expansion trend GNP. (The BEA estimates that in the post-1970 period each percentage point of unemployment is associated with 1.9 percent less of cyclically adjusted output. With productivity probably greater prior to 1970 it has seemed reasonable to round the 1.9 percent up to 0.02 in our formulation.) The mid-expansion trend GNP, unemployment rate and cyclically adjusted deficit are published in the December 1983, *Survey of Current Business*.

2 Price-adjusted surplus (and deficit)

The price-adjusted surplus is equal to the 6 percent high-employment surplus defined above plus price effects on the federal net debt. Price effects on the federal debt are in turn estimated as

$$PE_t = [(A - 1)D_{t-1} + (B - 1)(D_t - D_{t-1})]/B, \quad \text{where}$$

PE = price effects,
D = net federal debt at market value,
$A = P^e_t/P^e_{t-1}$,
$B = P^e_t/P_t$
P^e = end-of-year GNP deflator (taken as the mean of the fourth-quarter deflator and the deflator for the first quarter of the subsequent year) and
P = annual GNP deflator.

The deficit is of course simply the negative of the surplus.

3 Monetary base

The nominal monetary base is taken from the *Economic Report of the President*. The figures are averages for the month of December. The monetary variable used in the regression is defined as the change in end of period real stocks divided by real GNP. Algebraically, this may be written as

$$DMB_t = 100[(MB82_t - MB82_{t-1})/(GNP82_{t-1}],$$

where MB82 is the real monetary base and GNP82 is real GNP. The fourth-quarter implicit GNP deflator is used to deflate the monetary base.

4 Real exchange rate

The real exchange rate is a trade-weighted index of ten major trading partners of the US. The series is constructed by the Federal Reserve Board and published in the *Economic Report of the President*. The index is available for 1973 onwards. The index is assumed to be constant prior to 1973.

5 Investment measures

The abbreviation NIPA refers to the *National Income and Product Accounts of the United States*. The number following the NIPA designation refers to the table and line number.

Consumer durables	NIPA 1.2.3
Gross private domestic	NIPA 1.2.6
Net foreign investment	NIPA 4.1.22 deflated by GNP implicit price deflator
Net foreign, adjusted	Net foreign investment (NIPA 4.1.22) plus the difference between changes in the adjusted international investment position of the US at market value and changes in the official international investment position, from Eisner and Pieper (1990), table 8, columns 7 and 2, deflated by the GNP implicit price deflator
Federal tangible	NIPA 3.8.4 + 3.8.11 + 3.8.13 + 3.8.30
State and local tangible	NIPA 3.8.22 + 3.8.27
Research and development	NSF (1987), appendix table B.5, and for later years, *US Statistical Abstract*, deflated by GNP implicit price deflator
Education	
Federal	NIPA 3.15.20 + 3.15.48 + 3.15.78, deflated by deflator for non-defense government purchases constructed by dividing nominal by constant dollar purchases reported in NIPA 3.7 and 3.8
State and local	NIPA 3.16.9 + 3.16.50 − 5.5.47, deflated as above
Private	NIPA 2.5.85

140   Robert Eisner

Notes

William R. Kenan Professor of Economics, Northwestern University. Much of this chapter is based on or derived from joint work with Paul J. Pieper. I have borrowed most recently from Eisner and Pieper (1992). I have enjoyed the research assistance of John Applegate, Maurice Ewing, Oliver Haberstroh, Satish Reddy, Craig Safir, Marc Sokol, and Stacey M. Tevlin, and the continued financial support of the National Science Foundation, most recently through grant #SES-8909600, for the underlying research, but I alone am of course responsible for the contents of this chapter.

1 See Friedman (1983b and 1990), Summers and Carroll (1987), Gramlich (1989), Schultze (1990 and 1991), and Rivlin (1991), among many.

2 One might have thought that an appropriate theoretical formulation was given by Oskar Lange (1938) in his "Optimal Propensity to Consume . . ." article setting forth a model of Keynes' *General Theory*. There is a rate of consumption, private and public, that will maximize investment. On the one hand, increased consumption will raise the demand for capital to facilitate greater output. On the other, it will reduce investment by raising interest rates (or the supply price of capital goods, thus reducing the marginal efficiency of investment). If consumption is initially at or below this maximization point, reductions in consumption are likely to lower investment, not increase it.

3 Empirical confirmation that this may be so is found in the following AR(1) regression between federal grants in aid to state and local governments, GIA, and the price-adjusted high-employment deficit, PAHED6 (explained below), both expressed as a percent of GNP:

$$(2) \quad \Delta GIA_t = 0.142 \, X1 - 0.046 \, X2 + 0.083 \, \Delta PAHED6_t,$$
$$ (0.053) \quad (0.048) \quad (0.027)$$

$t = 1957\text{--}90$, $\hat{R}^2 = 0.367$, DW = 2.17, rho = 0.297.

This was estimated with a first-order correction for serial correlation, with rho the estimated autoregression coefficient. X1 is a constant term for the 1957–72 period while X2 is a constant for the 1973–90 period. The estimates indicate that each dollar more of the inflation and cyclically adjusted federal deficit was accompanied by 8.3 cents more in federal grants in aid to state and local governments.

4 These broader measures of national saving are presented in detail in Eisner (1991) which, with some updating, forms the basis of much of the first two sections of this chapter. A number of measures are taken or derived from the annual time series put together in my total incomes system of accounts (Eisner, 1989c). The net foreign investment adjustments are based on work in Eisner and Pieper (1990) and (1991).

5 We might suggest that here, as elsewhere, it is perfectly appropriate to include the total national income accounts surplus (or deficit) without distinguishing among surpluses in social security trust funds and deficits in the rest of the budget. The fact that politicians or others may choose to designate some revenues for one subaccount does not alter the relevant totality. They all go into the same pot. It may be added that what accountants designate as "in" the social security trust funds has nothing to do, in any economic sense, with what may be available to pay retirees or other beneficiaries in the future. That will depend upon the productivity of the people producing in the future, in turn related to the real wealth that has been accumulated. And this will relate to the real saving discussed in this chapter.

6 See Hayashi (1986) for an illuminating analysis of this.

7 This section, updated to 1990 where possible, draws heavily upon Eisner (1991), in which are to be found detailed series for all of the years from 1946 to 1989 for which they are

available. The underlying figures, in billions of current and constant (1982) dollars, are available on request to the author.

8 National saving in 1982 dollars is calculated, using the saving–investment identity, as NS0 = GPDI − CCA + (NFID − SD)/GNPDEF, where GPDI and CCA are gross private domestic investment and capital consumption allowances with adjustment, both in 1982 dollars, NFID and SD are net foreign investment and the statistical discrepancy, in current dollars, and GNPDEF is the implicit price deflator for gross national product.

9 From "Summary Fixed Reproducible Tangible Wealth Series, 1925–89," *Survey of Current Business*, October 1990, pp. 31–2, updated from tables furnished by John Musgrave, of the US Bureau of Economic Analysis.

10 Changes in the Federal Reserve's value of land at market prices in principle reflect: (1) general increases in land prices in excess of increases in all prices – what we refer to as net revaluations; (2) changes in the general level of all prices or gains corresponding to inflation; and (3) increases in the value of land as a consequence of investment expenses or development. With the available data, our measure of investment in land in fact cannot distinguish between (1) and (3) and hence includes both. In the measures of saving presented below including both investment in land and net revaluations, NS17D and NS17, we therefore include from TISA, as indicated below, total net revaluations *exclusive* of land.

11 See Eisner (1988 and 1989c). Kendrick (1976) laid foundations for much of the TISA accounts. Note also the work of Ruggles and Ruggles (1982), particularly with regard to revaluations and integration of stocks and flows.

12 A full description of sources and methods of TISA series is to be found in Eisner (1989c).

13 Eisner and Pieper (1984) and Eisner (1986), among others.

14 See Eisner (1986 and 1989b) and Eisner and Pieper (1988).

15 A brief, generally specified presentation of a relevant model of an economy with budget deficits is to be found in Eisner (1986), pp. 182–4. A full set of equations, of which some of the relations estimated in this chapter may be seen as reduced forms, is spelled out in Eisner and Hwang (1991).

The model underlying these equations is to be distinguished from that underlying Barro–Ricardian equivalence. According to the equivalence theorem, private agents would generally be indifferent to the financing of government expenditures by taxes or deficits, on the understanding that the present value of the taxes they would have to pay over their relevant horizons, including the lifetimes of successive generations, would be unaffected. The equivalence theorem would suggest that a larger deficit – reduced public saving – would induce greater private saving to pay anticipated larger future taxes. National saving would hence be unaffected. The model behind our equations – and the evidence presented in our estimates of parameters – suggest, however, that national saving may be increased by government deficits, particularly under conditions of less than full employment and excess capacity. Reductions of deficits, if they drive the economy away from full employment, may then reduce national saving.

16 See Eisner (1988a, 1989a, 1989c, and 1991), for example.

17 See Eisner and Pieper (1990) and (1991) for an explanation and presentation of necessary adjustments.

18 Summary descriptions of the various measures of national saving discussed here are presented in the "Definitions and Derivations of Saving Rates and Other Variables," above. Numerical designations correspond to those assigned in Eisner (1991), which offers complete series, in current and constant dollars and as percentages of GNP, of the measures of saving and their components, and an explanation of the sources and methods by which they were derived.

19 One should not be misled by the absolute size of the DMB coefficients. The standard deviation of the DMB variable – the change in the monetary base as a percent of GNP – is relatively small, some 11 percent of that of PAHED6. Large coefficients do not necessarily then imply correspondingly large effects of DMB on the various dependent investment variables.

20 Impulse response functions from VARs involving NS1, but otherwise similar to those with NS0 mentioned above, are again consistent with our ordinary regression results.

21 Eisner (1989c).

22 The absolute values of some of the coefficients, it should be noted, are awkwardly large. It is hard to see why each dollar of deficit should be associated with as much as eight or nine dollars of additional national saving, as some of the coefficients in table 4.8 would seem to suggest. There may be temporary accelerator effects and non-repeatable capital gains involved, indicating that not all of the estimated relationship can be taken as depicting states of long-run equilibrium. And there may, of course, be other, non-permanent and spurious effects that have been picked up in at least some of the estimates.

23 Some portion of the decline of conventionally measured national saving is indeed more imagined than real. Major portions, as we have indicated above and as further discussed in Eisner and Pieper (1991) and Goldstein (1990), relate to the measures of capital consumption allowances and net foreign investment, both of which are suspect.

24 See Aschauer (1989) for evidence that *non-military*, public tangible investment has proved a major contributor to private productivity. This suggests that reductions in military spending – including investment in weapons system and weapons research – associated with the end of the Cold War, might well be devoted to non-military public investment, rather than to deficit reduction.

5 Wages, aggregate demand, and employment in an open economy: an empirical investigation

Samuel Bowles and Robert Boyer

Cutting wages means only the cutting of buying power and the curtailing of the home market. . . . most of the people of the country live on wages. The scale of their living – the rate of their wages – determines the prosperity of the country.

Henry Ford, 1922

1 Introduction

Since the birth of economics as a distinct discipline, advocates of egalitarian economic policy have argued that increases in the real wage might promote employment and stimulate economic growth.[1] Not only the utopian socialist Robert Owen, but Adam Smith and Karl Marx, too, thought the idea had merit. In the modern context of liberal democratic capitalism, the political attractions of this position are clear: if wage increases induce higher levels of employment, then the economic interests of the vast majority of the society – the employed – are consistent with those of the poorest segment – the unemployed. Under these conditions the prospects for majoritarian support of egalitarian economic programs are considerably enhanced.

But is it true that an economy-wide real-wage increase will cause employment to rise? This is the question we will address.

Economists in the neoclassical tradition consider the answer to be obviously "no": the aggregate demand curve for labor is downward sloping. Wage increases entail reductions in employment for at least one of two reasons (in what follows we use the term wage to refer to the real wage). First, higher wages induce firms to substitute other inputs for labor, thus reducing the labor input for a given level of output. And second, higher wages entail cost increases which induce buyers to purchase goods from other producers, possibly from other countries, thus reducing the level of output.[2] While the magnitude of these effects – the

143

substitution effect and the scale effect – is a matter of debate, their existence and direction is thought to be the ineluctable result of the logic of profit maximization. The reason is that the aggregate demand for labor function is simply the summation of the demand for labor function of each employer, and if individual firms' demand for labor functions did not slope downwards there would be no profit-maximizing equilibrium.

Keynesian macroeconomics challenged this position: the wage rate is not only the cost of labor, it is also a determinant of the level of aggregate demand and hence of the demand for labor. While a wage increase will discourage employment by raising the cost of this input, it also may promote employment by supporting a higher level of demand. Thus, even if the individual firms' labor demand curves do slope downward, the aggregate demand curve for labor need not, as an economy-wide wage increase may shift each firm's demand curve to the right.

The key assumption of the Keynesian model is that firms are constrained by insufficient demand and thus each produces at a level below that dictated by the familiar neoclassical profit-maximizing condition according to which production should be expanded until price equals marginal cost. The importance of the assumption that firms are demand constrained is that otherwise they would not alter their outputs when the output demand curves facing them shifted to the right.

Even within the Keynesian model, however, the effect of wage variations on the level of aggregate demand cannot be determined a priori.[3] While a wage increase will increase the demand for consumer goods, it may be offset by other effects. A wage increase may reduce the expected future profit rate sufficiently to dampen the demand for investment goods even if firms are induced to substitute capital for labor; and it will raise the cost of goods, reducing the demand for net exports.[4] Which of these effects predominates is an empirical question, one, unfortunately which has not been adequately studied. While investigations of the demand for labor in the neoclassical framework abound – Hamermesh's recent survey presents well over a hundred of them – estimates of the effect of the wage on the demand for labor in a Keynesian aggregate demand model do not, to our knowledge, exist.[5]

In recent years attention has returned to a third aspect of the wage rate: the effect of the wage on labor motivation and labor discipline and hence on the level of output per hour of labor hired. Whether for the positive inducement of better motivation or the negative inducement of fear of job loss, wages have been shown in a number of studies to influence labor productivity.[6] The endogeneity of labor effort and the quality of work has attracted attention among macroeconomists primarily because it provides a microeconomic foundation for equilibrium unemployment: to induce higher levels of effort, employers' optimal wage offer exceeds the workers' next best alternative, thereby supporting a competitive equilibrium with involuntary unemployment. Less widely noted is the fact that the incentive incompatibility between employer and employee in endogenous effort models gives rise to a market failure with respect to the production process itself: cost-minimizing labor discipline strategies are typically inefficient in the sense that an increase in the wage rate above the profit-maximizing wage is efficiency enhancing.[7]

While this so-called efficiency wage or labor regulation approach would seem to support a positive assessment of the contribution of wage increases to productivity growth, it also highlights a negative influence of wage increases on employment, for if wage increases induce increases in labor productivity they must have negative employment effects *ceteris paribus*, albeit by a mechanism quite distinct from the factor substitution stressed by the conventional neoclassical model.

We will define a wage-led employment regime as an institutional structure within which an exogenous wage increase induces an increase in employment; the converse is termed a profit-led employment regime.[8] Correspondingly, under a wage-led aggregate demand regime an exogenous increase in the real wage increases the level of aggregate demand, with the converse being termed a profit-led aggregate demand regime. Where labor productivity is constant, of course, a wage-led aggregate demand regime is both necessary and sufficient for a wage-led employment regime. But with labor productivity endogenously determined by both substitution and labor effort effects, this is not the case: a wage-led aggregate demand regime is a necessary but not sufficient condition for a wage-led employment regime.

We may thus distinguish between two variants of wage-led economic policy prescriptions: those which focus on the possibly positive effects of the wage on aggregate demand and employment, and those which advocate wage increases as a means of supporting a higher level of output per unit of input. The first variant may be termed wage-led employment strategies, and the second wage-led productivity growth strategies. As is clear from the above reasoning, if productivity growth is strongly wage led, it is unlikely that employment will be wage led. In fact, a frequently heard objection to productivity-enhancing economic strategies is that if successful they would reduce employment; a fear particularly germane if the productivity growth is fostered by wage increases.

Following the above distinctions, we can identify four distinct approaches to modeling the effect of the real wage on the level of employment, as indicated in table 5.1. We also indicate which policy strategies are possible according to each modeling approach.[9]

Table 5.1. *Approaches to macroeconomic modeling and the possibility of wage-led productivity growth and wage-led employment*

		Firms demand constrained	
		No	Yes
Labor productivity endogenous	Yes	Efficiency wage model (wage-led productivity growth possible)	Labor regulation/Keynesian hybrid (both wage-led productivity growth and wage-led employment possible)
	No	Standard neoclassical model (neither possible)	Standard Keynesian model (wage-led employment possible)

In the pages which follow we seek to determine whether wage-led employment strategies are feasible. Because a necessary condition for a wage-led employment regime is that the aggregate demand regime be wage led, we will devote primary attention to estimating the effect of the real wage on the components of aggregate demand under the simplifying assumption that output per hour of labor hired is exogenously determined. In order to do this we econometrically estimate the determinants of investment, savings, and net export demand in France, Germany, Japan, the United Kingdom, and the United States over the post-World War II period.

In our next section we provide a simple model illustrating the logic of a wage-led employment strategy. Because the feasibility of a wage-led employment strategy depends critically on the possibility that income distribution affects the demand for consumer goods, and in particular that a larger wage share of income will support a higher level of demand for consumer goods, we explore the consumption function in section 3. In section 4 we address the relationship between profitability and investment demand. In section 5 we use the results of the previous sections as well as estimates of the determinants of net export demand to estimate the effect of a wage increase on aggregate demand. We address questions of stability in section 6; and in section 7 we summarize our results and conclude.

2   The logic of a wage-led employment regime in a closed economy

Consider a real private economy in which labor supply in hours, $\underline{H}$, is exogenously determined. A summary of our fully developed model (with

Table 5.2. *A summary of the model*

Employment	$h = H/\underline{H}$
Aggregate supply	$Q = qh = R + W$
Profits	$R = h(q - w)$
Wages	$W = wh$
Consumption demand	$C = (1 - s_w) W + (1 - s_r) R$
Investment demand	$I = i_0 + i_r R + i_h h$
Net exports	$X = x_0 + x_r R + x_h h$
Government borrowing	$B = b_0 + b_h h$
Excess demand	$D = I + X - S + B$
Product market clearing	$0 = D(h^*, w)$
Demand effect of wage change	$D_w = h(s_r - s_w - i_r - x_r)$
Demand effect of employment change	$D_h = i_h + x_h - s_h + b_h$
Employment effect of wage change	$h_w = - D_w/D_h$
Short-term stability	$D_h < 0$

Note: All aggregates are normalized on exogenously determined labor supply $\underline{H}$. $\underline{H}$ is the level of employment in hours, q is the level of output per hour.

endogenous government borrowing and net exports) appears for reference in table 5.2. Identical workers produce a single good according to the production function

$$Y = qH \tag{1}$$

where Y is total output (measured in physical units), $H = h\underline{H}$ is the number of hours of labor employed, and q is the units of output produced per hour of employed labor. We rewrite (1) dividing by $\underline{H}$, thus normalizing by labor supply.

$$Q = Y/\underline{H} = qH/\underline{H} = qh \tag{1'}$$

The critical simplifying assumption is that q is a constant.[10] Both the labor effort and input proportions effects of wage variations are suppressed so that variations in the wage rate or employment level do not affect output per hour.[11]

Aggregate supply (normalized) is determined by (1'), while aggregate demand is composed of the demand for consumption goods financed by wages and salaries, and an exogenously given level of autonomous demand (also normalized on $\underline{H}$,) which we can think of as investment demand, and hence denote by I.[12] We will presently relax the assumption that these elements of aggregate demand are exogenously determined. Workers receive an hourly wage, w, and spend a fraction of their income,

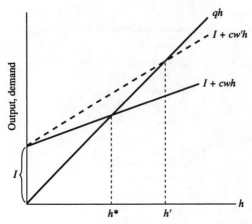

Figure 5.1   The logic of wage-led employment

c. Product market clearing will be determined by the equation of aggregate supply and aggregate demand, or

$$qh = I + cwh \tag{2}$$

Aggregate supply and aggregate demand are presented in figure 5.1, along with the market-clearing equilibrium represented by equation (2). We assume that firms are demand constrained and will thus hire more labor in the presence of excess demand and conversely. So equation (2) is a condition for the stationarity of h: if $qh < I + cwh$, then supply falls short of demand, generating excess demand in product markets, as a result of which firms cut back employment and $dh < 0$. The implied stationary (or equilibrium) employment level can be determined by rearranging terms, giving

$$h^* = I/(q - cw) \tag{3}$$

where h^* represents the equilibrium employment level, namely that for which the product market clears. We refer to (3) as the aggregate demand function for labor. Along this function product markets clear in the sense that the amount supplied is equal to the amount demanded, but the mechanism producing this equilibrium is not price adjustments, but rather firms' varying their levels of employment to accommodate to the demand constraints facing them.

It is clear from equation (3) that under the assumptions given an increase in the wage rate will increase equilibrium employment, or

$$dh^*/dw = cI/(q - cw)^2 \tag{4}$$

or using (3)

$$dh^*/dw = ch^*/(q - cw). \tag{4'}$$

Because the wage bill is just wh, h^* is the partial effect of a wage change on the total wage bill when employment is at its equilibrium level; thus the numerator of (4') is the direct effect of a wage change on aggregate demand for goods. One might think that the effect of a wage change on employment would be simply the wage effect on demand divided by the given level of labor productivity; and indeed this is the case if firms are assumed not to be demand constrained. By contrast to the neoclassical model, however, the denominator is not the level of output per hour, q, but the level of saving which results from the employment of an additional hour of labor, $q(1 - cw/q)$, obviously a far smaller quantity. Thus in the demand-constrained model of the aggregate labor market, employment effects are multiplied, exactly as output effects are expanded by the more familiar multiplier effect.

Equation (4) indicates that the effect of a wage change on equilibrium employment is greater, the larger is the fraction of the wage consumed and the smaller is the non-wage portion of hourly output $(q - w)$. The effect of a wage increase is indicated in figure 5.1 by the displacement of the initial equilibrium, the dashed line.[13]

Substantively, the mechanism producing the positive wage effect on employment is the fact that wage increases expand consumption demand (because consumption is financed entirely from wage income with all non-wage income being saved). The assumption that no demand for consumption goods arises from non-wage incomes is not crucial, as long as the savings propensities from the two types of income differ, with the propensity to spend from wage income being higher. However, an essential and suspect assumption in the above model is that wage increases do not reduce demand for investment goods; it is this assumption which guarantees that employment is wage led. (If the wage increase affected I negatively, the dashed line in figure 5.1 should shift downwards as it became steeper, yielding an indeterminate effect on h.)

Making investment demand endogenous will address this particular weakness of the simplified model. We represent investment demand as $I(w,h)$ now a function of both w and h, so as to allow consideration of the effect of wage variations on investment. The market-clearing condition can now be rewritten as investment demands equals savings, or, that excess aggregate demand D equals zero:

$$D(w,h) = I(w,h) - S(w,h) = 0. \tag{5}$$

As a wage increase will reduce profits (and presumably expected future

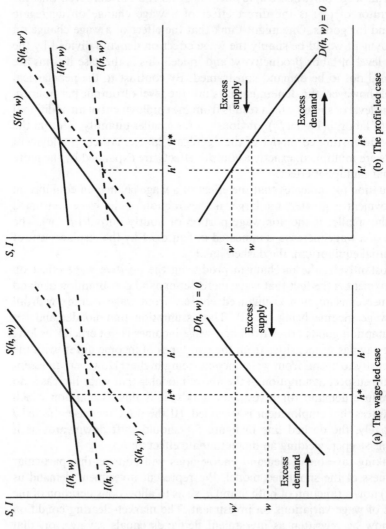

Figure 5.2   The aggregate demand for labor function

profits) the effect on investment may be expected to be negative. Hence I_w, the derivative of I with respect to the real wage, may be expected to be negative. As investment demand will most likely respond positively to the level of capacity utilization and hence to the level of employment we expect that $I_h > 0$. Given the consumption functions assumed in the simplified model, we know that savings will respond positively to the employment level and negatively to the wage rate so $S_h > 0$ and $S_w < 0$.

The result is a variant of the familiar IS diagram presented in figure 5.2, with the dotted lines indicating the effects of a wage increase. The equilibrium employment level is h^* for w and h' for w'. We have drawn the investment function flatter than the savings function, with the implication that at employment levels above the equilibrium level indicated by $D(h, w) = 0$, excess supply will exist, leading to cutbacks in employment, and conversely.[14] It is now clear that a wage increase can affect the equilibrium employment level in either direction. One's intuition is that the direction of the effect will depend on whether the shift in the savings function is more than offset by the shift in the investment function. We will see that this intuition is correct.

Because the excess aggregate demand function can be written as a function of both w and h, we can efficiently summarize the model of figure 5.2 by writing the zero excess demand condition in wage–employment space, as in panels a and b of the lower part of figure 5.2. Both represent aggregate demand for labor functions; like the traditional IS curve, they represent loci in combinations of w and h which satisfy the macroeconomic equilibrium condition of market clearing. The arrows in figure 5.2a and 5.2b indicate the out of equilibrium adjustment of the employment level given: above the equilibrium level (to the right of the demand function) excess supply exists, and firms hire fewer workers, reducing h. To the left of the demand function excess demand for goods exists as a result of which firms expand employment. Figure 5.2a is the wage-led case, and figure 5.2b the profit-led case; the slope of the demand function being the critical difference between the two. (Because productivity is constant wage-led aggregate demand implies wage-led employment.) Upon what does this slope depend?

The effect of the wage change on employment may be determined by totally differentiating the equilibrium condition (5) to get

$$dh^*/dw = -D_w/D_h = (S_w - I_w)/(I_h - S_h). \tag{6}$$

It is readily confirmed that (6) and (4′) are equivalent expressions for the effect of a wage change on equilibrium employment. Recalling that we have assumed that saving responds more to the employment level than does investment and hence an increase in employment will reduce excess demand, the denominator of (6) is negative.[15] The slope of the labor demand function thus depends on the effect of a wage increase on excess demand or D_w, which is equal to $I_w - S_w$, the (presumably negative) effect of a wage increase on investment minus its (presumably negative) effect on savings. If the wage increase reduces savings more than it reduces investment it will increase aggregate demand, and hence (with productivity assumed constant) will increase employment.

The existence of a stable wage-led aggregate demand regime thus depends on the sign of the numerator of (6), which we will presently estimate in an expanded model including net exports.

The first step in this empirical investigation is to determine if the distribution of income affects the level of savings.

3   Income distribution and the demand for consumer goods

The proposition that the rich save a higher fraction of their income than others both appeals to common sense and is supported by studies of family incomes and expenditures. Summarizing the data years ago, Simon Kuznets was unequivocal: "According to all recent studies of the apportionment of income between consumption and savings, only the upper income groups save; the total savings of groups below the top decile are fairly close to zero."[16] Kuznets' judgment is supported by more recent data; during 1983–6 the wealthiest decile of US households accounted for 98.4 percent of the total net real saving.[17] Among all but economists, the proposition that the rich save a larger fraction of their income has come to be taken as a sociological fact of life requiring little explanation.

Not surprisingly, the proposition that classes differ in their savings behavior has played a significant part in macroeconomic theory from the days of the classical economists to the present. In recent years models of the influence of income distribution on savings behavior have followed Kaldor's lead in postulating a savings function of the form

$$S = s_w W + s_r R = s_w wh + s_r h(q - w) \qquad (7)$$

where W and R are respectively total profits and total wages (which can be seen to sum to total output) and S is total savings, all of these aggregates being, like output and investment, normalized on $\underline{H}$. Ideally we would define both wages and profits on an after-tax basis, but data limitations do not permit this; as a result, here and below in our consideration of investment and export demand we are confined to before-tax measures. What may be termed the two propensity hypothesis holds that $s_r > s_w$.

Yet by contrast with family income and expenditure studies, aggregate econometric studies of household savings have yielded no consensus

Table 5.3. *Estimates of the two propensity household saving function*

Author	Country/period	Estimate of $(s_r - s_w)$
Marglin (1984)	US (1952–78)	Negative and/or insignificant
Malinvaud (1986)	US (1948–86)	0.60
Phan (1987)	France (1966–85)	0.40
Marglin and Badhuri	16 OECD countries	0.67 (gross saving)
(1990)	(1960–85)	0.37 (net saving)
Feldstein (1973)	US (1929–41; 48–68)	0.27
Gordon (1990)	US (1951–78)	0.37
Gordon (1993)	US (1955–89)	0.25

position. Stephen Marglin's exhaustive and careful study of US data failed to yield the expected differences in savings propensities between wage and salary income recipients and non-labor income recipients.[18] Our own econometric studies of household savings in France, Germany, Japan, UK, and the US over the period 1961–7 yielded similarly negative conclusions on the two savings propensity hypothesis.[19] Other researchers, however, have found evidence for the expected two propensity household savings function. Some of the relevant studies are surveyed in table 5.3.

The ambiguous econometric performance of the two propensity hypothesis when applied to household savings is surprising, but it is not directly germane to our model, as the relevant definition of savings in our context – total private savings – includes business savings which constitute a significant portion of gross private savings – about half – in all the economies under study.[20]

Our estimates of the effect of income distribution on private savings are based on a transformation of equation (7), taking account of the fact that wages and profits sum to total output, Q.

$$S/Q = s = s_w + (s_r - s_w)R/Q \qquad (8)$$

Equation (8) does not represent a behavioral model of individual or corporate savings decisions but rather is a way of summarizing the empirical relationship between aggregate savings and the distribution of income. We leave unexamined the precise microeconomic model underlying the observed regularities. Thus, the estimates of the parameters of (8) do not imply that individuals or families intend to save differing fractions of income from distinct sources, but only that under given institutional conditions, changes in the levels of wages and profits in the

Table 5.4. *The effect of distribution on private savings*

Country	s_w	$(s_r - s_w)$	Trend	r^2	dw
France	0.18	0.28	− 0.002	0.19	1.16
	(19.3)	(2.8)	(2.8)		
Germany	0.06	0.45		0.82	1.80
	(1.4)	(3.0)			
Japan	0.15	0.69		0.92	1.81
	(3.7)	(3.3)			
UK	0.10	0.40		0.65	1.41
	(4.6)	(2.8)			
US	0.11	0.46		0.60	2.10
	(3.6)	(1.8)			

Notes: The dependent variable is gross domestic private savings divided by gross domestic product or S/Q. The columns headed s_w and $(s_r - s_w)$ are the estimated constant and coefficient of R/Q, respectively (with t-statistics in parenthesis). The period of estimation is 1961–87. Equations for France and the UK were estimated using OLS, while for Germany, Japan, and the US, an ar1 adjustment was used.

aggregate yield different effects on total savings. As such referring to s_w and s_r as savings "propensities" may be misleading, but we will retain the conventional term for lack of a better alternative.

Our estimates of equation (8) for our five countries over the period 1961–87 appear in table 5.4. As in our investment and net export equations to be presented below, we have limited our investigation to estimating the effects of variables identified in our model. Beyond this we have experimented with various lag structures, where appropriate, as well as time trends and dummy variables. We have not sought to determine the influence of other variables. While the estimates of the difference in savings propensities is generally quite significant, the fact that we found no adequate correction for serially correlated error terms common to the five countries suggests caution in interpreting the results. The same caution applies to our subsequent estimates.

The estimated parameters of the savings function are consistent with the two propensity hypothesis. The average value of the estimate of $(s_r - s_w)$ is 0.46, suggesting a quite substantial influence of the functional distribution of income on the savings rate. (As the savings share of output S/Q is approximately equal to the profit share R/Q, the estimate of $s_r - s_w$ may be interpreted as an approximation of an elasticity; thus on average a 1 percent increase in the profit share is associated with slightly less than a 0.5 per cent increase in the savings share.) A redistribution from profits to wages would apparently support a major increase in the demand for consumer goods. The mechanism underlying the wage-led aggregate demand model is thus strongly supported.

4 Profitability and investment

Like the two propensity model of savings, the profit-driven model of investment has generated some debate and little consensus among economists. The profit-driven model posits that firms' investment decisions are influenced by expected future profits and by the firms' liquidity, both of which co-vary with current profits. Additionally, profitability may favorably influence firms' willingness to build new capacity in the face of uncertain product demand conditions. Other influences on investment typically included in profit-driven models are the level of expected future demand as measured by current capacity utilization or an accelerator term and the cost of borrowing (or relative input prices.)[21]

While measures of expected future demand typically dominate other variables in econometric studies of aggregate investment, measures of profitability, when included, are often significant explanatory variables. In a paper presenting estimates which provide little support for the profit-driven model, Ford and Poret comment: "Profit, or cash-flow, models have been found to perform no worse than and sometimes better than standard investment equations."[22] This assessment may be taken, however, as faint praise, given the generally poor econometric performance of most investment functions. Recent panel studies of firm-level data have provided further evidence for the role of expected profitability and cash flow in the investment decision. In this volume, Gordon's essay on savings and investment presents a compelling profit-driven model of investment, while Bhaskar and Glyn's essay suggests more caution. Nonetheless Bhaskar and Glyn conclude that "profitability had sizeable as well as statistically significant effects, comparable in influence on the decline of investment rate to both the output growth and relative cost variables."[23]

As our output and savings variables are in gross terms, and as our concern is with short-term variations in aggregate demand, not the long-run growth in capital stock, we seek to explain gross rather than net investment. Because we are interested in the direct and indirect effects on investment of changes in the profit rate and the employment level rather than in identifying structurally the mechanisms through which these influences work, our own estimation strategy is very simple. We introduce only the profit rate r and the employment rate h as explanatory variables, in most cases with lags both to address possible problems of simultaneity and to account for the process of expectation formation. A time trend is included to account for variations in the investment environment causally unrelated to r or h.

Our estimating equation is thus

$$I/K = I_0 + I_r(R/K)_{-1} + I_h h_{-1} \tag{9}$$

Because h is highly correlated with the activity level of the economy it may measure the influence of future demand expectations. But these, too, may be captured by the profit-rate term, which also co-varies with the level of employment and output. This can be seen from the expression for the profit rate implied by the model in section 2

$$r = R/K = h(q - w)/K. \tag{10}$$

As I_r is an estimate of the effect on investment of a change in the profit rate holding the employment rate constant, it may equivalently be interpreted as the effect of a change in the level of profits per hour of labor hired, expressed as a fraction of the capital stock. Note further that the total derivative of investment demand with respect to h taking account of the effects of the employment level on the profit rate is not I_h itself, but $I_h + I_r(q - w)/K$, from which it is clear that, while we expect the total derivative to be positive, I_h could be of either sign given that $I_r > 0$.

Our estimates appear in table 5.5. The coefficients of the profit term may be interpreted as the effect on the level of investment of an increase in the level of profits: thus, in Japan, for example, an additional 100 yen of profits yields the short-run result of an additional 25 yen of investment or (taking account of the implied inertia in the investment process measured by the coefficient of lagged investment) a long-run effect of 53 yen. As this example suggests, in those cases for which the estimated equation includes lagged investment on the right-hand side (France, Germany, and Japan) we need to convert the estimated parameters (which are instantaneous derivatives) to long-term or steady-state derivatives by multiplying them by $1/(1 - \lambda)$ where λ is the estimated coefficient of the lagged dependent variable. The transformed estimates, i_r, appear in table 5.5. For ease of reference we present in table 5.6 our estimating equations and the relationships they bear to the parameters of the theoretical model summarized in table 5.2.

As investment and profits are of approximately the same magnitude in the countries under study, these coefficients may be interpreted as elasticities. In the US, for example, a one dollar increase in profits is associated with a 16 cent increase in investment or, equivalently, a 1 percent increase in profits is associated with (approximately) a 0.16 percent increase in investment. The estimates yield quite different degrees of investment responsiveness to profitability with Japan at the high end and the UK and

Table 5.5. *Investment equations*

Country	λ	I_{r-1}	I_{h-1}	I_t	i_r	r^2	dw
France	0.68	0.08	0.17	0.05	0.25	0.96	2.31
	(12.0)	(3.6)	(4.9)	(4.8)			
Germany	0.37	0.21	0.13	0.02	0.33	0.96	1.34
	(3.1)	(4.7)	(2.6)	(1.2)			
Japan	0.53	0.25			0.53	0.91	1.84
	(4.0)	(3.0)					
UK		0.14	0.33	0.10	0.14	0.53	0.58
		(2.2)	(4.6)	(2.9)			
US		0.16	0.13	0.07	0.16	0.62	1.47
		(3.8)	(1.8)	(6.8)			

Notes: The dependent variable is the ratio of gross investment to the capital stock. The entries in each column are the estimated regression coefficients (with t-statistics in parentheses). The period of estimation is 1953–87. All estimates are by the ordinary least squares method. Each equation was estimated with a constant (not shown). The estimate for Germany includes a dummy variable for the years after 1973 (the coefficient of which is -0.53 (-1.9). The column headed i_r is the estimated coefficient of the profit term divided by unity minus the estimated coefficient of the lagged dependent variable, λ.

Table 5.6. *Estimating equations and parameters of the theoretical model*

$$S/Q = S_0 + S_1(R/Q)$$

$$s_w = S_0$$
$$s_r = S_1 + S_0$$
$$s_h = qs_r + w(s_w - s_r)$$

$$I/K = I_0 + \lambda(I/K)_{-1} + I_r(R/K)_{-1} + I_h h_{-1}$$

$$i_r = I_r/(1 - \lambda)$$
$$i_h = KI_h/(1 - \lambda) + i_r \partial R/\partial h$$

$$X/Q = X_0 + X_r(R/K)_{-n} + X_h h$$

$$x_r = X_r(Q/K)$$
$$x_h = X_h Q + x_r \partial R/\partial h$$

$$B/Q = B_0 + B_h h_{-1}$$

$$b_h = B_h Q$$

Note: The parameters of the estimating equations are in upper-case letters, those of the theoretical model are in lower case; the table indicates the relationship between the two.

the US at the bottom.[24] Taken as a whole these estimates indicate what may seem surprisingly little responsiveness of investment to profits; if all profits were invested, as in some very simplified macro models and linear growth models, the coefficient would be unity, yet the average of those estimated here is barely a quarter of that, 0.28.

5   A wage-led aggregate demand regime? Some empirical evidence

These estimates, along with the estimated difference in the savings propensities in table 5.4, allow a thought experiment: abstracting from net exports, does the relationship between savings and investment support a wage-led aggregate demand regime? As we have seen, answering this question requires that we estimate the derivative of the excess demand function D with respect to w, with a positive sign indicating a wage-led regime. Reviewing the entire model as summarized in table 5.2 we see that D_w is $(i_r - s_r)\partial R/\partial w - s_w \partial W/\partial w$ or $h(s_r - s_w - i_r)$ in this hypothetical "closed-economy" case.[25] Comparing the data in tables 5.4 and 5.5, it can readily be confirmed that all of the economies exhibit wage-led aggregate demand regimes under the hypothetical abstraction from the influence of net exports. In every case the difference in the savings propensities by income source exceeds the responsiveness of investment to variations in profitability.

Does the introduction of net export demand overturn this striking result?

As the rate of profit is strongly affected by the level of net output per hour relative to the wage rate and other determinants of competitive status, we use the profit rate as a measure of competitive strength and hypothesize (lagged) that profit rates and net export demand will be positively related. This does not imply that variations in profits (from whatever source) cause variations in net exports; a profit increase caused by an increase in the markup, for example, would presumably not increase net exports. But prices are not modeled explicitly here, consistent with the assumption each country faces given international prices for its exports and imports. Thus the effect of a real wage change operates solely on profits rather than prices, and profit effects on net exports must operate via non-price competition. (We consider the implications of a flexible price approach in section 7.)

Because import demand rises with employment and export demand is little affected, we expect net exports to vary inversely with h. Because structural shifts in trading relationships and exchange rates not causally affected by variations in h and r will also influence the level of net export demand, we have included time trends (or dummy variables) in the export equations.

Table 5.7. *Determinants of net exports*

Country	$X_{r(-t)}$	X_h	$d79$ (or t)	x_r	r^2	dw
France	0.06			0.07	0.04	1.30
	(1.4)					
Germany	0.32		0.015	0.30	0.23	0.84
	(2.3)		(3.2)t			
Japan	0.22	− 2.4	1.3	0.25	0.66	1.58
	(2.6)	(2.6)	(1.5)d			
UK	0.32	− 0.51	− 3.1	0.21	0.45	1.70
	(1.4)	(2.5)	(2.1)d			
US	0.24	− 0.44	− 2.7	0.16	0.78	1.23
	(3.4)	(3.6)	(9.1)d			

Notes: The entries in each column headed by a variable symbol are the estimated regression coefficients of the column variable (with t-statistics in parentheses). The dependent variable is net exports divided by gross domestic product or X/Q. Estimated constants are not shown. The method of estimation was OLS for France and Germany and AR1 for Japan, the UK, and the US. The period of estimation is 1961–87. Time trend coefficients are indicated by t, dummy variable coefficients by d. For the US, the UK, and Japan the estimate for the profit term is the sum of coefficients on a three-year third-degree polynomial lag. For Germany and France the estimates are for the contemporary profit rate. The estimate of x_r – the derivative of the level of net exports with respect to the level of profits – is the regression coefficient in the first column multiplied by Q/K (see table 5.6).

As in the case of investment we seek to estimate both the direct and indirect effects of variations in h and r and therefore we do not estimate a fully specified structural equation, but rather the following (suppressing the trend variables)

$$X/Q = X_0 + X_r(R/K)_{-t} + X_h h. \tag{11}$$

The resulting estimates appear in table 5.7.

Significant time trends (or time dummies) appear in four of the five equations, not surprisingly, indicating exogenous declines in the competitive position for the UK and the US, and improvements for Germany and Japan. The estimated effect of the profit rate is positive, as expected, although the estimates are of very poor quality for the UK and France. The equation for France is quite unsatisfactory, indicating little relationship between either the profit rate or the employment level and net exports. The very large estimated effect of the employment level in Japan is due to the quite restricted range of variation of the employment level in

Table 5.8. *The effect of a real wage increase on aggregate demand*

Country	$(s_r - s_w)$ (1)	i_r (2)	x_r (3)	h (4)	D_w (5)	$\underline{D}_w$ (6)
France	0.28	0.25	0.07	0.94	− 0.04	0.03
Germany	0.45	0.33	0.30	0.97	− 0.17	0.12
Japan	0.69	0.53	0.25	0.98	− 0.09	0.16
UK	0.40	0.14	0.21	0.94	0.05	0.24
US	0.46	0.16	0.16	0.93	0.13	0.28

Notes: Columns (1), (2), and (3) are from tables 5.4, 5.5, and 5.7. D_w is the estimated effect on aggregate demand, (5), is (4) $\{(1) - (2) - (3)\}$. Column (6) is a hypothetical estimate based on closed-economy assumptions modeled by simply abstracting from the effect of the wage increase on net export demand or (4) $\{(1) - (2)\}$.
Source: Tables 5.2, 5.4, 5.5, 5.6, and 5.7.

that economy, with very limited employment variations corresponding to quite significant output and income variations.

Taking account of the impact of net exports on aggregate demand dramatically alters the relationship between income distribution and aggregate demand. Using tables 5.2, 5.4, 5.5, 5.7, and recalling that $\partial R/\partial w = - h$, we can calculate the derivative of aggregate demand with respect to the real wage as

$$D_w = h(s_r - s_w - i_r - x_r) \tag{12}$$

estimates of which appear in table 5.8, using as an estimate of h the average employment rate in the economies in question for the period 1952–88. (The estimate of h clearly does not affect the designation of each country as either wage led or profit led, though because it represents the effect of a wage change on the level of profits and the total wage bill, it does effect the magnitude of the effect on aggregate demand.) Three countries – France, Germany, and Japan, now exhibit a profit-led aggregate demand regime, while the UK and the US remain wage led, though for the UK only marginally so.

Figure 5.3 summarizes the data in table 5.8. A comparison of the bars outlined with solid lines yields the estimate of D_w, while a comparison of the cross hatched bars indicates the estimate of $\underline{D}_w$, the hypothetical closed-economy wage effect on aggregate demand.

The importance of the degree of openness in determining the wage-led

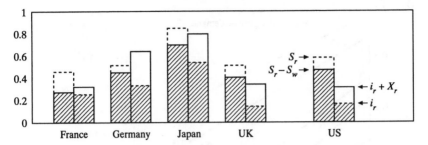

Figure 5.3   Saving, investment, and exports as determinants of demand regimes

or profit-led nature of the aggregate demand regime is suggested by the following hypothetical calculation. It seems reasonable to posit that the size of the export coefficient varies with the volume of imports and exports. Let us assume that x_r varies linearly with exports and imports as a share of full-employment output, and consider the effects of changing the size of the trade shares, assuming no other changes in the determination of net export demand. Define the degree of openness in each country relative to its current status over the period of estimation simply by the ratio of x_r to its estimated value appearing in table 5.8.[26] Figure 5.4 plots D_w for varying degrees of openness, thus defined. For example, for France, D_w changes sign at a level of openness of 0.57.

These estimates highlight the importance of the global integration of national economies in determining the nature of the aggregate demand regimes. Export and import shares of 10 percent or less – which characterized the advanced capitalist nations as a whole during the 1950s for example – would almost certainly have supported wage-led aggregate demand regimes in most economies. Under these conditions wage increases would trigger a virtuous circle of employment growth, providing the bargaining environment for yet additional wage increases. Similarly, expansions of unemployment insurance, by directly and indirectly supporting higher levels of demand for consumer goods would promote employment. The result, under these relatively closed-economy conditions, is that the negative impact on profits and investment of egalitarian and solidaristic social policies are partly attenuated by the induced increases in output.

Of course, these results are of little interest if our assumption of short-term stability is false, for under unstable conditions $D_w > 0$ would imply $dh^*/dw < 0$, thus reversing our results, and more importantly casting doubt on their relevance to any observed economy.

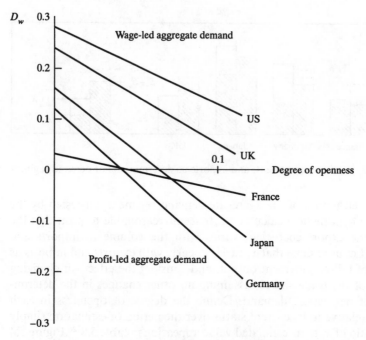

Figure 5.4   Demand regimes and the degree of openness

6   Government borrowing and stability

We have thus far assumed that the macroeconomic equilibrium defined by the absence of excess demand in product markets is stable. In the simple model of section 2, stability was guaranteed by the level of saving being more responsive than investment to variations in employment. In our more complete model stability requires that $D_h < 0$, or that increases in employment reduce excess demand. Our reasoning is as follows. Because employers increase hiring in the presence of excess demand and conversely, using $\dot{h}$ as the time derivative of h, we can write

$$\dot{h} = \rho(D) \text{ with } \rho' > 0 \text{ and } \rho(0) = 0 \tag{13}$$

from which it is obvious that if $D_h > 0$, a displacement of h from its equilibrium value h^* will be explosive, an increase, say, in h increasing excess demand, and this, by (13) increasing h, generating a further increase in excess demand, and so on.[27]

Because government demand financed by borrowing (or dissaving) exercises a major influence on aggregate demand and varies over the business cycle, we will need to take account of its influence in calculating

Table 5.9. *Estimated effect of employment variations on public sector borrowing*

Country	$B_{h(-1)}$	r^2	dw	Method
France	− 0.43 (8.1)	0.72	1.90	olsq
Germany	− 0.33 (2.6)	0.18	0.90	olsq
Japan	− 2.44 (4.1)	0.39	0.35	olsq
UK	− 0.05 (0.3)	0.65	1.29	arl
US	− 0.54 (2.4)	0.46	1.81	arl

Notes: The dependent variable is (net public borrowing)/GDP. The column headed $B_{h(-1)}$ presents the estimated coefficient of the lagged employment rate (with t-statistic in parenthesis). The period of estimation is 1962–87. The estimated constant is suppressed.

the effect of variations in h on excess demand. To do this we continue to abstract from taxation, and represent government borrowing as simply an autonomous component plus a component which varies inversely with the level of employment, higher levels of economic activity inducing lower levels of borrowing, and conversely, or

$$B = b_0 + b_h h \text{ with } b_h < 0. \tag{14}$$

Estimates of a version of (14) in table 5.9 suggest a significant negative impact of variations in h on net government borrowing in all countries except the UK.

Government demand financed by borrowing is an additional component of aggregate demand so the excess demand equation now becomes

$$D = I + X - S + B \tag{15}$$

with the resulting stability condition

$$D_h = i_h + x_h - s_h + b_h < 0 \tag{16}$$

Though we have not econometrically estimated s_h, it is simply the weighted average of the two savings propensities, weighted by the respective income shares, multiplied by hourly income, and hence can be inferred from the estimated values of s_w and s_r as well as w and q. This calculation, as well as the other transformations necessary to calculate the value of D_h from equation (16) appear in table 5.8. Calculations of this stability condition for the five countries under investigation indicate that all countries exhibit stability though in the absence of the built-in stabilizers implied by the public borrowing equation, France would be unstable. Thus our estimates of Dw are indeed estimates of the effect of a wage change on the level of aggregate demand.

7   Conclusion: one cheer for wage-led economics

In summary, our primary results are the following. First, the evidence suggests that the distribution of income affects the components of aggregate demand, though the effects are not uniformly strong or even statistically significant in all cases. Second, in each of the five economies studied differences in savings propensities from wages and from profits are sufficiently great to offset the effect of profits on investment. Thus, abstracting from the influence of international trade, each economy is characterized by a wage-led aggregate demand regime. Third, adopting the more institutionally realistic open economy assumption, however, three of the economies are characterized by profit-led aggregate demand regimes, wage increases entailing reductions in excess demand and hence in employment. Taking account of the effect of wage increases in inducing factor substitution in production and in providing the basis for work discipline – which we do not do – would, of course, support an even more pessimistic assessment of the likelihood of wage-led employment.

As one might expect, whether an economy exhibits a wage-led or profit-led aggregate demand structure appears to be quite sensitive to the institutional structure of the economy. This is in part the result of the fact that for all economies studied D_w is close to zero so it changes sign – shifting from wage led to profit led or vice versa – in response to quite minor changes in the estimates. This being the case and given the fact that our estimates are far from satisfactory, it would be best to conclude not that particular nations' aggregate demand structures are profit led or wage led, but rather that the effects on aggregate demand of an economy-wide change in the real wage are likely to be quite small.[28] The negative output effects of a wage change implied by neoclassical studies of the demand for labor, by contrast, are substantial, and are considerably larger (in absolute value) than the values in table 5.8 for the three countries with profit-led aggregate demand.[29]

Our estimates suggest that wage-led aggregate demand structures, if not prevalent, are at least distinctly possible where output per hour is exogenously determined. But even a positive effect of the wage on aggregate demand assuming constant labor productivity could be offset by a sufficiently large substitution or labor effort effect.[30] These results thus provide little support for the existence of a wage-led employment regime, at least under existing conditions of substantially open economies.

But this assessment of the prospects for a wage-led employment regime in open national economies does not extend to a world of coordinated economic policies. While the relatively closed economy conditions offering the possibility of wage-led aggregate demand regimes in the immediate post-World War II era clearly no longer exist, results very similar to the closed economy case would obtain, even under high levels of global economic integration, if wage increases were to take place throughout the world simultaneously. If the world economy taken as a whole even roughly approximates the five national economies under study in the relevant respects (and given the preponderance of the five in the global totals it would be surprising if this were not the case), then a simultaneous world-wide wage increase would certainly increase the level of global aggregate demand, and would quite likely stimulate employment as well. Given that our five countries account for well over half of all international trade, coordinated wage increases in these five economies alone might have analogous effects. Thus our estimates are not inconsistent at least with the short-term logic of the vision of globally coordinated demand expansion advocated by Willy Brandt, Michael Manley, Olaf Palme, and other internationalist socialists.

Yet for two reasons this observation cannot constitute an endorsement of a wage-led employment generating strategy. First, the coordination problems of agreeing upon and enforcing a common wage increase, even among a small number of countries, are daunting; the incentive for any single country to opt out of a wage increase agreement would be difficult to resist.

And second, the negative assessment of the prospects of wage-led employment growth in national economies taken singly must be considerably strengthened when a longer-run perspective is adopted. The reason is that, while theoretically possible, the empirical likelihood that a wage increase could foster a more rapid rate of accumulation is extraordinarily small, even in the extreme closed economy case: for this to be the case the positive effect of the wage increase on the level of activity in the economy, and the consequent effect on investment, would have to offset the negative effect of the wage operating via the profit rate.[31] For none of the countries under investigation is this even remotely likely as it would require a far greater responsiveness of investment to variations in the employment level than that observed. The long-term result of a real wage increase is thus likely to lower the rate of accumulation and hence to reduce the rate of productivity growth. Consequently wage increases –

even if employment inducing in the short run – may thus be unsustainable in the long run or if sustained compatible only with long-term declines in aggregate demand associated with reduced international competitiveness and a reduced investment incentive, or both.

It would be tempting to seek to explain the differences in our estimates among the five countries by reference to their institutional structures. Where a large fraction of private saving is done by corporations rather than households, for example, and where the effective management of corporations is highly insulated from stockholder accountability, we might expect to find a larger effect of profits on the savings rate. Similarly, where public provision of health insurance and other basic needs is assured, we might expect to see larger differences between the savings behavior of rich and other households. Under these conditions, the rich might prefer to save to support a living standard in old age at the level to which they are accustomed (presumably above the level supported by the state). Analogous speculations might propose institutional explanations of national differences in the responsiveness of investment and of net exports to variations in the profit rate. Where investment by firms is primarily internally financed, for example, we might expect to find a larger effect of the profit rate on investment via a cash-flow mechanism. And where the investment is dominated by monopolistically competitive globally oriented firms we would expect a greater responsiveness of both investment and net exports to the profit rate. A typology of institutions and macroeconomic regimes along the lines of table 5.10 might thus be developed.

Two considerations stemming from this empirical study, however, suggest that a sustained investigation along these lines might be premature. First, the estimates are not yet of sufficient quality to support anything but the most general of conclusions. And second, taking account of the quality of the estimates, one is struck not so much by national differences in the savings, investment, and export behavior relevant to the long-run demand for labor, but instead by how similar the five countries are, most apparently falling in the upper left quadrant of table 5.10. Analogous investigations in countries at differing levels of development and with more sharply differing institutional structures might, of course, yield less homogeneous results.

What remains, then, of the case for wage-led economic policies? Among the arguments often offered for an across the board wage increase, three are prominent: it fosters greater equality of income, it supports a higher level of employment, and it contributes to higher levels of productivity. Taking long-run effects into account, the second (wage-led employment) seems unlikely to be true under current institutional conditions in the

Table 5.10. *Institutional environments and possible macroeconomic*
regimes

Influences on: $S \rightarrow$ $(I + X) \downarrow$	Corporate firms, Welfare state	Simple proprietorship, little social insurance
Open economy	Either: $dh/dw \approx 0$	Profit led: $dh/dw < 0$
Closed economy	Wage led: $dh/dw > 0$	Either: $dh/dw \approx 0$

advanced (and probably other) capitalist economies. This being the case,
it is unclear whether the first is true. A wage increase resulting in a larger
fraction of the workforce being frequently without paying work could
well be disequalizing, given that a considerable fraction of the inequality
in the size distribution of income is attributable to the dispersion of
annual wages and salary income. Thus wage increases, even if economy
wide, may be neither employment generating nor income equalizing.

Yet strong arguments remain that wage increases may either directly or
indirectly contribute to higher levels of output per hour of labor. If true,
this claim provides support for wage-led economic policies as a generic
approach, but not for wage-led employment strategies. This conclusion
limits the types of gains that may be expected from policies to increase real
wages, but it does not suggest that wage-led policies should be abandoned.

Notes

We would like to thank V. Bhaskar, Gerald Epstein, Bill Gibson, Herbert Gintis, Andrew Glyn, David Gordon, Daniel Hamermesh, Mehrene Larudee, Stephen Marglin, Peter Skott, and William Milberg for help in preparing this paper.

1 The opening quote is from Ford (1924), p. 116.
2 The effect of the wage on the scale of output is clearly relevant at the level of the firm, but would be questioned at the national level by many neoclassical economists on the grounds that equilibrium aggregate output is determined independently of the real wage rate, the level of demand for the economy's goods accommodating the equilibrium output level through price and exchange rate adjustments.
3 Effects of income distribution on aggregate demand have been explored in a number of recent theoretical works, notably Rowthorn (1982), Dutt (1984), Taylor (1985), and Marglin and Bhaduri (1990).
4 The reader will note that a real wage increase will *ceteris paribus* increase the demand for investment goods in the neoclassical model as firms seek to substitute capital for labor; while the profit-driven model of investment common to Keynesian, post-Keynesian, and Marxian models implies the reverse.
5 The empirical study which comes closest is Blecker (1991) which provides an empirical test of Marglin and Bhaduri's "exhilarationist hypothesis" according to which a redistribution of income to profits will support a higher level of aggregate demand. He finds evidence of a shift from what he terms a wage-led to a profit-led aggregate demand structure in the US during the early 1980s. Symons and Layard (1984) provide tests of the effect of aggregate demand shocks on labor demand, but not on the effect of wage changes on aggregate demand.
6 Contributions to the theoretical literature on this approach is surveyed in Yellen (1984) and Stiglitz (1987). Tests of positive wage effects on productivity can be found in Bowles, Gordon, and Weisskopf (1983a) and Schor (1988).
7 See Bowles (1985) and Bowles and Gintis (1993).
8 Where the wage rate is endogenously determined, as in our 1988 and 1990 papers, for example, this formulation would refer to an exogenous upward shift in the wage function (rather than the wage itself).
9 In the standard neoclassical model a wage increase will induce factor substitution and support a higher level of output per hour of labor; we do not term this a case of wage-led productivity growth, however, because by contrast with the effect of an arbitrary wage increase in the labor regulation approach, it results in a decline in the productivity of at least one other factor of production and does not result in an increase in total factor productivity.
10 Let e be the level of effort performed per hour of work and t be the level of output per unit of effort; then $q = te$, from which it is clear that we assume both effort and what might be termed technical efficiency are constant.
11 A zero or very small substitution effect may be a reasonable assumption for the short run, but even in the very short run a considerable amount of labor–capital substitution is possible by varying the number of hours of work per unit of capital (double shifting and the like). However the effects on output per hour of cyclical variation in the ratio of labor hours hired to capital stock are quite different from the productivity effects of factor substitution based on the adoption of differing technologies. As it is the latter, and not the former which produces the productivity effects stressed in the conventional literature, and as this kind of technical choice-based factor substitution does not take place in

the very short run, abstracting from its effects in a short-run analysis seems legitimate. However, the studies of the cyclical relationship between the wage and the level of labor effort indicate a strong wage effect on labor effort and hence on output per hour of labor hired. It therefore seems questionable to abstract from variations in labor effort even in a short-run model. We relax the constant effort assumption subsequently.

12 We may assume (not unrealistically) that the workers' employer also works and like the workers spends cw on consumption goods, while saving from her property income.

13 Noting that the difference between the slopes of the aggregate supply function (q) and the aggregate demand function (cw) is the numerator of (4'), one can readily see why the size of the employment effect depends on the share of savings in income.

14 This is a condition of (short-term) stability. Our subsequent analysis of stability issues indicates that in our complete model, taking account of government borrowing and net export demand, the analogue of this stability condition empirically obtains in each of the five economies studied.

15 Indeed this is a condition for stability of the equilibrium, for if an increase in h increased excess demand, and if employers responded to increased excess demand by hiring more labor, the economy would not converge to an equilibrium.

16 Kuznets (1965), p. 263.

17 Avery and Kennickell (1990), table 11.

18 Marglin (1984), pp. 393–455. In some cases Marglin found statistically significant differences in savings propensities of the wrong sign.

19 In four of the five cases the estimated difference between the propensity to save from profits and from wages was of the wrong sign. If wealth effects on savings are important (and there is ample evidence that they are) econometric estimates which fail to take account of wealth may result in a downward bias in the estimate of the propensity to save from profits. The reason is that savings varies inversely with wealth and that wealth and profits generally co-vary. Similarly, because the propensity to consume from transfer income is apparently considerably higher than from wages (see Gordon's essay in this volume, for example) and because wages and transfer payments co-vary inversely, studies not taking explicit account of transfer payments will underestimate the propensity to consume from wages. We do not know, of course, if these possible specification biases account for our generally negative findings (and possibly Marglin's).

20 Over the years 1981–7, corporate sector savings constituted 61 percent of gross private savings in Germany and the U.K., and 48, 42, and 41 percent in the US, France, and Japan, respectively. Dean, *et al.* (1989), p. 68. Were it the case that households took full account of the effect of business saving on their asset position it might be argued that the business savings decisions would be fully offset by adjustments in household savings, but both the stringent theoretical requirements for this result and the lack of compelling empirical support for the proposition that business savings decisions have no effect on total private savings suggests that the business-saving decision may be considered as sufficiently independent of the household decision to warrant separate attention. The fact that we found quite different distributional effects on household savings and total private savings supports this position.

21 Studies of investment along these lines are Bowles, Gordon, and Weisskopf (1989) and Gordon, Weisskopf, and Bowles (1990) on the US, and Catinat *et al.* (1987) on Germany, France, and then UK, as well as Bhaskar and Glyn, and Gordon, both in this volume.

22 Ford and Poret (1990), p. 18. Ford and Poret survey a number of studies of profit-driven investment functions using both firm-level panel data as well as aggregate time series. See also Clark (1979).

23 Gordon (chapter 3, this volume) and Bhaskar and Glyn (chapter 6, this volume).

24 Directly comparable estimates are few, but Gordon's (chapter 3, this volume) estimate of a derivative of net investment (normalized on potential output) with respect to the after-tax profit rate is a highly significant 0.13, which implies an estimate comparable to our definitions of about 0.2. In order to compare these results with those of Bhaskar and Glyn one must transform their estimates to take account of the difference in the dependent variable (the natural logarithm of the rate of change of the capital stock and the level of gross investment divided by the capital stock) and the fact that their measure of profitability is the net profit share rather than the profit rate.

25 The mocking quotation marks are intentional, designed to draw attention to the hypothetical nature of this exercise, as there is no reason to expect that any of the basic equations of the model would remain unaffected were the economies in question to be substantially closed to international trade. In closed economies, for example, the responsiveness of investment to variations in the profit rate might be less than in open economies, as potential investors would not have the choice of investing abroad if the domestic profit rate were unsatisfactory.

26 A degree of openness of unity implies the values in table 5.8, while zero openness implies that $x_r = 0$. The degree of openness cannot be compared across countries, as the estimates of x_r themselves reflect the varying institutional situations of each economy. Thus the degree of openness is merely a measure to be compared with the conditions obtaining in each separate country over the time period in question.

27 If the wage is modeled endogenously, as in the next section, we would need a more complex stability condition taking account of the reciprocal effects of the wage rate and the employment level. Under conditions of wage-led employment, and where the equilibrium real wage, w^*, varies with the employment rate, for example, a displacement of h from its equilibrium value would generate an endogenous increase in the real wage which in turn would support an increase in the level of employment, possibly leading to a non-convergent series of effects. The relevant stability condition with the wage rate endogenous is that $D_h + (\partial w^*/\partial h)D_w < 0$, or that the total derivative of excess demand with respect to the employment rate is negative. As the labor discipline approach used to endogenize the wage implies that $\partial w^*/\partial h > 0$, $D_h < 0$ is a sufficient condition for stability unless $D_w > 0$. However, as $\partial w^*/\partial h$ rises to infinity as h approaches some limit less than full employment due to the high employment wage explosion (see Bowles and Boyer, 1990), any economy which exhibits a wage-led aggregate demand structure will be unstable at sufficiently high levels of employment.

28 To see how small, we can express D_w as an elasticity simply by multiplying the estimated values by w/Q, which given that Q is normalized on the level of labor supply is equal to w/qh, or the wage share of output divided by the employment rate. Thus we can represent the elasticity of output with respect to the real wage as approximately 0.9 times the values for D_w in table 5.8.

29 The sample mean of the over seventy available econometric estimates of the constant output elasticity of demand for homogeneous labor is -0.39. On the basis of a careful study of the existing research Hamermesh (1993) finds the best guess of this elasticity is somewhat lower, -0.30. This may be compared to the sample mean of the eleven estimates of the long-run (output endogenous) elasticity of demand for labor (those surveyed by Hamermesh as well as the individual country estimates of Symons and Layard (1984)) of minus two; the median value is -0.93. The difference between these two estimates, -1.7 or -0.63, is the implied estimate of the output effect $d \ln Q/d \ln w$. (The output endogenous elasticity is just the sum of the output effect and the constant output substitution effect.) This estimate is, of course, far in excess (in absolute value) of any of the estimates of the corresponding elasticities based on D_w in table 5.8.

30 This is obvious in the neoclassical framework for the substitution effect on employment and the demand or scale effect on employment are simply additive in natural logarithms; even a large positive demand effect could be offset by the substitution effect, which is negative. With demand-constrained firms the reasoning behind the statement in the text is explained in the previous section.

31 Formally it would have to be the case that $i_h dh^*/dw + i_r \partial R/\partial w > 0$, or that the (possibly positive) wage effect operating via the impact of the activity level of the economy on investment be sufficiently large to offset the (negative) effect of the wage on investment via its impact on the profit rate.

Part three

The determinants of investment: profits, demand, debt, and expectations

6 Investment and profitability: the evidence from the advanced capitalist countries

V. Bhaskar and Andrew Glyn

> The determination of investment decisions by, broadly speaking, the
> level and rate of change of economic activity . . . remains the *pièce de
> résistance* of economics
>
> M. Kalecki, "Trend and Business Cycle" (1971, p. 165)

Introduction

The idea that investment depends upon profits is amongst the oldest of
macroeconomic relationships to be explicitly formulated. The sharp fluctuations in profitability in the ACC's since the mid 1960s (see Glyn *et al.*,
1990) revived interest in this relationship and some accounts of the fall of
the golden age of the 1950s and 1960s (see Marglin and Schor, 1990)
placed considerable weight on the role of declining profitability via its
effect on capital accumulation. Yet the evidence for the impact of
profitability on investment is sketchy, with few attempts to test the effect
of profitability across a range of international experience.

The object of this chapter is to make use of an extensive data set for
investment and profitability for the major ACCs since the early fifties (see
Armstrong *et al.*, 1991) in an attempt to identify systematic relationships
between profitability and investment. Section 1 outlines a simple investment model, illustrating how output, profitability, and relative cost variables can be plausibly combined in a model designed to test their relative
importance. Section 2 describes the data which have been used, outlines
the patterns of accumulation and profitability, and confirms the results of
earlier studies that these patterns are correlated. Section 3 presents the
results of estimating a model which endeavors to evaluate the independent effect of profitability on investment by incorporating the other
explanatory variables (output growth and relative costs) suggested by the
simple investment model. We conclude that profitability must be regarded
as a significant influence on investment, though by no means the over-

whelming one. The Appendix discusses our choice of variables and some experiments with alternatives.

1   A basic model of investment

In this section we set out a basic model of investment where profitability, defined as the profit margin (or the share of profits in output), demand expectations and relative factor costs are the main determinants of investment. The approach in this section is related to the fix-price literature on investment such as Malinvaud (1980), Artus and Muet (1990), and Lambert and Mulkay (1987). The role for profitability arises in these models due to demand uncertainty. Higher profit margins make the firm more willing to invest in additional capacity in order to meet possible upward fluctuations in demand. The fix-price assumption in these models is convenient since it permits a simple separation of demand and profitability effects. The basic results can also be derived in a more traditional model of imperfect competition.

We assume a putty-clay technology, so that capital and labor are smoothly substitutable *ex ante*, but once capital is installed, there are fixed coefficients in production. The firm starts the period with an inherited capital stock (K), which defines its existing capacity. Let Y be the difference between current-period output and the existing capacity level. The *ex ante* production function for Y is assumed, for simplicity, to show constant returns to scale in gross investment (I) and labor (L).

$$Y = F(I, L) \tag{1}$$

The constant returns assumption implies that k, the incremental capital–output ratio, is a function of l, the labor requirement per unit of output on new capacity.

$$k = k(l), \quad k' < 0 \tag{2}$$

At the beginning of the period the firm must make its investment decision, thereby fixing both the addition to capacity output or potential supply (S) and its technique of production (k, l). We assume that there is no uncertainty about input costs. The price of output is taken to be given to the firm, and is normalized at unity. After the decisions regarding capital are taken, the level of demand for the firm's output (D) is revealed. Actual output is given by the minimum of capacity output (S) and demand (D), and the firm chooses the level of employment required to produce this output. Let demand be distributed with a density function $g(D)$ and a cumulative distribution function $G(D)$. The firm's assessment of additional profits from investment, π, is given by

$$\pi = (S - wlS)(1 - G(S)) + (D - wlD)g(D)dD - ckS \qquad (3)$$

where w is the wage rate and c is the cost of capital.

The firm chooses the optimal addition to capacity (S^*) and its technique (l^*) (and therefore $k(l^*)$) to maximize its expected profits. The first-order conditions are

$$\delta\pi/\delta S = (1 - wl^*)(1 - G(S^*)) - ck(l^*) = 0 \qquad (4)$$

$$\delta\pi/\delta l = - wS(1 - G(S^*)) - w\, Dg(D)dD - cSk'(l) = 0. \qquad (5)$$

The first-order conditions (4) and (5) may be differentiated with respect to the exogenous variables in order to derive comparative static results. This gives rise to an investment function

$$I = f(c/w, PS, g(D)) \qquad (6)$$

where PS is profitability on the existing capital stock,[1] c/w is the relative cost of capital and labor and $g(D)$ is the expected distribution of demand. Hence our basic investment function includes expected profitability, relative factor costs, and demand expectations. In the empirical estimations we take the net profit share as the profitability variable, real interest and depreciation relative to real labor cost to measure relative costs, and output growth as the indicator of demand expectations.[2] Since the first two variables are highly autoregressive – we are unable to reject the unit root in these variables for most countries – the future expected values are proxied by their lagged values.[3]

The static equation (6) has to be modified to allow costs of adjustment. We posit that there are costs in adjusting the rate of investment relative to the capital stock (I/K). If we further take this variable in logs, and assume that these costs of adjustment are quadratic, this gives rise to the usual partial adjustment mechanism, where $\ln(I/K)$ depends upon the forcing variables and upon its lagged value.

2 The data and trends in profits and investment

The data set covers the manufacturing and non-agricultural business (NAB, i.e., industry and non-government services) sectors in the biggest seven ACCs (Canada, France, Germany, Italy, Japan, the UK, the USA) from 1951 to 1988. The basic series culled from international and national account sources are:

(i) I Gross fixed capital formation (constant prices)
(ii) K Gross fixed capital stock (constant prices)
(iii) NPS Net profit share: operating surplus net of capital consumption as a ratio to net value added; for manufacturing and for

NAB (except in the USA, the UK, and Japan where data for
the corporate sector alone are available) operating surplus is
adjusted to exclude an average wage attributed to the self-
employed.

(iv) Y Output: value added at constant prices

(v) RC Relative costs (of capital to labor). This is calculated as the
ratio of real interest and depreciation costs to the real wage
adjusted for residual productivity. The former is the long-
term government bond rate less the expected increase in
investment goods prices (as "forecast" by past increases)
plus the depreciation rate implicit in the capital stock calculations. Real labor costs is average wages and salaries per
head deflated by the investment goods price index and
deflated also by a smoothed index of residual productivity
calculated from conventional Cobb–Douglas growth
accounting, using output, capital stock, employment, and
the NPS to weight inputs.

Trends in accumulation and profitability

The basic outlines of accumulation and profitability are contained in
figures 6.1–13 which plot the growth rate of the capital stock against the
(lagged) net profit share for NAB (except Canada where there were data
problems) and manufacturing. Since these trends have been discussed in
some detail already (see for example Glyn *et al.*, 1990), only the main
features need to be emphasized here. Capital stock growth in Europe
and Japan accelerated in the 1950s, was maintained at high rates in the
1960s, began to decline in the early 1970s, was sharply reduced in the mid
1970s, and in the 1980s fell further in Europe but recovered somewhat in
Japan. It is evident that there has been a very wide range of accumulation
rates within countries over the post-war period: Japan is the extreme
case; even in the USA where the variation in investment has been less
extreme there are still some important differences between high and
low accumulation periods (most strikingly the later and early 1960s
respectively).

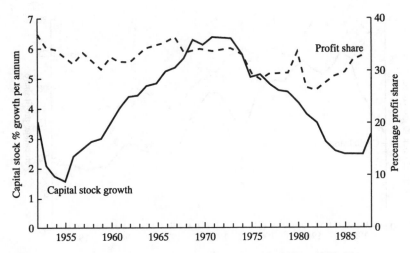

Figure 6.1   France business accumulation and profitability, 1952–88

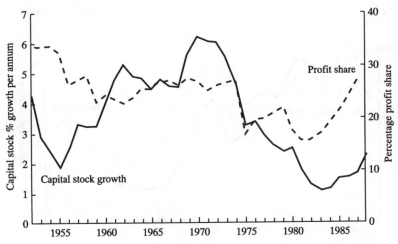

Figure 6.2   France manufacturing accumulation and profitability, 1952–88

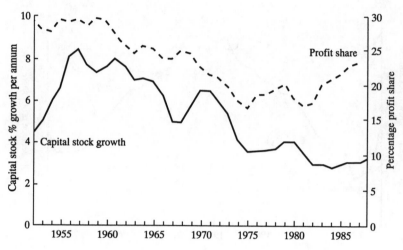

Figure 6.3   Germany business accumulation and profitability, 1952–88

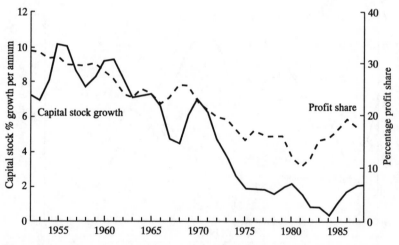

Figure 6.4   Germany manufacuring accumulation and profitability, 1952–88

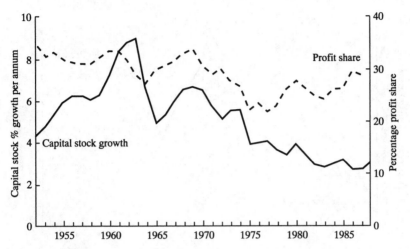

Figure 6.5   Italy business accumulation and profitability, 1952–88

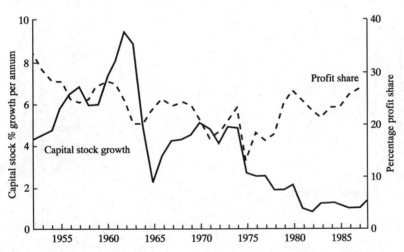

Figure 6.6   Italy manufacturing accumulation and profitability, 1952–88

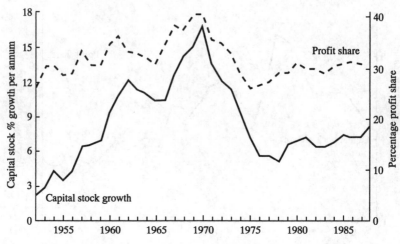

Figure 6.7   Japan business accumulation and profitability, 1952–88

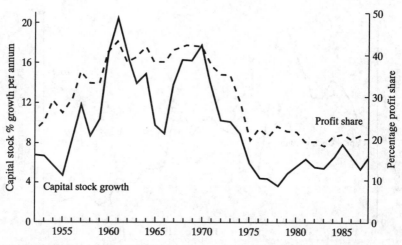

Figure 6.8   Japan manufacturing accumulation and profitability, 1952–88

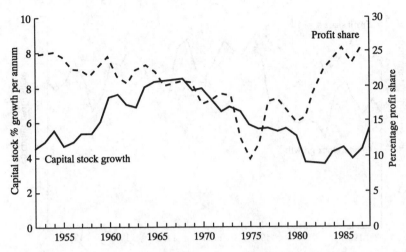

Figure 6.9   UK business accumulation and profitability, 1952–88

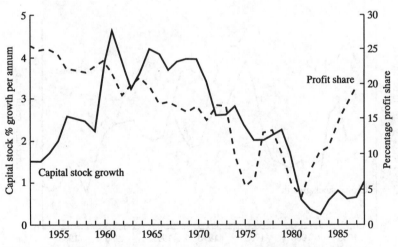

Figure 6.10   UK manufacturing accumulation and profitability, 1952–88

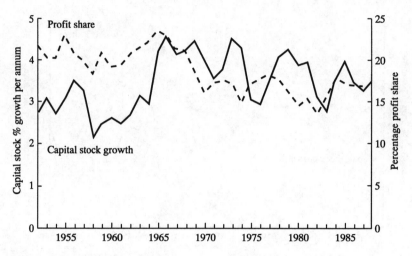

Figure 6.11   USA business accumulation and profitability, 1952–88

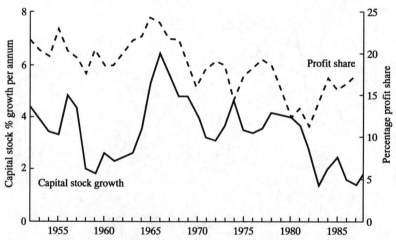

Figure 6.12   USA manufacturing accumulation and profitability, 1952–88

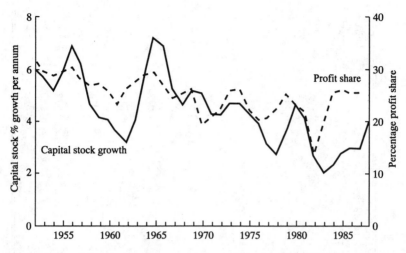

Figure 6.13   Canada manufacturing accumulation and profitability, 1952–88

The charts indicate some *prima facie* evidence of correlation of accumulation with profitability, but to very different degrees in different countries. To give this visual impression a bit more solidity, table 6.1 shows the results of some simple regressions when investment $(\ln(I/K))^4$ is regressed on its own lagged value and the lagged value of the net profit share. It can be seen that in nearly every case the net profit share is significantly correlated (at the 5 percent level) with the investment rate (for US business the significance level is 10 percent), even when the highly significant lagged dependent variable is included. The correlation with profitability seems rather similar in NAB and in manufacturing.

Not surprisingly with such a simple equation the test for autocorrelation (Durbin's t) frequently shows significant values. Nevertheless these results confirm the rather general finding of a consistent correlation of profitability with investment in equations which do not include accelerator terms (Bruno, 1986; Blanchard *et al.*, 1990; Poret and Torres, 1989, Glyn *et al.*, 1990). The issue, however, is whether profitability is affecting investment in its own right, or whether it is merely standing as a proxy for other variables (such as output growth).

3   Empirical results and interpretation

The analysis of section 1 suggests a basic investment model incorporating profitability, accelerator, and relative cost terms. Estimating this more comprehensive model results in the net profit share retaining statistical

Table 6.1. Simple investment and profitability equations
(time period 1955–88, dependent variable $\ln(I/K)$)

	Canada	France	Germany	Italy	Japan	UK	USA
NAB							
const		0.308	−1.312	−1.214	−1.066	0.468	1.313
		(1.7)	(4.4)	(3.7)	(2.8)	(1.7)	(2.3)
$\ln(I/K(-1))$		0.855	0.643	0.836	0.729	0.839	0.663
		(19.6)	(7.3)	(12.6)	(8.3)	(11.8)	(5.1)
$NPS(-1)$		0.012	0.016	0.024	0.016	0.008	0.006
		(3.6)	(4.3)	(4.0)	(2.3)	(4.0)	(1.4)
R^2		0.946	0.894	0.903	0.873	0.840	0.580
SE		0.044	0.060	0.104	0.096	0.046	0.057
Durbin's t		1.6	2.5	0.6	1.5	0.5	−0.78
Manufacturing							
const	−2.138	0.608	−1.927	−0.827	−1.481	1.048	1.572
	(5.9)	(2.2)	(5.3)	(3.0)	(2.5)	(4.0)	(3.7)
$\ln(I/K(-1))$	0.498	0.827	0.643	0.801	0.494	0.657	0.512
	(4.7)	(12.5)	(4.5)	(9.6)	(2.6)	(8.6)	(4.7)
$NPS(-1)$	0.029	0.005	0.024	0.015	0.015	0.015	0.026
	(4.9)	(1.8)	(5.0)	(2.6)	(2.0)	(4.9)	(4.6)
R^2	0.682	0.845	0.921	0.790	0.726	0.888	0.689
SE	0.116	0.074	0.080	0.116	0.181	0.080	0.092
Durbin's t	1.3	1.2	3.4	1.3	2.0	2.3	2.1

Table 6.2. *Basic investment model: non-agricultural business (NAB)* (*time period 1955–88, dependent variable* $\ln(I/K)$)

	Canada	France	Germany	Italy	Japan	UK	USA
const		0.765	-1.093	-1.265	-0.820	1.810	0.116
		(2.8)	(3.8)	(5.0)	(2.4)	(2.3)	(4.5)
$\ln(I/K(-1))$		0.827	0.596	0.791	0.720	0.709	0.906
		(42.6)	(7.3)	(15.6)	(10.4)	(6.7)	(4.5)
$NPS(-1)$		0.002	0.008	0.014	0.011	0.003	0.010
		(1.4)	(1.8)	(2.8)	(1.2)	(0.7)	(1.6)
$d\ln Q(-1)$		0.462	0.563	3.416	1.244	0.486	1.749
		(2.3)	(1.4)	(7.6)	(1.6)	(1.2)	(1.8)
$RC(-1)$		-0.037	-89.62	0.083	-0.025	-6.767	43.94
		(2.4)	(2.4)	(1.1)	(2.5)	(1.6)	(1.6)
R^2		0.990	0.912	0.964	0.955	0.845	0.774
SE		0.019	0.055	0.063	0.058	0.045	0.042
LM AR/MA(1)X²(1)		0.3	1.4	0.2	0.5	0	0.4
LM AR/MA(1)X²(2)		0.9	4.9	1.0	2.0	1.3	1.1
FRCST X²(3)		3.6	4.2	13.4*	2.2	18.5*	1.7
CHOW (split 1973)		1.2	2.7*	0.8	-2.6	0.2	3.8*
DF/ADF		1.9*	3.1	2.0*	1.9*	3.5	4.2

Notes: t values are bracketed. * indicate failure (at 5 percent confidence level) to pass the relevant test.
The relative cost variable is scaled differently for different countries.
The equations for France, Japan, and the USA use the current growth rate of output (instrumented), Japan the current profit share (instrumented), and Italy the second lag on the net profit share. The equation for Japan covers 1955–87 and for the UK 1956–88.

significance (at the 5 percent level) in six of the thirteen equations, including four in manufacturing (see tables 6.2 and 6.3). In Italy and Germany profitability is significant in both equations, in the USA significant in manufacturing and very nearly in business; in Japan there appears to be some influence in both sectors; in the UK the impact of profits is negligible and for France the two equations give contradictory results (including the only negative sign). Output growth shows up more consistently than profitability with no wrong-signed coefficient and no t-value less than 1, but there are again only six significant coefficients and no country displays a significant coefficient for both manufacturing and NAB. Relative costs also scores six significant coefficients (both sectors in France and Germany); in the USA both coefficients have the wrong sign.

The most comparable study to ours (Ford and Poret, 1991) considers only business investment in the biggest seven ACCs, where our results suggest that profitability has a less consistent role than in manufacturing. Thus their report of "little support for an independent role for profits in explaining investment" (p. 105) would be too negative a conclusion for our results.[5] Whilst there are inevitably differences in the patterns of results between different studies, our overall finding of mainly positive and quite often significant coefficients for profitability is broadly consistent with results reported in the scattered papers which include profitability together with demand and sometimes additional variables (Gordon *et al.* (1990) for the USA; Catinat *et al.* (1987) for the UK, Germany and France; Sneessens and Maillard (1988) and Artus and Muet (1990) for France; Lambert and Mulkay (1987) for Belgium).

Tables 6.2 and 6.3 also report equation diagnostics. These include the Lagrange Multiplier tests for first- and second-order serial correlation, the Chow test for parameter stability, and a test for forecast performance over the period 1986–8. These diagnostics are reasonably satisfactory given that we have estimated a single specification across thirteen equations. There is no evidence of significant serial correlation in any of the equations. Forecast performance is unsatisfactory in the case of Italian and Japanese business and the test value for Japanese manufacturing is almost insignificant. Parameter instability is indicated in the case of French business and Germany (both sectors). Where instrumental variables were used when current values of the variables were more significant, Sargan's test for instrument validity was satisfied. We also report the Dickey–Fuller/Augmented Dickey–Fuller tests for cointegration. We can reject the null of no cointegration for the manufacturing sector in all countries except France. For business only half the countries pass this test. However the cointegration tests lack power, so that being unable to

Table 6.3. *Basic investment model: manufacturing (time period 1955–88, dependent variable* $\ln(I/K)$*)*

	Canada	France	Germany	Italy	Japan	UK	USA
const	-1.817	1.724	-1.488	-1.113	-1.412	1.124	1.299
	(4.3)	(5.4)	(4.3)	(4.0)	(2.5)	(3.3)	(3.1)
$\ln(I/K(-1))$	0.541	0.654	0.470	0.609	0.457	0.699	0.569
	(4.3)	(9.9)	(5.3)	(5.7)	(2.6)	(9.4)	(5.0)
$NPS(-1)$	0.022	-0.004	0.013	0.011	0.010	0.002	0.025
	(2.7)	(1.3)	(2.5)	(1.8)	(1.4)	(0.5)	(1.9)
$d\ln Q(-1)$	0.560	0.611	0.897	0.545	1.261	1.769	0.553
	(1.3)	(1.3)	(2.3)	(1.0)	(2.3)	(5.1)	(1.3)
$RC(-1)$	-2.671	-0.089	-100.9	-0.027	-0.012	-5.858	23.22
	(0.3)	(4.0)	(2.5)	(2.0)	(0.9)	(1.1)	(0.7)
R^2	0.681	0.907	0.941	0.820	0.760	0.937	0.724
SE	0.112	0.057	0.069	0.107	0.169	0.060	0.086
LM AR/MA(1)X^2(1)	0.2	0.8	1.0	0.5	0.3	0	0.1
LM AR/MA(1)X^2(2)	0.3	1.4	3.3	2.4	2.0	0.3	0.4
FRCST X^2(3)	0.6	0.2	0.3	4.0	7.8	3.3	3.6
CHOW (split 1973)	1.0	3.4*	3.1*	2.1	1.5	0.2	2.5
DF/ADF	4.1	2.6*	5.8	3.2	4.7	3.4	3.4

Notes: t values are bracketed.
* indicate failure (at 5 percent confidence level) to pass the relevant test.
The relative cost variable is scaled differently for different countries.

Table 6.4. *Contributions to fall in manufacturing investment*

	Investment rates (I/K)			Attributable to change in		
	1960–8	1980–8	Change	NPS	$d \ln Q$	RC
Canada	0.068	0.054	− 0.014	− 0.013	− 0.005	− 0.004
France	0.078	0.057	− 0.022	—	− 0.009	− 0.023
Germany	0.094	0 058	− 0.036	− 0.023	− 0.008	− 0.013
Italy	0.110	0.072	− 0.038	− 0.004	− 0.012	− 0.028
Japan	0.191	0.102	− 0.089	− 0.059	− 0.035	− 0.009
UK	0.054	0.031	− 0.023	− 0.003	− 0.010	− 0.010
USA	0.075	0.060	− 0.015	− 0.024	− 0.004	—

Notes: Table 6.2 estimated coefficients plus average values of variables, refers to cases where coefficients had the "wrong" sign.

confirm cointegration raises a query over the relevant estimated equations rather than rendering them useless.

One response to the results in tables 6.2 and 6.3 would be to attempt to refine the models further by dropping insignificant variables from particular equations and including alternative measures and additional variables. In the Appendix we give a brief report on experiments with some alternative measures and variables which suggest quite strongly that the broad conclusions are not very sensitive to the particular formulation we have picked. In particular we may note here that indices of capacity utilization generally functioned less effectively than output growth as a proxy for demand expectations and that the valuation ratio, or Tobin's Q, performs poorly if added to our basic model. Since we are not primarily concerned to derive a "best" equation for each country and sector, but rather to assess the overall role of profitability in the context of a simple model incorporating the various influences on investment, the results in tables 6.2 and 6.3 provide the clearest basis on which to rest our conclusions.

As a way of disentangling the role of profitability we look at the extent to which, according to the coefficients from tables 6.2 and 6.3, the lower rate of accumulation in the 1980s, as compared to the 1960s, reflected the fall in the profit share between those two periods. Confining attention to manufacturing, where estimated equations are more satisfactory, table 6.4 shows the extent to which the shift in the average levels of the explanatory variables between 1960–8 and 1980–8 account for the decline in the investment rate.

It can be seen that in both Germany and Japan the fall in profitability appears to have been the most important influence on the very large declines in the investment rate between the 1960s and the 1980s.[6] For example, of the fall of 0.089 in the investment rate in Japan (i.e., from 19.1 percent of the gross capital stock to 10.2 percent), two thirds was accounted for by the fall in profitability. In North America as well, declining profitability appears to have been influential in the smaller declines in investment. Elsewhere the effect of profitability was small, either because the profit share was not much lower in the 1980s than the 1960s (Italy) or because the estimated effect of profitability on investment was small (UK and France). These results indicate that profitability had sizeable as well as statistically significant effects, comparable in influence to the decline in the investment rate to both the output growth and relative cost variables.

Conclusions

The basic conclusion from this analysis is support for the long-held belief that profitability affects the rate of accumulation. The impact varies in strength and statistical robustness from country to country and sector to sector but so does that of other variables. Thus profitability should take its place in investment models, alongside both demand and relative costs.

We should raise here an important further point about the use of output growth as an explanatory variable. Whilst there is obviously a good deal of purely cyclical fluctuation in output growth over the thirty-five year period we are examining, there is also (with the partial exception of the USA) a strong change in the trend of output growth after 1973. Most accounts of the slowdown in output growth would put considerable weight on the shift to more restrictive policies after 1973, and especially 1979 (see Marglin and Schor, 1990 for example). This shift was in response to the mounting difficulties encountered, including accelerating inflation *and*, we would emphasize, falling profitability. In this respect the falling profitability after the mid 1960s also contributed to the growth slowdown, and thus to lower investment via accelerator terms in our equations. It does not, however, appear that profitability often plays another indirect role via the valuation ratio – this variable's performance (even bearing in mind problems of measurement) is poor, confirming the results of Abel and Blanchard (1986) and Mullins and Wadhwani (1989).

High levels of manufacturing investment in both Japan and Germany played a decisive role in the most dynamic examples of the golden age; that profitability contributed importantly to the slowdown in investment in these countries during the 1980s underlines how this variable should be taken seriously in analyzing patterns of growth. However the behavior of manufacturing investment in these countries *during* the 1980s serves as a reminder of Kalecki's observation quoted at the start of this paper as to the complexity of investment modeling. Profitability recovered sharply in Germany and failed to do so in Japan, but the recovery of manufacturing investment was strong in Japan. It is hardly surprising that such simple models as those estimated here cannot capture the full complexity of expectation formation (see Heye's chapter).

More broadly our results do not show that enhanced profitability is always a necessary, let alone a sufficient condition for increased investment. Demand and relative costs are important as well, underlining how expansionary policies themselves can provoke a favorable investment response. A redistribution of income away from labor is not necessarily required, even though it would usually contribute to the strength of investment. Whilst having favorable effects via competitiveness on the constraints on expansion posed by the balance of payments, such a redistribution at the same time is likely to enhance distributional conflict and thus inflationary pressures. How these conflicting forces can best be balanced in an expansionary program is an exceptionally subtle question; confirming that profitability has a role in affecting investment, even if not an overwhelming one, adds a further piece to the puzzle without dictating how it may be solved.

Appendix: Alternative measures

Profitability

Both the net profit rate (net operating surplus as a ratio of net capital stock at current replacement cost) and gross profit share (both operating surplus and value added gross of capital consumption) were tried as alternatives to the net profit share. Neither substitution made a substantial difference to the results. Since there is some theoretical case for the profit share (see section 1), the net profit share was used in the equations reported here. Marglin and Bhadhuri (1990) argue for the profit share rather than the profit rate in an investment function which includes demand variables. Their point is that if the profit rate is included, the partial effect of demand upon investment is not necessarily positive (since the profit share must fall in order to offset the effect of higher capacity utilization on the output–capital ratio and thus the profit rate). Since our model in section 1 suggests a basic role for the profit share, and we do not want our profitability variable to pick up purely cyclical demand effects, we preferred to use the profit share.

Use of the log of the profit share gave similar, or on a few occasions, worse results, so the absolute level was used in all the equations reported here.

All these profits variables are measured pre-tax. In principle two different tax variables may be relevant. Average *effective* tax rates (T_e) which measure the proportion of profits taken in taxation and reflect tax rates, past patterns of investment, tax allowances, and financing patterns, might be expected to be significant if the profitability was important as providing internal finance. *Marginal* tax rates (T_m) on new investment reflect the impact of the current values of these variables on the profitability of new investment in the year in question; they would be expected to be important if profitability affects investment via expected returns of new investment. Series for T_e were assembled from various sources but did not prove significant when added to our model. King and Fullerton's estimates (1984) for T_m are available for 1960, 1970, and 1980 for Germany, Japan, the UK, and the USA. In order to obtain a *very rough* series these values for the manufacturing sector were interpolated and extrapolated. Alternative series were constructed adjusting for the impact of inflation (which usually reduces the marginal tax rate by reducing the value of tax offsets). Of the four countries in the King and Fullerton study only in the UK do there seem to have been significant changes in the tax system prior to the mid 1980s (in the UK the marginal burden fell sharply). These series for effective rates only showed a nearly significant effect on investment in the equation for Germany; since all the variance in this case came from fluctuations in inflation it is doubtful whether the impact being measured is really that of the tax system.

Demand expectations and capacity utilization

Capacity utilization is frequently suggested as a better measure of demand effects than output growth. Series for manufacturing from the IMF and for business from the OECD were extended, but on no occasion was capacity utilization clearly more significant than output growth and usually much less so (UK manufacturing and Italian business being isolated cases where capacity utilization performed as well as output growth). It may well be that the reason for the superior performance of output growth lies in the character of the period under scrutiny. In most countries (with the partial exception of North America) output grew much more slowly after 1973. Whilst at first leading to a drastic fall in capacity utilization, the decline in investment reduced the growth rate of capacity. By the late 1980s capacity utilization in manufacturing was as high as ever before, despite the slowdown in average growth. But it would be expected that, in the context of slower growth in the 1980s, a given level of capacity utilization would be associated with a lower investment level than the same level of utilization twenty years earlier. Output growth seems the fundamental variable determining demand expectations in a period when the trend of output growth shifted.

Relative costs

As well as the rather complicated variable described in the text some simpler components were tried – notably real interest rates on their own and the relative costs variable unadjusted for residual productivity. These variants were frequently wrongly signed and never significant. Without adjustment for residual productivity there tends to be a very strong upward trend in the relative costs variable as wages deflated by investment goods prices rise continuously, whilst the real interest and depreciation rate fluctuates.

Valuation ratio

The ratio of the market value of the sector to the replacement value of its assets is a popular substitute for profits (and in some formulations other) variables in investment equations. OECD series for this variable were available for a substantial part of the period covered (except for Italy). These were extended by regressing the OECD's series on the ratio of the index for industrial stockmarket prices to the net capital stock at current prices. Using this measure of $Q(-1)$ to replace $NPS(-1)$ in simple regressions, corresponding to table 6.1 in the text, yield significant coefficients everywhere except Japan; in France and Italy the coefficients on $Q(-1)$ for both sectors were more significant than those for $NPS(-1)$ shown in table 6.1. When added to our basic model of tables 6.2 and 6.3 $Q(-1)$ was only significant in Italian manufacturing (where it knocked out $NPS(-1)$), though it was not far from significant for both German sectors (leaving $NPS(-1)$ significant in both cases). The Q theory of investment suggests that Q alone should be used in investment equations, since it captures *all* variables which could affect the return to investment. This prediction is decisively falsified – one or more of our basic variables was almost always significant when added to an equation with Q. Further tests with alternative specifications suggested that only in Germany did Q robustly contribute to the explanation of investment (this is contrary to the finding of Mullins and Wadhwani (1989)). Our conclusion is that there is not a strong case for adding Q to our basic model nor substituting it for one of the included variables, particularly profits. Only in particular instances does the stockmarket valuation of companies seem to add to the "objective" variables included in our basic model.

Appendix   Data sources

Investment, capital stock	OECD, *Flows and Stocks of Fixed Capital*, 1962–87 plus earlier issues; EEC, *Indicators of Profitability, Capital, Labour and Output* plus national sources. See Armstrong *et al.* (1991), Appendix.
Profits, real output	OECD, *National Accounts of Member Countries*; EEC as above and national sources, see Armstrong *et al.*, 1991.
Capacity utilization	Manufacturing, IMF calculations; Business kindly provided by OECD spliced on to trend through peaks series kindly provided by Andrea Boltho.
Investment goods prices	Series for manufacturing were constructed from OECD *National Accounts* and national sources.
Valuation ratios	Partial data from Chan Lee (1986) were spliced on to ratios of stockmarket prices to net capital stock at current prices.
Interest rates, stockmarket prices	Long-term government bond rate, IMF, *Financial Statistics*.
Wages per head	OECD, *National Accounts*; EEC as above and national sources.

Notes

Our thanks to Philip Armstrong for his major contribution to putting together the data set, to Ha Won Jang and Giuseppe Mazzarino for help with computing, to Wendy Carlin and Kevin Denny for helpful comments and to Herb Gintis, Gerry Epstein, Robert Boyer, Sam Bowles, Steve Marglin and other members of the WIDER project on Savings and Investment for advice and encouragement.
1 More precisely, PS can refer to any measure of profitability at an exogenously given level of labor productivity. PS cannot refer to the profit share on new investment, $1 - wl^*$, since l^* is endogenously chosen by the firm via its choice of technique.
2 Profitability and current output are also likely to enter via their effect on the firm's cash flow if credit constraints are important, thereby reinforcing their effect in the basic model.
3 Average Q, the ratio of stock market valuation of capital to its replacement cost, may also reflect expectations regarding any one of these variables. However it is difficult to interpret Q in this framework and to identify its effect with any of the "structural" variables in the model. As reported later Q performs poorly in comparison with, or when added to, our model.
4 Gross investment is equal to the growth of the gross capital stock plus the retirements from the gross stock. The latter would be a constant ratio to the capital stock if an unchanged set of asset lives was used in constructing the gross capital stock series (as is

usually the case) and, since there will be variation in retirement rates for different assets, if the composition of the stock (as between buildings and machinery) was constant (which is not the case). It seems preferable to use gross investment as the dependent variable, rather than the change in the capital stock, since gross investment is the decision variable.

5 Ford and Poret's data cover a much shorter period than ours, 1968 to 1988, thus losing the experience of the golden age; they also use the profit rate as their profitability variable, whereas the profit share appears to be preferable (see Appendix); their data cover the whole of the business sector including agriculture where the measurement of profitability (by attributing an imputed wage to the self-employed) is especially tricky and their measure of business profits (though not investment) includes house rents which must weaken the accuracy of this measure. These differences (together with our use of a variety of lags) may account for the generally weaker effects of profitability in their table 9b as compared to our table 6.2. Nevertheless the main reason for our greater emphasis on profitability lies in our results for manufacturing where aggregation problems are somewhat less severe than for business.

6 These effects are calculated by simply applying the long-run coefficients implicit in table 6.3 to the change in the average values of the explanatory variables between the two periods (lagged one year). This is only an approximate estimate because of lags, but since two thirds to three quarters of the effect typically occurs in the first two years and since we are using averages for nine-year periods the inaccuracies should be small.

7 Expectations and investment: an econometric defense of animal spirits

Christopher Heye

1 Introduction

Few economic enterprises are at once as important and as poorly understood as the process of capital investment. The persistent empirical failings of conventional investment formulations have been both a conspicuous and disappointing development, prompting Blanchard (1986) to lament that "the discrepancy between theory and empirical work is perhaps nowhere in macroeconomics so obvious as in the case of the aggregate investment function." The disparity between theories of investment behavior and the historical record is not only rather obvious but also somewhat distressing, since few economic activities have as profound economic, social, and political consequences as the process of capital investment. In the long-run, the rate of investment expenditure significantly influences a society's level of worker productivity, degree of international competitiveness, and its overall standard of living. In the short run, investment outlays are crucial in determining the timing and duration of fluctuations in the aggregate business cycle. An inability to adequately characterize the investment process, therefore, necessarily implies a limited comprehension of a number of crucially important economic activities.

The failure of traditional economic theorizing to satisfactorily explain an economic function as important as capital accumulation suggests the need for alternative approaches. One strategy, adopted in this chapter, is to examine more directly the role played by business expectations in the non-residential investment decision making process. Since investment decisions are governed by considerations of what will transpire in the future, an investor's judgment of the viability of an investment project will be influenced by his or her expectations of prospective trends in economic activity. Many economists agree that this level of "business confidence" in the future economic environment is a crucial determinant of the rate of non-residential investment. It is widely accepted, however, that the independent variables currently employed in empirical research

197

on investment behavior do not adequately capture this kind of forward-looking characteristic necessary to effectively represent real-world investment behavior. With the partial exception of Q-based financial models, traditional investment formulations include data observations that reflect historical trends in the variables hypothesized as important for investment, measures that may or may not prove to be reliable proxies for their expected values. To model the non-residential capital investment decision, however, it is clear that a direct measure of the actual economic expectations of the investing individuals, usually firm managers, should be incorporated into the estimation procedures.

Surprisingly little research has been devoted to exploring the relationship between business expectations and capital investment. One reason for this situation is the absence of adequate times-series data on expectations. These measurement shortcomings, however, are now becoming less serious as business expectations data and data collection agencies proliferate. Now that a considerable amount of business survey data exists, both for the US and for other advanced industrial societies, there is no longer an excuse to ignore the issue of expectations and their relevancy for investment behavior and research. The inclusion of business survey data cannot solve all of the theoretical and technical problems associated with the study of investment behavior, but it can at least provide the analysis with an unambiguously forward-looking variable, absent in most previous empirical investigations.

In this chapter I explore some of the more significant properties of the available business expectations data for the United States, and to a lesser extent, for other large industrialized nations. Specifically, I investigate the ability of the expectations data to explain fluctuations in both physical investment spending and employment levels. The analysis is premised on the assumption that rates of capital investment and employment will respond positively to changes in the levels of confidence business managers possess in their outlooks for their firms, industries, and/or national economies. If the surveyed business expectations data prove to be reliable determinants of historical trends in investment outlays, I will have established an important link between expectations and action. In addition, I also analyze a second potentially significant property of expectations, namely their ability to predict future economic developments. In the debate over the "rationality" of expectations, there currently exists disagreement as to how well economic agents can successfully anticipate important future economic developments. As part of the inquiry into the dynamic properties of expectations, I will investigate the possibility that business managers tend to over- or underpredict trends in economic activity.

The remainder of the chapter is organized as follows. Section 2 tests the ability of business survey data to explain historical patterns of capital investment spending, and compares the explanatory power of the surveyed expectations measures to that of several other economic variables frequently employed in statistical analyses of investment spending. Section 3, explores the influence of expectations on a second measure of investment, namely that in total employment. Many business managers regard the hiring of human labor as an equally important business capital investment, and here too, expectations may play an influential role. To ensure that the expectations variables are not simply a function of the independent variables employed in the investment equations and therefore largely redundant, section 4 examines some causal relationships between the expectations measures and the other independent variables used in the previous regression equations. Finally, in section 5, tests of the "rationality" of business expectations are conducted. In this section, the propensity of business persons to consistently over- or underreact to changes in economic conditions is explored.

2   Expectations and capital investment

Model specification

The initial expectations models specified and tested possess a rather simple structure. In the first set of regression runs, only the expectations data and capital stock variables are included on the right-hand side of the equation in an attempt to see how well the business survey data alone can explain observed fluctuations in historical investment spending patterns. For the United States, this entailed employing several different expectations measures as independent variables, while also introducing a number of categories of non-residential investment spending on the left-hand side of the equation. The assumption underlying the expectations models is that higher levels of confidence amongst business managers concerning the future outlook for their firms, industries, or for the economy as a whole, will directly lead to higher levels of investment spending.

The initial test of the expectations model seeks to discern how well investment can be explained using only the results of the business survey data themselves. All estimated equations, therefore, assume the basic form

$$I_t = \sum_{s=1}^{N} k_s BEXP_{-s} \tag{1}$$

where $BEXP_t$ equals the surveyed level of business expectations in time t.

I assume that expectations will impact investment spending only after a delay, possibly of several quarters. I therefore incorporated a polynomial distributed lag function (sixteen-quarter lag, second-degree polynomial, no endpoint restrictions) into the expectations model equations in order to account for the lags in information processing and physical delivery associated with all investment projects.

It is not clear if a lagged capital stock figure, frequently utilized in more traditional investment formulations, should be included in the gross investment formulations of the expectations model. On the one hand, many economists believe that all types of investment, not just net, should appear as a function of expectations. The low levels of replacement investment observed in, for example, the 1930s would tend to support this thesis. On the other hand, one could argue that at least some replacement investment would occur even if the outlook for the economy were exceptionally weak. When expectations are held constant at a given level, one might expect a higher level of capital stock to still induce more (replacement) investment. My own tendency is to accept the former view, i.e., that all investment depends on expectations, though I will leave it as an empirical matter and test expectations models which include a lagged capital stock variable. The final form of the simple expectations equation therefore appears as

$$\frac{I_t}{GNP_t} = \frac{a}{GNP_t} + \sum_{s=1}^{N} k_s BEXP_{-s} + d\frac{K_{t-1}}{GNP_t}. \tag{2}$$

Subsequent regression runs incorporated other independent variables theorized as important for investment decision making – the rate of capacity utilization, capital costs, cash flow, and Q – along with the survey data to see if their inclusion acted to diminish the significance of the expectations data, or alternatively, to test whether the expectations data tended to reduce the significance of the more commonly included variables. (I assume that the reader is familiar with the more traditional investment models which hypothesize the importance of these variables. For detailed reviews of both theory and available evidence see Bischoff (1971), Clark (1979), and Jorgenson (1971).) These tests will help, I hope, to determine whether or not the expectations data contain additional information about investment propensities which is not adequately captured by the more traditional independent variables.

Data considerations

In recent years several national and international agencies have begun collecting business expectations data in a very rigorous and standardized manner. The Conference Board has been gathering business survey data for the United States, which has included responses to the same questions on a quarterly basis, for over fifteen years – certainly not an overwhelming volume of data, but enough observations to ensure reasonable statistical accuracy. The size (over 1,500 chief executive officers of large and small firms surveyed every three months), breadth (manufacturing, finance, and service industries), and detail (many surveys are industry specific) of the Conference Board's measures suggest they are potentially reliable indicators of actual business expectations.

The US business confidence data represent answers to questions asked by the Conference Board of hundreds of American chief executive officers (CEO's). Every quarter since 1976:2, the Conference Board has surveyed the business response to the following four questions (Question 4 was added in 1978:3)

1 In looking ahead 6 months as compared with now, do you think business conditions for the economy as a whole will be:
2 In appraising the prospects for your own industry, do you think business over the next 6 months, as compared to now, will be:
3 How do you rate the present business conditions for the economy as a whole, as compared with six months ago?
4 How do you rate present business conditions in your own industry, as compared with six months ago?

Five possible answers are allowed for each question – substantially better, moderately better, same, moderately worse, or substantially worse – and a score of 100, 75, 50, 25, and 0 is assigned, respectively, to each recorded response. An index, ranging from 0 to 100 is then created, reflecting the aggregate views of the business community. The answers to the second two questions, strictly speaking, do not represent expectations, but they do reflect an outlook similar to Keynes' concept of "business confidence," which may not be otherwise captured in the other economic variables. It is expected that each index will vary positively with changes in investment spending.

Estimation results

The results of the estimates for the expectations model appear in table 7.1. In general, the business survey data explain historical trends in investment fairly well. Judging by the size of the r-squareds, the significance of the coefficient estimates, and, in some cases, the lack of serial correlation, the expectations models (including its "current conditions" hybrids) appear to fit the data rather well. In three of the six estimated equations (two each

Table 7.1. Results of business confidence investment model estimations

Interval	Whole economy expectations 1976.2–1990.4		Own industry expectations 1976.2–1990.4		Whole economy current conditions 1976.2–1990.4		Own industry current conditions 1978.3–1990.4	
Dependent variable = Producers' durables								
Confidence measure	0.00041	(1.13)	0.00072	(1.38)	0.00048	(1.99)	0.00069	(2.18)
Capital stock	−0.014	(−0.15)	−0.013	(−0.13)	0.097	(1.07)	0.429	(6.78)
Constant	0.337	(0.05)	0.333	(0.05)	0.031	(0.34)	−0.158	(−3.68)
Rho	0.998		0.998		0.984		0.585	
r-squared	0.940		0.941		0.945		0.955	
Durbin–Watson	2.11		2.14		2.06		2.10	
First lag	−3		−3		−1		−2	
Dependent variable = Structures								
Confidence measure	0.00045	(1.98)	0.00069	(2.29)	0.00014	(1.07)	0.00065	(2.56)
Capital stock	−0.009	(−0.09)	−0.002	(−0.02)	0.043	(0.58)	−0.174	(−1.31)
Constant	0.006	(0.18)	−0.009	(−0.23)	0.001	(0.04)	0.045	(1.19)
Rho	0.937		0.932		0.974		0.913	
r-squared	0.967		0.970		0.965		0.961	
Durbin–Watson	1.67		1.81		1.49		1.86	
First lag	−3		−3		−2		−2	
Dependent variable = Office equipment								
Confidence measure	0.00025	(3.24)	0.00047	(4.82)	0.00023	(9.51)	0.00029	(6.22)
Capital stock	0.356	(16.9)	0.376	(20.7)	0.338	(48.7)	0.326	(28.4)
Constant	0.004	(0.69)	−0.010	(−1.61)	0.007	(5.86)	0.004	(2.01)
Rho	0.425		0.390					
r-squared	0.988		0.988		0.991		0.984	
Durbin–Watson	1.93		1.97		1.80		1.73	
First lag	−2		−2		−1		−1	

Notes: t-statistics are in parenthesis. All equations were estimated using a sixteen-period Almon lag, second-order polynomial, with no endpoint restrictions. Estimation periods differ slightly due to availability of data. Confidence variable values represent sum of coefficient estimates.

for producers' durables, structures, and office equipment) the expectations variable coefficient values appeared significant beyond the 0.05 level (two-tailed test), while a fourth proved just slightly less significant. The current conditions variable also performed rather well, with four of the six estimated coefficients appearing significant beyond the 0.01 level, and a fifth beyond the 0.05 level. The current appraisal survey variables seemed to better explain fluctuations in the producer durables dependent variables, though they were less capable of accounting for movements in non-residential structures. Expectations appear to be especially significant in the equations for both office equipment and non-residential structures, the latter being a measure of investment which in the past has proven particularly difficult to estimate. The decline in investment in structures since 1987, for example, is in fact closely paralleled by a similarly gradual decline in business confidence over the same period.

Judging by the magnitude of the estimated coefficients, expectations appear to more strongly affect investment decisions than appraisals of the current situation, though it is probably safe to say that investments are made based on evaluations of both the present and the future. Unfortunately, the two variables, being highly correlated, could not be combined in a single equation. One possible interpretation of the relative significance of the two is that expectations are more important for longer-term projects, such as the construction of new buildings, while current conditions are at least as or more important in shorter-term undertakings, such as the buying of new office computers.

Serial correlation was a problem in some equations, but not in all. In two of the equations for office equipment, no serial correlation was detected, while in three other equations the size of the autocorrelation coefficients (rho) appeared considerably less than unity. Still, most r-squared were artificially inflated by the autocorrelation adjustments applied to these equations. Capital stock coefficient estimates did not prove to be significant in either the producers' durable or structures equations. Excluding the capital stock variable did not change the value of the estimated expectations coefficient very much (though expectations coefficients t-stats frequently rose a little when the stock figure was excluded). The capital stock variable did however prove very significant in the office equipment equations. The significance of this estimate may say something about the "high-tech" nature of most of this equipment, which quickly becomes outdated with every new technological breakthrough and requires constant replacement.

Additional tests of the expectations models using European and Japanese data suggest the importance of business confidence in other countries as well. In the regression runs for Germany, Japan, and Italy, the expectations variables performed at least as well as, if not better than, they did in the equations for the United States. All estimated expectations coefficient values proved significant beyond the 0.05 level, with three of four exhibiting significance beyond the 0.01 level. The magnitude of the impact of the expectations variable on investment appeared particularly large in Germany. (The results of these additional regression estimates may be obtained from the author upon request.)

The results seem to suggest that all measures of expectations – whether based on one's own firm (as is the case for much of the non-US survey data), own industry, or whole economy – explain trends in investment rather well. The "own industry" variables appeared to explain movements in the dependent variables only slightly better than the "whole economy" measures. This may suggest that the narrower the focus (i.e., firm versus entire economy), the better the estimate, though the differences appear rather slight. This observed tendency toward convergence across expectations indicators is not difficult to explain. Theoretically, the outlook for any given firm will undoubtedly be influenced by the predicted outlook for that industry or the economy as a whole, particularly if that firm has a large national market or is sensitive to fluctuations in economy-wide indicators such as interest rates or domestic inflation levels. Statistically, individual responses which share divergent views about the prospects for their firm as opposed to their own industry or whole economy will in all likelihood tend to balance each other out – managers possessing an optimistic view of one and a pessimistic outlook for the other will tend to be balanced out by the reverse. One would therefore expect to find a high correlation across the different categories of surveyed responses, as is the case in the United States. In general, one would probably anticipate firm outlook responses to provide the best predictors of future investment activity, though it appears likely that the selection of any one particular expectations indicator over another will not crucially affect statistical analyses that attempt to assess the importance of expectations.

Multiple regressions

A skeptic might claim that the expectations model does not represent a valid alternative to the traditional investment formulations, at least not the way it has been constructed in the preceding analyses. One could argue that the answers to the survey questions merely reflect business managers' informal views on future profitability which are informed by movements in economic indicators (such as capacity utilization) which are already specified in the more conventional models. Adding the expectations variables to the standard investment formulations would therefore not improve the explanatory or predictive powers of these equations, since the existing variables already possess all the necessary information used by managers to make an investment decision. Under this scenario, the expectations variables could not be expected to exhibit significant coefficient estimates.

The counter argument to this claim is that the expectations variables do possess additional explanatory power because they contain information about factors important to the investment decision which is not captured in the traditional investment formulations. The obvious way to test for this is to devise multiple regression equations which include the business survey data along with the other variables which conventional economic theories suggest are important to investment. The inclusion of other variables theorized as determining investment expenditure helps to ensure that there are no (already identified) omitted variables in the equation and also allows for some comparison across the independent variables of the significance of each to observed movements in investment. If the expectations variables do not add to the explanatory power of the equation, then one would predict that the coefficient values for these variables would appear statistically insignificant. If, however, the survey data do possess additional information about investment prospects which is not captured in the more conventional formulations, then one would anticipate the coefficients for the business confidence data to exhibit positive and significant values.

The results shown in table 7.2 demonstrate that the expectations (and current condition) variables do in fact remain significant even after the inclusion of additional variables thought to be important for investment, suggesting that the expectations measures do provide the equation with additional explanatory power. In all equations, the coefficient estimates for the business survey variables appeared significant well beyond the 0.05 level (two-tailed test), while many coefficients demonstrated significance beyond the 0.01 level. In many cases, the significance level of the expectations variable coefficients emerged as considerably higher than those of the other more conventionally specified determinants of investment. In the equations for producers' durables, the expectations variables seem to explain fluctuations in the dependent variables considerably better than Q. (Other regression equation estimations for structures and office equipment yielded findings. The results of these regression runs are available from the author upon request.) Beta test analyses, moreover, continually revealed the expectations measures to be as, or more, important than any of the other variables in explaining historical trends in investment behavior.

Table 7.2. Results of composite regression estimations for producers' durable equipment (as a percentage of GNP) (Sample period 1976.2–1989.2*)

Independent variable	#1		#2		#3	
Constant	-0.162	(-4.99)	-0.197	(-5.84)	-0.117	(-5.83)
Expectations for whole economy	0.00021	(3.73)				
Expectations for own industry			0.00034	(3.84)		
Current conditions in whole economy					0.00032	(4.00)
Capacity utilization	0.192	(8.46)	0.204	(8.73)	0.158	(13.2)
Change in capital costs	-0.117	(-2.83)	-0.109	(-2.53)	-0.132	(-3.31)
Q	0.014	(3.53)	0.012	(2.97)	0.016	(4.90)
Net capital stock/GNP	0.149	(4.00)	0.190	(4.96)	0.097	(2.76)
r-squared adj.	0.964		0.963		0.968	
Durbin–Watson	2.22		2.25		2.4	

Notes: t-statistics are in parenthesis.
* All independent variables coefficient values (except capital stock) represent the sum-of-coefficients derived from a six-period Almon lag estimation calculation, employing a second-order polynomial with no endpoint restrictions.

Incorporating additional independent variables consequently did not improve the explanatory power of the equations much beyond the simple model which included only the expectations variables, though the presence of an autocorrelation correction term in the simple expectations models makes such a comparison somewhat problematic. In some cases, the presence of an expectations measure diminished the significance of other variables, though expectations models make such a comparison somewhat problematic. In some cases, the presence of an expectations measure diminished the significance of other variables, though including the survey data seemed in some cases to improve the overall performance of the other independent variables. This latter finding may imply that direct measures of business attitudes represent important omitted variables in most previously estimated investment equations.

What is less clear, however, is the nature of this missing information which the expectations data appear to be capable of providing. One interpretation of the continued significance of the expectations measures even after other influences are controlled for is that the expectations variables contain information about the *expected values* of indicators such as capacity utilization which the historical data cannot reflect. Business managers make decisions based on past as well as expected events, and the survey data accurately reflect their views concerning future trends in economic indicators such as capacity utilization or capital costs. A second interpretation, however, would suggest that the expectations variables furnish information on other factors beyond those which are normally specified in investment formulations which are nonetheless important for investment. The levels of the (historical) economic indicators reflect one kind of business concern, while the expectations data contain information about business managers' views regarding some other heretofore unidentified set of (political?) considerations. The fact that the current conditions variables remain significant even after the incorporation of other independent variables seems to support the second hypothesis, though the two explanations are not necessarily mutually exclusive.

On the basis of the foregoing analysis, two tentative conclusions may be drawn. First, business expectations, and to a lesser extent, current attitudes about the economy, as measured in survey data, are important determinants of investment. This importance has been establishing using not only US data, but business survey results from other major industrialized countries as well. As generally assumed, "business confidence" appears to be an important determinant of investment spending in advanced industrial societies – if business managers do not feel confident in the future, they will choose not to invest. A link between expectations and action has been established. Secondly, business survey data do appear to possess some additional information about the economy which the conventional investment determinants are failing to pick up on. Investment models which include only the expectations measures explain fluctuation in the dependent variable almost as well as more fully specified formulations, and the incorporation of variables such as capacity utilization or Q fails to undermine the significance of the expectations measures. The regression results suggest that business expectations are based on something other than an historical analysis of standard economic indicators such as capital costs or capacity utilization. These results may imply that past trends in conventionally specified variables do not proxy well for future values, or possibly, that expectations are being influenced by something other than strict economic considerations. In either case, it seems likely that including more direct measures of business expectations will substantially improve the explanatory power of investment equation estimates, and consequently improve our understanding of the capital investment process.

3   Expectations and employment

The model

In this section I examine the relationship between business confidence and an alternative measure of investment, i.e., that of labor requirements. Like capital, labor represents a primary input to the production process, and one might expect that trends in employment rates will also be significantly affected by movements in business expectations. If the total number of employed persons is considered the "employment" capital stock, then changes in that stock might be regarded as "investments." Accordingly, the dependent variable used in the following employment analysis represents the quarterly change in the level of (seasonally adjusted) total employed persons in private industry. The first set of regression runs therefore assumes the form

$$\Delta E_t = \sum_{s=1}^{N} k_s BEXP_{-s} \qquad (3)$$

where $BEXP$ equals aggregate whole economy expectations. Three additional equations were also estimated using the own industry expectations indicator and the two current conditions measures as well.

If one believes that employment and physical capital decisions are often determined jointly, then some of the same variables employed in the preceding physical investment analysis should probably be considered for inclusion in the employment equations. For example, most econometric models of employment growth (see Hamermesh (1986) and (1989)) include an accelerator type variable such as capacity utilization or sales. In addition, employment models usually include some measure of labor costs as well. Neoclassical economic theory argues that, like other commodities, employment demand should appear as a function of its price. As a measure of employment costs, I employed an index prepared by the Bureau of Labor Statistics, which expresses total employment costs (including all forms of compensation) as an index whose base value is 100 in June 1981. For the present study, these figures are divided by the GNP deflator, producing an index which measures the ratio of employment costs to all other economy-wide costs. I then introduced the rate of change of this deflated index as an employment "price" variable. It is assumed that higher compensation expenditures will have a negative impact on employment growth. Finally, because the lag time between a decision to hire and the actual hiring is expected to be shorter than the delay following a physical capital investment decision and actual outlays, I utilized a lag structure of shorter duration in the employment equations. (I employed a six-quarter, second-order polynomial Almon lag structure with no endpoint restrictions for the expectations variable, and a shorter three-quarter lag structure for the current conditions variable.)

Regression results

The regression results appear in table 7.3. As in the previous analysis, the business confidence variables emerge as highly significant determinants of employment growth. The "own industry" formulations tended to fare better than the "whole economy" equations, while the current conditions variables explained employment changes somewhat better than the expectations measures. The capacity utilization measure proved to be very significant in the expectations formulations, but considerably less so in the current conditions equations. The poor performance of the utilization variables in the current conditions formulations may be a consequence of multicolinearity – the current conditions (and to a lesser extent, the expectations) variables are moderately highly correlated with the capacity utilization measure. (More on this relationship in the next section.) The impact of employment "price" changes on job growth, on the other hand, did not appear very significant. The price variable appeared with the wrong sign in the expectations equations, and exhibited only a very small negative coefficient value in the current conditions equation. A beta weight analysis, moreover, suggested that the expectations and current conditions measures were by far the most important determinants of

Table 7.3. *Results of employment investment estimations*
(Dependent variable = quarterly change in total private employment (seasonally adjusted))

Interval	#1 1976.2–1990.4		#2 1976.2–1990.4		#3 1980.2–1990.4	
Own industry expectations*	0.00056	(2.28)	0.00084	(6.27)	0.00098	(6.27)
Capacity utilization$_{-1}$			0.111	(5.05)	0.117	(5.00)
Employment costs$_{-1}$					0.00009	(0.17)
Constant	−0.03	(−1.90)	−0.13	(−5.89)	−0.14	(−5.92)
Rho	0.547				0.487	
r-squared adj.	0.404		0.457		1.53	
Durbin–Watson	1.98		1.70			
	#4		#5		#6	
Own industry current conditions**	0.00063	(10.4)	0.00060	(9.55)	0.00063	(9.77)
Capacity utilization$_{-1}$			0.023	(1.44)	0.015	(0.89)
Employment costs$_{-1}$					−0.0004	(−0.97)
Constant	−0.03	(−8.68)	−0.04	(−3.57)	−0.04	(−3.01)
r-squared adj.	0.707		0.714		0.738	
Durbin–Watson	1.97		2.12		2.02	

Notes: t-statistics are in parenthesis. * Sum of coefficients estimate, based on a six-period (first lag = − 1) second-order Almon distributed lag estimation function, with no endpoint restrictions. ** Sum of coefficients estimate, based on a three-period second-order Almon distributed lag estimation function, with no endpoint restrictions.

changes in employment levels. The adjusted r-squareds imply that the estimators explain a considerable amount of the observed variance in the dependent variable, though there still seem to be additional omitted variables.

In contrast to the results obtained in the capital investment equations, the current conditions measure appears to be a more important determinant of fluctuations in the dependent variable than the expectations measure. Employment decisions seem to be influenced most by short-term considerations, and apparently as long as current conditions remain favorable, the hiring of new employees will require less confidence in the longer-term than the renting or purchasing of physical capital. This result may suggest that while employers regard their employees as "investments," they still view them as more short-term and variable than their longer-term capital commitments.

Summarizing the results for the employment growth equations, it is evident again that the expectations measures are capable of explaining a good deal of variation in the dependent variable. The expectations measures proved to be far and away the most important and significant determinants of total employment growth. In particular, the "own industry" current conditions indicator looks like it might be an excellent predictor of trends in US aggregate employment. Judging by the extremely large size of many of the t-stats, it appears that the expectations and current conditions measures are perhaps even better at explaining trends in employment than they are in explaining fluctuations in physical capital. This finding may be explained in part by the fact that the expectations variables reflect a rather short-term time horizon and consequently they emerge as more significant determinants of employment growth than physical capital outlays.

4   Expectations and causality

This section further explores the relationship between the business expectations survey data and some of the other variables believed to be important determinants of investment which were employed in the previous regression runs. It would be interesting to find out, for example, if fluctuations in economic indicators such as capacity utilization affected the state of business expectations, or conversely, if the level of expectations had any impacts on the rate of capacity utilization. Moreover, the results of such an inquiry may provide answers to the question raised earlier concerning the meaning of a significant expectations variable coefficient in an equation containing other frequently specified independent variables. If, for example, indicators such as capacity utilization could be shown to explain movements in expectations, then one might tentatively conclude that the expectations measures simply reflect their expected values, which bear some imperfect relationship to the historical values. (The absence of such a relationship, however, does not imply that the expectations variables do not reflect expected values. If expectations respond rapidly to changing external conditions, then there may not be any correlation between historical values of a given variable and its expected value.) If, however, variables such as capacity utilization cannot significantly explain movements in business expectations, and, furthermore, if the expectations variables are capable of describing fluctuations in other important economic indicators, then the possibility should be entertained that other factors beyond those currently specified in investment formulations may be influencing the rate of investment, as well as other important economic activities.

The model

The equations to be estimated were designed to jointly test two alternative hypotheses. The first hypothesis assumes the view that the independent variables shown to affect investment behavior in the previous equations will also influence the level of expectations. If this hypothesis proves to be correct, then one might assume that expectations are largely determined by movements in conventional economic indicators, and possibly that they merely reflect expected values of these variables. The competing hypothesis, on the other hand, implies that expectations will influence not only investment spending, but other economic decisions, such as the determination of the level of capacity utilization, as well. Arguably, both hypotheses may prove to be simultaneously true. However, if the first hypothesis is false and the second true, then the possibility exists that expectations are both important determinants of several economic activities and determined themselves by yet unidentified influences.

Measuring direct causality is a difficult thing, and the hazards associated with the currently accepted techniques have been dutifully noted (see especially Jacobi *et al.* (1979)). Nonetheless, I believe that some generalizations can be drawn from causality tests, particularly if the results suggest that the measured causality runs strongly in one direction. Two different tests, "Granger" and "Sims," were employed in the present study. (For an explanation of each approach see Granger (1969), Sims (1972), and Pindyck and Rubinfeld (1981).) The general idea behind these tests is to determine if and to what degree variable "A," say business expectations for the economy as a whole, can explain movements in variable "B," capacity utilization, and vice versa. If "A" is shown to be a statistically significant explainer of past and/or future trends in variable "B," then one might conclude that "A" "causally' determines "B." (The word "causally" remains in quotes because the technical problems associated with these types of tests suggests that the results should not be accepted as irrefutably valid.) Similarly, "B" may appear as causing "A." In general, "A" may cause "B," "B" may cause "A," or each (or neither) may cause the other.

Test results

The results from the causality tests are shown in table 7.4. In general, the hypothesis that changing levels of expectations cause significant fluctuations in the observed levels of the other independent variables commonly used in investment equations is confirmed. On the other hand, the hypothesis that expectations are themselves simply a product of these other variables receives little or no empirical corroboration. The results in table 7.4 imply that business assessments of current conditions in their own industries positively impact on levels of capacity utilization. (The joint F-tests designed to see if the current assessment variables were significantly different from zero could not be rejected at the 0.01 level.) Conversely, coefficient estimates measuring the possible effect of the capacity utilization on the business confidence variables consistently appeared with the "wrong" sign or proved to be insignificant (or both). The evidence provided by the capacity utilization tests, which imply that businesses' current evaluations of their own industries has a powerful effect on total capacity utilization, are rather striking (see figure 7.1). It is even more remarkable given that trends in capacity utilization have little or no impact on levels of current business confidence. These results seem to imply that not just investment plans but even everyday business decisions of how much to produce are substantially determined by prevailing business attitudes. They may also imply that expectations are influenced by other factors beyond those currently specified in conventional investment formulations.

5   A test of rationality

The final step in the analysis of the properties of business expectations entails a brief investigation of some of the dynamic characteristics of the US business survey data which appear to explain investment patterns quite well. Specifically, one possible test of the "rationalness" of business expectations is offered. In this section, I design and execute statistical tests which attempt to discern whether business persons tend to under or over predict trends in the economy.

Table 7.4. *Tests for causality: current conditions in own industry and capacity utilization*

"Sims" test results – Dependent variable: capacity utilization

Confidence measure (− 1)	0.000995	(3.23)
Confidence measure (− 2)	0.000009	(0.03)
Confidence measure (− 3)	0.000922	(3.01)
Confidence measure (− 4)	− 0.000095	(− 0.33)
Confidence measure (+ 1)	0.000213	(0.66)
Confidence measure (+ 2)	− 0.000847	(− 2.65)
Confidence measure (+ 3)	0.000052	(0.15)
Confidence measure (+ 4)	− 0.000817	(− 2.48)
Constant	0.767	(10.5)
Rho	0.947	(12.3)
r-squared adjusted	0.935	
Durbin–Watson	1.74	

Joint F-test that lagged variables are significant   4.72
Joint F-test that lead variables are significant   3.21*

	"Granger" test results – dependent variable			
	Capacity utilization		"Own industry" current conditions	
Confidence measure (− 1)	0.00169	(3.53)	0.937	(3.44)
Confidence measure (− 2)	0.00015	(0.32)	− 0.142	(0.00)
Confidence measure (− 3)	0.00130	(2.71)	0.497	(1.64)
Confidence measure (− 4)	− 0.00125	(− 4.08)	− 0.359	(− 0.10)
Capacity utilization (− 1)	0.690	(2.77)	− 7.41	(− 2.21)
Capacity utilization (− 2)	− 0.305	(− 0.98)	− 127.7	(− 0.05)
Capacity utilization (− 3)	0.095	(0.31)	− 5.61	(− 0.10)
Capacity utilization (− 4)	0.488	(2.05)	91.1	(0.12)
Constant	− 0.072	(− 1.49)	42.7	(1.46)
r-squared adjusted	0.947		0.720	
Durbin–Watson	1.84		1.84	

Joint F-test that current conditions are significant
   to capacity utilization equation   5.95
Joint F-test that capacity variables are significant
   to current conditions equation   0.94

Note: * Significant coefficients appeared with the "wrong" sign.
t-statistics are in parenthesis.

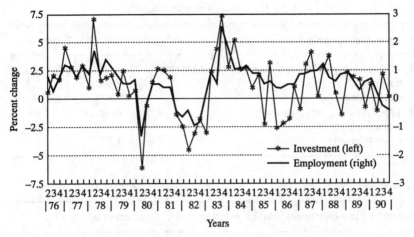

Figure 7.1 Employment and investment rates: quarterly changes

Many economists (Lovell (1986), Gramlich (1983), Frankel and Froot (1987)) have recently sought to directly test the "rationalness" of economic expectations using various types of survey data. In most cases, the rational expectations hypothesis has fared poorly compared to other models which assume adaptive behavior on the part of economic agents. In this section a similar test is conducted in order to see if business managers consistently over react to changes in the economic environment.

One way to test for possible over prediction is to choose a variable which should be important for expectations, e.g., profit rates, and see if business persons react with more vigor in their investment spending than is implied by the current level of profitability. In order to do this, the profit rate variable was regressed on past values of both itself and the expectations variable

$$\frac{\Pi_t}{GNP_t} = a + \sum_{s=1}^{N} p_s \frac{\Pi_{-s}}{GNP_{-s}} + \sum_{s=1}^{N} k_s BEXPO_{-s} \tag{4}$$

A new fitted variable was then created, calculated by using the parameter values obtained in the regression run. This fitted variable was then introduced into an investment equation for structures. This new variable should already control for the presence of expectations, and if managers correctly anticipate the future, then the "own industry" expectations variable should no longer appear significant. If however, business persons do over predict, or if their expectations are influenced by something other than profits, the expectations variable will remain significant.

Table 7.5. *Results of tests for possible overprediction*

Independent variables*	Period 1976.2–1990.4	
First stage – dependent variable = profit share (real after tax profits/real GNP)		
Constant	− 0.009	(− 1.75)
Lagged dependent	0.977	(28.2)
Expectations for own industry	0.00017	(2.16)
r-squared adj.	0.956	
Durbin–Watson	1.77	

Independent variables**	Period 1972.2–1990.4	
Second stage – dependent variable = investment in structures (as a % of GNP)		
Constant	− 0.179	(− 1.94)
Expectations for own industry	0.00135	(4.04)
Profits	− 0.607	(− 0.91)
Fitted profit variable	1.27	(1.81)
Change in capital costs	− 0.070	(− 1.68)
Capacity utilization	0.124	(2.01)
Rho	0.463	
r-squared adj.	0.973	
Durbin–Watson	2.02	

Notes: * Variables were estimated using a six-period Almon lag, second-order polynomial, no end-point restrictions. First lag = $t - 1$. ** Variables were estimated using a six-period Almon lag, second-order polynomial, no end-point restrictions. First lag = $- 1$. t-statistics are in parenthesis.

Test results

The results in table 7.5 clearly show that the expectations variable remains significant even after the new fitted variable is included. The t-stat for the expectations variable coefficient is significant beyond the 0.01 level. Interestingly, as is demonstrated in the top half of the table, the expectations variable positively influences profits, perhaps suggesting the possibility of investor self-fulfilling prophecies. Business optimism concerning the future seems to beget higher levels of profitability. Business attitudes about the future are clearly governed by more than is suggested by movements in known profitability. The potential for business managers' to over predict economic fluctuations is therefore strongly supported by the data. These results may also sustain another possible interpretation of the relationship between expectations and economic events suggested in the previous sections, namely that business expectations are determined by something other than objective economic measures.

Conclusions

Several tests were conducted with the goal of analyzing the importance of business expectations for various measures of economic activity. In virtually all cases, the expectations variables, and the current conditions evaluations as well, emerged as significant determinants of actual business behavior. Business confidence has been shown to be crucial in regulating not only the aggregate level of physical capital investment, but also in governing the overall rate of private industry employment and rates of manufacturing capacity utilization. The link between business expectations and their ensuing actions was firmly established. One possibly significant finding, or non-finding, of the research is that the expectations variables themselves do not seem to be particularly strongly influenced by at least one of the more commonly theorized determinants of investment. More analysis is necessary, but the initial results imply the need for widening the scope of research on investment to include other possible influences. For example, I suspect that the incorporation of political variables into the investment equation might significantly augment its explanatory power. Keynes, Kalecki, and others have frequently mentioned the potentially profound influence of political factors on the level of business confidence, and if some of these impacts could be quantified and brought into the analysis, a better understanding of investment decision making would likely be obtained.

Appendix A

The three most popular investment models – the "accelerator," neoclassical, and Q approaches – and most of their hybrids explicitly assume maximizing behavior. In the accelerator and neoclassical models, it is profits which are maximized, while in the Q models, a related concept, firm value, is the object of maximization. In each case, the future is believed to be known with probabilistic, if not perfect certainty, and the information which each individual needs to make investment decisions can be obtained without cost. It is assumed that this knowledge about the future allows the investor to make decisions which permit her to maximize profits (or firm value).

Despite their superficial similarities, the neoclassical, accelerator, and

Q models share a common basic structure. In all cases, investors seek to maximize profits by equating the discounted marginal costs of any investment with its expected discounted revenue stream. The differences across the models reflect variations in the way future revenues and costs are proxied, and differences in the number of relevant factors that are held constant. For example, in the accelerator model, total future revenues are taken as a given, and capital (rental) costs are held fixed, so investment depends solely on changes in output. Firms minimize costs by investing in new capital goods in order to optimize plant size, allowing them to reap the benefits of economies of scale. The neoclassical model, on the other hand, does not assume costs are fixed, and therefore includes a cost of capital term along with an output proxy. Finally, in the Q models, firms are assumed to own rather than rent capital, and their discounted revenue stream, rather than being taken as fixed, is proxied by securities' values. In all cases, the hypothesized maximization calculation (discounted marginal cost = discounted marginal revenue) is the same.

A closer specification of each model follows. The purpose of the more detailed analysis is to provide a clearer definition of the models to be estimated in the ensuing statistical tests.

Accelerator models

Perhaps the most widely employed model of investment demand is the well-known accelerator formulation, originally developed by Clark (1917) and later modified by Chenery (1952), among others. Under this interpretation, firms seek to adjust their current level of capital stock to the desired optimum level through additional expenditures on plant and equipment. This adjustment process is part of a cost-minimization strategy designed to effectively meet new demand while benefitting from economies of scale. Projected revenues, output prices, and capital costs are viewed as fixed. Usually, the adjustment period is expected to be non-instantaneous, implying that

$$K_t - K_{t-1} = \beta[K_t^d - K_{t-1}^d] \tag{1A}$$

where K_t is the actual level of the capital stock in time period t, K_t^d the desired level, and β a measure of the speed of adjustment. Since the desired capital stock is unobservable, an output measure is usually employed as a proxy for the desired stock

$$K^d = aO \tag{2A}$$

where O is some measure of output, usually sales. Inserting equation 2A into 1A, and replacing the left-hand side (of equation 1A) with the expression I^n, we get the generalized form of the accelerator:

$$I^n = a \sum_{s=1}^{N} \beta_s (\Delta O_{-s}) \tag{3A}$$

where I_t^n is a net investment in time period t.

Frequently, gross rather than net investment is the desired dependent variable, and an additional term dK_{t-1} is added to the net investment equation to produce a gross investment equation. When estimating gross investment, it is generally assumed that replacement investment will be equal to the amount of depreciated capital, which in turn is assumed to be a constant fraction d of the capital stock:

$$I_t = a \sum_{s=1}^{N} \beta_s \Delta O_s + dK_{t-1} \tag{4A}$$

In the actual specifications, output is usually proxied by sales figures, though increasingly, capacity utilization measures are used in econometric estimations of accelerator models. In order to correct for heteroskedasticity, both sides of the equation are frequently divided by a scale variable, usually real GNP, giving the final version

$$\frac{I_t}{GNP_t} = \frac{a}{GNP_t} + \sum_{s=1}^{N} b_s \frac{\Delta O_{-s}}{GNP_{-s}} + d \frac{K_{t-1}}{GNP_t}. \tag{5A}$$

Though output variables have shown themselves to be important determinants of investment in many statistical probes, accelerator models have been acknowledged as possessing two major shortcomings. One often noted defect of accelerator models is that they have very little to say about investor expectations. In all model specifications, past values of output are assumed to be accurate proxies for future levels. Investment decisions, however, are made based largely on predictions about the future, not on past events. While during times of steady, predictable growth, historical output values may effectively proxy for future levels of demand, under more realistic assumptions of shifting demands and irregular economic growth, the assumption that the past will provide a reliable guide to the future is clearly problematic. The inclusion of more forward-looking variables which rapidly adjust to these changing circumstances is therefore highly desirable.

The second major criticism made of accelerator models is that they effectively exclude, by holding constant, other theoretically important variables which might impact on the decision to invest. In particular, many economists feel that capital costs should somehow figure in the decision to invest. In short, the demand for investment goods should have some relationship to its price. The "neoclassical" adjustment to the basic accelerator model, which explicitly includes a price term, is discussed in the next section. A review of financial, or Q, models which introduce an explicit expectations component, is presented below.

Accelerator-cash flow: a hybrid model

One popular modification often made to the accelerator models is the inclusion of a cash-flow (profits) variable. Two reasons are generally given for introducing a measure of available cash. First, Miller–Modigliani notwithstanding, it is generally believed that internal funds are less costly than those obtained from outside the firm. Consequently, by lowering the costs of investment funds, a higher level of cash flow may positively impact on the decision to invest. The second argument for including a cash-flow variable rests on the belief that recent changes in profits convey information about the future which output or other cost variables fail to pick up on. Eisner (1978) among others has adopted this approach, and accelerator models which include cash-flow variables will be included in the statistical estimations. The model to be tested appears as follows:

$$\frac{I_t}{GNP_t} = \frac{a}{GNP_t} + \sum_{s=1}^{N} b_s \frac{\Delta O_{-s}}{GNP_{-s}} + \sum_{s=1}^{N} c_s \frac{\Pi_{-s}}{GNP_{-s}} + d \frac{K_{t-1}}{GNP_t} \quad (6A)$$

where Π equals real after-tax business profits (excluding inventory valuation adjustment).

Neoclassical models

The investment demand model developed by Jorgenson *et al.* (see for example (1967)) represent a modified version of the accelerator formulation in which capital costs are no longer held constant. Dubbed "neoclassical" because of its emphasis on factor prices, this model assumes that investment will respond to changes in factor prices as well as to fluctuations in output. Firms seek to maximize profits by equating marginal costs with marginal revenues, and their cost function (assuming, as Jorgenson does, that capital equipment is rented) is believed to be strongly dependent on the rental price of capital. In this formulation, the desired level of capital stock will respond to relative price movements in the required inputs as well as to changes in output

$$K^d = \psi \frac{pO}{C} \quad (7A)$$

where ψ equals the share of capital in output, p is the price of output, and C the rental price of capital. (Most neoclassical investment models, including Jorgenson's formulations, assume a Cobb–Douglas production function, though this supposition does not represent a crucial model assumption.)

As in the accelerator formulations, net investment represents the adjustment from the actual to the desired level of capital stock. Included in the adjustment process in the neoclassical formulation, however, is the explicit inclusion of a relative factor price variable

$$I_t^n = \sum_{s=1}^{N} \beta_s \left(\Delta \frac{pO}{C} \right)_{-s} \tag{8A}$$

where β equals ψ times the estimated parameter. Similarly, an estimate of the depreciated capital stock appears in the gross investment equation

$$I_t = \sum_{s=1}^{N} \beta_s \left(\Delta \frac{pO}{C} \right)_{-s} + dK_{t-1}. \tag{9A}$$

Dividing both sides by real GNP, we get

$$\frac{I_t}{GNP_t} = \frac{a}{GNP_t} + \sum_{s=1}^{N} b_s \frac{\left(\Delta \frac{pO}{C} \right)_{-s}}{GNP_{-s}} + d \frac{K_{t-1}}{GNP_t}. \tag{10A}$$

The so-called neoclassical model is therefore a simple variant of the accelerator model which allows investment demand to fluctuate inversely with changes in its price. It represents a version of the basic profit-maximizing model in which fewer values, i.e., output price and capital costs, are held constant. The inclusion of a price variable is generally recognized as an important theoretical contribution (though many econometric studies have shown its empirical underpinnings to be rather weak). This hypothesized improvement notwithstanding, the neoclassical model still shares a critical shortcoming with its accelerator cousin, namely an inability to properly capture the expectational components necessary for any realistic model of capital accumulation. Adjustments to desired levels of capital stock in the neoclassical model are again premised on past movements in output and prices, rather than on explicit expectations of price and output changes. One attempt to remedy this deficiency has been suggested by Tobin (1969) and others (Summers (1981), Abel and Blanchard (1986)), and the fundamental of Q-based financial models will be examined next.

Q models

Financial models based on Tobin (1969) continue to assume that investors seek to maximize profits by equating marginal costs with marginal revenues. The principal difference between the financial investment model and the neoclassical variant is that in the latter firms are assumed to rent capital, while in the former case they are assumed to own it. Hence, in the Q model, firms seek to maximize firm value, since this also guarantees in the long run the greatest level of return on invested capital. If capitalists indeed seek to maximize the value of their firm, then they should invest as long as the ratio of (marginal) equity values to (marginal) replacement costs exceeds unity. In other words, capitalists should invest as long as the marginal value of Q remains above one. In these models, revenues are no longer considered fixed, but fluctuate and are proxied with equity values, and costs are measured in terms of replacement values rather than rental expenditures.

The basic form of the financial model equation is therefore rather simple

$$\frac{I_t}{GNP_t} = a + \sum_{s=1}^{N} z_s Q_{-s}. \tag{11A}$$

Unlike output in the previously described models, Q does not really "cause" investment, but it is (or at least should be) correlated with capital spending, since both Q and investment are responding to the same set of expectations about the future. As long as holding physical capital is expected to be profitable in the future, both Q and real capital investment should increase.

One drawback to some of the earlier financial models was their inability to measure and include the proper value of Q. Though average Q is easily measurable, it is the more difficult figure to quantify, marginal Q, which remains relevant for any model of investment. In their maximization calculation, capitalists should seek to equate marginal costs and revenues, not average values. Predictably, previous research which incorporated only average Q (Summers (1981)), fared rather poorly. Fortunately, some attempts have been made to proxy for marginal Q (Blanchard, Rhee and Summers (1990)), and this will be the concept used in the empirical analysis. Looking to the more positive side, Q models are exceptional among profit-maximizing models in their ability to explicitly capture forward-looking values. Though the empirical record of marginal Q models over the years has been somewhat shaky (Abel and Blanchard (1986)), Q models remain popular amongst economists because of this expectational component.

Appendix B   Sources and notes

Capacity utilization: Quarterly data averaged from monthly figures of manu-facturing capacity utilization obtained from the Federal Reserve Board. Changes in sales: Change in real (1982) final sales as a percent of real GNP. Final sales figures were obtained from National Income and Pro-ducts Account (NIPA), table 1.4.

Change in capital costs: Rental price of capital deflated by the GNP deflator. Rental cost series furnished by Data Resources, Inc. (DRI model series IPDENRCOSTOTHR), and represents the rental price of capital for non-auto, non-office producer durable equipment. Costs are com-puted as a function of interest rates on debt, dividend payments, corpo-rate taxes, and inflation. The series is deflated by the GNP deflator (from NIPA) in order to obtain the ratio of capital to other production costs.

Cash flow as a percent of GNP: Change in real after-tax corporate profits as a percent of GNP. *Business Statistics* and *Survey of Current Business*.

Tobin's Q: The quarterly values of the Q variable utilized in this study were computed by Blanchard *et al.* (1990). See data Appendix in that paper for a fuller description.

Net capital stock: DRI quarterly interpolations of US Department of Commerce estimate of the total value of fixed non-residential private capital, constant cost valuation for all industries was utilized as a measure of the US gross capital stock. Net capital stock figures were computed by DRI for producers' durables (total), structures (buildings and other), and office equipment.

Investment and GNP: Obtained from Department of Commerce, NIPA, and are evaluated in 1982 dollars. All investment figures appear in NIPA, table 5.13.

Employment rate: Quarterly change in seasonally adjusted total private (excluding government) employment. Source: *Survey of Current Business*.

Employment costs: Quarterly change in (employment cost – total com-pensation index/GNP deflator). Source: *Monthly Labor Review*.

Business confidence indicators for United States: Conference Board, *Business Executives' Expectations*. See text for more detail.

Data for Germany: Business survey data obtained from IFO Institute in Munich, Germany.

Business expectations indicators for Japan and Italy: OECD, *Main Economic Indicators*, various years. See also OECD (1983) for a further description of the variables.

Note

I am grateful to Olivier Blanchard, Herb Gintis, Steve Marglin and Peter Skott for their helpful comments and support.

8 Private investment and debt overhang in Latin America

Manuel Pastor Jr.

Introduction

Since 1982, the debt crisis has dominated economic thinking and policy toward Latin America. In the initial years, analytical attention often centered on determining the conditions likely to produce repayment, rescheduling, or repudiation (see, for example, Bulow and Rogoff, 1989). US policymakers, recognizing the threat posed to the international financial system, leaned toward pressuring Latin American debtors to maintain payments despite the macroeconomic damage this caused throughout the region (see Sachs, 1986).

As the 1990s began, the analytical and policy focus started to shift. Low growth and macroeconomic instability in Latin America has led some observers to label the 1980s a "lost decade for development." Under the rubric of the 1989 Brady Plan, the US promised to work toward debt reduction in return for the continuation of orthodox policy measures. Despite flaws – the level of debt relief was insufficient, the expectation that banks would *voluntarily* grant relief to a large number of debtors was unrealistic, and the requirement of orthodoxy was problematic – the focus of debt relief signaled the beginning of a new awareness and understanding of the crisis.

That new understanding was based on one central insight: rather than a matter of finance and repayment, the regional crisis involved real sector costs, including slow growth, low investment, significant redistribution of income, and the political strains caused by all three of these economic phenomena. The economic trends are clear: while regional GDP growth averaged 5.4 percent in the 1970s, it declined to 1.2 percent in the 1980s; gross fixed capital formation as a percentage of GDP fell from 23.7 percent in 1978–80 to 20.1 percent in 1987–9; and a general index of equality (which takes into account worker share of income, distribution between different groups of workers, and the terms of trade between agriculture and industry) fell between 1978–81 and 1982–6 in seven of the nine countries for which such a measure can be constructed.[1] The political consequences remain unknown: while most countries were able to move toward more democratic political structures even as the economic situation deteriorated, many observers feel that this pattern may eventually become unsustainable.

In previous work, I have considered the growth and distributional aspects of debt and adjustment (see Pastor, 1987, 1989a). In this chapter, I explore what the debt crisis has meant for investment, particularly that of the private sector. The topic is timely since a renewal of investment is crucial to restoring growth and development in the region. Moreover, debt and investment have a particular linkage: high levels of debt in the region may reduce expected return and thereby dampen private investment. The negative effects of such a "debt overhang" imply that debt relief must be an important part of any growth-oriented alternative.

The first section of this chapter offers an overview of the general economic trends in Latin America in the late 1970s and 1980s. After noting the correlation between growth shortfalls, macroeconomic instability, debt problems, and the investment slowdown, I specify the concept of "debt overhang" and explain the mechanisms through which debt might constrain private investment. In the second section, I test a reduced-form equation for the private investment rate that includes proxies for the "overhang"; the results indicate that expected growth and public investment have positive effects on private investment while macroeconomic instability and the debt overhang have a negative effect. I also find that worker power has a negative impact on private investment while the presence of an IMF program has a positive impact, presumably because government adoption of a Fund program boosts capitalist confidence.

In the final section, I discuss the policy implications of this research. Debt relief, I argue, will be a key prerequisite for any new investment boom and can help with the macro stability and growth required for private capital formation. I warn against conditioning such relief on orthodox policy, particularly given the poor performance of "orthodox" hypotheses about the interest rate and public investment in the investment equations. I close by noting that the resurrection of private investment is fundamentally dependent upon the determination of a new set of social relations between workers, capitalists, and the state in Latin America, a topic of clear importance but one beyond the limits of this chapter.

General trends

A general overview

Table 8.1 offers a brief overview of the trends in Latin American growth, inflation, debt, and investment in the 1980s. Growth rates fell sharply in

Table 8.1. *Growth, inflation, debt, and investment in Latin America, 1978–89*

	Average 1978–80	1981	1982	1983	1984	1985	1986	1987	1988	1989
GDP growth (annual change)	5.4	– 0.2	– 1.1	– 2.8	3.4	3.5	4.0	2.9	0.3	0.9
GDP growth per capita (annual change)	2.5	– 2.2	– 3.4	– 4.8	0.9	1.3	1.9	0.8	– 1.8	– 1.1
Inflation (weighted average)	48.0	60.7	67.1	108.7	133.5	145.1	87.8	130.9	286.4	531.0
Total debt, excluding debt owed to Fund (billions of dollars)	191.7	288.8	331.2	344.4	359.0	369.1	383.6	415.9	401.3	398.6
Total debt (as % of GDP)	32.8	39.8	43.0	46.8	46.4	45.4	44.1	43.7	38.7	36.7
Total debt service (as % of Exports of Goods and Services)	36.9	43.9	53.1	42.7	42.1	41.3	44.8	35.9	44.9	35.1
Fiscal surplus (as % of GDP, weighted average)	– 1.1	– 5.6	– 5.8	– 5.8	– 4.9	– 6.8	– 9.1	– 9.3	– 9.3	– 12.9
Fiscal surplus (as % of GDP, median)	– 2.6	– 5.3	– 5.4	– 5.1	– 4.8	– 3.0	– 2.8	– 2.6	– 3.6	– 2.7
Gross capital formation (as % of GDP, weighted average)	23.7	23.3	21.2	17.4	16.6	17.4	17.9	19.8	20.8	19.6

Note: All series are for the Western Hemisphere, which includes the Caribbean.
Sources: 1982–9 figures from IMF, *World Economic Outlook*, 1990, pp. 123, 129, 130, 185, 191, 192, 142, 142, 131.
1981 figures from IMF, *World Economic Outlook*, 1989, pp. 73, 79, 80, 135, 141, 142, 92, 92, 81.
1980 figures from IMF, *World Economic Outlook*, 1988, pp. 59, 65, 66, 123, 129, 122, 78, 78, 67.
1979 figures from IMF, *World Economic Outlook*, 1987, pp. 117, 123, 124, 181, 187, 188, 137, 137, 125.
1978 figures from IMF, *World Economic Outlook*, 1986, pp. 179, 185, 186, 243, 249, 242, 199, 199, 187.

the early part of the decade, a result of the worldwide recession and austerity-oriented macroeconomic stabilization measures. The mid 1980s saw a brief recovery, although only to levels of growth which were below those posited in the latter part of the 1970s.[2] The final years of this decade brought another slowdown, and 1989 ended with regional per-capita GDP more than 8 percent lower than in 1980.

Macroeconomic instability was also a feature of the 1980s. Average regional inflation rates doubled between 1978–80 and 1983 and increased by almost another forty percentage points by 1985. While 1986 and 1987 brought a short-lived improvement, Latin America's 1989 average inflation rate was about 500 percent, driven largely by hyperinflationary pressures in Argentina, Brazil, Peru, and other debtor nations. The unfavorable macroeconomic scenario can also be noted in the fiscal measures listed near the bottom of the table; Latin America's fiscal balance showed a fairly steady deterioration through the decade, a trend which was both a cause and a consequence of the rising inflation.[3]

Debt measures follow a slightly different trend. Total nominal debt increased until a combination of private lender reluctance, limited debt–equity swaps, and some forgiveness produced dollar declines in 1988 and 1989. Debt as a percentage of GDP rose sharply through the middle of the decade, then fell slowly. The debt service ratio (principal and interest payments as a percentage of the exports of goods and services) rose sharply in the early 1980s, hovered between 40 and 45 percent through the middle of the decade, and showed some improvement in the last years of the decade.

Through the decade, gross capital formation (or investment) as a percentage of GDP fell, rose, then fell again, seeming to directly lag behind the movement of growth and debt measures. For example, when regional growth slowed and debt service and debt-to-GDP ratios rose through 1981–3, the rate of investment declined, hitting its lowest point in 1984, one year after the worst performance of regional growth. From 1984–7, as growth began to improve and debt service stabilized, investment followed with a slow recovery; when growth and debt service worsened in 1988, investment in the next year followed suit.

Recent policy discussions have centered on how to ensure that the Latin American investment trend moves upward, with particular focus on the resuscitation of investment by the private sector (Balassa *et al.*, 1986). Despite the voiced concerns with regard to the investment shortfall, the links between the debt crisis and investment performance have gone mostly unexamined.[4] I attempt to address the shortcoming below.

Investment trends and their determinants

The regional economic trends suggest a few determinants of the 1980s investment slowdown in Latin America: a lack of new capital flows, slow growth and hence poor demand conditions, macroeconomic instability, fiscal problems which constrain public investment, and a "debt overhang" which reduces investment incentives.

The pattern of declining capital flows is evident from the debt figures in table 8.1. After a growth rate of nominal debt averaging 23.5 percent between 1978 and 1982, post 1982 debt growth slowed to just over 4 percent.[5] In real terms, debt levels remained essentially the same during the 1980s; the Latin American public sector received mostly "involuntary" lending (designed simply to keep the country up to date on service payments) and the private sector was basically starved of new flows. The real-sector counterpart of this "capital shock" was the shift from modest trade deficits in the late 1970s (averaging less than $3 billion annually for the region in 1978–80) to massive surpluses in the late 1980s (averaging almost $25 billion in 1987–9).[6] The implied shortage of foreign savings was likely an important factor in constraining the level of investment.

Slow growth in the 1980s would also seem to be a culprit in the investment crisis. As noted, regional capital formation seems to follow regional growth with a short lag, a pattern which accords with a Kaleckian or "flexible accelerator" view that capital needs are essentially determined by expected output. Since the debt crisis brought a regional slowdown – attributable to reduced import capacity, mostly stagnant exports, and generalized adoption of macroeconomic austerity – investors trimmed investment plans in response to shrunken markets.

Macroeconomic instability throughout the decade also had a negative impact on investors. For many countries, inflation was both high and variable while exchange rate movements were sharp and sometimes quite erratic; both monetary phenomena made problematic the long-term projections necessary for investment plans. The fiscal deficits evidenced in table 8.1 led to government borrowing; this, in turn, created pessimistic expectations of future inflation as well as concerns about future budget correction and the fiscal drag this would induce.[7] The combination of instability and uncertainty kept annual capital flight from Latin America well above $10 billion annually in the second half of the 1980s, a phenomenon also indicative of reduced investment in the region.

Fiscal deficits contributed in another way to the investment slowdown. With tax revenues lagging and deficits widening, governments often sought to shrink spending. Public outlays on capital were sometimes easier to cut than politically sensitive subsidies and other current consumption items. These cuts in public investment reduced capital formation directly, and to the extent that public investment is complementary to private investment, reduced capital formation further through secondary effects on private investors' plans.

The gross capital formation figures of table 8.1 do not allow us to assess these effects since no distinction is made between public and private investment. Indeed, all the usual data sources for developing countries (the World Bank's *World Tables*, the IMF's *International Financial Statistics*, the UN's *National Accounts*, the Inter-American Development Bank's annual reports, and the UN Commission on Latin America's *Annual Statistical Yearbook*) lump together public and private capital spending under a measure for gross domestic investment.

To the rescue has come the International Finance Corporation (IFC). The IFC is a World Bank affiliate primarily concerned with promoting private-sector development in the third world, a task which requires that it actually know the level of private and public investment in the countries of interest. In a paper of great utility to researchers, Pfeffermann and Madarassy (1989) drew on World Bank Country Economic Memoranda, Public Investment and Expenditure Reviews, and other World Bank country studies to construct reasonably consistent series for public investment for thirty developing countries; private investment is then determined as a remainder. The problems with their methods are several: financial investment is not always excluded, changes in inventories are sometimes included and sometimes excluded, and some public enterprise investment is treated as private due to shortcomings in the data (see Pfeffermann and Madarassy, 1989, p. 2). Nonetheless, their work represents the first collection of more or less consistent private investment series covering the period since 1970 and hence serves as the basis for the breakdown employed here and in another empirical investigation of private investment by IMF staff economists (Greene and Villanueva, 1991).

Figure 8.1 uses this data base to calculate regional trends in private and public investment from 1970 to 1987. Twelve countries are included in the regional total: Argentina, Bolivia, Brazil, Chile, Colombia, Costa Rica, Ecuador, Guatemala, Mexico, Peru, Uruguay, and Venezuela.[8] Each country's investment as a percentage of GDP is weighted by its contribution to total GDP (in US dollars) for all twelve in the same year; since these twelve are only a partial list of Latin American countries, the gross domestic investment series does not exactly conform to the capital formation series in table 8.1 (although it follows a quite similar trajectory).

Figure 8.1 reveals that public investment rose slowly through the 1970s,

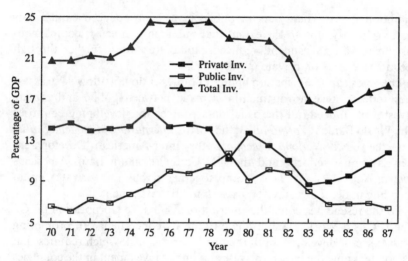

Figure 8.1   Private and public investment in Latin America, 1970–87

fell sharply from 1980 to 1984 (as fiscal retrenchment first set in), and remained stable at around 7 percent of GDP from 1984 to 1987. Private investment was more or less stable throughout the 1970s, fell steadily until 1983, then began a slow recuperation in the latter part of the decade. This pattern provides mixed evidence about the relationship between public and private investment. While the decline in private investment in the early years of the last decade does occur in tandem with the public investment slowdown, there were other factors (suggested above) operating in this period. Moreover, the post-1983 recuperation of private investment occurs on a non-growing base of public investment. Sifting through these trends to determine the relationship between public investment and private investment requires multivariate regression analysis, the focus of the subsequent section.

A final explanation for the lower levels of investment in the 1980s – and the one of most interest for this research – involves the stock of external debt. Some analysts suggest that when the level of debt exceeds repayment capacity, creditors are likely to condition payment upon output (Sachs, 1989). This imposes a sort of marginal tax, reducing expected return and thereby dampening investment. Some authors go on to suggest that both debtors and creditors might benefit from a debt writedown to more feasible levels; in this case, the debt burden is lump sum, disincentives are removed, investment is enhanced, and repudiation possibilities are reduced (see Krugman, 1988 and Sachs, 1989). Whether such a Pareto-optimal outcome is possible is not important to present purposes; the debt disincentive to investment exists even if only one party will benefit from debt reduction (International Monetary Fund, 1989, p. 63).[9]

Does this notion of a "debt overhang" explain some of the collapse in private investment evidenced in figure 8.1? Unfortunately, most overhang models assume a unitary borrower in which a social planner attempts to maximize country-wide utility by deciding when to invest or consume, repay or repudiate (Krugman, 1988 and Sachs, 1989). In this case, the link between debt and investment is clear since both are implicitly public sector. How, however, does Latin America's mostly public or publicly guaranteed external debt serve as a disincentive to *private* capital formation? The impacts likely occur through fiscal or exchange rate mechanisms: elites may fear that a large public debt means higher future taxes or worry that the hard currency requirement of public obligations will force up the exchange rate and hence the expected price of capital and intermediate imports.[10] Either chain of causation (or both) would curtail private investment.

The trends offer some causal support for the debt overhang proponents: private investment fell sharply during the emergence of debt-servicing difficulties in the early 1980s and subsequently improved as debt service and debt to GDP ratios were slightly reduced. Of course, other elements of the macroeconomic context were also in flux and debt may have worked indirectly through its effects on growth and inflation. Distinguishing the effect of a debt overhang *per se* requires a multivariate regression analysis of the determinants of private investment. I turn to this task below.

The determinants of private investment: an econometric investigation

In this section, I present the results of an econometric investigation of private investment in Latin America. I focus on private (rather than public) investment for several reasons. First, public investment is largely set by public policy rather than being determined by, say, profitability; while the policy decisions about public capital formation may be modeled as a reaction function to economic and political variables, the theory and empirics here are less clear and deserving of separate treatment.[11] Second, recent studies suggest that private investment may have a larger effect on growth than public investment (Khan and Reinhart, 1990); indeed, in the twelve-country set considered above, these economies with the highest output–capital ratios (a crude measure of productivity) also had a higher share of private investment in both GDP and total investment.[12] A third reason is rooted in the swing in regional policy toward resuscitating the private sector and its investment; a focus on private investment serves as an *entrée* into the current policy debate.

The section begins with a discussion of the determinants of investment and a review of the rather scanty existing literature. I then describe my own procedures and results, paying special attention to the debt overhang issue. I also investigate the effects of a distributional variable and IMF programs and explore what happens to regression coefficients if the sample is split to cover pre- and post-debt crisis periods.

The determinants of investment

The private investment decision is generally modeled as an attempt to achieve some desired level of capital stock adequate to service market demands for investors' output. This notion implies that the level of utilization of current productive capacity might drive investment demand (see, for example, Bowles *et al.* 1989). When such a measure (or a proxy such as the unemployment rate) is lacking, it seems best to adopt some variant of the "flexible accelerator" model in which desired capital stock for some future period is considered to be a function of expected output for the same period (see Blejer and Khan, 1984, p. 383). Naturally, adjustment to the desired capital stock takes time and some lag structure is appropriate; despite the complications, the basic insight here is that capital growth (or investment demand) is driven by expected growth.

The extent to which investors will actually adjust their capital stock depends on the confidence they have in their expectations; this, in turn, depends on past and present stability, particularly in the macro economy. The most evident sign of instability is inflation; high rates of inflation can also reduce firms' ability to predict relative prices and thereby increase the riskiness of long-term investment (Greene and Villanueva, 1991, p. 41).[13] On the other hand, moderate rates of inflation may enhance investment and growth by raising short-term profit expectations and shifting income toward capital (since nominal wages often lag, particularly in developing economies). Thus, the inflation–investment relationship may be that of an "inverted U" – moderate price hikes enhance investment while "excessive" inflation breeds visions of instability and therefore dampens investment.[14]

Investment is also determined by available financing. Analysts typically assume that investment is negatively related to the real interest rate, a measure which proxies both the ease of finance and the more neoclassical "user cost of capital." Some development economists have challenged this traditional role of the real interest rate, arguing instead that low (or negative) real interest rates are a sign of "financial repression"; the latter is said to dampen savings, financial accumulation, investment, and growth (see Fry, 1980).[15] In response, Dornbusch and Reynoso (1989) have suggested that real interest rates *per se* have less impact on growth than the sort of inflation-signaled instability discussed above.

Because of the debate, many analysts have thought it preferable to proxy available financing with some direct quantitative measure such as the level of, or change in, domestic credit granted to the private sector. This measure is flawed: if "financial repression" does exist, then it is likely that significant credit flows occur in informal markets, rendering data collected from the official banking system an unreliable indicator of total credit supply. Indeed, real interest rate measures determined with official nominal rates may also misrepresent the "true" ease of finance since such measures exclude costs in the curb market. This data problem is likely to prevent a definitive conclusion about either the effects of financial repression or the investment–interest rate relationship. In my view, credit availability – measured either directly or by lower real interest rates – should have a positive effect on private investment; given the data problems, however, one should hardly expect the relationship to be significant.

Public investment is also likely to affect private investment, although the direction of the effect is the subject of debate. The "crowding out" view suggests that public investment reduces its private-sector counterpart by either diverting scarce material and financial resources or by usurping the productive position of private capital. However, many observers argue that "crowding in" is more important: by providing infrastructure, critical intermediate inputs (from state enterprises), and a more buoyant aggregate market, public investment can actually enhance private investors' expectations (see Taylor, 1988, 1989 and Greene and Villanueva, 1991). Whether crowding in or out effects dominate may depend on the country and the time period, i.e., on the concrete relations between capital and the state in a particular social formation. For the purposes of the econometrics below, I assume that the complementarity of public investment dominates; as we will see, the results are supportive of this view.[16]

This brings us to the external constraints which may affect investment, particularly the so-called "debt overhang." As noted above, high levels of debt may lead private investors to fear that output gains from new investment will be taxed away. Most models of this effect are discontinuous; only when debt exceeds expected repayment capacity will debt payment become "linked to the economic performance of the country" (IMF, 1989a, p. 62) and hence act as a disincentive. In the real world, the effect is likely to be more continuous since there is always stochastic and informational uncertainty as to when debt becomes "unpayable," i.e., as to the exact level of external debt sufficient to transform payment obligations from a lump-sum burden to an effective marginal tax. Because of this,

I proxy the overhang with a continuous measure involving the expected burden of debt on future output, which in turn depends on the stock of debt, the expected international interest rate, and the level of GDP.

The overhang can also be proxied (although less "cleanly") by a measure of international capital flows. When an overhang exists – when obligations exceed capacity – lenders will offer only "involuntary" loans (or none at all). Any lender recognition of the adjustment disincentive posed by the overhang should also contribute to the reduction in new flows (see Krugman, 1988). Thus, lending levels indirectly signal whether the existing debt is "too large" and an overhang exists. The problem, of course, is that new loans also indicate foreign exchange availability and any such variable is therefore playing two explanatory roles.

It is important to distinguish between a debt overhang – that is, the expected "tax" on output if an historically given level of debt is fully serviced – and the *actual* level of debt service. The actual debt service ratio should also dent investment prospects, primarily because such service consumes scarce foreign exchange which might otherwise be directed toward the purchase of imported capital goods. Note, however, that shrinking current debt service through the sort of unilateral restrictions attempted in Peru in the mid 1980s does not affect the overhang threat: for this, debt relief and the reduction of *expected* payments is critical.

While the above variables are the basic expected determinants of private investment, there are a few others also investigated below. The first is the distribution of income between workers and capitalists. I assume that a reduction in wage share generally signals a reduction in workers' power, an increase in profitability, and a more favorable scenario for accumulation by private capitalists.[17]

The second variable of interest is the presence of IMF programs. In the orthodox view, an IMF program signals a return to "good" policy and positively affects expectations; from a radical perspective, an IMF program signals an increase in the power of capital and hence a more favorable scenario for accumulation (see the arguments and evidence in Pastor, 1987). Structuralists contend that IMF policies are inappropriate for the third world, and might lower investment by dampening growth and public investment. However, with macroeconomic variables held constant, an IMF variable as such is essentially capturing a "confidence" effect and a positive sign is therefore expected. The equation for private investment then is

$$PRIVGDP = f[EXPGRO(+), INFL(+), INFLSQ(-),$$
$$RI(-) \ (or \ CHCRED(+)), PUBIGRO(+),$$
$$DEBTOVER(-), LENDING(+), DSERV(-),$$
$$WORKERY(-), DUMIMF(+), GNPPC(+)]$$

where *PRIVGDP* is private investment as a share of GDP, *EXPGRO* is the expected growth rate, *INFL* is the inflation rate, *INFLSQ* is the inflation rate squared (which taken together with the previous variable should give the inverted U relationship discussed above). *RI* is the real interest rate (and *CHCRED* is the change in credit to the private sector), *DEBTOVER* is a measure of the expected debt burden which takes into account both debt levels and the international interest rate, *LENDING* is a measure of voluntary lending with both overhang and foreign exchange aspects, *DSERV* is a purer measure of foreign exchange drain which records actual debt service as a percentage of exports, *WORKERY* is a measure of worker income, and *DUMIMF* is a dummy variable indicating whether a country is under some sort of IMF supervision. The last variable, *GNPPC*, is a proxy for per-capita income; it is used, as in Greene and Villanueva (1991), on the grounds that higher-income countries have a greater ability to mobilize resources for investment. The signs in parentheses after the variables indicate their expected direction of influence; each sign should be clear from the discussion above.

Table 8.2 lists all variables and offers some more detailed explanations of their actual construction and lag structure. Before turning to the methodology used in testing the equation as well as the actual results, it is useful to discuss findings by others.

Other studies of private investment

Despite the importance of private investment, there have been few empirical studies of investment behavior in developing countries. The reasons partly lie in a lack of data: estimates of capital stock are virtually unobtainable for most of the developing world; capacity utilization, unemployment, and wage rates are also problematic; credit measures such as the real interest rate or the change in domestic claims are poor proxies for actual credit levels in the economy (for reasons discussed above); and even inflation and other politically sensitive variables can easily be "mismeasured" by domestic authorities. The most important data constraint, of course, has been the general absence of publicly available data on private investment. As a result, the two most relevant studies were done by staff economists at the IMF, an institution with access to the necessary unpublished data.[18]

Blejer and Khan (1984) examine the effects of government investment, domestic credit, and output (or more specifically, an output gap) on private investment. They proxy the capital adjustment mechanism with the lag of private investment, a technique which eliminates the problem of directly estimating the country's capital stock, and then apply the resulting

Table 8.2. *Variables in the investment equation: definitions and sources*

PRIVGDP	Private investment as a percentage of GDP. Taken from Pfeffermann and Madarassy (1989).
EXPGRO	Expected growth rate. Calculated as the average growth rate for the last *two* years to allow for slower adjustment in expectations and investment realizations. Growth rates taken from the World Bank's *World Tables, 1988–89*.
INFL	The inflation rate. Calculated using the GDP deflator from *World Tables 1988–89* since this price index proxies the producer price index most relevant to the investment decision better than a CPI-based rate. The lag of the rate is used because of adaptive expectations assumptions and to reduce either simultaneity problems or correlation with the real interest rate measure (see below); the variable is actually entered as a natural log on the assumption that the effects of higher rates decline as inflation rises.
INFLSQ	The inflation rate (as above) squared.
RI	The real interest rate. Nominal interest rates taken from Greene and Villanueva (1991) and inflation from above. Similar to the approach in Greene and Villanueva (1991), this variable is calculated as $[(100 + \text{the nominal interest rate})/(100 + \text{the inflation rate})]$. Greene and Villanueva use next year's inflation rate on the grounds that this is "conceptually the correct specification" for future expectations and because this specification yielded the "best" results (Greene and Villanueva 1991:46). Since it strains credibility to assume that economic agents in Latin America can actually predict future inflation, I use the current rate of inflation in calculating *RI*.
CHCRED	The change in credit to the domestic private sector as a percentage of GDP. Calculated by summing: (1) the change in domestic banking claims on the private sector, and (2) net flows (disbursements minus repayments) on long-term private sector non-guaranteed external debt, both as a percentage of GDP. The former is calculated using line 32d from various issues of the International Monetary Fund's *International Financial Statistics* and the latter is taken from the World Bank's *World Debt Tables 1988–89*; local currency GDP and dollar GDP (used in calculating the actual ratios summed) are taken from *World Tables 1988–89* with dollar GDP derived by multiplying per capita dollar GNP times the population times a GNP/GDP ratio figured from the constant currency series reported. This credit measure is similar to variables in Wai and Wong (1982) and Blejer and Khan (1984). The actual measure is entered as a lag.
PUBIGRO	The change in public investment as a percentage of GDP. Taken from data in Pfeffermann and Madrassay (1989). Entered as a lag.

DEBTOVER A measure of the percentage of GDP expected to be devoted to future debt service. Calculated by multiplying the lag of the ratio of total external debt to GDP by the lagged London Interbank Offer Rate (LIBOR) for three month deposits. Total external debt and dollar GDP are taken from *World Tables 1988–89* and LIBOR from *International Financial Statistics*. LIBOR is used because this is the benchmark rate for most third world lending; multiplication of debt by LIBOR may slightly overstate the expected GDP "tax" since not all Latin American debt was contracted at variable interest rates. The measure for 3-month deposits is employed since this was used to proxy the real interest burden in Khan and Knight (1983) and Pastor (1989c).

LENDING A measure of lending. Calculated as net long-term flows (disbursements minus repayments) divided by last year's stock of long-term debt; the actual variable is entered as a lag. All data from *World Tables 1988–89*. Long-term figures are used because this is more indicative of voluntary loan flows and it is such voluntary flows that would be negatively affected by the presence of an overhang.

DSERV Debt service (repayments plus interest) as a percentage of exports of goods and services. Only long-term debt service included because this was the only consistent series available for the whole time period. Data from *World Tables 1988–89*. Entered as a lag.

WORKERY Index of worker share of income or real unit labor costs. Measured as employee earnings as a percentage of value-added in the manufacturing sector. Taken from *World Tables 1988–89*. Entered as a lag.

DUMIMF A dummy variable which equals one when a country has an IMF Stand-by, Extended Fund, or Structural Adjustment Arrangement, and zero otherwise. Procedures for determining when a program begins and how long its effects last follow those in Pastor (1987) and Donovan (1982). Information about arrangements from the IMF's *Annual Reports* and *International Financial Statistics*.

GNPPC GNP per capita as a percentage of US GNP per capita. Calculated from data in *World Tables 1988–89*.

Data generally cover the period 1975–1987, a range dictated primarily by the coverage of the nominal interest rate series used in calculating the real interest rate. Countries in the regressions are Argentina, Brazil, Chile, Colombia, Mexico, Peru, Uruguay, and Venezuela. Private investment as a percentage of GDP is missing for Venezuela in 1987. The change in credit (CHCRED) is missing for 1987 in Brazil, 1986 and 1987 in Chile, and 1987 in Colombia (which implies that the raw series for domestic credit are missing for a year earlier since CHCRED is entered as a lag). WORKERY is missing for 1987 for all countries, and for 1975–76 for Peru (again, the raw series is missing for a year earlier since this variable is entered as a lag).

flexible accelerator model to a set of twenty-four developing countries for
1971–9. The econometrics are ordinary least squares with dummy variables, although there is a brief detour into a log-likelihood procedure to
estimate some adjustment parameters. The results support the positive
effects of output, domestic credit, and public-sector investment, although
there is also evidence of some "crowding out."[19] However, the pooling in
this work is somewhat problematic: the authors use the real levels of all
variables (rather than ratios), a strategy which generally introduces a high
degree of heteroskedasticity into the system. Moreover, the study does
not include the debt overhang variables of central importance in this
chapter.

   Greene and Villanueva (1991) do consider debt issues, testing private
investment (scaled by GDP) as a function of the real interest rate, the
growth of per-capita output (lagged), public-sector investment as a percentage of GDP, the current inflation rate, the dollar value of per-capita
GDP (lagged), and two "debt overhang" variables: the lagged debt
service ratio and the lagged debt to GDP ratio. The sample is a pooled
cross-section time series covering twenty-three countries from 1975 to
1987. Their results (like mine below) suggest that the debt overhang does
limit private investment.

   While my work parallels the Greene and Villanueva study, there are
several differences. They use two-stage least squares with inflation considered as the endogenous variable. While it is clear that the level of
private investment can affect inflation (by swelling the level of aggregate
demand), it is less obvious why the ratio of investment to GDP would
have a similar effect; for that reason, I simply use OLS.[20] To avoid
collinearity with the real interest rate measure and because investment
decisions may have been made in an earlier period and with earlier
information, I use the lagged inflation rate (and lags of most other
variables). Recall that I also use an inverted U functional form (lagged
inflation and its square) to reflect the notion that moderately higher prices
encourage investors (as in Fry, 1980) but very high inflation breeds
expectations of instability and deters investment.

   I also include three debt variables (*DEBTOVER*, *LENDING*, and
DSERV) rather than two. The new variable, *LENDING*, attempts to
capture Krugman's notion that creditor reluctance to lend may signal an
awareness that a debt overhang exists (in which case it is disadvantageous
to lend more).[21] Note also that my most direct "overhang" measure
multiplies the debt to GDP ratio by the expected interest rate in order to
fully calculate the potential "bite" of GDP taken by external debt; this
seems superior to Greene and Villanueva's simple debt to GDP ratio
although the latter also performs well. Finally, I also test for the effects of

two new variables, worker share of income (or worker power) and the presence of IMF programs.[22]

The results

The results of the regression exercise are listed in table 8.3. The procedure was OLS on a panel of eight larger Latin American countries (Argentina, Brazil, Chile, Colombia, Mexico, Peru, Uruguay, and Venezuela) for 1975–87. The time period was dictated by the coverage of the nominal interest series. The country set was limited to these eight primarily because they are a bit more homogenous and have been pooled before (see Pastor, 1990); the sign and significance pattern reported below is quite similar if we also include the four smaller Latin American countries for which private investment data exist. The dependent variable, private investment, was scaled by GDP to reduce heteroskedasticity; as in Blejer and Khan (1984) and Greene and Villanueva (1991), country dummies were introduced to account for intercountry differences. As usual, the results really describe an "average" Latin American country.[23]

For ease, I repeat the equation to be estimated below.

$$PRIVGDP = f[EXPGRO(+), INFL(+), INFLSQ(-), RI(-)$$
$$(or \quad CHCRED(+), \quad PUBIGRO(+), \quad DEBT\text{-}$$
$$OVER(-), \quad LENDING(+), \quad DSERV(-),$$
$$WORKERY(-), DUMIMF(+), GNPPC(+)]$$

Following usual practice, I conducted a "specification search" in which variables were added one by one to see if the introduction of certain variables significantly altered coefficient estimates of previous variables. The estimates were more or less stable and so I report just four equations: (1) private investment as a function of just domestic variables (*EXPGRO, INFL, INFLSQ, RI, PUBIGRO*); (2) private investment as a function of both domestic and debt overhang variables (*DEBTOVER, LENDING, DSERV*); (3) private investment as a function of domestic variables, debt overhang, and worker power (*WORKERY*); and (4) private investment as a function of domestic variables, debt overhang, and the presence of IMF programs (*DUMIMF*). All regressions also included the control variable *GNPPC*. The estimates for the constant and country dummies are not reported here in order to conserve space.

Scanning columns (1) and (2), we can see that the results are quite supportive for our hypotheses: while the real interest rate is anemic (as expected), every other variable is significant at the 1 or 5 percent level (two-tail) and the directions of causality are as expected. Inclusion of the debt overhang variables raises explanatory power by about 0.08, a

Table 8.3. Determinants of private investment in Latin America, 1975–87

$$\overset{+\quad+\quad+\quad+\quad+\quad\quad-\quad-\quad\quad+}{PRIVGDP = f(EXPGRO, INFL, INFLSQ, RI \text{ (or } CHCRED\text{)}, PUBIGRO, DEBTOVER, LENDING, DSERV,}$$
$$\overset{-\qquad\quad+}{WORKERY, DUMIMF, GNPPC)}$$

Time period Version	1975–87 (1)	1975–87 (2)	1975–87 (3)	1975–87 (4)
EXPGRO	0.414	0.320	0.350	0.379
	(5.224)***	(4.335)***	(4.637)***	(4.890)***
INFL	5.874	5.940	5.398	6.319
	(3.064)***	(3.437)***	(3.130)***	(3.712)***
INFLSQ	−0.684	−0.727	−0.722	−0.769
	(3.079)***	(3.616)***	(3.643)***	(3.886)***
RI	−2.202	−1.676	−3.477	−1.573
	(1.201)	(0.962)	(1.653)#	(0.922)
PUBIGRO	0.390	0.333	0.300	0.303
	(2.628)**	(2.454)**	(2.252)**	(2.267)**
DEBTOVER		−0.549	−0.580	−0.539
		(3.513)***	(3.750)***	(3.519)***
LENDING		0.039	0.042	0.041
		(2.150)**	(2.116)**	(2.302)**
DSERV		−0.050	−0.040	−0.057
		(2.139)**	(1.544)#	(2.495)**
WORKERY			−0.240	
			(2.932)***	

DUMIMF	0.251 (3.034)***			1.387 (2.122)**
GNPPC		0.125 (1.560)#	0.210 (2.401)**	0.159 (1.983)*
Adjusted R-squared	0.588	0.667	0.706	0.680
Number of obs.	102	102	93	102
F-value	12.087***	12.902***	13.256***	12.943***

Notes: All independent variables are defined in table 8.2. The countries included in these regressions are Argentina, Brazil, Chile, Colombia, Mexico, Peru, Uruguay, and Venezuela. The table includes coefficient values; below these values are the corresponding T-statistics with significance levels denoted as follows:

*** significant at the 0.01 two-tail level,
** significant at the 0.05 two-tail level,
* significant at the 0.10 two-tail level,
# significant at the 0.20 two-tail level.

reasonable contribution. Including worker income (*WORKERY*) in column (3) reduces the number of observations by nine, making direct comparisons with (1) and (2) difficult; note that *WORKERY* enters negatively at the 1 percent level while the real interest rate improves slightly and the coefficient for the debt service ratio declines and loses some significance. In column (4), I drop the distributional measure and include the IMF variable; it enters positively at the 5 percent level while the real interest rate regains its insignificance and all other variables are significant at the 1 or 5 percent level. Since there is a correlation between IMF programs and regressive redistribution (see Pastor, 1987), I also ran a regression including both *WORKERY* and *DUMIMF*; the signs and significance levels remain quite similar to those reported in table 8.3 and this regression goes unreported to conserve space.

To afford the reader a sense of the magnitudes of the coefficients and the realism of the model, I conducted various simulations to calculate the effects of various variables on private investment.[24] To raise private investment by 1 percent of GDP, for example, expected growth needed to rise by over three percentage points. A similar change in private investment could be stimulated by an increase in public investment by 3 percent of GDP, a reduction in debt by 15 percent of GDP, a decrease in LIBOR of nearly four and a half percentage points, an increase in new lending around 25 percent of existing debt, or a 15 percent decrease in real unit labor costs. The IMF variable proved to have a large impact; signing an agreement was, *ceteris paribus*, associated with an investment increase amounting to 1.4 percent of GDP. Finally, the inflation rate effect peaked to a 60 percent annual rate; below that level, rising inflation produced higher investment (again, probably because of rising short-term profits or "forced savings"), while above that level, the negative instability effect set in. While some observers may view such an inflation "peak" as high, recall that Latin Americans have learned to live with extraordinary levels of inflation and may therefore have a different definition of "moderate" price increases.

For policy purposes, the most important result is the statistically significant and quantitatively important impact of the debt variables. The estimated coefficients also allow us to explore the relative merits of new loan flows versus debt relief. Calibrating the model, I found that a $1 billion increase in long-term loan flows would have three times greater impact on private investment than a reduction in the debt stock by the same amount; note, however, that the loan adds to the debt stock and subsequently deters investment through this route. Even if we neglect that medium-term effect, the cumulative benefits of debt relief (which has a lasting impact on private investment) would exceed the short benefit of new flows within four years (assuming that future year benefits are discounted by less than 25 percent). To prefer new loans to relief, government planners would therefore need to have extremely short time horizons, a feature probably present in the short-lived regimes that frequently characterize Latin American politics. Those concerned with the longer run should opt for debt reduction (if it is possible) rather than to add to the existing burden.[25]

The results for *WORKERY* deserve further discussion, particularly since they may be interpreted as an open invitation for wage cutting in Latin America. The results indicate that, holding all other variables constant, enhanced worker income will slow investment. This unsurprising result does not capture the effects of higher wages on demand and growth as well as the implications of worker power on policy positions; for example, a government favoring workers' interests may be more likely to reduce debt service and thus promote private investment through this channel.[26] A similar caution should be issued about the IMF variable; while agreements with the Fund boost investment, they may also be accompanied by recession, inflation, and higher levels of debt service, phenomena which would effectively wipe out any gain from the confidence effect.

On a more technical side, dropping the country dummy variables altogether reduces the adjusted R^2 by a relatively small amount (0.14) leaving the same pattern of signs but with substantially reduced significance for the inflation variables and debt service; this relative robustness suggests that the dummies are not contributing excessively to the explanatory power of the regression. In addition, an alternative set of regressions which uses *CHCRED* in place of *RI* yields roughly the same results (including the relative unimportance of the credit availability variable); for the sake of brevity, I report only the results using *RI*.

An interesting issue is whether the variable coefficients and levels of significance change over the pre- and post-debt crisis period. Does debt, for example, exert a more or less negative influence now? To get at this sort of question, I followed Greene and Villanueva's procedure of estimating the equation with variables which have essentially been split into two: one with observations for the pre-crisis period and zero otherwise, and the other with observations for the post-crisis period and zero otherwise.[27] As in Greene and Villanueva (1991), the post-crisis period is dated as beginning in 1982. The results of this procedure are reported in table 8.4 for an equation not including the distributional or IMF variables.

The results may be summarized as follows. Inflation has a slightly stronger effect in the post-crisis period, the effects of expected growth and

Table 8.4. *Determinants of private investment before and after the debt crisis*

Variables	pre 1975–81 Coefficient	post 1982–7 T-value
EXPGRO		
pre	0.524	(4.078)***
post	0.163	(1.931)*
INFL		
pre	3.214	(1.574)#
post	4.540	(2.540)**
INFLSQ		
pre	− 0.408	(− 1.612)#
post	− 0.547	(− 2.563)**
RI		
pre	− 1.603	(− 0.699)
post	0.116	(0.052)
PUBIGRO		
pre	0.346	(2.345)**
post	0.193	(0.919)
DEBTOVER		
pre	− 0.310	(− 1.473)#
post	− 0.564	(− 2.489)**
LENDING		
pre	0.019	(1.010)
post	0.022	(0.547)
DSERV		
pre	− 0.060	(− 2.311)**
post	− 0.027	(− 0.897)
GNPPC		
pre	0.243	(2.690)***
post	− 0.025	(− 0.252)
Adjusted R-squared	0.746	
Number of obs.	102	
F-value	12.391***	

public investment fall sharply, and lending has roughly the same positive impact.[28] The debt overhang variable, *DEBTOVER*, rises in coefficient value and significance in the post-crisis period while the coefficient for actual debt service declines significantly. The rising importance of the overhang variable conforms to most notions that the overhang is most operative in the debt crisis period. The simultaneous decline in the significance of actual debt service suggests that the real impediment to investment is not the current foreign exchange drain but rather the fear of large future payments, i.e., the debt overhang. The sort of restrictions on debt service practiced by Peru in the mid 1980s are not enough; actual debt relief is necessary for a resurrection of private investment.

On the more technical side, note that both the GNP per-capita and real interest rate variables "flip" signs, although the significance for both post-crisis coefficients is exceptionally low. The former probably occurs because the richer countries had more debt problems and sharper investment cutbacks while the latter probably occurs because of a post-crisis reliance on internal financing. This latter interpretation was given credence when I replaced the real interest rate measure, *RI*, with a quantity-based measure of the change in credit to the private sector, *CHCRED*, and discovered that *this* credit variable does not switch signs although the significance of its coefficient does fall in the post-crisis period.

Taken together, the results of the regressions suggest that the crucial impediments to raising private investment are slow growth, macroeconomic instability, and high levels of expected debt service – exactly the factors pointed to in our general overview.

Table 8.4 (*cont.*)

Notes: All independent variables taken from those defined in table 8.2; the "pre" version of the variable takes on the value of the independent prior to 1982 (and zero otherwise) while the "post" version takes on the value of the independent after (and including 1982). The countries included in these regressions are Argentina, Brazil, Chile, Colombia, Mexico, Peru, Uruguay, and Venezuela. The table includes coefficient values; to the right of these values are the corresponding T-statistics with significance level denoted as follows:
*** significant at the 0.01 two-tail level,
** significant at the 0.05 two-tail level,
* significant at the 0.10 two-tail level,
\# significant at the 0.20 two-tail level.

Conclusions

In the 1980s, Latin American growth and development stagnated. One critical factor was the continuing fall in public investment as well as significantly lower levels of private investment. Both trends were problematic for a region whose most pressing task is the construction of a new and viable accumulation model.

Both an overview of the general trends and the more detailed regression analysis suggest that one critical impediment to restoring accumulation was the continuing debt problems of the region. Weak capital flows and excessive debt service conspired to directly and indirectly reduce incentives for private (and public) investment. Equally important was the debt "overhang" – the simple fact that large stocks of debt and hence looming future payments lead private investors to fear future taxes and exchange shortages.

The central policy implication of this research is that debt relief could help foster private investment in the region, both because of its possible direct effects and because such relief is likely to stimulate public investment, improve growth, and reduce inflation. The need to shrink debt *obligations* deserves emphasis. As noted in the econometric section, new loans can provide for a temporary boost in investment but longer-lasting change requires subtracting from, not adding to debt stocks. In addition, actual debt service became a less important constraint through the 1980s while the overhang (or *expected* payments) rose in importance.

One potential worrry is that debt relief could cause lenders to curtail all future flows of credit. History suggests, however, that capital markets have short memories; witness the resumption of lending to Latin America despite the widespread defaults and moratoria of the 1930s (Fishlow, 1985). Moreover, the flows that might be lost by a bolder debtor stance on relief may not be all that great given the banker reluctance that has characterized international credit markets since 1982. Perhaps more to the point is that a congenial debt relief program can offer potential benefits to all sides: under a reasonable set of conditions, debt reduction – which reduces the probability of default – can actually raise the expected return to lenders and, indeed, this is one reason why the US shifted to the Brady plan in early 1989.[29] The task for borrowers, however, is to discover the discount (or relief) rate at which lenders are exactly indifferent between granting a debt reduction and insisting on repayment; since banks have an incentive to hide their preferences and understate their willingness to reduce the stock of debt, a bit of non-congenial bluster – i.e., threats to suspend payments – may be an important part of Latin American bargaining.

Another set of implications of this research concerns the relationship between policy and theory. While a focus on private investment is often associated with orthodox economists, the model of investment tested here is more consistent with Kaleckian, structuralist, and Marxist insights than with neoclassical reasoning: output drives investment, savings implicitly adjust, public investment complements private investment, foreign exchange constraints are significant limiting factors, and rising worker power negatively impacts investor expectations. Private investment may need to be nurtured, but perhaps with means not usually associated with the conservative defenders of the private sector. In particular, con-ditioning debt reduction on orthodox-style policy could be counterpro-ductive (see also Pastor, 1987); incomes policy, enhanced public invest-ment, and other more interventionist strategies may be the best domestic complement to external relief.

A final note of caution is in order. Investment is determined by factors beyond the economic variables examined here; a complex web of social relations between workers, capitalists, and the state are also fundamental to capitalist expectations of the future. If conflict between these forces is the chief characteristic of a society, private investment will be in short supply. To the extent that either capital is dominant or the rules of intergroup relations are at least clear, capitalist confidence rises and investment follows. The toughest task for Latin America in the coming decade is not attainment of debt relief but agreement on a new social contract. For societies whose historic inequalities have worsened during the crisis, constructing a new and potentially successful social structure of accumulation is a tall order.

Notes

Thanks to the members of the WIDER project (especially Gerry Epstein) for their comments on the initial work; thanks also to Mike Conroy, Richard Feinberg, Jeff Freiden, Jamie Galbraith, John Sheahan, Jim Whitney and others who provided comments on subsequent drafts. This research was conducted with the financial support of UNU/WIDER and the Guggenheim Foundation and the research assistance of Tod Clark and Jo King.

1 The growth and investment figures are figured from data for the Western Hemisphere available in the International Monetary Fund's *World Economic Outlook*, various years. The measure of equality is developed in Pastor and Dymski (1990).

2 Table 8.1 shows averages for 1978–80 for *all* variables primarily because the Fund's *World Economic Outlook* did not report consistent series for debt ratios, debt service, gross capital formation, and fiscal surplus for earlier years. Averages for the whole decade of the 1970s were available for the growth and inflation measures; the 1978–80 averages for these variables were quite close to those for the previous decade taken as a whole, suggesting that the choice of 1978–80 as a benchmark does not make for unfair comparisons.

3 Traditional macroeconomics suggests that rising government deficits, particularly given underdeveloped financial markets in developing countries, can trigger inflation by swelling demand and monetary creation. At the same time, the "Tanzi effect," in which rising inflation reduces the real tax revenues collected, also suggests that rising deficits will be the *consequence* of higher inflation.

4 A notable exception is Biersteker (1989). In a wide-ranging essay, he attempts to shift focus (as in this work) from the financial aspects of the crisis to the real-sector declines in output and investment. He also deals explicitly with the question of a debt overhang and the investment decline; unfortunately, he indicates a correlation between the two without really specifying a chain of causation. The most interesting aspect of his work is an attempt to review "good," "bad," and "inconsistent" reformers in light of their investment performance in the 1980s; he finds little evidence to support the notion that "good" (or orthodox) reforms will actually rekindle investment, a point echoed in the conclusion to this chapter.

5 The 1977 external debt figure for the region (used to calculate the 1978 debt growth) was $124.1 billion (IMF, *World Economic Outlook 1985*, p. 262).

6 Data on the regional trade balance for 1978–80 from Pastor (1989a, p. 81) and data for 1987–9 from IMF *World Economic Outlook 1990* (1990, p. 161).

7 In Mexico, for example, extensive borrowing led to interest payments on the government's domestic debt which were roughly 8 percent of GDP in the late 1980s, twice as large a bite as that taken by external debt. To achieve the fiscal balance that the IMF and other international institutions generally require, Mexico had to run a primary (non-interest) surplus of more than 10 percent of GDP, a phenomenon sure to create a major fiscal drag on growth.

8 The investment series were missing for Costa Rica for 1970–5, for Peru for 1971–3, and for Venezuela for 1987. As a result, these data points were not included in the calculation of regional averages.

9 Pareto optimality obviously matters for political or bargaining concerns; banks are unlikely to grant relief if they are net losers.

10 The fear that high debts will generate high taxes is a straightforward "Ricardian" hypothesis. Whether this disincentive actually works depends on whether elites actually fear that future taxes will be imposed and whether capital flight to evade any higher taxes is relatively easy. The foreign exchange constraint argument carries through as long as the country's Central Bank retains some control over hard currency flows. The econometrics below do not distinguish between these alternative avenues of causation (although this is an interesting line of future research) but simply test for the overall effect of debt on private investment.

11 This notion that public investment might react to economic events also suggests that it might be appropriate to treat public investment as an endogenous variable in a simultaneous equations approach to private investment. Most of the literature on private investment in the developing world sidesteps this issue and treats public-sector investment as an exogenous or predetermined variable (see, for example, Blejer and Khan, 1984 and Greene and Villanueva, 1991); I follow that strategy here as well although the endogenous approach might be useful for future research.

12 The output–capital ratio is figured as the change in real GDP over the years 1971–87 divided by total investment flows over the same period. The countries are then ranked and a "natural" break is used to divide them into two groups: the first has seven countries (with an average output–capital ratio of 10.6) and second has five countries (with an average output–capital ratio of 20.7). For the second group, the average private investment rate for 1971–87 is higher by 2.3 percent of GDP and average private

investment as a share of total investment is also significantly higher. Causality is a problem here – private investment may be larger because capital is more productive and not the other way around. It may also be that public investment is necessarily less productive since it involves critical projects with low immediate returns. Despite these qualifiers, the correlation of private investment to productivity is suggestive. GDP figures come from the World Bank's *World Tables* while the investment data are from Pfeffermann and Madarassay (1989); for Costa Rica, the averages are for 1976–87, for Peru 1974–87, and for Venezuela 1971–86. The countries in the group with the "low" output–capital ratio are Argentina, Bolivia, Chile, Costa Rica, Peru, Uruguay, and Venezuela while those in the "high" group are Brazil, Colombia, Ecuador, Guatemala, and Mexico.

13 A negative association between high rates of inflation (in excess of 20 percent) and economic growth is also suggested by a simple econometric exercise in Dornbusch and Reynoso (1989).

14 I also assume that the negative effects of higher inflation decline as rates increase, primarily because economic agents have already adjusted; alternatively, one could simply note that an extra 50 percent inflation when the base is 100 percent is more disruptive than when the base is 300 percent. For this reason, I actually use logs of the inflation rate, making the curve not strictly an inverted "U" since the right-hand side declines slowly.

15 Both Dooley (1986) and Pastor (1990) present econometric evidence suggesting that "financial repression" (measured as the real interest rate accounting for exchange rate depreciation rather than simply inflation) does tend to enhance capital flight, a phenomenon generally associated with reduced domestic investment.

16 An interesting project would be to break up public investment into, say, infrastructure, public enterprises providing inputs to private production, and public enterprises directly competing in private-sector activities. Such sectoral disaggregation of public capital flows is beyond the scope of this chapter, partly because no standard data exist across countries. However, this would be a most interesting direction for future country-level research.

17 Note that a measure of wage share (rather than just wages) also captures the notion of worker power in the factory as well. This is because wages as a percentage of output can also be written as the real wage divided by worker productivity/effort; to the extent that workers can effectively combat "speed-ups" and other effort-enhancing measures, wage share swells even for the same real wage levels. For more on the notion of labor extraction in the workplace, see Bowles (1985); for more on wage share as a "record" of class conflict as well as an econometric investigation of its determinants in Latin America, see Pastor and Dymski (1990).

18 Studies of lesser relevance include Wai and Wong (1982) and Fry (1980). Wai and Wong use limited data to test private investment functions for five developing countries from the early 1960s to the mid 1970s; the study suggests an important role for government investment and private output but does not consider the debt issues central to this work. Maxwell Fry tests savings and investment functions for sixty-one developing countries over the period 1964–76; however, private investment is not singled out and debt issues are also not considered.

19 Blejer and Khan (1984) argue that while public investment *levels* might be important for private investment, increases in public investment may produce crowding out because such increases reflect the government stepping beyond traditional infrastructure expenses and into the sort of markets in which public enterprises compete with private-sector counterparts. In various runs, they test as regressors: (1) the change in public

investment *and* its level; (2) trend public investment *and* the difference between actual and trend public investment; and (3) expected public investment (determined through an autoregressive procedure) *and* the difference between actual and expected public investment. All runs provide some support for the notion that both crowding in and out occur although the evidence may be questionable in light of the econometric problems discussed in the text.

20 Another candidate for endogeneity is the real interest rate. In the developing-country context, however, nominal rates are more likely to be set by mandate than by markets.

21 Another overhang variable which might be appropriate is the presence of interest arrears, a variable now reported by the World Bank (in *World Debt Tables 1989–90*) and one which clearly indicates debt-servicing difficulties. Reportage in *World Debt Tables*, however, is only from 1980 on; a call to the World Bank for additional years produced a conversation in which I was warned that the variable was not very accurate and should not be used in regression procedures. As a result, my attempt to partially proxy overhang through lending levels seemed superior, although as noted in the text, the measure picks up the effects of capital flows *per se* and is also somewhat collinear with the domestic credit series (which includes flows associated with long-term non-guaranteed private debt).

22 There are other differences. Greene and Villanueva calculate the real interest rate using a future inflation rate, a procedure which is based on an heroic assumption of accurate forward-looking expectations; for my real interest rate, I simply use the current inflation rate. Greene and Villanueva use per-capita GDP growth rather than aggregate GDP growth, a choice which seems unnecessary since capitalists should be concerned with the overall market size. They use the dollar value of per-capita GDP in current dollars, a procedure which does not properly discount for world inflation; the lag also seems unnecessary since this is just a control variable and so I use current per-capita GDP as a percentage of US per-capita GDP. Finally, I proxy the effects of public investment with a measure which takes into account the growth of public investment rather than simply its level. I did try Greene and Villanueva's measure, current public investment as a percentage of GDP, obtaining a positive sign but only anemic significance. However, when I dropped the country dummies to check the robustness of my results, public investment turned out to have a positive and highly significant effect; that is, it distinguished between countries, a phenomenon which explained its strong performance in the "wider" (or more "cross-sectional") studies of previous researchers. To accurately capture the positive effects of public investment as well as to avoid co-linearity with the debt overhang variable (which is also scaled by GDP), I decided to use the change in public investment as a percentage of GDP (lagged), a measure which I assume investors use to derive trends and predict current public investment levels.

23 There is also a data dummy used to deal with the fact that total external debt before 1977 does not include short-term debt while total external debt after 1977 does. Since our variable, *DEBTOVER*, uses total debt figures actually entered as a lag, I include a variable which is zero for 1975–7, and one afterwards. Dropping the earlier years altogether is another strategy to deal with the discontinuity in the total debt series. While the sample size is considerably reduced, the pattern of signs holds and the T-values are mostly significant; the debt service variable weakens most, which is not surprising in view of the likely collinearity between actual payments and the expected payments represented by *DEBTOVER*.

24 Some of the results reported in the text are "state-dependent"; for example, the effect on investment of changes in the LIBOR rate depends on the level of the debt burden. For such state-dependent predictions, I needed to determine a reasonable starting point. To

do this, I took partial correlations of actual and predicted private investment rates to determine which countries enjoyed the "best fit." Argentina was one of the best and 1980 was a year in which predicted and actual values for Argentine investment were virtually identical; thus, I chose this as the base state and calibrated the model around the actual values for Argentina in 1980. The coefficients for most variables were taken from the regression in column (2) of table 8.3; for *WORKERY* and *DUMIMF*, I took coefficients from columns (3) and (4) respectively.

25 This discussion of short time horizons may offer some insight into why Latin American governments chose to borrow, rather than adjust during the late 1970s.

26 Bowles and Boyer (1988) suggest various macroeconomic regimes in which higher wages, higher investment, and faster growth are compatible. The regression exercise here cannot capture the complex simultaneity of their model.

27 I split the variables rather than the sample primarily because running separate regressions for the two samples would, in the context of the limited number of observations and high number of explanatory variables, result in very few degrees of freedom.

28 The weaker post-crisis link between growth and private investment may be due to increased idle capacity; when capacity utilization is low, producers may choose to first meet new demand by using old plant and equipment and will only invest after the recovery is more established.

29 Since its 1989 Brady-sponsored debt deal, for example, Mexico has experienced both faster economic growth and improved relations with its creditors.

Part four

Finance and accumulation: efficiency and instability

9   Financial innovation, deregulation, and Minsky cycles

Peter Skott

The 1980s and early 1990s was a period of spectacular changes in the financial markets. Deregulation and financial innovation blurred the distinction between different financial institutions; markets became increasingly international; trade in options, futures, swaps, and other sophisticated financial instruments grew explosively; mergers and acquisitions, buy-outs and buy-ins – many financed by "junk bonds" – flourished; stockmarkets boomed, crashed, and recovered and, having reached dizzying heights, the Japanese stockmarket – the most buoyant of all – plunged almost 30 percent during the first few months of 1990 and subsequently continued its violent gyrations.

These developments have led to widespread concern about the stability of the financial system. This concern is ubiquitous in the financial press; it has caused policymakers in a number of countries to ease monetary policy to avoid a credit crunch, and academic economists have also voiced their fears over recent developments (e.g., Friedman, 1990 and Bernanke and Campbell, 1988). This chapter considers some aspects of the observed changes in the financial sphere and their policy implications. It is argued, in particular, that Minsky's work offers a useful perspective on the evolution of the financial system and on the existence of endogenous tendencies to financial instability.

The chapter is in four sections. In order to understand the present fragility of the financial system section 1 takes a brief look at the historical evolution of financial markets and some of the major financial changes of the 1980s and early 1990s. Section 2 considers Minsky's "financial instability hypothesis," and section 3 presents a formal model of the interaction between real and financial variables. The model supports some of Minsky's claims but also raises a number of questions. Some of these questions and the policy implications of the theory are discussed in the final section of the chapter.

1   General perspective

The pace of change may have been particularly rapid during the 1980s, but it would be a mistake to assume that radical change in the financial markets is without precedent. As recently as the 1870s, for example, the London market, the most highly developed financial center in the world, dealt mostly in government bonds and railway securities. A specialist financial press, furthermore, did not exist until the 1880s and the information available to both managers and financial investors was extremely poor, as was the computational ability to analyze complex information. The existence of accurate company accounts, for instance, is essential to the decision making of both managers/entrepreneurs and financial investors (unless the decisionmaker has reasonable information about costs and revenues it is difficult to attach any meaning to notions of profit maximization) but "even in the late eighteenth and early nineteenth centuries many substantial partnerships did not use the double entry. The widespread adoption of double entry in England was a feature of the nineteenth century, probably the latter part of it" (Yamey, 1977) and in the UK, until the Companies Act of 1948, the state of a company's financial health was fundamentally the affair of those who ran it, and very little meaning could be attached to published profitability figures.

Accounting standards and disclosure requirements improved in the post-war period, but evidence of inappropriate procedures and irrationality still remained. Thus, Modigliani and Cohn (1979) argue that rising inflation in the 1970s led to major and systematic errors in the assessment of profitability and that as a result of these "inflation induced errors, investors have systematically undervalued the stockmarket by 50 per cent" (Modigliani and Cohn, 1979, p. 24).[1] And it is not obvious that the recent gyrations in international stockmarkets represent optimal forecasts of future dividends (Shiller, 1990).

These brief historical remarks suggest that it may be dangerous to view the upheavals of the 1980s in isolation. Financial innovation has been "to a great extent the continuation of post-war tendencies" involving the "spreading and universalisation of modern business practices and attitudes" (Auerbach, 1988, pp. 191 and 114). One of the most notable developments has been the increased aggressiveness of financial institutions. This aggressiveness has contributed to the breakdown of traditional boundaries between financial institutions, a breakdown which has proceeded to an extent such that "perhaps for the first time since the days of Shylock, it is necessary to stop to ask quite what is a bank" (*Economist*, April 7, 1990, "Survey of International Banking," p. 5). Traditional banking services are now being offered by other financial – and non-financial – institutions but, conversely, banks have branched into areas outside their traditional sphere.[2] Banks have also been extending loans of a duration and "quality" which would have been unthinkable just a few years earlier and they offer an array of new financial arrangements, some of which do not appear in their balance sheets.

The increased aggressiveness has left its mark on banks' own profitability and credit ratings. Provisions for third world debt as well as the need to write off unprecedented amounts of commercial and property loans have left many banks in a shaky position, and rating agencies have carried out a general downgrading of the banking sector.[3] Bank failures have also increased dramatically. From an average of less than ten commercial bank failures per year from 1945–80, the number of failures in the US reached about 200 per year in the late 1980s.

The weakening of banks has given added impetus to the process of securitization. Large industrial firms have become able to raise finance more cheaply than banks by selling bonds or commercial paper directly to financial institutions or other corporations,[4] but another factor behind the substitution of market-based relationships for administratively based financial relationships has been the greater aggressiveness and creativity of investment and merchant banks, who have been instrumental in the creation of these markets. It is not simply a case of preexisting "markets" coming into use.[5] A clear example is the development of the junk bond market which to a large extent has been attributable to the actions of a single individual, Mike Milken.

The adoption of a historical perspective and the emphasis on changes in attitudes and practices do not imply that financial innovation proceeds in a smooth and linear fashion. It clearly does not (neither does innovation in most other areas). The pace of change was quite explosive in the 1980s and early 1990s, and any explanation of this fact must take into account the interaction of the general trends in business behavior with both the growing possibilities of computer technology and regulatory reform.

Advanced computer and communication technology has been an essential prerequisite for many developments in the financial sphere; the internationalization of financial markets, for instance, depends on fast and inexpensive communications, and without computerized records the securitization of, say, credit card loans would never have been viable. It is also correct to say that the existence of regulation gives the regulated part incentives to innovate and thereby circumvent the regulatory restrictions. Changes in monetary policy in the late 1970s strengthened these incentives as monetarist attempts to control the money supply led to high and volatile interest rates. High interest rates undermined the existing restrictions on the deposit rates of banks and thrifts; banks and thrifts designed negotiable order of withdrawal (NOW) accounts and automatic-transfer savings (ATS) accounts, and money market mutual funds (which had existed since 1971 and which faced no restrictions on interest rates) became increasingly successful. The volatility of interest rates played a part in the innovation process too. It spurred the development of new financial instruments, including adjustable-rate mortgages, interest rate swaps, futures, and options, in much the same way that the earlier international upheavals associated with the breakdown of the Bretton Woods system and the OPEC oil price increases had stimulated financial change.

Technological progress, changes in monetary policy, and reforms of the regulating framework have thus been important elements in the process of innovation but these factors cannot be regarded as exogenous explanatory variables. Changes in regulation and economic policy, firstly, have often been introduced in response to financial developments. The weakening, for instance, of Glass–Steagall restrictions and of prohibitions against interstate banking in the US are governmental responses to pressure from banks to expand their activities both across financial categories and geographically; the deregulation of the S & L industry in the early 1980s and the subsequent reregulation were responses first to the erosion of the industry's competitiveness and then to the crisis of the industry; the Big Bang reforms relaxing participation in the Stock Exchange by foreigners and others in Britain in 1986 were part of an attempt to maintain London's attractiveness as an international financial center in the face of increasing competition. Furthermore, large parts of the regulatory framework which has been undergoing reform (or demolition) in recent years have their origins in past financial crises. The Glass–Steagall Act from 1933, for instance, with its separation of commercial and investment banking, control of interest rates (Regulation Q), and introduction of deposit insurance was a response to the experience of the previous four years.

Secondly, it is always difficult to explain innovation as the outcome of constrained optimization, and financial innovation is no exception. Would one explain innovation in, say, aviation or medicine as the simple effects on the optimal solution of changes in exogenous constraints (in regulatory frameworks and in technology)? Technical change within any one sector of the economy will be influenced by developments elsewhere but, almost by definition, it also involves the realization that practices within the sector, which were previously thought optimal, should be changed; that in fact it would have been beneficial to have carried out the changes earlier.[6] Established practices thus had not been optimal, and a perspective which a priori assumes fully rational and efficient behavior within exogenous technological and legal constraints will miss essential elements in the process of innovation.

2   The financial instability hypothesis

Endogenous changes in the institutions as well as the attitudes and practices of private and public decisionmakers are central to the work of Hyman Minsky, and his ideas on systemic financial fragility would seem to offer a promising overall theoretical perspective on the current problems and the developments leading up to these problems. According to Minsky, financial fragility is an inevitable consequence of prolonged expansionary periods. Financial fragility is "systemic" since "the development of a fragile financial structure results from the normal functioning of our economy" (Minsky, 1977, p. 140). Acceptable financing techniques, Minsky argues, are not technologically constrained but depend on the subjective views and expectations of the different agents in the economy. These views change endogenously over time since "the absence of serious financial difficulties over a substantial period of time leads to the development of a euphoric economy in which increasing short-term financing of long positions becomes a normal way of life. As a previous financial crisis recedes in time, it is quite natural for central bankers, government officials, bankers, businessmen, and even economists to believe that a new era has arrived" (Minsky, 1986, p. 213). As a result, Minsky argues, financial attributes that are essential to modern capitalism lead to recurrent crises.

Minsky does not provide a formal demonstration of the mechanism behind the pattern of recurrent crises, but the task of formalizing Minsky's ideas has been taken up recently by, among others, Taylor and O'Connell (1985), Lavoie (1986/7), Semmler (1987), and Delli Gatti and Gallegati (1990).[7] The model below differs significantly from these existing formalizations, and some preliminary remarks on the concepts of fragility and tranquility may be helpful before the presentation of the model.

The term fragility, first, refers to the state of the financial system. The system is fragile if small disturbances – an unforeseen drop in income, for instance, or a rise in interest rates – would make it difficult or impossible for a significant proportion of the financial units to meet their contractual obligations. Thus, an increase in the share of contractual commitments in expected cash flow would indicate a rise in fragility: it would make the financial unit more vulnerable to shocks. Since the failure of one unit will have repercussions on the financial position of its creditors, the fragility of the system depends on the complete network of financial commitments between firms, households, financial institutions, and the public sector.

This network in turn reflects the behavior of private agents as well as the influence of economic policy and regulation. High leverage and adventurous Ponzi-schemes may represent typical manifestations of a high degree of fragility, but the relaxation, for instance, of the constraints on the activities of the US S&L's in the early 1980s also led to an increase in fragility (which subsequently reduced the tranquility of the system).

The existence of a fragile financial system must be distinguished from the actual appearance of crises: a fragile system need not be characterized by a lack of "tranquility" *if* the optimistic expectations which prompted the risky positions turn out to be satisfied. Financial commitments are made on the basis of expectations, and tranquility, which reflects the ability to meet these commitments, depends on *realized* cash flow as well as on the amount of contractual payments (including the possibility of rolling over the existing debt or obtaining new loans). The degree of tranquility is determined by this interaction between financial and real factors. It is at its lowest during a full-scale financial crisis involving the collapse of key financial institutions, but variations in the degree of tranquility may also be observed during more normal times; default and bankruptcy rates, for instance, are among the obvious (inverse) indicators of tranquility.

Fragility and tranquility are multi-dimensional concepts, and financial innovation and institutional change imply that the precise definitions of these dimensions will be undergoing constant change. The significance of a given debt–equity ratio, for instance, depends on the institutional environment (What are the relations between firms and their banks? Who are the shareholders?, etc.), and "the rate of interest" may be of little importance if credit markets are characterized by (variable degrees of) quantity rationing.

This institutional contingency implies that a focus on concrete institutions and practices may be misleading and fail to reveal systematic patterns. A bird's eye view of the historical process, on the other hand, shows a pattern of recurring financial and economic crisis, and an explanation of these persistent tendencies must – implicitly or explicitly – disregard the transient institutional elements in the succession of booms and busts. The model in section 3 therefore makes use of abstract financial indicators rather than institutionally specific and concrete variables.

3   A formal model

Laxity and trouble

Minsky's theory describes the interaction between (changes) in financial behavior, on the one hand, and the extent to which past expectations have been fulfilled and thus allowed agents to satisfy existing financial commitments, on the other. The essence of this argument can be expressed in terms of two scalar variables, L and T. The variable L describes the degree of laxity in financial behavior. This behavioral variable is closely related to the fragility of the system: lax financial decisions are reflected in a fragile system. The second variable, T, captures the degree of trouble in financial markets, and T is thus inversely related to the tranquility of the system.

In accordance with Minsky's argument, it is assumed that both financial laxity and trouble change endogenously and that the change in laxity is a function of the degree of financial trouble. In the absence of trouble, agents happily adopt schemes of ever-increasing optimism, and algebraically this assumption yields the following simple expression

$$\dot{L} = \varphi(T) \quad \varphi' < 0 \tag{1}$$

where $\dot{L} = \dfrac{dL}{dt}$ is the rate of change L.

Financial trouble, on the other hand, is the result of an incongruence between the past expectations which gave rise to the current financial commitments and the actual outcome. Assuming that the business sector (and the exposure of financial institutions to bankruptcies and defaults in this sector rather than among households) is the main source of trouble, the value of T will depend on financial laxity (positively) and on realized profit rates (inversely): firms' ability to meet their financial obligations depends on their profit income and a higher level of obligations requires bigger profits if the degree of financial trouble is to remain constant. If the profit share is constant (or functionally related to the output–capital ratio) then the profit rate is determined by the output–capital ratio, and we get

$$T = \theta(\sigma, L); \quad \theta_\sigma < 0, \ \theta_L > 0 \tag{2}$$

where σ denotes the output–capital ratio.

Investment and saving

The two financial variables influence investment and saving and thereby interact with the real side of the economy. Laxity and easy finance stimulate investment while trouble has a depressing effect, and I shall use the following investment function

$$I/K = f(\sigma, T, L); \quad f_\sigma > 0, \ f_T < 0, \ f_L > 0. \tag{3}$$

The positive influence of the output–capital ratio on accumulation is a standard assumption,[8] and recent work on the influence of financial constraints on investment lends support to the inclusion of T and L in the investment function (see, e.g., Fazzari et al., 1988; Devereux and Schiantarelli, 1989; Gertler et al., 1990).

Saving may also be affected by the financial variables, but here the directions of the effects are reversed: lax finance reduces saving while troubled times are associated with high saving.[9] These effects could be included without affecting the qualitative analysis below, but to simplify the exposition I shall assume that saving is independent of the financial variables and that

$$S/K = g(\sigma); \quad g_\sigma > 0. \tag{4}$$

Equation (4) assumes a monotonic relation between income and saving, and the standard assumption of simple proportionality is obtained as a special case.

Short-run equilibrium

Ignoring the financial variables and assuming linearity, equations (3)–(4) generate an elementary Keynesian model of the real sector. Equilibrium in the product market requires

$$S/K = I/K \tag{5}$$

and if $S/K = s\sigma$ and $I/K = i_0 + i\sigma + B$, equation (5) yields the equilibrium solution

$$\sigma^* = (i_0 + B)/(s - i). \tag{6}$$

For this solution to be meaningful, however, we must have $\sigma^* > 0$, and stability of the equilibrium also requires that $s - i > 0$.

The introduction of the financial variables complicates the picture. Retaining, for simplicity, the linearity assumption but replacing the constant B by the influence of the financial variables, the short-run equilibrium condition becomes

$$S/K = s\sigma = i_0 + i\sigma + aL - bT = I/K. \tag{7}$$

If equation (2) linking T to σ and L is linear too, and T is given by

$$T = -a\sigma + \beta L \tag{8}$$

the solution for σ^* becomes

$$\sigma^* = (i_0 + (1 - b\beta)L)/(s - i - ba). \tag{9}$$

Using equation (8), the associated equilibrium value of T is

$$T^* = -ai_0/(s-i-ba) + [\beta(s-i) - aa]/(s-i-ba)L. \qquad (10)$$

Comparing equations (6) and (9) it is readily seen that the introduction of the financial variables have made the stability requirement more stringent: stability now requires that $s-i-ba > 0$. Furthermore, a distinction must now be made between the short-run equilibrium defined by equation (9) and the long-run evolution of the economy. The equilibrium in (9) is contingent on the value of L, and by assumption the change in laxity is determined by the value of T.

Unstable equilibria

The interesting cases arise when financial factors exert a significant influence on saving and investment, i.e., when the parameters a, β, a, b are relatively high. But these are precisely the cases where the stability condition fails to be satisfied: high values of a and b imply that the short-run stability condition $s-i-ba > 0$ will be violated even if $s-i > 0$.[10]

An unstable short-run equilibrium implies a tendency for σ and I/K to increase without bounds if the initial value of σ happens to be above σ^* and to decrease without bounds if σ is below σ^* initially. Unbounded divergence of this kind is clearly implausible. The one-to-one correspondence between local instability and unbounded divergence is a feature of linear models, and the simplest solution to the problem is to introduce a non-linearity in the form of upper and lower limits on I/K: gross investment cannot become negative and managerial constraints and prohibitive adjustment costs may impose an upper limit on the rate of accumulation.[11] These assumptions imply that the linear investment function in equation (7) is replaced by

$$I/K = \begin{cases} m & \text{if} & i_0 + i\sigma + aL - fT < m \\ i_0 + i\sigma + aL - bT & \text{if} & m \leq i_0 + i\sigma + aL - bT \leq M \\ M & \text{if} & i_0 + i\sigma + aL - bT > M \end{cases} \qquad (11)$$

Equations (2), (8), (11), and the equilibrium condition (5) generate short-run solutions for I/K, σ, and T, and, assuming that the financial variables are important and that $s-i-ba > 0$, there are three cases to consider:

Case 1 (illustrated in figure 9.1): If $(i_0 + (a-b\beta)L)/(s-i-ba) < m/s$ there is a unique, stable short-run equilibrium given by $\sigma^* = M/S$.
Case 2 (illustrated in figure 9.2): If $(i_0 + (a-b\beta)L)/(s-i-ba) > M/S$ there is a unique, stable short-run equilibrium given by $\sigma^* = m/s$.

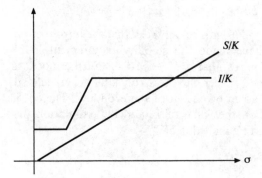

Figure 9.1

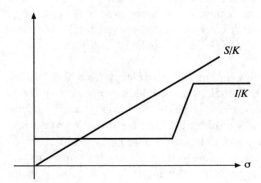

Figure 9.2

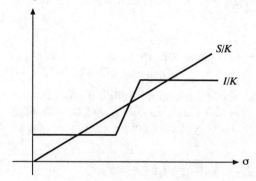

Figure 9.3

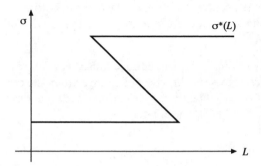

Figure 9.4

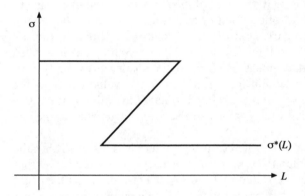

Figure 9.5

Case 3 (illustrated in figure 9.3): If $m/s \leq (i_0 + (a - b\beta)L)/(s - i - ba) \leq M/S$ then there are three short-run equilibria, an unstable central equilibrium flanked by two stable equilibria

$$\sigma^* = \begin{cases} m/s \\ (i_0 + (a - b\beta)L)/(s - i - ba). \\ M/S \end{cases}$$

The value of L determines which of the three cases obtains, and this dependence of the outcome on L is depicted graphically in figures 9.4 and 9.5. With L along the horizontal axis the $\sigma^*(L)$ curve shows the short-run equilibrium (equilibria) associated with any given value of L. Figure 9.4 corresponds to the case where $a-b\beta > 0$. This inequality implies an inverse relation between L and the value of the unstable, central solution for σ^*. A reversal of the inequality – so that $a-b\beta < 0$ – gives the configuration in figure 9.5. The instability of the central solution implies that in both cases the relevant positions of short-run equilibrium are along the horizontal segments of the $\sigma^*(L)$ curve.

By assumption the state variable L changes endogenously as a function of T, and the key question concerns the direction of change along the two horizontal segments. If $\bar{T} = \phi^{-1}(0)$ then the $\dot{L} = 0$ locus in (L, σ) space can be derived from equations (1) and (8), and we get

$$\sigma = -\frac{\bar{T}}{a} + \frac{\beta}{a}L \tag{12}$$

In figures 9.6 and 9.7 this upward-sloping $\dot{L} = 0$ locus has been superimposed on the $\sigma^*(L)$ curve. Since $\dot{L}$ is inversely related to L for any given value of σ, $\dot{L}$ is decreasing to the right of the $\dot{L} = 0$ locus and increasing to the left of this locus. It follows that intersections between the horizontal segment of the $\sigma^*(L)$ curve and the $\dot{L} = 0$ locus correspond to (locally asymptotically) stable equilibria. Thus, in figure 9.6 the plane is divided into three parts: initial values of (L, σ) in the shaded area imply convergence to the high equilibrium $(\bar{L}, \bar{\sigma})$, an initial value equal to the unstable equilibrium solution $(\tilde{L}, \tilde{\sigma})$ implies that (L, σ) will remain at this equilibrium, and initial values anywhere else give convergence to the low equilibrium $(\underline{L}, \underline{\sigma})$.

Figure 9.7 shows a more interesting case. Here it is assumed that the $\dot{L} = 0$ locus is flatter than the upward-sloping part of the $\sigma^*(L)$ curve (that $\beta/a < (a - b\beta)/(s - i - ba)$) and that the $\dot{L} = 0$ locus intersects the $\sigma^*(L)$ curve along the upward-sloping segment. These assumptions imply that there is a unique equilibrium solution for (L, σ) and that this equilibrium is unstable. The result is perpetual fluctuations. Assume, for instance, that initially the economy is at point A. This is off the $\sigma^*(L)$ curve and a fast adjustment process takes the economy vertically to the short-run equilibrium position at B. Since B is to the left of the $\dot{L} = 0$ locus the economy now travels slowly along the horizontal segment until point C. Laxity is still increasing at C, but as L moves above C the economy drops sharply to D on the lower arm of the $\sigma^*(L)$ curve. D is to the right of the $\dot{L} = 0$ locus, and L begins to decrease toward E where a new "catastrophe" takes the economy vertically to F. The cyclical process then starts all over again.

Figure 9.8 shows the associated time patterns of L, T, and σ. The model implies discontinuous shifts in I/K and σ as the economy alternates between periods of low growth with $I/K = m$ and high growth with $I/K = M$. The discontinuities in σ are reflected in T but T also changes – continuously – during the periods of constant growth. L finally exhibits

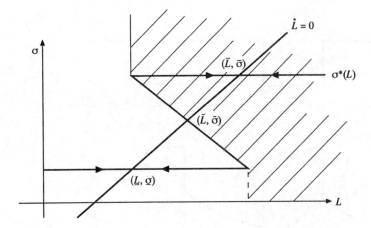

Figure 9.6

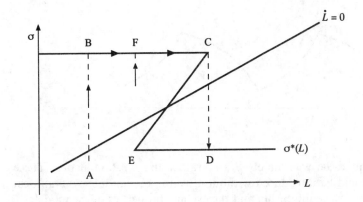

Figure 9.7

no discontinuities but rises (declines) during periods of high (low) growth with a discontinuity in $\dot{L}$ at the transition points between high and low growth.

These stark patterns with alternating periods of high and low growth could be softened. The ceiling and floor in the investment function could be replaced by a more general s-shaped specification thus removing the constancy of the accumulation rate along the upper and lower branches of the $\sigma^*(L)$ curve; allowing the financial factors to influence saving would modify the simple proportionality between the output–capital ratio and the rate of accumulation; the discontinuities would be eliminated if it were assumed that the adjustment of output toward its short-run

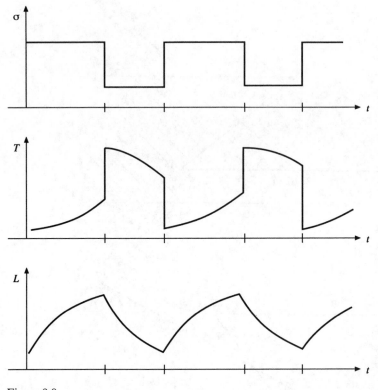

Figure 9.8

equilibrium value was merely "fast" rather than instantaneous. These changes could be introduced without affecting the uniqueness and local instability of the equilibrium and the cyclical properties of the model.

The qualitative picture in figures 9.7 and 9.8 does depend, however, on assumptions about the relative magnitudes of the different effects. Thus, it was assumed that $s - i - ba < 0$ and that $\beta/a < (a - b\beta)/(s - i - ba)$. The first inequality – the short-run instability condition – requires that the financial variables exert an important influence on real outcomes (a high value of ab). If this instability condition is satisfied, the second inequality becomes equivalent to the condition $\beta(s - i) - aa > 0$, and the second inequality therefore says something about the relative values of the financial coefficients: β must be high relative to aa. The plausibility of these parameter restrictions is an important empirical question, but one that is outside the scope of the present chapter.[12]

The analysis gives qualified support to the "financial instability hypothesis." The existence of feedback effects between real and financial variables may in some cases produce instability and recurrent crises. The parameter restrictions and non-linearities required to produce this outcome may be plausible, but other outcomes are possible: endogenous changes in financial behavior and the existence of feedback effects of the kind suggested by Minsky do not necessarily lead to a pattern of recurrent crises.

It should be noted, finally, that the model excludes a number of factors which affect the growth path of capitalist economies. The absence of a public sector, for instance, represents an obvious limitation of the model, but arguably the biggest problem is the neglect of the labor market: even as a first approximation it may be seriously misleading to disregard the interaction between capital–labor relations and the growth path of the economy.[13] The model may capture an important element of the interaction between financial and real factors but it gives a very incomplete picture of the causes of fluctuations in capitalist economies.

4   Concluding remarks

Historically, financial crises have been an important element in the cyclical path of capitalist economies and since the mid 1960s financial strains have again become increasingly visible. Financial institutions and practices evolve over time and the details of the cyclical pattern will be historically specific. But the long-term changes in financial structure may not be random. On the contrary, endogenous changes in both institutions and attitudes may lead to financial crises: the financial system may, in Minsky's words, be characterized by "systemic financial fragility."

This chapter has presented a simple formalization of Minsky's theory. It is central to this theory that economic agents are led to adopt increasingly risky practices during periods of tranquility. This argument has been dismissed by some commentators on the grounds that it implies an unexplained "irrationality": agents should learn from past mistakes and come to understand the dangers of financial fragility.[14] Knowledge about past financial crises may, however, provide little guidance for current behavior. Past crises will have led to changes in the institutional environment. As a result, new opportunities will have been opened up, practices that were highly risky in an earlier environment may have become safe, and previously safe procedures may have become recipes for disaster. Restrictions on the activities of commercial banks opened the door to mutual funds, finance companies, and other "non-bank banks," deposit insurance made it safe to place deposits with shaky S & L's which – because of their problems – offered high rates of interest to attract funds; non-innovating banks have faced trouble as their traditionally captive clients saw new opportunities in the form of interest-paying accounts for households and greatly expanded possibilities for firms to by-pass banks through direct securitization. Agents who simply extrapolate from past experience will be in the position of generals using the strategies of a previous war.

The continuous transformations of the institutional environment have influenced the modeling strategy in this chapter. The formalization of the theory has focussed on the hybrid variable "laxity" and "trouble" as indicators of a changeable and multi-dimensional set of variables. The simplification involved in this use of abstract indicators seems unavoidable given the complexity of the financial structure and the changes it has been undergoing. It would be possible, of course, to focus on one particular element of the financial structure, but the use of any such element instead of a hybrid indicator would represent an evasion of the aggregation problem rather than a solution to the problem.

The analysis has given some support to the "financial instability hypothesis." It has been shown how the introduction of financial variables into otherwise stable models may destabilize the system: the interaction between financial conditions and the real sector will, under certain conditions, generate recurrent crises and reduce the average growth rate of the economy. Considering the simplicity of the model, the picture presented in figures 9.7 and 9.8 fits the financial instability hypothesis remarkably well. Prosperity and tranquility gradually induce an increasingly risky financial behavior which at some point leads to a financial crisis. This financial crisis in turn has serious repercussions for real output and growth, and the resumption of fast growth has to await the restoration of a less fragile financial environment.

Insofar as fast growth is considered desirable, the theory implies a strong anti-laissez-faire position. Needless to say, the use of hybrid indicators like L and T precludes the derivation of operational policy rules for the regulation of the financial system, but the analysis indicates that without intervention increases in fragility will cause financial crises and real contraction. The analysis also implies that the stakes are high, and that it is misplaced to focus narrowly – as does much of the current debate – on the immediate costs to the tax payer of intervention: the potential costs of non-intervention may be of a different order of magnitude.

Intervention must take into account the particular institutional structures that exist, and the continuous evolution of the financial system implies that the design of policy intervention must change too.[15] Furthermore, successful intervention may encourage private agents to take on higher risks than they would have otherwise done. This change in behavior may happen simply as a result of lower assessments of the riskiness of the financial environment after a period without financial crisis. But intervention may also create "moral hazard" problems which imply that it will sometimes be desirable to maintain ambiguity about the precise policies of intervention. The present perspective cautions against the belief in simple rules and permanent solutions to the problems of regulation. The design of regulatory policies involves difficult questions, and these difficulties make policy mistakes inevitable. But the imperfections of regulation arise to a large extent for the same reasons that make regulation desirable: pervasive uncertainty and the existence of strong and complex externalities both invalidate laissez-faire and preclude the possibility of perfect regulation.[16]

It should be noted, finally, that the present chapter has focussed on the influence of financial innovation and of endogenous changes in attitudes to risk on the stability of the economic system. It might be argued, however, that even if the evolution of the financial system in the post-war period has led to increased fragility, there have been other benefits. Thus, a recent IMF report suggests that there is a trade-off between efficiency and stability and that "[a]s financial systems have become more competitive, more securitized, and more liquid, they have become more efficient. At the same time, such financial systems may be more susceptible to liquidity strains and crises than are less liquid, more bank-intermediated financial structures" (Goldstein *et al.*, 1992). The efficiency gains of financial innovation can be questioned, however. Traditionally the most highly developed and sophisticated financial centers have been found in the US and the UK, with Japan and the continental European countries appearing more "primitive" in this respect. Yet, the overall performance of the Japanese and the continental European economies has surpassed that of the Anglo-Saxon countries during the post-war period. Cosh *et al.* (1990), among others, have argued that financial short termism is part of the explanation for the relatively poor performance of the US and the UK.[17] The evidence on financial short termism may be mixed but so too is the evidence for greater "efficiency" of market-based system.[18] Certainly, the alleged efficiency benefits should not blind one to the effects of financial innovation on the stability of the system.

Notes

Earlier versions of this chapter have been presented at the WIDER conference on "Investment, Savings and Finance" in Amherst, August 1990, at the conference on "Analytical Political Economy" in Notre Dame, March 1991, and at a seminar at the Université Catholique in Louvain-la-Neuve. I am grateful to the participants in these meetings as well as to Paul Auerbach, Hyman Minsky and the editors of this volume for their constructive criticisms and suggestions.

272   **Peter Skott**

1 Modigliani and Cohn present both econometric work and anecdotal evidence in support
  of their theory. Brokerage firms, for instance, offer advice to clients but "in virtually
  every case, it was clear that analysts did not add back to earnings the gain or debt, and
  that they also relied at least partly on the capitalization of earnings at a nominal rate"
  (p. 35). Errors of this kind have also been noted by other observers. Carsberg and Hope
  (1976) found that sixty-three out of 103 large UK firms discounted *real* cash flow using a
  nominal discount rate.
      The Modigliani–Cohn argument has been challenged, and rival explanations of the
  observed decline in p/e ratios in the 1970s have been proposed. These explanations have
  been based on, *inter alia*, taxation effects and on changes in risk premia or in expected
  growth rates. The evidence in favor of these alternative explanations is weak, however
  (see Modigliani and Cohn (1985) and the references therein for discussion of the different
  theories).
2 In America and Japan some of these changes are still being hampered by regulatory
  measures but the restrictions have become progressively less important. Thus, in the US,
  Bankers Trust, Chase Manhattan, Citicorp, and J.P. Morgan have used loopholes in the
  Glass–Steagall Act separating commercial and investment banking to set up securities-
  underwriting affiliates. Rival institutions like investment banks, stockbrokers, and
  mutual funds in turn offer products which are virtually indistinguishable from bank
  accounts. Among non-financial companies General Electric has taken over the investment bank Kidder Peabody and become an important source of both consumer credit
  and funds for industry, and General Motors and Ford are building consumer finance
  businesses. Similar developments can be seen in other economies.
3 Initially, American banks were among the worst hit. European banks fared somewhat
  better in the 1980s but have suffered badly in the early 1990s, as have Japanese banks.
4 Regulatory requirements which raise the cost of capital to banks and, more importantly,
  the increased sophistication of bank customers may also contribute to this development.
  Thus, Auerbach emphasizes the "changes in the practices of borrowers, as corporations
  have refined their technique of cash management and for financing projects at minimum
  cost" (Auerbach, 1988, p. 198).
5 See Auerbach and Skott (1992) for further discussion of these issues.
6 Commercial banks in the UK, for instance, have not been subject to legal limitations on
  their investment bank activities (as in the US and Japan); their equity involvement was
  constrained only by custom and tradition.
7 The Taylor–O'Connell paper has been particularly influential. Taylor and O'Connell
  base their model on the dynamic interaction of two variables, the interest rate and the
  "state of confidence." The latter variable, ρ, is defined as the difference between the
  expected future return on capital and the current profit rate, and it is assumed that the
  change in ρ depends inversely on the current level of the interest rate. It seems strange,
  however, that expected profitability should evolve without any feedback from realized
  outcomes. If, for instance, the interest rate were maintained at a constant, low level then
  profit expectations would be *ever increasing* and with a constant actual profit rate,
  expectations would diverge further and further from actual outcomes.
      The choice of the interest rate as the other key variable can also be questioned.
  Movements in interest rates appear to be a poor indicator of the observed multi-
  dimensional changes in financial practices and institutions. The financial instability
  hypothesis suggests the endogenous evolution of new markets and new institutions (for
  example the junk bond market and mutual funds) as well as the importance of endogenous changes in attitudes and practices (for example with respect to corporate leverage
  and banks' lending policies), in the incidence of credit rationing, and in the structure of

interest rates (e.g., changing risk premia). It is clearly impossible to achieve a high degree of descriptive realism in a manageable and formal model. But it is not obvious that one should then focus on the bond rate of interest.

8 Consider, for example, the simple case where the optimal capital stock is proportional to output, $K^* = Y/\sigma^*$, and where σ^* is the desired output–capital ratio. Ignoring the influence of financial trouble and laxity, a model of partial adjustment suggests that

$$\frac{I}{K} = \lambda\left(\frac{K^*}{K} - 1\right)$$
$$= \lambda(\sigma/\sigma^* - 1)$$

where λ is the speed of adjustment.

9 The effect of liquidity constraints on household saving has received considerable attention recently, e.g., Zeldes (1989).

10 A standard short-run adjustment mechanism is assumed without output increasing (decreasing) when $I > S(I < S)$.

11 A similar non-linearity in the investment function is central to Kaldor's (1940) model of the trade cycle.

12 The use of abstract indicators does not preclude empirical analysis. If one considers a given economy during a particular period, then the abstract indicators can be given an operational definition in terms of well-defined elements of the financial structure. See Wolfson (1990) for an attempt to construct indicators of movements in financial tranquility and fragility in the US economy between 1946 and 1987.

13 This interaction holds center stage in Goodwin (1967) and Skott (1989).

14 This criticism has been raised by, among others, Tobin (1989). See Friedman and Laibson (1989), Guttentag and Herring (1984), Sethi (1992), and Skott (1994) for analyses of learning in relation to changes in financial behavior.

15 Current issues facing regulators include the potential but hidden problems of the broad range of financial operators who are subject to only limited regulation and the increasing importance of off-balance sheet business for the banking sector.

16 Lloyds, BCCI and Maxwell illustrate the dangers of the British strategy of making London an attractive financial center by having weak regulation.

17 It has been noted also that in a comparison of France, Germany, Japan, the UK and the USA, the UK and US stockmarkets have made the lowest net funding contribution; despite their highly developed financial markets both of these countries rely very heavily on retained earnings to finance investment (Mayer (1988)).

18 Auerbach and Skott (1992) discuss some of the issues involved.

10 Financial liberalization, capital rationing, and the informal sector in developing countries

J. Mohan Rao

1 Introduction

The search for an effective and broadly egalitarian macroeconomic policy requires an assessment of key questions concerning investment, saving, and finance. From the vantage point of less-developed countries (LDCs), two factors stand out in this connection. The first concerns international financial relations, including the problems of the debt overhang, capital flight, and limited foreign exchange earnings. The other relates to domestic financial arrangements as vehicles for mobilizing domestic resources. Diminished foreign capital inflow has increased the importance of domestic resources for financing growth. At the same time, the increasingly compelling problems of mass unemployment and inequality requires that attention be paid to the role of the so-called informal sector where much of the labor force is to be found. Of necessity, these concerns must be addressed from a theoretical position that incorporates the specificities of the domestic financial system of developing countries. Though established theories of capital accumulation are no doubt important, they do not or cannot provide a sufficient basis for the purpose.

Economists of orthodox persuasion, while recognizing some specificities of the LDC context, have nevertheless been content to focus on the consequences of so-called "financial repression" constituted by government-dictated ceilings on bank deposit and loan rates (McKinnon, 1973). For the persuaded, saving is fully realized as investment, the interest rate elicits ample responses in both, and financial intermediaries, when not held down by governments, do their job efficiently and stably. Orthodox policy prescription consists in deregulating intermediaries and lifting rate ceilings. Setting right interest rates on financial assets, of which bank deposits are the predominant form in LDCs, serves to mobilize a larger fraction of savings via the formal or organized financial system at the expense of self-financing thus raising the quality of investment. Together with a rise in saving, this is supposed to accelerate growth.[1]

To his credit, McKinnon recognizes the higher costs of finance in informal credit markets (or the dependence on self-financing) and the lack of free access to the banking system, attributing this partly to greater problems of moral hazard. But it is financial repression, whereby the cost of holding money is made inordinately high, that is held mainly responsible for the constriction of the banking system and for uneven access to its services. "Repressionists" contend that liberalization will not merely augment the scale of banking but also channel financial savings into the capital-starved sectors of the economy. As borrowing constraints are eased, returns to investment, like water, will reach a common level throughout the economy. With this, the vast differences among firms and sectors in technology, productivity, wages and investment opportunities will be reduced.

These claims are questionable not only because the problem of realization is a very real one in LDCs but also because significant responsiveness of deposits and formal-sector investments to interest rates is not demonstrated. There is little empirical basis to assert positive correlations between real loan rates and investment or real deposit rates and saving rates.[2] At best, low or negative real rates of return on financial assets have only a marginal negative impact on household or national savings (Giovannini, 1983).

Theoretical opposition to the repressionists has come from "neo-structuralists" who argue that raising formal rates may well reduce credit supply and thus slow the pace of growth. A larger flow of deposits due to higher rates may come either from dishoarding of inflation hedges such as gold or at the expense of the lending base in the unregulated informal credit market where reserve requirements are absent and lending out of equity is assumed to be the norm.[3] If the latter effect dominates, then, the reserve ratio requirement of formal banks implies an actual reduction in credit flow.[4] Hence, both rates rise and produce an inflationary impact via working capital cost–push. Lower real wages follow with a contractionary effect on effective demand. Thus, financial repression of the formal system serves to preserve and/or strengthen the more efficient informal system.

Repressionist and neo-structuralist models have a shared misconception of the nature and source of financial dualism that this chapter seeks to correct. While the financial system is divided into formal and informal (or organized and unorganized) markets, no attempt is made in the literature to differentiate the *borrowing* side. The wealthholding public allocates its funds between the two markets but a *homogenous* class of firms seeks finance in both these markets. With interest rate ceilings, formal credit is rationed and the spill-over is serviced by the informal financial system.[5] Implicitly or explicitly, then, the informal financial system is the result of rationing and, therefore, of authority-fixed deposit and loan rates. Hence, financial dualism is sustained by state policy.

To be sure, dualism is dysfunctional in the repressionist view because it signifies misallocated resources whereas it is functional in the structuralist analysis because it permits the equity-based (and quite competitive by agile) informal market to be larger than it would otherwise be.[6] But neither approach recognizes the links between financial dualism and a fundamentally heterogeneous *real* economy. By contrast, this chapter takes the view that real-side dualism is the norm in all late-industrializing countries. The formal sector is characterized by greater capital intensity and modern forms of large-scale organization while informal firms tend to be far more labor-intensive, traditionally organized, and of considerably smaller size. The bifurcation of the financial system doubtless mirrors "real-side" dualism:[7] financial markets specialized to each real sector arise for reasons related to the technology of processing, monitoring, and enforcing financial transactions. These differences sustain a high interest rate premium at which wealthholders reach portfolio equilibrium.

Informal and formal firms stand on a *struturally* unequal footing in the financial system. The formal real sector enjoys easy access to organized money, bond and equity markets whereas firms in the informal real sector can expect little financing from these sources but must rely instead on high-cost financing from informal intermediaries. Unequal access also has to do with the failure of cooperation among informal producers: although their investment demands are met only at very high interest rates, they collectively end up as net suppliers of saving, much of which is mediated by the banking system and funneled to formal firms at low rates.[8] While differential access is not unrelated to government policies or to bankers' unexamined assumptions about the relative reliability of small borrowers, we are persuaded that orthodox policy reforms or re-education camps for bankers will accomplish little.

Contrary to what is assumed in much of the literature – that the credit demands spill over into the informal sector – the reverse spill over appears to be the norm. Frequently, credit-worthy borrowers intermediate between banks and informal borrowers. Insofar as informal lending takes place out of non-equity sources, the main one appears to be the (secondary) mobilization of bank deposits (Christenson, 1993). This is driven by specialization and comparative advantage whose logic is no different from the sub-contracting relationships that prevail between formal and informal firms. Whereas neo-structuralists have insisted that the informal or curb market rate of interest is the relevant marginal rate for the whole economy, we propose a model in which, given structural fragmentation and credit rationing, this is the case only for the informal real sector.[9]

This chapter seeks an alternative framework to explore the implications of differential access to investment finance of the formal and informal sectors. Section 2 lays out the distinctions, between the two sectors relevant to such an investigation. These distinctions together with subsidiary assumptions concerning demand and production structures are incorporated into a macroeconomic model to explore the short-run interactions between real and financial variables. Section 3 extends the model to take account of investment responses, distinct for the two sectors, in the medium term. Section 4 studies medium-term reactions – of growth, employment, real wages, and the distribution of capital and bank finance between the two sectors – to a number of parametric changes around an initial equilibrium. Section 5 provides brief conclusions.

2 A macroeconomic model of formal/informal dualism

In order to explore the implications of differential access to investment finance, we propose a macroeconomic model. The economy is closed on both the real and financial sides. On the real side, it is aggregated into the formal and informal (or the F and U) sectors which may be distinguished along several dimensions:

First, firms in the F-sector are large in size and operate with modern, capital-intensive technologies. As a rule, capital hires labor and the wage system predominates. In contrast, large numbers of small firms employing relatively labor-intensive methods populate the U-sector. While capital[10] is present in informal-sector production, the capitalist may not be: the sector thus includes both small, labor-hiring firms, and a multitude of the "self-employed" working with their own or borrowed funds. Moreover, the average worker in the U-sector receives a wage that is significantly below the earnings of her F-sector cousin.

Second, while both sectors need to finance their investments, their sources of finance are markedly differentiated. Formal-sector firms have easy access to bank finance[11] sufficient to meet all their needs. The bulk of U-sector firms, on the other hand, must rely on open-market loans from the public to meet their needs though a privileged minority may, by luck or by pluck, gain access to bank funds. Privileged because the open-market loan rate tends to be substantially above the cost of bank finance.

Third, U-sector firms enjoy no normal surplus above labor and finance costs in the long run. This is ensured by the free entry and exit of firms. By implication, long-run movement to informal-sector investment are governed by the price of its output, labor costs, and the rate of interest, i.e., financing costs loom large in the investment calculus of U-sector producers. Financing costs play a comparatively lesser role in the behavior of formal-sector investment. Investment is governed mainly by the expected rate of profit with finance following capitalists' investment appetite. Thus, F-sector firms enjoy a normal surplus over costs even in the long run.

These distinctions form the theoretical core of the framework adopted here. They clearly center around production relations: capital/labor, capital/finance, and intercapitalist relations.[12] But other, arguably secondary, distinctions between the sectors are possible or become necessary. One pertains to the sources of demand for each sector. In practice, the two sectors produce for markets that run the gamut of possible intercommodity relations between strong substitutes and strong complements. The formal model can, in principle, accommodate the average relation that holds across the aggregated sectors. We present a case where the two aggregates are unrelated in price terms in order to focus on the capital–finance interconnections. This case also appears to be a plausible one in view of the facts that the informal sector includes food/agriculture, which is mainly a wage good, while the formal sector includes most investment goods. By assuming that all non-wage receipts are spent on the formal good, we consign all luxury goods production as well to that sector. Although the model ignores interindustry demands, it implies that these do not alter the basic assumption of independent demands. Thus, strong interindustry complementarity, as in some formal sector outsourcing or sub-contracting, or interindustry substitutability, as in construction, are aggregated away. The assumption of independent demands allows us to emphasize the links between the two sectors arising from the conditions of capital supply while keeping out demand links.

Another consideration suggests not so much a contrast between the two sectors as a distinction arising from the rule for price formation within the formal sector. U-sector firms, of course, are assumed to be price-taking competitors under all circumstances. As a norm, F-sector firms enjoy a measure of price-setting power governed by barriers to entry and, in the long run, by the level of investment demand. However, when market demand runs ahead of output capacity, the F-sector price becomes market determined.[13] These two variants of the basic model may be interpreted in alternative ways. One is that they refer to different economies (with competitive versus oligopolistic formal sectors). Another is that they refer to the same economy at different junctures (excess capacity versus full-capacity operation in the formal sector). At any rate, this suggests two notions of competition within the formal sector. One, which is secondary and conjunctural, refers to the price-setting rule. For the most part, the conclusions from the model are unaffected by the rule adopted. The other, which is primary and structural, refers to investment behavior. That investment is demand determined in the F-sector (but supply determined in the U-sector) implies a powerful constraint on competition in that sector.

To facilitate a focus on basic macroeconomic relations, microeconomic assumptions surrounding technology and consumption demand are kept as simple as possible. Fixed technical coefficients are assumed in both sectors: a and b denote the labor coefficients and c and k denote the capital coefficients, in the formal and informal sectors respectively. Nominal wages are assumed fixed in both sectors.[14] The informal-sector wage is denoted w while the formal-sector wage is a fixed multiple n of w.[15] Labor supply to both sectors is assumed to be perfectly elastic at their respective wage rates. On the consumption side, informal-sector workers are assumed to spend all their income on their own sector's good.[16] Formal-sector workers spend a fraction a of their income on the U good and the balance on the F good. Neither group of workers saves. Profit and interest incomes constitute the saving base and we make the simplifying assumption that a uniform rate of saving s applies to both. Consumption expenditures from these incomes are wholly directed to the formal sector. Observe that, in this formulation, the informal sector is essentially a wage-good producing sector. All investment and government demands, consumption out of surplus, and a portion of (formal-sector) workers' consumption are met by the formal sector.

Consider first the market for the informal sector good. Its supply N is fixed in the short run by the available capital stock K_U and the price p varies to clear the market. The market balance equation is given by

$$\frac{1}{p}(anwL_F + wL_U) - N = 0 \tag{1}$$

where L_F and L_U denote employment levels in the two sectors. Gross surplus per unit of output is $(p - bw)$ and the return to capital is $r_U = (p - bw)/qk$.

The formal sector, by contrast, is characterized by a fixed markup[17] μ over labor costs while output varies to clear demand under conditions of excess capacity. Its price q is thus given by $q = (1 + \mu)nwa$ where nwa is unit labor cost. Formal capital is entirely financed by bank finance at a fixed rate of interest i_b. The sector's (gross) profit rate r equals the product of the profit share, $\mu/(1 + \mu)$, and the output–capital ratio, X/K_F

$$r = \frac{\mu(nwaX)}{qK_F} = \left[\frac{\mu}{1 + \mu}\right]\frac{X}{K_F}. \tag{2}$$

Demand for F-sector output consists of consumption demand from formal-sector wages and from surpluses of both sectors, investment demands, and government expenditure. For convenience, we ignore both tax financing of government expenditures and possible technical interlinkages between public and private capital spending. This allows us to reduce the economic effects of government activity to those flowing from the level of the government deficit alone.[18] The demand–supply balance for the F-sector is thus given by

$$\frac{1}{q}(1 - a)nwL_F + (1 - s)\left[rK_F + \frac{(p - bw)N}{q}\right]$$

$$+ I_F + I_U + D - X = 0 \tag{3}$$

where X stands for formal-sector output. I_F and I_U, denoting F- and U-sector investment demand respectively, are taken to be exogenously given in the short run as is the fiscal deficit D. Substituting for r from equation (2) and simplifying (3) yields

$$\frac{(1 - s)(p - bw)N}{q} + I_F + I_U + D - \frac{(a + s\mu)X}{1 + \mu} = 0. \tag{4}$$

Clearly, formal-sector output is an increasing function of the gross surplus of the U-sector.

To complete the short-run model, the financial side of the economy needs to be specified. We work with a rather simple picture, yet one that we believe captures key features of the financial system. It is bifurcated from the supply side into the formal banking system and a non-bank or "informal" loans market. Banks receive deposits B from the public and make loans L_b to borrowers, the larger portion L_{bF} going to firms in the F-sector. There are no markets for either equity or government securities. Formal-sector profits accrue to their "owners" but their equity is suppressed in the model.[19] Government liabilities constitute all of the base money H and the deposit/base money multiplier, $\sigma = B/H$, is fixed by the central bank.

Total wealth equals the sum of capital stocks and base money, $W = q(K_F + K_U) + H$. Wealth owners choose to hold their wealth in the form of bank deposits or of market loans to informal-sector producers $W = B + L$. The proportion m of wealth held as deposits is: (1) an increasing function of activity levels – the transactions demand for money rises with the volume of trade; (2) a decreasing function of the interest rate i on informal loans – a rise in the loan rate prompts a shift of funds from banks to the informal market; and (3) an increasing function of the bank rate i_b – as the bank rate rises, wealthholders shift their portfolio in favor of bank deposits.[20] In all subsequent analysis, we shall assume that the elasticity of deposit demand for transactions is unity. The bank rate i_b is fixed by policy. The interest rate i varies to clear the demand and supply for informal loans. Since there are only two assets that wealthowners hold, the equilibrium condition for that market may be written (implicitly) as a condition for deposit equilibrium

$$(qK_F + qK_U + H)m = \sigma H. \tag{5}$$

Dividing through by H and writing in the m function gives

$$(\theta + 1)m\left[i,\, i_b,\, \frac{qX}{K_F} + \frac{p\Gamma}{k}\right] = \sigma \tag{6}$$

where the second argument in the m function is the value of total output $(qX + pN)$, normalized by K_F, $\theta = q(K_F + K_U)/H$ and $\Gamma = K_U/K_F$. θ and Γ serve as the state variables in the dynamic analysis of the following section. Note that θ is an *inverse* index of the degree of financial intermediation by banks.[21]

Several remarks are in order here. With regulated interest rates, neither lending nor deposit rates in the banking system are posited to equilibrate their respective demands and supplies. Rather, the above formulation implies an excess demand for bank loans/deposits and potential credit rationing within that system. As a rule, banks are assumed to cater first to the loan demands of firms in the formal sector. The reason for unequal treatment is a deep-seated one having to do with the unit size of loans, monitoring efficiency, and institutional affinities. Apart from larger administrative costs of making loans to informal borrowers, the similar internal structures of formal firms and banks allow for easier monitoring aided by the fact that formal firms are long-lived and have reputations to defend.

The excess of bank loanable funds over formal-sector demands is then rationed out to informal firms directly or, more often, indirectly through non-bank informal financial intermediaries specialized to the informal real sector. Such hierarchical rationing may also, to a varying extent, be regulated by the state to channel bank funds to specified segments of the informal sector. We assume that such rationing or directed allocation produces rents for those lucky enough to gain access to bank funds.[22]

Differential costs arising from hazards, both moral and otherwise, together with the much smaller size of loans account for the typically large informal market loan-rate premium over the bank lending rate. This is consistent, nevertheless, with non-bank lenders in the informal market having a decisive cost advantage in their dealings with informal borrowers. It must be recognized that the assumption of a unitary and competitive loan market outside the banking system is far from being descriptively apposite (Rakshit, 1989). Typically, the informal loan market is fragmented with substantial differences in rates and collateral requirements. The market is often spatially localized with rates related to the size of the loan, collateral offered, and non-credit relationships among borrowers and lenders. While these factors no doubt are descriptively relevant, they do not radically affect the propriety of our basic assumption that competitive forces act upon the informal loan market. At best, localized knowledge and other sources of fragmentation give rise to various forms of rent and affect the distribution of informal earnings between lender and borrower. The informal rate i is the relevant *marginal* cost of informal investment.

Finally, the model is assumed to operate within the range where the banking system is able to meet all the financing needs of the formal sector. Formally, this implies the restriction[23]

$$(qK_F + qK_U + H)m - H = L_b \geq qK_F \tag{7}$$

which can be restated, in terms of the state variables, as a lower bound on the deposit fraction m

$$m \geq \frac{1 + \Gamma + \theta}{1 + \Gamma + \theta + \Gamma\theta}. \tag{8}$$

The analysis to follow assumes that (8) holds with slack so that there are always some U-sector firms who receive bank loans at the bank rate.

Equations (1), (4), and (6) together determine the short-run equilibrium values of the U-sector price p, F-sector output X, and the interest rate i. The model is a variation on the IS–LM framework with two sectors one of which has a flexible output price. The simplifying assumptions on finance and investment behavior allow a convenient separation of the model's working: the only instantaneous effect of interest rate variations is a redistribution of U-sector profits between producers and informal lenders; their impact on activity levels and capital stocks become evident only in the dynamic analysis that follows. In particular, central bank relaxation of money supply (a rise in σ) reduces the interest rate facing the informal sector without affecting either p or X. Conversely, an increase in deposit demand (or a decrease in loan supply to the informal sector) raises the interest rate. Graphically, comparative statics for the two sectors can be represented on the p–X plane while interest rate effects may be read directly from equation (6).

The equilibrium relations (1) and (4) between p and X are shown in figure 10.1 by the lines marked UU and FF. From (1), a rise in formal-sector output X raises employment there. Hence, the demand for the informal sector's output rises and its price p must rise to restore

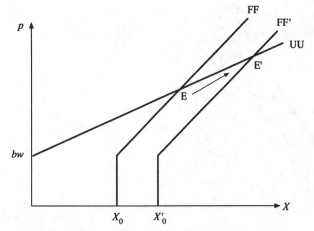

Figure 10.1   A rise in the government deficit

equilibrium. F-sector equilibrium also similarly requires a positive relationship between p and X: a rise in p raises U-sector profits which raises consumption demand for the F-sector. In consequence, output X rises in a multiplier fashion.[24] Closer examination of (1) shows that the p-intercept of UU is given by informal-sector wages per unit of output (bw): the value of U-sector output cannot fall below its wage bill since U-sector workers spend all their income on it. Below a price of bw, moreover, U-sector production in the short run ceases to be profitable. The relevant range of the model is therefore defined by $p \geq bw$. From (4), it is evident that at $p = bw$, X equals investment plus government demand times the multiplier,[25] and hence positive: $X_0 = (I_F + I_U + D)(1 + \mu)/(a + s\mu)$. The slopes of UU and FF are

$$\left.\frac{dp}{dX}\right|_U = \left[\frac{nwa}{N}\right]a \quad \text{and} \quad \left.\frac{dp}{dX}\right|_F = \left[\frac{nwa}{N}\right]\frac{a + s\mu}{1 - s} \tag{9}$$

so that the FF line is steeper than the UU line. It follows that FF must intersect UU from below establishing a stable equilibrium, given also that the interest rate i responds positively to an excess demand for deposits by wealthholders.

Figure 10.1 also demonstrates the impact of a rise in the government deficit D. In the dynamic analysis, a higher deficit will not only raise the flow of demand for X but also increase the stock of base money. Here we consider only the instantaneous responses. For any level of p, demand for X rises: the FF line shifts to the right and the equilibrium shifts from E to E'. The result is a rise in both p and X: the increased deficit is financed by a

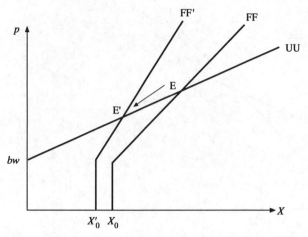

Figure 10.2   A rise in the saving rate

combination of forced saving out of wage incomes and a rise in capacity utilization. The transactions demand for money rises and, from (6), the loan rate i goes up. Hence, the return to U-sector capital $(p - bw)/qk$, goes up but so does the supply price of capital that it faces. Whether the return *net* of interest cost rises or not depends on the interest elasticity of deposit demand. The relevant computations show that net return will decline when the absolute value of the interest elasticity of deposit demand e is bounded from above as follows:

$$e < 1 - \frac{bwN}{qX + pN}.$$ (10)

When (10) holds, a higher government deficit has the potential for crowding-out private investment in the informal sector. A proper consideration of this issue must await the formulation of the dynamic relations.

A rise in the saving rate, on the other hand, has the opposite effects (figure 10.2). From (9), the slope of the FF line rises as the propensity to spend out of U-sector profits falls. At the same time, X_0 falls or FF itself shifts to the left as the multiplier declines. On both counts, p and X fall. As a result deposit demand for transactions falls so that i must fall to restore financial equilibrium. Once again, (10) defines the condition under which the net return to investment in the informal sector will *rise*: a higher propensity to save implies a relaxation of the capital constraint on the informal sector.

Consider next a rise in the F-sector wage with the U-sector wage

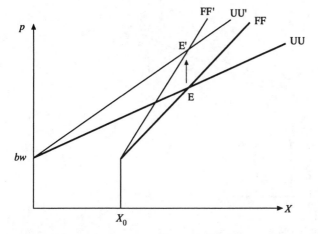

Figure 10.3   A higher formal-sector wage

unchanged. This is represented by a rise in the parameter n. The F-sector price q rises proportionately from the markup relation. From (9), it is clear that the slopes of UU and FF must rise proportionately so that UU and FF rotate toward the p-axis (see figure 10.3). Hence, p rises while X remains unchanged: while the rise in q neutralizes the increase in wage incomes of F-sector workers, the demand for X from U-sector profits remains similarly unchanged because of the mutually offsetting effects on the return to U-sector capital of the rise in p and q. From (6), however, the cost of loans in the informal sector rises as the rise in nominal income raises the demand for deposits. Thus, the principal effect of a rise in F-sector wages is a squeeze on the net return to U-sector capital. At least in the short run, F-sector workers' wages in terms of the U-sector good rises. Along the same lines, a rise in the wage rate w in both sectors has directionally identical effects on the endogenous variables and the return to capital in the U-sector as a rise in n. However, the rise in p is proportional to the rise in w so that real wages are unaffected in both sectors.

As a final experiment, consider the effects of a rise in the mark-up rate (see figure 10.4). The FF line rotates anti-clockwise as its slope, which is an increasing function of μ, rises in response. The multiplier $(1 + \mu)/(a + s\mu)$ is an increasing function of μ if and only if $a > s$. For plausible values of a and s, we expect this to hold so that X_0, the level of X due to autonomous demand when $p = bw$, rises. Hence, as shown in figure 10.4, FF shifts to the left at the same time that it gets steeper. The shift in the equilibrium values of p and X are ambiguous. However, total

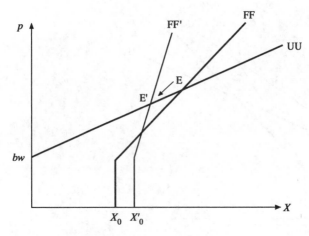

Figure 10.4   Impact of a higher mark-up

differentiation of (1) and (4) reveals that both p and X must fall whatever the values of a and s. As the profit share in the F-sector rises, workers' demand for its product falls. And, as X contracts, this reduces employment and hence the demand for the informal sector's product as well. The decrease in capacity utilization is less pronounced than the rise in the profit share so that the F-sector profit rate r rises. Note that while both p and X fall, the effect on total nominal income remains ambiguous on account of the rise in q. It can be shown that nominal income, and with it the interest rate, rises if and only if $(\mu + a)^2 > 1 - a$. Once again, for plausible values of a and μ,[26] this condition is sure to be satisfied so that a higher mark up leads to a rise in the informal-sector loan rate. Thus, a rise in the mark up not only reduces the gross return to informal-sector investment but also raises the cost of capital facing that sector.

3   A dynamic extension of the model

In this section, we extend the model to allow for changes over time in the capital and money stocks. Requiring all stocks to grow at a steady rate facilitates comparative static exercises around such a steady state within an analytically tractable model.[27] We pursue this approach in order to explore the impact of various changes, whether in policy or otherwise, on growth, income distribution, and the sectoral distribution of output, employment, and capital. The *access* of informal-sector firms to bank loans is also of special interest in this connection. U-sector firms obtain the excess of bank lending over F-sector loan demand which, from (7), equals $m(qK_F + qK_U + H) - H - qK_F$. Dividing through by total bank lending yields an expression for the informal sector's financial access to the banking system

$$\text{access} = 1 - \frac{1}{\sigma - 1}\left[\frac{\theta}{1 + \Gamma}\right]. \tag{11}$$

Turning now to investment behavior, we follow the neo-Keynesian tradition in supposing that K_F grows according to an investment demand function which, for simplicity, is given in linear form by the following equation

$$g_f = g(r, X/K_F, i_b) = \epsilon_0 + \epsilon_1 r + \epsilon_2 X/K_F - \beta i_b \tag{12}$$

where ϵ_0, ϵ_1, ϵ_2 and β are positive constants and g_f is the rate of growth of K_F. Demand for F-sector investment responds negatively to the cost of its financing (the bank rate of interest), positively to its profit rate, and, as in the accelerator model, to the rate of capacity utilization, X/K_F.[28] ϵ_0 reflects the part of investment demand that is unaffected by the profit rate or other economic variables. Since capacity utilization is a function of the rate of profit, (12) can be rewritten as a function of the interest and profit rates alone

$$g_f = \epsilon_0 + \epsilon r - \beta i_b \tag{13}$$

where

$$\epsilon = \epsilon_1 + \epsilon_2(1 + \mu)/\mu. \tag{14}$$

In light of the arguments of the previous section, we assume that U-sector investment demand is an increasing function of the difference between that sector's profit rate and the interest rate and that there is no surplus over costs, i.e., $r_U = i$, when sufficient time has elapsed to permit the free flow of investment into or out of the sector. Hence, deviations of informal investment demand outside of steady-state equilibrium will center around the formal-sector growth rate g_F. Accordingly, the investment function for the informal sector takes the form

$$g_U = g_F + \eta(r_U - i) \tag{15}$$

where η is a positive response parameter and g_U is the growth rate of K_U. It follows that steady-state equilibrium with a constant value of $\Gamma = K_U/K_F$ obtains when the informal sector's profit rate and interest rate are equalized as the differentiation of Γ with respect to time shows

$$\frac{\dot{\Gamma}}{\Gamma} = g_U - g_F = \eta(r_U - i). \tag{16}$$

In steady state, moreover, the stock of base money H must grow at the same rate as K_F. Recall that $\theta = q(K_F + K_U)/H$. In terms of growth rates, we have

$$\frac{\dot\theta}{\theta} = \frac{1}{1+\Gamma}(g_F) + \frac{\Gamma}{1+\Gamma}(g_U) - \frac{\dot H}{H} = 0 \tag{17}$$

Now the growth in base money supply equals the flow deficit of the government, i.e., $\dot H = qD$. Let δ denote the ratio of government deficit to the F-sector capital stock which we shall assume to be exogenously given[29] so that

$$\frac{\dot H}{H} = \frac{\delta q K_F}{H} = \frac{\delta\theta}{1+\Gamma} \tag{18}$$

Substituting (18) for $\dot H/H$ into (17) yields (for $\Gamma > 0$)

$$\frac{\dot\theta}{\theta} = g_F + \Gamma g_U - \delta\theta = 0 \tag{19}$$

Before considering the workings of the model, it is necessary to express the equilibrium relations (1) and (4) governing p and X in growth form. We normalize all flow variables in terms of the F-sector capital stock K_F and replace p by r_U using $r_U = (p - bw)/qk$. Accordingly, equation (1) may be rewritten as

$$\frac{ar}{\mu} - \Gamma r_U = 0. \tag{20}$$

For present purposes, it is also useful to restate equation (4) in terms of the saving–investment equality, their equivalence following from Walras' law. Total investment plus the government deficit must equal savings from the gross surpluses of the two sectors

$$E + I_F + I_U - srK_F - \frac{s(p - bw)N}{q} = 0. \tag{21}$$

Dividing through by K_F and substituting from equations (13) and (15), we have

$$\delta + (1 + \Gamma)(\epsilon_0 + \epsilon r - \beta i_b) + \Gamma\eta(r_U - i) - sr - \Gamma s r_U = 0. \tag{22}$$

The full model consists of equations (20), (22), and (6) which determine the equilibrium values of r_U, r, and i at each instant, and equations (16) and (19) governing the behavior of the state variables Γ and θ. For the reader's convenience, these equations are assembled together in table 10.1.

Local stability of equilibrium at each instant of time hinges on the responsiveness of formal investment to the formal profit rate and of

Table 10.1. *The full model*

$$\frac{ar}{\mu} - \Gamma r_U = 0 \tag{M1}$$

$$\delta + (1 + \Gamma)(\epsilon_0 + \epsilon r - \beta i_b) + \Gamma \eta(r_U - i) - sr - \Gamma s r_U = 0 \tag{M2}$$

$$(\theta + 1)m\left[i, i_b, \frac{qr(1 + \mu)}{\mu} + \frac{\Gamma}{k}(qkr_U + bw)\right] = \sigma \tag{M3}$$

$$\frac{\dot{\Gamma}}{\Gamma} = \eta(r_U - i) = 0 \tag{M4}$$

$$\frac{\dot{\theta}}{\theta} = (1 + \Gamma)(\epsilon_0 + \epsilon r - \beta i_b) + \Gamma \eta(r_U - i) - \delta\theta = 0 \tag{M5}$$

informal investment to the differential between informal profit and interest rates (ϵ and η respectively) relative to the saving rate. Sufficient conditions for stability are (1) that the response of aggregate saving to a change in the F-sector profit rate r exceeds the response of *total* investment

$$s > (1 + \Gamma)\epsilon \tag{23}$$

and (2) that the response of aggregate saving to a change in the U-sector profit rate exceeds η, the response of informal investment to a change in $(r_U - i)$

$$s > \eta. \tag{24}$$

Condition (24) ensures that an increase in U-sector profits will reduce the excess demand facing the formal sector. With these two conditions holding, it can also be shown that the dynamic equilibrium is locally stable. Hereafter, we shall assume that these restrictions hold to assure stability in the model.

The model is rather cumbersome to manipulate algebraically; rather more manageable is a graphical representation of it in reduced form. First, solve (M1) to get an expression for the U-sector profit rate r_U in terms of r and Γ

$$r_U = \frac{ar}{\mu\Gamma}. \tag{25}$$

A high F-sector profit rate (and employment) stimulates demand for the U-sector so r_U rises while a higher capital stock K_U will raise supply so r_U

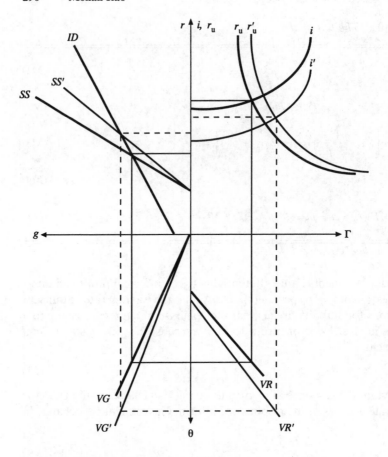

Figure 10.5   Changing growth equilibrium under monetary expansion

is inversely related to Γ. Equation (25) is represented, holding r constant, by the curve marked r_U in the northeast quadrant of figure 10.5 with Γ on the horizontal axis.

On the other hand, increases in K_U or Γ call forth higher interest rates from the financial equilibrium condition (M3). For ease of later exposition, we assume constant elasticities of deposit demand – $e < 0$ and $e_b > 0$ with respect to the two interest rates i and i_b, which allows an explicit expression for the deposit demand function

$$m = z(y/K_F)(i)^{-e}(i_b)^{e_b} \tag{26}$$

where y is nominal income $qX + pN$ and z is a shift parameter. Substituting for r_U from (25) and for m from (26), equation (M3) can be solved to yield the supply price of loans in closed form

$$i = \left[\frac{z(\theta + 1)}{\sigma} \left(\frac{q(1 + \mu + a)r}{\mu} + \frac{bw\Gamma}{k} \right) \right]^{1/e} (i_b)^{e_b/e}. \tag{27}$$

This equation makes it clear that the interest rate responds positively to changes in r, Γ and θ. An increase in r raises both real and nominal incomes causing the interest rate to go up. A higher Γ has the same effect. A rise in θ implies a fall in base money supply relative to capital stocks. Hence, the interest rate rises. The partial relationship between i and Γ appears as the curve marked i in figure 10.5. The equilibrium condition (M4) is satisfied at the point of intersection of the i and r_U curves. It should be noted that when the restriction (10) on the interest elasticity of deposit demand is met, then, from (25) and (27), this implies that, in graphical terms, a change in r will produce a larger shift in the i curve than in the r_U curve.

The demand for F-sector investment (equation (13)) is represented by the ID curve in the northwest quadrant.[30] After substituting for r_U from (25) and noting that $r_U = i$ in equilibrium, the saving–investment equality (M2) can be used to derive the supply of saving to the F-sector or the warranted rate of growth

$$g = \frac{1}{1 + \Gamma} \left[\frac{s(a + \mu)r}{\mu} - \delta \right]. \tag{28}$$

This is given by the SS curve in figure 10.5. At a low enough profit rate given by $\delta\mu/s(a + \mu)$, available saving is sufficient only to meet the government deficit so that the warranted growth rate is zero. Hence, SS has a positive r-intercept. It may be checked that the restriction (23) for stability implies that the SS curve has to be flatter than the ID curve.

Finally, the lower quadrants of figure 10.5 show the relationship between $\theta - g$ and $\theta - \Gamma$ that must, from equation (M5), hold in the steady state. These are represented by the curves marked VG and VR in the two quadrants. Faster growth reduces the ratio of money to capital so that θ must rise. Similarly, a higher ratio of K_U to K_F also raises θ since the deficit, and indirectly the money supply, is positively related to the F-sector capital stock.

4   Growth and other responses to parametric changes

Figure 10.5 has been constructed to yield an initial equilibrium at which the informal-market interest rate i exceeds the formal-sector profit rate r.

Table 10.2. *Comparative statics results*

Response	tog	Γ	θ	p	i	Real wage U	Real wage F	Total employment	Bank access
$\uparrow\sigma$	+	+	+	−	−	+	+	+	+
$\downarrow z$	+	+	+	−	−	+	+	+	−
$\uparrow\delta$	+	?	−	?	?	?	?	?	+
$\uparrow n$	−	−	−	+	+	−	?	−	+
$\uparrow s$	−	+	?	−	−	+	+	+	+
$\downarrow\mu$	?	?	?	?	?	?	?	?	?
$\downarrow a$	+	−	?	?	?	?	?	−	−
$\uparrow i_b$	−	?	?	?	?	?	?	?	+

This is only to emphasize the stylized fact that most informal borrowers have to pay a high rate of interest; the model itself implies no necessary relationship between the two profit rates. We now consider a number of parametric changes around an initial equilibrium to study the full responses of growth, employment, real wages, and the distribution of capital and bank finance between the two sectors (results appear in summary form in table 10.2).

Pure monetary policy

Consider first the effects of a relaxation of monetary control by the central bank. In the absence of securities markets, the only instrument of pure monetary policy available (barring the regulated bank interest rate which is considered separately below),[31] is the reserve requirement of the banking system so that σ, the deposit-base multiplier, rises. From (27), the *i*-curve in figure 10.5 shifts to the right and the interest rate falls at the initial level of Γ. That is, the excess supply of bank deposits is absorbed by means of a reduction in the loan rate *i*. As informal-sector investment rises in response, the capital stock ratio Γ begins to rise. The rise in I_U also raises market demand in the formal sector. The *SS* curve in the northwest quadrant rotates to the right which raises capacity utilization and the profit rate at the initial growth rate. As the profit rate *r* rises, there is a spurt in F-sector investment and growth accelerates.

The rise in the F-sector profit rate feeds back into the informal loan and U-sector commodity markets: as equations (27) and (25) reveal, both the interest rate and the U-sector profit rate rise. It can be shown, however, that the net effect of this feedback is only to dampen the initial stimulus to U-sector investment. Therefore, the new equilibrium must have a higher growth rate and a higher ratio of K_U to K_F. Both of these results entail a rise in θ, i.e., a rise in the capital-to-base money ratio. The rise in θ itself will further alter the values of all other variables since it raises the interest rate from (27). In the end, higher values for g, Γ and θ will all be sustained.

The possibility of a reversal of the initial impact on the interest rate cannot be ruled out. Although i falls initially, the rise in r (and in θ induced by the rise in r) serves to raise it in the sequel (see equation (27)). Total differentiation shows that the interest rate falls if and only if:

$$\delta + g > (1 + \Gamma)\epsilon r. \tag{29}$$

We shall suppose that formal-sector savings are insufficient to meet the fiscal deficit plus formal-sector investment, i.e., $\delta + g > sr$. From (M2), this is equivalent to the restriction $si > g_U$ so that the informal sector contributes more to saving than it uses by way of investment, i.e., it is a net source of savings for the rest of the economy. But when this restriction is coupled with the stability condition (23), we have:

$$\delta + g > sr > (1 + \Gamma)\epsilon r \tag{30}$$

which implies (29). The economics behind this result is as follows: as r rises, given the stability condition, saving out of F-sector profits rises more than total investment does. At the same time, the rise in Γ assures a rise in net (positive) savings supplied by the U-sector. Equilibrium is restored only if savings out of U-income falls which requires that the interest rate falls. Hence, around a stable equilibrium, the assumption that the U-sector is a net source of savings is *sufficient* to ensure that the interest rate falls with an easing of monetary policy.

A fall in the price of the informal good also then follows. Real wages of workers in both sectors rise. Total employment will rise on two counts: due to the rise in capacity utilization in the F-sector and, given that the labor–capital ratio is higher in the U-sector, due to the rise in the capital stock ratio in favor of that sector. Does the informal sector gain greater access to the banking system? The expansion of bank deposits assuredly increases the relative importance of bank intermediation and reduces the role of the informal credit market. However, the fact that the informal sector itself acquires a larger share of the capital stock entails that it also increases its share of bank loans.

Structural change

Virtually identical results obtain when the impulse producing the initial reduction in the informal loan rate is a fall in the parameter z in equation (26). A fall in z signifies a shift in wealthholders' preferences favoring informal investments/loans and away from bank deposits. This may be brought about by exogenous changes in the structure of the economy that reduce the risks or otherwise raise the attractiveness of informal-sector activity. It is easy to see, following the above analysis, that growth must accelerate and capital shift toward the informal sector. While the capital/money ratio rises, bank intermediation *declines* and a larger proportion of the increase in informal-sector investment is financed by the informal credit market, i.e., access to bank loans declines.

These results underline the significance of the structural determinants of the finance constraint on the informal sector. Gains in growth, employment, and real wages are obtainable however this constraint is relaxed, whether through an expansion of formal banking or the opposite. As we shall see, no generalization is possible linking changes in access to bank funds and changes in either overall growth or growth of the informal sector. Indeed, from the previous paragraph, it is legitimate to conclude that any increase in the ability of formal intermediaries to attract deposits can hurt rather than encourage the informal sector and overall growth.[32] There are obviously strict limits, dictated by prudential norms, to the efficacy of monetary policy in easing this constraint. Beyond that, the practice of "financial reforms" as a way of accelerating growth and employment appears to be of dubious value.

Fiscal expansion

The impact effects of a rise in government expenditure are considerably more complex than those due to an easing of monetary restraint. Fiscal expansion is the normal mode of expansion in the money supply – financial structure, in other words, typically renders the distinction between monetary and fiscal policies superfluous. On the real side, an immediate effect is to shift the SS curve up as the required saving to meet the deficit rises. Accordingly, F-sector utilization and profit rates go up. The higher demand for output raises the informal price p while also raising the interest rate: with a low enough interest elasticity of deposit demand (see restriction (10)), the net profit rate $(r_U - i)$ declines and, as noted in the earlier section, this impact alone will serve to crowd informal-sector investment out. On the financial side, however, a rise in the deficit spells a rise in the base money supply so that the capital–money ratio θ must also decline and, from equation (27), the interest rate will be pushed down as the supply of deposits increases. The overall impact on the interest rate of these conflicting influences may work out either way. Hence, which way Γ or i will shift is indeterminate. Differentiating the model with respect to δ shows that growth accelerates and the money–capital ratio rises (θ falls). It also shows that the necessary and sufficient condition for Γ to rise is:

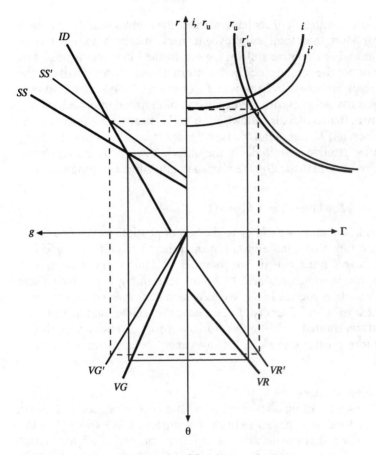

Figure 10.6   The consequences of fiscal expansion

$$e > 1 - \frac{bwN}{qX + pN} - \theta \left[\frac{\epsilon_0}{\epsilon_0 + \epsilon r} \right]. \tag{31}$$

With (10) holding, the higher the initial value of θ and the smaller the responsiveness (ϵ) of formal-sector investment to its profit rate, the greater the likelihood that condition (31) will be met and Γ will rise.[33]

Thus, in economies which have a relatively underdeveloped system of formal financial intermediation (high θ), we expect fiscal expansion to stimulate informal-sector accumulation. This is the situation depicted in figure 10.6: the i curve shifts to the right showing the dominance of the money stock effect over the flow demand effect. The rise in Γ also flattens out the SS curve and, together with the rise in the growth rate, dampens the shifts in the VG and VR curves. The figure only shows the final position after all these effects have worked themselves out. Assuming Γ rises, it follows that total employment rises due both to the rise in utilization and the relative shift of capital to the labor-intensive sector. Whether or not the capital stock in the informal-sector rises relative to the formal sector, its access to bank funds – or share of total bank lending – unambiguously goes up with the expansion of financial intermediation.

As drawn, figure 10.6 also shows a fall in the steady-state interest rate. However, even if Γ rises, a fall in i is not guaranteed: this is easy to see by reversing the relative magnitudes of the shifts in the i and r_U curves shown in the figure. Mathematically, the necessary and sufficient condition for i to fall is

$$\delta + g\Gamma + (1 + \Gamma)er < \theta[g - (1 + \Gamma)er]. \tag{32}$$

If this condition holds, we end up in the best of possible worlds as a fall in the interest rate also signifies a fall in the price of the informal good so that real wages must rise in both sectors. A fear of inflation and of crowding out is sometimes held to be the restraining factor over fiscal policy in countries such as India. We have seen, that in the short run, such fears appear to be well founded. But we have also shown that they are not necessarily warranted over a longer horizon. More definitive conclusions require more precise knowledge of investment behavior and economic structure.

Wage changes

We next take up a set of wage experiments. First, consider a rise in the formal-sector wage (a rise in the parameter n). We know from the previous section that this has a neutral impact on both F-sector output and on the U-sector profit rate. But from (27), as the wage increase is passed through in the formal-sector price q, the interest rate must rise at the initial Γ: the i-curve in the northeast quadrant of figure 10.7 shifts up. As informal-sector investment falls in response, the supply of saving curve SS in the northwest quadrant rotates anti-clockwise, capacity utilization drops, and growth is retarded along the investment demand curve ID. A stable dampening effect ensues in the market for informal-sector investment: the r_U and i curves must shift down without nullifying the initial downward push to Γ. As both g and Γ fall, the VG and VR lines become flatter and the capital stock is reduced in the new steady state relative to the stock of money. It also follows that total employment falls.

Figure 10.7 shows a steady-state rise in the interest rate commanded by informal loans. Along the same lines as before, total differentiation of the model with respect to n establishes this to be the case if (but not only if) the informal sector is a net source of savings. The same condition also

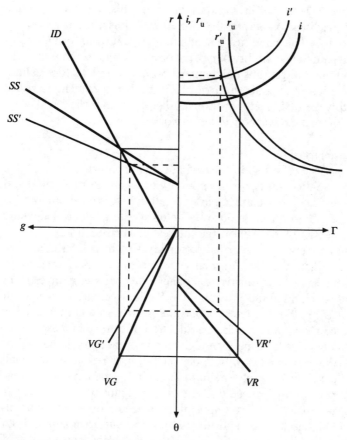

Figure 10.7   Impact of a rise in the F-sector wage

guarantees that the net dynamic effect of the fall in g, which reduces p, and the fall in Γ, which raises it, is to increase p. Clearly, then, real wages of U-sector workers must fall. To assess the effect on F-sector real wages requires consideration of the relative magnitude of the price response to the wage increase: the rise in wages is of course matched by a proportionate rise in the price q so that the real wage rises (falls) if the elasticity of the price response is less (more) than unity. This intriguing possibility – of a fall in the F-sector real wage in response to a rise in its nominal wage – is realized if a, the propensity of F-sector workers to consume the informal good, satisfies a lower bound.

Suppose now that the nominal wage rises proportionately in both sectors, i.e., that w rises. Much the same results, as with a rise in the formal-sector wage alone, i.e., the growth rate falls, Γ falls, and total employment declines. As before, the interest rate rises if the U-sector is a source of savings. This condition also guarantees that the informal-sector price rises. Again the possibility of p rising proportionately more than the rise in the nominal wage, thus reducing real wages in both sectors, cannot be ruled out. Finally, in contrast to the previous two experiments, a rise in the nominal wage of U-sector workers alone does raise their real wage while reducing the real wage of F-sector workers.

A rise in saving

The effects of a rise in the saving rate are shown in figure 10.8. Initially, the SS line shifts down as required saving to meet the fiscal deficit declines. The immediate impact is a fall in F-sector output and the U-sector price. Both effects reduce the interest rate as deposit demand falls. If the restriction in (10) on the interest elasticity e holds, then on balance, the net return to informal-sector investment rises: the interest rate falls more than does the informal-sector profit rate. As I_U responds, the capital–stock ratio Γ must rise. Higher informal-sector investment will stimulate demand in the F-sector – the SS line becomes steeper – but the initial *shift* in SS dominates so that the growth rate is permanently lowered. Since Γ rises and g falls, the direction of change in θ cannot, in general, be determined. A small enough responsiveness of formal-sector investment (the parameter ϵ) will render the fall in the growth rate small relative to the rise in Γ so that the ratio of capital to base money θ rises. The contrary case, of a reduced θ, is depicted in figure 10.8.

The steady-state interest rate and informal-sector price fall unambiguously: growth deceleration and the rise in informal-sector capital both reinforce the initial drop in the informal-sector price. Hence, real wages of workers rise. Total employment may well rise: while employment falls in the F-sector, capital is now weighted more heavily in favor of the labor-intensive informal sector. Although bank intermediation itself may decline (θ may rise), it is interesting to find that the growth in saving unambiguously raises the U-sector's access to the banking system. It is no surprise in the present model that a rise in thriftiness far from raising the growth rate actually reduces it. Nevertheless, it should be emphasized that the informal sector conforms, in this experiment, to the orthodox expectation of a fall in the cost of capital and a rise in its supply although income distribution shifts in favor of labor.

A fall in the mark-up rate

In the short run, we have seen that a fall in the F-sector mark-up rate μ (that is, a rise in the product wage of the F-sector) raises demand

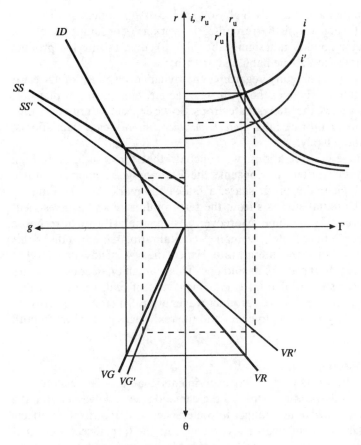

Figure 10.8   The dynamic effects of a rise in saving

and, as a result, both formal-sector output and informal-sector price go up. However, the profit share falls more steeply than the rise in capacity utilization so that r falls. Given that F-sector investment responds positively to both capacity utilization and the profit rate, the response of the growth rate to a rise in the product wage is ambiguous as it depends on the relative magnitudes of the response parameters ϵ_1 and ϵ_2. This ambiguity is not resolved merely by adding more plausible detail to investment behavior in equations (13) and (14). Thus, we may assume that ϵ_1 is not a constant but varies inversely with the profit share $\mu/(1 + \mu)$, i.e., that the profit share stimulus to investment is stronger the lower is the profit share itself. And that is not all. Regardless of the specific assumption on investment demand and of the initial level of the profit share, it is easy to see that a sufficiently high (low) value of a produces an "exhilar-ationist" ("stagnationist") response: if workers' consumption of the formal-sector good is not significant (high a), then raising the product wage cannot stimulate demand and growth.

There is less ambiguity regarding the dynamic response of U-sector investment: not only does the profit rate there rise but also, for plausible parameter values, the interest rate drops. So we expect I_U to rise over time when the mark-up rate falls. *Ceteris paribus*, this makes a stagnationist response more likely.

From these considerations, we conclude that for a sufficiently high propensity of workers to consume the F-sector good coupled with a relatively high initial profit share, a fall in the mark-up will stimulate growth. The initial stimulus from the rise in informal-sector investment will reinforce this outcome. Moreover, a stagnationist growth response will necessarily raise θ, i.e., the money–capital ratio assuredly falls in this case which will raise the interest rate. Hence, the new steady-state level of Γ may or may not be above the old one. This ambiguity, of course, carries over to the response of total employment and of real wages. In other words, a fall in the F-sector product wage, even if it stimulates growth, may well reduce total employment and the real wages of workers in both sectors.

Modernization

Next, we consider two experiments that can be related to a process of modernization. One, on the demand side, involves a fall in the parameter a: exogenous changes in preferences or demonstration effects serve to raise workers' propensity to consume the formal-sector good at the expense of the informal-sector good. Modernization and the growth of "consumerism" are, of course, associated with rising incomes but it is nevertheless relevant to relate them to such exogenous changes as well. Another, affecting supply, refers to technical improvements that raise labor productivity (a fall in the parameter a) and reduce the labor–capital ratio of formal-sector production. Again, this process is frequently linked with rising wages and capital–labor conflict but some of it appears exogenously as when firms devise new strategies to reduce their dependence on labor.

Take the latter change first. Closer inspection of the model shows that a enters the model exactly as does the wage parameter n. Conclusions for this case are therefore ready to hand. As a falls, the rate of growth rises, the informal sector's share of the capital stock rises and the money–capital ratio falls. The rise in Γ will produce higher employment and so will the rise in capacity utilization that accompanies the change. On the other hand, there is a direct loss of employment associated with modernization of the formal sector. On balance, total employment will rise provided the F-sector's initial share of employment is suitably small. The interest rate and the informal-sector price fall so that real wages rise in both sectors. These favorable results from a reduction in the formal sector's labor intensity may, at first blush, appear counter-intuitive in a model with a demand constraint. However, the fall in labor costs also reduces the price of formal-sector output and reduces the interest rate. Once again, it is the finance constraint on the informal sector that produces the clue to these surprising results.

A fall in a raises F-sector output and profits while reducing the U-sector price in the short run. Total differentiation of equation (M3) also shows that nominal income rises and, therefore, the interest rate rises. It follows that returns in the informal sector are doubly squeezed (on the price and cost sides). While capital accumulation in the formal sector is stimulated, it is retarded in the informal sector. It can be shown that while the capital stock unambiguously shifts away from the informal sector, the growth rate rises if (not only if) the informal sector is a net source of investible resources for the rest of the economy. These effects can be expected to reduce total employment. While the immediate impact on p is negative, the rise in capacity utilization and the fall in Γ serve to raise it. On balance, the full impact on the interest rate and the informal-sector price cannot be easily signed so that real wages may go either way.

The interesting outcome of this exercise is that the model associates faster growth with these changes in labor intensity or consumer preferences (reductions in a and α). In practice, of course, episodes of rapid growth are often associated with modernization which cannot be reduced to isolated changes in technology or preferences. Recognition that such episodes may also be accompanied by changing conditions of bargaining between capital and labor prevents any firm conclusion from being drawn as regards the overall impact on employment and income distribution.

Interest rate liberalization

Finally, consider a relaxation of the ceiling on the bank (lending and deposit) rate, i_b. As i_b rises, bank deposits rise at the expanse of funds supplied in the informal market causing the informal rate i to rise as well and, of course, formal investment declines. Graphically, the impact effect is to shift the i-curve in the northeast quadrant leftward and to shift the ID curve to the right. As investment is adversely affected in both sectors, formal-sector capacity utilization suffers a fall; demand and price for the informal good fall in consequence. From (25), it is clear that the decline in the formal profit rate must shift the r_U-curve downward causing a further loss of informal investment. It can be readily shown that the growth rate and formal profit rate fall unambiguously in the new equilibrium. Together with the decline in capacity utilization, this ensures that the informal sector's share of banking lending rises.

However, the final impact on both Γ and i is indeterminate. For one thing, the first-round cuts in activity levels and the price p reduce the transactions demand for deposits which would tend to reduce the informal interest rate from the supply side. For another, shrinking formal investment allows increased access to bank funds for informal investors which would reduce i from the demand side.[34] These effects will shift the i-curve to the right opposing the impact effect and leaving the net outcome ambiguous. Mathematically, Γ *rises* if and only if

$$\left[\frac{e_b}{i_b} - \frac{\beta\theta}{g(1+\theta)}\right][\delta + (1+\Gamma)\epsilon_0]$$

$$< \beta(1+\Gamma)\left[\frac{\theta\epsilon r}{g(1+\theta)} + 1 - \frac{bwN}{qX+pN} - e\right] \tag{33}$$

and i *falls* if and only if

$$\left[\frac{e_b}{i_b} - \frac{\beta\theta}{g(1+\theta)}\right][\delta + (1+\Gamma)\epsilon_0]$$

$$< \beta(1+\Gamma)\left[\frac{\theta\epsilon r}{g(1+\theta)} + 1\right] + \frac{e_b}{i_b}\Gamma g. \tag{34}$$

In the new equilibrium, a fall in i and a rise in Γ are more likely the larger the decline in formal investment (a large value for β) and the smaller the rise in bank deposits (a small value for e_b). Perhaps more to the point, for given values of β and e_b, these outcomes are more likely in an under-developed financial system, i.e., with a suitably large initial value of θ.

5   Conclusion

It is important to alert the reader about the limitations of the approach we have adopted. While focussing on the question of financial allocation, we have left out two important issues relating to financial policy: the nature and extent of instability originating from the financial system (liquidity and confidence crises) and the existence of hedge assets such as gold. Though liberalization remains the key word, caution and even ambivalence appear to have crept into orthodox prescriptions particularly after the adverse growth and destabilizing consequences of experiments in the Southern Cone of Latin America.[35] The latter omission may be justified on the assumption that the holding of hedge assets is relatively unresponsive to interest rates perhaps because of general lack of confidence in financial institutions (i.e., that this is a slow-changing variable).[36] Nor have we considered the complications arising from financial openness but this would properly be the subject of another essay. On the other hand, we believe that the model can be extended to include an inflation process, working capital financing, and cost-push pressures as in some neo-structuralist models, and a more complete account of the rationing process.

Within the approach adopted, the following conclusions emerge.

First, we contend that the liberalization debate has overblown the importance of finance, as opposed to real-side factors, in the accumulation and investment allocation process. The real side is of fundamental importance in structuring the financial system in the first place so that policies affecting the financial system are of second-order significance (at least as far as growth, as opposed to short-term macroeconomic objectives, is concerned).

Evidence from cross-country analyses of Africa and Asia shows that the volume of informal finance often rivals or surpasses that of formal finance (Tun Wai, 1980; see also World Bank, 1989, chapter 8).[37] Moreover, its relative importance is inversely related to the level of economic development and directly to the relative size of the informal *real* sector. This suggests that the dualism of real activity and of financial intermediation are closely related. Were financial dualism and the exclusion of small firms and producers simply the result of government policy, as previous theorizing has argued, then, we must assume that the degree of financial repression among LDCs varies inversely with income levels, an assumption that is scarcely tenable.

There is some support, based on Granger tests, for the view that financial development leads economic growth (Jung, 1986). However, besides the fact that the measures of financial development used are simply ones such as the currency–demand-deposit ratio, allowance has to be made for the fact that "the deliberate establishment and promotion of financial institutions in many less developed countries might reflect (a) belief in the 'supply-leading' relationships between the two developments." (Jung, 1986, p. 333) At any rate, the link between finance and growth must be separated from the link between financial structure and real structure. Even if finance leads growth as has traditionally been argued in the finance and development literature, the real structure may lead financial structure.

Second, the model establishes that even with a dualistic real side, lifting interest rate ceilings on banks causes the rate of growth to decline just as has been contended by neo-structuralists. This underlines the importance of the differences in investment behavior and finance constraints associated with dualism. On the other hand, liberalization also enhances the access of informal firms to bank finance. In fact, in a financially underdeveloped economy, we have argued that the informal interest rate falls, real wages rise and the informal share of the capital stock also rises, possibly aiding total employment. While regressionists might derive some comfort from this, it is more noteworthy that the fall in growth is associated with what might be termed (real) structural retrogression.[38]

Third, assessments of the *relative efficiency* of formal and informal finance cannot be divorced from the economic and non-economic factors supporting real-side dualism which is mirrored in financial dualism. Suppose, for example, that the criterion is capital productivity; then, the returns to capital should be equalized in the two markets, i.e. the formal profit rate r and the informal interest rate i should be equalized. But this is only a partial index of economic welfare in an economy where the relevant markets are distorted. Even ignoring such considerations as the promotion of employment, there are two targets (growth and efficient allocation) but only one instrument, the formal interest rate, which the literature has emphasized. By working with a single real sector, neo-structuralists are able to focus on the volume of finance to the exclusion of its allocation.[39]

The formal financial system has a strategic significance in economic development that economic historians have traditionally emphasised.[40] A low interest rate policy (as opposed to strategic credit allocation) may not be the most important element in effecting it. Nevertheless, the orthodox case for liberalization does not commend itself and its promise of a level financial playing field is illusory.

Notes

I am particularly grateful to Bill Gibson and Jong-il You who provided detailed and searching criticisms on an earlier version of this chapter. I would also like to acknowledge with thanks the comments I received from Gerry Epstein, Herb Gintis, Stephen Marglin, Lance Taylor, two anonymous referees and participants at the Amherst-WIDER conference. I have done my best to respond to them all.

1 The prescription is based on the theory of financial repression initially formulated by Shaw (1973) and McKinnon (1973). For a more recent exposition, see Fry (1988).

2 Gonzales Arrieta (1988) provides a thorough survey of the relevant empirical literature. Based on evidence for Turkey, Akyuz (1991) has argued that a higher interest rate, by redistributing income from high-saving corporate borrowers to low-saving household creditors, may well reduce the saving rate even though it deepens financial intermediation.

3 That is, lenders' own equity forms the credit base.

4 See Taylor (1983 and 1991), van Wijnbergen (1983a and 1983b), and Buffie (1984).

5 Repressionists often refer to political influences on the rationing process while neo-structuralists typically leave the process unspecified.

6 Repressionists justify their position by pointing out that (1) if informal lenders are in fact genuine *intermediaries*, then, they too must hold reserves to ensure liquidity: if anything, the lack of deposit insurance or access to the central banks makes required reserves greater; (2) informal credit allocation suffers from poor information, restriction to insiders, and the inability to offer anything but small, non-lumpy credits. On both counts, informal lending is comparatively inefficient (Cho, 1990).

7 For a theoretical analysis of the sources of real-side dualism, see Rao (1993b).

8 It is well known that agriculture (which we regard as part of the informal sector) is a source of saving for the rest of the economy. In most LDCs, it is equally evident that the formal sector (including the government) absorbs savings from the rest of the economy.

9 Although the direct conversion of saving into investment (including *physical saving*) remains noteworthy, it seems reasonable to suppose that self-finance is not the source of growth at the margin: the existence of a variety of loan markets attests to the importance of financial needs being met, however imperfectly, through market exchange.

10 We intend agriculture to be included in the U-sector. The formulation that follows ignores land rent; in effect, the supply of land is augmentable through capital investments.

11 The banking system is allowed to stand for all types of organized or formal financial intermediaries.

12 While both real and financial sides are thus isomorphically differentiated, we do not distinguish between fixed and working capital requirements nor assume that the formal sector is self-financing – either severally in respect of fixed capital or jointly (via the banking system) in respect of working capital. See Fitzgerald and Vos (1989) for a model formulated along these lines.

13 The price formation rule cannot, in the two-sector case, be simply re-interpreted in terms of the fixity or variability of the *real wage* and thereby reduced to the conditions of capital–labor bargaining.

14 A more complete model would incorporate an inflation mechanism whereby nominal wages respond to the real cost of living. This requires that the rate of inflation also enter the loan supply function as an argument.

15 As an alternative, it could be assumed that the U-sector product wage and, given the demand assumptions, the real wage of U-sector workers are fixed. Observe also that a fixed nominal wage in the F-sector, under conditions of oligopolistic price behavior, may be rationalized in terms of ability to pay or profitability as the determinant of wage bargaining.

16 Letting U-workers consume the F-sector good also will not alter anything essential in the model.

17 As noted above, excess capacity operation in the formal sector is treated as the normal case and will be the only case treated in this chapter.

18 The provision of public goods for agricultural production is an important instance where government expenditure drives private investment. The determinants of growth and distribution in such a context are examined in Rao (1993).

19 The implicit story here is that control, if not ownership as well, of F-sector firms is strongly concentrated in the hands of a small proportion of the wealthholding public.

20 Bank lending and deposit rates are taken to be identical thus suppressing bank profits and costs.

21 The money–wealth ratio is, in the context of the present model, close to Goldsmith's (1969) "financial interrelations ratio," a general measure of financial development.

22 With strictly regulated rates, some cross-subsidization between bank loans to formal and informal sectors is implied. Alternatively, if banks are permitted to compete freely with informal financial intermediaries, differentiated rates on bank lending for the two sectors will prevail. Bank funds may still be rationed among informal seekers of funds permitting rents to emerge as an enforcement device. The formal model here is more in keeping with the second of these two scenarios though the first one is not, in practice, without significance.

23 For the sake of algebraic simplicity, we ignore working capital needs in both sectors.

24 If there are strong Engel effects in workers' consumption and if workers' demand for the F-sector is suitably large, then, this $p - X$ relation may be negative. We do not pursue this possibility here noting only that it is of a piece with other possible demand linkages between the two sectors, indicated earlier, which run counter to the assumption of independent demands.

25 The output multiplier equals $(1 + \mu)/(a + s\mu)$. It is the reciprocal of the weighted sum of the propensity to save (s) out of profits and F-sector workers' propensity to consume the informal sector good (a), the weights being the profit and wage shares respectively.

26 Even for $a = 0$, this condition is satisfied for an initial profit share in excess of one half, which is likely to hold.

27 If divergent growth is allowed, we need to introduce real time, specify the initial values of θ and Γ, and study the evolution of the system.

28 In the short to medium run, the expected rate of profit is assumed to be a function of the realized profit rate r.

29 In practice, it is reasonable to take government revenues to be closely related to the formal-sector capital stock. If expenditure levels are also similarly related, then, the simple representation in the text follows. This assumption needs to be suitably modified where fiscal revenues and expenditures relate to the dualist structure in more complex ways.

30 Note that the intercept of this curve equals $\epsilon_0 - \beta i_b$, which we shall take to be positive which assures the existence of equilibrium.

31 It is the absence of open market operations due to the lack of private portfolios with securities, as distinct from *regulated* bank portfolios, that makes monetary policy distinctive in LDCs.

32 At least in this sense, enhanced *efficiency* in formal intermediation contributes neither to growth nor to a wider access by excluded borrower segments to formal finance.

33 This restriction is automatically satisfied when the "crowding-out" restriction (10) does *not* hold.

34 Shahin (1990) argues that raising the formal loan rate causes the informal loan rate to decline. As the supply of bank loans rises, unorganized loan demand falls and so does the unorganized loan rate. However, this is based on a model with a wholly exogenous and undifferentiated real side.

35 See McKinnon (1982), Diaz Alejandro (1985), and Grabel (1992).

36 At any rate, we believe that portfolio substitution occurs largely between formal and informal financial options. For a detailed consideration of these issues, see Danby (1992).

37 In the Indian case, for example, the size of the informal financial sector has been estimated at between 30 percent and 50 percent of total credit flows (Timberg and Aiyar, 1979 and NIPFP, 1988).

38 Though partial integration of the two financial markets permits substitution at the margin, the above two conclusions may be interpreted as reflecting financial complementarity on average. Ghate (1992) reaches a similar conclusion based on an empirical morphology of formal and informal financial markets.

39 An otherwise odd implication of the neo-structuralist position – that in the absence of a regulated bank lending rate, wealthholders would choose to allocate a *smaller* fraction of their portfolio to the informal credit market notwithstanding that market's lower reserve leakage and competitiveness – may be rationalized as an example of second-best logic.

40 See, for example, Lee (1992) on the South Korean case.

11 International profit rate equalization and investment: an empirical analysis of integration, instability, and enforcement

Gerald A. Epstein

1 Introduction

Few doubt that we now live in a global economy. Billions of dollars are traded on the foreign exchanges every day. Many major companies earn most of their profits overseas. World stock markets never close; they just follow the sun. And tardy conference papers can be FAXed across the ocean in a matter of minutes.

Yet there is little agreement among economists about the nature and implications of this globalism. Many economists argue that as communications and transactions costs have plunged, we are quickly moving to an integrated world that approximates the Walrasian ideal.[1] Here, product flows equalize prices, and capital flows equalize rates of return around the globe. In this world, nations and economic agents are price takers: governments, workers, and businesses have very few degrees of freedom to alter prices, wages, taxes, profit rates, or working conditions. They must take them as given – or see their markets, jobs, or investment vanish to some other locale.[2]

Other economists have raised doubts about the Walrasian view. One group suggests that, because of the high degree of instability that has characterized the global economy in the last several decades, the markets for goods and capital remain segmented, despite the decline in transactions costs. According to this argument, instability generates uncertainty, which reduces the responsiveness of agents to international profit differentials. Krugman (1989), Dixit (1988), Dumas (1988), and others have built models which show that in the presence of exchange rate instability (combined with sunk costs, transactions costs, or indivisibilities), goods (or capital) will not flow to equalize prices or profit rates. A decline in instability will increase the responsiveness of goods and capital flows to differentials. Gordon (1988a) attributes this lack of integration and increase in instability to a deterioration of the post-war Social Structure of Accumulation resulting from the decline of US hegemony.

A second view (Epstein and Gintis, 1992) argues that the Walrasian model is wrong because it assumes that transactions are costlessly enforced through third-party enforcement.[3] In fact, many domestic and virtually all international transactions lack such third-party enforcement. In its absence, international lenders will lend or invest only as much capital as their enforcement capabilities will allow. As a result, borrowers will be rationed. Thus, flows of goods and capital will be attenuated. Prices and profits will fail to equalize no matter how stable are exchange rates, interest rates and prices.

According to this enforcement view, while transactions costs may have come down in the post-war period, enforcement costs have not. The relative decline of US economic power since the middle 1960s and the (possibly related) reduced legitimacy of military intervention have resulted in enforcement problems which have inhibited the flows of goods and capital that would equalize prices and rates of return on capital investment internationally.

Thus, while the Walrasian view implies that declining transactions would lead to a higher degree of international integration over the post-war period, the instability and enforcement views doubt that such integration has proceeded so rapidly or so far. The instability and enforcement views differ, however. While the first suggests that stability in macroeconomic variables and low transactions costs are sufficient to integrate international capital and goods markets, the second argues that they are not. Enforcement power is also required.

A great deal of empirical evidence on some aspects of international integration has been generated over the last several years. Some of the evidence has led to increasing doubts that declining transactions and communications costs are resulting in an integrated, Walrasian world. Many studies have shown that the "law of one price" appears to fare, calling into doubt the degree of integration of goods markets.[4]

Short-term financial markets, on the other hand, appear to fare somewhat better. The covered-interest parity theorem appears to hold for short-term assets in major financial centers.[5] Yet, Zevin (1992) doubts that declining transactions and communications costs have much to do with it. Short-term financial markets, he argues, are no more integrated now than in the late nineteenth century. Moreover, on uncovered assets, where exchange risk is not eliminated, interest parity fails, even after trying to account for "time varying" risk premia.

Evidence against the integration of long-term financial markets is, perhaps, the most striking. Feldstein and Horioka (1980) and a host of other economists since then,[6] have shown that, even in advanced capitalist economies, there is a high correlation between domestic saving and domestic investment. This appears to contradict the Walrasian model which would predict that domestic investment draws on a pool of world savings and therefore should be independent of domestic savings.[7]

In sum, while there appears to be increasing integration of short-term financial markets over the post-war period (though, not, perhaps, relative to the late nineteenth century), the markets for goods, and savings do not seem to be highly integrated.

While there has been a good deal of research on the integration of financial markets, there has been relatively less research on the degree to which the markets for real investment are integrated internationally. The Feldstein–Horioka findings are suggestive, but they do not present direct evidence on the responsiveness of domestic investment to foreign factors, or on the degree to which profit rates equalize internationally in response to capital flows.[8]

Koechlin (1992) has estimated time-series and time-series cross-sectional investment equations for seven major OECD countries to assess the impact of foreign profit rates and other factors on domestic manufacturing investment. He found very little influence of foreign variables on domestic investment, and concluded that domestic manufacturing investment in the major OECD countries is primarily domestically determined.

On the other hand, Stevens and Lipsey (1988) estimated investment equations for a panel of US multinational firms.[9] They found that foreign investment displaced domestic investment in most of the firms in their sample.

In related work, numerous studies have been undertaken of the determinants of US foreign direct investment. While foreign direct investment (FDI) is essentially a financial flow and therefore does not constitute real investment, neither is it simply a portfolio investment. FDI confers an element of control, at least in principle. Evidence on the responsiveness of US FDI to relative rates of return, tax rates, and unit labor costs, though rather mixed, does indicate some degree of responsiveness.[10] But no study has assessed the degree to which responsiveness to foreign variables has increased over the post-war period.

Similarly, there have been very few studies of the tendency toward international profit rate equalization.[11] Harberger (1987) found large disparities in rates of return to capital in a sample of developed and less-developed capitalist economies. But he gave no estimates of the degree to which these returns were converging over time. Ando and Auerbach (1988, 1990) estimated the cost of capital in Japan and the US over the post-war period, and have found an increasing gap over time, at least by some measures.[12] McCauley and Zimmer (1989) similarly find large gaps in the cost of capital with no apparent tendency toward equalization. Gordon (1988a) estimated the coefficient of variation of domestic profit rates across a sample of countries, and found no tendency for the coefficient to decline.

In the next section I present new estimates of the degree to which rates of return to investment have equalized over the post-war period. I develop estimates of the rate of return to US foreign direct investment in different locales and analyze the trend in their dispersion and correlation over time. I find only modest support for the Walrasian view that international profit rates have tended toward greater equalization over the post-war period. While there was some decline in the dispersion of profit rates in the 1960s, by the 1970s and 1980s, dispersion increased or at least, failed to further decline, by most of the measures analyzed.

Correlations of profit rates suggest that in the 1970s and 1980s cross-country profit rates are more highly correlated than in the 1960s; however, in the latter period, they were no more correlated than they had been in the 1950s, once again calling into question the Walrasian view of international integration.

It is more difficult to distinguish between the enforcement and the instability view. I present some evidence that instability by itself cannot account for the absence of an increased international profit rate equalization in the 1970s and 1980s.[13]

In section 3, I present some estimates of the degree to which US foreign direct investment (US FDI) responds to international differentials in rates of return and relative rates of economic growth. I find that US FDI is responsive to both profit rates and relative economic growth, but that, once again, there is no apparent tendency toward an increased responsiveness over time, as the Walrasian approach would suggest.

In the last section, I discuss the policy implications of the enforcement approach.

2   International profit rate equalization

In this section I try to answer the question: have intercountry profit rates become more equal over the post-war period? The Walrasian view would suggest that, holding all else equal, the decline in transactions and communications costs should have brought about a decline in the variations in profit rates among countries. The instability view would imply that, in light of the increased international instability in the last several decades, one would not expect to find an increased tendency toward equalization. The enforcement view is more equivocal about the likelihood of such

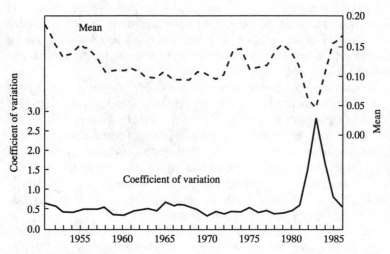

Figure 11.1   Coefficient of variation and mean of profit rates, 1951–86 (book values)
Sources: US Department of Commerce.

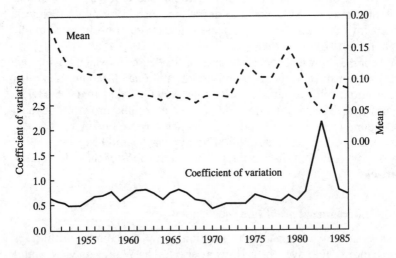

Figure 11.2   Coefficient of variation and mean of profit rates, 1951–86 (market values)
Sources: US Department of Commerce.

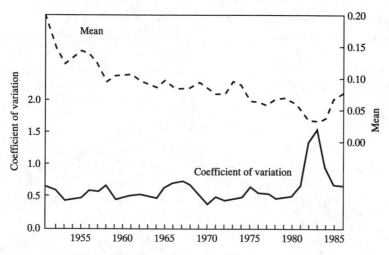

Figure 11.3 Coefficient of variation and mean of profit rates, 1951–86 (replacement values)
Sources: US Department of Commerce.

equalization. To the extent that there has not been a decline of enforcement costs, especially since the late sixties when US power began to seriously erode, one would not expect to find such a tendency toward equalization.

The major difficulty in assessing these views is the lack of comparable data on profit rates across a broad range of countries. Lack of good data for many countries, differences in accounting practices, and complications arising from estimating after-tax income, create tremendous difficulties in making such cross-country comparisons.

To try to overcome at least some of these problems, in this chapter I analyze the rates of return to US foreign direct investment abroad. The advantages of using these data are that they tend to be relatively comparable across countries and over time. Moreover, the data are available for a fairly wide range of countries over virtually the whole post-war period. Of course, these data have disadvantages as well. First, time series are available only for before-tax income.[14] Second, there are valuation problems since the direct foreign investment data are valued at book value. As discussed below, I have tried to correct for these valuation problems.[15]

Figure 11.1 presents data on the coefficient of variation and mean of rates of return to US FDI abroad for twenty-one countries from 1951 to 1986.[16] As figure 11.1 indicates, there has been no decline in the coefficient of variation since the early fifties. In fact, there was a large increase in the eighties!

Table 11.1. *Average coefficient of variation of rates of return: book, market, and replacement values selected periods, 1951–86*

	Book	Market	Replacement
1951–60	0.479	0.606	0.518
1961–70	0.507	0.677	0.553
1971–86	0.760	0.807	0.665
Memorandum			
1951–86	0.612	0.715	0.592

Notes: Book: Book value measure of foreign direct investment (FDI) position; Market: Market value measure of FDI; Replacement: Replacement value measure of FDI.

Figure 11.1 may be misleading however. One problem with the data in figure 11.1 is that the denominator, the FDI position, is measured at book values and therefore the ratios may be distorted by variations in inflation and exchange rates. To try to correct for these measurement errors, I have used two market-based estimates of the US FDI position: the first measures the US foreign direct position at market values and the second measures FDI at replacement cost.[17]

Figures 11.2 and 11.3 use foreign direct positions measured at market values and replacement costs, respectively. They present the coefficients of variation and mean profit rates from 1951 to 1986. The alternative measures appear to make little difference in the estimates of the coefficient of variation. As in figure 11.1, there is no apparent decline in variability of profit rates since the 1950s. Moreover, they show the same bulge in the early 1980s.

Table 11.1, which presents the averages of these coefficients of variation over selected time periods, confirms the impression given by the graphs: if anything, the variability in profit rates has gone up over time.

While the coefficient of variation is useful for standardizing the units in which one measures standard deviations, it has the problem that temporary changes in the mean may swamp changes in the standard deviation. For example, as figures 11.1–11.3 make clear, the plunge in the mean profit rate during the depression of 1982 generated a huge increase in the coefficient of variation during that period. To eliminate the sensitivity of the measures to short-term changes means one can examine the standard deviation of returns.

Figure 11.4 presents data on the standard deviation of the rate of return

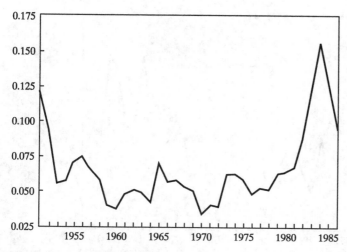

Figure 11.4   Standard deviations of rates of return to US direct investment abroad, 1951–86 (book values)
Sources: US Department of Commerce.

to US FDI across the twenty-one countries from 1951 to 1986. The figures are standard deviations of income to book values of the US FDI position. Figure 11.4 suggests that in the early post-war period, roughly until 1970, the standard deviation declined.[18] However, around 1970, the standard deviation of returns began to increase, and by 1985 the standard deviation was even higher than in 1951.

Hence far from exhibiting a steady decline associated with falling transactions costs, the variability in profit rates mirrors the ebbs and flows of US international power which, according to many observers, peaked in the late 1960s. Or perhaps, it reflects the fall and rise of international instability.

Figure 11.5 shows the standard deviation of rates of return, with FDI measured at market value. These data show the same basic pattern as the book value data. Once again, the standard deviations follow a U-shaped pattern, not a steady decline as suggested by the Walrasian transactions cost approach.

Replacement cost data, however, present a picture much more consistent with the Walrasian view. Figure 11.6 presents the standard deviation of rates of return, this time with FDI measured at replacement cost. The pattern of these data seems markedly different from the others. Rather than following the U-shaped pattern, they indicate a decline in variability, at least until 1970 or so.

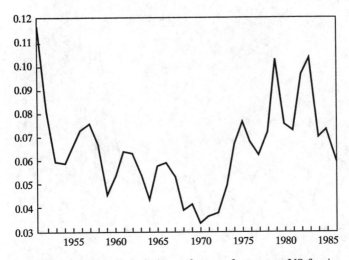

Figure 11.5   Standard deviations of rates of return to US foreign direct investment abroad, 1951–86 (market values)
Sources: US Department of Commerce.

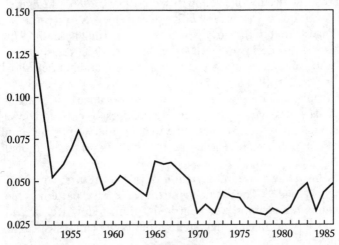

Figure 11.6   Standard deviations of rates of return to US foreign direct investment abroad, 1951–86 (replacement costs)
Sources: US Department of Commerce.

Table 11.2. *Average standard deviations of rates of return: book, market, and replacement values selected periods, 1951–86*

	Book	Market	Replacement
1951–60	0.067	0.069	0.069
1961–70	0.051	0.050	0.051
1971–86	0.074	0.069	0.038
Memorandum			
1951–70	0.059	0.060	0.060
1971–86	0.066	0.064	0.050

Notes: See table 11.1.

Table 11.2 presents data on averages of the standard deviations over selected time periods. The standard deviations of rates of return using book and market values fall between the 1950s and the 1960s, they rise again in the last period, 1971–86. In the latter period, variability was at least as great as it had been in the 1950s. However, rates of return using replacement data (column 3) show a very different pattern. F-tests confirm that over the three periods, variability of these rates of return did decline as the declining transactions costs view would suggest.

In sum, most measures of variability – the coefficients of variation and two of the three standard deviation measures – suggest that profit rate variability did not decline over the whole post-war period. However, one measure – the standard deviation of rates of return when the capital stock is measured at replacement value – indicates that profit rate variability has declined since the 1960s.

Implicit in the discussion so far has been the idea that profit rate variability reflects only transactions costs and enforcement costs. However, as the instability approach suggests, profit rates will also be more variable if factors which determine profit rates are also more variable. Casual empiricism suggests that shocks in the 1970s and 1980s were larger, if not more variable, than in previous periods. Perhaps variability of these shocks masked a decline in profit rate variability that would have occurred in their absence.

Table 11.3 suggests that, as expected, some shocks were more variable, particularly in the 1970s. The cross-country variation in inflation increased dramatically in the 1970s and again in the 1980s. On the other hand, there is no apparent increase in real GDP growth variability, as measured by standard deviations over time.[19] The intercountry standard deviation of exchange rate changes show the same pattern as inflation,

Table 11.3. *Standard deviations of inflation, exchange rates: real GDP growth, 1953–86*

	Inflation rate	Exchange rates	GDP growth
1961–70	0.16	0.11	0.03
1971–86	0.52	0.36	0.03
Memorandum			
1953–71	0.08	0.13	
1973–86	0.21	0.31	

Notes: The variables are the time period averages of the standard deviations across countries of the rate of change of the consumer price index (inflation), rate of change of exchange rates (exchange rate change) and the rate of real GDP growth (GDP Growth). See table 11.7 for sources.

with the 1980s and especially the 1970s showing large increases in variability. F-tests confirm that in the case of inflation and exchange rate changes, variability did increase in the 1970s and 1980s, relative to the previous period.

Can this variability in inflation and exchange rates account for the absence of the decline in profit rate variability by most of the measures? Would the coefficients of variation and standard deviations of profit rates measured by replacement cost have declined by even more if these "shocks" had not occurred?

To try to answer this question I performed a number of experiments. First, I regressed the coefficient of variations of profit rates by all three measures of profit rates against the coefficient of variations of the shock variables and a time trend.[20] The coefficient of variation of real GDP growth and inflation were significant determinants of the coefficient of variations of rates of return. However, in none of the cases, did the time trend show a decline in variability after 1970, after holding constant for variations in exchange rates, inflation rates, and real GDP growth. And in the case of book and market value calculations, the time trend remained positive and significant for the period 1964–86.

I performed the same tests for standard deviations of return. In general, standard deviations of exchange rate changes, inflation changes, and real GDP growth had very little explanatory power for standard deviations in rates of return by any measure. And, once again, there was no evidence of a negative time trend after 1970 for any of the measures after taking into account these shocks.

Table 11.4. *Average standard deviations of "shock free" residuals: market and replacement cost*

	Market	Replacement
1951–70	0.032	0.032
1971–86	0.038	0.020

Notes: The data are based on standard deviations of the residuals from regressions of profit rates, with FDI measured at market and replacement cost, against inflation, changes in exchange rates, the rate of growth of real GDP, and a time trend. The difference between the two replacement figures is significant at the 10 percent level.

Second, I regressed each country's profit rate (both market value and replacement value) against that country's inflation rate, exchange rate change, and real GDP growth. For most countries, exchange rates, inflation rates, and real GDP growth were important determinants of profit rates.[21] I then used the residual from each country's regression as a measure of the "shock free" rate of profit and took the standard deviation across countries of these residuals as a measure of the variability of the shock-free rates. If profit rate variability declined over time, holding constant for these shocks, then the variability of these residuals should have declined.

Table 11.4 presents averages of these "shock-free" standard deviations over selected periods. The data indicate that the standard deviations of profit rates, measured at replacement costs, did decline between 1961–70 and the 1970–86 period by almost one-third, while the "shock-free" market value variation did not decline over the period.[22]

Hence, accounting for shocks does not change the basic results. For one measure, standard deviation at replacement cost, there does seem to have been a decline in variability after 1970. On the other hand, the other measures show no such decline after 1970, and, in fact, many indicate a rise in cross-country variability in the 1970s and 1980s.

Is there a way to choose among the different measures? First, apart from short-term fluctuations in means, coefficients of variation seem to be a better measure of variability than the standard deviation because they are comparable across measures and time.

Second, book value measures seem definitely inferior to measures of investment position that attempt to account for changes in the value of the capital stock over time. The choice between market value and replacement value is less clear. Given data problems, it is probably safe to

Table 11.5. *Average pair-wise correlation coefficients: selected periods,*
1951–86

	Profit rates	Inflation	Real GDP growth
1951–60	0.38		
1961–70	0.03	0.24	0.13
1971–86	0.23	0.30	0.28
Memorandum			
1951–86	0.37		

Notes: Profit rate figures use replacement cost figures for FDI. All average
correlations are significantly different from zero. The differences among them are
also significantly different from zero.

conclude that replacement cost measures are more problematic than
market values. Unless market values are equal to replacement costs,
market values should more closely reflect marginal, as opposed to average
profit rates. However, given the high variability, and apparent irrationality in stock markets, replacement values may be a better reflection of
underlying rates of return.

Another measure of the degree of international integration is the degree
of correlation among returns in different countries.[23] I examined the
pair-wise correlations between the returns of the twenty-one countries in
the sample plus the United States to see whether there was a tendency for
the correlations to rise over time. Table 11.5 presents data on the averages
of these correlations. Between the 1961–70 period and the 1971–86
period, there was a dramatic increase in the average correlation coefficient
of profit rates (using replacement cost figures). This might seem to imply a
huge increase in integration. Part of the increase probably reflects the
increased correlation of inflation and GDP growth reflected in the second
two columns of the table.[24] However, the average correlation coefficient
for the 1971–86 period of 0.23 is lower than that for the 1951–60 period!
Table 11.5, then, does not provide support for the Walrasian view.

3   Foreign direct investment and profit rates: is there a relation?

The results of the previous section are easy to summarize. By most
measures, there was no discernible decline in intercountry variations in
profit rates, over the whole post-war period, even after accounting for
shocks. By one measure, the standard deviation of rates of return, with
FDI measured at replacement cost, there was a substantial decline over

the whole period. Can we find other evidence to distinguish between the Walrasian, instability and enforcement approaches? In this section I look at US FDI flows for additional evidence on the degree of integration of international capital markets. The Walrasian approach would suggest that declining barriers toward international investment flows would increase the rate of investment and, perhaps, the sensitivity of that investment to profit rate differentials, all else constant. Those increased flows, in turn, should bring about a reduced variability in intercountry profit rate differentials.

The enforcement model, on the other hand, suggests that, while capital might flow in response to profit rate differentials, declines in transactions costs would not, by themselves, lead to increased responsiveness to profitability if enforcement problems are on the rise. Finally, the instability approach would imply a *decline* in responsiveness to profit rates in response to increases in instability, holding all else constant.

The data on profitability and FDI in the sample of twenty-one countries used here should shed some light on the responsiveness of FDI to profitability. Of particular interest is the degree to which FDI flows respond to profit rate differentials between the home country (in this case, the United States) and the foreign country. Both neoclassical and non-neoclassical models of investment would suggest that the higher the differential between foreign rates of return and the US rate of return, the higher the rate of investment, holding all else constant.[25]

Keynesian and neo-Keynesian theories of investment suggest that the rate of growth of output is also a positive determinant of investment.

Finally, industrial organization models of oligopolistic rivalry and FDI suggest that FDI is motivated by the relative growth of foreign markets relative to the home market.

A general, extremely simplified model of FDI would suggest that

$$FDI^i = F(R^i - R^{US}, G\dot{D}P^i - G\dot{D}P^{US}) \tag{1}$$

where: FDI^i = rate of US foreign direct investment into country i
        R^i = rate of return to FDI in country i
        R^{US} = rate of return to investment in the US
        $G\dot{D}P^i$ = rate of real GDP growth in country i
        $G\dot{D}P^{US}$ = rate of real GDP growth in the US

In addition, the rate of FDI may change over time and the responsiveness of FDI to profit differentials may change over time as well. Hence I have included a time trend and an interactive variable for time and profit rates.[26]

Table 11.6 presents estimates of a version of equation (1). The dependent

Table 11.6. *Foreign direct investment, profit rates, and real GDP growth, 1954–86* (Dependent variable: change in the log of FDI measured at replacement cost)

	C	RP	RP × Time	GDP	Time	Rho	DW	R^2	F
1 Australia	0.10 (12.0)	0.92 (4.88)		-0.5E - 2 (-0.20)			1.67	0.41	12.0
2 Brazil (1962–86)	0.11 (0.60)	-7.8 (-2.7)	0.31 (2.47)	-0.4 (-3.4)	0.003 (0.33)	0.57 (2.62)	2.18	0.53	6.5
3 Canada	0.11 (6.77)	-0.29 (-1.03)		0.60 (2.07)	-0.003 (-3.07)		1.55	0.33	6.2
4 Chile (1962–86)	-0.05 (-0.40)	-0.47 (-0.27)		4.0 (1.6)			2.47	0.02	1.3
5 Colombia	0.05 (3.9)	-0.86 (-3.13)		0.02E - 2 (0.61)			1.64	0.20	6.0
6 France	0.13 (9.20)	1.34 (5.02)		-0.40 (-1.09)			1.83	0.43	12.9
7 Germany	0.12 (12.1)	1.03 (5.48)		-0.10 (-0.9)			2.48	0.47	15.2
8 India	0.03 (1.3)	-0.02 (-0.04)		-0.50 (-0.11)			2.03	-0.09	2.2
9 Ireland	0.04 (0.52)	5.63 (3.53)	-0.27 (-3.08)	0.20 (0.22)	0.007 (1.94)		1.48	0.26	3.7
10 Italy	0.16 (8.4)	1.53 (3.69)		-0.50 (-0.86)			2.02	0.29	7.5
11 Japan	0.12 (5.85)	0.49 (1.71)		0.20 (0.40)			2.35	0.10	2.9

12 Mexico	0.08 (3.1)	0.72 (1.8)		0.30 (0.77)			1.57	0.09	2.6
13 Neth.	0.19 (3.0)	−2.7 (−1.2)	0.16 (2.0)	−0.50 (−0.6)	−0.002 (−0.83)		2.32	0.08	1.7
14 Panama	0.07 (3.7)	0.66 (3.7)		0.30 (1.23)			2.42	0.29	7.6
15 Phillip.	0.04 (1.9)	0.35 (1.1)		0.50 (1.1)			2.45	0.02	1.4
16 S. Africa	0.07 (0.4)	−0.67 (−0.5)	0.065 (1.6)	1.11 (1.6)	−0.02E − 2 (−0.03)		1.64	0.26	3.9
17 Spain	0.05 (1.1)	2.29 (6.3)		0.2 (1.3)	0.006 (2.6)	−0.34 (−1.89)	1.96	0.52	9.0
18 Sweden	0.15 (6.9)	1.95 (4.6)		−0.05 (−0.38)			1.83	0.38	10.7
19 Switz.	0.11 (4.1)	1.45 (5.02)		−1.36 (−2.02)			1.90	0.42	12.6
20 UK	0.09 (9.2)	0.40 (1.87)		−0.40 (−0.83)			1.64	0.05	1.9
21 Venez.	−0.08 (−0.52)	1.46 (1.89)	−0.07 (−2.6)	−0.05 (−0.04)	0.08E − 2 (0.16)		1.97	0.14	2.3

Notes: Dependent variable: Change in the log of the US foreign direct investment (FDI) position. Independent variables: *RP*: Profit rate, with FDI measured at replacement cost, lagged one period; Profit rate measured relative to earnings price ratio (*EP*) in US stock market (*RP − EP*): *RPXTIME*: Relative profit rate lagged times a time index, lagged one period; GDP: Rate of real GDP growth, lagged one period, relative to real GDP growth in the US (*GDPUS*) (*GDP − GDPUS*). See table 11.7 for sources.

variable is the change in the log of the stock of FDI, which is a measure of the change in the rate of US FDI into each country. The independent variables are: (1) *RP*, the rate of return to US FDI minus the rate of return to investment in the US measured as the earnings price ratio in the US stockmarket, both lagged one period; here the stock of FDI is measured at replacement cost; (2) *RPXTIME*, the relative rate of return times a time index; this is one measure of the degree to which the sensitivity of foreign investment changes over time, lagged one period. (3) *GDP*, the rate of growth of real GDP in the host country minus the rate of growth of real GDP in the United States, both lagged one period. (4) *Time*, an index for time, to measure the degree to which the rate of growth of FDI changes over time.

Table 11.6 reports ordinary least-squares regressions for each of the twenty-one countries.[27]

The results indicate that for many countries, the relative rate of profit is a significant, positive determinant of FDI. Of the twenty-one countries, fifteen had coefficients of the expected sign that were significant at least at the 10 percent level. In very few cases did the sensitivity of the rate of investment to profit rates increase over time. (Only Brazil, the Netherlands, and South Africa have positive significant time/rate of profit interactive terms.) Similarly, very few of the time trends had significantly positive coefficients (only Ireland and Spain). A positive time trend would represent an increase in the rate of FDI. The relative rate of growth of GDP has a significant, positive effect on FDI in only a few of the countries. This result is puzzling, both theoretically, and in light of the results reported below. Finally, it is important to note that, for most countries, these regressions leave unexplained a good deal of the variation in changes in FDI rates.

Thus, while FDI does seem sensitive to profit rates, there is little evidence that sensitivity has changed over time. These results are basically confirmed by table 11.7 which presents a pooled cross-section/time-series analysis of the same data. The regression shows that for the pooled sample, the (lagged) relative profit rate is a significant determinant of FDI. At the same time, there is no evidence that the rate of FDI increased over time, or grew more sensitive to the profit rate differential between the US and the host country over the post-war period.[28]

Unlike the individual country regressions, relative real GDP growth was a positive and highly significant determinant of FDI in the pooled sample.[29]

As with the country regressions, a good deal of variation in FDI remains to be explained. Here, the adjusted R^2 is 0.13. Also, as indicated by the beta coefficients and elasticities, the impact of relative GDP growth is relatively small. The impact of the relative profit rate is larger. The

Table 11.7. *Cross-sectional time-series regressions: foreign direct investment, rates of return, and real GDP growth*
(Dependent variable: change in the log of FDI position, measured at replacement cost)

	RP	RP × time	GDP	Time	$\bar{R}^2$	F
RP relative to US	0.723	− 0.011	0.376	− 0.06E − 2	0.13	5.2
	(2.79)	(− 1.00)	(2.2)	(− 0.65)		
Beta coefficient	0.284		0.086			
Elasticity	0.004		0.057			

Notes: The regressions were run on a pooled sample of the 21 countries over the period 1951–86; however, the period started later for some of the countries because data on GDP were not available until later for some countries. The total number of observations was 672.

Dependent variable: Change in the log of US Foreign Direct Investment position.

Independent variables: *RP*: Profit rate, with FDI measured at replacement cost, lagged one period; profit rate measured relative to earnings price ratio (*EP*) in US stockmarket *RPXTIME*: Relative rate of profit, multiplied by the time index, lagged one period; *GDP*: rate of real GDP growth, lagged one period relative to real GDP growth in the US (*GDPUS*) (*GDP − GDPUS*); the equation also included an (insignificant) constant term and (mostly significant) country dummies.

Sources: US Department of Commerce, Bureau of Economic Analysis, various issues; US Department of Commerce, various issues; Eisner and Pieper, 1990; IMF, *International Financial Statistics Yearbook*, 1983 and 1988; US Council of Economic Advisers, 1990.

beta coefficient indicates that a one standard deviation increase in relative profit rates generates more than a quarter standard deviation change in investment rates. The effect is certainly not massive, but it is significant.

In sum, US FDI appears to respond to profit rate differentials between the US and "host" countries, and possibly, to differentials in real GDP growth. There is, however, no evidence of increased profit rate sensitivity or increases in the rate of flows over the post-war period as a whole. These results seem to provide little evidence in support of the Walrasian view. There is also little evidence that responsiveness has fallen over time, as the instability view would suggest. However, more work is necessary before we can clearly distinguish between the enforcement and instability view. Finally, there remains a large amount of unexplained variation in investment flows.[30]

Much work remains to be done to improve upon the estimates presented here. Most important would be to estimate domestic investment equations to see the degree to which they respond to foreign profit rates.

Elaborating on the panel data approach of Stevens and Lipsey (1988) would be particularly useful.

In terms of the estimates presented here, it would be useful to estimate after-tax rates of return for FDI and perform the analysis of section 2 on those estimates. One suspects, though, that tax rates have converged over time, so that, if anything, taking taxes into account would only increase the variability of returns. One can also include tax and political-economic variables in the FDI equations in this section.

Finally, in future work it would be important to better distinguish between the enforcement and instability explanations of segmented international markets.

4   Policy implications

The data presented here suggest that there is little tendency toward increased equality of profit rates to US FDI over the entire post-war period. This provides further evidence against the Walrasian view of increased international integration, at least since the 1970s. The data also suggest that increased instability, by itself, cannot account for the lack of tendency for profit rates to equalize over the entire period, raising some doubts about the instability argument as a complete explanation.

The data on investment also do not augur well for the Walrasian view; there has been no apparent increase in the responsiveness of US FDI relative profitability over the post-war period.

In short, there is little evidence that there has been an increased tendency for investment to move in response to international differences in profit rates.

What are the policy implications of this fact and of the support it lends to the enforcement approach to international capital movements?[31] The main implication is that, contrary to the global Walrasian view and much current thinking, progressive movements and policymakers may make policies which cause lower domestic profit rates relative to foreign profit rates without generating large and immediate capital outflows, *ceteris paribus*.[32] Does this mean that governments, labor unions, and citizens can act as if their economy is a closed economy, that the much ballyhooed trend toward "globalization" places virtually no constraints on national policy, as earlier "insular" macroeconomic models implied? For better or worse, things are not so simple.

More likely, the increasing integration of international financial markets do in fact place severe constraints on national policy, but not in the way and not of the same types as implied by the global Walrasian model. As Epstein and Gintis (1992) argue, any coherent analysis of the current international financial markets must be able to accommodate the fact that there can be sizeable international capital flows of great significance, but that there are also serious constraints on those flows. Along these lines, Epstein and Gintis (1992) develop what we call an "asset balance model" of international capital flows. The model starts from the simple idea that lenders want to be repaid and borrowers would rather not repay. Thus lenders need some type of enforcement of loan contracts if they are going to be willing to lend. In domestic lending there are various legal remedies which a lender can bring to bear to improve the chances of being repaid. In other words, there is exogenous enforcement of contracts, of which the legal system is a good example.

In international capital markets, however, there is no exogenous enforcement of that type. Credit contracts must be enforced through some other, endogenous mechanism – collateral, credit rationing, threatened economic sanctions, threatened economic or military sabotage.

In such markets, it is obvious that the neoclassical Walrasian ideal in which powerless individuals face a given interest or profit rate that will clear the market for lending or investment is incorrect. Instead, the asset balance model implies that power relations are central to international credit markets.

Given the need to enforce international credit contracts, lenders will be reluctant to lend enough that would equalize profit rates; some countries would face credit rationing. Similarly, other countries will be reluctant to borrow as much as they could because they may be worried that in the future their credit will be abruptly cut off. Thus, according to the asset balance model, the world will be filled with *reluctant lenders* and *reluctant borrowers* which will result in widespread credit rationing – far different from the Walrasian view that flexible interest rates will clear the market for international lending and borrowing.

Technically, this model implies that countries have what we call a target net asset (or debt) position, 1*, measured as a percentage of GDP or capital stock. These target positions, which are likely to be constant for significant periods of time, will represent the structural position of countries in the world economy.[33] Creditor countries, that is countries that have a large net asset target (and positions) are likely to be few and far between. They must have the international economic, political, and military power to enforce their international loans and investments. Great Britain and the US had such power in their heyday. Oil-producing countries, in contrast, have not had such structural power so their net asset positions quickly faltered. Lending by these creditor countries is thus limited by the extent of their enforcement power.

In order to attract loans and investment, debtor countries, by contrast, must make themselves vulnerable to potential creditor sanctions. For example, they must orient a large part of their economies toward exporting and make themselves dependent on imports; in this way, debtor countries expose themselves to potential creditor sanctions and thereby reduce the likelihood that they will renege on their loan commitments.

The model is thus consistent with the idea that countries can export and import huge amounts of capital on a net basis over a limited period of time. But then, eventually, their ability to export or import capital will be limited by their economic growth and the enforcement capacities of creditors. The model is thus also consistent with the Feldstein–Horioka (1980) result that over the long term, countries' investment and savings rates will be highly correlated since, over the long term, the amount that countries can lend and borrow is strictly limited. Finally, the model is consistent with high levels of gross mobility of short-term capital, a dominant feature of contemporary international financial markets. Such two-way flows of short-term capital do not raise the same enforcement problems as imbalanced net accumulation of credit or debt.[34]

The policy implications of this enforcement approach are quite different from either the "global Walrasian view" or the "insular economy" view. The global Walrasian view suggests that nations have no ability to set interest rates or profit rates differently from those abroad, though they do have the ability to borrow and lend as much as they would like at the market determined rate of return. The insular model, by contrast, argues that economies have wide latitude in setting interest and profit rates, but are rather constrained in their ability to borrow abroad.[35]

The asset balance model, by contrast, implies a set of opportunities and constraints on policy that are reducible to neither those of the Walrasian or the insular models. For the asset balance model, confidence in enforcement abilities is a much more important determinant of capital flows than are interest rate or profit rate differentials. In addition, the asset balance model is consistent with the important fact that, in the current period, the international financial markets are characterized by a high degree of gross mobility of capital combined with a relatively low degree of net mobility.

A number of important implications follow from these two considerations. In the short run, in contrast to the "insular model," countries may be severely constrained from undertaking policies which reduce "confidence in the enforcement" of credit contracts. Institutional, legal, or political changes which call into question the enforcement power of creditors are likely to engender short-term capital flight which is not easily combated by simple increases in interest rates, because the ability to borrow on a net basis becomes much more limited. In this sense, the danger of capital flight becomes more severe than recognized in either the insular or Walrasian models.

By the same token, however, the ability for countries to alter interest rates and especially profit rates (through monetary policy, tax, and other social and government policies) may well be much greater than the global Walrasian model implies because of the limits enforcement requirements place on capital mobility.

In the long run the differences between the asset balance model and standard models is even greater. Here the model suggests that for countries to remain net creditors or debtors, in the long run they must not simply choose to lend or borrow; they must create and maintain economic structures and institutions which will sustain their net asset positions. More specifically, creditors must possess institutions and behaviors that give them credible economic, political, and military power which will allow them to enforce their creditor position; and debtors must make themselves vulnerable to sanctions from creditors by, for example, making their economies open and dependent on exports and imports, and dependent on borrowing from abroad. Countries which want to be internationally unengaged and large creditors will not be able to do so; countries will, similarly, have to choose between being autonomous and independent, on the one hand, or borrow large sums on a net basis, on the other. Neither the Walrasian nor the insular models imply such severe institutional constraints for long-term international creditors and debtors (Epstein and Gintis, 1992).

Notes

The author thanks: Emily Kawano and Mehrene Larudee for research assistance; Samuel Bowles, Herbert Gintis, and Mehrene Larudee for very helpful discussions; Tim Koechlin, Robert Eisner and Paul Pieper for data; and WIDER, the University of Massachusetts Faculty Grants Office, and the University of Massachusetts Economics Department for financial assistance.

1 Ironically, both neoclassicals and some radicals share this image. For the neoclassical version of this model, see, for example, Frenkel and Razin (1992). For the radical version of this, see, for example, Wachtel (1990).

2 For example, progressive macroeconomic policy becomes highly problematic since globalization makes domestic investment more responsive to profit rates, and therefore makes "wage-led" growth less likely to succeed. See the papers by Blecker (1989) and Bowles and Boyer, this volume. For notions of wage-led growth and the related, but not identical notions of stagnationist growth see Bowles and Boyer (1990) and Marglin and Bhaduri (1990) and David Gordon's paper, this volume. For a general summary of the policy implications of these different approaches, see Epstein and Gintis (1992), as summarized there in tables 7.6 and 7.7.

3 Those papers build on the work of Bowles and Gintis; see, for example, their 1988 paper. See Eaton, Gersovitz, and Stiglitz (1986) for a survey of the extensive theoretical

literature on enforcement as applied to international lending. Also, see Lessard (1986) for a useful discussion of these issues and Lipson (1985) and Frieden (1989) for historical work along these lines.

4 See Krugman (1989) for a review of this literature.

5 See Gintis (1988) for an excellent survey. Also see Frankel (1993).

6 See Gintis (1986) and Frankel (1993) for reviews.

7 Epstein and Gintis (1992) argue that the high correlation of domestic saving and investment is explained by countries' having target net asset and net debt positions generated by creditors' enforcement capabilities and debtors' ability to attract capital by credibly committing themselves to repay. See more below.

8 The high correlation between domestic savings and investment could be explained by the low degree of substitutability between domestic and foreign real capital (Frankel, 1993, Krugman, 1989), by government reactions to external asset or debt accumulation (Bayoumi, 1989; Feldstein and Bacchetta, 1989), or both (Epstein and Gintis, 1992).

9 They were able to only get data for seven firms operating both domestically and abroad. Thus, their results are rather limited.

10 See Koechlin (1992), Hartman (1985), Slemrod (1989), Hines (1988), Jun (1989a, 1989b).

11 There have been numerous studies of equalization of real interest rates (e.g., Cumby and Obstfeld, 1984).

12 In the latter period, Ando and Auerbach (1988) find that including capital gains on land can bring up the rate of return in Japan to approximately US levels. However, it is not clear that such capital gains ought to be included.

13 However more work needs to be done to adequately distinguish these two views.

14 Precise after-tax data are available only for the relatively few benchmark years. It is possible to construct some estimates of after-tax returns (see Koechlin, 1992). Some economists (Hartman, 1985) claim that, because of the nature of the US tax structure, taxes do not affect FDI decisions of mature US firms. However, Hartman's view has been increasingly challenged. (See the papers by Jun, Slemrod, Hines, and Boskin and Gale, Grubert and Mutti).

15 See the data appendix for more details on the data set.

16 The coefficient of variation is the standard deviation divided by the mean. This is the measure used by Gordon (1988) in his analysis of international integration. The countries are: Australia, Brazil, Canada, Chile, Colombia, France, Germany, India, Ireland, Italy, Japan, Mexico, the Netherlands, Panama, Philippines, South Africa, Spain, Sweden, Switzerland, United Kingdom, and Venezuela. The list was determined by data availability over the 1951–86 period for both the income data and the capital stock data described below. The data are for all industries. Separate data for manufacturing are not available for the capital stock data.

17 Robert Eisner and John Pieper generously supplied these data. See Eisner and Pieper (1988) and the data appendix for a description of them.

18 The tendency still appears even if one excludes the period before 1954, when there was a precipitous decline.

19 The GDP data include all twenty-one countries only from 1964 on.

20 In most cases I used the coefficient of variation of the shock variable and its square. In several cases I also corrected for serial correlation.

21 A time trend was also included to account for the changes in countries' rates of profit over time.

22 The "shock free" coefficient of variation of returns measured at replacement values did not decline, however.

23 Zevin (1992), for example, focusses on correlations. See also King *et al.*, 1990 and the references cited there.

24 See Checci (1989) for further evidence on business cycle synchronization in the 1970s and 1980s. In fact, the major reason for the low correlation coefficient in the 1961–70 period is the fact that so many profit rates were negatively correlated. The absolute value of the correlation coefficient in the 1961–70 period was 0.45 versus 0.33 in 1971–86.

25 See Bhaskar and Glyn and Gordon "Horse Before the Cart . . ." both this volume for useful surveys of investment models.

26 In addition to these variables, one could include tax measures and political economic variables to measure enforcement power. See Koechlin (1992) for some interesting results along these lines. Koechlin's work does not look at the responsiveness to profitability per se; nor does it look at change in responsiveness over time. But it is a very useful complement to the work presented here.

27 I only report the "best" equation from a number of specifications for each country. I also estimated the system using "seemingly unrelated regressions" with similar results.

28 I also tested to see whether the relative profit rate between the host country and the mean of the other host countries was significant, but multicollinearity prevented good estimates of that relationship.

29 This raises a puzzle. The significance of GDP does not appear to be as robust to changes in the set of countries included as does the profit rate which is highly robust.

30 I also pursued an alternative test to see whether responsiveness to profit rate differentials increased over the post-war period. I estimated country regressions with polynomial distributed lags, over several different time periods to see whether the lags with which investment responded to profit rate differentials declined over time. However, there was no discernible pattern across countries. Finally, I estimated some regressions to test whether profit rate differentials declined in response to FDI flows, as theories that investment flows reduce profit rate differentials would imply. I estimated vector auto-regressions (VAR's) for FDI flows and profit differentials. In most cases, profit differentials declined (with a lag) to investment flows. More research is required, however, to determine how robust this relationship is.

31 See Epstein and Gintis (1992) for a more extended discussion of these points.

32 Note, however, that policies which reduce the profit rate may have negative consequences on the macro economy for other reasons (see Bowles and Boyer and Gordon, this volume, for example).

33 Epstein and Gintis (1992) present econometric evidence that countries have such net asset targets and that their net asset ratios adjust to these targets (1*) within three to five years, on average.

34 See R. Prem (1994) for further discussion of this point.

35 Interestingly, lending abroad is not seen as problematic.

Part five

Macroeconomic policy: new rules of the game

12 Growth, distribution, and the rules of the game: social structuralist macro foundations for a democratic economic policy

David M. Gordon

It is now widely recognized that most of the advanced macro economies have performed poorly for much more than a decade.[1] Despite the continuing ideological celebration of free markets and *laissez-faire*, the spread of right-wing economic policy during the 1980s failed to reverse and in some respects deepened this longer-term economic stagnation.[2] But what is the alternative?

This chapter outlines the promise and possibility of a democratic strategy for stronger macro performance in the advanced countries.[3] It builds upon the premise that a sound long-term macroeconomic strategy should contribute at least to the macroeconomic objectives of assuring employment opportunities for everyone and promoting high rates of environmentally sustainable productivity growth in ways which directly foster the broader social goals of greater equity and greater democracy. It outlines a strategic approach to macroeconomic policy which could serve simultaneously to achieve these macroeconomic objectives and social goals.[4]

This argument is developed here through application of a "social structuralist" model of the capitalist macro economy. This model, rooted in a burgeoning non-mainstream macro literature, highlights the relationships among power, distribution, utilization, and investment in a capitalist macro economy. I begin in section 1 with a small model emphasizing these core macro relations. In section 2 I outline some empirical evidence supporting a particular specification of key equations in that model for the case of macro economies like the United States, as well as briefly considering evidence on its applicability to a broader range of advanced economies. Section 3 applies that specific structuralist model to the consideration of macro policy, showing how democratizing the institutional rules of the game in many of the advanced economies, through greater equity of income distribution and greater democratic participation, could potentially enhance macroeconomic performance.

1   A social structuralist macro model

The spare macroeconomic model introduced in this section highlights the interaction among power, the factor distribution of income, the activity level of the economy, and the pace of accumulation. It builds upon a growing literature exploring a synthetic non-neoclassical macroeconomics, an alternative which can most compactly be characterized as "structuralist" macroeconomics.[5] A wide variety of contributions, building on a number of different traditions and camping under different nomenclatural umbrellas, have pointed over the past decade toward this kind of synthetic structuralist approach.[6] This brief section begins with a generic presentation of this kind of approach and then further specifies its relationships, in what I call a "social structuralist" model, to illustrate the determination of equilibrium in an economy with an institutional structure like that prevailing in the post-war United States economy.

A generic structuralist macro model

To keep the basic relationships as compact as possible, we can begin with a reduced-form model of a real open private economy. It is a *real* macro economy in the sense both that all variables are determined in real terms (and price determination is therefore set aside) and that credit- and money-market operations are left as exogenous to the model (leaving, for example, the real interest rate as an exogenous variable in the system).[7] It is a model of an *open* economy in the limited sense that at least one important reflection of international linkages, the net trade balance, is determined endogenously. It is a model of a *private* economy, finally, in the elementary sense that both government purchases and interest rates are determined exogenously.

This schematization involves a *reduced-form* model in a dual sense. First, it relies on an equation in which the profit rate, as a key measure of aggregate distribution, is determined directly in a behavioral equation rather than, more appropriately, as an algebraic function of the level of real productivity, of real wages, and of other deductions from total output; this equation therefore provides a reduced-form rather than a structural expression for the determination of the profit rate. Second, it implements the heterodox Cambridge savings hypothesis through a consumption function in which consumption is a negative function of the profit rate rather than a direct function of the (normalized) flows of wage and capital income; this involves the obvious assumption that the relative sizes of wage and capital flows are themselves a function, other things equal, of the aggregate profit rate and thus represent a reduced-form expression for aggregate consumption.[8]

In order to control for the relative size of the economy, all flow variables are normalized for scale by dividing them by potential output – rather than, for example, by expressing them as rates of growth. Aggregate output so normalized thus generates a measure of *capacity utilization* – defined as the ratio of actual to potential output and denoted as ϕ – to serve as a standard indicator of the level and relative vitality of macroeconomic performance.[9]

The core equations of this lean reduced-form model are presented in table 12.1, outlining the logic of the model in its most generic and generalized possible form.[10] In the functional representations of the behavioral equations ((1.2)–(1.5)), the expected signs of the respective first partial derivatives are printed above the independent variables.

Equation (1.1) is the standard product-market balance equation in which aggregate output is assumed to equal aggregate expenditures, expressed here as the sum of consumption, net investment, depreciation, net exports, and all other exogenous components of aggregate demand. Standardization of all aggregate flow variables results in a left-side variable for capacity utilization, defined as $\phi = Q/Q^*$, and all right-side variables divided by potential output.[11]

Equation (1.2) represents a generalized version of a structuralist aggregate consumption function. All the heterodox traditions share a common general approach to the determination of consumption and savings by households – even if the specifics of the saving parameters may vary across models.[12] It is assumed that there are two classes of households, those households of "workers" who depend primarily on wage and salary income and those households of "capitalists" who rely largely upon income from their owned capital assets. For somewhat obvious reasons, it is further assumed that "capitalists' households" have much higher savings propensities than "workers' households," or, at the extreme for the purposes of analytic convenience, that workers spend all of their income on consumption and that capitalists devote all of their income to savings. This approach deploys what is often called the "Cambridge" or "Classical" savings function.

In background work for the social structuralist model reviewed here, I have tried to ground this heterodox approach somewhat more formally (Gordon, 1994, chapters 4 and 6). I propose separate microbased models of consumption for two different groups of households – "working households" and "affluent households." In the former category, because it is assumed that there is virtually no discretionary income, working households seek to achieve a customary or "targeted" level of consumption

Table 12.1. *An illustrative reduced-form structuralist model of a real open private macroeconomy*

(1.1)	ϕ	$\equiv C + I^n + d_k + X^n + \mathbf{Z}\phi$

$$\qquad\qquad\qquad +\ -\ -$$
| (1.2) | C | $= C(\phi,\ r,\ i,\ \mathbf{Z}_C)$ |

$$\qquad\qquad\qquad +\ +\ -$$
| (1.3) | I^n | $= I^n(\phi,\ r,\ i,\ \mathbf{Z}_I)$ |

$$\qquad\qquad\qquad -\ ?\ -$$
| (1.4) | X^n | $= X^n(\phi,\ r,\ i,\ \mathbf{Z}_X)$ |

$$\qquad\qquad\qquad\qquad ?$$
(1.5)	r	$= r(\phi,\ \mathbf{Z}_r)$
(1.6)	S^n	$\equiv \phi - C - d_k$
(1.7)	π	$\equiv r/(\phi \cdot q_k^*)$
(1.8)	d_k	$\equiv \lambda \cdot K$
(1.9)	K	$\equiv K_{-1} + \cdot I \cdot Q^*$
(1.10)	g_k	$\equiv \dot{K}$
(1.11)	q_k^*	$\equiv Q^*/K$

where $\dot{X}$ $\equiv$ Logarithmic rate of change of X
ϕ $\equiv$ Aggregate capacity utilization ($\equiv Q/Q^*$)
C $\equiv$ Real consumption expenditures
I^n $\equiv$ Real net investment
d_k $\equiv$ Real depreciation
X^n $\equiv$ Real net exports
r $\equiv$ Rate of profit
π $\equiv$ Profit share
i $\equiv$ Real interest rate
S^n $\equiv$ Real saving (net of depreciation)
q_k^* $\equiv$ Potential -output–capital ratio
K $\equiv$ Real fixed capital stock
g_k $\equiv$ Rate of growth of real fixed capital stock
Z_i $\equiv$ Vector of exogenous variable(s) affecting endogenous variable i
and flow variables (C, I^n, d_k, X^n, $\mathbf{Z}\phi$, S) normalized on potential output

and adjust to recent deviations of actual consumption from this target.[13] In the latter category, precisely because affluent households are definitionally assumed to have access to discretionary income, they are presumed to choose between present and future consumption through the optimization highlighted by the standard mainstream "life-cycle" model of consumption. The relative importance of these two behavioral representations in the determination of aggregate consumption is conditioned by the relative proportion of income flowing to these two groups of households. In the aggregate, summing over the consumption of these two categories of households, consumption is then determined by the union of the variables appearing in the respective household models as well as the distribution of income affecting the relative importance of those variables.

Equation (1.2) thus expresses (normalized) consumption as a function of (normalized) total income (ϕ), affecting both working and affluent household consumption, the interest rate (i) as an influence on affluent household intertemporal substitution, and the profit rate (r) reflecting the distribution of income between the two classes of households.[14]

Equation (1.3) represents a comparably synthetic structuralist investment function. It is presupposed in the recent heterodox literature that the distribution of income affects not only consumption and savings but also aggregate (net) investment.[15] This leads to the formal conceptualization of an aggregate investment function in which investment is determined jointly (a) by some measure of the robustness of aggregate demand, usually an index of aggregate capacity utilization, and (b) either the rate of profit or the profit share as a measure of distribution.[16] The ultimate effect of factor distribution on macro dynamics then depends on the strength of its impact on savings, through the Cambridge savings function, relative to its impact on investment.

One problem with these recent formulations, however, is that they neglect the potential influence of the rate of interest on investment.[17] The influence of profitability on investment is presumably a measure of *relative profitability* – the expected rate of return on fixed investment *relative* to the opportunity cost of some alternative uses of those available funds. It seems more appropriate, therefore, to write a (simplified) aggregate net investment function as

$$I^n = I^n[(r^e/i_0), \phi^e, \mathbf{Z}_I] \tag{1}$$

rather than simply as $I^n = I^n(r^e, \phi^e, \mathbf{Z}_I)$, where I^n is (normalized) net investment, r^e is the expected rate of profit on fixed investment, i_0 is the opportunity cost of investment, such as the financial rate of return, ϕ^e is the expected level (or rate of change) of aggregate capacity utilization, and $\mathbf{Z}_I$ incorporates other exogenous influences on investment.[18] I adopt this augmented approach in equation (1.3) in table 12.1, writing it in the most general possible functional specification, as $I^n = I^n(\phi, r, i, \mathbf{Z}_I)$, to allow for alternative possible specifications of the determination of "relative" profitability and of expectations on profitability and demand factors.[19]

Equation (1.4) integrates the determination of the net trade balance within the same structuralist framework, similarly expressing (normalized) net exports as a function of utilization and profitability. Although earlier structuralist models dealt with closed economies, more recent analyses have explored the open economy properties of models emphasizing distribution–accumulation interactions.[20] The effect of capacity utilization on net exports draws on standard analytic expectations: since imports are assumed to be much more income elastic than exports, it is expected that an increase (decrease) in the level of economic activity will result in a deterioration (improvement) of net exports.[21]

The relationship between profitability and the net trade balance is more ambiguous. In one direction, if an increase in the profit share or profit rate results from a higher markup, international competitiveness is likely to erode and net exports to decline. In the other direction, if an increase in profitability results from a reduction in unit labor costs, accompanied by a less than proportionate reduction in unit prices, competitiveness is likely to improve and net exports to increase. The sign above the profit rate in equation (1.4) reflects this theoretical uncertainty in the determination of net exports. In a flexible exchange-rate economy, finally, we would expect a negative relationship between the rate of interest and net exports – since, other things equal, higher interest rates would increase the value of the domestic currency, making imports relatively less expensive.

Equation (1.5) then expresses profitability as a function of the level of aggregate demand and a vector of key exogenous variables affecting profitability (Z_r), the choice of whose elements may vary across the structuralist literature. In the post-Keynesian/Kaleckian tradition, the key exogenous variable is likely to be one or another index of monopoly power. In the classical Marxian tradition, the key exogenous variable would probably be some independent measure of the intensity of competitive pressure. In the version of the social structuralist model more fully specified in the next section, the key exogenous variable is an index of capitalist power as developed in my joint work with Bowles and Weisskopf (see Bowles, Gordon, and Weisskopf, 1983a, 1983b, 1986, 1989, 1990).

Sign expectations about the influence of capacity utilization on profitability are in general ambiguous. Much of the structuralist literature would expect a neutral or positive relationship between utilization and the profit *share*, depending on whether the mark-up is assumed constant or whether prices are allowed to vary pro-cyclically with variations in demand pressure. One would further expect an amplifying positive effect in moving from the profit *share* to the profit *rate*, since the output–capital ratio would vary directly with the utilization rate (see the identity (1.7)).

In contrast, the high-employment profit-squeeze literature (Glyn and Sutcliffe, 1972; Boddy and Crotty, 1975) would lead one to anticipate the possibility of a more than offsetting decrease in profitability at high levels of economic activity. Within the structuralist literature taken as a whole, therefore, the net effects of utilization on the profit rate remain uncertain.

The remaining identities in table 12.1 close the system. The definition of aggregate (normalized) net saving in (1.6) permits the translation of the general product-market balance relation in (1.1) into an explicit relationship between net investment and net saving. Equation (1.7) establishes the algebraic relationship between the profit share and the profit rate; although the profit rate is exclusively deployed as an index of distribution in the model outlined here and the profit share is therefore redundant, the definition of the profit share in (1.7) permits commensuration with other formulations in the heterodox literature. Since (1.3) determines net rather than gross investment, (1.8) is necessary to derive depreciation – itself also a component of aggregate (normalized) expenditures in (1.1) – endogenously within the model. Equations (1.9)–(1.10) establish definitionally the link between the determination of the level of utilization in (1.1)–(1.5) and the long-term rate of accumulation, central to considerations of the longer-term performance of the macro economy; these identities underscore the relevance of such models not merely for the determination of the level of activity of the economy but also for its longer-term growth and accumulation performance. For the sake of completeness, equation (1.11) reminds us of the relationship between the potential-output–capital ratio and the endogenously determined level of the capital stock – although most of the heterodox literature is inclined to assume that potential output grows proportionately with the capital stock and that the potential-output–capital ratio can therefore be treated as (approximately) a constant parameter.

There are eleven endogenous variables and eleven equations – with four central behavioral relations ((1.2)–(1.5)), two key accounting identities ((1.1), (1.6)), and five auxiliary definitional relationships ((1.7)–(1.11)). There are only seven exogenous variables – the interest rate (i), the level of potential output (Q^*), and the five vectors of exogenous variables $[Z_i]$.[22]

The system is not only complete but also generates a determinate equilibrium. Treating the standard product-market balance relation as an expectation about balance between net saving (leakages) and net investment (infusions), we can substitute from (1.2)–(1.4) and (1.6) into (1.1), giving us one equation in two unknowns (ϕ, r)[23]

$$S^n(\phi, r, i, \mathbf{Z}_C) \equiv I^n(\phi, r, i, \mathbf{Z}_I) + X^n(\phi, r, i, \mathbf{Z}_X) + \mathbf{Z}_\phi \tag{2}$$

The meaning of this expression is perhaps more clearly captured by expressing it as an "excess demand" function. Subtracting the left-hand side from both sides, we arrive at a functional expression for excess demand, ϕ^y

$$\phi^y \equiv \phi^y(r, \phi)$$
$$\equiv I^n(\phi, r, i, \mathbf{Z}_I) + X^n(\phi, r, i, \mathbf{Z}_X) + \mathbf{Z}_\phi - S^n(\phi, r, i, \mathbf{Z}_C) \quad (2a)$$

A condition for balance in the macro system, indicating equality between aggregate expenditures and income, is that $\phi^y(r, \phi) = 0$, implying that $\dot{\phi} = 0$.

The determination of equilibrium in the model is completed by incorporating the profit equation (1.5) into the analysis, resulting in a compressed system with two equations and two unknowns. Simultaneous solution of those two equations yields equilibrium values for profitability and utilization $\langle r^*, \phi^* \rangle$. In referring to the logic of this model, I shall sometimes refer to the product-market balance relation in (2) as the utilization function, writing it as $\phi(r)$, and to the expression for the profit rate in (1.5) as the profitability function, writing it as $r(\phi)$.

As much of the heterodox literature has made abundantly clear, the logic and dynamics of this determinate equilibrium are not at all clear on a priori grounds.[24]

In the first and simpler instance, the shape of the profitability function is itself uncertain, given the ambiguous sign of the relation between utilization and profitability in (1.5).

The second and somewhat less transparent problem involves the utilization function in (2). Formulating this expression with utilization as a function of distribution, the slope of $\phi(r)$ is determined by the sign of the derivative of utilization with respect to the profit rate. Totally differentiating (2), writing the partial derivative of X with respect to Y as X_y, and then rearranging, we get

$$d\phi/dr = -\frac{S^n_r - (I^n_r + X^n_r)}{S^n_\phi - (I^n_\phi + X^n_\phi)} \quad (3)$$

The sign of the denominator is expected to be positive, both because of the usual assumption necessary for "Keynesian stability" that saving is more responsive to variations in aggregate demand than is investment (see Marglin and Bhaduri, 1989, pp. 164–5) and because of the further presumption that $X^n_\phi < 0$. But the sign of the numerator cannot be determined a priori, since we have no way of anticipating in the abstract the relative magnitudes of S^n_r, I^n_r, and X^n_r. The expected slope of $\phi(r)$ is therefore indefinite.

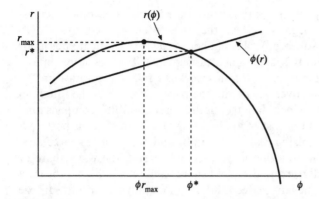

Figure 12.1 Equilibrium in a social structuralist model

Further specification: a social structuralist model

In the abstract, faced with this indeterminacy, the structuralist literature has tended to elaborate a variety of alternative possibilities for the behavior of a macro economy governed by this set of interrelations among distribution, utilization, and accumulation, remaining agnostic about which possibility is likeliest to apply to what situation.

I am not inclined toward such agnosticism. Based on joint work with Bowles and Weisskopf (1983a, 1986, 1989, 1990) and my own separate explorations, I am persuaded that we can more precisely stipulate the characteristics of advanced economies such as the United States and, with those stipulations, can specify a more determinate logic and dynamics for the generic model elaborated in table 12.1. This further specification of what I am calling here a "social structuralist" model is illustrated in figure 12.1.[25]

Our joint work suggests that, at least for the United States and probably also for macro economies "like" it, the profitability function assumes the non-linear inverted-U shape illustrated by $r(\phi)$ in figure 12.1: r first rises with ϕ (at low levels of ϕ) and then falls with ϕ (at high levels of ϕ).[26] This non-linear profit function can be derived formally from either atomistic or bargaining models of firm-level capital–labor relations in which the threat of job loss is the ultimate source of labor discipline.[27] The intuitive logic of such a curve is easily outlined: At low levels of economic activity, firms can increase their levels of operation without having to pay substantially higher real wages because labor markets remain characterized by substantial excess supply; higher ϕ means higher output and higher profits with the same capital stock, and thus higher rates of profit. Although this positive capacity-utilization effect continues to contribute to higher firm rates of profit as ϕ rises, it becomes increasingly offset by a negative effect that has been labeled the "high-employment profit squeeze."[28] The higher the level of ϕ, the tighter labor markets become. But this is not a neutral tendency: the rate of unemployment is a critical determinant of the worker's fallback position in the capital–labor conflict over wages and the pace of work. As the rate (and duration) of unemployment falls, so, in the absence of fully compensating wage increases, does the cost of job loss to workers; this means both that owners' profit-maximizing real wage climbs and that unions' bargaining power rises. Whether for the first or second reason, the wage share of national income will rise and the profit share will fall. The higher the level of ϕ, the greater the negative effect of the high-employment profit squeeze on r. At some level of ϕ less than the full capacity-utilization (full employment) level, this negative effect will overcome the positive utilization effect; the profit function will then turn downward.[29]

At least in the short run, profit-maximizing owners will clearly prefer the point r_{max} on the profit function $r(\phi)$.[30] Referring as well to the short run, we can reasonably assume that workers will prefer higher levels of ϕ, since the real wage rises, the level of labor effort falls, and employment rises with higher levels of economic activity. At rates of capacity utilization below that which maximizes the profit rate (ϕr_{max}), both capital and labor benefit from increases in ϕ. But at higher levels of economic activity, their interests conflict. Whether or not there will be conflict over the directions in which economic policymakers push the economy will therefore depend on where the $r(\phi)$ curve intersects with the utilization function.

This will partly depend on the slope of the utilization function. If the numerator in (3) $[S_r^n - (I_r^n + X_r^n)]$ is negative, the $\phi(r)$ function will slope upward. Although speculative theorizing on this count should largely await the concrete empirical evidence presented in the following section, there are several a priori grounds for suspecting that an upward-sloping $\phi(r)$ function has grown more and more likely in many contemporary advanced capitalist economies in an increasingly integrated world economy.

Considerations affecting all three terms in the numerator of (3) seem pertinent: (a) In an increasingly open global economy, the elasticity of private domestic investment with respect to the domestic profit rate is likely to rise as investors become more and more sensitive to the choice between investing at home and the alternative of investing either abroad or in financial assets.[31] (b) As international competition among firms intensifies and flexible exchange rates pertain, movements in unit labor costs are likely to become increasingly important – with counter-competitive, discretionary shifts in the mark-up becoming correspondingly less important – in regulating the relative competitiveness of domestic producers, with net exports varying inversely with real unit labor costs. This would mean, other things equal, that the positive statistical association between profitability and net exports would be amplified since the profit share itself varies directly (and inversely) with real unit labor costs. (c) The mounting push in many countries toward fiscal austerity, regardless of the short-term state of the economy and of profitability, may have served to weaken the linkages between total net (public and private) saving and net private profitability; if that linkage has been weakened, it would be likely to have resulted in a diminishing (positive) value for S_r^n, reducing its weight relative to $(I_r^n + X_r^n)$ and thereby increasing the likelihood of a positive-sloping utilization function.

All of these speculations refer to *changes* in the level of the derivative of utilization with respect to profitability and do not directly stipulate on a priori grounds the *level* itself. Let us nonetheless presume, for the purposes of discussion and pending review of available empirical evidence in the next section, that it is plausible to draw the utilization function in figure 12.1 as upward sloping. Given the shape of the profit function as well, it is reasonable to assume that the equilibrium at $\langle r^*, \phi^* \rangle$ exists at positive levels of the profit rate and capacity utilization.[32] It also seems plausible to presuppose that the point of intersection between the two curves will tend to fall somewhere to the right of $\langle r_{max}, \phi r_{max} \rangle$ – given (a) the arcs on the profitability functions, in relation to the point r_{max}, where the preferences of owners and workers about the preferred level of economic activity coincide (to the left of r_{max}) and conflict (to the right of r_{max}); (b) the possible role for exogenous government influence over i and Z_ϕ in affecting the position of $\phi(r)$; and (c) the likelihood in democratic societies that workers' preferences will exert at least some influence over public policy outcomes and therefore that owners will not succeed in effecting an equilibrium at r_{max} which unilaterally satisfied their interests.

Short-term displacement and long-term growth

Two final theoretical questions remain about the logic and dynamics of a macro economy governed by the social structuralist relations illustrated in table 12.1 and further specified in figure 12.1 – the first involving short-term comparative statics and the second concerning longer-term growth prospects.[33]

Displacement of equilibrium

In the short-term, we need to consider two questions about the equilibrium set $\langle r^*, \phi^* \rangle$.

First, is the equilibrium illustrated in figure 12.1 stable? Referring back to the excess demand function in equation (2a), the economy will return to equilibrium from an initial displacement of capacity utilization if, for example, conditions of excess demand lead to a reduction in utilization. This would require, for example, that an increase in utilization (when $\phi^y(r, \phi)$ is positive) lead to a fall in the value of ϕ^y. Since the profit rate is endogenous in this system and would react to changes in utilization, we must totally differentiate (2a) in order to assess its response to changes in utilizaton; full stability, encompassing the endogeneity of profitability, therefore requires that the total derivative of ϕ^y with respect to ϕ be negative.[34] Totally differentiating ϕ^y in (2a), and again writing the partial derivative of X with respect to Y as X_y, the stability condition can be expressed as

$$\phi^y_\phi + \phi^y_r \cdot (dr/d\phi) < 0, \qquad \text{or} \qquad dr/d\phi < -\frac{\phi^y_\phi}{\phi^y_r}. \tag{4}$$

As figure 12.1 is drawn, at equilibrium the slope of the profit function $dr/d\phi$, is negative, while the slope of the utilization function, the inverse of $-(\phi^y_\phi/\phi^y_r)$, is positive, ensuring that the stability condition is met.[35]

Second, what kinds of changes in economic conditions could produce displacement of the equilibrium position itself?

In some of the heterodox literature, especially that rooted in post-Keynesian/Kaleckian perspectives, there is a tendency to assume that the *profitability function* would be fairly inertial. In a standard Kaleckian formulation, for example, the profit share at a given level of utilization would be primarily conditioned by the mark-up, the wage, and technically determined hourly output. The mark-up would be unlikely to change (at given levels of utilization), at least in the short run, and the real wage is often treated as either constant, slowly drifting, or modulated by a targeted (constant) wage share – none of which assumptions would be likely to result in much movement in the profitability function. This would leave us with exogenous technical change as a potential source of shifts in $r(\phi)$. But in a model with wage bargaining over the productivity dividend, real wages are likely to grow approximately in proportion to hourly output, maintaining a more or less constant profit share.

In our joint work, Bowles, Weisskopf, and I have taken a broader and more social view of the determination of profitability (Bowles, Gordon, and Weisskopf, 1986, 1989). We argue that profitability, reflecting the interrelationships among utilization, productivity, wages, and prices, is conditioned by the relative power of capital in its relationships with workers, citizens, foreign buyers and suppliers, and other capitalists. The relative power of capital is in turn a function of a complex web of social, political, and economic relationships, grounded in the sometimes enduring and sometimes eroding institutional environment of the economy. The full logic of this perspective is detailed elsewhere (see, especially, Bowles, Gordon, and Weisskopf, 1989). For the purposes of discussion here, our perspective can be represented by two equations. First, we rewrite equation (1.5) from table 12.1 with the generic vector of exogenous variables Z_r replaced explicitly by a vector of "social" variables (**P**) conditioning capitalist power as well as an exogenous index of disembodied technological innovation, Ψ

$$r = r(\overset{+}{\phi}, \overset{+}{\mathbf{P}}, \overset{+}{\Psi}). \tag{1.5a}$$

Second, we observe that capital's relative power can be increased either by changes in regulating macro conditions, represented by the levels of both capacity utilization and the real interest rate, and/or by changes in the "underlying" or structurally determined level of capitalist power, represented by the vector $\mathbf{P}^\mu$ and defined as that level of observed capitalist power (**P**) at given benchmark levels of our indicators of the state of the economy. Given that we hypothesize (and subsequently affirm empirically – see below) that sustained higher levels of utilization erode underlying capitalist power (the "high-employment profit squeeze") while higher interest rates enhance it (through the favorable impact of higher interest rates on the terms of trade and thus on the cost of imported inputs), we can therefore write this second equation as[36]

$$\mathbf{P} = \mathbf{P}(\overset{-}{\phi}, \overset{+}{i}, \overset{+}{\mathbf{P}^\mu}) \tag{5}$$

By substituting (5) into (1.5a), this allows us, finally, to write a reduced-form expression for the profitability function as

$$r = r(\overset{?}{\phi}, \overset{+}{i}, \overset{+}{\mathbf{P}^\mu}, \overset{+}{\Psi}) \tag{1.5b}$$

where the uncertainty about the derivative of profitability with respect to utilization, retained from the original formulation of (1.5) in table 12.1, is now seen explicitly to reflect the indeterminacy of the countervailing positive effects of utilization on the profit rate (in (1.5a)) and negative effects of utilization on observed capitalist power (in (5)).

This analysis helps clarify the potential sources of shifts in the profitability function, $r(\phi)$. Setting aside the question of disembodied technological innovation, it would appear that the major potential source of enduring shifts in the profit function would come from movements in underlying capitalist power, $\mathbf{P}^\mu$. In our research on the United States, indeed, we conclude that the principal source of the initial onset of stagnation in the US economy in the mid 1960s stemmed from a sharp and substantial downward shift in the profit function.[37]

Moving from the profitability function to the *utilization curve*, three main potential sources of shifts in the $\phi(r)$ curve may also be identified.

First, and obviously, the utilization function might shift as a result of changes in discretionary government fiscal or monetary policy. One such change could affect equilibrium through increases or decreases in the level of exogenous components of aggregate expenditures, Z_ϕ – foremost among which, of course, would be increases or decreases in the level of (normalized) government purchases. Alternatively, variations in monetary policy could potentially affect equilibrium combinations of net saving (leakages) and investment (infusions), with reductions in interest rates presumably shifting the utilization function down and to the right.

Second, shifts in other among the exogenous variables Z_i in behavioral equations (1.2)–(1.4) might effect displacement of the utilization function. For example, an exogenous deterioration in the terms of trade would be likely directly to diminish net exports – without obvious counter-balancing effects on net saving or net investment – leading to a leftward movement in $\phi(r)$.

Third, and less tangibly, changes in expectations may result in evolving parameters in the saving, investment, and/or net export functions, affecting the elasticity of those endogenous variables with respect to any given combination of utilization and profitability. A surge in investors' "animal spirits," for example, might result in both an expansionary shift in the utilization function as well as a change in its slope.[38]

Long-term growth performance

All of these possible kinds of displacements may have more or less promising implications for macro policy. But their potential implications will depend in part on the relationship between short-term equilibrium and long-term growth performance.

The long-term rate of growth of a macro economy will depend in large part on the rate of growth of potential output: If the activity level increases without increases in potential output, the economy will bump up against inflationary or political barriers to sustained growth in actual output. Assuming for the purposes of discussion that the rate of growth of potential output is a positive monotonic function of the rate of growth of the real fixed capital stock and referring back to the generic model represented in table 12.1, we can see that the long-term rate of growth of the economy, regulated by the pace of accumulation (g_k), will be a direct monotonic function of the pace of investment (see equations (1.9)–(1.10)).

What levels of investment are consistent with the macro equilibrium

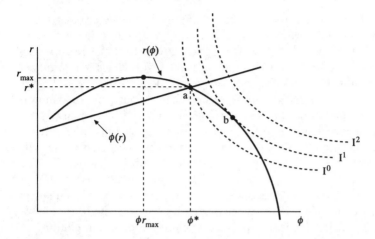

Figure 12.2   Equilibrium and investment in a social structuralist model

sketched in figure 12.1? Our discussion of investment to this point, exemplified by equation (1), has implicitly focussed on private investment and the optimizing decisions of private investors. But a broader view of the pace of accumulation needs to take public investment into account as well. We can therefore conceive of a simple composite investment function

$$I = I(r, \phi) = I^{P}(r, \phi) + I^{G} \tag{6}$$

where $I^{P}{}_{\phi}$ and $I^{G}{}_{\phi}$ are (normalized) private and public investment, respectively, with positive first derivatives of the aggregate I function (with respect to r and ϕ) following directly from the positive first derivatives of the I^{P} function established above.

As a function in r and ϕ, this generalized investment function can be represented in the profit/utilization space of figure 12.1 by a series of iso-investment curves reflecting ever-higher levels of investment as r and ϕ increase, as added in figure 12.2 to the original graph in figure 12.1.[39] The point of tangency of $r(\phi)$ with the isoquant I^{1}, at point b, represents the point of maximum investment I^{1} attainable under conditions depicted by the profit frontier $r(\phi)$.

Note that this maximum point would coincide in general neither with the preferred position of owners nor with that of workers – with owners preferring a position to the left, at lower levels of output closer to ϕr_{max}, and workers preferring a position to the right providing even higher levels of utilization, employment, and wages. Note also that this point of tangency, at point b, is not a system equilibrium, which has already been established to occur at point a.

Rather than adding to our understanding of the determination of macro equilibrium, these iso-investment loci can remind us in the present context of three simple but central conclusions about the relationship between the short-term equilibrium established within this macro model at point a and the long-term rate of growth it implies. First, *all other things (including public investment) equal*, there is only one (maximum) rate of accumulation and productivity growth consistent with any given equilibrium combination, $\langle r^*, \phi^* \rangle$, because there is only one rate of investment generated by that combination; in this particular sense, this apparently short-term model, establishing the equilibrium activity level of the macro economy, can also serve as the basis for analysis of long-term growth prospects as well. Second, this warranted rate of accumulation would only coincidentally reach the maximum rate of growth *sustainable* by the prevailing technical and social conditions of accumulation (as reflected by the level and shape of the profitability function $r(\phi)$) if point b happened to coincide with point a in figure 12.2; in this sense, this model in no way guarantees enjoyment of a "golden age." Third, these iso-investment loci also underscore that demand-side expansion by itself will not *necessarily* increase either the rate of investment or the long-term rate of growth. This simple point can be illustrated in two ways: First, given the logic of the investment function in (6), a rightward (expansionary) shift in the $\phi(r)$ curve would move the point of equilibrium downward along the profitability function; it is perfectly possible, in such an instance, for the positive effects of higher utilization on investment to be more than offset by the negative effects of a lower rate of profit (necessitated by the negative slope of the $r(\phi)$ curve). Or second, imagine that in figure 12.2 the point of equilibrium a coincided with (or fell to the right of) the maximum attainable investment point b. In this case, we can see that a rightward (expansionary) movement in the utilization function would necessarily result in a lower level of investment, given the shapes drawn for the profit curve and the iso-investment loci, because the new point of equilibrium to the right of b would intersect with an investment locus reflecting a lower level of investment than at I^1.

This last reminder leads us to one last, relatively more technical point. Bhaduri and Marglin (1990) warn of a potential confusion lurking in the (private) investment function originally introduced in equation (1), in which the influence of distribution on investment is filtered through the profit rate rather than the profit share. They show (appendix A), for such an investment function in a closed-economy model, that the assumption of a positive derivative of investment with respect to utilization ($I_\phi > 0$) is inconsistent with an "exhilarationist" regime characterized by an upward-sloping utilization function. Were this logic binding on the model presented here, we would need either to relax the assumption that $I_\phi > 0$ or conclude this theoretical exposition with greater logical agnosticism about the slope of the utilization curve traced in figures 12.1 and 12.2.

Three quick responses to their warning should allow us to move ahead. First, their conclusion does not strictly hold in the case of an open-economy model in which (at least) net export demand also appears in the product-market balance equation; in such cases, the twin presumptions of a positive I_ϕ and an upward-sloping $\phi(r)$ curve are mutually consistent.[40] Second, anticipating some of the discussion in section 3 below, the slope of the $\phi(r)$ function is much less important than the slope of the $r(\phi)$ function for the policy exercises to which this model is applied here; as long as the utilization function cuts the profitability function from below, ensuring a stable equilibrium, most of the policy discussion in section 3 would be consistent with a flat or even a gently downward-sloping utilization function. Third, and perhaps more important, their reminder helps underscore the critical importance of avoiding *purely* abstract debates about the theoretically "likely" or "warranted" values of individual parameters or slopes of specific functions in this model. There are dangers to some apparently innocent assumptions, as Bhaduri and Marglin (1990) demonstrate. Wherever possible, as a result, we should try to ground our discussion in at least proximate efforts to establish empirically plausible bounds or ranges for critical model parameters for the class of macro economies under discussion. Presumably inferences about the "real" world can help steer us among the wide range of possible model configurations which theory without empirical escort is capable of generating. And it is precisely a quest for such empirical grounding to which we now turn.

2   Social structuralist theory confronts "the facts"

It is hardly the intention of this section to provide an exhaustive empirical "test" of the compact social structuralist model introduced in the previous section. I hope much more modestly to consider the *empirical plausibility of the particular specification of the social structuralist model* introduced in the previous section and illustrated by figure 12.1, since it is that particular specification on which much of the policy discussion in the following section rests. What can we learn about the properties of the model from available empirical evidence about the advanced macro economies? Because of my own experience and comparative advantage, the most detailed evidence will be reviewed or presented for the case of the United States, limiting myself to considerably more general comments about the available evidence for other advanced macro economies.

The profitability function

As anticipated briefly above, it will turn out in section 3 that the shape of the profitability function matters more to the policy applications of this social structuralist model than the shape of the utilization function. So it makes sense to begin this brief empirical review with that relationship expressing the profit rate as a function of the level of capacity utilization (and other factors).

The United States

If one ignores the influence of "social" variables on the rate of profit or the implications of micro models focussing on the logic of labor extraction, there seems to be little doubt that the profitability function would slope upward in profit-rate/utilization space: Even if the profit share, and particularly its component element, the mark-up, does not itself increase at higher levels of activity, the profit rate is algebraically expressed as the product of the profit share and the utilization rate (adjusted, with the normalization used here, by the potential-output–capital ratio); *ceteris paribus*, a positive relationship between the profit rate and the level of utilization is therefore virtually guaranteed.[41]

But this appears to be one case in which *ceteris* is clearly not *paribus*. Bowles, Weisskopf and I have argued (1986, 1989) that some crucial trade-offs exist between various social and political economic determinants of the profit rate, on the one hand, and crucial indices of the level of economic activity, on the other.

One example of such a trade-off between the level of economic activity and an important determinant of the profit rate strikes us as particularly illuminating. It involves a conflict between (1) the desirability of having a high level of capacity utilization to translate a high profit share into a high profit rate and to stimulate investment, and (2) the desirability – from capital's stand-point – of having a low level of capacity utilization to sustain high unemployment as a way of maintaining labor discipline and thereby contributing to a high profit share.

We have found reasonably clear empirical evidence supporting such a trade-off between the cost of job loss, one of our key measures of employer control over workers (see Bowles, Gordon, and Weisskopf, 1986), and the rate of capacity utilization. (The importance of the cost of job loss as a determinant of the profit rate is highlighted in the regression results reported in table 12.2 opposite.) Regressing the cost of job loss against the level of capacity utilization in the US economy between 1957 and 1979, we find both a negative slope, indicating that higher capacity utilization is associated with a lower cost of job loss and therefore with

Table 12.2. *The profitability function: net after-tax rate of profit, non-financial corporate business sector, United States*

	(1) ln(r) Annual 1955–86	(2) ln(r) Annual 1955–86	(3) ln(r) Quarterly 55.1–88.4	(4) r Quarterly 55.1–88.4
Constant	− 9.48	− 8.94	− 5.74	− 0.19
	(11.61)	(11.54)	(17.14)	(5.06)
Capacity utilization	5.47	1.45	3.38	0.19
	(9.96)	(3.07)	(19.25)	(8.01)
Past capacity utilization/	—	− 3.42	− 5.34	− 0.11
utilization squared		(6.27)	(21.80)	(6.99)
Real federal funds rate	—	3.06	0.05	0.01
		(5.73)	(4.90)	(0.69)
Product market tightness	0.31	0.17	—	—
	(4.66)	(3.21)		
Cost of job loss	0.66	0.58	—	—
	(5.88)	(4.14)		
Worker resistance	0.14	0.08	—	—
	(3.21)	(1.70)		
Trade power	6.01	9.63	—	—
	(4.66)	(4.24)		
Government regulation	− 0.98	− 0.95	—	—
	(3.78)	(4.61)		
Capital's tax share	− 2.94	− 2.67	—	—
	(7.79)	(8.45)		
Import penetration	− 1.65	− 1.52	—	—
	(9.03)	(9.03)		
Price controls dummy	− 0.09	− 0.04	− 0.22	− 0.01
	(2.02)	(1.14)	(2.16)	(2.63)
Technological innovation	0.51	0.64	0.78	− 0.01
	(1.54)	(2.54)	(3.29)	(1.04)
Underlying capitalist power	—	—	1.02	0.06
			(9.19)	(6.33)
Dummy variable, 1966–88	—	—	—	− 0.005
				(2.35)
MA(1)	—	—	0.75	0.80
			(9.63)	(11.17)
MA(2)	—	− 0.78	0.38	0.60
		(2.52)	(4.94)	(8.12)
AR(3)	—	—	0.26	0.81
			(3.80)	(13.90)
$\bar{R}^2$	0.91	0.96	0.94	0.95
DW	2.25	2.25	1.89	2.09

Notes: Numbers in parentheses are t-statistics.
Sources and variable definitions: Columns (1), (2) from Bowles, Gordon, and Weisskopf (1989), table 3, cols. (1), (2). Columns (3), (4) based on same data and variable definitions, with quarterly interpolations of annual variables where necessary. Lags for (1)–(2) as reported in ibid.; lags for (3)–(4) approximate quarterly equivalents of the annual lags for (1)–(2).

the prospect of diminished profitability – and a negative shift in this trade-off after the mid 1960s – suggesting that combinations of capacity utilization and cost of job loss that were possible during the 1960s were unattainable during the 1970s.[42]

Such illustrative results lead us to expect a contradictory relationship between profitability and capacity utilization when we turn to econometric estimation of equation (1.5) in table 12.1. Table 12.2 illustrates a sequence of tests exploring these relationships. It provides regression results seeking to explain variations in the net after-tax non-financial corporate business (NFCB) rate of profit for the United States from the mid 1950s through the late 1980s.[43]

Column 1, reproduced from table 3 of Bowles, Gordon, and Weisskopf (1989), represents a direct estimation of the structural equation (1.5a), with the profit rate expressed as a function of the level of capacity utilization, seven indices of "observed" capitalist power, an index of technological innovation, and a dummy variable for the Nixon Round of price controls in 1971–3. As expected for the structural formulation in equation (1.5a), the coefficient on capacity utilization in column (1) of table 12.2 is positive.

The problem with that estimated coefficient, however, is that many of our indices of capitalist power are themselves functions of the level of capacity utilization (or, closely related, the real interest rate), creating collinearity among the independent variables. The equation reported in column (2) (table 12.2) addresses this problem by moving to the reduced-form profit equation introduced above as (1.5b). This involves working with estimates of $\mathbf{P}^\mu$, our respective indices of "underlying" capitalist power. In this equation, we have substituted for the indices of "observed" capitalist power deployed in column (1) our estimates of the elements of $\mathbf{P}^\mu$, which are derived by purging the P_i of their covariation with either the level of capacity utilization or the real rate of interest.[44] By construction, these variables capture variations in observed capitalist power which remain after controlling for the influence on those indices of utilization or the interest rate. To remain faithful to the construction of this reduced-form equation (1.5b) (through algebraic substitution from (5) into (1.5b)), we must include the "state" variables used in our estimation of equation (5) – in this case an index of past (trend) capacity utilization and the real interest rate.

In column 2 (table 12.2), all the coefficients on the indices of capitalist power retain the signs and significance shown in column (1) (with only the worker resistance coefficient dropping to roughly 5 percent significance on a one-tailed test). The large negative coefficient of trend capacity utilization reflects the corrosive effects of sustained high levels of economic activity on observed capitalist power. Summing the two capacity utilization coefficients, we can see that a steady-state increase in capacity utilization has a negative effect on the profit rate, consistent with the negative slope of $r(\phi)$ in figure 12.1 to the right of ϕr_{max} and the kind of trade-off discussed above involving one of the key power indices, the cost of job loss. The sign on the real interest rate (measured here by the real federal funds rate), similarly, is positive because of its positive effect on our index of (measured) trade power – reflecting the advantages to owners (through lower imported input costs) of high interest rates and the more favorable terms of trade which result.

At first blush, then, this evidence tends to affirm the logic behind the partly negative slope of the profitability function in the social structuralist model illustrated in figure 12.1. But two empirical issues remain.

First, the estimates reported in columns (1) and (2) of table 12.2 are for annual data. Because the index of capacity utilization is so cyclically sensitive, is it possible that quarterly data might reveal a different inter-relationship between r and ϕ?

The estimates reported in column (3) consider this possibility, present-ing a version of the equation in column (2) estimated on quarterly data and extended through 1988. To simplify the estimation and presentation, the individual elements of $\mathbf{P}^\mu$ are combined into a single composite index of underlying capitalist power by weighting each index of underlying capitalist power by its respective regression coefficient in an updated (annual) version of the equation in column (2). (This method of construc-tion implies that the estimated regression coefficient on the composite variable should (roughly) equal one.) This composite index $\mathbf{P}^\mu$ literally represents the variations in the after-tax profit rate which are associated with changes in this composite index of the underlying power of the capitalist class, according to the results of the equation in column (2) and holding constant the levels of the remaining state and exogenous variables which also influence profitability.[45]

The estimates in column (3) are consistent with those in column (2) (including a regression coefficient on $\mathbf{P}^\mu$ approximately equal to one). Once again, we find that the sum of the coefficients on the two capacity utilization terms is negative, reaffirming the relevance of the kind of negative trade-off between profitability and utilization which we emphasize.

The second question involves the issue of non-linearity. I have drawn the profitability function in figure 12.1 as a non-linear, inverted U-shaped curve, first rising with ϕ and then falling at higher levels of utilization. On purely theoretical grounds, given the micro foundations for this analysis (see discussion above, and especially note 29), this idea of an inflection from a positive to a negative slope makes sense. But the estimates reported in column (3) (table 12.2) reflect a purely linear specification. Is our theoretical conception of a non-linear profit function consistent with the evidence?

Column (4) reports one test of this possibility. It reproduces the equation in column (3) with only three exceptions: First, in order to allow direct translation of the non-linear estimates into the units of measurement of the index of capacity utilization itself, the equation is estimated in levels of the variables rather than in logs. Second, and critical for this exercise, the square of capacity utilization is substituted for trend capacity utilization, creating the possibility of a second-order polynomial expression; if our graph in figure 12.1 were consistent with the evidence, we would expect a positive coefficient on the level of capacity utilization and a negative coefficient on the level squared. Third, it introduces a dummy variable for the period after the post-war profit peak in 1966, allowing for the possibility of estimating and plotting a downward shift in the profit function resulting from a deteriorating economic environment after the mid 1960s.

The estimates reported in column (4) confirm our expectations.[46] Given those results, by solving for the peak of the second-order polynomial in ϕ, we can then derive an empirical estimate of the level of capacity utilization corresponding to ϕr_{max}. During the period of estimation, from 1955.1 through 1988.4, our index of capacity utilization ranged from a trough of 0.862 to a peak of 1.025. The estimated value of ϕr_{max} derived from the equation in column (4) is 0.855, just to the left of the lower band of the range of values for ϕ. Across the 136 quarters in the period of estimation, in other words, the level of capacity utilization was consistently above (to the right of) this estimated value of ϕr_{max}.

Figure 12.3 illustrates these results. It explicitly graphs the implied shape of the profit function projected by the estimated equation in column (4) (table 12.2), setting the exogenous variables at their mean values for the full period of estimation. The two levels of the profit function are estimated respectively for the period of the boom, from 1955 to 1966, and for the period of stagnation, from 1966 to 1988; the position of the two curves is based on the different mean values for our index of underlying capitalist power between those two periods as well as the negative coefficient on the 1966–88 dummy variable (with all other exogenous variables at their means for the full period). The cross-hatched area maps the domain of effective variation for the two endogenous variables over this period of estimation, with the horizontal boundaries corresponding to the minimum and maximum quarterly values for capacity utilization between 1955.1 and 1988.4 and the vertical boundaries repre-

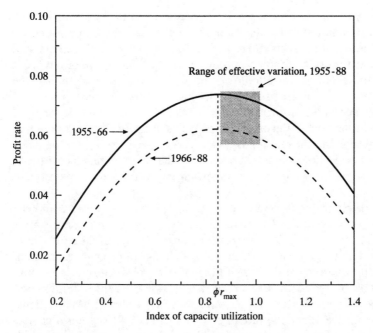

Figure 12.3   Estimated profitability function
Sources: Slope and position of profit function based on estimated equation in table 12.2, column 4, evaluated at mean values for exogenous variables. Curve for 1955–66 based on mean value for "underlying capitalist power" for that period; curve for 1966–88 based on mean value for underlying capitalist power and dummy variable for 1967–88.

senting the range of cycle averages for the profit rate across the same period.[47] The value of ϕr_{max} represented on the graph corresponds to the maximum profit rate implied by the coefficients on ϕ and ϕ^2 in the equation in column (4).[48]

Still referring only to the case of the United States, in short, these provisional estimates support two aspects of the specification of the model represented in figure 12.1: (a) it is plausible on empirical as well as theoretical grounds to specify a profitability function with a non-linear inverted-U shape; and (b) it is further plausible on empirical grounds to presume that the center of gravity of real-world values for $\langle r, \phi \rangle$ will lie to the right of the point ϕr_{max} in figure 12.1.

One final question remains. As noted at the beginning of the previous section, the profit function studied here is a reduced-form expression: Rather than deriving the profit rate algebraically from an identity implied by (1.7) in table 12.1, with the profit share in turn derived from an identity expressing it as a function of real hourly output and the real hourly wage, the profit function directly determines the profit rate through a structural behavioral equation such as (1.5). But fluctuations of productivity and wages over the cycle are somewhat more familiar than those of the profit rate or the profit share. Should it not also be possible to confirm the high-employment profit squeeze by looking at the relationship between the real wage and real productivity, on the one hand, and the level of capacity utilization on the other? Standard expectations are that both real hourly output and the real hourly wage vary pro-cyclically. But the kinds of labor extraction models underlying the high-employment profit squeeze would lead us to expect somewhat more complicated patterns of interaction.[49]

We can test for consistency between the results in table 12.2 and the behavior of productivity and wages over the cycle with some simple regression experiments. If we regress the rate of change of the profit share on current and lagged values of the rate of change of capacity utilization, we find (in equations not reported here) an echo of the results in column (2), with a positive coefficient on the current rate of change of utilization and negative coefficients on lagged values – and the sum of the coefficients sharply negative. Since the rate of change of the profit share is algebraically equal to the rate of change of real hourly productivity *minus* the rate of change of the real hourly wage, we ought to be able to account for these results with comparable regressions of productivity growth and wage change, respectively, on current and lagged values of the change in utilization. We find, indeed, that the sum of the positive coefficients on (the rate of change of) utilization in the wage-change equation strongly dominate the corresponding sum of coefficients in the productivity-change equation – in large part because lagged utilization-change has strong negative effects on productivity growth but not on real wage growth – resulting in a negative relationship between the rate of change of the profit share and the rate of change of utilization. This implies that the high levels of utilization squeeze the profit share primarily through their corrosive effect on labor effort and, in turn, hourly output. Labor extraction models are instrumental, it would appear, in helping us understand the sources of the empirical evidence for a negatively sloped profitability curve.

The advanced economies

The micro analysis underlying the kind of profit function illustrated in figure 12.1 emphasizes the critical role of the threat of job dismissal in the arsenal of labor-extraction techniques deployed by firms in such an economy. This would lead us to expect significant differences in the shapes of such profitability functions across the advanced economies if there were substantial cross-country variations in the degree to which firms in those economies indeed relied upon job dismissal as a labor incentive/extraction mechanism. It should not be surprising that we would find (provisional) empirical evidence of a pronounced negative relationship between the profit rate and capacity utilization at high activity levels in the United States because, we have argued, US firms rely heavily on the "stick" as a labor discipline device (Bowles, Gordon, and Weisskopf, 1990, chapters 6 and 11). It should be equally unsurprising if we were to find some economies, notably those in which the "carrot" tends to replace the "stick" in labor relations, in which the profit function did not slope downward so decisively at high utilization levels and in which, indeed, the $r(\phi)$ curve was either relatively flat or even upward sloping as the economy moved toward "full" employment.[50]

Direct detailed comparative analyses of the profit/utilization relation in advanced economies remain scant. But a few recent studies suggest a pattern of variation in the relevant macro relationships which are consistent with the speculative expectations of the preceding paragraph.

Weisskopf (1992) conducts a comparative study of the determinants of profitability in manufacturing across eight leading advanced countries. He finds that there is a negative steady-state relationship between utilization and the profit share across all of those economies. He finds, however, that the sources of declining profitability in the sample (from the 1960s through the 1980s) vary among countries, requiring a much more detailed look at some of the institutional factors affecting the components of profitability.

Pursuing one such investigation, Weisskopf (1987) studies the relationship between productivity growth and the unemployment rate, as a proxy for threat of job dismissal, across eight advanced economies (while controlling for the rate of capacity utilization). If the high-employment profit squeeze argument based on labor-extraction models were valid, we would expect to find a positive relationship between unemployment and productivity growth, reflecting the disciplinary impact of slack labor markets on work incentives. In contrast, we might expect to find the opposite relationship in countries with relatively more cooperative labor relations in which economic insecurity compromised the capital–labor accord and served to undermine labor incentives. His econometric results provisionally support these expectations. He finds (1987, table 1) some evidence of the "stick" effect in the United States and the United Kingdom and some suggestion of the "carrot" effect in Germany and Sweden. He concludes (1987, p. 149):

Among the eight countries in my sample the US is surely the one with the lowest degree of worker security, and it is arguably also among the ones with the most antagonistic capital–labour relations. Among the other countries in my sample, Canada may be the closest to the US in these respects, with the UK and Italy and France somewhere in the middle, Germany and Japan further away, and Sweden at the opposite end of the spectrum . . . [T]he finding of some evidence that the UK and Italy share with the US a positive work-intensity effect of unemployment on productivity, and the finding that Germany and Sweden are most at variance with the US model, is encouraging.

Based at least on these two studies, then, it seems reasonable to conclude that the shape of the $r(\phi)$ function may vary substantially across countries and that its shape may depend centrally on the institutional rules of the game which prevail in any given economy.[51]

The utilization function

We have seen in section 1 that the shape of the $\phi(r)$ function will depend on the relative magnitudes of the derivatives of saving, investment, and net exports with respect to the profit rate and to utilization. Econometric specification and estimation of such relationships can be so contingent that one could hardly expect to derive precise point estimates of those elasticities. One would hope, much more modestly for our purposes here, to be able to reach some tentative conclusions about the range of plausible values for those functions and the relative likelihood that the utilization function will slope upward as drawn in figure 12.1.

The United States

A few estimates for these functions for the United States, specified in different ways, are scattered throughout the literature. Rather than engage in a detailed survey here, I limit myself to some compact direct estimates of the functions as specified in the preceding section.

For ease of estimation, I have expressed all three functions in linearized form.[52] Following the standardized formulations represented in table 12.1, this results in three simple linear equations:

$$S^n = a_0 + a_1 \phi + a_2 r + a_3 i = \epsilon_1 \qquad a_1, a_2, a_3 > 0 \qquad (1.2a)$$

$$I^n = b_0 + b_1 \phi + b_2 r + b_3 i = \epsilon_2 \qquad b_1, b_2, > 0 \, b_3 < 0 \qquad (1.3a)$$

$$X^n = c_0 + c_1 \phi + c_2 r + c_3 i = \epsilon_3 \qquad c_1, c_3 < 0, c_2 > 0 \qquad (1.4a)$$

I have estimated these three equations on quarterly data for the period 1955.1–1988.4 for the US economy, estimating them with two-stage least squares (since utilization is endogenous to the system from which they are derived).[53] All of the equations suffer from serious autocorrelation; I have chosen a standard ARMA adjustment for all three equations which comes closest to allowing us to confirm the null hypothesis of white-noise residuals across all three estimated equations.[54] However simplified the equations, they can at least give us some impression of the range of values plausible for the relationships hypothesized by the social structuralist model.

The upper panel in table 12.3 presents the results of those estimations. All of the relevant sign hypotheses are confirmed, particularly including the positive relationship hypothesized between each respective dependent variable and the profit rate. The bottom panel in table 12.3 adjusts the regression coefficients by the respective estimated AR(3) coefficient(s) to produce long-term or "steady-state" estimates of both the coefficients and the relevant composite sums necessary for evaluating the slope of the utilization function. The steady-state estimates strongly support the hypothesis of an upward-sloping utilization function. We can see the critical importance of situating this analysis in the context of an open-economy model, since the estimated coefficients from the net-export equation are instrumental in determining the final sign of the slope of the utilization function.

Two other essays in this volume contain overlapping estimates for the US. In my own separate essay on saving and investment (Gordon, this volume), tables 5 and 6 present estimates of much more complexly specified saving and investment equations on the same quarterly data set (although the saving variable here is total net private saving and there it is personal saving). There, the relative magnitudes of the coefficients across the saving and investment are roughly comparable to the estimates reproduced in table 12.3. Bowles and Boyer (chapter 5, this volume) also present estimates for the United States. Although their data are annual and some of their definitions are different, they also conclude that in such an open-economy model the utilization function for the United States is upward sloping.

The advanced economies

Only a few relevant comparative studies exist. With somewhat different specifications than mine, Bowles and Boyer (this volume) find relatively common patterns of variation across countries in the relative magnitudes of the respective coefficients and conclude that all the economies in their sample have upward-sloping utilization functions. Bhaskar and Glyn (this volume) also find relatively little variation across countries in the effects of profitability on investment, with only France and the UK manifesting very small and/or insignificant effects; they do not directly

Table 12.3. *The utilization function*

	(1) S^n 55.1–88.4	(2) I^n 55.1–88.4	(3) X^n 55.1–88.4
Constant	− 0.16	− 0.12	0.08
	(5.95)	(11.10)	(5.54)
Capacity utilization	0.21	0.14	− 0.10
	(8.08)	(13.03)	(6.86)
Rate of profit$_{-9|-1|-5}$	0.13	0.23	0.18
	(1.91)	(7.74)	(4.50)
Real interest rate$_{-3|-2|-12}$	0.11	− 0.02	− 0.08
	(3.38)	(1.65)	(4.66)
MA(1)	0.72	0.96	0.82
	(10.73)	(16.36)	(14.74)
MA(2)	0.66	0.75	0.67
	(9.47)	(12.86)	(11.21)
AR(3)	0.68	0.61	0.76
	(13.99)	(14.79)	(22.93)
$\bar{R}^2$	0.81	0.94	0.90
SER	0.006	0.002	0.004
DW	2.05	1.59	1.74

Notes: Numbers after profit rate and interest rate names indicate the length of the lags for those variables in columns (1)–(3) respectively. Numbers in parentheses are t-statistics.

Sources and variable definitions: (a) From *National Income and Product Accounts*: Saving: real net private saving divided by potential output. Investment: real net fixed non-residential investment divided by potential output. Net exports: real net exports divided by potential output. (b) Documented in Bowles, Gordon, and Weisskopf (1989, data appendix): Potential output: method of estimation detailed. Capacity utilization: real private non-residential business output divided by potential output in that sector. Rate of profit: Net after-tax rate of profit, non-financial corporate business sector. Real interest rate: cols. (1)–(2), cost of capital services; col. (3), real federal funds rate.

study saving or net exports in the same context. Catinat *et al.* (1988) and Andersen (1987) also find relatively common elasticities of investment with respect to profitability across several OECD countries.

It would appear, then, that two highly provisional conclusions about the logic and shape of the utilization function in the social structuralist model are warranted. First, it appears that there is probably less variation across countries in the shape of the utilization function than in the profitability function. Second, especially if we endogenize net exports in an open-economy model, it does not seem unreasonable to conclude that the utilization function may be upward sloping, or at least not dramatically downward sloping, in many of the advanced countries.

In commenting on the policy implications of the social structuralist model, in short, it appears plausible to conclude – modestly and provisionally – that the specifications represented in figures 12.1 and 12.2 are reasonable for the United States; that the $r(\phi)$ curve will be likely to differ (from the US case) across countries more than the $\phi(r)$ function; and that those critical variations across countries in $r(\phi)$, where they exist, are likely to reflect differences in the institutional rules of the game in those respective societies.

3 Foundations for a democratic economic strategy

Two of the key challenges for macroeconomic policy in the 1990s are to raise the rate of capacity utilization (hopefully also reducing unemploy-

Table 12.3 (*cont.*)

Composite estimates of slope of utilization function

	"Steady-state" estimates	
	$X_r/(1 - \rho)$	$X_\phi/(1 - \rho)$
Saving	0.40	0.64
Investment	0.60	0.37
Net exports	0.75	− 0.43
$-[S_r - (I_r + X^n_r)]$	0.95	—
$[S_\phi - (I_\phi + X^n_\phi)]$	—	0.70
$d\phi/dr$		1.36

ment and improving employment security) and to raise the rate of investment (as one important step toward more rapid productivity growth). Under what circumstances might it be possible, indeed, to improve macro performance (by these criteria) in ways which also foster greater equity and greater democracy? I discuss in this section what we can learn from the social structuralist model illustrated in figures 12.1 and 12.2 about alternative policy approaches to achieving those twin objectives. I first consider its implications for conventional right-wing and Keynesian policy initiatives and then apply it to lay the conceptual foundations for a democratic economic strategy.

Conventional economic strategies

If we view conventional economic policy approaches through social structuralist lenses, do right-wing and Keynesian strategies show promise of achieving higher utilization and enhanced investment?

Right-wing initiatives

Economic policy in many advanced countries since the late 1970s has been dominated by a right-wing agenda. At least for the case of the United States, to whose experience this model has already been informally applied (Bowles, Gordon, and Weisskopf, 1990, chapters 8–10), we can use the model of table 12.1 and figure 12.1 to provide a fairly compact summary of the consequences of right-wing policies during the 1980s.

Refer back to figure 12.1. Let us take $\langle r^*, \phi^* \rangle$ as the equilibrium which prevailed during the prior 1973–9 business cycle, before Reaganomics arrived with thunderous impact.[55] The profit curve $[r(\phi)]$ had already declined to its new and lower position after the heyday of the long post-war boom (see the shift reflected by the lower of the two curves in figure 12.3), confronting capital and policymakers alike with a considerably less favorable menu of combinations of profitability and utilization. Along that frontier, relatively restrictive fiscal policy had kept utilization levels fairly low (at ϕ^*_1) with average profit rates both below their peak levels of the mid 1960s and below the potential maximum at the peak of the prevailing profitability function.

Business and their right-wing allies in government had sought since the early 1970s to restore corporate power through aggressive offensives against the challengers who had eroded corporate power since the mid 1960s. The intensified business offensive beginning in the late 1970s sought to break the political stalemate of the Ford–Carter years and to restore corporate advantage in their push for profits. Through a wide variety of political and policy initiatives, we argue (Bowles, Gordon, and

Weisskopf, 1990, chapter 8), this offensive effectively involved an effort to push the profitability function back up toward its levels of the post-war boom.

This political effort failed. Despite all the political battles won by business and its right-wing allies in government, we find no evidence that "underlying capitalist power" increased during the 1980s.[56] This meant, referring back to figure 12.1, that the frontier of possible profit/utilization combinations remained lodged at the position of $r(\phi)$ in the graph. The net effect of right-wing economic policies, primarily as a result of the sharply restrictive monetary policies applied in late 1979, was to shift the utilization function in a contractionary direction, moving it up and to the left from $\langle r^*, \phi^* \rangle$, resulting in a new equilibrium with somewhat lower utilization rates during the 1980s than in the previous cycle and faintly higher profit rates.[57]

Right-wing policies won their political battles in short, but they lost the war. They failed to restore underlying capitalist power and, as a result, had only marginal impact on the underlying macro performance of the US economy. In the meantime, of course, the vast majority of workers and households in the United States paid the price of these right-wing policy failures.

This is not to say that right-wing strategies could never possibly work. Perhaps if a monetarist cold-bath were applied long enough and frigidly enough, the profit function might eventually shift upward through a re-constitution of capitalist control. Such an outcome cannot be ruled out in principle. All we can say from the experience of the late 1970s and 1980s, in the case of economies like the United States and the United Kingdom, is that such a hallowed moment had not yet arrived and that, in its absence, some of the political consensus which had made right-wing initiatives possible had begun to unravel.[58]

Keynesian interventions

Many liberals and progressives have traditionally hoped to promote fuller employment and more rapid growth through government demand-side interventions or support for higher wages. But the social structuralist model illustrated in figure 12.1 casts serious doubt upon the political economic promise of such policy strategies.

Suppose, referring back to equation (1.1) in table 12.1, that the central government sought to improve macro performance through expansionary fiscal policy. Assuming that such policies resulted in higher normalized government purchases of goods and services, the utilization function would shift down and to the right from $\langle r^*, \phi^* \rangle$ in figure 12.1. Since it is clear that any strategy affecting only the $\phi(r)$ curve can at best move macroeconomic equilibrium along the profit function, this means that higher levels of ϕ can be achieved only at lower levels of r.

The social structuralist model suggests that such expansionary initiatives are likely to be problematic on several grounds.

First of all, because of the shape of the profit function, any gain in capacity utilization benefits workers at the expense of lower profits for owners, and for this reason is likely to encounter intense political opposition from the latter, often expressed in the guise of the need to avoid "overheating" or excessive inflation. Because it is likely in many advanced capitalist economies that business interests will be able to assert their interests vigorously, it is further likely that expansionary efforts which result in lower profit rates will be opposed and successfully rolled back. The social structuralist model thus highlights potential dimensions of class conflict over economic policy initiatives which more conventional models tend to obscure.

Second, the gains in capacity utilization from expansionary macro policy become increasingly limited as ϕ rises because of the increasingly negative slope of the non-linear $r(\phi)$ curve. Whereas traditional Keynesian and post-Keynesian models have highlighted such barriers to sustained expansion at or above the level of full utilization, the social structuralist model suggests that such diminishing returns are likely to kick in considerably below full-utilization levels.[59]

Third, as already noted in the previous section, the trade-off between r and ϕ reflected in the relevant portion of the $r(\phi)$ curve means that any expansionary shift of the utilization function will do little to raise private investment (and may actually decrease it), since the investment gain due to an increase in utilization will be offset by the investment loss due to the decrease of profitability – providing little or no comfort for long-run growth prospects. Indeed, other countries' experience with populist or left-Keynesian economic policies indicates that this dampening profit squeeze on investment is often a decisive obstacle (see Sachs, 1990).

Because of these barriers to effective Keynesian expansion, many in the heterodox tradition have hoped that "wage-led growth" might be possible, that direct (and in this context exogenous policy) support for wage expansion might help boost macro performance. Suppose that trade union bargaining power were enhanced in an advanced economy and that they were able to bargain for higher wages. All other things equal, many have hoped that such increases in the wage share (and corollary reductions in the profit share) would improve macro performance by increasing utilization.

Such policy interventions would take effect in the structuralist models discussed here through an exogenous downward shift in the profit function. But as figure 12.1 shows and as both Marglin and Bhaduri (1990) and Bowles and Boyer (1990; this volume) make clear, such "wage-led" expansion would require that two conditions hold in the economy: both (a) a negatively sloped utilization function and (b) system equilibrium in a positively sloped portion of the profit function. If one or the other or both of these conditions does not pertain, then a reduced profit share would not be likely, all other things equal, to result in a higher level of utilization. But the empirical evidence outlined both in this chapter and in Bowles and Boyer (this volume) suggest that such strategies build on wishful thinking – that in open advanced macro economies, at the least, such negatively sloped utilization functions are relatively unlikely to pertain.[60] The evidence sketched in the previous section further anticipates that in economies such as the US, equilibrium is not likely to occur in an upward sloping portion of the profit curve. For both reasons, I would have strong reasons for anticipating that Keynesian wage-led strategies would be unlikely to produce the "wage-led" outcomes which their proponents anticipate.

Toward a democratic strategy

It follows from the preceding discussion that policies seeking fuller employment and enhanced investment probably ought to look elsewhere. In terms of the social structuralist model outlined above, more precisely, it would appear that macroeconomic strategy should seek to shift or alter one or both of the two remaining curves in figure 12.2, the profit function or the iso-investment loci. I review here the logic of democratic policy approaches which could potentially both enhance macro performance and advance the broader social goals of greater democracy and equality. The point of this final section is not to provide a detailed blueprint of policy initiatives but rather to illustrate the *types* of strategic alternatives which – when viewed through the lenses of this social structuralist model – would appear to hold considerable promise. It is important to note in advance, further, that the effectiveness of some of these potentially promising strategies could not easily be realized within the current institutional context of economies such as the United States but would depend on changes in their institutional rules of the game.

Shifting the iso-investment loci

Clearly any policy that served to increase the rate of investment forthcoming at given levels of profitability and capacity utilization would be desirable. Such an upward shift in the $I(r, \phi)$ function would serve effectively to relabel the iso-investment curves of figure 12.2, increasing the rate of investment associated with each such curve; a higher rate of investment would then be attainable at the macroeconomic equilibrium at point a in figure 12.2.[61]

This would require autonomous shifts in the generalized investment function in (6). Two primary sources of such shifts flow most transparently from the logic of the social structuralist model: an increase in public investment, I^G; and an auspicious change in expectations producing a favorable shift in the parameters of the investment function with respect to either or both profitability and utilization.

The former case seems relatively promising; all other things equal, increased I^G would have positive effects. But how is such spending financed? Three fiscal alternatives can be envisioned: (a) One path would involve a change in the composition of government expenditures from non-investment to investment categories, holding tax rates constant. As long as the categories from which expenditures were transferred were relatively unproductive, such as defense spending in the United States, then such changes would help boost the longer-term rate of growth of potential output without other potentially serious economic reverberations. (b) Alternatively, at constant levels of utilization, such increased public expenditure would need to be financed by increased taxes. At this point, the potential net impact of such a program cannot be fully anticipated without specification of the character and distributional impact of the higher taxes. If the increased taxes fell disproportionately on capital, for example, then potentially diminished profitability might offset the higher government investment in (6) by lower private investment. If the higher taxes fell disproportionately on employee compensation, higher investment might still result but in ways which did not foster greater economic equity – an outcome corrosive of a democratic strategy's ambitions. (c) Or, finally, increased public investment could be financed by increased government borrowing. In the context of this model, however, two additional problems could ensue. First, it might be that increased government borrowing tended to "crowd out" private investment by putting pressure on credit markets; despite conventional fears about the strength of such effects, however, available evidence suggests that such crowding out would have marginal impact, at best, on private investment.[62] Second, deficitary stimulus would potentially encounter some of the more general problems facing Keynesian demand-side strategies, as reviewed above; these political and economic barriers would be likely to limit the potential short-term stimulus afforded by sustained increases in government borrowing, at least beyond the very short term, and would be likely to encounter resistance from capital if, as anticipated in the previous discussion of such interventions, they resulted in a short-term decline in the profit rate.

Some (but probably not all) forms of increased public investment seem promising, in short, but more because they would be likely to enhance long-term growth prospects than because they would have favorable impact on short-term economic well-being.

What about shifts in the parameters of the private investment function which served to increase private investment at a given equilibrium combination $\langle r^*, \phi^* \rangle$? If "animal spirits" soared, all other things equal, it would appear from this model that long-term growth prospects would unambiguously improve. But could such increased private investment be financed? Without credit explicitly incorporated into the model, by definition, the higher desired investment levels could not be directly financed out of profits since our thought experiment here presupposes a constant level of profitability and utilization. We would thus need to expand the model, considerably beyond the scope of this chapter, in order to integrate credit and borrowing into the analysis. Whether the expanded investment would enhance profitability enough to cover the increased service charges of higher accumulated debt would need to be modeled explicitly. Short of that extension, the possible returns to enhanced animal spirits must remain uncertain.[63]

Other less transparent strategies for shifting the investment curves also flow from the logic of the model.

One alternative approach to stimulating investment recognizes that a major obstacle to capital formation is the uncertainty surrounding future market demand conditions. If each firm could be assured that other firms were also intending to expand their level of economic activity through new capital formation, then each firm could be more confident that its own expansion of productive capacity would encounter a corresponding expansion of demand for its output. At issue here is the classic Keynesian coordination-failure problem: new hiring and investment decisions by individual firms fail to take account of the benefits of expanding markets for other firms. One way to resolve this Keynesian coordination-failure problem is to increase the predictability and certainty of market growth by reducing the volatility of aggregate demand over time.

Such reduced volatility can potentially be achieved through standard Keynesian means – by conventional automatic stabilizers (such as progressive taxation or public unemployment compensation) and by discretionary stabilization policies. At the microeconomic level, the same effects could be achieved by providing greater cyclical job security for workers; in this event, when demand falls, individual firms maintain higher levels of employment (presumably by borrowing), providing in effect a private unemployment compensation mechanism.[64] It is interesting in this regard to note one result from Weisskopf's (1992) comparative study of profitability across some of the leading advanced economies. He finds that the profit rate is much more cyclically volatile, other things equal, in economies such as the United States which feature relatively more conflictual capital–labor institutions. In economies such as Germany and Sweden, where greater employee security is forthcoming, it appears that conditions more conducive to stability in the level of warranted investment also pertain.

Raising the profit function

An even more effective macroeconomic policy intervention would be one that served to shift the profit function $r(\phi)$ upward. In the context of the social structuralist model specified above, the effects of this strategy are illustrated in figure 12.4. Holding the utilization function fixed at $\phi(r)$, the profit curve shifts upward from $r(\phi)_1$ to $r(\phi)_2$, raising the rate of profit at every level of capacity utilization and resulting in a new equilibrium at point b. Given the slopes of the curves in this specification of the social structuralist model, this new equilibrium would yield an unambiguous Pareto improvement for the economy, with a higher profit rate, a higher rate of capacity utilization, and a higher rate of investment. In addition to these economic advantages, such a shift also has obvious potential political advantages in advanced capitalist economies as well, since it would serve to forestall potential capitalist opposition to expansionary policies.

Progressives typically wince at such prospects, however, for a number of obvious and valid reasons: (a) The strategy overlaps with the objectives which right-wing forces have pursued in economies such as the United States since the mid 1970s, potentially tainting the strategy with guilt by association. (b) People on the left are habitually suspicious about the effects of policies which would increase the rate of profit. (c) Within the structure of more traditional macro models, virtually the only way to shift the profit function upward would be to reduce the wage share by putting downward pressure on wages, an approach which would both isolate the left from its traditional political allies and appear to confound the background premise introduced at the beginning of this chapter – that a democratic macro strategy should pursue ways of improving macro performance which fostered greater economic equity rather than trampling on it.

But traditional analyses have been too restrictive. Within the framework presented here, there are some plausible paths toward raising the

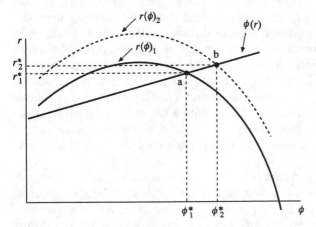

Figure 12.4 Shifting the profit function upwards

profit function about which progressives might conceivably feel much less squeamish.

One promising approach to shifting the profit function upward is suggested by the critical role of public capital goods and services in private-sector production. Many of the capital inputs required for efficient productive activity in a modern economy – education, training, communications, transportation, and other elements of an economy's infrastructure – have a significant "public good" character that precludes their being supplied in adequate amounts by private firms. Here lies another coordination failure, in that it is optimal for each private enterprise independently to underinvest in such capital goods and services. Only the economy-wide public sector can be expected to solve the coordination failure problem and undertake the needed infrastructural investment. Note that public investment thus contributes both directly to higher levels of overall capital formation, through shifts in the iso-investment loci, and indirectly to higher levels of private-sector productivity and profitability.[65]

Perhaps even more promising, the profit function could also potentially be raised by institutional changes at the enterprise and economy level which helped to moderate capital–labor conflict. Imagine, for example, that macroeconomic conditions assured employment for every worker – whether or not they retained their specific job in a particular enterprise; workers would have much less to fear from labor-saving innovation within their own enterprise. Imagine further that enterprise property rights were restructured so that the costs and benefits of capital formation were shared with workers; owners and workers would confront more similar risks and payoffs in investment decisions, reducing investors' skepticism about potential worker erosion of the expected returns to innovation and investment. If, as a result of such institutional changes, higher levels of investment and innovation became a cooperatively repro-duced equilibrium outcome, it would take much less in the way of enforcement costs to ensure that these higher levels of investment and innovation were reproduced. The resulting boost to organizational and technological innovation would increase economy-wide productivity, all other things equal, and lift the rate of profit attainable at any given rate of utilization.

Why might such democratic strategies succeed in raising the profit function when right-wing strategies in the 1980s, as noted above, appear to have failed at achieving precisely the same objective. We encounter here what Bowles, Weisskopf, and I call the "costs of keeping people down" (Bowles, Gordon, and Weisskopf, 1990, chapters 12–13). Raising the profit function by wielding the stick bears considerable auxiliary costs – the costs of supervisors (or what we more generally call "guard labor"), of high-employee turnover, and of employee resistance (however inter-mittent). Even though profits might be enhanced through lower wages or higher labor intensity as a result of right-wing strategies, many if not most of these potential increases in profitability would be likely to be offset by the added costs of keeping people down. Because democratic strategies, relying on the carrot rather than the stick, are in principle self-monitoring and self-reproducing (see Bowles, this volume), they are likely to avoid many of these additional costs incumbent in the right-wing stick-wielding approach.

This sounds perilously like the "free lunch" whose existence econo-mists deny. But in economies such as the United States, the meal would not be *gratis*. Such a cooperative solution would hinge on institutional and policy changes which served to promote long-term employment relations and the sharing of profits and decision making between workers and owners. In the case of the US macro economy, for example, it would require, *inter alia*, dramatic improvements in workers' ability to organize unions, significant increases in employment security (at least as perceived by workers), and dramatically enhanced opportunities for worker partici-pation and control at the enterprise level.[66] These institutional changes would involve the start-up costs of any sort of major institutional restruc-turing – the costs of coalition-building, legislative activity, and education – and would in this sense hardly be free. The potential appeal of the democratic strategy, however, rests on the probability that such fixed costs of institutional restructuring would be easily amortized over time

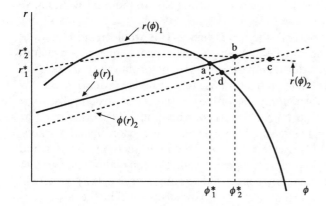

Figure 12.5   Flattening the profit function

through the steady and presumably handsome returns to raising the profit curve.

Flattening the profit function

Alternatively, comparably enhanced macro possibilities could be achieved by means of new policies that served to flatten out the profit function, reducing its curvature around the same average profit rate. This approach is illustrated in figure 12.5 by the shift from curve $r(\phi)_1$ to $r(\phi)_2$. With such a flattened profit curve, which would involve an attenuation of the high-employment profit squeeze, the macro economy would settle at a new and unambiguously more favorable equilibrium $\langle r^*_2, \phi^*_2 \rangle$ at point b.[67]

This approach would also have additional advantages over the strategy of raising the profit function – advantages which would result from improving the trade-off between profitability and capacity utilization along the profit function. This would increase the effectiveness of expansionary macroeconomic policies designed to shift the product-market function to the right (as with curve $\phi(r)_2$), for such shifts would then result in larger increases in capacity utilization and smaller decreases in profitability than if such expansion were undertaken in the absence of a flattening of $r(\phi)$; this possibility is illustrated by the difference between the movement from b to c and the movement from a to d in figure 12.5. Perhaps more important, on a political plane, such a curve flattening would tend to moderate capital's opposition to expansionary policies, since the profit rate at point c would be only marginally lower than at the previous point b.[68] Thus the objections raised earlier to a traditional, demand-side expansionary policy of shifting $\phi(r)$ to the right would have considerably less force.

How does one "flatten" the profit curve? This would require ways of reducing the salience of the high-employment profit squeeze – which in turn underlies the critical downward trend of profitability as rates of employment and capacity utilization rise to ever higher levels. Unemployment in a capitalist economy, according to the social structuralist logic outlined here, is not just a Keynesian coordination failure occasioned by the mismatch of aggregate supply and demand in uncoordinated markets. Unemployment also arises because of the conflict between owners and workers and the role of unemployment in disciplining labor. The greater the importance of unemployment as a disciplining device, the greater will be the persistence of unemployment and the steeper will be the downward slope of the profit function.

Flattening the profit function thus requires that reliance on the threat and cost of job loss be reduced in favor of reliance on alternative means of worker motivation, which hinge less on negative sanctions associated with unemployment and more on positive incentives undiminished by higher rates of employment and capacity utilization. That such changes are plausible, *even within a capitalist context*, is illustrated by Weisskopf's finding (1987) that there appears to be a positive relationship between productivity growth and high-employment rates in Germany and Sweden, inverting the relationship which appears to prevail in the United States and the United Kingdom.

Such transformations would call for changes in the institutional structure of relations between owners and workers, at the level of the individual enterprise, which would reduce conflict and enhance cooperation. But such changes cannot simply be invoked. They are likely to require changes in enterprise property rights. If workers are to be motivated positively, they must have a meaningful stake in the residual income generated by their joint productive activity. When workers are residual claimants on the firm's income they have a strong motivation to engage in mutual monitoring of their workmates in order to foster high standards of work quality and effort. This suggests at least that profit-sharing mechanisms should be encouraged, and more strongly that democratically organized worker-owned cooperatives may be the most promising form of enterprise organization.[69]

In economies such as the United States, where production relations fall far short of these desiderata, there could be two principal routes toward greater worker participation and ownership, one direct and the other indirect.

The direct approach lies through encouragement of worker-owned and

Table 12.4. *Democratic strategies for improved macro performance*

	Type of effect in social structuralist model		
	Investment loci	Raise profit function	Flatten profit function
Public investment	√	√	
Reduce demand volatility			
Automatic stabilizers	√		
Job security	√	√	
Promote firm democracy			
Democratize property rights		√	√
Subsidize democratic firms		√	√
Enhance workers' voice			√
Reduce reliance on dismissal			√

managed cooperatives. Because cooperative work places find it difficult to borrow the funds necessary to start up, a key to their success would be the provision of credit to these democratic enterprises on terms as favorable as those accorded their corporate competitors. Other forms of support to enterprises that foster positive work motivation through some kind of direct worker and/or community involvement or control would include subsidized training in business management and democratic decision making for new worker-owners.

The indirect approach lies through union collective bargaining. Where workers can count on securing a large share of productivity gains through collective bargaining, and where unions give workers what Freeman and Medoff (1984) call a "voice" in the management of the firm, some of the effects of democratic participation and ownership may redound. They conclude (1984, p. 180) that "higher productivity appears to run hand in hand with good industrial relations and to be spurred by competition in the product market." A democratic economic strategy for the United States would help promote positive union effects on productivity through labor law reform to remove the formidable obstacles now blocking workers' paths toward unionization, through promotion of fuller employment to enhance workers' bargaining power, through industrial policies that would seek to promote direct union involvement in programs to enhance enterprise efficiency, and through expanded federal monitoring of union elections to help reduce infringements on union democracy.

There appear to be, in conclusion, several promising policy options for promoting stronger macroeconomic performance in the advanced economies. It further appears that pursuit of these policies would increase employment levels and productivity growth in ways which simultaneously promote greater equality and democratic participation. Table 12.4 provides a compact summary of this review of democratic policy initiatives, indicating down its rows the kinds of policy initiatives and institutional changes which would seem desirable and locating for each row the type of effect they would be likely to have on the relationships stipulated by the social structuralist model.

Such enticing promises can often appear soft-headed and utopian. I hope that the analysis outlined in this chapter has avoided such illusory argument. Deriving potentially promising democratic strategic orientations from the social structuralist macro foundations presented in this chapter should help to remind us of three important final conclusions.

First, the model serves to highlight some important differences between more traditional Keynesian demand-side strategies and the kind of democratic supply-side strategies emphasized here. In the absence of critical interventions to moderate the high-employment profit squeeze, traditional demand-side policies to promote full employment in the future are likely to founder on exactly the same kind of combination of inflationary barriers and political opposition which plagued and increasingly eviscerated those strategies in the 1970s and 1980s.

Second, it serves equally to highlight the critical importance of changes in the institutional rules of the game regulating capitalist economies. As long as we remain locked in the kind of counter-productive conflictual capital–labor relations which characterize economies like the United States, we are likely to remain trapped in the stagflationary quagmires into which many advanced economies plowed in the early 1970s. Cooperative relationships appear to have great promise; the handshake appears to have considerably greater appeal than the fist. Democratization of the economy makes sense, but democratization will not fall from the sky. Concrete, in some cases far-reaching changes in the rules of the game will apparently be necessary to reap its potential harvest.

Third, even though it may appear that pursuing macro policies which would serve to raise and/or to flatten the profit function could advance everyone's interest, such policies are nonetheless likely to encounter stiff opposition in some quarters. Whereas it might appear that wages and employment could be enhanced without necessarily cutting into profits through such strategies, some economic agents would suffer a substantial loss of prestige and status from economic democratization. It is a common experience in the United States, for example, that middle-level managers resist enhanced workplace participation, even though they realize such institutional changes can potentially improve productivity and profitability, because their own economic roles would be undermined. Such resistance may not always be easy to overcome; some arm-twisting may be necessary. It may be necessary, for example, to institute substantial penalties against firms which do not join in a process of democratization – precisely in order to encourage them to institute changes which may, in the long run, serve their own interests.

Such changes may seem daunting, and they are. But the possibilities are real. One can compactly and simply formulate the lessons of this essay: Cooperative handshakes are good for macroeconomic performance, democracy and equality are good for handshakes, but some arm-twisting and rule changes may be necessary to get everyone playing the game. That a democratic macroeconomic strategy reflecting these imperatives and possibilities would require significant changes in the institutional "rules of the game" merely underscores both the challenging opportunities before us and the scale of political mobilization which will undoubtedly be necessary to realize those prospects.[70]

Notes

The author would like to thank Sam Bowles, Robert Eisner, Steve Marglin, Lance Taylor, Tom Weisskopf, the editors of this volume, and participants in the political economy seminar at the University of California–Riverside for helpful suggestions.

1 See Glyn *et al.* (1990), Epstein and Schor (1990), and Glyn (this volume) for useful background on macro performance and economic policy through the successive stages of boom and stagnation in the post-war period.
2 See Bowles, Gordon, and Weisskopf (1990, chapters 9–10) for a detailed review of the record of right-wing economic policy in the United States, Green (1989) for the UK, and both Armstrong, Glyn, and Harrison (1991, chapters 17–19), and Glyn (this volume) for a broader review of economic policy and macro performance in the advanced countries.
3 This chapter builds closely on joint work with Samuel Bowles and Thomas E. Weisskopf. In particular, it represents a direct expansion and elaboration of sections of Weisskopf, Bowles, and Gordon (1992).
4 The chapter does not directly address the problem of the *environmental sustainability* of long-term growth. For some further (though only skeletal) discussion of this issue, see Bowles, Gordon, and Weisskopf (1990, chapters 12–13).
5 Some explanation of nomenclature: I prefer *not* to work with some combination of the usual Ricardian/Marxian/Keynesian/Kaleckian/Sraffian labels – whether "neo" or not – in order to emphasize the synthetic character of the approach represented here, with feet firmly rooted in many of those traditions. I deploy the generic term "structuralist" for four reasons: (1) to emphasize the structures of determination and effect of economic

classes, thus building on the concerns with distribution of all of the heterodox traditions and on the importance for some, especially within the Marxian tradition, of class conflict; (2) to stress the importance, highlighted particularly by the social structure of accumulation and regulationist approaches (see Gordon, Weisskopf, and Bowles, 1987 and Boyer, 1990), of the institutional structures (or regimes) whose configurations condition different logics and dynamics of accumulation and growth in different capitalist economies; (3) to emphasize important communalities with the tradition of "structuralist" macroeconomics focussing on problems and possibilities within the developing world (see Taylor, 1983, 1991); and (4) to underscore the inclination of this literature *not* to insist on explicit micro foundations for every macro relationship it explores (even though micro foundations have been formulated for many of those relationships). I use the modifier "social" to designate the particular implementation of structuralist macro economies presented in this chapter in order to stress its roots in the "social structures of accumulation" perspective as well as in the kinds of "social" models of macro relationships which Bowles, Weisskopf, and I have emphasized (see for example, Weisskopf, Bowles, and Gordon, 1983).

6 Some of the earliest explorations are represented by Rowthorn (1982), Marglin (1984), and Taylor (1985). More recent developments, again using a variety of labels to describe their work, are pursued and reviewed in Bhaduri and Marglin (1990), Bowles and Boyer (1990), Skott (1989), Bowles, Gordon, and Weisskopf (1989), Dutt (1990), Taylor (1991), and Gordon (1994).

7 It would need to be shown, in a more complete model, that a reasonable approach to price determination would be consistent with the logic of the real model introduced here. For the connections between this real model and an expanded model taking price determination into account, see Gordon (1994, chapter 5).

8 For the steps required to move from this double reduced-form representation to a fuller structural model, see Gordon (1994, chapters 4–6).

9 Many alternative normalizations are consistent with the recent heterodox literature. My own choice of normalization here relies on two main justifications: (a) Recent literature on the dynamic properties of alternative macroeconomic models has focussed explicitly on the relationship of capacity utilization to other critical macro barometers; my normalization, resulting in a simple indicator of capacity utilization, permits easy comparison with much of that literature (see, for example, Taylor, 1985 and Marglin and Bhaduri, 1990). (b) My recent joint work with Bowles and Weisskopf has also relied explicitly on capacity utilization as a measure of the activity level of the economy as well as an instrument for "purging" the effects of the macro economy from our "underlying" power variables (see, in particular, Bowles, Gordon, and Weisskopf, 1989). Use of capacity utilization as a measure of aggregate performance thus allows for direct incorporation of our joint results where appropriate.

10 Among the presentations in the recent literature, the model in Taylor (1991, table 2.1) is probably closest in dimensions and internal logic to the formulation outlined here in table 12.1, although Taylor's model does not propose the more particular "social structuralist" specifications which follow toward the end of this section.

11 Output is not separately determined in this model because it is assumed a priori that output equals expenditures and therefore that the balance condition represented by (1.1) strictly holds. Potential output remains exogenous to the model.

12 Marglin (1984, chapters 6–7) provides a useful review of the analytic foundations of this heterodox approach.

13 This follows the suggestions of Marglin's "disequilibrium" hypothesis in ibid., chapter 6.

14 In Gordon (this volume), a purely macro path toward derivation of a structuralist consumption function is followed which results in an alternative, more complex version of equation (1.2) in which the profit share, rather than the profit rate, captures the influence of distribution. Either formulation is consistent with the logic of the model presented here in table 12.1.

15 See, for example, Rowthorn (1982), Taylor (1985, 1991), and Marglin and Bhaduri (1990).

16 Although such an approach to aggregate investment is not particularly controversial, it is hardly a trivial matter rigorously to derive such an aggregate investment function from micro foundations. One useful approach is suggested by Skott (1989, appendix 6A).

17 Both Marglin (1984) and Taylor (1991) note, for example, that they set aside interest rate effects on investment for reasons of analytic convenience.

18 This approach is explicitly developed and applied in Gordon, Weisskopf, and Bowles (1993).

19 Bhaduri and Marglin (1990, p. 380 and appendix A) raise questions about an investment function incorporating the profit rate rather than the profit share; see below for further discussion of this issue.

20 See, for example, Blecker (1989), Bhaduri and Marglin (1990), and Taylor (1991, chapters 7–9).

21 See, for example, Dornbusch (1980, chapter 3).

22 In a more complete, longer-term model, both the interest rate and potential output would be endogenized, leaving only the Z_i as exogenous variables. I should note, as well, one additional dimension of simplification in this model. In both (1.2) and (1.3), the effects of some of the independent variables should be taken *after taxes*, such as the effect of the rate of profit on investment. I have abstracted from tax effects in this simplified presentation, as well as in the econometric estimates presented below; in a more complete model, tax rates would be added to the list of exogenous variables. (See Gordon, this volume, for estimation of consumption and investment equations taking taxes and transfers into account.)

23 This is the structuralist equivalent of the Keynesian I-S relation, specified here in utilization/profitability (rather than output/interest-rate) space.

24 See, in particular, Marglin and Bhaduri (1990) and Bowles and Boyer (1990, this volume).

25 In the discussion which follows, I write occasionally as if the rate of capacity utilization and the employment rate were closely correlated. This may or may not be the case, of course, depending on output–employment effects and labor supply effects. See Bowles and Boyer (this volume) for more discussion of this issue. See also Gordon (1994, chapters 5–6) for a full set of relationships connecting the rates of capacity utilization and employment.

26 The formulation in this paragraph is based primarily on theoretical expectations. In the next section, I review empirical evidence for the United States which is consistent with these expectations.

27 The logic of such expectations, although their model is formulated in wage-rate/employment-rate space, is illustrated in Bowles and Boyer (1990).

28 See Glyn and Sutcliffe (1972), Boddy and Crotty (1975), and Bowles, Gordon, and Weisskopf (1986).

29 These expectations can be elaborated more formally. Following (1.7) in table 12.1, accepting the functional dependence of the profit share on the level of capacity utilization, and setting the potential-output/capital ratio equal to one, the profit rate can be written as $r(\phi) \equiv \pi(\phi) \cdot \phi$. It follows that the rate of change of the profit rate with respect

to utilization, in this simplified functional relationship, can be expressed as $dr/d\phi = \pi + \phi\pi'(\phi)$. Using an atomistic model of capital–labor relations, Bowles and Boyer (1990) show that the level of the profit share becomes negative at levels of utilization close to but less than full employment; that $\pi'(\phi) < 0$; and that $\pi'(\phi)$ approaches negative infinity as ϕ approaches full capacity from below. Consider, then, the sign of $dr/d\phi$ as ϕ ranges between 0 and 1. At $\phi = 0$, the profit share will be positive if the profit share is anywhere positive (since $\pi'(\phi) < 0$) while the second term drops out (since $\phi = 0$). We thus begin at low levels of utilization with $dr/d\phi > 0$. At levels close to full utilization, by contrast, π has turned negative while $\pi'(\phi)$ is approaching negative infinity. Even though ϕ is approaching one, both the first and second terms will clearly be negative and $dr/d\phi$ will have become negative. We can therefore conclude on these simplifying theoretical grounds that the profit rate first rises and then falls as utilization rises from zero to one and that the maximum of the profit rate falls somewhere in the $0 < \phi < 1$ interval. (I am grateful to Sam Bowles for suggesting this formulation.)

30 In the long run, they may also take heed of the point on the profitability function coinciding with the maximum rate of accumulation; more on this below.

31 See Gordon, Weisskopf, and Bowles (1990) for evidence of the inverse relationship between the foreign rate of profit and the US domestic rate of investment. In the limiting case of what might be called "global hypermobility," where capital can move without barriers from one country to another in search of higher profitability, the elasticity of investment with respect to profitability approaches infinity. As I argue elsewhere (Gordon, 1988), reports of such hypermobility have probably been exaggerated in recent years.

32 As the shapes of the curves in figure 12.1 suggest, this equilibrium need not be unique. Given the non-linear configuration of the profitability function, there could potentially be a second equilibrium at very low levels of capacity utilization (depending on the vertical intercepts of the two curves). The empirical evidence reviewed in the next section, which suggests that the economy spends most if not all of its time to the right of the maximum of the profit curve, leads me to elide this second possible point of macro equilibrium.

33 In the context of this model, I define "short-term" as the period within which it is reasonable to treat the level of potential output (Q^*) as exogenous and the longer-term as the period during which the pace of investment begins endogenously to feed back on the level of potential output.

34 Strictly speaking, this is a necessary but not a sufficient condition, since it is also necessary that vertical displacements of profitability result in a return to equilibrium. In equation (1.5), as represented on figure 12.1, points above (below) the $r(\phi)$ curve represent situations in which profits are too "high" ("low") given the prevailing constellation of technical and social conditions affecting the supply side of the economy; according to the models underlying this expression, in conditions of excess (inadequate) profitability, labor extraction and bargaining relations will tend to push profits back down (up) toward the optimal level of profitability at prevailing levels of utilization. Since these conditions are less likely to change in the short run, I have concentrated in the text on the requirements for stability in the excess demand function.

35 Note that a second possible equilibrium at low levels of economic activity, not explicitly represented in figure 12.1, would be unstable, since at such an equilibrium the positive slope of the profitability function would be greater (steeper) than the positive slope of the utilization function and the stability condition in (4) would not be met.

36 The logic and details of these theoretical expectations are elaborated in Bowles, Gordon, and Weisskopf (1989; 1990, chapter 10).

37 This argument is developed in Bowles, Gordon, and Weisskopf (1990, chapters 5–6, 10). See also an empirical illustration of this effect in figure 12.3 below.

38 Marglin and Bhaduri (1990) provide a useful discussion of these potential effects.

39 These iso-investment curves correspond to the growth loci sketched in Marglin and Bhaduri (1990). They are drawn here as convex to the origin to reflect the assumption of diminishing marginal contributions of each factor to investment as well as a positive effect of increases in each factor on the marginal contribution of the other – for example, the effect of profitability on investment is greater at higher levels of capacity utilization.

40 For further clarification on this point, see Blecker (1989) and Taylor (1990).

41 Based mostly on these considerations, for example, Marglin and Bhaduri (1990) consistently draw their PE curve, analogous to $r(\phi)$ here, with an upward slope. They refer tangentially to the possibility of a downward-sloping profitability function in a footnote (ibid., note 4).

42 In our joint work we also illustrate a second trade-off involving a conflict between (1) the desirability of having a low real interest rate to promote investment, and (2) the desirability of having a high real interest rate to maintain the value of the domestic currency as a way of lowering the real price of imports and thereby contributing to a high profit share. High real interest rates, in short, are good for profits but not so hot for the level of economic activity. For discussion and evidence supporting this hypothesis, see Bowles, Gordon, and Weisskopf (1990, chapter 10 and especially figure 10.4).

43 These results are either reproduced from or closely replicate previously published equations; readers are referred to the sources cited in the table for complete explanation and documentation of the variables and estimation procedures.

44 See Bowles, Gordon, and Weisskopf (1989, pp. 123ff.) for the "purging" procedure.

45 The composite index was estimated with annual data and then interpolated to produce a quarterly estimate. See Gordon (1994, chapters 3–4) for explanation of the interpolation procedure.

46 The squared term for utilization is included as a *polynomial distributed lag* in the estimation of (2.4), with the sum of the lag coefficients reported in the table. This is necessary both to avoid strong collinearity between the level and the squared values of the contemporaneous term but also to capture, as is true with the (lagged) trend term in (2.3), the effects of sustained utilization pressure.

47 I represent the range of variation for the profit rate by its cycle averages to abstract from the wide cyclical variation in the rate of profit.

48 I should add one note of clarification about the graph in figure 12.3: Since the observed values for capacity utilization for the period of estimation fall uniformly to the right of the imputed ϕr_{max}, we do not technically speaking observe *in the data* the actual inflection point in the non-linear curve. But the inflection point ϕr_{max} is consistent with the estimated curvature of that curve, reflected in the coefficients on the first- and second-order terms in capacity utilization. It is thus reasonable to assume that, were the level of economic activity to shift substantially to the left in figure 12.3, it would "encounter" the positively sloped portion of the curve.

49 For application of such labor extraction models to the case of the United States, see Bowles (1991) for an empirical study of the case of the real wage and Weisskopf, Bowles, and Gordon (1983) for the case of hourly output.

50 For general analyses of important institutional differences between the United States and many other advanced economies which are consistent with and help support the inferences in this sub-section, see the useful comparative analyses in Esping-Andersen (1990) and Pekkarinen, Pohjola, and Rowthorn (1992).

51 For additional analysis which extends and deepens Weisskopf's comparative findings on productivity, see also Buchele and Christiansen (1992). For some further reflections on similarities between the US and the UK, at least during the 1980s, see Green (1989).

52 As noted above, these formulations abstract from the effect of taxes. See Gordon (this volume) for estimated consumption and investment equations which take taxes and transfers into account.

53 The instruments used in the estimation included normalized government purchases, normalized change in business inventories, normalized gross residential investment; the profit rate and interest rates included in each of the three behavioral equations; as well as the exogenous variables in the profit equation in table 12.2.

54 I preferred to use the same ARMA correction across all three equations in order to simplify comparison rather than varying the form of correction across the equations, as would have been warranted on strict econometric grounds. While the magnitude of the estimated coefficients in the respective equations is sensitive to common or varying corrections across the equations, the final composite conclusion empirically affirming a positive slope for the utilization function is robust across all the alternative corrections I tried.

55 This characterization of conditions at the beginning of the 1980s relies on Bowles, Gordon, and Weisskopf (1990, chapters 5–6).

56 This argument is presented in some detail in ibid (chapter 10) as well as in Bowles, Gordon, and Weisskopf (1989). Referring to simple quantitative measures, our index of "underlying" capitalist power averaged 2.86 in the 1973–9 business cycle and declined slightly to 2.80 in the 1979–88 cycle.

57 Using the data definitions deployed in the previous section, the average index of capacity utilization declined from 0.952 in 1973–9 to 0.943 in 1979–89 while the after-tax rate of corporate profit increased from 5.5 percent to 6.0 percent over the same interval.

58 For further comment, see Armstrong, Glyn, and Harrison (1991, chapters 17–19), Bowles, Gordon, and Weisskopf (1990, chapters 8–11), and Green (1989).

59 See Bowles' and Boyer's discussion (1990) of their "wage explosion" point for elaboration of this likelihood.

60 Bhaduri and Marglin (1990) also anticipate this possibility about open economies on theoretical grounds, but do not ground their conclusions in the empirical evidence.

61 Such a favorable shift in the investment function would also result in a rightward shift of the $\phi(r)$ curve, pushing the equilibrium point along the downward-sloping profit function. The additional effects on investment from this secondary displacement of equilibrium would be likely to be small, however, since the positive effects of higher utilization would be approximately offset by the negative effects of a lower rate of profit. Furthermore, the shift in the investment function itself might be resisted by owners who feared its potentially negative effect on profitability; this once again illustrates the crucial importance of potentially conflicting macro objectives highlighted by the model's attention to distribution.

62 See, for a brief review of these problems of financial-market reverberation, Gordon (this volume). See also Bernstein and Heilbroner (1989).

63 See Gordon (this volume) for some further discussion of the possibility that increased investment can be self-financing. See also Gordon (1994, chapter 7) for extension of the left structuralist model to incorporate credit and borrowing.

64 See Bowles (this volume) and Epstein and Gintis (this volume) for further discussion of some of the kinds of policy changes which might result in such micro transformations.

65 A wide variety of recent empirical work on the US economy has highlighted the deterioration of the US infrastructure, the increasing inadequacy of public investment,

and the extent to which enhanced public capital formation can be expected to increase the profitability of private-sector economic activity. See, for example, Aschauer (1989).

66 Bowles, Gordon, and Weisskopf (1990, chapters 12–14) discuss the logic and possibilities for many such institutional changes in the US case.

67 The curve $r(\phi)_2$ in figure 12.5 is drawn as if the relationship between profitability and utilization at low levels of utilization, below the peak in the profit curve, was also flattened, reducing the rate at which the profit rate drops as utilization falls to the left of $\phi r_{\max}$. This aspect of the illustration is not necessary for the policy points which follow, since they focus exclusively on the possible moderation of the high employment profit squeeze as utilization approaches full employment. The curve was drawn with the shape presented in figure 12.5 in order to underscore graphically the idea that the curve flattening along the profit curve is being supposed to occur, in this thought experiment, at more or less the same average rate of profit as in $r(\phi)_1$ over the relevant range of the respective curves.

68 The same logic applies to the issue of inflationary pressure resulting from expansionary government policies. All other things equal, expansion in the context of $r(\phi)_1$ is likely to generate inflationary price increases as firms seek to protect the profit margins eroded at higher levels of utilization. In the context of profit curve $r(\phi)_2$, by contrast, firms will feel much less pressure to engage in price hikes as the economy moves toward "full" utilization.

69 See several of the essays on worker participation and productivity growth in Blinder (1990). See also the discussion in Bowles (this volume). It is also important to note that there are some offsetting shortcomings of the democratic firm; many of these are explored in Bowles and Gintis (1993).

70 In Bowles, Gordon, and Weisskopf (1990), chapters 12–14, we discuss at length the specific policy directions implied by and the political changes necessary for such a democratic macroeconomic strategy in the United States.

13 Macroeconomic policy after the conservative era: a dual agency approach to state and market

Gerald Epstein and Herbert Gintis

1 Introduction

At least since the Great Depression economic policy analysis has been marked by the persistent opposition of two divergent philosophies, one based on faith in markets and the other on the virtues of the state. Robert Dahl and Charles Lindblom long ago recognized the futility of this opposition, arguing in *Politics, Economics and Welfare* (1953), that market and state are complementary rather than competing instruments in the coordination of economic activity.

The evidence clearly supports the notion of state–market complementarity. Among the strongest economic performers of the 1960s and 1970s were the Northern European countries, which applied a social democratic model involving market competition, Keynesian stabilization, and centralized policy coordination among highly organized labor, business, and government organizations. More recent strong economic performers include the Japanese, Korean and other Pacific Basin economies following a "conservative interventionist" model involving entrepreneurial, business-oriented government control of the economy. Even more recent evidence favoring the thesis of state–market complementarity lies in the collapse of the state socialist economies of Eastern Europe and the former Soviet Union, which had staked out a polar position in the state versus market spectrum. Moreover England and the United States, lying at the opposite end of this spectrum, have experimented in the past dozen years with economic policies geared to limiting state intervention to the absolute minimum. The improvements in economic performance promised by the proponents of *laissez faire* markets have not materialized.

Theoretical considerations also support the notion of state–market complementarity. Traditional arguments for state intervention to redistribute income, regulate decreasing cost industries, and correct market externalities have been supplemented in recent years by an approach to market coordination failures based on transactions costs, asymmetric information, and the inadequacy of third-party contract enforcement.

Moreover, while the Walrasian model provides no coherent defense of market as opposed to state implementations of efficient allocations, contemporary game-theoretic modeling of economic interaction does explain the disciplining and information-revealing efficacy of competition, and agency theory explains the ineffectiveness of the state in supplanting market interactions.

The progressive vision of an egalitarian society that recognizes human dignity and rewards merit rather than privilege has traditionally hitched its wagon to the state model, and hence has come to lose its moorings in the contemporary social arena. With the state socialist model out of the running, progressives have turned to the Nordic social democratic and the Asian conservative interventionist models for inspiration in providing alternatives for the United States, Europe, and the developing countries. Yet as we suggest below, these models of corporatist intervention may not transplant well to other soils, and may not be easily turned to purposes other than those for which they were created.

This chapter explores an alternative conception of progressive economic policy. Whereas corporatist intervention, be it of the Nordic or Asian variety, relies on the *discretionary judgment* of a few powerful groups in state and economy to correct market inefficiency and inequity, our conception stresses the state as the source of *new rules of the game* that, along with markets, provide a context for the interaction of private agents in a manner conducive to egalitarian and meritocratic social goals. In any real economy both rules and discretion must be judiciously deployed, but we hope our focus on rule-based policy can serve as a partial corrective to the widespread hostility toward rule-oriented economic policy on the left.[1]

Our analysis is based on a *dual agency* model of the interaction of state and private economy. Roughly speaking, an *agency problem* exists when agents agree to coordinate their activities in a particular way, but it is difficult and costly for one party to the agreement (the *principal*) to ensure that other parties (the *agents*) will honor their commitments. In the dual agency perspective, both public and private sectors (state and market) contribute positively to the attainment of economic objectives, but both exhibit important agency problems that must be directly confronted in implementing macroeconomic policy.

To implement a policy, agency theory suggests, the principal must not only select a set of coordinated actions that, if followed, will achieve the policy objective in a cost-effective manner, but must also supply the proper incentives ensuring that agents find it in their interest to behave as prescribed by the policy. A policy implementation is *incentive compatible* if it includes rewards, penalties, and a structure of accountability (i.e., a monitoring system) that ensure that agents responsible for implementing the policy will act appropriately. From an agency-theoretic perspective, the principal is the public (or a democratically constituted majority thereof), the agents are state managers, elected public officials, and private firms, and the central challenge to policy formulation is to achieve policy objectives through a cost-effective and incentive compatible mix of policy instruments in the public and private sectors.

The characteristic prejudices of conservative policy flow, we will argue, from its recognition of agency problems in the state but not in the economy. This selective application of agency theory leads to the conservative policy view of the state as hopelessly Machiavellian and the economy as perfectly Walrasian, a view from which exclusive reliance upon the market ineluctably follows.

Keynesianism, by contrast, has traditionally ignored agency problems, relying on stylized facts concerning "sticky prices," "money illusion," and "liquidity traps," or "true uncertainty" and "money contracting" to justify aggregate demand management, and "increasing returns" and "market externalities" to justify state intervention and provision of public goods. New Keynesian theory uses agency-theoretic analysis to provide micro foundations for traditional Keynesian concepts but, as we shall argue, New Keynesian theory does not recognize the constraints placed on macroeconomic policy by distributional conflicts among powerful economic groups, and hence does not provide a political and structural analysis of the determinants of long-term full employment and economic growth.

The dual agency perspective holds that economies are successful to the extent that they develop political and economic institutions that adjudicate the interests of major economic actors in a manner consistent with the key agency problems of state and private economy. Moreover, a new progressive macroeconomic policy must be more sensitive to problems of incentive compatibility than in the past, when productivity growth was taken for granted and the environmental costs of growth were unrecognized.

We suggest three such principles. The first is reliance on a *public infrastructure/private initiative* conception of long-term economic growth, in which the major role of the state is the financing of investment in social and environmental infrastructure, as well as the promotion of rules ensuring competition, democratic accountability, and egalitarian asset distribution in the private sector. This contrasts with the conservative contempt for social infrastructure, and the socialist prejudice against an independent private sector.

Long-term growth, no less today than in capitalism's golden age, requires a commitment to the development of human, social, and environmental resources, and hence to egalitarian social policy, broadly defined. Yet egalitarian programs, to a greater extent than deemed necessary in the high-growth years following the Second World War, must be incentive compatible. Hence our second principle is *asset-based redistribution*, in which egalitarian social policy takes the form of redistributing private assets to the asset-poor (e.g., promoting human capital formation, home ownership, community ownership of natural resources, democratically controlled, worker-owned enterprises, and extensive estate taxation) rather than attempting to extend its traditional price, quantity, and income instruments (minimum wage, rent control, highly progressive income taxation, international protectionism). The concept of asset-based redistribution flows naturally from an agency-theoretic view of the economy, in that asset redistribution avoids the incentive incompatibilities that arise when implementing redistributive goals involving separating residual claimant status (ownership) and decision-making authority (control).

The third principle is reliance on *incentive compatible discretionary policy* in which decisionmakers are subject to incentive compatible systems of reward and accountability, in place of the unconstrained discretionary policy characteristic of Keynesian and social democratic approaches. This requires, in particular, democratically accountable central bank and financial regulation institutions relatively impervious to influence by the economically and politically powerful.

The principle of incentive compatibility in discretionary policy also suggests that public services, such as education, health, day care, and communications services be provided in a context of competition and incentive-compatible rewards broadly characteristic of the private sector, and where feasible, in competition with the private sector. Incentive-compatible discretionary policy avoids the problem of mandating that a certain policy be implemented without ensuring that the conditions for its implementation, in terms of the incentives facing decisionmakers, exist or are in place. It also locates the source of bureaucratic inefficiency in improper incentive systems and focusses on the transformation of incentive systems in improving the institutional response of public agencies.

These policy prescriptions, the reader will note, contrast sharply with the approaches favored by many opponents of conservative and neo-Keynesian policies: the Nordic social democratic and the Asian corporatist models, which rely on the formally institutionalized power and discretionary intervention of powerful groups (government, labor, industrial capital, and/or financial capital) to set major macroeconomic policy variables. Why might a "rules of the game" approach be preferred to such discretionary systems?

Questions of agency aside, discretion is favored over rules when purposeful deliberation can produce higher quality decisions than the rote application of pre-given criteria, because decision criteria are sufficiently complex that valid categorical standards cannot be explicitly formulated. However, we argue in this chapter in favor of an agency-theoretic approach to policy, in which agents act to achieve their own objectives, subject to the constraints placed upon them by socially imposed incentive mechanisms. In such a framework, discretion is preferred to rules only if reliable incentives can be constructed leading decisionmakers to act in the public interest.

While there is to our knowledge no systematic theory of rules versus discretion in the public choice literature, it is not difficult to argue on general grounds of democratic accountability that where feasible rules should be preferred to discretion. A rule-based system demands relatively simple incentives systems to ensure its proper operation – general principles of responsibility and criteria of malfeasance tend to suffice. A discretionary system, by contrast, imposes two burdens on the public. The public must be mobilized not only to choose delegated decisionmakers (e.g., through periodic elections), but also to construct incentive systems to which such delegates are to be subject. Only if such incentive systems are concrete and well defined (e.g., legislators' pay is a specific function of the behavior of economic indicators) is discretion likely to produce publicly desired outcomes.

While a system based on discretion benefits the groups who control the incentives, in general, well-defined incentives for discretionary decisionmakers cannot be specified by a democratic process. Where incentive systems are relatively undefined, groups with special interests can gain by imposing their own incentives upon decisionmakers. As Mancur Olson has stressed, such groups are likely to be effective in direct proportion to the material resources they control and inversely proportional to their size (Olson, 1975) – the elites of political and economic life. Discretionary decisionmakers of course remain accountable to the public by virtue of the threat of removal from office, but this threat in many cases is considerably offset by the structure of rewards and penalties in day-to-day decision making.

Discretionary economic policy, then, tends to benefit powerful elites, and is thus likely to benefit the public only when such elites view their own success as predicated on the well being of society as a whole. One condition under which this would occur is where the public has single-peaked preferences regarding social policy, creating a degree of public agreement that simply cannot be ignored by public-sector decision-makers. A second condition involves social elites so powerful that they behave as residual claimants on society, in a context where economic growth opportunities render a smaller part of a growing pie more attractive than a larger part of a stagnant pie. If a significant degree of economic equality fosters rapid economic growth, and we shall argue that this is indeed the case, then modernizing elites can use their discretionary power to further the public good.

It should be noted that both these conditions are more likely to obtain *the more homogeneous is social life.* The success of discretionary policies in the corporatist intervention systems of Northern Europe and Asia is likely not independent of their extreme degree of social homogeneity in racial, ethnic, cultural, and religious terms, and the extent to which they have a relatively small number of hegemonic economic groups. Where such homogeneity is lacking, the development of centralized corporatist institutions that internalize the diverse needs and interests of the public are not likely to occur. In its place arise the corrupt, particularist, predatory governments that are the rule rather than the exception in corporatist intervention systems around the world.

The social democratic model, for instance, has always depended on a unified and hegemonic organization of labor that would be unsustainable and politically infeasible in less culturally homogeneous societies. Moreover, while in the past it was virtually axiomatic that the political base of the left lay in the organization of producers, labor is now, and probably will continue in the future to be, both internally fragmented and only one of several complementary and equally important bases of support for progressive social change, others pursuing the struggle for citizens' rights, community power, and environmental integrity, as well as gender, racial, ethnic, and national equality (Bowles and Gintis, 1986). Since the political bases of a progressive economic policy are socially or structurally heterogeneous and have diverse interests, and since they tend not to have direct power in the economy, it is likely that a progressive model of corporatist intervention would empower a coalition consisting of an aristocracy of capital and labor that would act more or less the way ruling groups do in the corrupt right-corporatist systems.

This state of affairs is true of the United States, Europe, and much of the third world, where labor is but one of several basic social groups having an independent and at times conflicting interest in progressive macroeconomic policy. Even where organized labor is a central actor in the economy, it would be politically unacceptable to other groups in a progressive coalition to extend its influence to the governmental sphere to the extent required for a successful implementation of social democratic macroeconomic policy. Social democratic corporatism is, according to this reasoning, a successful but historically non-generalizable phenomenon.

Thus the notion of importing the social democratic model to the rest of the world, or copying the conservative interventionist strategies of Asian capitalism with "labor" as opposed to "capital" in control, may then be infeasible. We do not propose, however, merely to take over one or another of the existing policy alternatives. Rather, we attempt to identify the key weaknesses of the conservative and Keynesian approaches, and apply the results to a formulation of an alternative policy perspective for the left.

2   Conservative macroeconomic theory

The conservative policy consensus of the 1980s, encouraged by electoral successes in the United States and Great Britain, developed in major research universities, and implemented by international lending agencies around the globe, holds that government is the obstacle, not the facilitator of economic growth, while increased economic equality and democratic accountability are achievable, if at all, only as a by-product of free-market competition.

Since intervention in product, financial, and labor markets is ineffective, conservative policymakers argue, deregulation and privatization provide potent opportunities for increasing allocational efficiency and restoring productivity growth. Similarly, according to this view, government support of labor and collective bargaining have retarded innovation and raised the rate of unemployment, and should be replaced by measures to foster a "non-collusive" labor-market environment.

There is indeed evidence that conservatives have identified certain key weaknesses of the Keynesian model. The shift in the 1980s to tighter fiscal and monetary policies, and the slowdown in the rate of increase of social spending contributed to the dramatic reduction in inflation rates and helped to restore profitability in virtually all advanced capitalist countries (Glyn, this volume). In several countries that adopted conservative policies, notably the United Kingdom and New Zealand, during the 1980s dramatic increases in productivity growth also occurred (Glyn, this volume). Yet at the same time, these policies did not appear to generate large increases in productivity growth in many other countries.

However, even where these policies were successful, they came at the expense of increases in inequality. For the OECD as a whole, for example, there was a 1.2 percent increase in the share of the top 20 percent of the income distribution between the late 1970s and the middle 1980s. In countries where conservative policies were most thoroughly implemented the shift to inequality was even greater: there was a 2 percent increase in the United States and a 3 percent increase in the United Kingdom, in the share of the top 20 percent. In addition, there are reasons to believe that the increase in productivity associated with conservative policies in several countries are not sustainable in the long run, both because they took the form of eliminating antiquated firms rather than promoting new technologies, and because they represent short-run gains ignoring social infrastructure and the environment. Finally, the long-run record of *laissez-faire* policies is not promising. Over the period 1950–90, for example, those among the advanced capitalist countries that pursued the most extreme *laissez-faire* policies tended to have the lowest rates of productivity increases and GDP growth rates (Bowles and Edwards, 1993).

The objective of a progressive alternative is to exploit the productivity-enhancing capacity of market competition in a more efficient, egalitarian, and environmentally sustainable manner. Conservative policy exaggerates agency problems in the state, while treating market exchange as an ideal Walrasian system. Three key, and closely interrelated, policy guidelines follow from this biased treatment of public and private sectors. First, egalitarian policies interfere with healthy economic performance. Second, the public sector is a drain on investment funds and discourages private initiative, thus impeding economic growth. And third, the capitalist economy has an automatic tendency toward full employment, rendering Keynesian policies of unemployment insurance and demand management unnecessary, and exacerbating the macroeconomic adjustment process by burdening the economy with government deficits and inflation, while weakening the incentives for dislocated workers to adjust to new labor-market conditions.

A considerable body of evidence contradicts these three propositions. Concerning the link between inequality and economic performance, international comparative data exhibit no inverse relationship between social indicators of economic equality and rates of growth of output or productivity.[2] Indeed, the implication that progressive governments and strong labor organization harm economic performance is not empirically supported. Lange and Garrett (1985, 1989) present evidence that a strongly unified labor organization is positively associated with growth when accompanied by left control of government, and that left governments promote economic growth only when labor is tightly organized. This strong relationship has been overlooked, they suggest, because investigators had previously used either the government or the labor variable, but not both. When either variable is only weakly present, they found, the impact of the other on economic growth is negative, supporting the conservative analysis.

Lange and Garrett's finding has been explained by the fact that a unified labor organization reduces the ability of particular unions to implement relative wage increases (Calmfors and Driffill, 1988), while at the same time increasing labor's time horizon, so they are willing to accept short-term costs for long-term gains (Przeworski and Wallerstein, 1982). Their results, moreover, have been confirmed by Hicks (1988), who corrected econometrically for the effect of energy prices (especially the 1970s oil boom in Norway), and Hicks and Patterson (1989), who extended the analysis to the eighteen largest industrialized democracies in the period 1961–84.

This analysis, which questions the traditional "trade-off between efficiency and equality" is not likely to be an aberration of the historical period studied. A recent review of the historical evidence covering England and the United States by Peter Lindert and Jeffrey Williamson (1985) concurs with this position. "American and British history," they write

suggests that more inequality does not raise accumulation by much, and that more accumulation contributes little to inequality . . . the "growth-versus-equality" view is in retreat, and a previously closed debate remains open. (p. 370)

The conservative paradigm also maintains that public-sector expansion is detrimental to economic growth, as egalitarian redistribution of income crowds out business investment and weakens individual incentives to enhance income-earning capacity. However redistribution in the form of investment in human capital (especially health, education, and stable family life) has a high social rate of return (Chenery et al., 1974; Adelman and Robinson, 1978). Moreover, non-military public infrastructure investment (schools, hospitals, parks and forests, streets and highways, water, sewer, and mass transit systems, airports, energy generation facilities, recycling and refuse disposal) is a significant portion of total social capital, and is complementary to private capital.

According to Commerce Department data, non-military public capital amounted to almost half the size of private capital in the United States in 1988 (Munnell 1990b). Aschauer (1990a,b) suggests that if public infrastructure investment in 1970–90 had maintained the share of GNP it enjoyed in the period 1950–70, the rate of return to private capital would have been 22 percent higher, the investment rate would have been 20 percent higher, and productivity growth would have been 50 percent higher. Ford and Poret (1991) replicate this finding for eleven OECD countries, using Aschauer's econometric methodology. Aaron (1990) suggests that these estimates are too optimistic, and others find the cross-sectional results highly sensitive to the countries included. In respecified equations, Munnell (1990a) finds similar results to Aschauer's. However, using state and local data, Munnell (1990b) finds the contribution of public capital to be 43 percent as large as found by Aschauer and in Munnell (1990a). These results suggest that a 1 percent increase in public capital would raise national output by about 15 percent. Munnell's results also suggest that the marginal productivity of non-military public capital is equal to that of private capital.

Has the public sector in fact been a drag on economic growth? Again the empirical evidence does not support the conservative analysis. Ascertaining causality in the relationship between growth and the size of the public sector is complicated by the fact that a decline in growth may directly induce public-sector growth as social services expand to counter the negative effects of a weak economy. Nevertheless several recent studies (Gemmell, 1983; Landau, 1983, 1986; Singh and Sahni, 1984; Ram, 1986) have used cross-sectional country data to test the proposition that the expansion of the public sector entails a decline in the rate of growth of national income. The results have been diverse and inconclusive.

In a more comprehensive analysis, Conte and Darrat (1988), studied twenty-two OECD countries with consistent time-series data on government outlays for the period from 1960 to the early 1980s, using Granger causality tests to handle the problem of mutual dependence. They conclude that "public sector expansion is not generally accountable for the decline in real economic growth among OECD countries" (p. 322). Indeed, they provide evidence that the form and quality of public expenditure may be critical to policy effectiveness, public-sector expansion causing growth rates to decline in four of the twenty-two countries, and to increase for three countries.

The conservative argument that a competitive market system has an automatic tendency to full employment has also not stood up to the empirical evidence. The central message of Keynesian economics is that unemployment is caused by inadequate aggregate demand. The widespread critique of this notion among economists in the 1980s, as Keynesians point out (Blinder, 1987, 1988; Gordon, 1990), was based not on the inadequate empirical support for the Keynesian demand-side position, but rather on the theoretically shoddy micro foundations of the Keynesian model – including in particular the heresy that competitive labor markets are compatible with the existence of involuntary employment.

Several alternative theories have been offered to account for the observed pattern of employment fluctuation. Search theories (Lippman and McCall, 1976; Mortensen, 1986) suggest that unemployment is frictional and reflects job search activity. Sectoral shock theories (Hall, 1979; Diamond, 1981; Lilien, 1982; Diamond and Fudenberg, 1989) argue that sectoral shifts lead to excess demand for labor in some areas and excess supply in others, and that observed underemployment reflected a search process culminating in the reassimilation of workers in the expanding sectors. Real business cycle theory (Long and Plosser, 1983; Plosser, 1989) relies on the intertemporal substitution of leisure for income to explain changes in employment over the business cycle; i.e., when the demand for labor declines, the resulting fall in the wage rate leads agents to take more leisure. This leisure, while really a voluntary withdrawal from the labor market, is then treated in Keynesian theory as involuntary unemployment.

These alternatives have fared poorly under empirical scrutiny. Contrary to search models, quits are strongly procyclical rather than countercyclical, unemployment is concentrated among the long-term unemployed, and the unemployed average only four hours per week on search activity (Blinder, 1987). Moreover, while the sectoral shock approach predicts countercyclical movements of labor between sectors, measured intersectoral mobility is strongly procyclical (Murphy and Topel, 1987), and high unemployment rates coincide with low levels of help-wanted advertizing (Mankiw, 1989). The intertemporal substitution theory is contradicted by the fact that real wages are not highly correlated with the business cycle, and econometric studies show an extremely low elasticity of substitution between income and leisure (Altonji, 1986; Mankiw, 1989).

3   New Keynesian macroeconomics

The popularity of conservative policy has not been based on evidence of its effectiveness. Rather, it came into favor as a reaction against the liberal Keynesianism that had held sway from the conclusion of the Second World War to the mid 1970s.

For Keynesian policymakers, government is a proactive policy instrument: government spending sustains full employment, automatic stabilizers dampen the cyclical fluctuations, egalitarian redistribution promotes economic growth, high wages spur aggregate demand and promote human capital formation, organized labor fosters economic stability and controlled productivity growth, regulation of domestic financial markets prevents financial crises and channels credit in socially productive directions, and the regulation of international capital movements expands the repertoire of effective policy instruments.

Disenchantment with conservative policies are likely to lead to a reassertion of these Keynesian tenets. Indeed, the conceptual and empirical foundations for such a reassertion are already visible (see, for instance, Blinder, 1988; Gordon, 1990; Mankiw and Romer, 1991a,b). A considerable body of research indicates that Keynesian models of employment, wage, and price-level dynamics hold up well to empirical scrutiny. Most important in this respect is the short-run Phillips curve, which indicates the ease with which increases in aggregate demand induce increases in the level of employment. New classical theories, of course, maintain the verticality of this curve, and have supported this claim by noting the breakdown in the explanatory power of the Phillips curve in the "stagflationary" 1970s.

Prior to this period, however, Keynesians had simply ignored supply-side variables in their price determination equations, and consequently underestimated inflation in a period dominated by food and energy price increases. But by the mid 1980s it was well documented that, so augmented, the Phillips curve equation fits the data well (Friedman, 1983; Perry, 1983; Gordon, 1985). In addition, the relevant elasticities indicate that monetary and fiscal policy can have potent stabilizing effects (Blanchard, 1990).

The central assertions of the conservative perspective thus generally do not withstand critical scrutiny, while the Keynesian alternative generally emerges with strong empirical support. Commenting on this state of affairs, Alan Blinder (1988) recently wrote

the ascendancy of new classicism in academia was . . . a triumph of *a priori* theorizing over empiricism, of intellectual aesthetics over observation and, in some measure, of conservative ideology over liberalism . . . macroeconomics is already in the midst of another revolution which amounts to a return to Keynesianism – but with a much more rigorous theoretical flavour. (p. 278)

This confidence is, we believe, nevertheless not fully justified: New Keynesians capably defend their turf in the realm of short-term demand management, but have abandoned their claim to possessing a compelling long-run approach to macroeconomic policy. Yet it is precisely in this area that most pressing macroeconomic problems lie, including growth rates, average rates of factor utilization, and the distribution of income and wealth.

An important example of this "retreat to the short-run" is the abandonment by New Keynesians of the traditional Keynesian notion that proper macroeconomic policy can achieve full employment. In the post World War II era this notion took the form of assuming a stable negatively sloped long-run Phillips-curve trade-off between inflation and unemployment. This assumption was disputed by Phelps (1968) even before the inflationary experience of the 1970s decisively discredited the Keynesian position, and even Keynesians began assuming long-run money neutrality in the mid 1970s (Gordon, 1972, 1975; Laidler and Parkin, 1975; Blinder, 1988). But the *coup de grace* and a central rallying-point for the New Classical school, was the defense of the natural rate hypothesis in the critique by Lucas and Sargent (1978).

Keynesians appear to believe that abandoning the commitment to achieving full employment is a minor concession. Blinder (1988) characteristically asserts:

Since about 1972, a Phillips curve that is vertical in the long run has been an integral part of Keynesian economics. So the natural rate hypothesis played essentially no role in the intellectual ferment of the 1972–1985 period. (p. 281)

It would indeed suffice to know that traditional Keynesian demand management can keep an economy near its natural rate, were this rate really "natural." But in view of the fact that the "natural" rate varies widely across time and space (Bowles, Gordon, and Weisskopf, 1990), the Keynesian concession amounts to a serious retreat.[3] Moreover, there are compelling reasons for believing that the inflation–unemployment trade-off is not a technical problem, but rather reflects the precise way an economic system resolves the conflict over distributional shares among industrial capital, finance capital, and labor.[4] If this is so, demand management becomes a deeply political issue, so state policy cannot be treated as autonomous and unconstrained.

A second indication of this retreat to the short run is the trivialization of the Keynesian notion that investment creates its own saving, and hence that the long-run growth potential of an economy depends on the conditions underlying the "animal spirits" of investment. It remains a tenet of the New Keynesians that a downward shift in the savings schedule can increase aggregate demand and investment, and hence increase aggregate savings (Friedman, 1977, 1978; Haliassos and Tobin, 1990), but it is just as strongly argued that faltering growth is caused by inadequate savings (Friedman, 1988; Hatsopoulos, Krugman, and Summers, 1988).[5]

4   The social democratic model

It might be argued that New Keynesian short-run macro policy and the apparently successful Northern European social democratic model of long-run growth together form a cogent progressive policy alternative. This argument is strengthened by the Lange-Garrett (1985, 1989) analysis demonstrating the general viability of a combination of progressive government and centralized labor organization. Moreover the successful economic performance of the European countries conforming to the social democratic model is evident (Bowles, Gordon, and Weisskopf, 1990).

However for reasons suggested above this model may not be generalizable. Indeed, social democracy appears to be declining even in the countries where it has been historically most successful. Thus even such sympathetic social scientists as Moene and Wallerstein (1993) report that "[T]he social democratic model of industrial relations . . . has completely disappeared in Sweden." The bargaining environment has become decentralized, the dynamics of wage inflation now approximate that of the more traditional advanced capitalist economies, and even the last Social Democratic government announced its intention to use a policy of monetary austerity to discipline the labor market.

The reasons for this decline in social democracy have not, to our knowledge, been systematically explored, but Moene and Wallerstein (1993) present arguments supporting our general conclusion that corporatist intervention cannot operate in a heterogeneous, multi-centered economic system. First, the unity of the labor movement in social democratic countries has been based on a degree of ethnic and social class homogeneity that is breaking down under the pressure of increasing labor force differentiation and expanded international labor movements, and which simply does not exist in the rest of the world. Second, and perhaps more important, the integration of the Nordic countries in the European community, with its multiculturalism, heterogeneous labor and capital organizations, and multiplicity of local centers of economic power, precludes the corporatist planning that is key to social democratic success. The notion that social policy can be implemented by representatives of the major interest groups sitting down at a table and "working it out" is increasingly unrealistic and untenable. A rule of law must replace a rule of persons.

It is important, then, to explore new avenues for progressive economic policy. Our "dual agency" approach to economic policy captures, we believe, the valid insights of older approaches, while avoiding some of their more obvious shortcomings.

5   The agency-theoretic model of individual action

The agency-theoretic model of individual action is a thorough implementation of the neoclassical notion that agents maximize an objective function subject to constraints. By a "thorough implementation" we mean that we drop what we term the *integrity principle*: the assumption of traditional social theory (economics included) that among the constraints on individual behavior is the *obligation to keep promises and honor agreements*.[6]

The integrity principle presumes not only that agents honor their commitments, but that (a) most agents are honest most of the time – i.e., they honor their agreements and tell the truth through inclination and moral commitment; (b) it is not excessively costly to devise laws and social norms which enforce and encourage such behavior, at least when such laws and norms enjoy widespread legitimacy; and (c) it is not excessively difficult to identify honest individuals, and to detect the malfeasance that may arise in the course of their performing their social functions.

The integrity principle is incorrect for two reasons. First, it incorporates an inadequate conception of individual behavior, which may be termed the *normal-deviant opposition*. The "normal" individual in this conception has been properly socialized to operate according to approved norms, and the contrasting "deviant" individual has imperfectly incorporated social norms.[7] In place of this normal-deviant opposition, agency-theory models the agent as treating laws and social norms as *obstacles to* and *tools for* the achievement of a set of goals which are influenced by, but not reducible to, the socially approved. The major implication of this change in perspective is that, from the system standpoint, we expect agents to fulfill their roles not when they have the proper set of personal values, but when they are exposed to the proper set of incentives.[8]

The integrity principle, second, underestimates the extent to which the character of individual action is *opaque and private*. Laws cannot adequately specify social obligations because, except in the most egregious cases (theft, murder, embezzlement, falsification of documents, fraud, and the like), the criteria of "socially correct" behavior are both more subtle than can be captured in a regulation, a contract, or a law, and are highly susceptible to dissimulation (Becker and Stigler, 1974; Gintis, 1980). Thus where the integrity of principle assumes that information is passed among agents according to moral and scientific conceptions of veracity and truth, in fact agents tend to pass information to one another to best achieve their personal goals subject of course to whatever constraints are imposed by society and their own ethical standards (Laffont and Maskin, 1982).

If our description of the integrity principle seems to set up a straw man, consider the traditional theory of socialist planning (Barone, 1935; Lange, 1937). In the state socialist economy, planners are expected to act in the public interest, managers are expected to innovate and produce efficiently, and workers are expected to do their best on behalf of the enterprise and in the larger interest of society (Meurs, forthcoming).

When asked, planners are supposed to reveal their actions and intentions to government authority, managers are supposed to divulge the true conditions of production and opportunities for innovation, and workers are supposed to reveal both the actions they have taken and the personal goals which motivate their choices. Were the integrity principle correct, and in the presence of the proper system of laws, regulations, and internal checks and balances, this might be sufficient to ensure the accountability of economic agents.[9] But it is not.

6   Public agency, the state, and economic policy

We may analyze the state as a principal agent problem in which the public is the principal and state officials are the agents responsible for implementing collectively established objectives. Since the public cannot write enforceable behavior-specifying contracts, state officials must be exposed to incentive compatible conditions of employment and office holding to elicit their proper performance. The central enforcer in such cases is *contingent renewal*: holders of political and administrative office are given high salaries and perks, with the threat of their withdrawal (by removing the politician from office, or replacing the administrator) in case they do not "deliver the goods."[10] As conservative policy analysis has traditionally stressed, this incentive mechanism is in many key cases insufficient to ensure compliance with the public mandate.[11]

There are two basic reasons for the weakness of contingent renewal in the public sector: first, it is difficult to measure the quality of the agents' behavior; and second, it is difficult to ensure that public agents remain subject to incentives compatible with the execution of their duties. The first of these difficulties is common to all situations in which the agent's behavior cannot be assessed by the agent's *inputs* (e.g., hours worked, energy expended, ulcers contracted) but only by the agent's *outputs* (number of widgets produced, level of nuclear safety achieved). Where an objective standard for output is not available (the general case) the most effective way to assess an agent's output is often to subject several agents to the same incentives under conditions preventing collusion among the agents, and use the results of their parallel and non-collusive actions to set minimum acceptable standards and to reward their relative performance. *Contingent renewal in the public sector is ineffective when the state holds a monopolistic position in decision making.*[12] As a result the electoral success of public officials depends only weakly on their performance, administrators are sheltered from all but the most egregious performance-related dismissal, and public enterprises normally face "soft budget constraints" (Kornai, 1986; Putterman, 1991).

The second reason for the difficulty in instituting efficient incentives is that particular groups with an especially strong stake in the public agent's decisions have an interest in constituting alternative incentives to influence the public agent's behavior (e.g., electoral contributions, promise of lucrative non-government employment in the future, pecuniary bribes, threats to have the agent removed from office). Moreover the theory of rent-seeking behavior (Buchanan, Tollison, and Tullock, 1980) suggests that in general only small and influential groups (such as organized business and labor) are likely to have the long-term interest and means to impose such alternative incentives (Olson, 1975). The rent-seeking behavior of such "special interest groups" thus tends to replace socially desirable mechanisms with others that favor whatever groups currently have access to positions of political power. Hence government failure, like market failure, is the rule rather than the exception (Epstein and Schor, 1990a, 1992).

Marxists have also traditionally rejected the notion that state policy reflects the public interest, in favor of the notion that the state either represents the ruling class in society or reflects the dominant class struggle in society. The socialist experience in the Soviet Union, Eastern Europe, China, and elsewhere, however, indicates that the class analysis of the state alone is insufficient, and must be complemented by agency-theoretic considerations. Critical flaws in traditional socialist planning have agency-theoretic roots, the understanding of which is a prerequisite to the success of socialist initiatives in the future (Bowles and Gintis, 1986; Brus and Laski, 1990; Estrin and Le Grand, 1989; Putterman, 1991).

7   Agency and power in the market economy

The traditional Walrasian model assumes that market exchanges consist of legally enforceable contracts. Where writing such a contract is impossible or excessively costly, an agency problem exists, in which the *de facto* terms of an exchange result in part from endogenous claim enforcement: the parties to the exchange themselves adopt sanctions, surveillance, and other strategic enforcement activities to improve their exchange position. We term a transaction a contested exchange.[13]

The two most important contested exchanges involve labor, in which a wage is exchanged for a promise to work faithfully on behalf of the enterprise, and capital in which funds today are exchanged for the promise of repaying a larger amount in the future. Since the worker's promise cannot generally be enforced by the state or other third party, it must be enforced by whatever system of control the enterprise may devise. Similarly, since the promise to repay can be enforced only for fully collateralized loans (and not at all for equity transactions), the lender must devise incentive mechanisms and forms of private enforcement that induce borrowers to act in a manner consistent with the lender's interests.

Such agency problems and their associated coordination failures have been at the center of the New Keynesian project of providing a theoretically satisfactory microeconomic basis for those Keynesian concepts that have traditionally appeared incompatible with a competitive market system: non-clearing labor and capital markets in equilibrium, sticky prices, non-neutrality of money, and the causal role of expectations in investment (Shapiro and Stiglitz, 1984; Stiglitz and Weiss, 1981; Mankiw and Romer, 1991a,b; Woodford, 1991b). Conservative policy theorists, by contrast, have generally either ignored these agency problems (most prominently the New Classical school and the rent-seeking literature in the Buchanan-Tullock tradition), or have argued that competitive markets adequately overcome them (Coase, 1960; Alchian and Demsetz, 1972; Fama, 1980; Jensen and Meckling, 1976; Williamson, 1985).

There is one fundamental attribute of contingent renewal-based contested exchanges of key importance for macroeconomic theory: markets fail to clear in equilibrium, with power lying on the long side of the market (i.e., with non-quantity-constrained agents). The power of employers over their employees, and of lenders over borrowers, lies precisely in the fact that jobs and credit are rationed in equilibrium, and thus long-siders can exercise credible threats over their exchange partners. In particular, the contested exchange model of the labor market, which we term the "labor discipline model," explains why Keynesian attempts at creating full employment are consistently thwarted, and suggests key economic variables responsible for the location of the long-run Phillips curve.

The labor discipline model is a variant of efficiency-wage theory, which has been widely studied in the past decade (Akerlof and Yellen, 1986), and has considerable explanatory power. Bulow and Summers (1986), for instance use a labor discipline model to explain the effect of unionization on productivity, the effect of firm size on wages, why firms oppose job sharing and advanced notification of plant closings, and the preference of employers for full-time rather than part-time workers.[14]

The major prediction of the labor discipline model for macroeconomic theory is that the level of worker productivity, unit labor costs, and the profit rate, depend on the cost of job loss, which is in turn a function of the unemployment rate and the level of income-replacing social services (Bowles and Gintis, 1982). Several studies have provided empirical support for this model, including Bowles, Gordon, and Weisskopf (1983a, b), Schor (1985), Weisskopf (1987), Tsuru (1987, 1988, 1989), and Green and Weisskopf (1989).

The dual agency approach provides insights into the political economy of macroeconomic policy that escape the more traditional classical and Keynesian approaches. Most important, it supports the interpretation of liberal Keynesian policy as fundamentally supportive of labor, both by its commitment to maintaining a low unemployment rate and to providing high levels of social and unemployment insurance (Bowles and Gintis, 1982, 1986).[15] Moreover, it argues that the "missing variable" underlying the wage elasticity of unemployment is the cost of job loss, and thus explains the shift of the Phillips curve over time and across countries in terms of differences in the institutional conditions affecting the cost of job loss (Bowles, Gordon, and Weisskopf, 1990). It thus explains the ability of Nordic social democracy to achieve very low unemployment rates: centralized wage policies and non-dismissal-based labor discipline institutions detach the cost of job loss from labor productivity and wage inflation.

Keynesian theory, while affirming the failures of competitive markets, has not integrated an endogenous enforcement analysis of labor and capital markets into its framework. This accounts, we believe, for its unwillingness to recognize its *parti pris* in the political economy of contemporary capitalism, and hence its underestimation of the structural impediments to the deployment of Keynesian policy, as well as its excessive faith in the ability of the government, with little structural innovation, to produce full employment through demand management, and to generate an acceptable rate of growth of income and productivity.

8   Asset-based redistribution

Economic policies desirable on distributional grounds may be excessively costly to implement and may have unacceptable social side effects. The political success of conservative economic policy in recent years is due in part to the opinion that the costs of Keynesian policies in many cases outweigh their benefits. Progressives can promote a renewed commitment to egalitarian programs by developing egalitarian programs with lower costs. The concept of asset-based redistribution is one means of lowering costs of redistributional policies.

Asset-based redistributions conform to an important agency principle: where the contribution of one party to a market exchange is difficult to monitor, residual claimancy and control should *ceteris paribus* reside with this party. Where the transaction involves the exchange of an easy-to-monitor claim (e.g., money) for a difficult-to-monitor service (e.g., labor or entrepreneurial initiative) the party supplying the latter service should, on efficiency grounds, be the residual claimant. On these grounds, there is a *prima facie* case for individuals to own and control their human capital, for families to own and control their homes, and for workers to own and control the firms in which they are employed.

In traditional economic models, no such presumption exists. According to the famous Fundamental Theorem of Welfare Economics, in a Walrasian economy any attainable distribution of welfare can be achieved by an initial lump-sum redistribution of assets, followed by competitive equilibrium. In this ideal context, redistribution costs are zero and issues of control do not arise. The problem with the Fundamental Theorem is that the lump-sum redistribution of *ownership* rights in a productive asset (raw material inputs, physical and human capital, talent) has strong implications for the assignment of *control* rights in this factor. In the Walrasian model no such implications exist, since there always exist competitive markets through which any agent can rent the productive services of any asset. In real market economies, by contrast, the rental of such services is normally a contested exchange. We shall give several examples.

The human capital and talents of a worker can be redistributed by assigning to another agent residual claimancy on the earnings of the worker. But the contested nature of the labor exchange implies that such a reassignment involves significant, often insurmountable, incentive incompatibilities, since the worker continues to control his labor, even as he relinquishes residual claimant status on his earnings.[16] Our asset-based approach suggests in this case that redistribution costs can be reduced by stressing an egalitarian distribution of human capital through a public commitment to universal education, training, and basic health and nutrition. This conclusion is of course not controversial, although its agency-theoretic basis is normally not stressed.

The difficulty of separating ownership and control in housing assets is considerably less severe, but still significant. The exchange between landlord and tenant is a contested exchange because the obligation of the tenant to maintain and improve the capital value of the asset cannot be contractually specified. In particular, improvements by tenants, both through individual and community initiative, benefit the landlord, and hence are not generally undertaken. Traditional public programs promoting affordable housing, which have stressed rent control, subsidies to the construction of low-rental housing, and public housing, thus tend to have high costs of implementation and generally unsatisfactory results. The asset-based redistribution approach suggests that the asset rather than its service be redistributed; reliance on such traditional public programs would be reduced in favor of providing widespread financial opportunities for home ownership.

A final example is financial assets, especially claims on the profits of enterprise. The efficiency of a Walrasian economy is independent of the distribution of these claims, since competition forces firms to maximize profits, factors of production (including physical capital) are rented at a competitive rate, and the expected value of the residual is zero. In real market economies, by contrast, the contested character of credit markets implies that the link between residual claimancy and control of the firm cannot be arbitrarily ruptured. Indeed, firms in capitalist economies are generally controlled by agents with residual claims to the profits of the enterprise (through ownership or managerial incentives) or who hold their positions only with approval of owners and creditors.

Agency problems are thus at the root of the difficulty in redistributing financial assets. When ownership is transferred away from agents who monitor and control the enterprise, control must also be relocated or the mechanisms that induce firms to produce and invest efficiently will become inoperative. The communist regimes in the Soviet Union and Eastern Europe foundered on this issue, failing to institute efficient non-capitalist forms of enterprise control. But the issue is no less valid when applied to the taxation of wealth in the capitalist countries: high tax rates on wealth are incentive incompatible with control of investment and production.

The most natural solution from the asset-based redistribution perspective is to link the redistribution of wealth to a redistribution of control of the enterprise to workers. The worker-controlled enterprise is attractive on grounds of democratic accountability: as a contested exchange, the employment relationship involves the exercise of power; hence its governance ought to be accountable to its membership. Of course no more than in the capitalist case can the ownership and control of democratic firms be arbitrarily ruptured. Thus a prerequisite for the democratic firm's efficient operation is that its membership enjoy significant residual claimancy status: worker control requires a significant degree of worker ownership. Indeed, a key attraction of workplace democracy is its capacity to coordinate a redistribution of economic power and a redistribution of wealth in a potentially incentive compatible manner (Bowles and Gintis, this volume).

Whereas our previous examples of asset-based redistribution clearly accord with the principle of locating residual claimancy with the difficult-to-monitor service, the case of the democratic firm is more problematic. It is true that labor services in the enterprise are typically more difficult to monitor than other inputs. The capitalist firm, which allocates residual claimancy to the most easily monitored input of all (financial capital), is thus *ceteris paribus* inferior to a firm in which residual claimancy is allocated to those who participate directly in the firm's production and investment activities.

We expect the efficiency gains associated with the democratic firm to arise from a correct social accounting of the costs of regulating the intensity of labor and consequently an optimal mix of monitoring costs and wage incentives, an increased effectiveness of monitoring due to the incentive for workers to report private information on the activities of their fellow workers, and improved incentive compatibility concerning the intensity of labor (Bowles and Gintis, this volume). There is evidence that such efficiency gains exist (Estrin, Jones, and Svejnar, 1987; Ben-Ner, 1988; Weitzman and Kruse, 1990). In response to the argument that such firms, were they efficient, would emerge autonomously in a competitive capitalist framework, we note that contested exchange models of capital markets attribute the bias against democratic firms to wealth constraints faced by workers and the difficulty of passive investors controlling the behavior of democratic majorities (Gintis, 1989).

The general presumption in favor of the efficiency of the democratic firm does not extend, however, to one key area of enterprise performance: optimal risk-taking. While it is socially optimal that firms act risk-neutrally, economic agents tend to be risk averse, and more so the larger the portion of their wealth involved in a particular project. Capitalist firms mitigate this problem by being controlled by wealthy and hence relatively less risk-averse agents, and by being financed through relatively risk-neutral institutions, such as stockmarkets, that induce firms to innovate and take risks.

In a purely worker-owned democratic firm, members are neither wealthy nor are compelled by outside interests to take risks. They can thus be expected to engage in a socially suboptimal level of risk taking and innovation.[17] Indeed, since workers earn employment rents, they incur additional costs of failure (the loss of job rents) not imposed on their capitalist counterparts thus inducing even more risk-averse behavior on democratic firms (Gintis, 1989). It follows that the optimal ownership structure of the democratic firm, taking account of the tendency of external ownership to promote innovation and risk taking, and of worker ownership to promote productive efficiency, involves a balance of internal and external residual claimancy and control (Bowles and Gintis, this volume).

9   Conclusion

Economies develop durable, sophisticated, and historically specific institutional forms to resolve the disputes and coordinate the actions of economic agents. The ensemble of such institutions at a point in time have been called a *social structure of accumulation* (Gordon, Edwards, and

Reich, 1982). The dual agency perspective suggests that a major role of such institutions is the effective resolution of agency problems in state and economy. We thus suggest that *chronic economic problems generally reflect a structural failure in these resolution mechanisms*, rather than the simple mismanagement of macroeconomic policy. Macroeconomic policy thus involves a strong element of institutional innovation. Our support of rule-based economic policy, which holds that the government should primarily institute and enforce the long-term rules that empower and constrain economic actors, rather than intervening to affect short-run economic outcomes, is motivated in part by the necessity of thinking more clearly about the development of new *rules of the game* rather than new, or increasingly empowered, *corporate decision-making bodies* for public policy.

Notes

The authors thank Kevin Crocker for his excellent research assistance, and Samuel Bowles, Stephen Marglin, Peter Skott, and participants in the Political Economy Seminar at the University of Massachusetts for helpful comments on the previous draft.

1 Our notion of a 'rules of the game' approach to economic policy should not be confused with the rules versus discretion debate in short-run stabilization policy (Friedman, 1968; Kydland and Prescott, 1977), which involves a generally distinct set of issues. We do not deal with short-run stabilization policy in this paper.

2 Persson and Tabellini, 1991; Bowles and Edwards, forthcoming. Persson and Tabellini find that inequality and GDP growth are *inversely* related.

3 Keynesians have carefully documented the tendency for the long-run natural rate to differ across countries (Johnson and Layard, 1986), and to have strong structural elements (Blanchard and Summers, 1986). But there is no Keynesian policy corresponding to this appreciation.

4 For theoretical and empirical treatments along these lines, see Rowthorn (1977), Bowles and Gintis (1982), Benassy (1982), Boyer and Mistral (1983), Gordon (1988), Marglin and Bhaduri (1989), Bowles (1989), Epstein and Schor (1990b), and Epstein (1991).

5 Of course an outward shift in the savings schedule increases the full-employment growth rate of the economy, but if savings are investment driven, the savings schedule cannot explain short-run weakness in the propensity to invest.

6 We do not, however, assume that individual objectives are selfish, or that preferences are fixed and preconstituted. For a more complete discussion, see (Bowles and Gintis, 1993b).

7 This notion was formalized in structural-functional sociology. For a critique, see Gintis (1975), and Bowles and Gintis (1981).

8 This of course does not imply that the personal values of incumbents are unimportant, but rather stresses that proper incentives both lead to filling positions with individuals holding appropriate values, and are not unreasonably demanding of personal integrity.

9 Other coordination problems, among them information overload, severely degrade the performance of central planning, but agency problems dominate in socialist economies that allow the market to determine the majority of prices.

10 Other enforcement mechanisms have been tried sporadically (e.g., executing, or tar and feathering, unpopular politicians and their families), but these have been found ineffective or undesirable.

11 The original conservative critique of state intervention was couched in information-theoretic terms: since economic knowledge is necessarily diffuse, incommunicable, and decentralized, the state has no empirical basis for correct decision making (Hayek, 1945). Recent contributions (Downs, 1957; Krueger, 1974) follow our agency approach, arguing that public officials, rather than maximizing social welfare, will generally follow their personal interests, subject to the reward structures they face and the constraints that can be placed upon them.

12 Private markets generally judge agent performance by fostering "tournaments" among competing agents. Indeed, it may be argued that the economic value of markets lies not so much in "getting the prices right," but in deterring malfeasance by forcing economic actors to compete in a common environment (Holmstrom, 1979; Lazear and Rosen, 1981). When public organizations are compelled to compete with private counterparts, accountability can be secured through contingent renewal (e.g., private and public hospitals).

13 See Alchian and Demsetz (1972), Gintis (1976), Bowles (1985), Stiglitz (1987). The term is from Bowles and Gintis, 1990.

14 Additional support for labor discipline models of wage dispersion include Krueger and Summers, 1988; Groshen, 1988; and Dickens and Katz, 1987a, b. Other studies empirically support the proposition that the cost of job loss predicts productivity. See Oster (1980), Stern and Friedman (1980), Rebitzer (1987), Schor (1988), and Holzer (1989).

15 For additional support, see Haveman, 1978; Sachs, 1980; and Schultze, 1981.

16 The taxation of worker earnings is, of course, a partial redistribution of ownership rights, and implies similar redistribution costs at sufficiently high tax rates.

17 Of course there is no presumption that the level of risk-taking in capitalist firms is optimal. Managerial control can lead to insufficient risk-taking, and bank finance can entail excessive risk-taking.

14 Escaping the efficiency–equity trade-off: productivity-enhancing asset redistributions

Samuel Bowles and Herbert Gintis

No society can surely be flourishing or happy, of which the far greater part of the members are poor and miserable.

Adam Smith, *Wealth of Nations*

1 Introduction

The optimism of the golden age of egalitarian economic policy, roughly the first three decades following World War II, was fostered by the belief that wage increases and the expansion of publicly funded social services and transfers would promote economic growth. This belief gained coherence from the rapid growth in living standards in many countries pursuing egalitarian economic policies during the period. Nor was theoretical support lacking. Particularly prominent was the variant of Keynesianism that held that output is limited by aggregate demand, and that egalitarian policies increase aggregate demand by redistributing income to those with a high marginal propensity to spend. According to this view, egalitarian policy is doubly blessed, addressing the needs of the less well off, and, by stimulating economic growth, promoting abundance for all. Under this rubric, policies to promote high employment or to expand unemployment insurance easily won support from all strata of workers, from those with secure and well-paying positions to the unemployed, and even from significant numbers of employers as well.

As the century draws to a close, however, heightened international competition, environmental constraints, and other supply-side limits to growth have clouded the optimism of the golden age and disrupted once powerful egalitarian coalitions. The once secure faith that government redistributive expenditure and wage increases will promote full employment and economic growth has been shaken. Recent econometric studies suggest that while this might be the case for a hypothetical economy without international trade, the optimistic "wage led growth" program is infeasible in highly open economies.[1]

In response to the changed circumstances, attention has shifted from the effect of egalitarian policies on aggregate demand to their effect on "competitiveness" which is to say on costs and productivity. Students of the social democratic economies of Northern Europe have convincingly argued that the success of egalitarianism in these countries depended on the long-term productivity effects of active labor-market policies, human resource development, wage equalization, and high levels of trade union membership (Moene and Wallerstein, 1993a and 1993b). But in policy circles the supply-side successes of egalitarian policies are given little attention, and the growing focus on questions of wages and productivity under the general rubric of competitiveness has supported a near consensus that wage restraint and the limitation of social expenditures are necessary conditions for adequate economic performance. Society might still opt for egalitarian measures on moral grounds, many now believe, but at a cost leaving even the poor to suffer in the long run.

While recent attention on issues of productivity is entirely welcome, we believe that abandoning the egalitarian project is theoretically ill-founded and empirically unsupported: the concern with supply-side problems does not preclude egalitarian solutions. There is no simple correspondence between demand-side economics and egalitarian policy, on the one hand, and supply-side economics and inegalitarian distributional policies on the other. Figure 14.1 illustrates a richer menu of choices. Demand-side considerations can as easily justify not only egalitarian demand-expansion policies but inegalitarian policies as well, for example in the form of low-wage export-led growth (the "Demand side" row in figure 14.1).[2] Conversely, solving supply-side problems need not involve "structural adjustments" that increase inequality: the experience of social democracy during its heyday shows that egalitarian economic policies can be productivity enhancing (the "Supply side" row in figure 14.1). Our main claim in the pages that follow is that *egalitarian redistribution, if properly designed, can attenuate many of the costly incentive problems facing modern economies and hence can be productivity enhancing.*

2   Equity and efficiency: an overview

Inequality fosters conflicts ranging from lack of trust in exchange relationships and incentive problems in the workplace to class warfare and regional clashes. These conflicts are costly to police. Also, they often preclude the cooperation needed for low-cost solutions to coordination problems. Since states in highly unequal societies are often incapable of or have little incentive to solve coordination problems, the result is not only the proliferation of market failures in the private economy, but a reduced capacity to attenuate these failures through public policy. Economic

Distribution aspect of policy

		Egalitarian	Inegalitarian
Economic problem	Demand side	Left Keynesianism	Low wage export-led growth
	Supply side	Productivity-enhancing redistributions	IMF "structural adjustment" policy

Figure 14.1   Economic problems and policies

performance depends on the *structure of economic governance*: the institutions, norms, and conventions that regulate the incentives and constraints faced by economic actors, and hence which determine the nature of coordination problems and their solutions. Ideally, a structure of governance is a means of avoiding or attenuating the coordination failures that arise when economic actors' interactions lead to such collectively irrational outcomes as unemployment and environmental degradation. If the above argument is correct, the structure of economic governance critically influences both the level of productivity and the degree of inequality, and is itself strongly influenced by the degree of inequality. Thus the relationship between inequality and economic performance is mediated by the structure of economic governance: *inequality impedes economic performance in part by obstructing the evolution of productivity-enhancing governance structures.*

Three arguments may be offered in support of this position. First, institutional structures supporting high levels of inequality often prove costly to maintain. Solving coordination failures often requires an effective and activist state. But a state so empowered is also capable of redistributing income in response to populist pressures. For this reason the wealthy may well prefer a weak state in an inefficient economy to a strong state in an efficient economy. Indeed, under even autocratic political regimes, increased inequality heightens the probability that the rich would be unable to contain the populist potential of an activist state. Moreover states in highly unequal societies often commit a large fraction of the economy's productive potential to enforcing the rules of the game from which the inequalities flow.

The maintenance costs of inequality are not confined to the private sector. Enforcement activities in the private sector may also be counted as costs of reproducing unequal institutions. Enforcement costs of inequality may thus take the form of high levels of expenditure on work supervision, security personnel, police, prison guards, and the like. Indeed, one might count unemployment itself as one of the enforcement costs of inequality, since the threat of job loss may be necessary to discipline labor in a low-wage economy. In less conflictual conditions, unutilized labor might have been allocated to productivity-enhancing activities. In the United States in 1987, for example, the above categories of "guard labor" constituted over a quarter of the labor force, and the rate of growth of guard labor substantially outstripped the rate of growth of the labor force in the previous two decades (Bowles, Gordon, and Weisskopf, 1990).

In short, enforcement costs rise with the level of inequality, crowding out productive investment and other productivity-enhancing policies. It may well be, for example, that the sharply contrasting economic performances of the very unequal Latin American and less unequal East Asian economies over the 1980s and early 1990s is related to the high enforcement cost of economic inequality.

Our second reason for a positive relationship between efficiency and equality is that more equal societies may be capable of supporting levels of cooperation and trust unavailable in more economically divided societies. Both cooperation and trust are essential to economic performance, particularly where limited or asymmetric information make both state intervention and market allocations inefficient.

A time-honored prejudice among economists holds that economies may be organized by one of two means: competition or command. Yet a third mode of organization is no less important: cooperation for mutual benefit, or to continue the metaphor, the handshake. Neither hierarchical command nor atomistic competition captures the range of economic relationships essential to high levels of economic performance. In any economy, a third type of relationship is ubiquitous and essential: bargaining over the creation and sharing of the results of collaborative efforts is no less important than the giving and taking of orders or the buying and selling of commodities on markets. Kenneth Arrow writes (Arrow, 1969, p. 22)

It is useful for individuals to have some trust in each other's word. In the absence of trust it would be very costly to arrange for alternative sanctions and guarantees, and many opportunities for mutually beneficial cooperation would have to be foregone . . . norms of social behavior, including ethical and moral codes (may be) . . . reactions of society to compensate for market failures.

One of the possible positive productivity effects of greater equality thus may operate through the political and cultural consequences of redistribution. A well-run welfare state or a relatively equal distribution of property holdings may foster the social solidarity necessary to support cooperation and trust. Marshall Sahlins (1972, p. 186) writes: "If friends make gifts, gifts make friends," and the same might be said of egalitarian redistribution: it is both the result of and the support for feelings of solidarity and social connection.

These and related sentiments such as trust frequently provide the basis for low-cost solutions to coordination problems. A critical example of a coordination problem of this type is, of course, the distribution of income and opportunity. It is perhaps not surprising in this regard that in the more advanced welfare states and more egalitarian capitalist economies, Sweden, Netherlands, Denmark, and Germany, for example, the fraction of workdays lost to strikes in the post-World War II era has averaged less than a third of the level in countries with less well-developed welfare states, the United States, Canada, Australia, and Italy.[3]

By providing the cultural and political preconditions for bargained solutions with sufficient legitimacy to require little enforcement, egalitarian distributions of assets and income may contribute to the solution of complex problems that would otherwise be highly costly to solve.[4]

A third source of equality–productivity complementarity concerns the inefficient incentive structures that arise in economies with highly unequal asset distributions. An example may make this clear. Consider an agrarian economy of a hundred households and in which most of the land is owned by a single landowner who hires labor and/or leases land under share-cropping tenancy. Both of these forms of employment have adverse incentive effects. Wage workers have little intrinsic work motivation, since they do not own the results of their work. As a result, the costs of supervising agricultural labor may be considerable. Share-croppers, too, have diluted incentives as they are only partial owners of the results of their work. They will thus allocate less effort and care to their rented land than they would if they owned it themselves.[5]

A simple fixed-sum rental contract in which the renter were the residual claimant on the entire income stream resulting from her work would avoid these incentive problems, of course.[6] But this solution to the labor effort incentive problem would simply displace the incentive problems to the issue of the treatment of the asset – in this case concerning issues of land improvement and over-exploitation.[7]

The result of these incentive problems is that the concentrated distribution of land is inefficient: there exists a more egalitarian distribution which, by supporting a set of employment relationships that more efficiently address the incentive and monitoring problem, allows general improvements in well being (including compensation for the erstwhile landlord).

This being the case, one might wonder why the redistribution does not come about spontaneously, for if dispersed land ownership avoids incentive problems and supervision costs, land will be worth more to the land poor than to the landlord, and so each land poor or landless household would profit by borrowing to purchase land from the landlord. But the propertyless cannot generally borrow large sums at the going rate of interest. For this reason inefficient distributions of property rights may prove dynamically viable despite the existence of other more efficient (and also dynamically viable) distributions.

The generic problem here is that behaviors critical to high levels of productivity – hard work and risk-taking, for example – generally are sufficiently difficult to monitor that they cannot be fully specified contractually. As a result key economic actors, workers and managers, for example, cannot fully capture the productivity effects of their activities, as they would for example if they were the residual claimants on the resulting income stream or asset value. The result is an *incentive incompatibility*: the residual claimant has an incentive to enhance productivity, but key actors whose behaviors affect productivity are not residual claimants. Where asset holdings are highly concentrated, those who bear the costs of undertaking productivity-enhancing activities often have little claim on the resulting benefits, the result being costly incentive incompatibilities.

The agrarian example thus supports a more general conclusion, one developed by the modern economic theory of principal–agent relationships. A principal–agent relationship arises when the objectives of A (the principal) are affected by some action of B (the agent) which is costly for B to undertake and costly for A to monitor. An important and uncontroversial proposition in the theory of principal–agent relations is this: *where a risk-neutral agent supplies a costly-to-monitor good or service to a principal who is the residual claimant in the transaction, efficiency would be enhanced by transferring residual claimancy from the principal to the agent.* This is simply a generalization of the commonsense adage that jobs are better done if the persons doing them own the results, for better or worse, of their own effort. Our argument to follow is in the spirit of this proposition, and demonstrates the possibility of attenuating the resulting incentive incompatibilities through reallocations of residual claimancy accomplished by redistributing assets.

Modern economies, of course, cannot avoid incentive incompatibilities by restoring the simple property ownership structures of the world of the yeoman farmer. The economies of scale that characterize all contemporary economies make team production ubiquitous. Thus free riding and related agency problems will arise under any conceivable set of property distributions and institutional arrangements. Nonetheless structures of economic governance will differ markedly in the costliness of the incentive incompatibilities to which they give rise.

These three reasons perhaps explain why the efficiency–equity trade-off has been so difficult to document empirically. A comparison of income inequality and rates of investment or productivity growth across nations reveals no trade-off: countries with more equal distributions of income appear to perform if anything better on standard macroeconomic measures. Persson and Tabellini (1991), for instance, find that inequality and growth in gross domestic product are negatively correlated in a cross section of sixty-seven nations as well as in long time series for nine advanced capitalist nations.[8] Moreover, Japan, South Korea, and Taiwan, among the fastest growing countries in the 1980s, appear to have distributions of income dramatically more equal than most Latin American economies, which were not.[9]

Equally suggestive of a positive relationship between egalitarian institutions and policies, on the one hand, and economic performance, on the other, is the fact that the advanced capitalist countries, taken as a whole, have grown faster under the aegis of the post-World War II welfare state than in any other period for which the relevant data exist. In historical retrospect, the epoch of the welfare state of social democracy was also the golden age of capitalism.[10] We conclude not that egalitarian distributions generally induce strong economic performance, but that at least under some institutional circumstances the two objectives are not inconsistent.[11]

3   Productivity-enhancing redistributions

In this chapter we develop the economic logic underlying the third of the above reasons, exploring the positive incentive effects of egalitarian asset redistributions. We use an agency-theoretic argument for the existence of a class of egalitarian productivity-enhancing asset redistributions, we give some examples of feasible redistributions of this type, and we explain why these redistributions do not take place spontaneously in a market environment.

Ours is a contribution to the growing literature asserting that the distribution of control rights over assets and residual claimancy on income streams have efficiency effects.[12] Some have stressed the improved nutritional and other health-related effects of economic equality. Others have developed models to show that the misassignment of control rights over productive resources leads to inefficiencies. Our analysis here is complementary to this second body of research.[13]

We consider a redistribution to be "productivity enhancing" if it increases technical efficiency, raising output for unchanged inputs, for example. We then consider a redistribution "egalitarian" if it shifts wealth from more to less wealthy agents.[14]

Our claim is that where complete contracts are infeasible, so that the claims arising from exchanges are enforced by the parties to exchange, egalitarian productivity-enhancing redistributions are possible. Among the reasons for the infeasibility of complete contracts are asymmetric information (as in variable labor effort models), the unenforceability of claims (as in the promise to repay a loan), and the absence of a sovereign body with appropriate jurisdiction (as in the case of international debt).

Where these characteristics of an exchange preclude contracting for such productivity-relevant behaviors as working hard and well, maintaining complex assets, or taking risk, a reallocation of the residual claimancy status associated with ownership will generally have productivity effects. Reallocating residual claimancy on income streams without reallocating asset ownership generally displaces the incentive incompatibility from such income-determining behaviors as labor effort to behaviors directly affecting the value of the asset, such as maintenance. Thus where claim enforcement is endogenous, asset redistributions to active owners may be productivity enhancing.

As we have seen, redistribution of agricultural land may raise productivity for three reasons. Variations of this model apply whenever impediments to third-party claim enforcement give rise to incentive problems. Relocating residual claimancy from a single owner/principal to members of a team of agents raises more complex issues than in the single-agent case, as team members may free ride on each other, whatever the ownership of the asset. But even here the logic of redistribution to the tiller applies. We will see, for example, that redistribution of a productive asset to members of a work team gives the members an incentive to engage in mutual monitoring, a productivity-enhancing strategy that is otherwise infeasible or prohibitively costly. Similarly, relocating ownership from landlord to tenant in a residential community may induce agents to maintain property values and to cooperate in effecting community improvements, the bulk of the benefits of which would otherwise accrue to the landlord.

The absence of third-party enforceable contracts governing agent behavior is of course a market failure.[15] But in a competitive economy one might expect the ownership of assets (and hence residual claimancy) to accrue to those who can use the assets most efficiently, thus attenuating this market failure. Were credit markets not themselves subject to agency problems, asset transfers might arise spontaneously to resolve the agency problems surrounding ownership and control. But because credit markets are also subject to problems of endogenous enforcement, asset-poor agents are typically credit constrained, and hence unable to acquire assets through borrowing. Thus these spontaneous productivity-enhancing redistributions will not occur even under competitive conditions (Stiglitz and Weiss, 1981).

4   Passive ownership: a contingent renewal model

Before addressing real world cases concerning the governance of firms and residential communities, we consider a principal–agent relationship between the owner of an asset who is also residual claimant to the returns generated by the asset, and the individual members of a team of agents upon which the present and future income flow of the asset depend. We subsequently consider a relationship in which the team of agents become the owner, thereby incurring financial obligations equal to capital costs of the asset. We call the former *passive* and the latter *active* ownership.

Suppose the asset yields net income per time period $q(\Sigma_j c_j)$, a stochastic function of the actions c_j, $0 \leq c_j < \infty$, of a team of one or more identical agents, $j = 1, \ldots, n$, where q is increasing and concave in the relevant region. The utility $u_j = u_j(c_j, w_j)$ of agent j depends on action c_j and the salary w_j, with the action being negatively valued and the salary positively valued on the margin. We assume the action c_j, while known to the agent, is observable by the asset owner only at a cost. The resulting asymmetry of information is critical to our argument. We refer to c_j as the *level of care* bestowed by agent j on the asset.

The interaction between the owner and each agent is the following. The owner maximizes the net income associated with the asset, employing a monitoring mechanism to assess the level of care taken by agents, using the threat of contract termination to motivate a high level of care. Knowing the attributes and utility functions of each agent, the owner infers the agents' best response functions $c_j(w, m)$, selecting a level of payment w, and of monitoring, m, as well as the size of the work team n, in hours of services purchased. Each agent selects the level of services to perform that maximizes the present value of expected utility, taking account of both the disutility of care and the effect of care on the probability of retaining the relationship.

We call this a *contingent renewal* model of endogenous contract enforcement.[16] The situations that the contingent renewal model plausibly represents include the employer–employee relationship where contracts cannot specify work effort, the residential landlord–tenant relationship where contracts cannot specify property maintenance, creditor–debtor relationships where the risk taken by the debtor cannot be specified, and the owner–manager relationship where managerial behavior cannot be formally specified.

We model the contingent renewal relationship as an infinite-horizon repeated game, in which the owner in each period pays the monitoring cost and pays the agent the salary w. Each agent then chooses care c_j, a stochastic return $q(\Sigma_j\, c_j)$ then accrues to the owner, who observes the results of the monitoring system, and decides which agents to renew. Omitting subscripts signifying individual team members, we can summarize the incentives facing the agent by the salary w and the probability $f(c,m)$ of termination, with $f_c < 0$ and $f_m > 0$ (we denote partial derivatives by subscripting functions).[17]

To derive the agent's best-response function, we define v^P, the *value of tenure* for the agent as the discounted present value of net benefits from the relationship, including the utility effects of the salary w and of care c (the superscript "P" refers to the passive ownership situation we are analyzing). Because care is valuable to the owner, and at sufficiently high levels care is subjectively costly to the agent, the marginal utility of providing care will be negative in the neighborhood of any equilibrium. The agent's *fallback position* z is the analogous present value of net benefits upon termination, including the cost of search, the startup costs in another endeavor, and the discounted present value of that endeavor. We call the difference between the value of tenure and the fallback position, $v^P - z$, the *enforcement rent*, or the *cost of termination*. Clearly the owner's threat of termination affects the agent's behavior only if the enforcement rent is non-zero.

The agent's utility in any period depends on the level of care expended and the salary: $u = w(w,c)$. Given the discount rate ρ and fallback z, the agent will maximize

$$v^P = \frac{u(w,c) + [1 - f(c,m)]v^P + f(c,m)z}{1 + \rho}$$

where the first term in the numerator is the current period utility, assumed for convenience to accrue at the end of the period, and the others measure the expected present value obtainable at the end of the period, the weights being the probability of retaining or losing the position. Simplifying, we get

$$v^P = \frac{u(w,c) - \rho z}{\rho + f(c,m)} + z. \tag{1}$$

The term ρz in the numerator is the forgone flow of utility from the fallback, so the numerator is the net flow of utility from the relationship, while $f(c,m)$ in the denominator is added to the discount rate, reflecting the fact that future returns must be discounted by the probability of their accrual as well as by the rate of time preference.

The agent varies c to maximize v^P, giving the first-order condition

$$u_c - f_c(v^P - z) = 0 \tag{2}$$

which says that the agent increases care to the point where the marginal disutility of care is equal to the marginal reduction in the expected asset loss occasioned by dismissal. Solving (2) for c gives us the agent's passive ownership best-response function

$$c = c^P(w,m). \tag{3}$$

We now define the *reservation salary–care pair* $(\underline{w}, \underline{c})$, a point on the agent's best-response function at which the agent is just indifferent between being in the relationship and her next best alternative. The salary $\underline{w}$ is the reservation salary, and $\underline{c}$ is the reservation care level, which clearly must be that for which the marginal utility of care is zero.[18]

Given the agent's best-response function, the owner maximizes profits, that is he solves

$$\max_{w,m,n} \pi = q\left(\sum_j c_j(w,m)\right) - n(w + m). \tag{4}$$

Abstracting from the owner's choice of the optimal size of the work team, n^*, which we assume to have no effects on the agents' actions, and dropping the subscripts indexing each agent, this yields the owner's first-order conditions

$$c_m = c_w = \frac{c}{m + w} \tag{5}$$

the marginal effects of both monitoring and salary on care must be equal to the average level of care per unit of cost.

The best-response function and (part of) the owner's choice of an optimal enforcement strategy (w^*, m^*) is shown in figure 14.2, which plots care against the salary, holding the level of monitoring constant at its optimal level m^*. The iso-v^P function v^{P*} is one of a family of loci of care levels and salaries that yield identical present values to the agent. Their slope, $- v_w^P/v_c^P$, is the marginal rate of substitution between wage and care in the agent's objective function. Preferred iso-v^P loci lie to the right.

By the agent's first-order conditions (2), the iso-v^P loci are vertical where they intersect the best-response function (because $v_c^P = 0$). The negative slope of the iso-v^P functions below $c^P(w,m^*)$ results from the fact that in this region (by construction) the tenure effects of an increase in care (via $f_c(v^P - z)$) outweigh the care-disutility effects. Above $c^P(w,m^*)$,

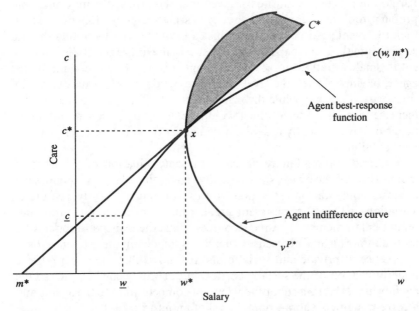

Figure 14.2   The agent's best-response function $c(w,m^*)$

the care-disutility effects predominate. Because v^P rises along $c^P(w,m^*)$, the agent is unambiguously better off at a higher salary.[19] Assuming the level of monitoring to be selected at the optimal level, we can identify one of the owner's iso-cost loci, labeled C^*. Given $m = m^*$, for all points on C^* the cost per unit of care provided $(w + m^*)/c$ are equal. The owner's first-order condition (5) identifies the equilibrium salary w^* as the tangency between the owner's iso-cost function, C^*, with slope of $c/(w + m^*)$, and the agent's best-response function, with slope c_w, or point x in the figure.

Pareto efficiency in this case requires that the slope of the owner's iso-cost function $c/(w + m^*)$ and each agent's iso-v^P function be equal. That this is not the case at (w^*,m^*) with care $c^* = c^P(w^*,m^*)$ is clear, since the agent is indifferent to any point on the iso-v^P locus v^{P*} and prefers outcomes to the right of v^{P*}, while in the neighborhood of the equilibrium the owner is indifferent to any point lying along the iso-cost function and prefers points above it. The shaded lens in figure 14.2 indicates Pareto improvements over the equilibrium outcome.

The assumption that m remains fixed at m^* allows this particularly simple depiction of the Pareto-inferiority of the passive ownership equilibrium, but it plays no role in generating the result. The lens of potential

Pareto improvements must exist given that the principal's maximization problem took as a constraint the agent's best-response function rather than the agent's iso-v^P function. This case can be seen by noting that in equilibrium the principal, having varied w to maximize profits, is indifferent to small variations in w, while the agent is not. Correspondingly the agent, having selected the level of care to maximize v^P, is indifferent to small variations in c, while the principal is not. Clearly there exists some increase in both c and w which would render both principal and agent better off. We presently ask whether an asset transfer could remedy this market failure.

A second market failure arises in the determination of the level of monitoring. Of the owner's two incentive costs, the salary and monitoring expenses, only the latter entails the use of socially costly resources. Variations in the salary represent a redistribution of claims on output, but do not entail the use of scarce resources. Thus the owner's selection of a cost-minimizing enforcement structure is made in the presence of a divergence of private and social costs. It follows that there is a relative underutilization of the socially costless but privately costly input, so the equilibrium exhibits a suboptimal level of compensation to the agents and a correspondingly supra-optimal level of monitoring.

Figure 14.3 depicts the equilibrium enforcement structure of the firm as a tangency between an iso-cost function labeled C^* and an iso-care function labeled $c^*(w, m)$. The owner's iso-cost function is the locus of equally costly enforcement strategies. The optimum is at point x defined by the owner's first-order condition $c_w = c_m$ (the location of this optimum cannot be read from the figure; it could be at a level of cost and care higher or lower than C^* and c^*). To demonstrate the inefficiency of the equilibrium outcome under passive ownership, imagine an arbitrary increase in the salary above its equilibrium level w^*, accompanied by a reduction in monitoring just sufficient to maintain the agents' level of care. The result, at point x', is that the same level of output is maintained (care is unaffected) but one of the inputs, monitoring, has been reduced by an amount $m^* - m'$: the result is an increase in technical efficiency. In addition, agent welfare has risen because care is unchanged, monitoring and the probability of termination are reduced, and the salary is higher.

We can confirm this result by inspecting the implied agent's iso-present value schedules in figure 14.3. These must be upward-rising in the region of the passive ownership equilibrium, since the slope of the iso-v^P locus (labeled v^{P*}) is $-v_m^P/v_w^P$, and $v_m^P < 0$ since increased monitoring implies an increased probability of termination for a given level of care, in the absence of income satiation, $v_w^P > 0$. Hence a reduction in monitoring and an increase in salary along a given iso-care function must enhance the

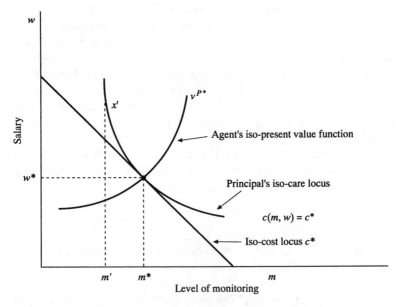

Figure 14.3   Equilibrium enforcement structure of the organization

agent's welfare. But, while the increase in efficiency and in agent well being are both unambiguous, the welfare of the owner has fallen, as costs are clearly higher and the return profile of the asset is unaffected. Thus a redistribution of income has induced an unambiguous productivity improvement that nonetheless is not a Pareto improvement.

However a salary increase of this type can be shown to be at least hypothetically Pareto-improving. Because the principal has chosen both m and w to minimize costs, at the passive ownership equilibrium (w^*, m^*) a small variation in w and m yields variations of second-order magnitude in costs to the owner, and hence to owner profits. But, as we have just seen, a small increase in w and decrease in m effect a first-order gain in agent welfare. Thus there exists some small increase in salary and decrease in monitoring that yield sufficient benefits to agents that a lump-sum tax could be levied on them sufficient to compensate the principal for the cost increase while leaving the agents better off. This hypothetical lump-sum compensation may well be infeasible and it may be objectionable on moral grounds, but this does not affect our argument, as our productivity criterion does not require that the better off be compensated.

This demonstration that by comparison with the competitive equilibrium, there exists a Pareto-improving increase in the salary and a compensating reduction in monitoring does not apply to comparisons among out-of-equilibrium points, as it makes use of the results of both the agent's and the owner's first-order conditions. But the initial demonstration that technical efficiency gains are generated by salary increases and compensating monitoring reductions makes no use of the first-order conditions, and hence applies throughout the range of possible wages.

It follows that at any salary level short of income satiation, there is a salary increase and a monitoring decrease that improve efficiency. For increases in salary incur no social cost and allow reduction in a socially costly input, while monitoring reflects a real social cost. We will see presently, however, that this may not be true in a model including a broader range of team decision variables, in particular those concerning risk taking.

5   Active ownership

Consider now a shift to active ownership, in which the same team of homogeneous agents are owners of shares of the asset and residual claimants on its income streams.[20] Ownership of a share is a necessary condition for team membership and conversely; those joining or leaving the team are presumed to buy or sell their share.[21] We assume, initially, that agents are not credit constrained and can transact loans at interest rate ρ, assumed in equilibrium equal to the rate of time preference. If the value of the asset divided by the number of agents is k_0, the per-period opportunity cost of purchasing a share is ρk_0.

Like the passive owner, the team uses contingent renewal to motivate care levels among team members. Team members terminated for insufficient care sell their share of the asset without penalty other than the loss of the enforcement rent $v - z$.[22]

The decision facing team members (again abstracting from changes in the size of the team, which we assume remains fixed at n^* members) is to select a level of monitoring to maximize team members' present value of tenure. Each team member receives an income from the team equal to $q(\Sigma_i c_i)/n - m$. Thus the net payment taking account of the member's forgone interest income, ρk_0, is $w = q(\Sigma_i c_i)/n - m - \rho k_0$. Thus the team must select m according to

$$v^A = \max_m \frac{u(w,c) - \rho z}{\rho + f(c,m)} + z \tag{6}$$

where the superscript "A" refers to the active ownership situation.

Given that the agents' best-response function is still of the form $c = c^A(w,m)$, we interpret the problem as follows: the team collectively selects a level of monitoring and agrees to pay the residual income of the organization to members as a salary equal to w plus the forgone return on assets ρk_0. Each team member j then selects c_j to maximize v_j^A.

The first-order condition for the team's choice of m then becomes

$$u_w \frac{dw}{dm} = f_m(v^A - z) \qquad (7)$$

This says that the marginal utility of gains from the higher care levels induced by additional monitoring (the left-hand side of (7)) equals the increased expected asset loss associated with the higher probability of non-renewal that results from more intensive monitoring.[23]

There are four reasons to think that active ownership may be more efficient than passive ownership. First, as one of the residual claimants, the team member captures part (albeit possibly a very small part) of the returns from greater care, so the member's best-response function shifts upward, thus entailing greater care for given levels of salary and monitoring. The strength of this *direct residual claimancy effect* declines with increasing team size: if the asset is a single-family home, the direct residual claimancy effect is probably large, but in a large firm with no internal decentralization of teams, the effect is negligible.

For very large teams, it might be thought that free riding is no less a problem for the active ownership team as for the passive owner. But this is not the case. The residual claimancy status of agents provides active ownership with monitoring mechanisms unavailable under passive ownership. This is our second reason. Team members frequently have virtually costless access to information concerning the activities of fellow members. In the passive ownership case members have an interest in colluding to thwart the owner's monitoring strategy. By contrast, under active ownership each agent, as a residual claimant, has an interest in the care taken by others. Unless the cost of reporting information is high, the result will be an improved monitoring system, and hence less resource use, to motivate the same level of agent care. We refer to this as the *mutual monitoring effect*.

To see that the mutual monitoring effect does indeed generate gains in productivity, consider figure 14.4, which compares the best-response functions under passive and active ownership, $c^P(m^*, w)$ and $c^A(m^*, w)$, assuming for ease of comparison that the level of (non-mutual) monitoring inputs remains m^*. The best-response function under active ownership lies above that of passive ownership because, for a given level of j, of the effect of variation in care on the probability of detection, due to the greater accuracy of the monitoring system. The increased efficacy of the monitoring system rotates the best-response function upward (improved monitoring does not alter the reservation position as the agent is indifferent to

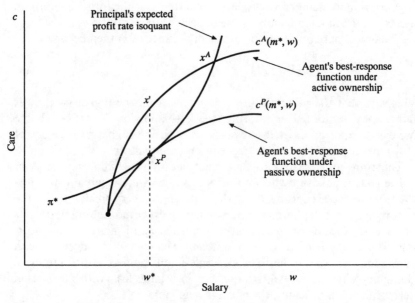

Figure 14.4   The mutual monitoring effect generates gains in technical efficiency

termination of membership at that point). The passive ownership equilibrium previously analyzed occurs at point x, where the owner's profit rate isoquant

$$\pi^* = \frac{1}{k_0} \left(\frac{1}{n} \left(q(\sum_j c_j) \right) - m - w \right)$$

is tangent to the best-response function $c^P(w,m)$.[24] Assuming that in equilibrium $\pi = \rho$, what was the passive owner's optimal profit isoquant is now identical to the active ownership organization's budget constraint, or

$$w = \frac{1}{n} q(\sum_j c_j(m,w)) - m - \rho k_0.$$

Because v^A rises along the agents' best-response function, and the team maximizes v^A subject to the budget constraint, the active ownership equilibrium occurs at x^A. The new equilibrium entails a higher payment and a higher level of care, even holding the level of monitoring constant at its passive ownership optimum. By comparison with the passive ownership equilibrium at x^P, we cannot of course directly say that point x^A represents an efficiency gain, as agents are exerting more care at x^A. But considering point x' corresponds to the level of care forthcoming in the active ownership team at the equilibrium salary under passive ownership, we could hypothetically reduce the level of (non-mutual) monitoring inputs, lowering the agents' best-response function sufficiently so that points x^P and x coincide (w^* entails the same level of care). Under active ownership, the team could thus choose to pay the same salary as in the passive ownership case, and elicit the same level of care, with a lower level of monitoring inputs. But this is true for every salary level greater than $\underline{w}$, so the active team's best-response function reflects an unambiguous technical efficiency gain. The mutual monitoring made possible by active ownership thus allows an increase in technical efficiency.

Our third productivity effect results from the difference in the objective functions of the active and passive owners: under active ownership the point chosen on the best-response function better reflects the social opportunity costs of wages and monitoring. This occurs because active owners distribute as salaries the entire income of the asset, net of monitoring costs. This attenuates the suboptimal level of salaries relative to monitoring which we have previously identified as a source of market failure under passive ownership. As the active owners regard the payment of salaries as a benefit rather than a cost, their evaluation of the costs and benefits of monitoring and salary payments induces them to select a more salary-intensive and monitoring-saving enforcement strategy. We call this the *salary effect*.

A fourth productivity effect is that the redistribution of property and control rights is likely to alter agents' preferences in a productivity-enhancing manner. Under active ownership, the agent is both a claimant on a share of the return to the asset, and a member of a sovereign decision-making unit. Agents thus integrated by both property and control may experience their activity as less onerous on the margin and therefore, if faced with a given salary and monitoring structure, would exercise more care than under passive ownership. Just as the exclusion of the agent from decision making and residual claimancy is socially alienating, so the contrasting integration of the agent under active ownership, even if highly imperfect, may give active ownership important motivational advantages. The improved incentives may be of the carrot variety, as when the agent identifies more strongly with the organization, or more stick-like, as when the agent fears termination more since the activity is more pleasurable or less onerous.[25]

Active ownership, while improving productivity, does not result in a social optimum level of monitoring and care in the active ownership equilibrium. Indeed, under some conditions they might not even enhance overall economic efficiency, when the possibly adverse effects of active ownership on the interests of non-team members are considered. Because the members of the pool of potential team members are less wealthy than actual team members (i.e., $z < v$), we cannot even say that the shift from passive to active ownership is egalitarian in its broader consequences. Thus in the absence of additional policies to rectify the possibly inegalitarian implications of team members' choices, the efficiency gains outlined above may not constitute productivity enhancements as we have defined them. If, as we suspect, these additional policies are feasible, the case of active ownership is still compelling, if a bit more complicated.

6   Impediments to the spontaneous emergence of active ownership

Why might active ownership, even when productivity enhancing, nonetheless fail to emerge from competitive market exchange? We will analyze one substantial impediment to active ownership: the fact that credit markets use equity requirements to resolve the agency problem surrounding loan repayment.[26] Because of these requirements, in many cases the capital needed for active ownership exceeds the financial capacity of capital-poor team members. Even when this is not the case, risk-averse agents would not choose to concentrate their wealth in a single asset. We refer to this as the *wealth constraint*.

An active ownership organization is viable only if, in a competitive environment, it is able to recruit members, taking account of the opportunities available in passive ownership organizations. We thus have the following *viability condition*: given the structure of financial markets and the wealth position of potential worker-members (in an economy composed solely of passive ownership teams), active ownership must increase the wealth position of an agent currently enjoying the present value v^P of tenure in the passive ownership organization.[27] Assuming that active ownership is productivity enhancing, then, it is clear that with either Walrasian credit markets allowing workers to borrow large sums at the going interest rate, or sufficiently wealthy agents, active ownership would not only be viable, but would displace passive ownership.

Let k^+ be a wealth level (possibly infinite) such that team members are risk neutral and sufficiently wealthy to fund active ownership, and let ρ be the risk-free interest rate – the opportunity cost of investing capital in the team's asset. Let $v^A(k)$ be the present value of belonging to an active ownership organization in which each member has wealth k. Thus $v^{A*}(k^+)$ is equal to the active team member's present value defined in (6). On the basis of our reasoning in the previous section we have $v^{A*}(k^+) > v^P > z$.

To illustrate this condition, suppose a team of agents attempts to form an active ownership organization enjoying the same asset return structure $q(\Sigma_i c_i)$ as passive ownership teams. Since agents are identical and team size is fixed, we can simplify this to $q(n^* c)$, and consider the case of a single agent. Each agent contributes an amount k_e of equity to the team, which then borrows an amount $k_f = k_0 - k_e$. We take agents as decreasingly risk averse as their wealth rises, while passive owners are risk neutral (capital markets allow them to diversify fully).

An active ownership team fails if it cannot repay its loans in full. In this case we assume that its net revenue is dissipated in bankruptcy liquidation. The active ownership team can lower its probability of failure by partially self-financing its debt. If the probability of success is p, it is easy to see that $p = p(k_e)$ is an increasing function, since the larger the capital invested, the lower the debt/income ratio of the firm, and hence the lower the probability of default.[28]

While the team lowers the probability of bankruptcy by increasing member equity, this increases members' exposure to risk. To see this, suppose the nominal interest rate paid to active agents on their invested capital k_e is $r_e(k_e)$, the expected rate of return at which members are indifferent between leaving k_e in their risk-free portfolio and contributing to the team. It can be shown that under reasonable conditions $r_e(k_e)$ is increasing, as higher levels of k_e entail greater risk exposure. To determine the optimal level k_e^* of equity, we note that the members' relationship with the project may be terminated either as the result of failure of the project or non-renewal of membership in a successful team. Thus the probability of termination can be written as $(1 - p) + pf$ where $f = f(c, m)$ is the probability of non-renewal. Note that $r_f k_f = (1 + p)k_f/p$ is the nominal debt service for risk-neutral lenders when the risk-free interest rate is p. Then (6) can be written as

$$v = \frac{u(y, c) - \rho z}{\rho + 1 - p + pf(c, m)} + z \tag{8}$$

where y is now given by

$$y = q(c) - m - \frac{(1 + \rho)(k_0 - k_e)}{p(k_e)} - r_e k_e. \tag{9}$$

This gives rise to a best-response function $c^A = c^A(y, m, p)$, and it can be shown that c is an increasing function of p, and hence of k_e: the more equity one has invested in the project, the more care one provides, *ceteris paribus*.

The active ownership team now chooses m and k_e to maximize (8) with $c = c^A(y, m, p(k_e))$ and y given by (9). The team must weigh the positive impact of greater equity on the project's probability of success and hence on the levels of care against the members' rising opportunity cost of providing additional equity and incurring increased risk exposure. The determination of k_e is depicted in figure 14.5, the optimal level of equity

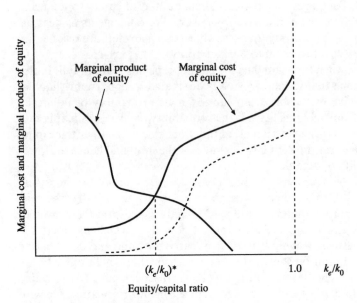

Figure 14.5   The internal finance of the active ownership team: effect of an increase in wealth on the equity/capital ratio

k_e^* occurring where the "marginal product of equity" and the "marginal cost of equity" schedules intersect.[29]

How does wealth k affect the present value v^A of being a member of the active ownership team? We have already seen that unless k is sufficiently large, the active ownership is not viable at all, since in general we expect a positive equity/capital ratio. Moreover, it is clear that the optimal equity level is an increasing function of wealth, since when worker wealth increases, the risk exposure entailed by any given level of equity falls and hence the opportunity cost to members on their equity, $r_e(k_e)$ shifts down, as indicated in figure 14.5. The higher level of k_0 lowers both borrowing costs and the probability of failure.

This relationship is depicted in figure 14.6, which shows v^A as a function of wealth. The active ownership team is clearly not viable if $v^A < v^P$, for in this case the active ownership firm would prefer to sell out to a passive owner. Thus member wealth must be such that $v^A \geq v^P$. The minimum wealth at which this occurs is labeled k^*, below which, despite the superior care regulation of the active ownership team, none will exist.

Note that at some level of wealth, labeled k^+ in figure 14.6, agents can borrow and supply equity on the terms equivalent to that of passive owners. Thus the difference $v^A(k^+) - v^P$ is a measure of the superior care

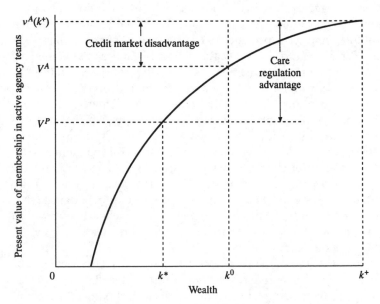

Figure 14.6   Agent wealth and viability of the active ownership team

regulation capacities of the active ownership team. Consider k^0, some level of wealth such that $k^* < k^0 < k^+$. We can decompose the advantage of the active ownership team in expected utility terms, $v^0 - v^P$, into its care regulation superiority, $v^A(k^+) - v^P$ minus its credit market disability, $v^A(k^+) - v^0$, as shown in figure 14.6.

7   Asset redistribution to active owners: housing and production

Housing is a prime target for productivity-enhancing asset redistribution, since active ownership organizations (individual home ownership, cooperatives, and condominiums) are widespread and successful economic forms, while passive forms (private and public rental units) tend to involve non-wealthy agents for whom credit constraints apply. Currently in the United States, over a third of all housing units are rental units. Doubtless some renters are asset rich, but prefer renting. But much tenancy is no doubt related to wealth constraints. As an indication of this, the rental rate for non-white families (whose average wealth is below that of white families) is 56 percent, while the rental rate for white families is 32 percent.

A passive ownership relationship in housing is an agreement between landlord and tenant in which the landlord (the principal) agrees to lease to the tenant (the agent) the services of a capital good, the domicile, for a period of time and to deliver a set of auxiliary services, such as maintenance, utilities, and security associated with the proper functioning of the domicile. Tenant behavior (care of the physical facilities, maintaining or enhancing neighborhood amenities, monitoring and disciplining the behavior of residential community members and political representatives), in turn, can increase the asset value of the domicile. As in our general model, it is infeasible to contract for tenant care, which is costly to observe. Transferring residual claimancy to the tenant is infeasible given the degree of risk aversion for asset-poor tenants. But bargaining over each of the myriad of contingencies that arise in the course of tenancy involves excessive transactions costs. The tenant may pay a security deposit that insures against certain types of damage to the domicile, but this covers only a small part of the costs and benefits involved. The landlord uses the threat of not renewing the tenant's lease to secure a profitable level of tenant care.

The value of tenure in the passive ownership model here becomes the *value of tenancy*: the discounted present value of the flow of housing services $v(w)$ to the tenant, net of rental payments w, taking into account the possibility of tenancy being terminated. Here the tenant's utility varies inversely with w, of course. The tenant's fallback position z includes the costs of relocation, and the expected value of the tenant's tenure at a new domicile should the lease be terminated. The landlord's threat of non-renewal is costly to the tenant only if $v(w) > z$, and $v(w) - z$, the difference between the value of tenancy and the fallback, is the *tenancy rent*.

As in the general case of passive ownership, the landlord can induce greater compliance of the tenant by "increasing the salary" (i.e., reducing the rental rate w), and may use monitoring to assess the tenant's level of care. In this case the value of tenancy is $v(w,m,c)$. The tenant chooses to maximize welfare, as before setting $v_c = 0$, giving rise to a best-response function $c = c(w,m)$. Thus $c(w,m)$ is the level of tenant care that maximizes the value of tenancy for each rental rate w and level of landlord monitoring m. The landlord then chooses w and m to maximize profits subject to this tenant's best-response function. If the landlord selects an optimal rental rate w^* lower than the reservation salary $\underline{w}$ the tenancy rent will be positive.

With suitable simplification it can be shown that agents will fall into four classes: the wealthiest will be landlords who own their own domicile, the middle range of wealthholders will be owners of their domicile, and among the least wealthy will be tenants and the housing rationed (possibly homeless) who would be willing to rent quarters at the going rate w^*, but are unable to find a willing landlord.

In coping with the agency problems surrounding the care of the domicile, active ownership has significant advantages over a rental relationship. To see this, consider a residential community consisting of cooperative or condominium units. We assume the community of owners can impose termination on their own members in the same manner as the landlord *vis-à-vis* the tenants.[30] In the housing case the direct residual claimancy effect is likely to be particularly strong. Homeowners, as individual residual claimants, will take account of the effect of their contribution to the capital value of their domicile, thereby avoiding the incentive incompatibility that arises in the landlord–tenant relationship. This effect is likely to be large, since a relatively small portion of owner effort is likely to take a "public good" form, in which the benefits are shared by other residential community members. The mutual monitoring effect is also likely to be powerful in this case, since individual property values depend strongly on common amenities and the quality of community life. Community members frequently have virtually costless access to information concerning the activities of their neighbors relevant to the supply of community amenities (e.g., which residents contribute to noise pollution, environmental destruction, or engage in illegal commercial activity). The strength of the direct residual claimancy effect thus provides a strong motive for mutual monitoring, cooperation, and informal sanctions among community members, particularly with respect to the actions of team members that affect the value of members' assets. Perhaps the most likely form of such mutual monitoring would be in the collective effort to solve asset value reducing public good problems (crime, noise, unfavorable treatment by social service delivery agencies, poor schools, and the like). Note that while tenants also have incentives to engage in such collective efforts, these incentives are attenuated by the fact that permanent improvements to the community add to the capital value of the property, thus increasing the landlord's wealth rather than the tenants, and even entailing higher rental costs for the tenant.

In short, our model suggests that communities in which active ownership predominates will be more productive in the delivery of residential services. But because the asset poor are risk averse and equity requirements are prevalent as a means of endogenous enforcement in the housing market, passive ownership and relatively inefficient delivery of services will dominate in asset-poor communities.

While housing provides an important example of the inefficiency of passive ownership, by far the best-studied case of passive ownership with contingent renewal is the firm. Here the profit of the passive owner of the firm depends upon the level of effort workers devote to their assigned tasks. The promise to work hard is, however, for the most part legally unenforceable. Work is thus subjectively costly for the worker to provide, valuable to the employer, and difficult to measure.

The endogenous enforcement mechanisms of the enterprise, including the contingent renewal threat, are thus directly responsible for ensuring the delivery of any particular level of labor services per hour of labor time supplied. In terms of our model in section 4, the salary w becomes the wage, the care c_j becomes the level of effort of worker j, and the return to the asset $r(\Sigma_j\, c_j)$ is the value of the firm's output as a function of total worker effort. Contingent renewal takes the form of the employer incurring a monitoring cost of m per hour of labor, while paying a wage yielding the worker a per-period flow of benefits $[u(w,c) - \rho z]$ net of the imputed returns to the fallback position, z, which is the present value of net benefits if the job is terminated – perhaps a stream of unemployment insurance as well as the non-pecuniary benefits and cost associated with joblessness, followed by the stream of benefits from another job. Here the enforcement rent $[u(w,c) - \rho z]/[\rho + 1 - p(c,m)]$ is the cost of job loss, the difference between asset values v^P and z.

The active ownership alternative to the capitalist firm is the democratic firm, in which workers are owners of shares in the firm and residual claimants. While firms of this type have been extensively modeled, most approaches have both abstracted from the problem of endogenous enforcement of effort, and attributed to the worker-owned firm forms of property rights ("collective ownership" for example) which militate against efficient decision making.[31] The more balanced treatment of the worker-owned firm along the lines of our generic active ownership team supports a more positive evaluation, consistent with recent empirical studies.[32]

While the direct residual claimancy effect is likely to be weak in all but the smallest firms, the mutual monitoring effect in the democratic firm is likely to be powerful. Under passive ownership, workers typically have little incentive to reveal private information concerning the level of effort of fellow team members to the employer, while under active ownership they do have such an incentive, provided only that the cost of revealing information is less than the direct residual claimancy gain from doing so. This is likely to be the case in many circumstances. The reduction in inefficiently high levels of monitoring associated with the salary effect is also likely to be operative. Thus the shift from passive to active ownership in work teams is likely to be productivity enhancing.

However, even when more efficient in regulating work than their capitalist counterparts, democratic firms nonetheless operate at a competitive disadvantage and hence do not flourish in a capitalist economy since, as our general argument has shown, wealth constraints inhibit the formation and lower the profitability of such firms. This credit-market disability of worker-owned firms obviously has greater force the larger is the firm's capital requirement.[33] Two additional considerations may apply to this specific case. First, learning to govern a firm effectively through democratic means requires a workforce schooled in common deliberation and decision making. Unless the efficiency gains associated with the democratic firm are considerable, the costs of learning and the lack of a pool of workers experienced in democratic management may be prohibitive. This constraint may be a particularly strong impediment to the proliferation of democratic firms to the extent that the experience of work in capitalist firms and the process of formal schooling orients human development toward capacities that are more functional in the context of authoritarian rather than democratic relationships and that discourage the development of capacities for the governance of production (Bowles and Gintis, 1976).

Second, where organizational forms generate positive external economies for like institutions and diseconomies for unlike institutions, the conditions favoring the competitive viability of the democratic firm may be more likely to obtain in an economy with many such firms, and similarly for the capitalist firm. Thus an economy composed primarily of capitalist firms might sustain and foster general economic conditions precluding the viability of the democratic firm, while an economy of democratic firms would also preclude the viability of the capitalist firm.

Examples of what may be termed this *ecological constraint* abound. Levine and Tyson (1990) and Levine and Parkin (forthcoming) argue that because democratic firms are less likely to alter their own employment over the business cycle, the variability of demand differentially favors the capitalist over the democratic firm in a capitalist economy. But the variability of demand itself depends on the fraction of firms that are worker-owned, for their lesser propensity to lay off workers during downturns reduces the value of the autonomous expenditure multiplier, resulting in a lesser response of aggregate demand to exogenous shocks.

8   Conclusion

We have offered three interrelated reasons why the efficiency–equity trade-off might be less ubiquitous than often suggested. First, the costs of enforcing highly unequal distributions of income and wealth may be high. Second, great inequality fosters conflict and mistrust, while the solution of coordination problems often requires their opposites: cooperation and trust. Finally, economies with highly unequal asset distributions give rise to inefficient structures.

Our analysis has addressed the third of these reasons, demonstrating that under plausible conditions the parallel redistribution of property titles and control rights in productive assets is both egalitarian and productivity enhancing. Indeed, in appropriate circumstances the shift from passive to active asset ownership is productivity enhancing even in cases where the asset must be worked by a multi-agent team rather than a single agent. Moreover, unregulated market activity cannot achieve these productivity gains due to coordination failures in capital markets.

We have also suggested that there may be public interventions into credit markets that increase the share of active ownership assets in the economy, at the same time as increasing economic efficiency and improving the distribution of wealth. The prospects appear to be particularly promising in the housing market and in productive enterprises involving low capital per worker.

While egalitarian policy in these areas would plausibly enhance efficiency, we have not yet provided any reason why public interventions which realign residual claimancy and control rights to attenuate incentive incompatibilities arising from agency problems should generally be egalitarian. One can readily imagine situations in which highly concentrated assets provide solutions to otherwise intractable agency problems. Where ownership of a firm is widely dispersed, for example, no single owner may have sufficient incentive to adequately monitor the management of the firm; a greater concentration of assets would attenuate this familiar free-rider problem.[34] On what grounds do we claim that efficiency-enhancing asset redistributions will on balance be egalitarian?

Not surprisingly, our answer invokes the credit constraints facing the asset poor. In relationship to the capital needs of most projects, substantial asset holders, unlike the asset poor, are not generally credit constrained. Thus transfers of residual claimancy to the wealthy generally take place spontaneously if they are productivity enhancing while, by our above argument, this is not the case for the asset poor. Thus to the extent that potential but unrealized productivity-enhancing asset redistributions exist, they will be preponderantly egalitarian. Credit constraints of this sort support a major conclusion: *productivity-enhancing redistributions not implemented through private exchange are likely to be egalitarian, and to be achievable only through government intervention.*

A more adequate model would take account of the possibly adverse innovation-reducing effects of a redistribution of residual claimancy and control over assets to the asset poor. It is socially optimal that risk and innovation be handled in a close to risk-neutral manner, while economic agents tend to be risk averse, and more so the larger the portion of their wealth involved in a particular project. Passive ownership mitigates this problem by vesting control in relatively wealthy, highly diversified and hence less risk-averse individuals and institutions. The internally financed team of active owners can be expected to act in a more risk-avoiding manner, since its members are neither wealthy nor capable of diversifying their asset portfolio. Moreover in the case of productive teams and residential communities, active owners have an additional reason to shun high-risk high-return projects: since active owners enjoy enforcement rents, they incur bankruptcy costs (the loss of job rents or rents of tenancy) not imposed on their passive owner counterparts (Gintis, 1989).

Such socially non-optimal risk-avoiding behavior can be attenuated if adequate insurance is available protecting active owners against adverse outcomes. Such insurance may require state provision to avoid an obvious adverse selection problem when participation in an insurance plan is voluntary: active teams with a high probability of loss would want to purchase more insurance. The moral hazard problems associated with such insurance can be handled to the extent that it is possible to distinguish between risks resulting from choices made by agents and those independent of their choices, and insuring as fully as possible the risk unassociated with the choice of care. Consistent with this principle is the practice of extending the duration of unemployment insurance in periods of high general unemployment rates. Under reasonable assumptions it can be shown that the reduction in exposure unassociated with the agents' actions induces greater risk taking on the part of the agent. The contribution of policies based on asset redistribution to active owners to long-run productivity growth may depend strongly on the existence of insurance programs that approximate this ideal.

Interventions to attenuate the market failures we have identified could range from providing publicly funded partial loan insurance to foster the extension of credit to asset-poor borrowers incapable of posting sufficient collateral, to more directly redistributive measures such as direct subsidies to the asset-poor members of efficient but credit-market penalized active ownership teams financed by inheritance taxation on large estates.[35]

While attenuating market failures in credit markets will contribute to the evolution of technically efficient solutions to the types of agency problems we have identified, in the absence of directly distributive measures the result need not be greater economic equality, and hence by our criterion could not be deemed productivity enhancing, even if technical efficiency gains did result.

There are two reasons for this counter-intuitive result. First, assuming there is a continuum of wealthholdings from negative amounts to k^+ (the level beyond which credit constraints now do not occur) the capacity of individuals to take advantage of the benefits of active ownership will continue to be wealth related unless all agents can borrow at the same rate. As it seems inconceivable that any set of desirable public policies would achieve this result, a more nearly (but not perfectly) Walrasian credit market would extend to the middle ranks of wealthowners some of the opportunities now enjoyed by the wealthy. The result need not be egalitarian by any reasonable standard. Second, while active ownership improves the well being of team members it may well reduce the well being of non-members, and these include not only passive owners but potential team members unable to secure membership.[36] As we have no reason to believe that the latter group, which includes the unemployed, is well off economically, the net effect of the proliferation of active ownership teams could be to increase inequality.

Thus productivity-enhancing redistributions of assets to active team members need not be egalitarian in this case. This underscores the need to address egalitarian asset redistribution as an objective in its own right rather than one that is subordinate to the goal of efficiency.

The notion of productivity-enhancing asset redistribution suggests an approach to public policy: level the playing field by redistributing wealth while enhancing productivity through a more appropriate alignment of incentives and by fostering competition. Opponents of the inegalitarian outcomes generated in capitalism have sometimes attributed these outcomes to competitive processes, and have sought the attenuation of inequality by suppressing the market. Yet as conservatives have often cogently argued, and as market socialists from Oskar Lange to Pranab Bardhan and John Roemer have long recognized, in the absence of equivalent new market allocational and incentive mechanisms, suppressing competition may entail the inefficient production and delivery of goods and services. Egalitarian asset redistribution to active owners, aimed at attenuating incentive incompatibilities arising from the agency problems associated with highly unequal wealth distributions, borrows the traditionally progressive notion of redistributing wealth. But it hitches this notion to the operation of competition, thus offering the possibility of enjoying the benefits of both.

Thus, while global competition challenges many conventional redistributive policies, it does not preclude a recasting of the egalitarian project consistent with the new economic realities. An economically viable new egalitarianism would rely substantially on the kinds of productivity-enhancing asset-based redistributions to simultaneously promote equality and strengthen the economy's competitive position. The chief impediments to egalitarianism in the globally integrated economy may not be a dirth of economically viable programs, but rather a surfeit of political obstacles. There are three reasons for this.

First, by enhancing the degree of competition in most markets, international integration reduces the effectiveness of demand expansion policies which once helped to secure the support of disparate elements in the egalitarian coalitions. Second, the more highly competitive situation has heightened a divergence of interest between public-sector and private-sector workers, between the employed and the unemployed, between workers, farmers, and those in the informal sector, and between other groups whose unified endorsement of egalitarian policies was often critical. Owners of firms in consumer goods industries, for example, may be less likely to join workers in support of wage increases and other domestic demand-enhancing policies and look instead to the world market.[37] Finally, to the extent that new policies require asset-based redistributions, they are likely to incur strong opposition by an anti-egalitarian coalition which in many countries can readily unify under the banner of the defense of the existing distribution and definition of property rights.

On the other hand, a broader dispersion of asset holdings in the population and the close association of property holdings with both residence and workplace entailed by the asset-based redistribution strategy would reduce the global mobility of capital and thereby might relax one of the major constraints on egalitarian policy.

Notes

We would like to thank Kenneth Arrow, Charles Blackorby, James Crotty, Nancy Folbre, David Kotz, Mehrene Larudee, Paul Malherbe, John Roemer, Amartya Sen, Peter Skott, Joseph Stiglitz, Elisabeth Wood, members of the Political Economy Workshop at the University of Massachusetts, and members of the Workshop on Economic Theory and Inequality, Stanford Institute for Theoretical Economics, Stanford University, for helpful comments.

1 A study by Bowles and Boyer (this volume) of the US, France, the UK, Japan, and Germany, and by Gordon (this volume) of the US suggest that under prevailing conditions, aggregate demand is as likely fostered by a redistribution from wages to profits as the reverse. Smaller and more internationally open economies are unlikely to be exceptions to these findings. The econometric evidence presented in both studies indicates that the positive effect of real wage increases on the level of aggregate demand posited in the Keynesian wage-led growth model is likely to obtain in closed economies but quite unlikely in economies with the degree of openness exhibited by most advanced capitalist economies. In the two cases identified by Bowles and Boyer as examples of a positive effect of the real wage on aggregate demand, the US and the UK, the wage effect on aggregate demand is small, and insufficient to support a positive relationship between the real wage and the rate of accumulation. Thus even where an increase in real wages supports a higher level of aggregate demand, it is unlikely to foster economic growth. Thus there is some doubt concerning the relevance, even in the heyday of social democracy, of a Keynesian wage-led growth regime.

2 To complicate matters, as Bhaduri and Marglin (1990), Rowthorn (1982), Taylor (1985), and others have shown, policies to expand aggregate demand need not be egalitarian.

3 US Department of Labor, Bureau of Labor Statistics, Office of Productivity and Technology (1990).

4 Singleton and Taylor (1992) argue that the failure to solve coordination problems of the common property type dramatized by the tragedy of the commons often stems from the lack of community, defined as a set of people with shared beliefs, stable membership, and ongoing, relatively unmediated interaction: "The more a group resembles a community, the lower are the transactions costs which it must meet in order to solve a given collective action problem" (p. 319).

5 On the incentive effects of concentrated land ownership see Stiglitz (1989) and Eswaran and Kotwal (1989).

6 The "residual claimant" owns whatever remains (the residual) after all fixed claims (in this case the rent paid to the landlord) are settled.

7 If the renter is risk averse and if the income stream is variable (in response, say, to variations in the weather) the share-cropping contract may be attractive to the renter as a risk-sharing mechanism. It may be that with sufficient ingenuity economists could design contracts and monitoring mechanisms that would eliminate the resulting incentive problems. However, none of the optimal contracting designs of this type are of practical relevance.

8 See also Bowles, Gordon, and Weisskopf (1990), Alesina and Rodrik (1992), and Glyn (this volume). Alesina and Rodrik find that a measure of asset (land) inequality is inversely associated with economic growth in a sample of thirty-nine countries. Glyn surveys the impact of the 1980s shift in economic policy in most of the advanced capitalist nations toward less egalitarian objectives. Bowles, Gordon, and Weisskopf find a negative association between income inequality and both the long-term rate of growth of output per employed person and the investment share of output in ten advanced capitalist economies.

9 See, for example, Choo (1991) and World Bank (1989). Hong Kong, by contrast, has combined a very unequal distribution of income with rapid economic growth (Terasaki, 1991).

10 Growth rates of both capital stock and gross domestic product per capita for thirteen advanced capitalist countries during the period 1950–79 were double their (unweighted average) values for the periods 1820–1950 (for GDP per capita) and 1870–1950 (for capital stock). The data are from Maddison (1989).

11 One can readily imagine productivity-enhancing inegalitarian redistributions: an increase in the degree of concentration of asset holdings may be productivity enhancing if it attenuates the free rider problem among a team of principals in monitoring a single agent, such as a manager, for example. However such redistributions, we shall argue, are generally effected without policy intervention.

12 Eaton and White (1991) develop a model in which inequality reduces productivity by fostering insecurity of property rights, and hence weakens the incentive to invest.

13 For health-related effects, see Dasgupta and Ray (1986) and Moene (1992). For control-related effects, see Eaton and White (1991), Milgrom (1988), Grossman and Hart (1986), Moene (1989), Hart and Moore (1990).

14 The compensation criterion based on the concept of Pareto efficiency deems a reallocation "superior" only if it is possible to compensate the losers without dissipating the gains to the winners. Since asset transfers are central to the effectiveness of the mechanisms analyzed in this chapter, in general no feasible compensation can be designed. The compensation criterion is thus ill-suited for the efficiency analysis of redistribution.

15 The underlying problem is analogous to missing markets in such agent behaviors as risk-taking, labor effort, and tenant care, which are thus similar to environmental externalities and other non-market interdependencies as sources of market failure.

16 The analysis of contingent renewal is developed in Gintis (1976), Calvo (1979), Shapiro and Stiglitz (1984), Bowles (1985), and Gintis and Ishikawa (1987).

17 The owner will select an optimum termination schedule to maximize profits. For the derivation of the optimal termination schedule with an unbiased, normally distributed signal, see Gintis (1994).

18 The reservation pair is thus defined by the two equations, $v^P = z$ and $u_c - f_c(v^P - z) = 0$, which together imply that $u_c(\underline{w}, c) = 0$.

19 In general $c^P(w, m^*)$ is increasing and concave only in a neighborhood of the passive ownership equilibrium (by the second-order conditions of the owner's maximization), but we have drawn it so throughout for simplicity.

20 In some cases "team ownership" is likely to involve collective property, as in the ownership of a firm by its employees. In other cases, it is likely to involve individual property, as in the case of home ownership in a community or apartment ownership in a condominium or cooperative. Of course in the latter case the simple additivity of care effects implied by our assumption $q = q(\Sigma_j c_j)$ is unrealistic.

21 The market value of shares could perhaps be determined on a pseudo-stockmarket of the type described by Bardhan and Roemer (1992). See also Bowles and Gintis (1990).

22 By assumption, on the sale of their shares, agents retain the same fallback position, z, as in the passive ownership case.

23 In equation (7), we have $dw/dm = (q' c_m - 1)/(1 - q' c_w)$.

24 The iso-profit function is not identical to the iso-cost function in figure 14.2 as the size of team membership is assumed to vary in figure 14.1, but we have assumed (for ease of comparison) that the active team will be of whatever size was optimal under passive ownership. Our comparative results follow *a fortiori* for the case where the active team can alter the size of its membership.

25 Taking account of excluded members would require a general equilibrium approach beyond the scope of this chapter. Even without this more complete treatment, the logic of our caveat is clear. In maximizing v^A subject to an income constraint, team members take account not only of the effects of their choice of monitoring and care on output but also on the likelihood that they will be terminated from the team. Termination results in an asset loss of $v^A - z$, and a corresponding gain for a currently excluded potential member. While from an individual standpoint it would be irrational to ignore the termination probability, the retention of the enforcement rent by any particular agent is not of concern to a social optimizing process. For this reason the levels of c and m chosen by the team and its members are socially non-optimal.

This is readily apparent from the first-order condition determining the level of m chosen by the team. The social optimum would be attained by maximizing net income, w, which would of course imply $dw/dm = 0$, rather than the team's first-order condition $dw/dm = f_m(v - z)/u_w$. Taking account of termination probability leads the team to adopt too little monitoring from a social standpoint. Analogously the social optimum level of care is dictated by equating the marginal rate of substitution in each agent's utility function to the marginal rate of transformation of care into income. But agents seek to avoid termination (a private not a social cost), which affects their choice of a care level.

26 Another impediment is the lack of experience in management and democratic business decision making among workers. See also Levine and Tyson (1990) and Levine and Parkin (1994).

27 It may be argued that agents without contracts would agree to form an active ownership organization as long as the present value of belonging exceeds their fallback position z. However were such a firm viable, its members would prefer to sell it to, and become agents of, a passive owner.

28 We forgo a full mathematical model here. For details, see Bowles and Gintis (1993a).
29 The "marginal product of equity" is defined as the rate at which increases in agent equity lower the cost of external finance, and the "marginal product of equity" is the rate at which increases in equity raise the amount of agents must be compensated to be willing to bear the increased risk exposure.
30 This assumption is probably unduly strong, and is doubtless inappropriate where the community consists of individual homeowners, where means of legal redress by the community are quite narrow. On the other hand, in such cases the direct residual claimancy effect is correspondingly more powerful.
31 Ward (1958), Domar (1966), Vanek (1970), Meade (1972), Furubotn and Pejovich (1974), Jensen and Meckling (1979).
32 Levine and Tyson (1990), for instance, surveyed fourteen studies of worker cooperatives and found positive effects on productivity in thirteen of them, with no negative effects in any. Craig and Pencavel's recent (1992) study of worker-owned plywood firms, however, suggests that labor productivity is lower in the coops than in classical firms. Weitzman and Kruse (1990) surveyed sixteen econometric studies of the effects of profit sharing on productivity and found that of the total of 226 estimated regression coefficients for variables measuring profit sharing 94 percent were positive and 60 percent were twice or more than their standard errors, while no negative coefficient estimates were statistically significant by this standard. For related studies supporting this research, see Cable and Fitzroy (1980), Ben-Ner (1988), Ben-Ner and Estrin (1988), Conte and Svejnar (1990). Worker participation in decision making and residual claimancy status appear to be complementary in that their joint effects exceed the additive effects of each factor separately. For a recent review of the evidence, see Bonin, Jones, and Putterman (1993).
33 For a rough sense of the relevant wealth constraints consider that in 1988 the average wealth (including car and home) of the least wealthy 80 percent of US families was about $64,000 (half of which was house and car). The capital stock in the US economy per employee (roughly our k_0) was about $95,000 (Bowles and Edwards, 1993, p. 257), and the number of employed workers per family was about 1.3. Thus total net worth of a typical worker is about half the value of the capital stock they typically work with.
34 See, for example, Shleifer and Vishhny (1986).
35 Where they are heterogeneous with respect to risk aversion, members of teams might contract for variable amounts of risk exposure with voting rights being exercised in proportion to their residual claims. This would allow a Pareto-improving allocation of risk within the team, and would give greater decision-making influence to less risk-averse members.
36 Moene (1992) observes an analogue to this phenomenon in which land is transferred from large to small landowners and in equilibrium the landless may be worse off as a result.
37 Trade liberalization might enhance the viability of egalitarian coalitions in other respects. Gerschenkron (1944) argues that conflicts over tariff policies obstructed a potentially egalitarian farmer–worker alliance in pre-World War I Germany, for example. A general argument might be made that tariff and other policies which politicize the relative prices of commodities tend to favor vertical alliances within industries rather than cross industry coalitions; and it may be the latter type of coalition which is more viable as a vehicle for egalitarian policy.

References

Aaron, Henry J., 1990. "Discussion," in Alicia H. Munnell (ed.), *Is There a Shortfall in Public Capital Investment?*, Boston: Federal Reserve Bank of Boston.

Abel, A. and O. Blanchard, 1986. "The Present Value of Profits and Cyclical Movements of Investment," *Econometrica*, 54: 249–73.

Adelman, Irma and Sherman Robinson, 1978. *Income Distribution Policies in Developing Countries: A Case Study of Korea*, Stanford: Stanford University Press.

Aglietta, M., 1976. *Theory of Capitalist Regulation*, London: New Left Books.

Akerlof, George and Janet Yellen, 1986. *Efficiency Wage Models of the Labor Market*, Cambridge University Press.

Akyuz, Yilmaz, 1991. "Financial Liberalization in Developing Countries: A Neo-Keynesian Approach," Discussion Paper, Geneva: United Nations Conference on Trade and Development.

Alchian, Armen and Harold Demsetz, 1972. "Production, Information Costs, and Economic Organization," *American Economic Review*, 62 (December): 777–95.

Alesina, Alberto and Dani Rodrik, 1992. "Distribution, Political Conflict, and Economic Growth," in A. Cuckierman *et al.* (eds.), *Political Economy, Growth, and Business Cycles*, Cambridge, MA: MIT Press.

Altonji, Joseph G., 1986. "Intertemporal Substitution in Labor Supply: Evidence from Micro Data," *Journal of Political Economy*, 94(2) (June): S176–S215.

Amsden, Alice, 1989. *Asia's Next Giant: South Korea and Late Industrialization*, New York: Oxford University Press.

Andersen, Palle S., 1987. "Profit Shares, Investment and Output Capacity," Bank for International Settlements, Basle, Working Paper No. 12 (July).

Ando, Albert and Alan J. Auerbach, 1988. "The Cost of Capital in the United States and Japan: A Comparison," *Journal of Japanese and International Economies*, 2: 134–58.

1990. "The Cost of Capital in Japan: Recent Evidence and Further Results," National Bureau of Economic Research, Working Paper, No. 3371 (May).

Armstrong, Philip, Andrew Glyn, and John Harrison, 1991. *Capitalism Since 1945*, Oxford: Basil Blackwell.

Arrow, Kenneth, 1969. "Political and Economic Evaluation of Social Effects and Externalities," in M.D. Intriligator (ed.), *Frontiers of Quantative Economics*, Amsterdam: North-Holland.

Artus, P. and P. Muet, 1990. *Investment and Factor Demand*, Amsterdam: North-Holland.

Aschauer, David Alan, 1989. "Is Public Expenditure Productive?," *Journal of Monetary Economics*, 23(2) (March): 177–200.

1990. "Why is Infrastructure Important?" in Alicia H. Munnell (ed.), *Is There a Shortfall in Public Capital Investment?*, Boston: Federal Reserve Bank of Boston.

Atkinson, A., 1993. "What is Happening to the Distribution of Income in the UK," STICERD Discussion Paper No. 87.

Auerbach, P., 1988. *Competition*, Oxford: Blackwell.

Auerbach, P. and P. Skott, 1992. "Financial Innovation and Planning in a Capitalist Economy," *Metroeconomica*, 43(1–2) (February–June): 75–96.

Avery, Robert and Arthur Kennickell, 1990. "Measurement of Household Saving Obtained from First Differencing Wealth Equations," Paper presented at the Twenty First General Conference of the International Association for Income and Wealth, Lahnstein Germany, February.

Balassa, Bela, Gerardo M. Bueno, Pedro-Pablo Kuczynski, and Mario Henrique Simonsen, 1986. *Toward Renewed Economic Growth in Latin America*, Washington, DC: Institute for International Economics.

Bank for International Settlements, 1988. *Annual Report 1987/8*, Basle.
    1993. *Annual Report 1992/3*, Basle.

Banuri, Tariq and Juliet B. Schor, 1992. *Financial Openness and National Autonomy*, Oxford: Clarendon Press.

Bardhan, Pranab and John Roemer, 1992. "Market Socialism: A Case for Rejuvenation," *Journal of Economic Perspectives* (Summer).

Barone, Enrico, 1935. "The Ministry of Production in a Collectivist State," in Friedrich A. Hayek (ed.), *Collectivist Economic Planning*, London: Routledge, pp. 245–90.

Barro, Robert J., 1974. "Are Government Bonds Net Wealth?" *Journal of Political Economy*, 82(6) (November/December): 1095–117.

Baveja, Roohi Prem, 1993. "International Currencies and Endogenous Enforcement: An Empirical Analysis", mimeo, University of Massachusetts, Amherst, December.

Bayoumi, Tamin, 1989. "Saving-Investment Correlations: Immobile Capital, Government Policy or Endogenous Behavior?" International Monetary Fund Working Paper, WP/89/66 (August, 22).

Bean, C., 1989. "Capital Shortages and Persistent Unemployment," *Economic Policy*, 8 (April): 11–53.

Becker, Gary S. and George J. Stigler, 1974. "Law Enforcement, Malfeasance, and Compensation of Enforcers," *Journal of Legal Studies*, 3: 1–18.

Benassy, Jean-Pascal, 1982. *The Economics of Market Disequilibrium*, Orlando, FL: Academic Press.

Ben-Ner, Avner, 1988. "Comparative Empirical Observations on Worker-Owned and Capitalist Firms," *International Journal of Industrial Organization*, 6: 7–31.

Ben-Ner, Avner and Saul Estrin, 1988. "Unions and Productivity: Unionized Firms versus Union Managed Firms," mimeo, University of Minnesota.

Bernanke, B.S and J.Y. Campbell, 1988. "Is There A Corporate Debt Crisis," *Brookings Papers on Economic Activity*, 1: 83–139.

Bhaduri, Amit and Stephen Marglin, 1990. "Profit Squeeze and Keynesian Theory," in Juliet Schor and Stephen Marglin (eds.), *The Golden Age of Capitalism: Reinterpreting the Post War Experience*, Oxford: Oxford University Press.

Bhaskar, V. and A. Glyn, "Investment and Profitability: The Evidence from the Advanced Capitalist Countries," this volume.

Bernstein, Peter M. and Robert L. Heilbroner, 1989. *Debt and the Deficit: False Alarms and Real Possibilities*, New York: W.W. Norton.

Biersteker, Thomas J., 1989. "Reform Without Relief: From the Debt Crisis to the Investment Crisis in the Developing World," mimeo, School of International Relations, University of Southern California (December).

Bischoff, Charles W., 1971. "Business Investment in the 1970s: A Comparison of Models," *Brookings Papers on Economic Activity*, 1979(1): 13–63.

Black, F. 1974. "International Capital Market Equilibrium with Investment Barriers," *Journal of Financial Economics*, 1(4) (December): 337–52.

Blanchard, Olivier J., 1986. "Comment on paper, 'Investment, Output and the Cost of Capital'," by Matthew Shapiro in *Brookings Papers on Economic Activity*, 0(1): 153–8.

1990. "Why does Money Affect Output? A Survey," in B.M. Friedman and F.H. Hann (eds.), *Handbook of Monetary Economics*, Amsterdam: North-Holland.

Blanchard, Olivier J., C. Rhee, and L. Summers, 1990. "The Stock Market, Profit and Investment," National Bureau of Economic Research, Working Paper No. 3370.

Blanchard, Olivier J. and Lawrence Summers, 1986. "Hysteresis and the European Unemployment Problem," *National Bureau of Economic Research Macroeconomics Annual*, pp. 15–77.

Blanchard, Olivier Jean and Stanley Fischer, 1989. *Lectures on Macroeconomics*, Cambridge, MA: MIT Press.

Blecker, Robert A., 1988. "Alternative Models of North-South Capital Mobility and Unequal Growth," mimeo, November, American University.

1989. "International Competition, Income Distribution and Economic Growth," *Cambridge Journal of Economics*, 13(4) (December): 395–412.

1990. *Are Americans on a Consumption Binge? The Evidence Reconsidered*, Washington, DC: Economic Policy Institute.

1991. "Profitability and Saving-Spending Behavior in the US Economy: A Test of the Exhilarationist Hypothesis," American University Department of Economics Working Paper (January).

Blejer, Mario I. and Moshin S. Khan, 1984. "Government Policy and Private Investment in Developing Countries," IMF *Staff Papers*. 31 (June): 379–403.

Blinder, Alan S., 1987. "Keynes, Lucas, and Scientific Progress," *American Economic Review*, 77(2) (May): 130–6.

1988. "The Fall and Rise of Keynesian Economics," *Economic Record*, 64 (December): 278–94.

Blinder, Alan S. (ed.), 1990. *Paying for Productivity: A Look at the Evidence*, Washington, DC: Brookings Institute.

Block, Fred, 1990. "Bad Data Drive Out Good: The Decline of Personal Savings Reexamined," *Journal of Post Keynesian Economics*, 13(1) (Fall): 3–19.

Boddy, Raford and James Crotty, 1975. "Class Conflict and Macro-Policy," *Review of Radical Political Economics*, 7(1) (Spring): 1–17.

Boltho, A., 1990. "Macroeconomic Trends and Household Welfare," in G. Cornea (ed.), *Child Poverty in Industrialized Countries*, Macmillan.

Bonin, John P., Derek C. Jones, and Louis Putterman, 1993. "Theoretical and Empirical Studies of Producer Cooperatives: Will Ever the Twain Meet?" *Journal of Economic Literature*, 33(3) (September): 1290–320.

Boothe, Paul, Kevin Clinton, Agathe Cote, and David Longworth, 1985. "International Asset Substitutability: Theory and Evidence for Canada," Bank of Canada (February).

Boskin, Michael J. and William G. Gale, 1987. "New Results on the Effects of Tax Policy on the International Location of Investment," in M. Feldstein (ed.), *The Effects of Taxation on Capital Accumulation*, Chicago: University of Chicago Press.

Bowles, Samuel, 1985. "The Production Process in a Competitive Economy: Walrasian, Neo-Hobbesian, and Marxian Models," *American Economic Review*, 75(1) (March): 16–36.

1989. "Contradictory Optimizing Rules: Optimal Pricing and Wage Setting in a Model of Employment and Aggregate Demand," University of Massachusetts Department of Economics Working Paper.

1991. "The Reserve Army Effect on Wages in a Labor Discipline Model: US, 1954–1987," in T. Mizoguchi (ed.), *Making Economies More Efficient and More Equitable*, Oxford: Oxford University Press, pp. 385–406.

Bowles, Samuel and Robert Boyer, 1988. "Labor Discipline and Aggregate Demand: A Macroeconomic Model," *American Economic Review*, 78(2) (May): 395–400.

1990. "A Wage-Led Employment Regime: Income Distribution, Labor Discipline, and Aggregate Demand in Welfare Capitalism," in Stephen A. Marglin and Juliet B. Schor (eds.), *The Golden Age of Capitalism: Reinterpreting the Post-war Experience*, Oxford: Clarendon.

Bowles, Samuel and Herbert Gintis, 1976. *Schooling in Capitalist America: Educational Reform and the Contradictions of Economic Life*, New York: Basic Books.

1981. "Contradiction and Reproduction in Educational Theory," in Len Barton (ed.), *Schooling, Ideology, and Curriculum*, Sussex: Falmer Press.

1982. "The Crisis of Liberal Democratic Capitalism," *Politics and Society*, 11: 51–93.

1986. *Democracy and Capitalism: Property, Community, and the Contradictions of Modern Social Thought*, New York: Basic Books.

1988. "Contested Exchange: Political Economy and Modern Economic Theory," *American Economics Association Papers and Proceedings*, 78(2) (May): 145–50.

1990. "Contested Exchange: New Microfoundations of the Political Economy of Capitalism," *Politics and Society*, 18(2): 165–222.

1993a. "The Democratic Firm: An Agency-Theoretic Evaluation," in Bowles, Gintis and Bo Gustafsson (eds.), *Markets and Democracy: Participation, Accountability, and Efficiency*, Cambridge University Press.

1993b. "The Revenge of *Homo Economicus*: Post-Walrasian Economics and the Revival of Political Economy," *Journal of Economic Perspectives*, 7(1) (Winter): 83–102.

This volume. "Productivity-Enhancing Redistributions."

Bowles, Samuel, David Gordon, and Thomas Weisskopf, 1983a. "Hearts and Minds: A Social Model of US Productivity Growth," *Brookings Papers on Economic Activity*, 2: 381–450.

1983b. "Long Swings and the Nonreproductive Cycle," *American Economic Review*, 73(2) (May): 152–7.

1986. "Power and Profits: The Social Structure of Accumulation and the Profitability of the Postwar US Economy," *Review of Radical Political Economics*, 18 (1 and 2) (Spring and Summer): 132–67.

1989. "Business Ascendancy and Economic Impasse: A Structural Retrospective on Conservative Economics, 1979–87," *Journal of Economic Perspectives*, 3(1) (Winter): 107–34.

1990. *After the WasteLand: A Democratic Economics for the Year 2000*, Armonk, NY: M.E. Sharpe.

Bowles, Samuel and Richard C. Edwards, 1993. *Understanding Capitalism: Competition, Command and Change*, 2nd edition, New York: Harper-Collins.

Boyer, Robert, 1990. *The Theory of Regulation: A Critical Introduction*, New York: Columbia University Press.

Boyer, Robert and J. Mistral, 1983. *Accumulation, Inflation, Crises*, Paris: Presses Universitaires.

Bradford, David F., 1989a. "Market Value versus Financial Accounting Measures of National Saving," National Bureau of Economic Research, Working Paper No. 2906, Cambridge, MA (March).

1989b. "What is National Savings?," National Bureau of Economic Research, Working Paper No. 3341.

Bridel, P., 1987. "Saving Equals Investment," in J. Eatwell, *et al.* (eds.), *The New Palgrave Dictionary of Economics*, vol. IV, London: Macmillan, pp. 246–8.

Brumbaugh, D., A. Carron, and E. Litan, 1988. "Cleaning Up the Depository Institutions Mess," *Brookings Papers on Economic Activity*, 1.

Bruno, M.,1986. "Aggregate Supply and Demand Factors in OECD Unemployment – An Update," *Economica*, 53 (210), Supplement: 533–52.

Brus, Wlodzimierz and Kazimierz Laski, 1990. *From Marx to Market: Socialism in Search of an Economic System*, New York: Oxford University Press.

Buchanan, James, Robert Tollison, and Gordon Tullock, 1980. *Toward a Theory of the Rent-seeking Society*, College Station: Texas A&M University Press.

Buchele, Bob and Jens Christiansen, 1992. "Industrial Relations and Productivity Performance," unpublished paper, Smith College.

Buffie, E., 1984. "Financial Repression, the New Structuralists, and Stabilization Policy in Semi-Industrialized Economies," *Journal of Development Economics*, 14: 305–22.

Buhmann, B. *et al.*, 1988. "Equivalence Scales, Well-being, Inequality and Poverty," *Review of Income and Wealth*, 34(2) (June): 115–42.

Bulow, Jeremy I. and Lawrence H. Summers, 1986. "A Theory of Dual Labor Markets with Application to Industrial Policy, Discrimination, and Keynesian Unemployment," *Journal of Labor Economics*, 4(3): 376–414.

Bulow, Jeremy and Kenneth Rogoff, 1989. "A Constant Recontracting Model of Sovereign Debt," *Journal of Political Economy*, 97(1): 155–78.

Cable, John and Felix FitzRoy, 1980. "Co-operation and Productivity: Some Evidence from West German Experience," *Economic Analysis and Worker's Management*, 14: 163–80.

Calmfors, Lars and John Driffill, 1988. "Bargaining Structure, Corporatism, and Macroeconomic Performance," *Economic Policy*, 3: 13–61.

Calvo, Guillermo, 1979. "Quasi-Walrasian Theories of Unemployment," *American Economic Review*, 69(2) (May): 102–7.

Carsberg, B. and A. Hope, 1976. "Business Investment Decisions under Inflation: Theory and Practice," Institute of Chartered Accounts in England and Wales.

Catinat, M., R. Cawley, F. Ilzkovitz, A. Italianer, and M. Mors, 1987. "The Determinants of Investment," *European Economy*, 32 (March).

1988. "Investment Behavior in Europe: A Comparative Analysis," *Recherches Economiques de Louvain*, 54(3): 277–324.

Chan Lee, R., 1986. "Pure Profit and 'Tobin's q' in Some OECD Countries," *OECD Economic Studies*, 7.

Checchi, Daniele, 1989. "Economic Interdependence and Structural Change: An Investigation on Business Cycle Transmission," *International Review of Applied Economics*, 3(1) (January): 57–88.

Chenery, H.B., 1952. "Overcapacity and the Accelerator," *Econometrica*, 20(1) (January): 1–28.

Chenery, Hollis *et al.*, 1974. *Redistribution with Growth*, London: Oxford University Press.

Chirinko, Robert S., 1987. "The Ineffectiveness of Effective Tax Rates on Business Investment," *Journal of Public Economics*, 32 (April): 369–87.

Chirinko, Robert S. and Robert Eisner, 1983. "Tax Policy and Investment in Major US Macroeconomic Econometric Models," *Journal of Public Economics*, 20 (March): 139–66.

Cho, Yoon Je, 1990. "McKinnon-Shaw versus the Neostructuralists on Financial Liberalization: A Conceptual Note," *World Development*, 18: 477–80.

Choo, Hakchung, 1991. "A Comparison of Income Distribution in Japan, Korea and Taiwan," in Toshiyuki Mizoguchi, Tsuyoshi Tsuru *et al.* (eds.), *Making Economies More Efficient and More Equitable*, Oxford: Oxford University Press, pp. 3–24.

Chow, Gregory C. and An-Loh Lin, 1971. "Best Linear Unbiased Interpolation, Distribution and Extrapolation of Time Series by Related Series," *Review of Economics and Statistics*, 53(4) (November): 372–6.

Christensen, Garry, 1993. "The Limits to Informal Financial Intermediation," *World Development*, 21: 721–31.

Citibank, various years. *Citibase.*

Clark, J.M., 1917. "Business Acceleration and the Law of Demand: A Technical Factor in Economic Cycles," *Journal of Political Economy*, 25(1): 217–35.

Clark, Peter, 1979. "Investment in the 1970s: Theory, Performance, and Prediction," *Brookings Papers on Economic Activity*, 1.

Coase, Ronald, 1960. "The Problem of Social Cost," *Journal of Law and Economics*, 3 (October): 1–44.

Coe, D., M. Durand and U. Stiehier, 1988. "The Disinflation of the 1980s," *OECD Economic Studies*, 0(11) (Autumn): 89–121.

Congressional Budget Office, 1991. *How Federal Spending for Infrastructure and Other Public Investments Affects the Economy*, Washington, DC: Government Printing Office.

Conte, Michael A. and Ali F. Darrat, 1988. "Economic Growth and the Expanding Public Sector," *Review of Economics and Statistics*, 70: 322–30.

Conte, Michael A. and Jan Svejnar, 1990. "The Performance Effects of Employee Ownership Plans," in Alan Blinder (ed.), *Paying for Productivity: A Look at the Evidence*, Washington: Brookings Institute, pp. 95–142.

Cooper, Ian and Evi Kaplanis, 1986. "Costs to Crossborder Investment and International Equity Market Equilibrium," in Jeremy Edwards *et al.* (eds.), *Recent Developments in Corporate Finance*, Cambridge University Press, pp. 209–40.

Cosh, A., A. Hughes, and A. Singh, 1990. "Analytical and Policy Issues in the UK Economy," in *Takeovers and Short Termism in the UK*, London: Institute for Public Policy Research.

Craig, Ben and John Pencavel, 1992. "The Behavior of Worker Cooperatives: The Plywood Companies of the Pacific Northwest," *American Economic Review*, 82(5) (December): 1083–105.

Crotty, James and John Goldstein, 1992. "Financial Fragility, Competitive Regime Shifts and the Investment Decision: Empirical Evidence," mimeo, University of Massachusetts.

Cumby, R.E. and M. Obstfeld, 1984. "International Interest Rate and Price Level Linkages under Flexible Exchange Rates: A Review of Recent Evidence," in J.F.O. Bilson and R.C. Marston (eds.), *Exchange Rate Theory and Practice*, Chicago: University of Chicago Press.

Cutler, D. and L. Katz, 1991. "Macroeconomic Performance and the Disadvantaged," *Brookings Papers on Economic Activity*, 0(2) 1–61.

Dahl, Robert and Charles Lindblom, 1953. *Politics, Economics and Welfare*, New York: Harper & Row.

Danby, Colin, 1992. "Financial Liberalization in Mexico," mimeo, University of Massachusetts, Amherst.

Dasgupta, Partha and Debraj Ray, 1986. "Inequality as a Determinant of Malnutrition and Unemployment: Theory," *Economic Journal*, 96 (December): 1011–34.

Davidson, Paul, 1978. *Money and the Real World*, London: Macmillan.

Davis, S., 1992. "Cross-country Patterns of Change in Relative Wages," *NBER Macroeconomics Annual*, 239–300.

Dean, Andrew, Martine Durand, John Fallon, and Peter Hoeller, 1989. "Saving Trends and Behaviour in OECD Countries," OECD Department of Economics and Statistics Working Paper No. 67 (June).

Deaton, Angus, 1987. "Consumers' Expenditures," in J. Eatwell *et al.* (eds.), *The New Palgrave Dictionary of Economics*, vol. I, London: Macmillan, pp. 592–607.

Desai, Meghnad, 1987. "Profit and Profit Theory," in J. Eatwell *et al.* (eds.), *The New Palgrave Dictionary of Economics*, vol. III, London: Macmillan, pp. 1014–21.

Devereux, M. and F. Schiantarelli, 1989. "Investment, Financial Factors and Cash Flow: Evidence from UK Panel Data," National Bureau of Economic Research, Working Paper No. 3116.

Dewald, William G. and Michael Ulan, 1989. "The US Net International Investment Position: Misstated and Misunderstood," in James A. Dorn and William A. Niskanen (eds.), *Dollars, Deficits, and Trade*, Norwall, MA: Kluwer Academic Publishers for the Cato Institute.

Diamond, Peter, 1981. "Mobility Costs, Frictional Unemployment, and Efficiency," *Journal of Political Economy*, 89: 789–812.

Diamond, Peter and Drew Fudenberg, 1989. "An Example of Rational Expectations, Business Cycles in Search Equilibrium," *Journal of Political Economy*, 97 (June): 606–19.

Diaz Alejandro, Carlos, 1985. "Good-bye Financial Repression, Hello Financial Crash," *Journal of Developmental Economics*, 19: 1–24.

Dickens, William T. and Lawrence F. Katz, 1987a. "Industry Wage Differences and Industry Characteristics," in Kevin Lang and Jonathan S. Leonard (eds.), *Unemployment and the Structure of Labor Markets*, Oxford: Basil Blackwell, pp. 48–49.

1987b. "Industry Wage Differences and Theories of Wage Determination," National Bureau of Economic Research, Working Paper No. 2071 (July).

Dixit, Avinash, 1988. "Entry and Exit Decisions Under Uncertainty," mimeo, Princeton University, July.

Domar, Evsey, 1966. "The Soviet Collective Farm as a Producer Cooperative," *American Economic Review*, 56 (September): 743–57.

Donovan, Donal J., 1982. "Macroeconomic Performance and Adjustment Under Fund-Supported Programs: The Experience of the Seventies," IMF *Staff Papers*, 29 (June): 171–203.

Dooley, Michael P., 1986. "Country-specific Risk Premiums, Capital Flight and Net Investment Income Payments in Selected Developing Countries," mimeo, International Monetary Fund.

Dornbusch, Rudiger, 1980. *Open Economy Macroeconomics*, New York: Basic Books.

Dornbusch, Rudiger and Alejandro Reynoso, 1989. "Financial Factors in Economic Development," National Bureau of Economic Research, Working Paper No. 2889.

Downs, Anthony, 1957. *An Economic Theory of Democracy*, New York: Harper.

Dumas, Bernard, 1988. "Pricing Physical Assets Internationally," National Bureau of Economic Research, Working Paper No. 2569 (April).

Dumenil, G. and D. Levy, 1992. "The Historical Dynamics of Technology and Distribution: The US Economy Since the Civil War," *Review of Radical Political Economics*, 24(2) (Summer): 34–44.

Dutt, Amatava Krishna, 1984. "Stagnation, Income Distribution and Monopoly Power," *Cambridge Journal of Economics*, 8: 25–40.

1990. *Growth, Distribution, and Uneven Development*, Cambridge University Press.

Dymski, Gary, Gerald A. Epstein, and Robert Pollin, 1993. *Transforming the U.S. Financial System; Equity and Efficiency for the 21st Century*, Armonk, NY: M.E. Sharpe.

Eaton, B. Curtis and William B. White, 1991. "The Distribution of Wealth and the Efficiency of Institutions," *Economic Inquiry*, 29(2) (April): 336–50.

Eaton, Jonathan, Mark Gersovitz, and Joseph E. Stiglitz, 1986. "The Pure Theory of Country Risk," *European Economic Review*, 30: 481–513.

Eichengreen, Barry and Peter H. Lindert, 1989. *The International Debt Crisis in Historical Perspective*, Cambridge, MA: MIT Press.

Eisner, Robert, 1978. *Factors in Business Investment*, Cambridge, Ballinger.

1986. *How Real is the Federal Deficit?*, New York: The Free Press.

1988. "Extended Measures of National Income and Product," *Journal of Economic Literature*, 26 (December): 1611–84.

1989a. "Divergences of Measurement and Theory and Some Implications for Economic Policy" (1988 Presidential Address to the American Economic Association), *The American Economic Review*, 79 (March): 1–13.

1989b. "Budget Deficits: Rhetoric and Reality," *Journal of Economic Perspectives*, 3 (Spring): 73–93.

1989c. *The Total Incomes System of Accounts*, Chicago: University of Chicago Press.

1991. "The Real Rate of US National Saving," *The Review of Income and Wealth*, 37(1) (February): 15–32.

Eisner, Robert and Sang-In Hwang, 1993. "Self-Correcting Real Deficits: A New Lesson in Functional Finance," manuscript copy, 3/16/91, for F. van Winden and H.A.A. Verbon (eds.), *The Political Economy of Government Debt*, Amsterdam: Elsevier, pp. 255–94.

Eisner, Robert and Paul J. Pieper, 1984. "A New View of the Federal Debt and Budget Deficits," *American Economic Review*, 74 (March): 11–29.

1988. "Deficits, Monetary Policy, and Real Economic Activity," in Kenneth J. Arrow and Michael J. Boskin (eds.), *The Economics of Public Debt,*, London: Macmillan Press in association with the International Economic Association, pp. 3–40.

1990. "'The World's Greatest Debtor Nation'?" *The North American Review of Economics and Finance*, 1 (Spring): 9–32.

1991. "Real Foreign Investment in Perspective," *Annals, American Academy of Political and Social Science*, 516 (July): 22–35.

1993. "National Saving and the Twin Deficits: Myth and Reality," in James H. Gapinski (ed.), *The Economics of Saving*. Recent Economic Thought Series, Norwell, MA and Dordrecht: Kluwer Academic: 109–33.

Englander, S. and A. Mittelstadt, 1988. "Total Factor Productivity: Macroeconomic and Structural Aspects of the Slowdown," *OECD Economic Studies*, No. 10.

Epstein, Gerald A., 1990. "Endogenous Enforcement and Debt Repayment in Latin America," mimeo, University of Massachusetts at Amherst, May.

1991. "Profit Squeeze, Rentier Squeeze, and Macroeconomic Policy under Fixed and Flexible Exchange Rates," in *Economies et Sociétés*, 8 (November–December): 2319–57.

Epstein, Gerald A. and Herbert Gintis, 1988. "An Asset Balance Model of International Capital Market Equilibrium," University of Massachusetts Working Paper, September. Forthcoming in the *Review of International Political Economy*.

1992. "International Capital Markets and the Limits of National Economic Policy," in Tariq Banuri and Juliet B. Schor (eds.), *Financial Openness and National Autonomy*, Oxford: Oxford University Press.

This volume. "A Dual Agency Approach to State and Market."

Epstein, Gerald A. and Juliet B. Schor, 1990a. "Macropolicy in the Rise and Fall of the Golden Age," in Stephen A. Marglin and Juliet B. Schor (eds.), *The Golden Age of Capitalism: Reinterpreting the Post-war Experience*, Oxford: Clarendon Press, pp. 126–52.

1990b. "Corporate Profitability as a Determinant of Restrictive Monetary Policy: Estimates for the Post-War US," in T. Mayer (ed.), *The Political Economy of American Monetary Policy*, Cambridge University Press, pp. 51–63.

1992. "Structural Determinants and Economic Effects of Capital Controls in the OECD", in Tariq Banuri and Juliet B. Schor (eds.), *Financial Openness and National Autonomy*, Oxford: Clarendon Press.

Esping-Andersen, Gosta, 1990. *The Three Worlds of Welfare Capitalism*, Princeton: Princeton University Press.

Estrin, Saul, Derek Jones, and Jan Svejnar, 1987. "The Productivity Effects of Worker Participation: Producer Cooperatives in Western Economies," *Journal of Comparative Economics*, 11: 40–61.

Estrin, Saul and Julian Le Grand (eds.), 1989. *Market Socialism*, Oxford: Clarendon Press.

Eswaran, Mukesh and Ashok Kotwal, 1989. "Credit and Agrarian Class Structure," in P. Bardhan (ed.), *The Economic Theory of Agrarian Institutions*, Oxford: Oxford University Press.

Executive Office of the President, 1993. *A Vision of Change for America*, Washington, DC: US Government Printing Office (February).

Fair, Ray C., 1984. *Specification, Estimation, and Analysis of Macroeconometric Models*, Cambridge, MA: Harvard University Press.

Fama, Eugene F., 1980. "Agency Problems and the Theory of the Firm," *Journal of Political Economy*, 88(2): 288–307.

Fazzari, Steven, R. Glenn Hubbard and Bruce C. Petersen, 1988. "Financing Constraints and Corporate Investment," *Brookings Papers on Economic Activity*, 1: 141–95.

Feldstein, Martin, 1973. "Tax Incentives, Corporate Savings, and Capital Accumulation in the United States," *Journal of Public Economics*, 2: 159–71.

1983. "Domestic Saving and International Capital Movements in the Long Run and the Short Run," *European Economic Review*, 21: 129–51.

Feldstein, Martin and Phillipe Bacchetta, 1989. "National Saving and International Investment," National Bureau of Economic Research, Paper No. 3164 (November).

Feldstein, Martin and Charles Horioka, 1980. "Domestic Saving and International Capital Flows," *Economic Journal*, 90(2) (June): 314–29.

Fishlow, Albert, 1985. "Lessons From the Past: Capital Markets During the 19th Century and the Interwar Period," *International Organization*, 39,3: 383–439.

Fitzgerald, E.V.K. and Rob Vos, 1989. *Financing Economic Development*, Aldershot: Gower.

Ford, Henry, 1922. *My Life and Work*, Garden City: Doubleday, Page, and Co.

Ford, R. and P. Poret, 1990. "Business Investment in the OECD Economies," OECD Department of Economics and Statistics, Working Paper No. 88 (November).

1991a. "Business Investment in the OECD Countries: Recent Performance and Some Implications for Policy," *OECD Economic Studies*, 16.

1991b. "Infrastructure and Private-Sector Productivity," OECD Department of Economics and Statistics, Working Paper No. 91 (January).

Frank, Ellen Tierney, 1994. *Three Essays on Key Currencies and Currency Blocs*, unpublished Dissertation, University of Massachusetts, Amherst.

Frankel, Jeffrey A., 1985. "International Capital Mobility and Crowding Out in the US Economy: Imperfect Integration of Financial Markets or of Goods Markets?," National Bureau of Economic Research, Working Paper No. 1773 (December).

1993. "Quantifying International Capital Mobility in the 1980's," in Jeffrey Frankel, *On Exchange Rates*, Cambridge, MA: MIT Press.

Frankel, J.A. and K.A. Froot, 1987. "Using Survey Data to Test Standard Propositions Regarding Exchange Rate Expectations," *American Economic Review*, 77(1): 133–53.

Freeman, Richard B. and James L. Medoff, 1984. *What Do Unions Do?*, New York: Basic Books.

Frenkel, Jacob and Assaf Razin, 1987. *Fiscal Policies and the World Economy: An Intertemporal Approach*, Cambridge, MA: MIT Press.

Frieden, Jeffrey A., 1989. "The Economics of Intervention: American Overseas Investments and Relations with Underdeveloped Areas, 1890–1950," *Comparative Studies in Society and History*, 31(1) (January).

Friedman, Benjamin, 1977. "Financial Flow Variables and the Short-run Determination of Long-term Interest Rates," *Journal of Political Economy*, 85: 661–89.

1978. "Crowding Out or Crowding In? Economic Consequences of Financing Government Deficits," *Brookings Papers on Economic Activity*, 9: 593–641.

1983a. "Recent Perspectives In and On Macroeconomics," National Bureau of Economic Research, Working Paper, No. 1208.

1983b. "Implication of the Government Deficit for U.S. Capital Formation," in Federal Reserve Bank of Boston, *The Economics of Large Government Deficits*, Proceedings of a Conference Held in October.

1988. *Day of Reckoning: The Consequences of American Economic Policy Under Reagan and After*, New York: Random House.

1990. "Views on the Likelihood of Financial Crisis," National Bureau of Economic Research, Working Paper No. 3407.

Friedman, B. and D. Laibson, 1989. "Economic Implications of Extraordinary Movements in Stock Prices," *Brookings Papers on Economic Activity*, 0(2): 137–72.

Friedman, Milton, 1968. "The Role of Monetary Policy," *American Economic Review*, 58: 1–17.

Fry, Maxwell J., 1980. "Saving, Investment, Growth and the Cost of Financial Repression," *World Development*, 8: 17–327.

1988. *Money, Interest and Banking in Economic Development*, Baltimore: The Johns Hopkins University Press.

Furubotn, Eirik G. and Svetozar Pejovich, 1974. *The Economics of Property Rights*, Cambridge, MA: Ballinger.

Gatti, F. Delli and M. Gallegati, 1990. "Financial Instability, Income Distribution and the Stock Market," *Journal of Post Keynesian Economies*, 12(3) 356–74.

Gemmell, Norman, 1983. "International Comparison of the Effects of Non-Market Sector Growth," *Journal of Comparative Economics*, 7: 368–81.

Gerschenkron, Alexander, 1944. *Bread and Democracy in Germany*, Berkeley: University of California Press.

Gertler, M., R.G. Hubbard, and A. Kashyap, 1990. "Interest Rate Spreads, Credit Constraints, and Investment Fluctuations: An Empirical Investigation,' National Bureau of Economic Research, Working Paper No. 3495.

Geweke, John, Richard Meese, and Warren Dent, 1983. "Comparing Alternative Tests of Causality in Temporal Systems: Analytic Results and Experimental Evidence," *Journal of Econometrics*, 21(2) (February): 161–94.

Ghate, P.B., 1992. "Interaction between the Formal and Informal Financial Sectors: The Asian Experience," *World Development*, 20: 859–72.

Gilbert, C., 1990. "Primary Commodity Prices and Inflation," *Oxford Review of Economic Policy*, 6(4).

Gintis, Herbert, 1975. "Welfare Economics and Individual Development: A Reply to Talcott Parsons," *Quarterly Journal of Economics* (June).

1976. "The Nature of the Labor Exchange and the Theory of Capitalist Production," *Review of Radical Political Economics*, 8(2) (Summer): 36–54.

1980. "Theory, Practice, and the Tools of Communicative Discourse," *Socialist Review*, 50–1 (March–June): 189–232.

1986. "International Capital Markets and the Validity of National Macroeconomic Models," University of Massachusetts, June.

1988. "Savings, Investment, and the Interest Rate: Credit Rationing in Competitive Equilibrium," Working Paper, Department of Economics, University of Massachusetts (February).

1989a. "The Principle of External Accountability of Financial Markets," in Masahik Aoki, Bo Gustafsson and Oliver Williamson (eds.), *The Firm as a Nexus of Treaties*, New York: Russell Sage.

1989b. "Financial Markets and the Political Structure of the Enterprise," *Journal of Economic Behavior and Organization*, 1: 311–22.

1994. "Optimal Dismissal Functions in Labor Discipline Models," University of Massachusetts (May).

Gintis, Herbert and Tsuneo Ishikawa, 1987. "Wages, Work Discipline, and Unemployment," *Journal of Japanese and International Economies*, 1: 195–228.

Giovannini, A., 1985. "Saving and the Real Interest Rate in LDCs," *Journal of Development Economics*, 18(2–3) (August): 197–217.

Glyn, A. 1992a. "Corporatism, Patterns of Employment and Access to Consumption," in J. Pekkarinen, M. Pohjola, and R. Rowthorn, *Social Corporatism: A Superior Economic System?*, World Institute for Development Economics Research Studies in Development Economics, Oxford; New York; Toronto; Melbourne: Oxford University Press, Clarendon Press.

1992b. "The 'Productivity Miracle,' Profits and Investment," in J. Michie (ed.), *The Economic Legacy 1979–92*, London: Academic Press.

This volume. "Stability, in Egalitarianism and Stagnation: An Overview of the Advanced Capitalist Countries in the 1980s."

Glyn, Andrew, Alan Hughes, Alain Lipietz, and Ajit Singh, 1990. "The Rise and Fall of the Golden Age," in Marglin and Schor, pp. 39–125.

Glyn, Andrew and Robert B. Sutcliffe, 1972. *British Capitalism, Workers, and the Profit Squeeze*. London: Penguin.

1992. "Global But Leaderless?," in R. Miliband and L. Panitch (eds.), *Socialist Register 1992*, London: Merlin Press.

Goldsmith, Raymond W., 1969. *Financial Structure and Development*, New Haven: Yale University Press.

Goldstein, Henry N., 1990. "Should We Fret About Our Low Net National Saving Rate?," *The Cato Journal*, 9 (Winter): 441–62.

Goldstein, M. and M.S. Kahn, 1984. "Income and Price Effects in Foreign Trade," in *Handbook of International Economics*, Amsterdam, North-Holland, pp. 1042–105.

Goldstein, M., D. Folkerts-Landau, Mohamed El-Erian, S. Fries, and L. Rojas-Suarez, 1992. "International Capital Markets: Developments, Prospects, and Policy Issues". World Economic and Financial Surveys, IMF.

Gonzales Arrieta, Gerardo, 1988. "Interest Rates, Saving and Growth in LDCs: An Assessment of Recent Empirical Research," *World Development*, 16: 589–605.

Goodwin, R.M., 1967. "A Growth Cycle," in C.H. Feinstein (ed.), *Socialism, Capitalism and Growth*, Cambridge University Press.

Gordon, David M., 1978. "Up and Down the Long Roller Coaster," in Lourdes Beneria *et al.* (eds.), *US Capitalism in Crisis*, New York: Union for Radical Political Economics, pp. 22–35.

1988a. "The Global Economy: New Edifice or Crumbling Foundations?," *New Left Review*, No. 168 (March–April), pp. 24–64.

1988b. "The Un-natural Rate of Unemployment: An Econometric Critique of the NAIRU hypothesis," *American Economic Review Papers and Proceedings*, May, pp. 117–23.

1989. "What Makes Epochs? A Comparative Analysis of Technological and Social Explanations of Long Economic Swings," in M. Di Maltes *et al.* (eds.), *Technological and Social Factors in Long Term Fluctuations*. New York: Springer-Verlag, pp. 267–304.

1992. "Kaldor's Macro System: Too Much Cumulation, Too Few Contradictions," in E.J. Nell and W. Semmler (eds.), *Nicholas Kaldor and Mainstream Economics: Confrontation or Convergence?*, London: Macmillan.

1994. "Power and the Macroeconomy: Comparing Social Structuralist Models with Neoclassical, Post-Keynesian and Marxian Alternatives," manuscript in progress, New School for Social Research.

This volume. "Growth, Distribution and the Rules of the Game: Social Structuralist Macro Foundations for a Democratic Economic Policy."

This volume. "Putting the Horse (Back) Before the Cart: Disentangling the Macro Relationship between Investment and Saving."

Gordon, David M., Richard Edwards, and Michael Reich, 1982. *Segmented Work, Divided Workers: The Historical Transformation of Labor in the United States*, Cambridge University Press.

Gordon, David M., Thomas E. Weisskopf, and Samuel Bowles, 1987. "Power, Accumulation and Crisis: The Rise and Demise of the Postwar Social Structure of Accumulation," in R. Cherry *et al.* (eds.), *The Imperiled Economy: Macroeconomic Perspectives*, vol. I, New York: Union for Radical Political Economics, pp. 43–57.

1990. "Power, Profits and Investment: An Institutionalist Explanation of the Stagnation of US Net Investment since the Mid-1960s," October, University of Michigan.

1993. "Power, Profits, and Investment: The Social Structure of Accumulation and the Stagnation of Net Investment since the Mid-1960s," Working Paper No. 16, Department of Economics, New School for Social Research, October.

Gordon, Robert J., 1972. "Wage Price Controls and the Shifting Phillips Curve," *Brookings Papers on Economic Activity*, 2: 385–421.

1975. "The Impact of Aggregate Demand on Prices," *Brookings Papers on Economic Activity*, 3: 613–62.

1985. "Understanding Inflation in the 1980s," *Brookings Papers on Economic Activity*, 0(1) 263–99.

1990. "What is New-Keynesian Economics?," *Journal of Economic Literature*, 28 (September): 1115–71.

Grabel, Ilene, 1992. *Essays on Optimal Financial Market Regulation in Open Economies*, Amherst: University of Massachusetts, dissertation.

Gramlich, Edward M., 1989. "Budget Deficits and National Saving: Are Politicians Exogenous?," *The Journal of Economic Perspectives*, 3 (Spring): 23–35.

Gramlich, L., 1983. "Models of Inflationary Expectations Formation: A Comparison of Household and Economic Forecasts," *Journal of Money, Credit, and Banking*, 15(2): 155–73.

Granger, C.W.J., 1969. "Investigating Causal Relationships by Econometric Models and Cross-Spectral Methods," *Econometrica*, 37: 424–38.

Green, Francis, 1988. "Neoclassical and Marxian Conceptions of Production," *Cambridge Journal of Economics*, 12(3) (September): 299–312.

Green, Francis (ed.), 1989. *The Restructuring of the U.K. Economy*, New York: Harvester Wheatsheaf.

Green, F., A. Henley, and E. Tsakalotos, 1992. "Inequality in Corporatist and Liberal Economies," University of Kent, Studies in Economics, 92/13.

Green, Francis and Thomas Weisskopf, 1990. "The Worker Discipline Effect: A Disaggregative Analysis," *Review of Economics and Statistics*, 72(2).

Greene, Joshua and Delano Villanueva, 1991. "Private Investment in Developing Countries: An Empirical Analysis," *IMF Staff Papers*, 38(1): 33–58.

Gregg, P. and S. Machin, 1993. "Is the Rise in U.K. Inequality Different?" Centre for Economic Performance, mimeo, LSE.

Groshen, Erica L., 1988. "Why do Wages Vary Among Employers?," *Federal Reserve Bank of Cleveland*, own publication, 19–38.

Grossman, Sanford J. and Oliver D. Hart, 1986. "The Costs and Benefits of Vertical and Horizontal Integration," *Journal of Political Economy*, 94(4) (August): 691–719.

Grubert, Harry and John Mutti, 1989. "Taxes, Tariffs and Transfer Pricing in Multinational Corporation Decision Making," mimeo, Department of the Treasury, March 21.

Guttentag, J. and R. Herring, 1984. "Credit Rationing and Financial Disorder," *Journal of Finance*, 39(3) (December): 1359–82.

Haliassos, Michael and James Tobin, 1990. "The Macroeconomics of Government Finance," in B.M. Friedman and F.H. Hahn (eds.), *Handbook of Monetary Economics* II, Amsterdam: North-Holland, pp. 889–959.

Hall, Robert E., 1979. "A Theory of the Natural Unemployment Rate and the Duration of Unemployment," *Journal of Monetary Economics*, 5: 153–69.

Hamermesh, Daniel, 1986. "The Demand for Labor in the Long Run," in O. Ashenfelter and R. Layard (eds.), *Handbook of Labor Economics*, vol. I, Amsterdam: North-Holland, pp. 429–71.

1989. "Labor Demand and the Structure of Adjustment Costs," *American Economic Review*, 79(4): 674–89.

1993. *Labor Demand*, Princeton: Princeton University Press.

Harberger, Arnold C. 1987. "Perspectives on Capital and Technology in Less-Developed Countries," in M.J. Artis and A.R. Nobay (eds.), *Contemporary Economic Analysis*, London: Croom-Helm, pp. 14–40.

Hart, Oliver and John Moore, 1990. "Property Rights and the Nature of the Firm," *Journal of Political Economy*, 98(6) (December): 1119–58.

Hartman, David G., 1985. "Tax Policy and Foreign Direct Investment," *Journal of Public Economics*, 26: 107–21.

Hatsopoulos, George N., Paul Krugman, and James M. Poterba, 1989. *Overconsumption: The Challenge to U.S. Economic Policy*, New York: American Business Conference and Thermo Electron Corporation.

Hatsopoulos, George N., Paul Krugman, and Lawrence H. Summers, 1988. "US Competitiveness: Beyond the Trade Deficit," *Science*, 241 (July 15): 299–307.

Haveman, Robert H., 1978. "Unemployment in Western Europe and the United States," *American Economic Review*, 68(2) (May): 44–50.

Hayashi, Fumio, 1986. "Why is Japan's Saving Rate So Apparently High?," in Stanley Fischer (ed.), *NBER Macroeconomics Annual 1986*, Cambridge, MA: MIT Press, pp. 145–210.

Hayek, F.A., 1945. "The Use of Knowledge in Society," *American Economic Review*, 35(4) (September): 519–30.

Hicks, Alexander, 1988. "Social Democratic Corporatism and Economic Growth," *Journal of Politics*, 50(3) (August): 677–704.

Hicks, Alexander and W. David Patterson, 1989. "The Politics of Economic Growth in Industrialized Democracies," Emory University Working Paper.

Hines, James R., Jr., 1988. "Taxation and US Multinational Investment," in Lawrence H. Summers (ed.), *Tax Policy and the Economy*, vol. II, Cambridge, MA: MIT Press: 33–61.

Holloway, Thomas M., 1989. "Measuring the Cyclical Sensitivity of Federal Receipts and Expenditures: Simplified Estimation Procedures," *International Journal of Forecasting*, 5: 347–60.

Holmstrom, Bengt, 1979. "Moral Hazard and Observability," *Bell Journal of Economics*, 10(1) (Spring): 74–91.

1982. "Moral Hazard in Teams," *Bell Journal of Economics*, 7: 324–40.

Holzer, Harry J., 1989. "Wages, Employer Costs, and Employee Performance in the Firm," National Bureau of Economic Research, Working Paper No. 2830 (January).

Inter-American Development Bank (IDB), 1989. "Savings and Investment in Latin America," in IDB, *Economic and Social Progress in Latin America, 1989 Report*, Washington: Inter-American Development Bank, pp. 89–106.

International Monetary Fund, 1989a. "Investment and Growth in Heavily Indebted Countries," in *World Economic Outlook, April 1989*, Washington, DC: International Monetary Fund, pp. 61–7.

1992. *World Economic Outlook* (May).

various years. "International Financial Statistics," Data Tape.

various years. *International Financial Statistics Yearbook*.

Jacobi, L., E. Leamer, and M. Ward, 1979. "The Difficulties with Testing for Causation," *Economic Inquiry*, 17, pp. 401–13.

Jensen, Michael C. and William H. Meckling, 1976. "Theory of the Firm: Managerial Behavior, Agency Costs and Ownership Structure," *Journal of Financial Economics*, 3: 305–60.

1979. "Rights and Production Functions: An Application to Labor-Managed Firms and Codetermination," *Journal of Business*, 52: 469–506.

Johnson, G.E.R. and P.R.G. Layard, 1986. "The Natural Rate of Unemployment: Explanation and Policy," in O. Ashenfelter and R. Layard (eds.), *Handbook of Labor Economics*, Amsterdam: North-Holland.

Jorgenson, D., 1971. "Econometric Studies of Investment Behavior: A Survey," *Journal of Econometric Literature*, 9(4): 1111–42.

Judge, George *et al.*, 1985. *The Theory and Practice of Econometrics*, New York: John Wiley & Sons, 2nd edn.

Jun, Joosung, 1989a. "What is the Marginal Source of Funds for Foreign Investment?," National Bureau of Economic Research, Working Paper No. 3064 (August).

1989b. "Tax Policy and International Direct Investment," National Bureau of Economic Research, Working Paper No. 3048 (July).

1989c. 'US Tax Policy and Direct Investment Abroad," National Bureau of Economic Research, Working Paper No. 3049 (July).

Jung, Woo S., 1986. "Financial Development and Economic Growth: International Evidence," *Economic Development and Cultural Change*, 35(2) (January), 333–46.

Kaldor, N. 1940. "A Model of the Trade Cycle," *Economic Journal*, 50: 78–92.

Kalecki, M., 1971. *Essays on the Dynamics of the Capitalist Economies*, Cambridge University Press.

Kelly, Patricia M., 1990. "Ability and Willingness to Pay in the Age of Pax Britannica, 1890–1914," mimeo, University of Massachusetts, Amherst, 1992.

Kendrick, John W., 1976. *The Formation and Stocks of Total Capital*, New York: National Bureau of Economic Research.

Keynes, John Maynard, 1964 [1936]. *The General Theory of Employment, Interest, and Money*, New York: Harcourt, Brace & World.

Khan, Mohsin S. and Malcolm D. Knight, 1983. "Determinants of Current Account Balances of Non-oil Developing Countries in the 1970's: An Empirical Analysis," IMF *Staff Papers*, 30(4) (December): 819–42.

Khan, Mohsin S. and Carmen M. Reinhart, 1990. "Private Investment and Economic Growth in Developing Countries," *World Development*, 18(1): 19–27.

Kindleberger, Charles P., 1978. *Manias, Panics, and Crashes: A History of Financial Crises*, New York: Basic Books.

King, M. and D. Fullerton (eds.), 1984. *The Taxation of Income from Capital*, Chicago: University of Chicago Press.

King, Mervyn, Enrique Sentana and Sushil Wadwani, 1990. "Volatility and Links Between National Stock Markets," National Bureau of Economic Research, Working Paper No. 3357 (May).

Koechlin, Timothy, 1989. *The Globalization of Investment: Three Critical Essays*, Unpublished PhD. dissertation, University of Massachusetts Amherst.

1990. "Accumulation and the Nation State: An Analysis of the Location of Investment," mimeo, Skidmore College.

1992. "The Responsiveness of Domestic Investment to Foreign Economic Conditions; An Analysis of Seven OECD Countries," *International Review of Applied Economics*.

Kornai, Janos, 1986. "The Soft Budget Constraint," *Kyklos*, 39(1): 3–30.

Krueger, Anne, 1974. "The Political Economy of the Rent Seeking Society," *American Economic Review*, 64 (June): 291–303.

Krueger, Alan B. and Lawrence H. Summers, 1988. "Efficiency Wages and the Interindustry Wage Structure," *Econometrica*, 56: 259–93.

Krugman, Paul, 1988. "Financing vs. Forgiving a Debt Overhang," *Journal of Development Economics*, 29: 253–68.

1989. *Exchange Rate Instability*, Cambridge, MA: MIT Press.

Kuznets, Simon, 1965. *Economic Growth and Structure*, Cambridge, MA: Harvard University Press.

Kydland, F.E. and E.C. Prescott, 1977. "Rules Rather than Discretion: The Inconsistency of Optimal Plans," *Journal of Political Economy*, 85: 473–92.

Laffont, J.-J. and Eric Maskin, 1982. "The Theory of Incentives: An Overview," in Werner Hildenbrand (ed.), *Advances in Economic Theory*, Cambridge University Press, pp. 31–94.

Laidler, D.E.W. and J. Michael Parkin, 1975. "Inflation – A Survey," *Economic Journal*, 85(340) (December): 741–809.

Lambert, J. and J. Mulkay, 1987. "Investment in a Disequilibrium Context or Does Profitability Really Matter?," CORE Discussion Paper No. 8703.

Landau, Daniel, 1983. "Government Expenditure and Economic Growth: A Cross-Country Study," *Southern Economic Review*, 49: 783–92.

1986. "Government and Economic Growth in the Less Developed Countries: An Empirical Study for 1960–1980," *Economic Development and Cultural Change*, 35: 35–75.

Landefeld, J. Steven and Ann M. Lawson, 1991. "Valuation of the US Net International Investment Position," Survey of Current Business, 71 (May): 40–9.

Lange, Oskar, 1937. "On the Economic Theory of Socialism," *Review of Economic Studies*, 4 (October): 53–71, and (February): 123–42.

1938. "The Rate of Interest and the Optimal Propensity to Consume," *Economica* (February), New Series, 5: 12–32. Reprinted in American Economic Association, *Readings in Business Cycle Theory*, Philadelphia: Blakiston, 1944, 169–92.

Lange, Peter and Geoffrey Garrett, 1985. "The Politics of Growth: Strategic Interaction and Economic Performance in the Advanced Industrial Democracies, 1974–1980," *Journal of Politics*, 47(3) (August): 792–827.

1989. "Government Partisanship and Economic Performance: When and How does 'Who Governs' Matter?," *Journal of Politics*, 51(3) (August): 676–93.

Lavoie, M., 1986/87. "Systemic Fragility: A Simplified View," *Journal of Post Keynesian Economics*, 9(2) (Winter): 258–66.

Lazear, Edward and Sherwin Rosen, 1981. "Rank-Order Tournaments as Optimum Labor Contracts," *Journal of Political Economy*, 89(5) (October): 841–64.

Lee, Chung H., 1991. "The Government, Financial System and Large Private Enterprises in the Economic Development of South Korea," *World Development*, 20: 187–97.

Lessard, Donald R., 1986. "Country Risk and the Structure of International Financial Intermediation," MIT Sloan School of Management (November).

Levine, David I. and Laura d'Andrea Tyson, 1990. "Participation, Productivity, and the Firm's Environment," in Alan Blinder (ed.), *Paying for Productivity*, Washington, DC: Brookings Institute, 183–244.

Levine, David and Richard Parkin, 1994. "Work Organization, Employment Security and Macroeconomic Stability," *Journal of Economic Behavior and Organization*.

Levy, F. and R. Murnane, 1992. "US Earnings Levels and Inequality," *Journal of Economic Literature*, 30: 1333–81.

Lilien, David M., 1982. "Sectoral Shifts and Cyclical Unemployment," *Journal of Political Economy*, 90 (August): 777–93.

Lindert, Peter H. and Jeffrey G. Williamson, 1985. "Growth, Equality, and History," *Explorations in Economic History*, 22: 341–77.

Lippman, S.A. and J.J. McCall, 1976. "Job Search in a Dynamic Economy," *Journal of Economic Theory*, 12: 365–90.

Lipson, Charles, 1985. *Standing Guard: Protecting Foreign Capital in the Nineteenth and Twentieth Centuries*, Berkeley: University of California Press.

Long, John B. and Charles I. Plosser, 1983. "Real Business Cycles," *Journal of Political Economy*, 91(1): 39–69,

Lovell, M., 1986. "Tests of the Rational Expectations Hypothesis," *American Economic Review*, 76(1): 110–24.

Lucas, Robert E. and Thomas Sargent, 1978. "After Keynesian Macroeconomics," in *After the Phillips Curve: Persistence of High Inflation and High Unemployment*, Conference Series 19, Federal Reserve Bank of Boston.

MacKinnon, J.G., 1990. "Critical Values for Cointegration Tests," Working Paper, University of California at San Diego (January).

Maddison, Angus, 1989. *The World Economy in the 20th Century*, Paris: OECD.

Malinvaud, Edmond, 1980. *Profitability and Unemployment*, New York: Cambridge University Press.

1986. "Pure Profits as Forced Savings," *Scandinavian Journal of Economics*, 88: 109–30.

1987. "Capital productif, incertitudes et profitabilité," *Annales d'economie et de Statistique*, No. 5: 1–36.

Mankiw, N. Gregory, 1989. "Real Business Cycles: A New Keynesian Perspective," *Journal of Economic Perspectives*, 3(3) (Summer): 79–90.

1991. "Macroeconomics in Disarray," *NBER Reporter* (Summer).

Mankiw, N. Gregory and David Romer, 1991a. *New Keynesian Economics, Volume I: Imperfect Competition and Sticky Prices*, Cambridge, MA: MIT Press.

1991b. *New Keynesian Economics, Volume II: Coordination Failures and Real Rigidities*, Cambridge, MA: MIT Press.

Marglin, Stephen A., 1984. *Growth, Distribution and Prices*. Cambridge, MA: Harvard University Press.

1987. "Investment and Accumulation," in J. Eatwell *et al.* (eds.), *The New Palgrave Dictionary of Economics*, vol. II, London: Macmillan, 986–91.

Marglin, Stephen A. and Amit Bhaduri, 1989. "Profit Squeeze, Stagnationist Models, and Keynesian Theory" in Stephen Marglin (ed.), *The Rise and Fall of the Golden Age; Lessons for the 1990s*, Oxford: Oxford University Press, pp. 153–86.

1991. "Profit Squeeze and Keynesian Theory," in E. Nell and W. Semmler (eds.), *Nicholas Kaldor and Mainstream Economics*, London: Macmillan, pp. 123–63.

Marglin, Stephen A. and Juliet B. Schor (eds.), 1990. *The Golden Age of Capitalism: Reinterpreting the Post-war Experience*, Oxford: Clarendon.

Mayer, C., 1988. "New Issues in Corporate Finance," *European Economic Review*, (32) (June): 1167–89.

McCauley, Robert and Steven Zimmer, 1989. "Explanations for International Differences in the Cost of Capital," Federal Reserve Bank of New York, Working Paper.

McKinnon, Ronald, 1973. Money and Capital in Economic Development, Washington, DC: Brookings Institute.

1982. "The Order of Economic Liberalization: Lessons from Chile and Argentina," in K. Brunner and A.H. Meltzer (eds.), *Economic Policy in a World of Change*, Amsterdam: North-Holland.

Meade, James E., 1972. "The Adjustment Processes of Labour Co-operatives with Constant Returns to Scale and Perfect Competition," *Economic Journal*, 82: 402–28.

Meurs, Mieke, 1993. "Agency Problems and the Future of Comparative Systems Theory," in Samuel Bowles, Herbert Gintis, and Bo Gustafsson (eds.), *The Microfoundations of Political Economy: Participation, Accountability, and Efficiency*, Cambridge University Press.

Milgrom, Paul R., 1988. "Employment Contracts, Influence Activities, and Efficient Organization Design," *Journal of Political Economy*, 96(1): 42–60.

Minsky, Hyman P., 1977. "A Theory of Systemic Fragility," in E.I. Altman and A.W. Sametz (eds.), *Financial Crises: Institutions and Markets in a Fragile Environment*, New York: John Wiley and Sons.

1986. *Stabilizing an Unstable Economy*, New Haven: Yale University Press.

Modigliani, F. and R.A. Cohn, 1979. "Inflation, Rational Valuation and the Market," *Financial Analysts Journal*, 35 (March/April): 24–44.

1985. "Inflation and Corporate Financial Management," in E.I. Altman and M.G. Subrahmanyam (eds.), *Recent Advances in Corporate Finance*, Homewood, Ill.: Irwin.

Moene, Karl Ove, 1989. "Strong Unions or Worker Control?," in John Elster and Moene (eds.), *Alternatives to Capitalism*, Cambridge University Press.

1992. "Poverty and Land Ownership," *American Economic Review*, 81(1) (March): 52–64.

Moene, Karl Ove and Michael Wallerstein, 1993a. "Egalitarian Wage Policies," mimeo, University of Oslo, July.

1993b. "What is Wrong with Social Democracy?," in Pranab Bardhan and John Roemer (eds.), *Market Socialism: The Current Debate*.

Moore, Basil, 1988. *Horizontalists and Verticalists: The Macroeconomics of Credit Money*, New York: Cambridge University Press.

Mortensen, Dale T., 1986. "Job Search and Labor Market Analysis," in Orley Ashenfelter and Richard Layard, *Handbook of Labor Economics II*, Amsterdam: Elsevier.

Mullins, M. and S. Wadhwani, 1989. "The Effect of the Stock Market on Investment," *European Economic Review*, 33: 939–61.

Munnell, Alicia H., 1991a. "Why Has Productivity Growth Declined? Productivity and Public Investment," *New England Economic Review*, (January/February): 3–22.

(with the assistance of Leah M. Cook), 1990b. "How Does Public Infrastructure Affect Regional Economic Performance?," *New England Economic Review*, September/October.

Murphy, Kevin M. and Robert H. Topel, 1987. "The Evolution of Unemployment in the United States: 1968–1985," *National Bureau of Economic Research Macroeconomics Annual*.

NIPFP, 1988. *Urban Informal Credit Markets in India*, New Delhi: National Institute of Public Finance and Policy.

OECD, 1983. *Sources and Methods*, Business Surveys, No. 37 (April).

1988. *The Future of Social Protection*, Paris.

1989. *Economies in Transition*, Paris.

various years. *Historical Statistics*, Paris.

1990. *The Income Tax Base*, Paris.

1990. *Economic Outlook*, Paris, various issues.

1990. *Employment Outlook*, Paris, various issues.

1990. *National Accounts, 1960–1988*, Paris: Organization for Economic Cooperation and Developments, vol. I.

O'Higgins, M. and S. Jenkins, 1990. "Poverty in the EEC," in R. Teekens and V. van Praag, *Analysing Poverty in the European Community*, Brussels.

Olson, Mancur, 1975. *The Logic of Collective Action*, Cambridge, MA: Harvard University Press.

Oster, G., 1980. "Labour Relations and Demand Relations: A Case Study of the Unemployment Effect," *Cambridge Journal of Economics*, 4: 337–48.

Oulton, N., 1990. "Labour Productivity in UK Manufacturing in the 1970s and 1980s," *National Institute Economic Review*, No. 132.

Oxley, H. *et al.*, 1990. "The Public Sector: Issues for the 1990s," OECD Working Paper No. 90.

Pastor, Manuel Jr., 1987. "The Effects of IMF Programs in the Third World: Debate and Evidence from Latin America," *World Development*, (15)(2): 249–62.

1989a. "Latin America, the Debt Crisis, and the International Monetary Fund," *Latin American Perspectives*, 60 (16)(1): 79–110.

1989b. "Debt, Stabilization, and Distribution in Latin America," paper presented at the American Economics Association meetings, Atlanta, Georgia in December.

1989c. "Current Account Deficits and Debt Accumulation in Latin America," *Journal of Development Economics*, (31): 77–97.

1990. "Capital Flight from Latin America," *World Development*, 18(1) (January).

Pastor, Manuel Jr. and Gary Dymski, 1990. "Debt Crisis and Class Conflict in Latin America," *Review of Radical Political Economics*, 22(1): 155–78.

Pechman, Joseph A., 1987. *Federal Tax Policy*, Washington, DC: Brookings Institute, 5th edition.

Pekkarinen, Jukka, M., Pohjola, and R. Rowthorn (eds.), 1992. *Social Corporatism: A Superior Economic System?*, Oxford: Oxford University Press.

Perry, George L., 1983. "What Have We Learned About Disinflation?," *Brookings Papers on Economic Activity*, 587–602.

Persson, Torsten and Guido Tabellini, 1991. "Is Inequality Harmful for Growth? Theory and Evidence," *National Bureau of Economic Research*, Working Paper No. 3599 (January).

Pfeffermann, Guy P., and Andrea Madarassy, 1989. *Trends in Private Investment in Thirty Developing Countries*, International Finance Corporation Discussion Paper No. 6 Washington, DC: World Bank.

Phan, D., 1987. "Un modèle econometrique pour la France," mimeo. R.

Phelps, Edmund S., 1968. "Phillips Curves, Expectations of Inflation and Optimal Unemployment over Time," *Economica*, 34: 254–81.

Pieper, Paul J., 1989. "Why Net investment Has Fallen," paper presented to Western Economic Association Meetings (June 20).

Pindyck, R. and D. Rubinfeld, 1981. *Econometric Models and Economic Forecasts*, New York: McGraw-Hill.

Plosser, Charles I., 1989. "Understanding Real Business Cycles," *Journal of Economic Perspectives*, 3(3) (Summer): 51–77.

Poret, P. and R. Torres, 1989. "What does Tobin's Q Add to Modelling of Investment Behavior," in M. Funke (ed.), *Factors in Business Investment*, Berlin: Springer-Verlag.

Poterba, James M. and Lawrence H. Summers, 1987. "Recent US Evidence on Budget Deficits and National Savings," National Bureau of Economic Research, Working Paper No. 2144 (February).

Prem, Roohi, 1994. "Three Essays on the Key Currency Question". Unpublished PhD dissertation, University of Massachusetts, Amherst. (See also, Prem Baveja).

Przeworski, Adam and Michael Wallerstein, 1982. "The Structure of Class Conflict in Democratic Capitalist Societies," *The American Political Science Review*, 76: 215–36.

Putterman, Louis, 1991. "Incentive Problems Favoring Noncentralized Investment Fund Ownership," Brown University.

Rakshit, Mihir, 1989. "Underdevelopment of Commodity, Credit and Land Markets: Some Macroeconomic Implications," in M. Rakshit (ed.), *Studies in the Macroeconomics of Developing Countries*, Delhi: Oxford University Press.

Ram, Rati, 1986. "Government Size and Economic Growth: A New Framework and Some Evidence from Cross-Section and Time Series Data,' *American Economic Review*, 76: 191–203.

Rao, J. Mohan, 1993a. "Distribution and Growth with an Infrastructure Constraint," *Cambridge Journal of Economics*.

1993b. "Labor and Liberalization in Developing Countries," Geneva: International Labour Organization, mimeo.

Rebitzer, James B., 1987. "Unemployment, Long-Term Employment Relations, and Productivity Growth," *Review of Economics and Statistics*, 69: 627–35.

Reitzes, James D. and Donald J. Rousslang, 1988. "Domestic Versus International Capital Mobility: Some Empirical Evidence," *Canadian Journal of Economics*.

Rivlin, Alice M., 1991. Statement Before the Committee on Ways and Means, US House of Representatives (December 17).

Romer, P., 1989. "Crazy Explanations of the Productivity Slowdown," *NBER Macroeconomics Annual*.

Rowthorn, R., 1977. "Conflict, Inflation, and Money," *Cambridge Journal of Economics*, 1(3): 215–40.

1982. "Demand, Real Wages and Economic Growth," *Studi Economici*, 18: 3–53.

1992. "Social Corporatism, Wage Dispersion and Labour Market Performance," in Pekkarinen, Pohjola, and Rowthorn, *Social Corporatism: A Superior Economic System?*, Oxford: Oxford University Press.

Rowthorn, R. and A. Glyn, 1990. "The Diversity of OECD Unemployment," in Stephen A. Marglin and Juliet B. Schor (eds.), *The Golden Age of Capitalism: Reinterpreting the Post-war Experience*, Oxford: Clarendon.

Ruggles, Richard and Nancy D. Ruggles, 1982. "Integrated Economic Accounts for the United States, 1947–1980," *Survey of Current Business*, 62 (May): 1–53.

Sachs, Jeffrey, 1980. "The Changing Cyclical Behavior of Wages and Prices: 1890–1976," *American Economic Review*, 70(1) (March): 78–90.

1986. "Managing the LDC Debt Crisis," *Brookings Papers on Economic Activity*, 2: 397–431.

1989. "The Debt Overhang of Developing Countries," in Calvo, Guillermo, Ronald Findlay, Pentti Kouri, and Jorge Braga de Macedo (eds.), *Debt, Stabilization and Development: Essays in Memory of Carlos Diaz-Alejandro*, Oxford and Cambridge: Basil Blackwell.

1990. "Social Conflict and Populist Policies in Latin America," in R. Brunetta and

C. Dell'Aringa (eds.), *Labour Relations and Economic Performance*, London: Macmillan, pp. 325–52.

Sahlins, Marshall, 1972. *Stone Age Economics*, Chicago: Aldine.

Saunders, P. and F. Klau, 1985. "The Role of the Public Sector," *OECD Economic Studies*, 5.

1992. *World Development Report*, Washington.

Schor, Juliet B., 1985. "Changes in the Cyclical Pattern of Real Wages: Evidence from Nine Countries: 1955–1980," *Economic Journal*, 95(378) (June): 452–68.

1988. "Does Work Intensity Respond to Macroeconomic Variables? Evidence from British Manufacturing, 1970–1986," Harvard Institution of Economic Research, Discussion Paper No. 1379, April.

1992. "Introduction," in Tariq Banuri and Juliet B. Schor, *Financial Openness and National Autonomy*, Oxford: Clarendon Press, pp. 1–14.

Schultze, Charles L., 1981. "Some Micro Foundations for Macro Theory," *Brookings Papers on Economic Activity*, 2: 521–92.

1990. "Cut Defense to Increase Saving," *Challenge*, 33 (March/April): 11–17.

1991. Statement Before the Committee on Ways and Means, US House of Representatives (December 17).

Semmler, W., 1987. "A Macroeconomic Limit Cycle with Financial Perturbations," *Journal of Economic Behaviour and Organization*.

Sethi, R., 1992. "Dynamics of Learning and the Financial Instability Hypothesis," *Journal of Economics*, 56(1): 39–70.

Shahin, Wassim N., 1990. "Unorganized Loan Markets and Monetary Policy Instruments," *World Development*, 18(2): 325–32.

Shapiro, Carl and Joseph E. Stiglitz, 1984. "Unemployment as a Worker Discipline Device," *American Economic Review*, 74(3) (June): 433–44.

Shaw, Edward S., 1973. *Financial Deepening in Economic Development*, New York: Oxford University Press.

Shiller, R., 1990. *Market Volatility*, Cambridge, MA: MIT Press.

Shleifer, A. and R.W. Vishny, 1986. "Large Shareholders and Corporate Control," *Journal of Political Economy*, 94(3): 461–88.

Sims, Christopher A., 1972. "Money, Income and Causality," *American Economic Review*, 62(4) (September): 540–52.

1980. "Macroeconomics and Reality," *Econometrica*, 48(1) (January): 1–48.

Singh, Balvir and Balbir S. Sahni, 1984. "Causality between Public Expenditure and National Income," *Review of Economics and Statistics*, 66: 630–44.

Singleton, Sara and Michael Taylor, 1992. "Common Property, Collective Action, and Community," *Journal of Theoretical Politics*, 4(3): 309–24.

Skott, Peter, 1989. *Conflict and Effective Demand in Economic Growth*, Cambridge University Press.

1994. "Minsky Cycles and the Rationality of Increasing Financial Fragility," mimeo, University of Massachusetts, Amherst.

Slemrod, Joel, 1989. "Tax Effects on Foreign Direct Investment in the US: Evidence from a Cross-Country Comparison," National Bureau of Economic Research, Working Paper No. 3042 (July).

Sneessens, H. and B. Maillard, 1988. "Investment, Sales Constraints and Profitability in France," Recherches Economiques de Louvain, 2.

Stern, D. and D. Friedman, 1980. "Short-run Behavior of Labor Productivity: Test of the Motivation Hypothesis," *Journal of Behavioral Economics*, 9: 89–105.

Stevens, Guy V.G. and Robet E. Lipsey, 1988. "Interactions Between Domestic and Foreign Investment," Board of Governors of the Federal Reserve System, International Finance Discussion Papers, No. 329 (August).

Stiglitz, Joseph, 1987. "The Causes and Consequences of the Dependence of Quality on Price," *Journal of Economic Literature*, 25 (March): 1–48.

　　1989. "Rational Peasants, Efficient Institutions, and a Theory of Rural Organization," in P. Bardhan, *The Economic Theory of Agrarian Institutions*, Oxford: Oxford University Press, pp. 19–29.

Stiglitz, Joseph E. and Andrew Weiss, 1981. "Credit Rationing in Markets with Imperfect Information," *American Economic Review*, 71 (June): 393–411.

Summers, L., 1981. "Taxation and Corporate Investment: A Q-theory Approach," *Brookings Papers on Economic Activity*, (1): 67–140.

　　1988. "Tax Policy and International Competitiveness," in Jacob A. Frenkel (ed.), *International Aspects of Fiscal Policies*, Chicago: University of Chicago Press, pp. 349–75.

Summers, Lawrence, and Chris Carroll, 1987. "Why Is US National Saving So Low?," *Brookings Papers on Economic Activity*, 2: 607–35.

Symons, J. and R. Layard, 1984. "Neoclassical Demand for Labour Functions for Six Major Economies," *Economic Journal*, 94 (December): 788–99.

Taylor, Lance, 1983. *Structuralist Macroeconomics*, New York: Basic Books.

　　1985. "A Stagnationist Model of Economic Growth," *Cambridge Journal of Economics*, 9(4) (December): 383–403.

　　1988. *Varieties of Stabilization Experience*, Oxford: Clarendon Press.

　　1989. "Gap Disequilibria: Inflation, Investment, Saving and Foreign Exchange," WIDER Working Paper No. 76.

　　1990. "Real and Money Wages, Output and Inflation in the Semi-Industrialized World," *Economica*, 57(3) (August): 329–53.

　　1991. *Income Distribution, Inflation, and Growth: Lectures on Structuralist Macroeconomic Theory*, Cambridge, MA: MIT Press.

Taylor, L. and S.A. O'Connell, 1985. "A Minsky Crisis," *Quarterly Journal of Economics*, 871–85.

Terasaki, Y., 1991. "Distributional Consequences of Laissez Faire Policy and Inequality Structure in Hong Kong, 1976–1986," in Toshiyuki Mizoguchi, Tsuyoshi Tsuru, *et al.*, *Making Economies More Efficient and More Equitable*, Oxford: Oxford University Press.

Timberg, T. and C.V. Aiyar, 1979. "Informal Credit Markets in India," mimeo, The World Bank, Washington, DC.

Tobin, J., 1969. "A General Equilibrium Approach to Monetary Theory," *Journal of Money Credit and Banking*, 1 (February): 15–29.

　　1989. "Review of Stabilizing an Unstable Economy," *Journal of Economic Literature*, 27(1) (March): 105–8.

Tsuru, Tsuyoshi, 1987. "Wage Deceleration in the Long-Term Crisis: Developments in the U.S. Economy, 1955–85," *Institute for Policy Research*, Hitotsubashi University, May.

　　1988. "Change in the Wage-Unemployment Relation," *The Economic Review*, 39(3) (July).

　　1989. "The Reserve Army Effect, the Collective Bargaining System, and Nominal Wage Growth," *Institute for Policy Research*, Hitotsubashi University, March.

Tun Wai, U., 1980. *Economic Essays on Developing Countries*, The Hague: Sijthoff and Noordhoff.

US Department of Commerce, various years. *Survey of Current Business*.

　　various years. *National Income and Product Accounts*.

　　Bureau of Economic Analysis, various years. *Selected Data on Direct Foreign Investment Abroad, 1950–1976*, Washington, DC: Department of Commerce.

　　"US Direct Investment Abroad," computer printout, Department of Commerce, *Survey of Current Business*, various issues.

United States Department of Labor, Bureau of Labor Statistics, Office of Productivity and Technology, 1990. "Industrial Disputes, Workers Involved, and Worktime Lost, 15 Countries, 1955–1989" (November).

US Council of Economic Advisers, 1990. *Economic Report of the President*, Washington, DC: Government Printing Office.

Vanek, Jaroslav, 1970. *The General Theory of Labor-Managed Market Economies*, Ithaca: Cornell University Press.

Vanek, J. and A.H. Studenmund, 1968. "Towards a Better Understanding of the Incremental Capital-Output Ratio," *Quarterly Journal of Economics*, 82 (August): 452–64.

van Wijnbergen, Sveder, 1983a. "Credit Policy, Inflation and Growth in a Financially Repressed Economy," *Journal of Development Economics*, 45–65.

1983b. "Interest Rate Management in LDCs," *Journal of Monetary Economics*, 433–52.

Wachtel, Howard, 1990. *The Money Mandarins*, Armonk, NY: M.E. Sharpe.

Wai, U. Tun and Chorng-huey Wong, 1982. "Determinants of Private Investment in Developing Countries," *Journal of Development Studies*, 19: 19–36.

Ward, Benjamin, 1958. "The Firm in Illyria: Market Syndicalism," *American Economic Review*, 48 (September): 566–89.

Weisskopf, Thomas E., 1987. "The Effect of Unemployment on Labour Productivity: An International Comparative Analysis," *International Review of Applied Economics*, 1(2) (June): 127–51.

1992. "A Comparative Analysis of Profitability Trends in the Advanced Capitalist Societies," in Fred Moseley and Edward N. Wolff (eds.), *International Perspectives on Profitability and Accumulation*, Aldershot: Edward Elgar, pp. 13–41.

Weisskopf, Thomas E., Samuel Bowles, and David M. Gordon, 1992. "We Need Handshakes and Arm-Twisting to Mobilize Our Recovery," *Challenge*, 35(2) (March–April): 48–54.

1983. "Hearts and Minds: A Social Model of US Productivity Growth," *Brookings Papers on Economic Activity*, 2: 381–441.

Weitzman, Martin and Douglas Kruse, 1990. "Profit Sharing and Productivity," in Alan Blinder (ed.), *Paying for Productivity*, Washington, DC: Brookings Institute, pp. 95–142.

Williamson, Oliver, 1985. *The Economic Institutions of Capitalism*, New York: The Free Press.

Wolfson, M.H., 1990. "The Causes of Financial Instability," *Journal of Post Keynesian Economics*, 333–55.

Woodford, Michael, 1991b. "Self-Fulfilling Expectations and Fluctuations in Aggregate Demand," in Mankiw and Romer: 77–110.

World Bank, 1989. *World Development Report*, Washington, DC: Oxford University Press.

1991. *World Development Report; The Challenge of Development*, New York: Oxford University Press.

Yamey, B., 1977. "Some Topics in the History of Financial Accounting in England, 1500–1900," in W. Baxter and S. Davidson (eds.), *Studies in Accounting*. The Institute of Chartered Accountants in England and Wales.

Yellen, Janet, 1984. "Efficiency Wage Models of Unemployment," *American Economic Review*, 74 (May): 200–5.

You, Jong-Il, 1990. "Income Distribution, Growth and Economic Openness," mimeo, Harvard University.

Zeldes, S.P., 1989. "Consumption and Liquidity Constraints: an Empirical Investigation," *Journal of Political Economy*, 97(2) (April): 305–46.

Zevin, Robert B., 1992. "Are World Financial Markets More Open? If So, Why and With What Effects?," in Tariq Banuri and Juliet B. Schor, *Financial Openness and National Autonomy*, Oxford: Oxford University Press.

Subject index

Name index